OHIO ART AND ARTISTS

The Whistling Boy. Frank Duveneck. (Cincinnati Museum of Art).

OHIO ART AND ARTISTS

By

EDNA MARIA CLARK, M. A.

RICHMOND
GARRETT AND MASSIE, PUBLISHERS

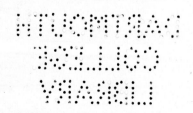

In the Hope That the Wealth of a
Rich Artistic Inheritance
May be More Fully Enjoyed by the
People of That State Whose
Name Signifies
The Beautiful River
This Book is Dedicated to the
People of Ohio

Preface

THE time seems to demand that some attempt should be made to set forth clearly the wonderful things that have been accomplished in the field of art in Ohio. The justification of this book is the growing pride which the citizenry of the state is taking in its art history—a pride which advances *pari passu* with an understanding of the heritage of Ohio art, and its present development. Thomas B. Macaulay said: "A people which takes no pride in the achievement of remote ancestors, will never achieve anything to be remembered by remote descendants."

The need of a volume of this kind was brought forcefully to the author's attention during an eight-year period of service as chairman of art for the Ohio Federation of Women's Clubs, when club women made frequent requests for information regarding Ohio artists. It was a matter of deep regret to be able to give them only a few scattered references for a small number of artists of the state. If this book fills, even partially the need that arose at that time, it will have justified its publication.

It is the hope of the author that this book will promote clear thinking as to the place of art in Ohio, and make the thoughtful reader acquainted with some of the men and women who have created works of art in this commonwealth. The book is not primarily a work of art criticism, but it is hoped, nevertheless, that it will help to build up a greater appreciation of what constitutes beauty in the abstract sense.

In the side pocket of every automobile should be the handbook published by the American Federation of Arts, Washington, D. C., called *Art in Our Country*. It lists the works of art in each city, so that the passing tourist may stop and investigate what the cities on his route have to offer. Many citizens of the Middle West do not realize that now, right in our midst, are art treasures to be admired—they are not all in the East. Furthermore, a knowledge of the art of Ohio would give tremendous encouragement to the artist himself.

In the research entailed in the preparation of this volume, necessarily covering so many phases of art, a voluminous amount of material has been unearthed. The difficulty has not been in the gathering, but in deciding what to omit. The demands for space were greater than an ordinary volume affords.

During the course of preparation, among the many kindnesses extended that the author takes pleasure to acknowledge, the principal debt of gratitude is owing to James R. Hopkins, A.N.A., for valuable assistance in planning the book and for many suggestions furthering its development. Acknowledgments are also due to Miss Alice Robinson, Professor Ralph Fanning, Professor Erwin Frey, Professor Arthur Baggs, Dr. Tom B. Haber, Professor Thomas E. French, and Professor Charles St. J. Chubb, all of the Ohio State University; also to Mr. H. C. Shetrone, Director of the Ohio State Museum; W. A. Ireland and Ray O. Evans, of the *Columbus Dispatch,* for reading the manuscript of different chapters and giving helpful criticisms and suggestions; the American Federation of Arts, for permission to use many names and data from the *American Art Annual;* the A. N. Marquis Company, for the use of sketches in *Who's Who in America;* Mantle Fielding, for biographical information in the *Dictionary of American Painters;* and to many friends, artists, museums, and libraries, for helpful coöperation. In the matter of illustrations, specific acknowledgment is made in connection with each one. The author has a genuine appreciation of all the aid in this undertaking given by these people who have made possible this record of Ohio art, and wishes to extend hearty thanks to them. The author also asks the reader's indulgence for any errors which may have been overlooked, especially omissions in compiling the biographical list of Ohio artists. It was not possible to obtain complete data in many instances.   E. M. C.

Columbus, Ohio
August, 1932

CONTENTS

PLATES

PLATES

PLATES

OHIO ART AND ARTISTS

CHAPTER I

The Art of the Mound Builders
and the Indians

WHO were the mound builders? Why did they build mounds? What were the artistic instincts of these primitive peoples? Some threads of their romantic story have been unraveled by the pick and shovel of the archæ-ologist, who has bared the secrets of the ancient mounds and brought to light the remains of the implements and utensils used. The old-fashioned method of teaching history was to require the pupils to memorize dates of decisive battles and concluding treaties of peace; but now it is agreed that the social life of a people constitutes their real history. We want to know how a people lived; how they worked and how they played; how they entertained their guests and were entertained in return; how they made love and were married; how they worshipped; and how they were buried. The objects they used become the artifacts that tell the story of their lives, and so make real history.

What records are there that will convince one that the mound builder lived in Ohio in prehistoric times? Ohio has many mute evidences of these mysterious people just beneath the soil. The First Americans wrote their history vividly, though unintentionally, in the soil of their native land. First, there are the mounds, piles of earth that usually cover human remains and various relics. However, it is necessary to know the topography of a country to be able to distinguish between mounds and common knolls. For example, in Logan County there are many knolls that might be called mounds, but they are not; they are only glacial remains. A mound is nothing more nor less than a monu-ment to the dead, and the site of a mound is usually a sacred place which the builders wished to preserve. The Scioto Valley is full of mounds. Butler County was one of the earliest in which interest in Ohio archæology was awakened, as it was one of the best suited in the state for primitive man; that county furnished an abundance of food and water, the mound builder's primary needs, so all he had to do was to accept conditions and make use of nature's bounty.

The first thing primitive man used as a tool was something he could pick up, as a club or a stone to hold in the hand and strike with or throw. Consequently he was interested in the terminal moraine because the detritus brought stones somewhat rounded by wearing and shaped almost ready for his use. The

1

PLATE 1—Fig. 1, Indian stone ax. Fig. 2, Stone celt. Fig. 3, Specimen of flint chipping. (Ohio State Museum)

terminal moraine begins in America on Long Island, runs west, and enters Ohio in Columbiana County, and goes thence southwest to Brown County on the Ohio River. Of the stones that came down in the drift, quartzite was preferred and best adapted to the use of the aborigines, though granite and diorite were also used. The round stones needed some change but could be shaped easily and used as hammers. Then the hammer stone was used to make other implements, such as the grooved hammer, to be used with a handle for striking at a little distance. Next came the grooved ax of stone, with many localities having their own types, the Wisconsin ax differing greatly from the Ohio type. The Ohio State Museum, at Columbus, which has the largest collection of mound-builder artifacts in existence, has more than three thousand of these Indian stone axes.[1] Two granite implements universally used and found all over the country were the celt, or ungrooved ax, having a keen-cutting edge, and the mortar and pestle, important implements for grinding grain into meal. The celt was used in the hand or had a handle attached by means of a green skin which, when it became dry, was a secure fastener (Figs. 1, 2, Plate 1).

The flint implements of the chase and of defense are equally interesting. In Hopewell Township, Licking County, is the largest quarry of flint in the world. This flint ridge is a point never gone over by a glacier, so the round hammer stones had to be carried thence and used to break up the flint after it had been quarried. Arrow points, spear points, drills and blades for cutting, were deftly chipped out of the flint. The chipping of flint is an interesting process: a piece of buckskin is placed in the palm of the hand, the piece of flint put on the buckskin, then a deer horn is used for chipping the flint into shape, the flint breaking with a conchoidal fracture and with sharp edges. Knife blades were made very sharp, and arrow points could be sharp enough to pierce the body and stick deeply into the vertebræ. No people within the horizon of barbarism have shown such versatility in stone. The darts are chipped with precision, there is a noticeable rhythm in the flakings, and the shapes have a graceful line and proportion. Arrow and spear points are frequently turned up in ploughing Ohio's soil (Fig. 3, Plate 1).

*   *   *   *   *

Can we not truthfully say that Ohio art begins here? These primitive implements were probably made with little conscious feeling of esthetic principles, yet they possess the important qualities upon which beauty depends: balance,

---

[1]It may be well to state here that the archæologist uses the words "mound builder" and "Indian" interchangeably, but with caution, for while the mound builders were part of the Indian family, yet other tribes of Indians did not build mounds at all.

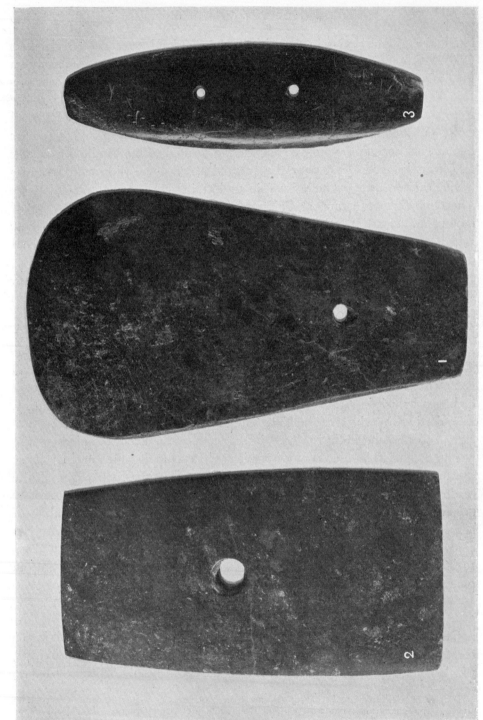

PLATE 2—Pendants and Gorgets. (Ohio State Museum)

rhythm, symmetry, regularity, and proportion. A suitability for the function they were intended to perform unites their practical and esthetic values. We are prone to think of art as the exclusive product of the painter or the sculptor or the architect, but it may belong to a worker in any material whatever that is adaptable to artistic expression.

The Indian wished to adorn himself just as we do; human nature changes little in the course of the ages. He was fond of enhancing his appearance with a ceremonial or banner stone, shaped like a double crescent or double triangle, with a hole through the middle into which a staff was put and carried in some way. Most of these pieces were made of Laurentian slate, carefully chosen examples characterized by layers of various shades running through it, some light, some dark; it is foreign to Ohio, being brought in by the glacier in the drift, but is found in abundance. Pendants to be suspended around the neck, usually oval at one end, but sometimes spear-shaped or rectangular, were cut from the specimen of the slate with beautiful markings. The gorget, also made from Laurentian slate, was probably the first ornament. It was always worn with a cord around the throat, though its use is not definitely known; thousands of these, probably lost in the chase, have been found in Ohio right on the surface of the ground. These ornaments were all shaped with a careful feeling for symmetry (Plate 2).

In primitive life, the first occupation was necessarily the quest of food and clothing, protection from the elements, and fashioning tools for defense. People who live out-of-doors, in the wilds, are extremely careful observers of what is taking place around them; every changing mood of nature is noted accurately. The mound builder was obliged to know the plants well in order to choose the edible ones from the poisionous ones, and he was obliged to know every trait of the animals in order to trap them for food, and to defend himself from their attacks. We have only to study the mound builder's pipes to realize how thoroughly he knew the animals and how amazingly well he could carve them in stone. The opossum, the frog, the hawk, fox, otter, fish, dog, bear, squirrel, raccoon, eagle, and many other animals were faithfully cut in most characteristic actions and attitudes; the plumage of the hawk and other birds was very meticulously cut, all in a surprising fashion to show the overlapping effect of the feathers (Fig. 2, Plate 3). Early man's contact with nature was responsible for all the motifs used in the decoration of his crafts. The lone pine, the cottonwood and the willow impressed him greatly, but the animals gave the zest and fire to his life. The realism of these first Ohio sculptors is remarkable. They had a keen sensitiveness to the decorative possibilities of animal forms, chose their most significant aspects, with the result that realism is the most striking quality of their sculpture. An almost startling piece is a small stone image, a ceremonial stone, or boat stone as it is called because it is hollowed out, about three inches long; it represents a wild duck asleep with its head twisted around on top of its back, a characteristic posture (Fig. 1, Plate 7). As a mass it is perfect, being just the effect the modern sculptor strives to attain; this carver had the rare good judgment not to mar the mass with petty detail.

The mound builder also attempted the sculpture of the human form with unusual success. A good example of the carved human head is one forming the bowl of a tobacco pipe found in what is called Mound City, a remarkable group of twenty-six mounds on the Scioto River, three miles from Chillicothe. The character of the person is well portrayed, even the tattooed adornment of the face being shown. The head is covered with a Hopewell type of headdress, having small antlers; while forming a wreath on the forehead and on each side of the face is a row of pearls set into the stone from which the pipe is made. A tubular pipe representing a full-length figure of a man was found in the Adena Mound near Chillicothe, by Dr. W. C. Mills, Ohio's pioneer archæologist (Plate 4). The scant drapery, the spool ornaments in the ears and the elaborate headdress should be noted.

There is a great difference in mounds in Ohio. There are two distinct cultures, the Fort Ancient culture and the Hopewell culture, besides several minor ones. We can differentiate them by the artifacts. The Fort Ancient culture left fortified hills surrounded by walls, as exemplified by fortified Spruce Hill, in Paint Creek Valley, Ross County, where hoes, fishhooks, arrow points, awls, scrapers and bodkins were found, all made of bone. As bone was strong and hard, the ulna of most animals was used, especially that of the deer and elk. Bone pins and needles were found in every tepee; the awl, made from the tarsus or the metatarsus of the wild turkey, was a most useful instrument, being used as a fork or as a tool for making perforations; scrapers made from the leg bone of a deer were used for removing flesh from the pelts in preparing them for tanning; an instrument for cutting corn from the cob was made from the lower jaw of the deer; bone fishhooks were usually found along the streams where there had been villages. These may seem small things, but they give us glimpses of aboriginal man and his activities (Fig. 1, Plate 3).

Of all the art found in the mounds, perhaps nothing is more remarkable than the precise engravings of animals on human bones. Every line is made to count in these conventionalized but recognizable cuttings. Much engraving on shell has been found, and it is equally meritorious.

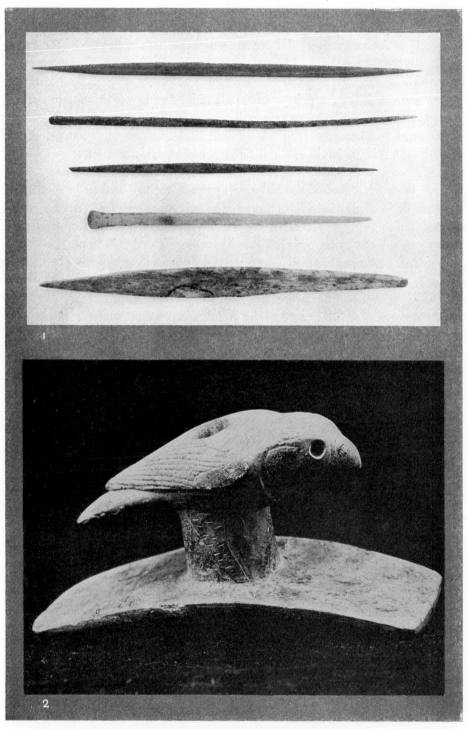

PLATE 3—Fig. 1, Bone implements, needles and bodkins. Fig. 2, Stone pipe
representing a hawk. (Ohio State Museum)

The Fort Ancient culture did not approach the high sculpture of the Hope-well culture. The latter had obsidian (volcanic glass), which is never found among the Fort Ancient artifacts. To transport obsidian more than half way across the continent from its source of origin, the Rocky Mountain district, must have been a tremendous task as it was probably carried in bags of skin by man-power and by canoe through the long, arduous journey. Three hundred pounds of obsidian in chunks and flakes were found in one of the Hopewell mounds.

The mound builders of the Hopewell culture are believed to have attained a higher degree of artistic development than any other strictly stone-age people of the earth. Through the exploration of a Hopewell mound, near Anderson, Ross County, in 1924, many beautiful objects were brought to light. The burial of a couple—a young man and a young woman—was unearthed. The profuse ornaments and decorations placed around the bodies reveal real pomp and splendor. At the shoulders, hips and knees of each body were large, shield-like plates of copper, carefully made, with perforations for attachment to the cloth-ing; at the ears were spool-shaped ornaments made from meteoric iron covered with thin sheets of hammered copper and silver, while at one end and side of the grave were upwards of a hundred similar copper ornaments placed in rows; around the neck of each was a necklace of grizzly bear tusks cut into fanciful form and set with large pearls; on the woman's arm were two copper bracelets. Literally covering and surrounding the two bodies, especially that of the woman, were thousands of pearls, varying in size from the small seed pearl to specimens as large as the end of the finger. Some of the pearls had been strung as necklaces and others sewed to the garments, portions of the cloth being still present, as were the imprints of bird feathers and of fur which had formed parts of the elaborate costume.

In a small mound near the one containing the double burial was disclosed another burial with which were placed many fine pearls, of both the smooth and the so-called node pearls, the latter having uneven or nodular surfaces which reflect the light in a pleasing manner. These pearls comprise what is believed to be the finest and best preserved prehistoric necklace in existence (Plate 5). The strand measures more than three feet and contains over three hundred pearls, and while they have suffered from their long burial under-ground, they still retain much lustre and beauty. Pearls must have been a regular fetish with the mound builder, since such great quantities of them have been found in the mounds. If all the fine pearls found in the Ohio mounds were in good condition they would rival in value the crown jewels of many a monarch.

PLATE 4—A tubular pipe sculptured to represent a human figure. (Ohio State Museum)

The quest for pearls must have been an intriguing pursuit for the primitive man in Ohio.

The skeleton in the burial place last described was supplied with other rich personal adornments: a very interesting copper helmet-like headdress, pearl-set bear tusks, and a carved stone tobacco pipe. Another copper headdress was found which may be said to resemble Lindbergh's plane, but which without doubt was meant to represent a conventionalized bird, perhaps the eagle (Plate 6). The body portion of the bird was curved to fit the head of the wearer, with the large wings drooping on each side; around the body of the bird were placed designs cut from silvery mica, apparently to represent feathers, while to the whole had been attached a bonnet-like drapery of woven cloth. Parts of this fabric had been preserved by the oxidation of the copper, and to it were sewed bear claws, bird talons, and a number of unusually large pearls. It would require very little imagination to picture this man as a chief of the Hopewell tribe, bedecked in as much fine raiment as the Indian in "Hiawatha:"

> "He was dressed in shirt of doe-skin,
> White and soft, and fringed with ermine,
> All inwrought with beads of wampum;
> He was dressed in deer-skin leggings,
> Fringed with hedgehog quills and ermine,
> And in moccasins of buck-skin,
> Thick with quills and beads embroidered.
> On his head were plumes of swan's down,
> On his heels were tails of foxes,
> In one hand a fan of feathers,
> And a pipe was in the other."

The Hopewell group had much copper which, it is supposed, they obtained in trading. Rings, bracelets, anklets, breastplates of copper, and wood or stone buttons covered with copper foil, were found in many mounds. The art of working in metal is most noticeable in the profuse use not only of copper as ornaments and implements, but also, to some extent, of silver, meteoric iron, and gold. The various methods of working the metals are worth our attention, all of the artistic *repoussé* and cut-out work being accomplished without the melting of the metal—certainly an industrial achievement. In the Ohio State Museum, Columbus, is a splendid piece of hammered copper in the design of a double eagle (Fig. 2, Plate 7). The greatest economy of line is observed, but each line is very significant. This is a good example of the way the animal

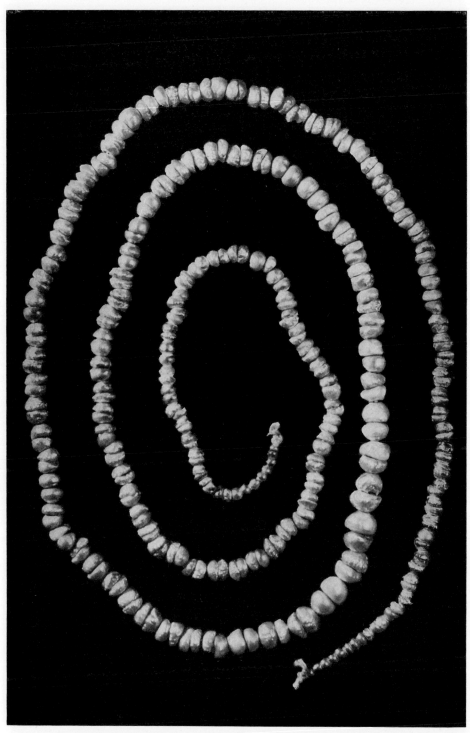

PLATE 5—Necklace of fresh-water pearls. (Ohio State Museum)

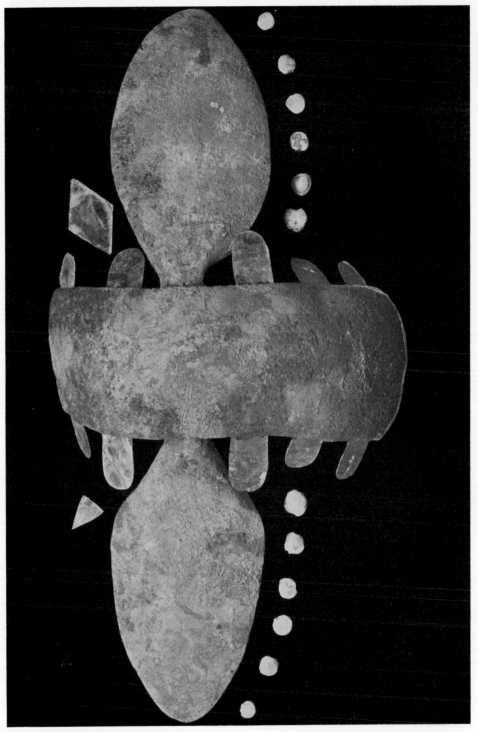

PLATE 6—Copper headdress. Triangle, diamond, and rows of pearls were originally attached to the copper. (Ohio State Museum)

designs of the Hopewell tribe became conventionalized, as can be seen readily by comparing this with the realistically carved pipes. Sheets of mica cut into beautiful scrolls are also owned by the museum.

The pottery is of great interest. The manufacturing process is thought to have been discovered by accident through the baking of clay in a primitive altar, or in the use of clay covering the flat baskets to protect them when used for cooking. It seems certain that many pieces of pottery were modeled inside baskets, which were burned off in the firing, as the impressions of basketry on the outside are very regular. There were large semi-globular pieces for holding salt, vessels containing from two to ten gallons for storing dried corn, pitchers for carrying water, bowls and basins and jugs for preserving bear oil. Shaped entirely by hand, the rotundity unproportioned except by the keen eye, the Hopewell pottery possesses a high esthetic value.

The decoration of the pottery was largely of a highly developed linear pattern, with flowers and animals conventionalized until they became purely geometric designs. The decoration was varied by the use of concentric circles, dotted bands, zigzags, crosshatchings, triangles and dogtoothing; some of these motifs no doubt representing the sun, clouds, lightning, and other phenomena of nature. There was a feeling then that the everyday things of life must be embellished, which makes one realize that the process of the growth of the esthetic idea is long and obscure. Hopewell pottery was well made and symmetrical. There is an unusual square form of jar with feet, having for its decorative motif a highly conventionalized wild duck, in the act of swimming, which is remarkably well adapted to the shape of the jar (Fig. 3, Plate 7). The plastic art is to be seen further in pipes and in terra-cotta images of various animals, birds and even the human form, all probably having a function to perform in some religious rite.

H. C. Shetrone, Director and Archæologist of the Ohio State Museum, Columbus, in his new book, *The Mound Builders,* tells us that: "The textile art, including the making of cloth or woven fabric, basketry, needlework, and quillwork, is the art which affords the primitive artist his greatest opportunity for detailed and ingenious application. . . . . Archæological evidences within the mounds indicate a remarkable development of the textile art among the mound builders, but since the materials of the craft are mostly of a perishable nature, the extent to which it was developed can only be conjectured. Woven fabric of good quality, some of it with colored designs, has been recovered from the ancient tumuli."[2]

---

[2] *The Mound Builders,* H. C. Shetrone, p. 115.

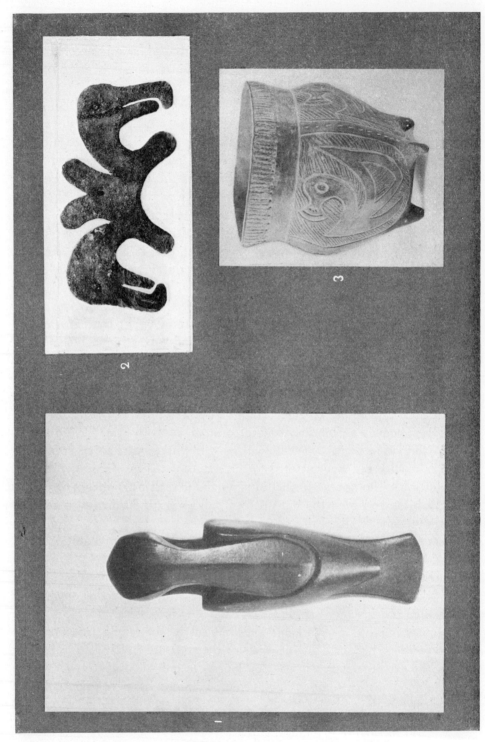

PLATE 7—Fig. 1, Duck image in stone. Fig. 2, Double-headed eagle design in hammered copper. Fig. 3, Pottery jar or ceremonial vessel of the Hopewell culture (Ohio State Museum)

The mound builder used colored pigments for many purposes: to paint his pottery and ornaments, and for tattooing his own body. The universal motif of the swastika was used over and over again in various modifications; so was the common sun pattern, but seldom were the conventionalized life-forms found in pigment.

Afer all, the most distinctive art of the mound builder was the construction of the mounds which have given him his title, "Mound Builder"; his practice of the minor, or allied, arts being somewhat similar to that of most primitive peoples. The Great Serpent Mound, situated in Adams County, in the picturesque hill country of southeastern Ohio, is the most wonderful effigy mound in the world. It fills every visitor with awe; and if one is basking in the very comfortable feeling of the superiority of modern man, it will prove wholesome to be humbled in the presence of this marvelous earthwork creation on a spot that must have been sacred to its people. One is forced to stop and think (Plate 8).

On top of a high, steep cliff overlooking a small creek and a beautiful valley, lies the embankment representing the huge serpent in graceful curves, seeming to uncoil itself as it creeps stealthily along the crest of the cliff. The serpent's jaws are open ready to grasp the egg, as the oval work in front of the jaws is usually called. From the jaws the neck extends for more than a hundred feet, then the body makes one convolution after another, in a singularly lifelike manner, until it is terminated by the triple coil of the tail. Some dimensions may be interesting: the concavity of the oval is eighty-six feet long, and thirty feet in its greatest width, measured from the inner edge of the surrounding bank; the ridge, or pile of earth, averages three feet in height and eighteen feet in thickness. The extended jaws of the serpent measure thirty feet across; the entire length of the serpent following its convolutions, from the oval to the tip of the tail, measures thirteen hundred and thirty feet. The body measures from four to five feet in height.

A transverse section of the serpent gives evidence that it has been built up of yellow clay and stones on a foundation of decayed grayish rock. During the centuries—who knows how many?—since its construction, a foot of dark soil has formed over the top of the stones and yellow clay; a well-kept sod now covers and softens the whole effect, making the serpent even more snake-like in its ensemble.

It is scarcely possible to conceive of any motive other than a religious one for the building of this mound. Here, on the Western continent, may we interpret this as a symbol of the old serpent faith of the East, which influenced

PLATE 8—Serpent Mound, Adams County. (C. L. Young)

people from the earliest time, and played such a part in the formation of succeeding religions? The mound and several acres surrounding it are owned, fortunately, by the Ohio State Archæological and Historical Society, which will maintain and preserve it forever as a free public park.

Ohio is exceedingly rich in mound-builder remains: there is another serpent mound in Warren County, lacking, however, the gracefulness of the Great Serpent; while hundreds of conical mounds, varied in size, are scattered through the Scioto Valley.

For a full appreciation of the art of the mound builder, we need to quote again Mr. Shetrone, than whom there is no greater authority on this subject: "The origin and development of conventional and symbolic design and of sculpture and the graphic arts are particularly well illustrated, or at least strikingly suggested, in the old mound art, as are also such interesting other aspects of art history as the influence of available materials on esthetic expression and the relation between utility and artistic treatment."[3] Continuing, he says: "Certain small sculptured productions, as the effigies of birds, animals, and the human form, and conventional designs engraved on bone and other materials, found in the mounds of the Hopewell and more southerly cultures, have been pronounced the artistic equals of any similar objects produced by stone-age peoples at any time or place, not excepting the highly evolved cultures of middle America or even those of ancient Egypt."[4]

To forge a connecting link between the prehistoric mound builder and the historic Indian is not at all difficult. The anthropologist thinks that the red man who was here when the first white settlers came was a direct descendant of the primitive mound builder, and consequently the Indian art is only a survival of the earlier mound-builder art. Naturally there have been some changes in the transition; while many patterns and decorative motifs used by the earlier artists remain the same, yet here and there patterns have been modified, or dropped out, or lost altogether and discontinued in the Indian art.

It has not been possible, nor to our purpose, to give here an exhaustive treatment of Ohio's primitive art, but even this rapid sketch of the art of the mound builder and the Indian is sufficient to prove that they deserve a clearly defined place in the genesis of Ohio art.

---

[3] *The Mound Builders*, H. C. Shetrone, p. 111.
[4] *The Mound Builders*, H. C. Shetrone, p. 123.

CHAPTER II

Pioneer Crafts

THE things of the present do not constitute the entire wealth of a nation. There is an inestimable value in the arts of a period gone by. At present the interest in every form of early American life is at white heat, so one finds a supreme desire to make real again the arts and customs of the pioneer. The public has been brought to an appreciation of the inevitable, strong, subtle influences which pass from material things through the eye to the brain, affecting our actions; and it is now being realized that the beauty and simplicity of the early crafts are conducive to high thinking and wholesome living. The deadly dullness, elegance, and artificiality of Victorian objects have passed forever, it is hoped! One must be surrounded with beautiful things if he intends to become cultured and possess an appreciation of the best the world has to offer.

Following the arts of building the home and tilling the soil, the pioneer turned to the arts of carving, weaving, metal-working, and so on, for the convenience, the enrichment, and the embellishment of the home. The discussion of crafts here will be confined to products in which skill and taste have been applied according to esthetic principles, the crafts that give the real emotion experienced by the maker, as he puts himself into his work, by means of honest workmanship and artistic expression.

WOOD CARVING

Wood, with its possibilities for expression, was the material ready and at hand. Our forefathers turned first to carving the homely implements and utensils for daily use. No doubt ax handles and mauls demanded first attention as aids in building and in clearing the land. To turn out an ax handle meant very deft handling of the wood, and it is doubtful if a man could be found today who knows how to produce an ax handle with the right curve. There were wooden hoes for digging, wooden scrapers to use on the hides before tanning, and wooden plows. For the household, there were ladles carved from wood, bowls for mixing bread and working butter, butter paddles and butter markers, potato mashers, large mixing spoons, and many other articles. In a common churn one can find the elements of beauty. The simpler the lesson, the clearer the sermon. Of course there are more important productions in the

world of art, but in a very humble utensil there is a note from a master craftsman who followed the impulse for beauty and has given the fundamentals of
artistry to his work.

Perhaps the more decorative carving has a greater interest. Chests were
ornamented with the flat or gouged-out sort of carving. It is said that all furniture evolved from the chest; it is easy to believe such a logical conclusion, as
a box to hold one's belongings was surely the first portable furniture. Beadings
and elaborately carved and twisted posts were common decorations of furniture, each craftsman working out his own ideas as to proportions.

In any consideration of early American crafts, whether in Ohio or any other
state, one pertinent fact must be kept in mind constantly: they were a distinct
echo of what was going on across the Atlantic. The antiquarian has a strong
interest in early carving, for in no other field are the Old World traditions
continued and perpetuated to such an extent, though the American artisan put
his own individuality into whatever he produced. The crafts show the oneness
of the traditions prevailing on both sides of the Atlantic. The influences were
mainly English and Dutch, since these settlers came here as homemakers, not
as adventurers, like the Spanish and the French. The French influence is mani-
fested very little until after the Revolution, when sympathies naturally became
stronger for the French than the English. There is much unnecessary worry
that American arts and letters are not what is called "pure American," for being
distinctively American is not itself a merit.

The greatest contribution in decorative carving was wrought as an architectural accessory. Interior woodwork consisted largely of well-devised moldings
and carefully proportioned panels, an occasional egg-and-dart molding, a
buxom rosette, or acanthus leaf, or sunburst. Upon the mantels and chimney
pieces the carvers focused greater skill than elsewhere in the house, because
there were greater opportunities in this center of the home life. The central
panels of the mantelpiece were often little masterpieces of relief; reeded
colonettes formed the fire frame, and frequently hand-carved eagles made a
decoration. Exterior decorations were brackets, corbels, pendants, and molds
showing a boldness of sweep. The main entrance received rich and choice
bits of carving.

Considering the tools of those days, the precision with which the fine-scale
detail was cut in truly remarkable, comparing favorably with the achievements
of the most painstaking workmen of today. It is not easy to carve wood into
a thing of beauty. Have you ever tried to make a basket from a peach seed, a
feat which was one of the favorite pastimes of the early days? Few people

can sharpen a pencil, even. The public seems to be awakening to the fact that there is much artistic salvage to be picked up if eyes are kept open and alert. Many old houses, pulled down to make way for some modern structure, could furnish a finely carved mantel, some nicely proportioned paneling, a graceful balustrade, or a door, pilasters, or some bit of carving, which could be incorporated into a new house and add that touch of beauty which only time can give.

METAL WORK

An Ohio farm was a self-supporting domain during the first half of the nineteenth century—yes, even much later than that. The farm owner produced enough food for his family, bred sheep to yield the wool which his wife spun and made into clothes; he raised hogs to be butchered for meat that was preserved in the smokehouse, and cattle whose hides were tanned and made into boots and shoes and harness.

Some larger farms had their own blacksmith shops. In communities of small farms the village blacksmith held sway. He was an important personage in the community. He was a craftsman indeed, for he wrought on his anvil not only the nails and hardware for each new house, but a variety of farm tools and kitchen utensils, as well as andirons, fire sets, and shoes for the horses of the whole countryside. And he toiled with much care and originality, as his handiwork shows. Iron, the least promising material in its crude state, has usually come to the hands of the man who must build as utility points the way. More credit to the blacksmith. It is only the valiant who can work in iron, only he who can laugh at the obstacles presented by the stubborn material. These virtues, coupled with a sense of design and the soul of an artist, may make of any man a smith. Well may Longfellow sing his praises!

In making objects of iron, two methods—cast and wrought—were used. Cast-iron is brittle, owing to the process by which it is made; it can not be bent, and breaks easily. The term "wrought" iron of course simply means "worked" iron, and might properly, as far as the actual meanings of words go, be applied to iron shaped by any process, but by usage it has come to be narrowed to denote the craftsman's actual contact with the material in his hands. Wrought iron is pliable, bends easily, and shows the irregularity of the hammer marks.

In the required hardware for the houses the craftsman in iron found an almost unlimited field to display his cunning, and the resourceful wealth of his art found play in hinges, locks, keys, bolts, bars, and latches. Early latches and knockers were admirably suitable; they belonged to their doors, and their simple lines were consonant with the architecture. The separate iron door handle with a latch was commonly used. It was finely wrought, altogether graceful, and nicely tapered to fit the hand. It terminated at each end in a triangular piece of thin hammered iron which was often given an extra twist or fanciful curve in keeping with the blacksmith's humor of the moment. A decoration occurred in the center of the handle, a series of ridges or the initials of the owner impressed with a chisel. About 1830 cast handles riveted to plates came into favor, and from that time on nothing at all worthy was produced; the modern door knob came into fashion everywhere. The finest examples of latches were on church doors where the latch was large enough to allow very bold design and to be visible from some distance.

While modern hinges are sunk into the wood and almost entirely concealed, the early hinges were placed on the outside of the doors, so that there was no doubt of the function they were intended to perform. The common kind was the strap hinge, though there were also the angle-, T-, and H-hinges. The expanse of iron offered an invitation for beautiful design and decoration; the motifs used were borrowed largely from wood carvings. Iron, as one of the baser metals, demands a close following of conventionalized treatment, and its forms should suggest strength. Keys reached enormous size; they were leviathans compared to the present ones. Some fine examples of early ironwork are also to be found in balusters, screens, transom traceries for doorways, gates, and railings. A bit of usually despised iron may be made vastly precious.

In the muddy days, when paved sidewalks were the exception, every home had a foot scraper. They ran the gamut from very plain to quite elaborate; there were chair-shaped scrapers, heart-shaped ones, and fanciful scrolls, or urns for upright posts. Weather vanes, too, received much attention from the ironworker who made them with a date, or name, a rooster, sheep, or other animal forming the design.

Heating and lighting made heavy demands on iron. Most persons are sensitive to the charm of an old fireplace; it lurks in the shadows surrounding the radiance; in the sooty bricks which have a hidden depth; in the rugged, uneven joints of lime and mortar. Cranes and hooks, and kettles of many sorts were necessary accessories to the fireplace, to say nothing of andirons and fenders, tongs, spiders, shovels, and pokers.

A popular heating arrangement was the Franklin stove. This was an open stove of cast-iron, with a raised hearth, and andirons like a fireplace. It was intended to save the fuel, which was wood, and to increase the warming of the room. Benjamin Franklin, by borrowing and bettering the ideas of the

French and the English, worked out the idea, but he did not patent it. He gave the model to a friend, Robert Grace, who cast and sold the stove and its parts. All modifications of the stove, even the mere fire frame, with or without a raised hearth or iron legs, became dignified with the name of Franklin. He had little to do with the ornamental part of the cast-iron frame and back. A strong Adam influence is seen in many of these stoves; sunbursts, urns, colonettes, well-turned finials, small bosses, and other characteristics are seen in extreme refinement. Later stoves show the Empire influence: finely executed grapevine decorations on the side columns, large corner medallions, and some-times a brass rail at the top.

Iron seems to have been the first metal to be used for lamps, candle holders, and other lighting devices. The Betsy or "Betty" lamp was so simple that any blacksmith could make it, and it was virtually indestructible. The "Betty" lamp is in fact nothing less than the ancient Grecian lamp, with a long, curved handle connected by a swivel to a short bar of iron. This device enabled it to be carried in the hand, or hung from a rafter or chair back, or stuck into the wall or a crevice of the chimney, or again, placed upon a table. It required only some grease, and a twisted rag for a wick; kerosene caused it to become obsolete.

As the pioneers prospered and their worldly goods increased so that they could keep herds of cattle, candles of beef tallow came more and more into general use. Various forms of candle holders were fashioned by the local blacksmiths and ironworkers. Many of these show much skill in the formation of the candle sockets, in twisted stems and arms, and a fine appreciation of line and balance in design. While wrought iron is indeed fit for the most elaborate treatment, we no doubt reverence it in the hardy vigor of the earlier and ruder days, because they seem best typified in such a sturdy metal.[1]

The candle molds in most homes were made of tin, usually of a size to make a dozen candles at one pouring. In appearance the mold was somewhat like a small radiator, the top being shaped like a dish, into which the melted tallow was poured so it would run into each of the slender barrel-like molds for shaping the candle. The wicks were fastened at the top on a small stick, which was an aid in pulling the candles from the mold after they were set. The women

---

[1]Iron, a metal not usually thought of as delicate, entered the field of the fine arts centuries ago, and it has a fascination for the modern craftsman. Andirons, to mention but one wrought-iron object, have been successfully designed by present-day artists, among them Stanley-Brown, of Cleveland, and by an outstanding Columbus craftsman, Don Jefferson Sheets. Wrought iron in screens, stair railings, and other adornments, most certainly bestows individuality to any interior decorative scheme. Special commendation was expressed for the screen designed by Paul Feher, Cleveland, when it was displayed at the 1930 annual show in Cleveland.

of the home were faithful in the production of light. In the fall their deft fingers began making the supply of candles for use in the long winter evenings. Tin boxes, cylindrical in shape, held the supply of candles. Candle sconces of simplest form had the tin edges pressed into scallops; *repoussé* effect of hammering, punch-work in designs, or a figure of copper set in silhouette, were other forms of decoration.

Tin lanterns embodied the idea of enclosing a candle, thus protecting it from the wind and making it more steady. The tin, pierced lanterns are called Paul Revere lanterns, since it is supposed that was the kind used to give the signal to the patriot who made the dashing ride for his country.[2] The feeble rays of a candle filtering through the pierced holes would not seem to have carried very far. Foot warmers added much to the comfort of the traveler on a long ride, or to the worshiper in a cold meetinghouse. This convenience consisted of a tin box which held hot coals from which radiated heat. A wooden frame held the tin box, the sides of which were punctured in designs; spindle posts were at each corner of the frame, and a wire bail served for a handle. Tea caddies, trays, teapots, coffeepots, and other tin utensils received stenciled decoration, a poor relation of japanning. Tin trays were handsomely japanned from about 1825 to the mid-Victorian period; rococo borders and flower centers were carried out in beautiful colors and arrangements.

Domestic utensils of copper and brass are so far forgotten as to render curious those once common objects of daily use. If the process of making some of these old things is understood, it gives them an added interest. Such brasses as old andirons and candlesticks are hollow cast, then turned to a smooth surface on a lathe and burnished. Kettles are either "spun" or hammered from sheet metal. If hammered, the surface shows innumerable round spots, all so smooth as scarcely to be seen. "Spun" brass was worked in this fashion: a sheet of brass, rolled thin, was held against a wooden mold, and by the pressure of smooth tools was rounded into shape while mold and brass were spinning at great speed. In globe-shaped pieces, such as teakettles, there is a fine line to be seen where the two spun hemispheres have been brazed together.

Among kitchen utensils of copper and brass, the most common were teakettles and kettles of various sizes (Fig 1, Plate 9). There were brass skimmers, with wrought-iron handles, to meet every need: to skim cream from the milk; to remove scum from boiling cider or jelly; to lift the cracklings from frying lard; and so on and on. Above all in importance was the brass candlestick.

---

[2]The tin, pierced lanterns have long been called, erroneously, Paul Revere lanterns; it is now definitely known that the kind used was a larger lantern with four sides of glass.

PLATE 9—Fig. 1, Early Ohio brass and copper utensils. Fig. 2, Glass goblets and saltcellars. (Author)

The more practical candlestick had a saucer base with a ring on the side for a handle. Then there were the very ornate candlesticks of the baluster type in many varieties of turnings, usually with the square or rectangular base with the corners cut off. Brass, funnel-shaped candle extinguishers, and brass snuffers to clip the charred wick and make the flame burn brightly were devices accompanying the candlestick.

Some of the most decorative early brass work was done upon the fireplace accessories; the proportion of the turnings on the andirons, the lace-like openwork of the fenders, the elaborate sets of shovel and tongs and poker to match. The polishing of the metal work throughout the house in the good old days was a considerable item in the program of work, but the result from the reflected lights must have been a satisfactory reward for the arduous task. The copper or brass warming pan held an honored place in the chimney corner. It was used for warming the beds in those heatless rooms on severely cold winter nights. Hot coals were first placed in the pan, then by means of its long handle, the pan was pushed around between the sheets to take off the icy chill. Warming-pan lids furnished the opportunity for the metal worker to display his skill and inventive powers in decoration; scrolls, foliage, and flowers were chased on the lids (Fig. 1, Plate 10).

Door knobs and latches were cast in brass, but the old knocker is the most romantic of the door hardware. It seems more hospitable than the electric bell! The early knockers were cast in sand molds from wood-carver's models; thus the touch of the craftsman persists, as the carvings were not absolutely symmetrical. Brass knockers were hand-chased in scrolls or engraved with the name of the owner. The eagle, a motif common in all the early crafts, formed many of the door knockers. Through the Georgian and classical periods of architecture, knockers were so varied in design, and hence in cost, that they frequently revealed much of the social, political, and economic life of the people on whose houses they appeared. The urn shape appeared in connection with shells, garlands, lions, lyres, and other items of classical ornament which the brothers Adam had done so much to popularize.

Copper and brass tips were put on the toes of the boots to make them wear indefinitely. The brass swan's-necks on the little sleds took the skin from the tongue of many an unsuspecting youngster when dared by the older boys to stick his tongue to the swan's-neck on a frosty morning. Brass buckles, chains, and trappings on harness were no doubt relics of medieval times when the horses were gaily caparisoned. Harness brass was produced by casting and stamping, thus multiplying the designs, and it was very handsome when

PLATE 10—Fig. 1, Five-ladder-back rocker and brass warming pan. Fig. 2, Cherry Hepplewhite desk and Windsor chair. (Author)

polished. There was a medallion of brass where the forehead strap met the cheek strap, an ornament on the forehead, and on the martingales, and the blinders bore the initials of the owner, or other decoration in brass. The crescent symbol brought back by the Crusaders was still used. Brass sleigh bells gave the "sounding of brass and the tinkling of cymbals" to the winter night. Brass hardware on old furniture is a factor in its value and its beauty. Brass eagles screamed from the tops of clocks and mirrors.

Pewter was in all probability a household product in the early days, serving the needs afterward filled by silver, pottery, and china. The composition of pewter has a base of tin with a small quantity of other metal (usually lead or antimony, sometimes copper or zinc), used as an alloy to give it greater wearing quality. The comparative ease with which the alloy was prepared and managed made it a simple matter to produce the ware at home. Spoons and other objects that wore out quickly with constant use, could be melted and remolded. Perhaps a spoon mold would be passed around for the use of the whole neighborhood. Think of the economy in making over your old spoons, and the help-each-other spirit of a community owning such utensils in common!

A little later, pewter was made by the itinerant craftsmen who traveled about the sparsely settled country with their molds and metals. They stopped at each house several days or long enough to make the supply of pewter each household needed. When pewter came to be manufactured in the larger towns, it was distributed through the outlying districts by peddlers traveling in carts, whose stock included also brass, tin, iron, and copperware. Cincinnati became one of the greatest centers in the whole country in the manufacture of pewter. All pewter bearing the mark of Homans and Company, Cincinnati, is highly prized; another pewter firm of that city, William Sellew and Brother, founded in 1836, made ware that the collector covets. The subject of pewter-marks is an intricate one, and offers many unsolved problems to the collector, as much of the American pewter bears no mark at all.[3]

There is scarcely an article for table, toilet, kitchen or church which cannot be found in pewter. Its manifold uses are suggested by the following list: candle molds, candlesticks, oil and grease lamps, teapots, coffeepots, measures, jugs, and ladles for the kitchen; plates, spoons, cups and saucers, pitchers, platters, porringers, chargers, sugar bowls and creamers, for the table; washbowls for the toilet; and for the church, Communion sets, baptismal bowls, and alms dishes.

The simple, massive forms are what constitute the beauty of pewter, which

---

[3]A fine collection of early Ohio pewter is owned by Mrs. A. V. Donahey, Indian Lake, Ohio.

at its best is plain; the very sturdiness of its structure allows for little super-fluity or ornament in design. Ornamentation consisted of distribution of lines, decorative but simple moldings, to a small extent engraving, and in a few instances "wriggling," a surface decoration of broken or wavy lines. Moldings and rims cast in a mold are necessarily simple, and characterized by restrained convexity of proportion rather than by complexity of members, concavity, or undercutting. The unobtrusive contours of the moldings and rims do not inter-rupt the beauty of the metal's surface in the plain portions. The large ears or handles of punched work adorning the porringers are truly decorative, and dis-play Dutch ancestry. The early spoons were known as "rat-tail" spoons, from the resemblance to a rat's tail of the raised decoration on the bottom of the bowl; other spoons show the shell form at the end of the handle on the bottom of the bowl. The rims of plates form their chief decorative feature. By the middle of the nineteenth century there was a decided decadence in regard to shape; pewter was obviously molded in imitation of silver, losing its simple beauty.

All through the Victorian period of artificiality pewter was relegated to the woodshed or some other out-of-sight place. At the present its very soberness and beautiful proportions satisfy an esthetic taste, and a saner appreciation of it is felt generally.

FURNITURE

Early Ohio furniture was made for use, not for adornment of the home, nor for sale; therefore, it was very sturdily made and expected to last a lifetime. Its honest workmanship is one of its chief merits. Glue was not depended upon in joining as it is in present-day furniture; the old reliable wooden pin was indispensable.

The furniture used in Ohio was far more simple than that of the Colonial and Southern states. There are two divisions that must be considered. On the one hand, there was the furniture brought into Western Reserve by the settlers from Connecticut, and that of the Virginia type found in southern Ohio. Both were of high quality, and closely approached the styles of the English cabinet-makers in the use of the Gothic arch, or the Chinese pierced fret splats, in the chair backs of Chippendale design. The early American cabinetmakers also introduced the cabriole legs which Chippendale had continued from the Queen Anne style; they also used the square, tapered legs and straight, structural lines of the Adam and Sheraton styles, and the shield-back chair of Hepplewhite. Then there was the simpler type, rather provincial in origin, and made for

PLATE 11—Group of early Ohio crafts. (Author)

people of modest means, which only approximated in some ways the fully developed style. The more simple type seems more truly Ohioan, and in the fitness of things it was more appropriate.

In the ornamental features of chests is found the first European influence, the Jacobean. When reference is made to the Jacobean period in England, it means reckoning from 1603, when the Stuarts came in with James I, through Cromwell's time and the Restoration, to their exit with James II in 1688, who gave way to William of Orange. Of course, an English style carried over for many years, and then many more years were required for it to reach this country. The characteristics of Jacobean furniture are heaviness and clumsiness; in form and line it was severe, even though much ornamented. Chests and cupboards were decorated with glued-on split turnings, and geometrical designs in moldings until they were weighted down with them. Chairs were almost square, with straight lines, high and very straight backs, seats high from the floor, with heavy stretchers near the floor. Long, heavy tables had bulbous legs, a characteristic carried over from the Elizabethan style; the gate-leg table was in vogue at this time, and there are still many variations of it, such as the butterfly table.

After the Restoration, English styles were affected by Dutch, Flemish, French, Spanish, Portugese, and Italian influences; the furniture of the Colonies, except New York, which was predominantly Dutch, exactly reproduced the styles of the mother country. Thus the early Ohio furniture was a composite type, gradually merging the older forms into a simple unity. Two types of chairs developed: the slat-back (or ladder-back) type, and the turned spindle type. They were of rectangular construction, with straight back and front posts, the tops of the back posts finished with a finial, often beautifully designed and turned. Between the back posts of the ladder-back type were fitted the slats, three, four, or five in number, varying in width and (in the best examples) curved slightly in their top line (Fig. 1, Plate 10; Plate 11; Plate 13). For the spindle type, two horizontal spindles were set into the back posts, and the vertical spindles set between them. These two types of chairs run down almost to modern times, with many varieties in the turning of tops of back posts, in the shape and number of the slats, or ladders, and in the spindles. The old chairs were light in weight, but sturdy in construction.

The period of William and Mary was short, only fourteen years, from 1688 to 1702, but with it came a very definite change from straight to curved lines; ogee and flat arches, scroll stretchers, double-hood backs on cabinets and settees, and trumpet turnings, were the characteristics. One contribution of the period was the highboy, consisting of two parts, a chest of drawers and a stand. The chest part was divided into drawers, usually four, the top drawer being cut into two or three short ones. Sometimes the stand or table, which furnished a base, had one or two drawers with a shaped apron below. Lowboys were small dressing tables much like the stands used as bases of highboys, with similar drawers, aprons, and stretchers. While the highboy was not common in Ohio, the chest of drawers was in every home. They were made of cherry, curly maple, walnut, or mahogany veneer; many a chest was ornamented with exquisite inlay borders and beautifully carved posts. Three-cornered cupboards were exceedingly popular, with much variation in wood, style and size, from the small, elaborate one to be used in the parlor to the large, simple, and heavy ones for kitchen use.

With the reign of Queen Anne a distinctive type of furniture developed and continued for many years afterward, finally merging into the Georgian period and the styles of the English cabinetmakers. It brought in the cabriole leg and more carving than had been used before, so that craftsmen turned their efforts to the embellishment and refinement of the designs handed down to them.

The bedsteads of the period had tall, slender, round, square, or octagonal posts that held a tester for curtains; early Georgian bedposts were carved with the back posts almost always plain, because they were concealed by the curtains. Great height and slenderness of posts indicate age; later ones became shorter and heavier (Plate 13). Low, trundle-beds (Plate 12), that were pushed under the high bed during the day, were commonly used by the children of the household; small and few rooms made it necessary to economize space for living quarters during the day.

In the rush-bottom armchairs with straight, turned legs, the arm support was an extension of the front leg. Split hickory or slippery elm made chair seats equal to the rush-buttoms. The most striking of all the chairs was the Windsor, which appeared in Philadelphia in 1763, and was adopted by the settlers of the West later. Its wood was oak, ash, hickory, and pine, combined in different parts, and the design was little influenced by the stylistic quality of the finer furniture. The back was all spindles; the seat was thick and deep, fully shaped; the legs were sharply raked or splayed; these characteristics give the charm to the Windsor. The Windsor chair could be made in its best style only by specially trained men who could obtain the proper slants of the legs, seat, and arms. New England added the arm to the Windsor chair. The Philadelphia comb-back was a fine, man's chair; the end of the comb was generally carved with a strong spiral, having one more whorl than the other types.

PLATE 12—Interior of log cabin. (Ohio State Museum)

The so-called flareback was secured by springing out the spindles after they left the arm rail (Fig. 2, Plate 10). Early Windsors were painted green, to use as garden chairs; later ones were generally black. Charming, long settees often had Windsor backs.

Drop-leaf tables were made and used for dining tables from the earliest days. They would seat six or eight people comfortably. Most of them were of cherry or walnut, simple in design, with turned legs. Drop-leaf tables of Queen Anne and early Georgian styles had cabriole legs, claw-and-ball feet, and ogeed aprons at the ends. Small, bedside stands or tables with shallow drawers were made by every cabinetman. It is strange that of the thousands of these two-drawer stands now extant in Ohio, never are there two alike—every home cabinetmaker had his own ideas of turnings and proportions; surely the product was individual and the more interesting on that account (Plate 13).

Books were not numerous enough to demand many bookcases, though in combination with writing desks there were many composite pieces, called secretaries. Such pieces had an upper section serving as a cabinet or bookcase, and a slant-top desk for the lower portion. There were also slant-top desks without the upper section, but with drawers below, and these form some of the finest pieces of Ohio furniture.

In the early nineteenth-century furniture of Ohio there is a blending of the treatments which are associated with Hepplewhite and Sheraton. Thomas Sheraton, the last of the great English cabinetmakers, was a devotee of straight lines in furniture, and drew largely from the classic forms of the Louis XVI style, transforming them into English style. Hepplewhite got his ideas from the same source, so there is often confusion in attributing work to the proper craftsman. The influence of Sheraton was for greater simplicity, vertical flutings, and inlay for decoration. Many desks followed the style of Hepplewhite, using the tall, French foot, which he popularized, with its refined proportions and graceful outward curve, and often the serpentine front and inlaid borders (Fig. 2, Plate 10).

Mirrors not infrequently had two sections, the upper one devoted to a painted-on-glass picture, the lower portion for the mirror (Plate 11). The frame for such mirrors had pilasters or columns at the sides, rosettes at the corners, a cornice at the top, and was properly called the architectural frame. The painted-on-glass pictures of flowers, or a Jeffersonian house with a roadway, were quaint and primitive-looking. The mirror, with a Chippendale frame of thin walnut cut into scrolls, was a very elegant one, as was the convex mirror

PLATE 13—Early bedroom furnishings. (Author)

in a circular, gold frame. Tilt-top tables on tripod pedestals served as tea tables, around which centered the social life of the day.

Empire furniture was long fashionable in the United States, since France was bound to this nation by so many ties. When President Monroe refurnished the White House in 1818, the handsome furniture made in Paris was in this taste. But the bombastic French style degenerated into exaggeration, and there followed the Victorian period, when good taste was assassinated. Duncan Phyfe, the New York cabinetmaker, actually redeemed some of the disagreeable features of the Empire style of the French. He curved the front legs of the chairs forward and the back legs backward, in much the same manner as the old Roman curule chairs. Head- and footboards of bedsteads and ends of sofas were scrolled over with a Greek curve; such beds were frequently called "sleigh beds" from their contour. Backs of chairs were rolled back, too; the much-discussed Hitchcock chair may be said to belong to the Empire period, as it has the characteristic roll at the top of the back. Card tables with turn-over hinged tops were a fashion of the day; these were made of crotched walnut or mahogany veneer, and belonged to the Empire style, some of them graceful, others heavy and clumsy. The Empire mirror frame was of crotched mahogany in the form of an ogee molding (Plate 13). The strength and beauty of the early furniture were an expression of the splendid character of the pioneers.

GLASS

The latest fad of the antiquarian is for old glass bottles and dishes. Ohio has proved the richest field for the collector in the last five years. Collectors, ten years ago, would designate every swirled flat or bulbous bottle as a Stiegel, but now attributions are made more carefully, and it is certain that most of the ones found in Ohio were made at Zanesville.

Surveying the history of old glass, one finds that its need brought about its manufacture, as is true of most other commodities. In 1815, a group of Zanesville citizens decided that a glassmaking industry could operate with profit there, supplying the need for bottles of the traveler on the National Road. In 1822 the plant bore the name of Shepard and Company, though it was commonly referred to as the White Glass Works; with some changes in ownership, it operated until 1851.

"This house," Mrs. Knittle tells us, "made bottles and flasks and domestic hollow ware for thirty-four years, unquestionably turning out much of the fine, early glass which is now being found in Ohio, and evolving types and designs

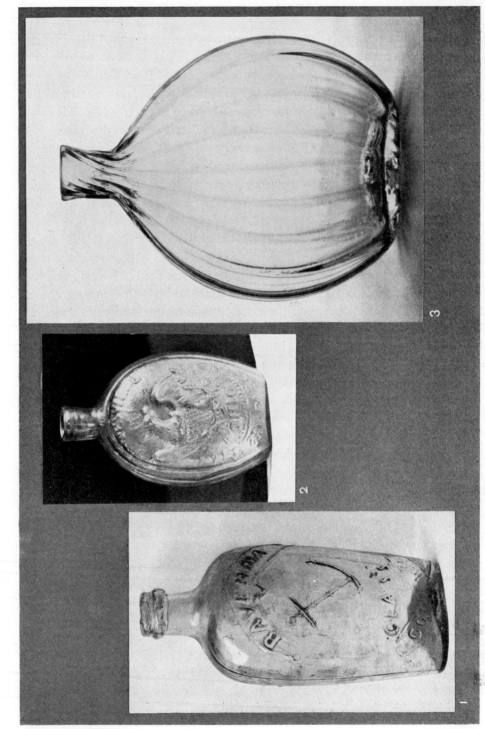

PLATE 14—Early Ohio glass bottles. Fig. 1, Ravenna bottle with anchor and Ravenna Glass Company. Fig. 2, Zanesville eagle flask; reverse, Masonic emblem. Fig. 3, Zanesville perpendicularly fluted bottle. (Rhea Mansfield Knittle)

which differed from the blown flint glass and flasks of other furnaces . . . . It has now been proved that this house produced the mid-Western type of bowl, pitcher, cruet, and pan, in some respects similar to the production of the Greensboro (Pennsylvania) Glass Works; and that it frequently expanded types from pattern molds. Zanesville's output, like that of Keene, Cambridge, and Greensboro, has until very recently never been adequately appreciated."[4] Mrs. Knittle has recently discovered that another important glass factory was incorporated in Zanesville in 1816.

The bulbous swirled bottles are beautiful in line and color. Those early glassblowers were certain and confident as to grace of line. The old glass may have bubbles or other imperfections, but they really enhance its beauty, the bubbles or tears breaking up the light just that much more. One of the Shepard and Company bottles eagerly sought is the one bearing the Masonic arch and other emblems on one side, and the eagle on the other. It was made in pint and half-pint sizes, and in several shades of green and amber colors, sometimes blue or purple. The ever-popular motif in the early crafts, the cornucopia, was the decoration used on another of their bottles, with the basket of fruit on the reverse. The bottles having such raised patterns were made by blowing the molten glass into iron molds on the inside of which the patterns was incised. The chestnut-shaped flask, and the more common eagle bottles were also made by this firm. The great need for bottles is understood when it is recalled that they were used for many more purposes than at present. Every corner cupboard had its quota of "bitters" bottles, and macasser oil for the hair, and even spices and other supplies were kept in bottles in the absence of paper cartons (Plate 14).

Zanesville had several other glasshouses. One of them was the firm of Murdock and Cassel, which made window glass primarily, but some bottles as well. The Putnam Flint Glass Works put out "Milk pans with reamed edges, wide-necked and rather straight-sided pitchers, chemical apparatus, druggists' supplies, pickle and capers bottles, candlesticks, cruets, sugar bowls, glass balls, hollow glass dippers, glass globes, bottles and many other commodities."[5]

At Ravenna there developed a glass concern, the Diamond Glass Company, which became noted for window glass and bottles. Again Mrs. Knittle gives this information: "The windows in the Ohio building at the Philadelphia Centennial Exposition of 1876 were furnished by this works."[6] They made an unusual bottle, long-necked and bulbous in shape, known as the calabash. Jenny

---

[4] *Early American Glass,* Rhea Mansfield Knittle, p. 374.
[5] *Early American Glass,* Rhea Mansfield Knittle, p. 378.
[6] *Early American Glass,* Rhea Mansfield Knittle, p. 384.

Lind's portrait decorated one of their calabash shapes, and was one more souvenir of the triumphant tour of this country by the Swedish singer; everything from beds to bottles was named for her.

Steubenville became a center for glassmaking, probably for the same reason that Sandwich, Massachusetts, did—because of the location of sand and fuel, and the opportunity for cheap transportation by water. About 1850, the A. J. Beatty glass factory boasted of a flourishing business in blown and pressed glass tableware, specializing in tumblers and goblets. The physical advantages of the site of Steubenville made it possible for this factory to produce a high-grade glass goblet that could be sold cheaply, and soon this factory was producing enough to supply the whole country, becoming the leader in the manufacture of goblets. The Beatty Company made almost every known design in goblets (Fig. 2, Plate 9). Most of the early glass tableware is much heavier than the modern. The goblets seem as steady and stable as the people of the time. They seem to have the Puritanical solidity that goes with pewter, and spinning wheels, and coverlets. The sheer weight of the salt cellars give them stability, and there would be little danger of "upsetting the salt." The early pressed glass has a laciness in pattern that is very attractive. Because it was inexpensive, it was carelessly handled, and perfect pieces that have been handed down are not abundant.

NEEDLEWORK AND WEAVING

When thoughts revert to the pioneer women, one pictures them with their spinning, knitting, weaving, or sewing; and around them are grouped their daughters or servants, whom they are instructing in these utilitarian crafts.

The wife of the pioneer had to face the problem of seeing all her family respectably clothed. This problem could not be met by going to the shop and buying every necessary garment. No — she had to card the flax and the wool first, spin them into thread, then dye it and weave it into cloth, before she was ready even to begin a garment. It is difficult for one to realize that the whole textile industry that today keeps thousands of mills and tens of thousands of workers busy, was once, in this country an entirely domestic function.

Vast quantities of the linen-thread output of the spinning wheel were woven into sheets, towels, tablecloths, and bolts of cloth to be made into garments as needed. The quality of the cloth varied from that of the fine tablecloth to the coarse straw tick or grain sack. If the weaving could not be done by the family, the raw material was taken to a weaver; or the work was done by an itinerant weaver who went from house to house and did the stock of weaving for the household. Few decorative effects were attempted in weaving; plain homespuns were the principal products. The spun woolen thread was woven into blankets and flannel for wearing apparel. Occasionally, one can find such a blanket yet: the threads are uneven, but the fabric is soft and lovely. Linsey-woolsey was a coarse cloth of cotton and wool, or linen and wool, and had splendid wearing qualities.

The woolen thread was twisted into hanks and hanks of yarn which had to be knitted into socks, stockings, wristlets, hoods, mittens, garters, and long nubias, to say nothing of old socks that needed new toes and heels! It is no surprise that the women never sat down without picking up their knitting. A decorative element entered into the knitting in borders and purling, in intricate shell patterns on the mitten backs, and in beautiful, knitted laces either of linen or wool. An accomplishment to be proud of was the knitting of the dainty silk reticules and purses. Crocheting had fewer votaries than knitting, though it is closely allied to it; in some instances the effect is so similar that it is difficult to say whether it is one or the other.

The ornamentation of wearing apparel with embroidery was only another phase of turning to advantage everything they had, and in the absence of any other means of embellishment they turned to what they had, the needle. Many a waistcoat and petticoat were elaborately embroidered. When the polonaise was in fashion, petticoats were exposed to view and needed much decoration. Baby clothes came in for lavish adornment, most meticulous work in bands of embroidery, fine edgings, and rows of tiny ruffles and plaits. Needlecases were delicate, beautiful little book-like affairs, covered with embroidery. It was the fashion to be an expert needlewoman, and fashion played just as important a part in the affairs of the day as it does now.

Poorly heated log houses made it necessary to have a bountiful supply of warm bedding; the comfort of the family depended on the women making these things, so they were a natural development. The stern and rugged life of the pioneer woman did not crush her love for color; it found expression in the making of quilts which contained combinations of bright-colored "oil-boiled" calicoes, and quaint prints. The interest in quilt-making was intense, from the beginning of collecting the "pieces," making the blocks, setting them together, and through the patient hours of tedious quilting, to the completed product displayed for admiration.

There are between three and four hundred patchwork patterns with specific names, such as "Four-patch," "Nine-patch," "Ocean Wave," "Monkey-wrench," "Star of Bethlehem," "Anchor," "Log-cabin," and so on to an infinite variety.

The "Nine-patch" was by far the most common of all the patterns for cotton quilts, while the "Log-cabin" found greatest favor in making silk and wool quilts. Some of the quilts were made in the manner of appliqué, especially where the design called for curved lines that could not be managed in piecing (Plate 12). The pieced blocks were usually quilted in parallel diagonal lines; the plain blocks and borders offered an opportunity for much fancy quilting in designs of feathers, shells, fans, pineapples, diamonds, ocean wave, hearts, and many other motifs. The making of bedcoverings was universally engaged in, so the artistic touch to be found in quilting is thoroughly representative of folk art.

Perhaps no output of the early craftswomen carries so much romance and so much genuine interest as the coverlet (Plate 15). Coverlet weaving seems to be a purely American art expression, though the weaves came from the early European forms. The making of a coverlet represented a year of labor. Flax had to be grown, hackled and spun into thread for the linen warp; sheep must be raised, sheared, and the wool washed, carded, spun for the weft of the coverlet; roots and the barks of trees must be gathered to produce the dyes; then came the joy of expressing herself in the weaving. The Ohio woman was as faithful to her loom as was Penelope to hers.

What is known as the four-harness loom was the typical household loom, and on it the interesting overshot patterns were made. The complexity of a harness loom depends on the number of harnesses it carries; two-harness makes the plain, or tabby weave of coverlet. The overshot patterns were produced by skips or floats in colored material, usually dark work over a tabby weave of cotton or linen. The overshot patterns were never ugly.

In the double-weave coverlet there are two distinct and separate webs (one of white cotton or linen, the other usually of dark-blue wool), that lie one above the other and interlace along the edges of the figures composing the pattern. The two webs may be pulled apart over the blocks in the pattern. Only the more skilled weavers could make the double-weave. The "summer-and-winter" weave resembles the double-weaving in that it is double-faced, the pattern being reversed, but it does not have the two webs. It is one of the most beautiful weaves, and apparently an American development.

In the second quarter of the nineteenth century, the professional weaver became established, sometimes permanently, or again as a wanderer. The Jacquard apparatus to use on looms in weaving figured goods was too complicated for the domestic weaver, so the housewife took her wool, all spun and dyed ready for the weaving, to the professional weaver, often a foreigner, who wove his

PLATE 15—Ohio coverlets. Fig. 1, Simple overshot weave. Fig. 2, Double weave with popular pine tree border. Fig. 3, Elaborate flower and wreath pattern of professional weaver. Fig. 4, Birds in nest and town border much used in Ohio. (Ohio State Museum)

name, county, state, and date into the corners of the coverlet. This was the period of the gorgeous coverlet, the conventional and geometric designs of the home weaver being replaced by the rather florid designs of the professional. Schoolhouses, steepled churches, flying eagles waving *"e pluribus unum,"* scrolls, tulips, medallions, and roses were placed satisfactorily in borders and allover patterns.

The names of the designs are as poetic and fantastic as one can imagine. A lovers' knot with a pine-tree border was the favorite pattern for the double-weave coverlets. For the single weave, the "chariot wheel" circle predominates; it consists of a circle having two diameters crossing each other at right angles and resembling the Greek letter theta. After all, certain forms are common to all art through all the ages. Some of the small, geometric designs of the home weaver bear quite prosaic names, such as "Cat Track," "Double Chain," "Snow Storm," "Hen Scratch"; a little more impressive are "Rising Sun," "Blazing Star," "Ocean Wave"; there are historical ones made by the professional weaver —"Lafayette's Victory," "Perry's Victory," "Bonaparte's March," "Boston Town," "Whig Rose," "Rose Eagles"; the list could be extended to a hundred at least, all reflecting certain influences of the time.[7]

The resourcefulness of the pioneer housewife is again demonstrated in making the vegetable dyes which she used; one can never mistake the coverlet colors, for they are always the same. She knew how to obtain several colors from the same ingredients, using a mordant such as copperas, alum, blue vitriol, and cream of tartar. In her three-cornered cupboard could be found madder, turmeric, indigo, and other dyestuffs, but she was not dependent upon them, for she could gather peach leaves and swartweed for yellow, butternut hulls and hemlock bark for brown, wax myrtle for blue, pokeberry root for a magenta red, and many other things for substitutes as good as anything she could buy.

Aside from the coverlet, there is probably no single object of needlework that holds so much glamour as the sampler (Plate 16). It is a piece of needlework made to preserve the patterns of the letters and numbers used in marking the linens. The making of a sampler was no small part of a young woman's education, for she was expected to spin the flax and weave the linen for her masterpiece. There were orderly rows of the letters of the alphabet, small, capital, and script, then the numbers, and little figures of trees, houses, or

[7] Weaving, perhaps the oldest of all the arts, has woven for itself a colorful history. The making and the decoration of textiles has interested human ingenuity since the dawn of history. It is no matter of surprise, therefore, that there are in Ohio today splendid artists fascinated with weaving; a few of them are Anna Riedel of Yellow Springs, Sophia Flurschutz of Newark, Mary Gale and Margaret Fisher of Columbus, and Gunhild Tiberg who does Swedish weaving in Cleveland.

PLATE 16—Sampler. Note economy of space in the lettering. (Author)

baskets to fill in the vacant spaces; the whole enhanced by a surrounding border. After the influence of Isaac Watts resulted in theological discussion everywhere, pious verses were worked upon the samplers, and they gradually degenerated into moral and religious doggerel almost entirely.

Still another phase of needlework was the making of carpets and rugs. In the colored stripings of the rag carpets much ingenuity was shown, both in the stripes of the chain or warp, and in the stripes made by the rags, but more often the carpets were the familiar hit-and-miss pattern. The rag sewings and quilting parties were the social events of the community, and here tongues wagged as industriously as needles. Rugs represented a gain in luxury and comfort, and so became ornamental as well as useful. The size, proportions, and the stripes of the braided rug were carefully calculated. The hooked rug was a place for the imagination to run riot in an effort to make a decorative pattern of the design (Plate 17). The process of making was very simple. By means of a hook, strips of cloth were pulled through the meshes of a coarse cloth, such as burlap, which had been stretched and tacked to a wooden frame. Loops of the cloth pulled through were left to make the surface of the rug. The rug makers made their own designs: flowers, animals, geometrical figures, and scrolls, were the favorite motifs. Red roses seemed most popular of the flowers, since the remnants of the red-flannel underwear could be worked up in them. Animals as mythical in anatomy as the phœnix bird were seen; tawny lions, black cats, shepherd dogs, antlered stags, and spotted horses were attempted with more or less success in the drawing. Allover floral effects were satisfactory in design, so were the basket patterns.

The women attained a higher degree of proficiency in needlework than in any other of the minor arts. One is likely to lose sight of the absorbing interest which needlework held for them, since all the needs are met now by the manufactured article. Should not they be envied for the joy which they must have experienced in creating things? Does not the modern woman fail to receive such pleasure in buying everything she needs just ready to use? It is not so long ago, either, that everything in use was manufactured in the home and thus stamped with a rare and individual value. The days of our beginnings are not far away.

It is because the pioneer craftsmen endeavored to create beauty in the common objects of daily use, and found happiness in such self-expression, that they are considered early American artists.

PLATE 17—Old hooked rugs. (Author)

CHAPTER III

A Panoramic View of Architectural
Movements Before 1900

ARCHITECTURE, like all art, never stands still, but constantly evolves. The difficulty in following it makes the pursuit even more intriguing. It is always interesting to trace the architectural developments in a new land; especially is this true of Ohio, where one can note the transplanted tendencies over long periods.

Ohio, the pioneer state in the great Northwest Territory, has little architectural heritage. The Indians who inhabited this area were not a building race and left no remains of architecture. The French missionaries left little influence on building activities; nor did the Moravians, who made the first settlement in Ohio, at Schoenbrunn, Tuscarawas County, in 1772. A group of small log dwellings were clustered about two larger log houses: the one of sufficient size to shelter most of the small community when they congregated for worship, the other a building large enough to accommodate the children who went to school. Thus the first church and schoolhouse in Ohio were erected at Schoenbrunn. The Moravians were a peace-loving sect who held conscientious objections to war; consequently their position became embarrassing during the Revolution. Fearing for the safety of the whole settlement, they decided to abandon it and start a colony elsewhere. The town disappeared in 1780, and for more than a century the very location of Schoenbrunn, "Beautiful Spring," was unknown. By means of an old surveyor's chart found in Pennsylvania, in 1923, it was possible to find the exact original site and rebuild the first town in Ohio. The cabins have been rebuilt as nearly as possible like the original ones, the ancient log church accurately restored, and the crude log schoolhouse reconstructed. The Ohio State Archæological and Historical Society preserves for future generations the rebuilt town as a state park.

The first permanent settlers came from New England, and the neighboring states on the east—New York, Pennsylvania, and Virginia. A simple building to furnish shelter was naturally their first architectural problem. There was no money nor need for pretentious buildings. The land was covered with thick woods, and since the land had to be cleared before the pioneers could begin to cultivate their farms, they used the resources at hand, the cut timber, for building purposes. The forests furnished many fine woods — walnut, maple, oak, poplar, and other useful varieties for building. The long winter months gave the husbandmen a chance to fell the trees and get the logs ready for their rude log cabins. There was plenty of stone for foundations and plenty of good clay and fuel to make bricks for the fireplaces and chimneys.

The splendid community spirit of the time evidenced itself when the logs for the cabin were prepared and all was in readiness. Mr. Howells gives an interesting description of the raising of a log cabin: "Their houses and barns were built of logs, and were raised by the collection of many neighbors together on one day, whose united strength was necessary to handling of the logs. As every man was ready with his axe and understood this work, all came together within the circle where the raising was to be done, and all worked together with equal skill. The best axman was given charge of the placing of the logs on the wall, and some one of experience took the direction. The logs of the width and length of the house were usually of different lengths. Those intended for the two sides were placed in a convenient place, some distance from the foundation; those for the ends, in another place. The two side-logs were put in place at the back and front; the end logs were notched down in their places. At the corners, the top of the log, as soon as it was put in place at the back and the front, would be dressed up by the corner man, and when the next logs were rolled up they would be notched, which notch would be turned downwards upon the saddle made to receive it, where the corner man would saddle the log ready for the next. This kept the logs in their place like a dovetail and brought them together so as to form a closer wall. The ends of the skids would be raised on each new log as it was laid down to make a base for the next. The logs on these skids would be rolled as long as the men could handle them from the ground, but when the wall was too high, then they would use forks, made by cutting a young notched tree, with which the logs could be pushed up. By using a fork at each end of the log, it could be pushed up with ease and safety. The men understood handling timber, and accidents seldom happened, unless the logs were icy or wet, or the whiskey had gone around too often."[1]

All the spaces between the logs were filled with chinking, of mud and chips. The roofs were of clapboards. Often a lean-to was added in the rear. Sometimes the floor was only the bare ground, or again it was a puncheon floor of smoothed slabs. Seldom were there more than two windows and one doorway. The cabin consisted of one room, which served all purposes of cooking, dining, sleeping, and living. At one side of it was a great fireplace, around which hung the iron kettles and pans, and other cooking utensils; in a corner was a bed

---

[1] *Life in Ohio, 1813-'40,* William Cooper Howells, p. 145.

PLATE 18—Log cabin still standing in Coshocton County. (M. B. Binning)

with a trundle-bed shoved under it (Plate 12); while the center of the room was graced by a homemade table and chairs. There are very few original log cabins remaining in Ohio, but these few make it possible to visualize the homes of the early settlers (Plate 18). Common to almost every community was a log cabin which took on aspects of defense: the blockhouse. It was a two-story structure, in which the second story projected several feet beyond the first story in order to combat the hostile Indian more effectively. An original blockhouse is preserved in Sherman-Heineman Park, Mansfield.

When General Rufus Putnam and his band made the first permanent settlement in the state at Marietta in 1788, they proceeded at once to build the first stockade fort. General Putnam knew too well the fighting nature of the Indian to place much confidence in the seeming friendliness with which he and his men were greeted upon their landing. General Putnam wrote to his friends in the East that this fortification, which they called Campus Martius, was the "handsomest pile of buildings west of the Allegheny Mountains, and would soon be the strongest fortification in the United States."[2] The Rufus Putnam house is all that remains of Campus Martius and is said to be the oldest house in the Northwest Territory, though that honor is also claimed by the Ohio Land Company office just across the street. Leading authorities hold that the Putnam house was erected in 1788, and that the land office could hardly have been built before 1790. The latter building contains priceless historical records, as all of the land grants in the original Northwest Territory were made in this office. They are both very simple frame buildings. The Rufus Putnam house was built by erecting a skeleton frame of large timbers and filling in the spaces between with upright boards. This was all covered with clapboards on the outside, but on the inside the walls were veneered with vertical boards about six inches wide and two inches thick, with a little bead at the joint. The doors were of the six-panel type, the hinges were strap or L, and the latches were simply cut out of sheet brass.

Settlements did not become in any degree permanent until the power of the Indian was broken in the victory of General Anthony Wayne, and the treaty of Greenville in 1795. Up to this time architecture could scarcely be classed as a fine art because it was concerned only in the creation of a shelter. Naturally such early building was engulfed by the tide of civilization. It leaves little impression upon Ohio architecture, though it was the first and most natural manifestation.

Since most of the early settlers in Ohio came from eastern states, one

---

[2] "Marietta," A. B. Barnard, *Columbus Motor Travel,* May, 1930.

may expect to find a reflection of the styles predominating in those states from 1788 to 1875. Each of the following stylistic waves passed over the eastern states, and each in turn was carried later into the Ohio country: Colonial, Post-Colonial, Georgian, Classical (Roman), Greek Revival, and Romantic, which includes successively Gothic and Romanesque.

COLONIAL AND POST-COLONIAL WORK

Theoretically, the style of Colonial architecture was developed by the colonists and, accurately speaking, ended with the Declaration of Independence. The style continued, however, for some time; people went on building in much the same manner as they were accustomed to before the Revolution. Within a generation or two, conditions were changed, and a different spirit crept into the old Colonial-like work. It was but natural that the settlers in Ohio should erect the same style of houses in which they had lived in the East, so a direct influence of Colonial resulted. Most of the early work extant in Ohio may be called Post-Colonial.

Until the sawmill was established in the new land, progress was very slow, but as soon as it brought proper materials to hand, effective work immediately became apparent.

New England Colonial building was of English extraction, but it developed under changed conditions in a new country and became a distinct style. It was largely a simple, wooden architecture. The cottage type seems to have been one of the earliest phases of domestic architecture in America. It was not based on models drawn from the mother country; it was characterized by a long, sweeping roof sloping down in the rear and cutting a corner off each story on its way. This type persisted and formed the basis of later interesting designs.

The Ohio pioneers were mechanics and carpenters as well as farmers. With the tools they brought with them they constructed simple buildings, utilitarian in character, in the straightforward, honest manner of craftsmanship that is evidenced in the New England buildings. There is no doubt that they made use of Asher Benjamin's practical books for carpenters. Many moldings with the same profiles as the ones in his books, as well as fan lights, mantels, and other details and motifs that are similar, are found on the early buildings in Ohio. The carpenters displayed much skill in all steps of their work, from the foundation to the finishing.

Usually the houses were frame, one-story, or one-and-a-half, or two-story structures, though occasionally there were two-story brick houses. The plan generally followed was to have a chimney in the middle of the house. Against the center chimney, and starting from a small vestibule, was a winding stairway. To the right were two rooms, and upon the left were two more. The second floor was very similar. In some of the early houses there was only one room on each side of the chimney. For the larger houses the hall was carried through the house, and there were two chimneys, one at each end of the house, built on the outside. The upstairs rooms had smaller fireplaces. Frequently the ground floor space was enlarged by placing a lean-to or shed with a single-pitched roof against one wall of the gable-roof structure. Several old houses show the frequent, though unattractive custom of extending the lean-to far enough beyond one end of the main house to permit a side-door facing the front and opening into the rear part of the dwelling. This addition, known as a "jut-by," gained some room, but at the expense of severe, ugly angles. This arrangement was an infraction of the first rule of Colonial building, namely, that the two halves of a building must perfectly balance on each side of a perpendicular line drawn in the center of the elevation. The one-story wing with a recessed porch was a feature of many early Ohio farmhouses.

As in the New England Colonial, there was always an attempt to enhance and beautify the front doorway. Frequently the doorway was the one spot of ornamentation. The first trim was the simple flat casings; then the architrave came into frequent use; next, flat pilasters, and soon complete entablatures and pediments. Vertical side-lights and fan-lights over the doors were often quite elaborate, with a Palladian three-part window over the doorway. The gable-roof porch over the doorway made use of interesting columns and other architectural forms. The front doors of the better houses were deeply recessed. The old Buckingham house in Zanesville has a recessed porch which, according to local tradition, was copied from one in Boston, Massachusetts. The limited extent of this work makes it impossible to cite many examples.

In driving along any of the state's highways, one may see occasionally a fine old Post-Colonial doorway. The formative architecture of Ohio has not received much attention, either in writings or in upkeep. Most of the early houses have become neglected and decayed structures, or restored beyond all semblance of their original quality and homelikeness. When one comes upon a fine example of an old house, there is a thrill and romance lingering around it that no new house can furnish. John Burroughs said: "The older the house, the more genial nature looks around it." The longer a house stands, the greater the harmony between it and nature. One of the stateliest of all early homes in Ohio, is Adena, built in 1798, at Chillicothe, for the residence of Governor

PLATE 19—Adena, Governor Worthington's home, Chillicothe. (Hathaway Art Studio)

Worthington (Plate 19). The solid stone walls are three feet thick. A magnificent view from the terraced garden at the side of the house, presents the scene that is used for the Great Seal of Ohio.

In the northeastern section of Ohio, known as the Western Reserve, there are examples of early architecture that compare favorably with those of New England. This is not surprising, for the population of that section was drawn largely from Connecticut. Especially fine in their Colonial character are several churches with towers suggesting the Christopher Wren types. The old Congregational Church in Atwater, with its classic portico and belfry tower, recalls the best traditions of the New England meetinghouses. The Congregational Church at Tallmadge has a similar tower and a classic façade (Plate 20). It was built by Colonel Lemuel Porter, who came to the Western Reserve from Waterbury, Connecticut, and after completing this edifice, took the contract for building some of the halls of Western Reserve College. The fine old church at Tallmadge stands in the central circular commons of the town, eight roads meeting at this point. One interesting feature of it is the variation in the placing of the volutes of the Ionic columns. It is curious that from soil that hitherto had not known anything more pretentious than a log cabin, there should suddenly spring, like Minerva from the head of Jupiter, these beautiful edifices. The early settlers in the Western Reserve secured a refinement in these old structures that seldom has been equalled since.

The Capitol of Virginia was the measuring-stick, or norm, for all Post-Colonial work, and the date of its completion (1789) marks the beginning of Post-Colonial architecture. Thenceforward the proportions became more slender and less consistent, giving way to forms more closely approaching the ancient Roman, and the French of the day. The portico, seldom used before 1790, became a characteristic feature.

It could not be expected that there would be found in early Ohio great houses like those that gave distinction to such old, historic towns as Salem and Boston, where opportunities for acquiring wealth were much greater than in a new country remote from the coast. Though not so pretensious, the majority of the houses followed closely the fashions prevailing in the section from which the builders came.

GEORGIAN STYLE

The Georgian style was, in reality, the classic architecture revived in England during the reigns of Kings George I, II, and III; hence the name Georgian. It was a type far more pretentious and stately than the Post-Colonial. The style

PLATE 20—Church at Tallmadge. Etching by Rudolph Stanley-Brown. (Artist)

was used in the New England states and spread to the South, where it developed to its best. The wealthy Englishmen who settled the southern states built palatial and substantial manor houses. They frequently brought with them from England, not only a knowledge of the true Georgian style, but also plans and the builders for their homes. Because of its extreme formality, the style required radical modifications to make it suitable for domestic architecture in the southern colonies. There were three phases of Georgian, which may be briefly characterized thus: the first phase used a great deal of paneling; the second used very little paneling, but added a large overmantel as a prominent architectural feature; the third used no overmantel. It is the last phase that may be traced in Ohio, finding its way through western Virginia and Kentucky.

Several houses of south-central Ohio, which was the old Virginia Military Land grant, suggest Georgian style. A typical one is the old Renick house, built in 1832, between Circleville and Chillicothe. It has many features that make it an unusual building—a low roof, broken by a single dormer, corner pavilions, and recessed porches with supporting stone columns. The brick walls have a trim of cut stone. The plan consists of a large room, twenty-five feet square, in the center. At three corners are small rooms, ten feet square, which give to the exterior the appearance of projecting pavilions; between them, on two sides, are recessed porches. The exterior walls of the pavilions rise above the roof and thus give a false-front effect. The interior trim shows the handiwork of the skilled craftsman. The spaciousness of the central room, its interesting paneled doors, mantel with as fine ladder carving as can be made today, and moldings, give it unusual beauty.

The inspiration for the handsome old Buckingham house, in Newark, must have come from the Carolinas or Virginia. It is a well-preserved house, which retains the slender, graceful proportions of the early Colonial work. The tall columns, and the delicate wrought-iron railing guarding the second-floor balcony, are distinctly Georgian features. The imposing Reeves home in Lancaster also reflects Georgian influence. It was built in 1833 by John Graybill Reeves, and is today occupied by one of his descendants. The house was built after duplicate plans drawn up by an English architect for the home of an English banker. It is claimed that this house is one of the earliest Ohio buildings (if not the first) to use Ionic columns. The interior contains a round staircase well of great beauty. There is a brick residence of the Georgian style on what is now called the Bryn Mawr farm, just south of Granville. This residence was erected in 1847, by Elias Fassett, the first president of the Baltimore and Ohio Railroad. It has the true charming Georgian air of hospitality.

The paneling, and the woodwork generally, of the Georgian houses, as of the old Colonial, exhibits many irregularities and often a lack of symmetry. These carpenters did not hesitate to make one panel deeper than another and, generally speaking, exhibited a marked freedom in the working out of their designs, in which respect their work seems to us to be decidedly modern. The two-story porch with full-length columns was a feature of the Georgian style.

Occasionally a bit of Dutch influence is seen in Ohio farmhouses. It is always individual and bears little relation to the Georgian. One feature is the reduction of the cornice projection. Sometimes the gable-end wall extends above the roof and is finished in steps. The theory of Dutch moldings is to make fine parallel lines and shadows, beads and fillets, all in delicate scale; they give a striking effect to the framing of the openings.

CLASSICAL AND GREEK REVIVAL STYLES

The Colonial, Post-Colonial, and Georgian styles met all the requirements of the American people, architecturally, before the Revolution and during the early federal period. As the wealth of the country increased, there was a feeling aroused for a more elaborate building program. There was an extreme consciousness of the new republic, and with it arose a wish to symbolize it on every hand; for instance, note the use of the eagle as a decorative motif in all the crafts.

A prevailing sentiment urged the need of a kind of architecture worthy of the new American Republic. The leaders realized that the Colonial style was provincial. Thomas Jefferson was one of the first leaders in this movement. He felt there was a close analogy between the new American Republic and the old Roman Republic, and that the national style of architecture in America might very fittingly be based upon the ancient Roman. Jefferson was in a position to have his wishes considered when commissions for buildings were awarded. When he was in France, as ambassador from the United States, he became enthusiastic over the remains of Roman architecture there, especially the Maison Carrée at Nîmes. He made many drawings of this building and used them later as an aid in designing the Virginia State Capitol.

The result was a veritable wave of classicism in American architecture. Stone was more generally used, and colonnades, domes, and cupolas were adopted as indispensable features of public buildings and churches. Residences felt its influence too. The movement soon found its way into Ohio, and there reached its climax about 1835-'40. The classical style is characterized by extensive use of the Roman orders, massive porticos, pediments, entablatures, and Roman moldings and ornaments. Ohio has many buildings bearing these Roman attributes. The American-Classic revival, as differentiated from the Georgian-Classic, came about largely through the development of friendly relations with France, and a distaste for things English during the War of 1812.

That the Romans borrowed the orders and other classic forms from the Greeks, who were the originators of them, had long been known through the ancient writings of Vitruvius, in the first century B.C. Stuart and Revett, two English architects, made an extensive first-hand study of Greek ruins, and in 1732 published volumes of measured drawings of the Greek orders and other architectural forms in their true proportions. These books were brought to America, and used by such architects as Benjamin Latrobe, whom Jefferson made the Surveyor of Public Buildings in the United States. Thus, the first professional office of architect was established in this country. Robert Mills and William Strickland, pupils of Latrobe, carried on the traditions of the Greek revival. Soon the Greek classic forms were the fashion, and the old Roman forms were supplanted by them. The Greek Revival style was sustained past the middle of the nineteenth century. There were evidences everywhere of the Classical and Greek Revival phases of architecture in Ohio. It is only a natural consequence, since the early work in Ohio dates from 1800 to 1850, contemporary with the same movements in the East.

One of the finest existing examples of the Greek Revival in American architecture, is the Ohio State Capitol, in Columbus. The story of the construction of the Capitol, is a long series of delays, changes of plans, and complications. The State Legislature, on January 26, 1838, passed an act providing for the erection of a new State House. Prizes were offered for the best plans submitted; the plan adopted was a modification of the three prize winners. The estimated cost of the building was $450,000, but it seems that estimates then, as now, were far short of the actual cost, which was $1,359,121.45.

The employment of two hundred convicts from the State Penitentiary was recommended, and the building commission contracted for the stone to be brought from a quarry three miles above the city, on the Scioto River. People were much gratified at the prospects of a new State House. Work began in the spring of 1839, and proceeded so rapidly that the corner stone of the building was laid on July 4, 1839. The laying of the corner stone was made an important occasion, with speeches, martial music, a military force, and a good dinner. Five or six thousand people were present, and even the weather was favorable for the event.

Plate 21—Ohio State House, Columbus. (Author)

The next ten years saw very little accomplished, and the patience of the people was very nearly exhausted. The legislature repealed the act providing for the new Capitol, in spite of the fact that forty thousand dollars had already been spent upon it. Then an agitation to remove the Capitol from Columbus suspended work for almost six years. A second act for the erection of a state house was passed in February, 1846. In 1848 the work was pushed with considerable energy. *The Ohio Statesman* of June 15, 1853, said: "The stone-cutters make the yard ring with the clink of their chisels. The hewn stones rise upward to their places. The oxen and the locomotives are busy at work. The boys in stripes move pretty briskly for the warm weather. The central columns are rising upward."

On January 6, 1857, there was a formal opening of the building. It combines "that sublime massiveness, that dignity of form and features, that beautiful symmetry of proportions, which constitute architectural excellence in a high degree." The building, one hundred and eighty-four feet wide and three hundred and four feet long, covers an area of a little less than one and one-third acres. It is surrounded by wide stone terraces, reached by flights of stone steps on all four sides. The east and west sides each have eight splendid Doric columns (Plate 21), the north and south sides each have four columns. The height of the columns is forty-two and a half feet, their diameter at the base is six and a half feet. The height of the building to the top of the cupola is one hundred and fifty-eight feet. The height from the rotunda floor to the eye of the dome is one hundred and twenty feet; the diameter of the rotunda is sixty-five feet.

In the center of the marble mosaic floor, immediately under the dome, is a circle. From the edge of the circle start the points of thirty-two pieces of marble representing the thirty-two states in the Union at the time the State House was built. In the center are thirteen blocks of marble symbolizing the original thirteen states, surrounding them are successive circles denoting territories added later, and the whole is enclosed by a circle representing the Constitution. In the original design of the Capitol a serious difficulty was encountered in determining the form and proportions of the dome or cupola. The architect had to avoid the erection of a spherical dome on the Grecian Doric order; however, he had it worked out satisfactorily, when a cry of economy frustrated his plans, and a poor makeshift of a cupola was added. *The Cincinnati Gazette* in 1849 calls it a "Chinese hat." The question thus raised in 1849 as to the fashion of the dome has been intermittently discussed ever since, without satisfactory results, and the Capitol of Ohio remains surmounted by a nondescript structure wholly out of keeping with the grand Grecian Doric style of the

PLATE 22—Sandusky County Courthouse, Fremont. (Finch Studio)

main part of the building. Historically, the building has great value as an example showing the development of American architecture.

Many county courthouses in the Greek Revival style were erected following the State House. Two notable ones were the Ashland County Courthouse at Ashland, and the Sandusky County Courthouse at Fremont. The former was a beautiful example, but unfortunately has been demolished to make way for a more modern structure. The latter may still be seen at Fremont, standing with dignity in the midst of new architectural styles (Plate 22). A worthy effort is being made to preserve another fine example of Greek Revival style, built in 1836, the Lafayette-Franklin Bank, Cincinnati.

Domestic architecture responded to the fashion of the Greek Revival to such an extent that Ohio has many examples, and one yields to the temptation to enumerate several of them. As "Westward the course of Empire takes its way," so does fashion, in this instance perhaps stirred by the classic home of Thomas Jefferson, Monticello. The notable characteristics of these residences are the fine, high-columned porticos, surmounted by a plain or ornamented pediment; columns of wood or stone; the main body of the house of simple, dignified design; and the utter lack of delicately detailed ornamentation so popular in the Georgian period.

A magnificent example in Cincinnati is the Charles P. Taft residence built *circa* 1830. Four stately columns support a portico with a pediment embellished by an elliptical window. The doorway, approached by a sweep of steps bordered with wrought-iron railings, is excellent; so, too, are the moldings around the pediment and along the cornice.

The first building in Columbus to lay claim to architectural pretensions was the residence, 306 East Broad Street, of Honorable Alfred Kelley, a man who left a strong impress upon the pioneer history of the state. This old mansion of Berea sandstone (Plate 23) was built about 1838. The approach to the house, set in spacious grounds and surrounded by shrubbery and forest trees, is one of dignity and grandeur. The façade, on the south side, has a portico consisting of four Ionic columns supporting a pediment. The well-proportioned columns are of solid stone, giving a real classic atmosphere. The three remaining sides of the house have recessed porticos with two Ionic columns each. The floors of the porticos are made of stone slabs, two and one-half by seven feet in dimensions. An unusual roof line is made by the attic over the central part of the building.

There is an interesting variety in the arrangement of the windows, which are set in sunken panels, with a plain panel sunk into the stone above the

PLATE 23—Kelly house, Columbus. (Author)

windows; the second-story windows are quite short. The interior presents much of its first magnificence: twelve-foot ceilings, wide hall, walnut stairway leading all the way to the attic, and fireplaces in every room. The mantels are crude imitations of classic motifs, but are pleasing, nevertheless. The cellar furnishes a real thrill; from it opened an underground railway tunnel used during the War by runaway slaves. The tunnel is about three feet wide, paved and arched over with brick, just high enough for a man to crawl through it. The cellar also furnishes a view of the massive foundation walls two and a half feet thick. This old house kept the escutcheon of Ohio stainless when Mr. Kelly pledged it for the payment of his note for some thirty thousand dollars, for money borrowed in New York to pay the overdue interest on the bonds of the state issued to build the Ohio canal system.

Nestled at the foot of the Welsh Hills, in Licking County, is the beautiful little town of Granville, renowned as a seat of learning since 1832, when Denison University was established there. The very atmosphere of the town reflects the subtle influence of culture and refinement emanating from its educational background. One would expect to find here the best in any field of endeavor, so it is no surprise to meet such a splendid example of classical influence in Ohio architecture as the old Alfred Avery House. The English architects, Benjamin Morgan and Son, built this house in 1841, at a cost of six thousand dollars. The house faces north, and is of frame construction, having very wide boards for siding. The façade presents a portico with four Ionic columns, undoubtedly inspired by the north porch of the Erechtheum, in Athens; the original columns were marvelous ones of black walnut. The akroterion (an ornament placed at the apex of the pediment) topping the gable is unusual and interesting, while the doorway copied from the Temple of the Winds, in Athens, is a delight. Surely, here the architect has successfully recaptured ancient beauty! Wings on the east and west sides of the house have been skilfully handled in the lower and less ornate Doric order. President McKinley, a connoisseur of architecture, pronounced it one of the most unique examples of architecture west of the Alleghanies (Plate 24).

The residence known as the George N. Guthrie homestead, Zanesville, is typical of the true Doric temple type of architecture as applied to residence work (Plate 25). From the foundation wall of huge stones rise the brick walls, thirteen inches thick. The façade consists of an imposing colonnade of four Doric columns, measuring twenty-one feet in height, and twenty-nine inches in diameter at the base. Entering the large living room, twenty-nine by seventeen feet, one is impressed with the ten-foot ceiling, beautifully paneled doors, the

PLATE 24—Avery house, Granville. (Author)

black marble mantel, original oak floor of hand-planed boards, and the ornate chandelier. The chandeliers caused much comment at the time, as they were the first ones for using gas to be installed in Zanesville.

The Wolverton home in Mount Vernon is one of the most attractive houses developed from the Greek Revival style. Tall, Ionic columns form a central portico, with a lower order on each side. An old stone house in Newark, now occupied by the Christian Science Church, is extremely simple, but perfect in proportion. Four heavy Doric columns support a pediment and make an effective façade. The Joseph Swift house at Vermilion, near Cleveland, is a fine Greek revival, one-story house built in 1841.

At Lancaster, are fine old houses similar, architecturally, to the ones already mentioned. However, the Ewing house, Lancaster, perhaps surpasses the others in historical significance. On the crest of a hill stands the handsome old brick house built by Thomas Ewing, United States Senator. Successive generations of the Ewing family have lived in the house. Scions of this family have been prominent in the national and state history; three sons born in the house became generals in the Union army. Here William Tecumseh Sherman was given a home and brought up by Thomas Ewing, who sent him to West Point. Sherman married the daughter of Thomas Ewing.

When compared with the famous mansions of New England, Pennsylvania, and Virginia, the Ohio houses may be simple and unpretentious, but designs were in most cases appropriately fitted to the sites, and the construction was substantial, the workmanship excellent. For several years, before and during the Civil War, and for a number of years afterward, very little building of architectural merit was done in Ohio. Conditions were so unsettled during this period that any style tendency was of short duration, and little of architectural quality developed.

THE ROMANTIC MOVEMENT: THE GOTHIC REVIVAL AND THE ROMANESQUE STYLE

The beginning of the Gothic Romantic movement may be traced back to England. Such romances as Sir Walter Scott's novels, *Waverley* and *Kenilworth,* were factors in turning the mind away from the classic ideals to the romantic. The pre-Raphaelite painters, Rossetti, Holman Hunt, and John Millais, exercised a strong influence toward the Romantic movement. Perhaps the greatest factor was the praise of the English and Italian Gothic styles by Ruskin, who claimed that the only true arch was the pointed arch.

In this country the Gothic developed into a hybrid style, denominated by some authorities as the Victorian Gothic. Many technical abuses were over-shadowed by a certain picturesqueness of towers and other features, and by an adaptation of the ideas of Mansard, the French architect.

The Smithsonian Institution at Washington is a notable example of this English Gothic influence. In Ohio there are many examples in county court-houses, a great many state institutions (among them the Columbus State Hos-pital, and the Institution for Feeble-Minded, Columbus) a few hospitals (one is the St. Francis Hospital, Columbus), and college buildings on nearly every campus, all built about 1870.

There is one notable variation of the style—University Hall, on the Ohio State University grounds, Columbus. On July 6, 1871, it was resolved that a college building be located "south of two walnut trees at the edge of the old orchard at the end of Neil Avenue." University Hall is the tangible result of this resolution. It is remembered by the old graduates as the building with the clock tower, and commonly called U Hall. J. Snyder was the architect. The characteristics of the building are its many towers; the central one containing the clock, and dominating many small ones, all of them square, and with very sharply pitched gable roofs. The roof of the building proper, with its many dormers, indicates a lingering Mansard influence (Plate 26).

Among residences, Mac-o-chee Castle, the old home of Colonel Don Piatt, near West Liberty, is a noted variant of this style. It is a stone building with those characteristic high, sharp-gabled, roofed towers. The most blasé person is thrilled by the associations connected with this castle, and the romantic his-tory of the Piatt family, which traces its family tree back to the Crusaders. The Piatts established themselves in this fertile valley in 1817. An old house of the cottage type, built by Judge Ben H. Piatt, in 1824, and a grist mill operated long before the Civil War, are still standing there. The Crusader traits made members of the Piatt family soldiers, jurists, poets, and leaders in every line of activity.

To obtain a comprehensive idea of the Romanesque movement in Ohio architecture, one must take a long look backwards, even to the eleventh and twelfth centuries in Southern France. The arts of the Middle Ages had long ceased to have any connection with the classic Greek and Roman art. In Italy, the ancient buildings were not used as models, but were pillaged and demolished as quarries for new edifices, chiefly of the medieval type, called the Romanesque.

Elie Faure describes the French Romanesque thus: "On this burnt earth of Southern France, which outlines itself against the sky with the sure lines that

PLATE 25—Guthrie house, Zanesville. (H. F. Parkins)

one finds again beside the bays of Greece, Gallo-Roman art united quite naturally the positiveness of Rome, Hellenic elegance, and the fresh vitality of the Gauls. It declined but little, if at all, upon the passage of the Arabs, who were adopted by this burning soil. Nothing could arrest the fever. Under its violent sun, the blood of nomadic Asia mingled with that of Greco-Latin Gaul."[3]

The Romanesque style was succeeded in France by the Gothic. It was not until a wave of Romanticism swept over France after the Revolution, that architecture turned again to the French Romanesque and adopted a free version of it. A people that had suffered the horrors of the Reign of Terror and endured so many drastic changes in government could not express its feelings in the calmness of classic art. It is well to recall that the term "romantic" was first adopted in literature as meaning opposed to classic, that is, not written in Latin, but in the Romance language, and from that came to be used to describe literature that was impassioned and demonstrative; in contrast, the classic examples were characterized by cold, unemotional representation.

The details of French Romanesque architecture varied considerably in the separate provinces, according as classic, Byzantine, or local influences prevailed, but usually one finds in this type pepper-pot turrets at the corners, projecting stories, painted or dentelated gables, painted or carved beams, and diamond windowpanes set in lead.

This fantastic style of the Romanesque was introduced into America about 1870 by a young American architect, Henry Hobson Richardson. Its introduction was a distinct surprise to people, and it created a furor. The love of novelty made the people grasp the Romanesque eagerly. Richardson was born in New Orleans in 1838. After finishing school at Harvard he went to Paris and entered the École des Beaux Arts. He remained there for six years, until 1865. This long and thorough training enabled him to rise far above his contemporaries, and to win commissions through competition because he could furnish good drawings and specifications. He worked with the state architect of France, from whom he acquired technique and rapidity.

Richardson's masterpiece is Trinity Church, Boston, It rises like a pyramid from every side. Its deep, round arches are based on the French Romanesque; the richness of the foliature and moldings compares favorably with some features of the old churches of Europe. The Romanesque has produced nothing better than Trinity Church.

The Romanesque style spread itself all over the country, to and beyond the Mississippi. Richardson himself carried it to Pittsburgh. One of the last

[3] *Medieval Art,* Elie Faure, p. 268.

PLATE 26—University Hall, Ohio State University, Columbus. (F. H. Haskett)

plans he drew was for an Ohio building, the Chamber of Commerce, Cincinnati (Plate 27). It had an animated sky line, a tall, picturesque tower, and dormers recalling those of the Albany Capitol. The dormers continued the same plane as the wall. It was a massive building, resembling some great and imposing castle built to outlast the centuries. It was built in 1887-'89, at a cost of $675,000. The material was undressed, pink Milford granite of severe aspect. The walls were rounded to a tower at each corner. The arcades of the main hall were powerful and impressive. The building burned in 1911, leaving only a shell; efforts to preserve it by making it into an observatory were never consummated, so the walls were razed.

At Dayton is an interesting library in the general style of Romanesque. Peters and Burns of Dayton were the architects. It is built of Dayton limestone laid in random range work, with Marquette red sandstone trimmings freely used, giving a very rich contrast. In Toledo is another very good Romanesque library. Orton Hall, Ohio State University, Columbus, is a good example of the style. It was built in 1891. The contrast of buff Amherst stone and dark Hocking Valley stone is very interesting. Some of the finest material to be quarried in Ohio is in the columns, walls, and ceiling of the vestibule. A striking feature is the round tower flanking the entrance; near the top are interlaced, carved arches; gargoyles are at regular intervals around the tower.

All the pretentious residences built about 1890 were of the Romanesque style. They are everywhere. The features were deep, round arches, heavy construction, and at one corner the inevitable tower much resembling the modern farm silo. A fine example is the building (once a residence) now occupied by the Massillon Women's Club, Massillon. It is built of rough, hewn stones; it has an interesting porch formed by deep, round arches, one at each end and three in front. The interior is decorated with heavily carved woodwork and dust-catching grilles that belong to that style. Cleveland showed a distinct preference for the Romanesque style, attested by many such residences on Euclid Avenue. In commercial architecture nearly every city affords one or more examples of Romanesque.

Richardson died nine years after the completion of Trinity Church, in 1877. His career lasted only a little more than ten years; but in that brief period he exerted an influence upon architecture which has not been equalled by any other artist, with the natural exception of Sir Christopher Wren. The public generally believes that Romanticists, in whatever field, refuse to bear the yoke of rules either because they have never learned them, or because they feel fettered by them. That is an erroneous opinion. A man must know before he can reform, and Richardson was one of the men who knew.

PLATE 27—Old Chamber of Commerce Building, Cincinnati. (Rombach and Groene)

The followers of Richardson were not so fortunate, for they made his ideas over-elaborate, especially in ecclesiastical architecture. The less skilled followers admired and exaggerated the most unsuitable features, until the country was filled with churches having towers *ad nauseam;* profiles lost refinement; columns became swollen ready to burst, and rough-hewn walls were everywhere. It is a safe assertion to make, that every county seat town in Ohio has a Richardsonian church. In connection with the Romanesque style, there developed a plan for Sunday school rooms known as the Akron Plan, because it was first used at Akron. Its invention is generally ascribed to Bishop Vincent of the Methodist Church. Classrooms, by this plan, were arranged around the floor and balcony of a high and large assembly room; they could be closed for class study or opened for general worship. Usually, this assembly room could be opened into the main auditorium of the church by means of folding or sliding doors or some ingenious device operating as a movable wall. The round-arched windows were filled with stained glass of garish color. Yellow woodwork of golden oak, curved pews, highly decorated organ and walls were other notes in bad taste. People turned back to the pointed Gothic as more "churchly" than the Romanesque, though that revulsion was based on over-elaboration and not on Richardson's real work.

The World's Fair at Chicago, 1893, proclaimed the death knell for the Romanesque style. For that exposition "The White City" was built in the classic style. It was so beautiful that people returned to their homes convinced that Greece and Rome furnished the best models in architecture, and the whole country selected the classic for all new buildings. One of the earliest results of this was the imposing railway station erected in Columbus in 1896. It was designed, with the Roman arch as the principal motif, by Daniel H. Burnham & Company, architects of the Chicago Fair.

The close of the century also marked the pathetic close of the story of the Romanesque style. It burst with brilliance like a summer morning, lived through a heyday of glory, then gradually fell into the shadows and died out. The modern mind is more interested in the real and the accurate than in the fanciful flights of the Romanesque.

CHAPTER IV

Development of Painting in Cincinnati up to 1900

EVERY one concedes the preëminence of Cincinnati over other western cities, during the middle and late nineteenth century, in the fields of art, literature, and public spirit. There are many valid reasons for this supremacy. Cincinnati was older than the other cities; for instance, Chicago was a mere fort and trading post when Cincinnati was a city of twenty-five thousand people with a definite social culture. Cincinnati and the Ohio River Valley had a slow, steady growth. To this region came settlers from Virginia, eastern Pennsylvania, and New England, bringing with them their culture and the ideals of the eastern states. This population had become thoroughly blended when it was followed in the forties by an influx of the best of the early German immigration. There had also been a smaller immigration of French settlers drifting down from Gallipolis. They all came West to establish homes. Cincinnati was never a land-speculating center, but from the beginning took on a permanent character.

Art in Cincinnati appears on the very early pages of the city's history, and runs like a romance through the entire chronicle. It is surprising to find a painter there as early as 1792, George Jacob Beck, who served with the scouts of Wayne's army in the Maumee campaign and the Battle of Fallen Timbers. After his military career, he lived in Cincinnati until 1800, being well known for his landscapes of the Ohio Valley, and it is maintained that he decorated the noted barge of General Wilkinson. Then for a time the New England portrait painter, John Neagle, painted in Cincinnati, his reputation being based largely on a picture called "Pat Lyon the Blacksmith," which was frequently reproduced in engraving and lithography.

"In 1817, there came to the city a gentleman by the name of Aaron H. Corwin, whose talent led many of the principal citizens to permit him to paint their portraits. At the suggestion of Dr. Drake (who thus became the first patron of art), Corwin was paid in advance in order that he might take a course of instruction to improve his style. Besides Corwin, another portrait painter, Edwin B. Smith, flourished at that time."[1]

---

[1] *Cincinnati, Queen City*, by Rev. C. F. Goss, vol. I, p. 236.

The master portrait painter of the Blue Grass State, Matthew Jouett, was painting the portraits of the fine ladies and gentlemen of Kentucky, and the influence of his work was beginning to be felt in Cincinnati about 1820. A child prodigy in art, he came forth a full-fledged artist without any instruction in painting. Disappointing his father by having no interest in law as a profession, he engaged in art as a serious vocation. Then he felt the need of some training, and went to Boston to study with Gilbert Stuart. Jouett, with only four months of study under Stuart, painted almost exactly as his master did. Stuart painted Dolly Madison, and Jouett painted her sister, Mrs. Todd; it is puzzling to attempt to tell which is by Stuart and which is by Jouett.

The influential Kentuckians of his time were the subjects of his portraits. His grandson, Richard Jouett Menefee, catalogued three hundred and thirty-four Jouett paintings. He was equally at home in delineating infancy, childhood, adolescence, manhood, or old age. Very few painters have possessed such rare ability in portraying children. He pictured the child mind on canvas. Simplicity of composition, beauty of pose, strength of drawing, charm of color, and directness of execution contribute to the portrait of his wife and child the qualities of a masterpiece.

"He separated the dominant traits of his sitters, and then combined them to bring out the strong points and make his portraits likenesses. Considering his lack of opportunities his work borders on the marvelous. It is difficult to believe that the great masters were not known to him. Honors came too late for him to reap the fruits of appreciation."[2] Jouett's fame began to spread in 1893 when his portraits were displayed in an historical group of American paintings at the World's Fair, Chicago; the hanging committee gave his portraits the best place in the gallery.

An early history, *Cincinnati in 1826,* by Drake and Mansfield, informs us that: "Mr. F. Eckstein, an intelligent and highly ingenious artist of this city, is about to commence the formation of an academy of fine arts, on a plan well calculated to ensure success. His skill in sculpture and taking plaster casts, his taste in painting, and his enterprising industry will, even with a moderate amount of patronage, ensure the permanence of the institution." In spite of the faith of the historian in this enterprise, it did not endure, though Mr. Eckstein did so much to awaken an interest in the beautiful among the citizens that he gained the distinguished title of the "Father of Cincinnati Art." He has one enduring claim to fame, that he was the instructor of Hiram Powers, the most notable figure among the artists in the early thirties.

---

[2] *Harper's Magazine,* May, 1899. "Matthew Harris Jouett," by C. H. Hart.

Cist, in his *Cincinnati in 1841* and in his *Cincinnati in 1851,* gives a long list of artists of the time. It is a matter of much astonishment to find so many who at that time supported themselves wholly or partially by their art. However, most of them were so obscure that they exerted no formative influence upon the artistic development of our state.

During the forties there were several painters who deserve consideration: James H. Beard, Miner K. Kellogg, William H. Powell, T. Buchanan Reid, William L. Sonntag, and the Frankenstein brothers.

James H. Beard, when a lad only six years old, came from New York state to Painesville, Ohio, with his father, an old lake captain. His first impulse toward art arose from watching the making of the figurehead for the first steamboat that sailed on Lake Erie. This boat was called *Walk-in-the-Water,* and was launched May 28, 1818. He made rough drawings of it on all the scraps of paper he could find. About 1834, before he was twenty-one years of age, he settled in Cincinnati, where he lived forty-two years. He sold his early attempts at portraiture for four or five dollars each; his mature work earned him the sum of thirty-six hundred dollars. Subjects for his portraits include such men as Henry Clay and Presidents John Quincy Adams, Taylor, and Harrison. His first ambitious composition was "The Deluge," which hung in the old Burnet house for twenty years. He made a picture of a child and dog that became so popular that parents besieged him to paint their children with dogs; endeavoring to meet this demand, he devoted his efforts to animals, principally dogs, so that he earned the title of the "Landseer of America."

Collaborating with his brother, William H. Beard, he made many comic pictures of bears; "Bears on a Bender" and "Bears and Bulls of Wall Street" are examples. "If any artist has yet (1886) lived who can paint bears better than Wm. H. Beard, he has not yet made himself known. James H. Beard makes his animals command our sympathy and affection, and instructs us in the graver lessons of human existence and truth. He is a moralist with some of the qualities of Æsop and La Fontaine. This is true of a picture of a monkey of Central Park, 'Jerry Crowley,' puzzling his brain over Darwin's descent of man, with a human skull on his right hand and a monkey's skull on his left, he seems quite as unable to solve the problem as Darwin himself."[3]

Miner K. Kellogg was a native Cincinnatian, spending many years in Paris and Florence; he became distinguished for painting types of different nationalities, the Circassian, the Greek, the Jew, and the Moor. Oriental life interested

[3] *Magazine of Western History,* June, July, August, 1886. "Art and Artists of Ohio," Francis Sessions.

PLATE 28—The Battle of Lake Erie. William H. Powell. (Webster P. Huntington). (Copyright by John W. Newton)

him: in Constantinople he painted a portrait of Raschid Pasha, prime vizier of the Sultan of Turkey. He was a recognized expert on the old masters, owning a valuable and extensive collection which he sold to L. E. Holden, of Cleveland, where Mr. Kellogg lived the later years of his life.

William H. Powell began his career in 1833. He came with his parents from New York state to Cincinnati when he was seven years old. At fifteen he produced his ideal picture of the Scottish chief, Roderick Dhu. In 1837 he completed a series of four allegorical pictures for a Cincinnati theater; these were suggested by Byron's "Siege of Corinth." In 1838 he was a pupil of Henry Inman; in 1845 he went to Europe and studied for four years. Washington Irving gave such unstinted praise to Mr. Powell's "Columbus Before the Council at Salamanca" that, upon returning to America, he received from the national government the commission, sought by over sixty competitors, to paint "De Soto Discovering the Mississippi" for the rotunda of the Capitol at Washington. Mr. Powell received ten thousand dollars for this work, which he painted in Paris. The "Burial of De Soto" and "Washington Taking Leave of His Mother" were painted soon afterward. His next important commission was "The Battle of Lake Erie," sometimes called "Perry's Victory," which hangs in the Ohio state capitol (Plate 28). This picture was authorized by the Ohio General Assembly in 1857, the joint resolution providing for a painting "not less than twelve by sixteen feet, to cost not more than five thousand dollars." In 1865, Powell presented a statement to the General Assembly, to the effect that he had spent over two years studying historical data and in other preparations for the work, and that five years had been required for its completion. He asked that the original sum be increased to fifteen thousand dollars; he was awarded ten thousand dollars. Subsequently, Powell produced an enlarged replica of the picture for the Capitol at Washington. Eventually he established a studio in New York, and painted portraits of Washington Irving, Peter Cooper, General McClellan, Peter Stuyvesant, Lamartine, and others; his last work was a full-length portrait of Emma Ames Abbott.

Thomas Buchanan Reid, like Washington Allston, was famous both as a poet and a painter. He is ranked among Cincinnati's illustrious painters because he began his career there. For his excellence in poetry we need only mention "Sheridan's Ride." In painting, most of his works have a literary interest, as these titles will suggest: "Milton Dictating to His Daughters," "Loves of the Zephyrs," "Jephthah's Vow," and the "Waterfall." A group picture that was exceedingly popular, photographed and seen in almost every family album, was his portrait of Longfellow's children.

PLATE 29—Landscape. W. L. Sonntag. (Cincinnati Museum of Art)

William L. Sonntag painted landscape much in the manner of the painters of the Hudson River school, though his work surpassed theirs (Plate 29). The Frankenstein brothers are considered in the section dealing with Springfield, though they belonged to Cincinnati nearly as much as to Springfield. Godfrey N. Frankenstein served as president of the Cincinnati Academy of Fine Arts when it was organized in 1835. This organization had a short existence, but it cultivated public taste and paved the way for future art organizations.

The Western Art Union was organized in Cincinnati in 1847, being inspired by the founding of the American Art Union in New York the previous year. Cole's "Voyage of Life" was exhibited in the Art Union building, a favorite resort of the artists; Worthington Whittredge, James H. Beard, T. Buchanan Reid, William Miller, the miniature painter, and J. O. Eaton were some of the painters who had their studios there. Eaton became widely known as a portrait painter; many of his portraits are to be found in Cincinnati, and some in European collections. The Western Art Union, organized by patrons of art for "the encouragement of the fine arts," disbursed all its funds for the purchase of American works of art. Charles Stetson was president.

A little later there entered upon the scene one who must be considered the pioneer patron of art in Cincinnati, Mrs. Sarah Worthington King Peter. In 1854, under the leadership of Mrs. Peter, there was formed the Ladies' Gallery of Fine Arts, to teach the arts of design by which women might earn a living. These women raised seven thousand dollars to purchase copies of masterpieces, and to this sum Mr. Charles McMicken added one thousand dollars for the purchase of plaster casts, which were to belong to the gallery until a school of design should be founded. Mrs. Peter went to Europe and selected the paintings and collection of casts. While the copies may not have had the highest artistic merit, yet until 1881, when the Lessing collection of studies and paintings was given to the Museum by Mr. Joseph Longworth, they were the only copies for students to study, and in connection with the casts they were of immense value in forming the taste of thousands of pupils of the School of Design. These women builded better than they knew, and deserve an honored place in the art annals of the city.

The rôle that women played in the development of the Queen City culture was significant. The poems of the Carey sisters were brought out in 1850. Their genius was nourished on a hillside overlooking the city, and their home was given the name of Clovernook in Alice's stories. Whittier referred to that home in this fashion:

PLATE 30—The Return of the Shrimp Fishers. Henry Mosler. (Cincinnati Museum of Art)

"Years since (but names to me before)
Two sisters sought at eve my door,
Two song birds wandering from their nest,
A gray old farmhouse in the West."

Alice's poem, "Beautiful Pictures That Hang on Memory's Wall", and Phoebe's hymn, "One Sweetly Solemn Thought", are known wherever English is spoken. In May, 1903, Wm. A. Proctor presented to the Misses Trader, trustees, Clovernook as a home for blind girls; so the beautiful thoughts of the Carey sisters of the mid-nineteenth century are perpetuated today in this altruistic effort of making happier the lives of the blind.

In a few years the Civil War was brewing, financial difficulties with attendant hard times were rife; the women were not able to obtain the necessary support for the gallery, and it had to be abandoned. The pictures and casts were stored, to serve later as the nucleus of the McMicken School of Design. It is interesting to note that this effort of the women in 1854 corresponds closely in time to the movement that was going on in England that crystallized in the founding of the South Kensington Museum in London in 1857. The idea of museums is believed to have had its inception in South Kensington Museum.

The next decade produced little in the field of art. It was the period when there was an evolution of the social leader into the champion of human rights. Cincinnati was fortunate in having the Beecher family as residents for twenty years, and they were closely connected with its educational history. It is said that no American family influenced American thought so much as the Beechers; it used to be a common expression that Ohio had two boasts: the American flag and the Beechers. Lyman Beecher gave utterance to more piquant expressions than any other American except Benjamin Franklin. His daughter, Harriet Beecher Stowe, met in Walnut Hills, Cincinnati, the originals of the characters in *Uncle Tom's Cabin*.

Cincinnati had such men as Chief Justice McLean, Salmon P. Chase, Jacob Burnet, Dr. Dan Drake, James C. Hall, Nicholas Longworth, Nathaniel Wright, Nat G. Pendleton, Charles Hammond, Henry Starr, Bellamy Storer, Larz Anderson, Bishop McIlvain, D. K. Este, John P. Foote, Nathan Guilford, General William Lytle, General W. H. Harrison, and Colonel Jared Mansfield, Surveyor General of the Northwest Territory, and professor of mathematics at West Point. "There was a mysterious and powerful foment at work in the soul of the city in these two decades. In every sphere of life there was progress. Politically, morally, religiously, intellectually, esthetically, the city grew. But when we come to a careful analysis, it was the discussion of the question of human rights and duties with regard to the slave traffic, that most powerfully affected the inner and higher life of the community."[4]

In the early seventies art life began to manifest itself again. Mr. Charles T. Webber, an artist, obtained from the members of the Ladies' Gallery of Fine Arts and from the trustees of the McMicken estate, to which the casts had reverted, the permission to use the pictures and casts for the purpose of a class. There was great interest in the class, and there were some who saw in this enthusiasm the possibilities of valuable results; among them were Mr. Joseph Longworth and Mr. Thomas S. Noble. In the course of time this class became known as the McMicken School of Design, as it was founded on a bequest of Mr. Charles McMicken. It was organized under a regular staff of instructors in 1869. Thomas S. Noble was a most successful executive and teacher, and later was instrumental in establishing the present Academy and Museum in Eden Park.

Early training in Cincinnati gives that city a valid claim upon Henry Mosler, who studied there with James H. Beard. He was especially successful in pictures telling a story of Breton peasant life. "The Prodigal's Return" pictures the old, old story of a young man coming home to find his mother on her deathbed, too late to obtain her forgiveness. It is full of pathos, arousing one's sympathies for the youth. The drooping head of the priest, the kneeling, contrite boy, the richly-carved Breton bed, the fireplace and all details are carefully and truthfully rendered. This was the first picture purchased by the French government from an American artist; it hangs in the Luxembourg, Paris. "The Return of the Shrimp Fishers" (Plate 30), and "The Wedding Feast in Brittany", are other charming. genre scenes of Brittany, sincerely portrayed by Mosler, who was the recipient of several gold and silver medals and honorable mention in at least a score of instances.

The formation of the Old Sketch Club was one of the art activities of 1860. Among its members were men known all over the country. Perhaps foremost in the group was the elder Beard (James H.) ; other members were T. Buchanan Reid, J. O. Eaton, Alexander Wyant, Chas. T. Webber, Thomas Noble, Insco Williams, Tom Lindsay, John Frankenstein and others.

About 1874 several women became interested in overglaze work, wood carving, embroidery, and other branches of applied design. Mr. A. T. Goshorn, for years active leader in the important industrial expositions held in Cincinnati, was chosen as the Commissioner-General of the Centennial Exposition in Philadelphia, in 1876. He persuaded the women to display their work at Philadel-

---

[4] *Cincinnati, Queen City,* by Rev. C. F. Goss, vol. I, p. 172.

PLATE 31—Professor Ludwig Loefftz. Frank Duveneck. (Cincinnati Museum of Art)

phia, and they assembled a splendid exhibit. The overglaze painting on china created much comment, and later developed into the Rookwood pottery, which is treated more fully in the chapter on Ceramics (see chapter VII). Mrs. William Dodd carved a table that was awarded a silver medal at the Philadelphia Centennial Exposition.

The Philadelphia Exposition had a profound effect upon American art, bringing before the eyes of the people, as it did, the best of the Old World art, notably that of England, France, and Japan. This effect was largely felt in Cincinnati, with a result that in 1878 the women who had been experimenting in overglaze founded the Loan Exhibition, renting a house and filling it with borrowed treasure of all kinds. The movement caused intense interest throughout the city, and out of it grew the Women's Art Association, with Mrs. Aaron F. Perry, president.

It is almost impossible to enumerate all the influences on art that operated at this period, but the influence of wood carving must be mentioned. The popularity of this form of art was due to the work of an English wood carver, Henry L. Fry, who settled in Cincinnati. His family records note the fact that he carved the throne chair used by Queen Victoria. He was very modest about his efforts; when friends told him that he was the greatest wood carver in the country, he would laughingly reply, "That is because I am the only wood carver here". The son, William H. Fry, was brought up in the traditions of the father, and they had a studio together. They were close friends of Nicholas Longworth, Sr. William H. Fry taught at the Cincinnati Art Academy for about fifty years. Cincinnati is rich in the possession of most of his work, especially the carved decorations on Music Hall organ. The majestic eagles that topped the old Pike Theater had a wing spread of twelve feet. Many homes are decorated with his carved mantelpieces of acanthus leaves showing a breadth of conception and fine sweep of line. His daughter, Laura Fry, has a collection of twenty-three paper knives, all carved after he was eighty-five years old. Fry has been termed the Ghiberti of American decorative art.

Cincinnati has probably produced more men of artistic ability than any other Ohio city, and in the history of the art of the state it is in a way comparable to the position of Florence, in Italy, during the high renaissance. From 1870 to 1890 may be properly called the golden age of art in Cincinnati. Here is the list of men born in or near Cincinnati and working there during that period: Frank Duveneck, John Twachtman, Joseph DeCamp, Robert Blum, Henry Farny, Charles Niehaus, Robert Henri, J. H. Sharp, Clement J. Barnhorn, L. H. Meakin, and William Forsyth.

This unusual array of talent can be accounted for principally by the encouragement given to young artists on all hands. Cincinnati seemed to take the lead in its gifts from its public-spirited citizens to found art institutions and to promote art by providing for their maintenance.

Frank Duveneck was the source of inspiration and leader of the group of artists just mentioned. "It is doubtful if an artist ever lived who exerted more influence on the art of his country than Mr. Duveneck. When Sargent was admitted to the Royal Academy in London, his toast was, 'Gentlemen, here's to the health of Frank Duveneck, the greatest of us all.' Later he said that Duveneck was the greatest talent of the century."[5]

Though born in Covington, Kentucky, Duveneck's fame falls on both sides of the river, as he gave his best endeavor to Cincinnati, and his greatest contribution to art was in Ohio. His family, of German descent, settled in Pittsburgh; his mother, Elizabeth Seimer, as a little girl, coming down to Cincinnati on a raft. When her father met with a fatal accident, she was taken into the home of James Beard, the painter, until the time of her marriage to Frank Decker, a native of Holland. In 1848, a son was born whom they named Frank; when the boy was only a year old his father died. In course of time his mother married Squire Duveneck, so the boy assumed the name of Duveneck as a matter of convenience. His mother took the precaution in her will to refer to her son Frank Decker, known as Frank Duveneck.

Norbert Heermann, the biographer of Duveneck, gives this account of his training: "During the Civil War, the Benedictine Friars were making altars for Catholic churches in Covington, and they employed Duveneck, still a mere boy, in his first artistic work. The varied work which followed proved important in Duveneck's development; he painted, modeled, carved, decorated churches in many places, even as far away as Canada."[6] There still exists an altar in a Kentucky convent that he did when he was fourteen. In 1866 he became the assistant to Lamprecht, the mural decorator. "After the close of the war, when the ebb and flow of the rougher element discharged from both armies made life colorful, but rather dangerous for a youth with a spirit of adventure, young Duveneck was placed in the home of a Catholic priest, who had in his possession a number of plates that outlined the features of the face at various angles. It was his pupil's task to do a number of careful copies of these drawings before going to breakfast each morning. Though this seems to have been for

---

[5]"Cincinnati's Preëminence in Painting and Sculpture," W. P. Teal. Paper read at School-master's Club, Cincinnati, December 9, 1922.

[6]*Frank Duveneck*, Norbert Heermann, p. 13.

PLATE 32—Tomb of Elizabeth Boott Duveneck, Florence, Italy (Cincinnati Museum of Art)

the sole purpose of keeping this young man off the street, he once confessed that his knowledge of the construction of the eye dated from that time."[7]

In 1870 Duveneck managed to get to Munich, which had at this time taken the place of Düsseldorf as the leading art school in Germany. Many transitions were taking place then. He painted under Wilhelm Dietz, who was following a course similar to Courbet, observing nature, pure and simple. Duveneck immediately aligned himself with the naturalists. The first year at Munich, he won most of the prizes offered, and in 1872 won the prize of a studio for himself. It was at this time he painted "The Whistling Boy" (Frontispiece).

"In this picture are fully evident the qualities which startled and quickly attracted the other painters and students to him. Foremost among these is the expressive use of the paint itself, an astonishing virtuosity of brush work closely related to Frans Hals, in which the daring and yet perfectly controlled hand defines planes, textures, and colors with an unhesitating brush loaded with paint. Even to the amateur this method makes an appeal, its chief merit being liveliness and force with rich, vibrant color. The fact that Duveneck at that time used to take his pictures to the Pinakothek, set them beside the old masters, the Dutch and Flemish ones being his favorites, makes us understand an inspiration that comes straight from the Netherlands. In later years Duveneck came under the spell of the French painters."[8]

In 1873 when cholera broke out in Munich, he returned to America. With only this short training in Munich, less than three years, when he was not yet thirty, he was bold enough to exhibit in Boston these five canvases: "The Old Schoolmaster", "The Woman With the Fan", "Portrait of William Adams", "Portrait of Professor Loefftz" (Plate 31), and "The Whistling Boy". William Morris Hunt, recognizing his ability, did much to help him. The one-man show was an immediate success: he was compared to Velasquez, and all the canvases were sold. "A new era in American art was proclaimed."[9]

When Duveneck went back to Munich, he started a school which became immensely popular, so that when he went to Florence the next year, his students followed him there. Men who later were important figures in the development of American art were enrolled in his class. This is the class roll of the famous "Duveneck Boys": John W. Alexander, John Twachtman, Frank Benson, Edmund Tarbell, Joseph DeCamp, Julius Rolshoven, Oliver Dennett Grover, Otto Bacher, Theodore Wendell, Louis Ritter, Ross Turner, Harper Pennington, Charles Forbes, George E. Hopkins, Charles E. Mills, Albert

[7] Manuscript by Ernest Bruce Haswell.
[8] *Frank Duveneck,* by Norbert Heermann, p. 22.
[9] *Frank Duveneck,* by Norbert Heermann, p. 9.

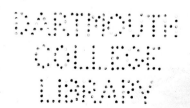

Rheinhardt, Charles H. Freeman, Henry Rosenberg, John C. Anderson, Charles Abel Corwin, and Julian Story. These boys were well known in Florence and Venice, where they went in summer, and they actually became a feature of Florentine life, as related by William Dean Howells, who called them the "Inglehart Boys", in his story, "Indian Summer".

For almost a year William M. Chase lived with Duveneck and Twachtman in Venice, each undoubtedly influencing the others, but each retaining his own individuality. It was with no disrespectful spirit that Duveneck, Walter Shirlaw, and Chase were nicknamed "The Father, Son, and Holy Ghost" by the students. These young Americans exhibited for the first time in New York, in the spring of 1877, the works made in Paris, Munich, and Venice. Duveneck's "Turkish Page" was in that exhibit. According to Haswell's account, "'The Turkish Page' (1876) was painted in the studio with Chase, who did a smaller canvas of the same model and background from a slightly different position. 'The Turkish Page' is done with what was for him an unusual regard for detail, but the figure assumes the place of importance. In the Chase canvas there is evidence of his growing interest in still life. It is in an excellent state of preservation, but the Duveneck is cracked and inclined to scale. Not many years before he died, he said as he watched James R. Hopkins carefully applying color: 'I wish I had thought more of the chemistry of color when I was painting.' He used carriage varnish on some of his larger canvases, and his reckless use of bitumen has darkened some of his best heads. His one thought was the building up of color spots of different value into a correctly-felt head or figure."[10]

From Venice, Duveneck sent remarkable exhibitions of the work of his students to New York, where they created a sensation. "It was the brush work instead of the carefully finished charcoal or crayon drawing that he insisted upon with his pupils as the real foundation of a picture; he imparted the painter's rather than the draughtsman's point of view in teaching the student, once the rough outlines were suggested in charcoal, to cover his canvas quickly with paint, boldly blocking in the large masses. Duveneck addressed his class thus: 'Now, I don't want any geniuses in this class; I don't care for students who claim an abundance of talent; but what I do want is a crowd of good workers.'"[11] About 1880, he became interested in etching through some experiments of his pupil, Otto Bacher. (See page 238.)

Duveneck married one of his pupils, Elizabeth Boott, of Boston, in 1886.

---

[10] Manuscript by Ernest Bruce Haswell.
[11] *Frank Duveneck,* by Norbert Heermann, pp. 50-53.

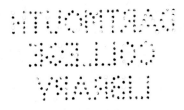

PLATE 33—Fig. 1, Moods of Music. Fig. 2, Flying Swallows. Robert Blum.
(Cincinnati Museum of Art)

She lived only two years after their marriage, and was buried in the Allori
Cemetery, Florence, Italy, where is placed the superb memorial he made for
her. While he was assisted in this sculpture by his friend, Clement J. Barnhorn, yet it clearly demonstrates his great versatility as an artist. It is a reclining
figure of his wife, simple and classic in its beauty, and not unlike the tomb of
Ilaria del Caretto, by Della Quercia (Plate 32).

After his wife's death he could not be persuaded to complete an order for
fourteen portraits to be made in London; he was always a procrastinator, and
money did not interest him. He returned to Cincinnati, and there spent many
years in teaching, painting, and giving advice on all matters pertaining to art.
In 1900 he was made head of the faculty at Cincinnati Art Academy. "At one
time he was persuaded to give several criticisms in Chicago each week. He
did not go to Chicago many times, for he preferred the quiet and uneventful
routine of teaching his class in the morning, having lunch with L. H. Meakin,
the landscape painter; C. J. Barnhorn, the sculptor, and William H. Fry, the
wood carver. Then, later in the day, it was his custom to stop at Foucar's for
his stein of beer before going to his home in Covington. It was impossible to
induce him to attend even the most informal social function."[12]

About the time Duveneck returned to Cincinnati, the paintings of H. F. Farny
were very much in vogue there, and it is said that he was quite jealous of Duveneck's unusual ability. However, it was not until the Panama-Pacific Exposition
at San Francisco, in 1915, that Duveneck came into full appreciation by the
people. He had an exhibit of thirty pictures there. Strange to say, it was the
foreign members of the art jury who suggested that a special, grand gold medal
be made to reward his great genius. Most of these thirty pictures, with others
to the number of almost a hundred, together with much sculpture and many
etchings, be bestowed upon the Cincinnati Art Museum in 1915, "for the benefit
of students of art in Cincinnati." It makes a unique representation of his work,
all in one museum.

He drew with the brush and scumbled up the paint afterward with his thumb.
In "The Girl With the Muff", we see the inheritance of the French palette of
David; in the portrait of "John Alexander", we note the Munich influence; in
some of his pictures of Italy we are aware that he painted sunlight before the
impressionists did; in his figures we always feel his living eyes; and in all his
work, his rich, full brush drawing compels our awe and admiration. His work
stands as an example of technical excellence and dexterity for all time. The
inspiration that he gave to his pupils and associates was such that we find the

---

[12] Manuscript by Ernest Bruce Haswell.

PLATE 34—The Waterfall. John H. Twachtman. (Cincinnati Museum of Art)

Duveneck tradition and teaching spreading year by year. If any one artist deserves an illuminated page in the history of Ohio art, it is Frank Duveneck.

Robert Blum, when a very young man, became interested in Japanese art. The Japanese display at the Philadelphia Centennial of 1876 fanned into white heat his wild desire to go to Japan. He went to New York before he was twenty years old and began to study. His success was instantaneous; after two years' study *Scribner's Magazine* sent him to Japan to illustrate Sir Edwin Arnold's "Japonica", with the result that he has given us the most picturesque records of Japan. A critic has said of his work: "His Venice is a dreamy pageant, a place of such scenes as only an observer of imagination and skill could have arrested upon canvas. Holland he has given reality which is none the less real, because it is streaked with vague suggestions of a colorist's enthusiasm and a draughtsman's passion for what is quaint and effective in a pictorial sense; and his Japan brings to the eyes of the West one of the most convincing and beautiful interpretations of the East which American art has shown."[13]

He had a complete mastery of the medium of pastel; he has presented in these colored crayons many charming little geisha girls making their toilets in bare rooms. They are done with an adorable lightness of touch yet with curious solidity; seldom has this delicate medium been used with more charm, enhanced by a sensitive feeling for color and strengthened by good drawing.

He had the honor of being the youngest member of the National Academy of Design. His "Lace Maker", now in the Cincinnati Museum, merited him the election to associate membership; and his "Ameya" ("The Candy-blower")[14] earned him the full membership. His most pretentious pieces of work were two murals in Mendelssohn Hall, New York City. One of these friezes, "Moods of Music" (Fig. 1, Plate 33), has an unreserved movement and a sweeping grace in the dancing figures; the turn of an arm, the swing of a drapery, the poise of a head, the effective accent of a shadow, are all rendered with the quick sureness of an expert brush man. It represents the rhythm of music itself. It is superior to his later frieze on the east wall of Mendelssohn Hall.

Many remnants of his work that were in his studio at the time of his death are now in the Cincinnati Museum; among them is one of the finest drawings in American art, the "Flying Swallows" (Fig. 2, Plate 33). As in "Moods of Music", there is a sensitiveness about the drawing that commands our attention. In the subject and the treatment, the influence of Japan is noticeable, but not

---

[13] *Scribner's Magazine,* April, 1893.
[14] In the Metropolitan Museum, New York City.

PLATE 35—Woman Drying Her Hair. Joseph DeCamp. (Cincinnati Museum of Art)

unduly in the manner of his work. He made many trips to Europe, in addition to the one to Japan, yet he remained his own master in his work. From the portrait of "Robert Blum", by John Alexander, in the Cincinnati Museum, we can gather that those dark eyes could reason, and analyze, and absorb, but never become dominated by an outside influence.

From Royal Cortissoz we quote: "I recall some consummate pen drawings of his, a portrait of Irving as Vanderdecken, and one of Joe Jefferson as Bob Acres. What a draftsman he was! But he could handle any medium—oils, water color, pastel. Also he etched some superb plates. In short, Blum had a flair for pure craftsmanship. We have never had any artist more imbued than he was with enthusiasm for technic, technic animated by a blithe and fascinating vivacity."[15]

Another artist of German origin (as were most of the Cincinnati artists born about the time of the Civil War) was John H. Twachtman, who was brought up in the same neighborhood as Robert Blum. The Duveneck and Twachtman families were old friends, both hailing from Hanover, Germany.

Twachtman began his career by decorating the window shades then so fashionable. Feeling the need for study, he enrolled in the Mechanics Institute, and later at the school of design where Frank Duveneck was instructor. Duveneck was only five years older than Twachtman. After Duveneck's immediate success with his exhibit at Boston, in 1875, he decided to return to Munich, and persuaded Twachtman to go with him. Twachtman found the atmosphere of Munich very sympathetic and stimulating. A new spirit was stirring, that of realism, a demand for painting a subject directly with first-hand information and observation.

He followed Duveneck and Chase to Venice two years afterward. The year 1880 found him one of the "Duveneck Boys" in Florence. We are told this by Norbert Heermann: "The advice of John Twachtman, of the Cincinnati contingent, one of the older ones, whose knowledge was wide, was appreciated next to that of the 'Old Man', as they lovingly denominated Duveneck."[16]

Returning to America in the spring of 1881, he married Martha Scudder. The couple went to Holland, where he profited by the encouraging criticism of Anton Mauve and the friendship of J. Alden Weir and Walter Shirlaw. He made many pictures of Holland, with the windmill figuring conspicuously. Up to this time his work reflected the bituminous palette of Munich, painting in grays and browns, in flat reaches of color without liveliness or detail. He settled in Paris in 1883, and then came a decided change in his manner of

[15] *Personalities in Art,* Royal Cortissoz, p. 409.
[16] *Frank Duveneck,* Norbert Heermann, p. 46.

PLATE 36—Ohio Valley and Kentucky Hills. L. H. Meakin.
(Cincinnati Museum of Art)

painting. An appreciation of light and values was awakened; he became preoccupied with the play of light under various conditions and upon various surfaces. Twachtman was considered the equal of Manet and Monet when the work of the three was exhibited in New York. His work is subjective, showing a poetic, often a fanciful impressionism with thoroughly felt underlying construction. "The Waterfall" (Plate 34), owned by the Cincinnati Museum, is carried further than any of his other paintings, and is said by most critics to be his best work; a similar painting, owned by the Metropolitan Museum, New York, is not so fine.

Planning to return to the United States, he shipped many of his canvases home. Unfortunately, the ship was wrecked, and his paintings executed during his years on the continent were lost. Not discouraged by this ill luck, he began again, locating on a small farm near Greenwich, Connecticut. Here he spent ten years doing his best work in his mature style. He went back and forth to New York City, teaching at the Art Students' League, associating at the Players' Club with his intimate friends, Weir, Hassam, Metcalf, Reid, Simmons, Carlsen and others.

Robert Reid has thus happily summed up his impressions: "Twachtman was of those to whom the subtle beauties of nature, which, though not hidden, have been seen only by the few, appealed most strongly; and it was the element in his nature which responded to that appeal that gave the charm to his work. Enthusiasm seems to have been the keynote of his character. A singularly gentle enthusiasm, a smiling rather than a laughing sympathy with his work, his family and his friends pervaded all he did, from the pastel note of a wild flower on a bit of tinted paper to his completest painting."[17]

He was essentially a painter's painter. He gained only slight appreciation from the public until after his death, in 1902, when the money value of his work advanced with great rapidity. While Mr. Gest was director of the Cincinnati Museum, he purchased in 1900 "The Waterfall" for something less than five hundred dollars. When Twachtman died, his pictures were not thrown upon the market as a whole, but were sold separately and at widely divided intervals. His widow and five children would live for a year upon the price received for one picture, then would sell another. The St. Louis Museum recently purchased a Twachtman, "The Rainbow's Source", at a figure reported to be very high, and seventeen thousand five hundred dollars was offered for a quick pencil drawing of Twachtman's wife and two children. Here is another instance in the history of art showing that rewards came too late for the artist to benefit from them.

---

[17] *John Twachtman,* by Eliot Clark, p. 16.

One of the "Duveneck Boys" of Florence, whose work extended well into the twentieth century, was Joseph De Camp. He often expressed his debt of gratitude to Duveneck, combining it with a sincere love for the man and a splendid loyalty to him. His portrait of Duveneck is one of the great portraits in America. For many years after his return from Europe, De Camp resided in Boston, serving as a member of the faculty of the Boston Museum of Fine Arts. He had technical equipment that was unsurpassed. His knowledge of anatomy and construction was thorough, his drawing academically correct, with remarkable ease in rendering surfaces and textures (Plate 35). He used rather heavy color and allowed it to flow freely. Some of his figures may be in unnatural positions, but one can never question his methods of work. His pictures show no hesitation nor difficulty, he is perfectly sure of himself. De Camp was a member of that noted group organized by Twachtman and known as Ten American Painters, and his associates were Frank W. Benson, Wm. M. Chase, Thomas W. Dewing, Childe Hassam, Willard Metcalf, Robert Reid, Edward Simmons, Edmund C. Tarbell, and Julian Alden Weir. They separated themselves from the National Academy in 1888 and began exhibiting together. It takes some boldness and foresight to break away from an old order and develop independent work as they did, without losing the fundamentals.

Although De Camp painted figures with much charm, and landscapes no less charming, it was mostly in portraiture that he won renown; distinguished soldiers, statesmen, musicians, artists, writers, and educators gave him steady patronage. He was chosen by the Harvard Class of 1880, President Roosevelt's class, to paint a portrait of Roosevelt to be placed in Harvard Union. This commission was executed in 1908-'9. He went to Washington for the purpose of the sittings, and an interesting story is told of his meetings with the President.

"Roosevelt did not take the matter of his portrait very seriously, and gave very little time to the sittings. Finally De Camp became discouraged and cleared up the situation with this pointed speech: 'Mr. President, this is a fine commission these Harvard men have given me, and I realize it will add not a little to my reputation to have been selected to paint the President of the United States. If you cannot give me the proper sittings, I must shut up my paint box, go back to Boston, and give up the whole affair.' Roosevelt appreciated De Camp's position and said, 'You're right!' After that all went well, the portrait was a speaking likeness, the delight of the class of 1880."[18]

Cincinnati Museum was the first of the American museums to buy pictures by American artists. The first picture by an American that the Chicago Art

[18] *Arts and Decoration,* April, 1911. "DeCamp, Master of Technique," by Arthur Hoeber.

PLATE 37—The Song of the Talking Wire. Henry F. Farny. (The Taft Museum)

Institute purchased was a landscape by the Cincinnati painter, L. H. Meakin. He belonged to a family that for generations had been connected with the pottery industry in England, in fact related to the Wedgewoods by marriage. His father and mother brought their family to Canada and thence to Ohio, settling definitely in Cincinnati.

After Meakin's first trip to Europe for study at Munich, he began teaching in the Cincinnati Art Academy, and was a member of the faculty until his death, in 1917. "No one could be more responsive to every promise of artistic capacity the individual art student might reveal. No one could more carefully search out the possible talent in the students' personality, provided they were willing to work patiently and incessantly."[19] In the galleries of the Cincinnati Museum he for many years rendered distinguished service in the selection, the care, and the hanging of its pictures. His work has a great range and variety; his art has a many-sided beauty, power, subtlety, and above all it is sincere. The Ohio River hills and valleys were his favorite subjects (Plate 36).

On several occasions special exhibitions of Mr. Meakin's work were held in the Cincinnati Museum, and in connection with the catalogues, he wrote each time, by request, an introduction or foreword in which he expressed with rare clearness and charm his conception of his art.

We quote from one of them as follows: "Whether I have found in nature a song loud enough to be heard above the hum of everyday life, and, if heard, whether it is worth listening to, is a question that cannot be decided by myself. I have always the hope, however, that something of the varied impressions made upon me by the different moods and aspects of nature may be felt by the observers of my pictures, and I have endeavored to render in each, as well as I could, the truths that impressed me as the most valuable and characteristic of the time and place. Corot is said to have told a lady who asked a question about some part of a picture, 'Madame, I pay you the compliment of taking for granted that you have an imagination', and the painter is very conscious that without imagination on the part of the observer the most important and essential part of what he has or hopes he has put into his picture is likely to be lost."

An artist who enjoyed a widespread fame as a painter of Indians and western scenes was Henry F. Farny. His youth was spent in Erie County, Pennsylvania. The Seneca Indians who came from their reservations in New York state to the neighborhood where Farny's father lived, taught him the lore of the woods and gave him a permanent interest in the red man. The story is told of how the father tried to make an office clerk of young Henry, but all to no

---

[19] Memorial folder published by Cincinnati Museum.

avail; he was interested only in making on the margins of his ledger sketches of every one who entered the office.

The Farny family moved to Cincinnati in 1859. *Harper's Magazine* had its attention called to the boy's sketches, and the outcome was their employment of him to illustrate for them during the Civil War. Then T. Buchanan Reid became interested in him and took him to Rome. Afterwards, Farny studied in Munich, where he and Munkacsy, who painted "Christ Before Pilate" and other familiar pictures, were classmates and roommates; it is said that Farny was always considered the more talented of the two.

Farny became more or less the victim of commercialism when he returned to America, where he devoted much time to the illustration of books, and this work influenced his art the rest of his life. "It was by his genius that the whole method of illustrating schoolbooks was revolutionized. Before his day the schoolbooks had contained unreal and impossible pictures. He made real children, engaged in real labors and amusements. The children of Cincinnati soon came to know him in person and hailed him on the streets, to his delight, as the man who made the pictures for their schoolbooks. Perhaps he never enjoyed quite as thoroughly his great fame as a painter of pictures that are to be seen in public and private galleries as he did his reputation among the children."[20] He made very beautiful illustrations for Professor Venable's poem, "The Teacher's Dream."

His painting of Indians was the fruit of a life of absorbed and concentrated interest. He spent several years among the Indians, studying their modes of life and appearance. Theodore Roosevelt said to him: "Farny, the nation owes you a great debt. It does not realize it now, but it will some day. You are preserving for future generations phases of American history that are rapidly passing away."

Mrs. Larz Anderson, of Cincinnati, has the finest and largest collection of Farny's pictures. The Charles P. Taft collection, Cincinnati, has "The Song of the Talking Wire" (Plate 37). It is a winter landscape. An Indian, facing us, wearing the costume of his tribe, is leaning against a telegraph pole in the foreground as if listening to the hum of the wires. Farther back, on the right, stand two horses, the carcass of a deer hanging from the saddle of one of them; half-embedded in the snow, at the left, are the decaying skull and horns of an ox. When Farny was at the height of his popularity abroad as well as at home, the late Kaiser of Germany wanted one of his pictures. Farny had none ready to send, so borrowed this one from Mr. Taft to send; of course, then the Kaiser

---

[20] *Cincinnati, Queen City,* by Rev. C. F. Goss, p. 449.

was eager to buy it, but Mr. Taft would not part with it, so the Kaiser had to content himself with another one.

Farny never had to seek a market for his pictures—customers were always waiting. "Coming of the Iron Horse" is a picture that gives us, in a breath, the full force of Farny's dramatic feeling and his ability to paint and compose something beautiful which is historically true. The picture shows a puffing, steaming locomotive with its trail of cars just emerging from a pass in the mountains. In the open valley in front of the train is a band of Indians making a desperate effort to run away from this frightful monster.

His last picture, "La Salle", shows the daring explorer standing on a drift of logs at the falls of the Missouri River with a spring forest for a background. This study has the same careful handling and sure knowledge that Farny gives us in his Indian portrayals.

One of the powerful influences exerted upon art in Cincinnati was the teaching of Vincent Nowottny, who became a member of the faculty of the Cincinnati Art Academy in 1885 and remained there many years. He was remarkably successful as a teacher, especially of the human figure, to which he gave years of thorough and exhaustive study. His knowledge was supplemented with an unflagging interest and enthusiasm. We regret that teaching allowed him little time to develop his own painting.

One can understand why Longfellow gave to Cincinnati the poetic appellation, "Queen City of the West". One must make obeisance to a city that made such sincere efforts towards the promotion of a general esthetic spirit and the appreciation of beauty in all forms.

> "To the Queen of the West
> In her garlands dressed,
> On the banks of the beautiful river."

CHAPTER V

Scattered Art Activities Prior to 1900

STEUBENVILLE

IN so far as one is able to ascertain from all available records, Steubenville has the honor of being the home of the first young man in Ohio to become a professional artist. He was Thomas Cole, nationally known as a member of the Hudson River school, and painter of "The Course of Empire". He was born in England in 1801, but his family were Americans, who returned and settled in Steubenville in 1819. The father was a wall-paper maker, and Thomas was a valuable assistant to his father in designing and coloring the blocks from which the paper was printed. His first work was the decoration of the old-fashioned window shades, the painting being done on specially prepared muslin. "A portrait painter named Stien coming along fascinated Cole, and he at once with such rude colors as he could command, began to paint, and was soon able to establish himself as a portrait painter."[1]

Cole started on a tramp to find patrons, going on foot to St. Clairsville where he proposed to set up a studio. But Ohio, at that time, offered little encouragement to one starting upon an artistic career. At St. Clairsville, Zanesville, Chillicothe, and in Harrison and Columbiana Counties where he sought commissions, he not only failed, but was at last obliged to return to Steubenville much poorer than when he left. Undaunted, however, he spent the spring and summer of 1823 making careful studies from nature. His powers developed rapidly; soon he was established as a landscape painter in Philadelphia. Thence he went to New York and began painting the scenes which gave him a national reputation: views of the Hudson River, the Catskills, Niagara Falls, and the White Mountains. Only a few years of his brilliant career were spent in Ohio, yet it is for us to glory in the fact that he received his first inspiration from the Ohio River and its hills and valleys; the landscape portions of his series of five pictures called "The Voyage of Life" were developed from sketches he made along the Ohio River. He is generally credited with being the originator of the American school of landscape painting.

William Watkins, another artist who went out from Steubenville, came with his family from England or Wales, about 1840. He made a specialty of minia-

---

[1] William Cullen Bryant made this statement in the oration he delivered at Cole's funeral. *History of Jefferson County*, Joseph B. Doyle, p. 329.

ture portraits, and is said to have been unexcelled in his day. He moved to Cincinnati, where he flourished for several years.

A native son of Steubenville to gain distinction as an artist, was Eliphalet Frazer Andrews, who had the advantage of study in Düsseldorf, later with Bonnat in Paris, and with Lüdwig Knaus in Berlin. He returned to the United States when his friend, Rutherford B. Hayes, was elected to the presidency, becoming a leading figure in the rather provincial art world of the capital city. The social position he enjoyed gave him additional power; so it seemed very fitting that W. W. Corcoran should select him as director of the School of Art in connection with the Gallery which Mr. Corcoran had founded. He was a great instructor, and his students adored him; many of the most successful artists of this generation received their training under him at the Corcoran School of Art, where he guided its activities from 1887 to 1902.

As a painter, Andrews did not do himself justice. He knew more than he painted. He was scrupulously accurate, an academician, a student of the classical idea, and often lost the charm and quality because of this conscientiousness. Much praise was given his "Garfield", of which he made a replica and presented it to the city of Steubenville, where it hangs now in the City Building. He was at his best in portraits. In the White House is a beautiful full-length portrait of Dolly Madison, and a very fine full-length portrait of Thomas Jefferson (Plate 38), by Andrews. In the galaxy of portraits of governors of Ohio, hanging in the State House, Columbus, are those of Foster and Hoadley, by Andrews. His portrait of Andrew Johnson is considered the best existing portrait of that president. Mr. Andrews, through his teaching, made a real contribution to American art.

MARIETTA

Marietta, named for Marie Antoinette, queen of France, is proud, and rightly so, of the foundation of historical events amid which the city was built. We are prone to think of Marietta as connected with "firsts" in the state, being the first permanent settlement in Ohio, in 1788; therefore it is not surprising to find some of our first artists there. "Firsts" in any realm have a perennial interest for most people.

Among the early settlers was the Bosworth family from Massachusetts. Their son, Sala, was only eleven years old when they settled on a farm a few miles east of Marietta. The meager school facilities of the time were all he enjoyed, but being an ambitious lad and a tireless worker, he supplemented his school work until he became a classical scholar. His strong inclination to put his impressions upon canvas made him resourceful in selecting the stones from the brooks, grinding them, and preparing his colors from them. The young man was able to support himself, and when he was twenty-two years old he found a way to go to Philadelphia to study at the Art Academy, then the best place in the United States to study art.

Bosworth became such an excellent portrait painter that he was in great demand when he returned to Ohio two years later. He painted portraits in Athens, Zanesville, Columbus, Circleville, Chillicothe, Marietta, Belpre and other towns in that section of the state. He was called upon to paint an oil portrait of General Rufus Putnam from a silhouette, which was the only likeness of General Putnam in Marietta. At this time there were several persons living in Marietta who remembered General Putnam, and their descriptions aided him greatly. An amusing controversy arose among these acquaintances of Putnam, some saying that he wore his hair in a queue, others that he did not; Bosworth first painted the queue in, and then painted it out.

The pictures painted by Bosworth of scenes around Marietta, "Farmer's Castle at Belpre", "Wolf Creek Mills", "Blennerhassett Mansion", are all valuable sources of history today, as they followed descriptions given him by the pioneers themselves, and were corrected by their criticisms. Late in life he took up the painting of landscape in water color, and this work is said to have the same clearness and transparency of color that marks the complexions in his portraits. For nine years, from 1861 to 1870, he served as postmaster at Marietta, receiving his appointment from President Lincoln.

Charles Sullivan was an artist who shared honors with Mr. Sala Bosworth in reproducing historical views of Marietta. The most important and valuable of these paintings is "The Mound Builder's Earthworks in 1788". The original is in New York, but several copies of it are in Marietta and vicinity. It was reproduced in *Ancient Monuments of the Mississippi Valley,* by Squier and Davis, published in 1848, one of the earliest archæological treatises of Ohio. "This picture is as correct as if the artist saw the scene himself, for it was painted under the careful direction of Colonel Ichabod Nye, who sat by the artist and directed him in all details. Colonel Nye, having been a pioneer of 1788, knew these earthworks perfectly well before their destruction began."[2]

Mr. Sullivan was a Pennsylvanian by birth. He studied at Philadelphia with Thomas Sully, who was his personal friend, and whose style of portrait painting is to be seen in Sullivan's portraits, though Sullivan was first and foremost a landscape painter. He spent several winters in Georgia and Tennessee, as

---

[2] Manuscript by Miss Rowena Buell, Marietta.

PLATE 38—Thomas Jefferson. E. F. Andrews. White House, Washington.
(Harris and Ewing)

the guest of Major Gordon and other prosperous planters, going from one plantation to another, painting landscapes, and portraits of Southern beauties. James K. Polk and Mrs. Polk were portrayed by him during one of these winter sojourns in the South. He came to Marietta in 1833 and lived there until his death, in 1867.

One of the Frenchmen who came to Marietta in 1833, was Giles Martin, father of Lily Martin, the child prodigy in art. From childhood the girl had shown a talent for drawing. The means of this French farmer's family were probably very limited, as the child's only materials for drawing seem to have been the walls of the house and pieces of charcoal which she picked up from the wood fire. Though she worked without instruction, it could not have been without encouragement, for her father could draw and was a great lover of nature. She worked until the walls of the Martin home were covered with her drawings. The story of them became bruited about, and the citizens of Marietta drove out to the Martin farm to look at them. One picture of her mother spinning, and one of Lily herself peeping through an open door, were much admired. In 1841, with the help of Charles Sullivan, she had an exhibit of her work in the home of Judge Nye, of Marietta. In three years she executed nearly fifty paintings, and it is most astonishing that a girl of eighteen, without ever seeing a masterpiece or receiving any instruction, could do so well as she did in handling light and shade.

Mr. Nicholas Longworth, of Cincinnati, heard of Lily Martin, and offered to help her to obtain an art education in Cincinnati. Her oil painting was very successful, and soon she was famous. In Cincinnati she met and married a Mr. Spencer; soon after they went to New York, and she opened a studio there. Her pictures were exhibited at the Philadelphia Centennial, in 1876, and many were reproduced as popular chromos. The painting which attracted most attention was "Truth Unveiling Falsehood", for which Senator Sprague, of New Jersey, paid $20,000. Her masterpiece is considered to be "Algeria", painted according to Byron's interpretation of it in *Childe Harold's Pilgrimage*. In the latter part of her working life she painted many splendid portraits of noted people: Mrs. Benjamin Harrison, Mrs. Elizabeth Cady Stanton, Mr. Robert Ingersoll and others. She kept a little gallery of her paintings at her home on the Hudson, near Poughkeepsie.

SPRINGFIELD

The city of Springfield was famed as the home of the Frankenstein family of artists, though they were closely identified with Cincinnati art activities.

PLATE 39—Portrait Bust of Judge McLean. John Frankenstein.
(Cincinnati Museum of Art)

"In 1831, John A. Frankenstein and Anna C. Frankenstein, the parents of John, Godfrey N., Marie M. C., George L., Gustavus, and Eliza, emigrated from Germany to America. They were shipwrecked on the coast of Virginia, but were more fortunate than some others in saving all their belongings. Some time during the year, they arrived at Cincinnati, a little later making Springfield their home. John A. Frankenstein was a professor of languages, also a thorough musician, but, those fields not being very remunerative at this time, he turned to cabinetmaking."[3]

The oldest child, John, was considered a prodigy. He drew with pencil or pen and ink, and painted portraits in oil from the time he was fifteen years of age, using color that was said by competent judges to be excellent. He began modeling in clay very early. He was self-taught, except for his father's help, and the study of anatomy, which he mastered at Ohio Medical College, Cincinnati. He went to Philadelphia when about eighteen years old and painted many portraits there. Going on to New York, he became intimate with the family of William H. Seward, painting his portrait, and making a portrait bust of Mrs. Seward. He returned to Cincinnati about 1843, and a few years later he painted two religious pictures that made him celebrated. These were called, "Isaiah and the Infant Savior", and "Christ Mocked in the Prætorium"; the latter contained several figures, Christ being the central one. Thousands and thousands of people went to his studio to see these pictures, which were later purchased by a Canadian connoisseur. The portrait bust of Judge McLean, in the Cincinnati Museum of Art, illustrates his ability as a sculptor (Plate 39).

It is related of Godfrey N. Frankenstein that when quite a little boy he painted a whole village, church and all, using coffee for the straw-colored houses, hog's blood, obtained on butchering day, for the red tiles of the roofs, and diluted ink for the slate roof of the church.[4] He worked as a sign-painter at the age of twelve, making beautiful letters on the signs, and carried on the business on his own resources, much to the astonishment of the customers who came and found such a youthful proprietor. Determined to give all his time to art, he opened a studio in Cincinnati, in June, 1839, and made many sketches in the vicinity of Cincinnati, Yellow Springs, and on the Little Miami, near Clifton, Ohio. Then he visited Niagara Falls and was so impressed with their beauty that he spent the greater part of the time between 1844 and 1866 picturing them on canvas at all seasons of the year, at all times of the day and night, and from every point of view (Plate 40). He is claimed to be the first

[3]History of Clark County, Ohio, by W. H. Beers & Co., Chicago, publishers, p. 493.
[4]History of Clark County, Ohio, by W. H. Beers & Co., Chicago, publishers, p. 494.

PLATE 40—Niagara Falls. Godfrey Frankenstein. (Cincinnati Museum of Art)

artist to paint Niagara Falls on the spot and to call attention to their great
beauty, painting them with faithfulness and delicacy. "The coloring of Niagara
by Frankenstein was better than Church's, and it was a bolder and stronger
picture, though less elaborately finished."[5]

Having already painted many pictures, on a small scale, of Niagara, he made
a panorama of it, an immense canvas that was exhibited all over the country
in 1853. At the time of his death, in 1873, he left the finest collection of oil
paintings of Niagara in the world. He parted with very few of his original
paintings, but Jenny Lind purchased a few from him when she spent several
weeks at the Falls the summer following her first concert tour in America. In
1849 he moved back to Springfield, and when he was not at Niagara he was
painting scenes on the Lagonda Creek, Mad River, and other places in the
neighborhood of Springfield. He painted portraits of J. Q. Adams, Charles
Francis Adams, Abbott Lawrence and many distinguished men, and probably
the first portrait ever made of the poet, William Cullen Bryant. He spent two
years, 1867-'69, in Europe, and while there painted Mont Blanc, Chamonix
Valley and other views of the Alps near Geneva "as they had never been
painted before". The Frankenstein sisters, Eliza and Marie M. C., were also
gifted in landscape painting; Gustavus painted pictures of heather in Wales,
and George was a painter of merit, making six artists in the Frankenstein family of Springfield.

S. Jerome Uhl, a Holmes County portrait painter, maintained a studio in
Springfield about 1880. No Ohio painter was more popular than he; his
portraits are numerous in central Ohio; the one of Henry Howe, the Ohio
historian, which hangs in the State Library, Columbus, is universally admired.
It is a clear, straightforward piece of portrait painting. Mr. Uhl had another
studio in Washington, and one in New York, where many notables sat for
their portraits.

DAYTON

Dayton, on account of its proximity to Cincinnati, was fortunate in being
able to bask in the art atmosphere radiating thence in the early years.

One of Dayton's earliest artists was Charles Soule, Sr., who was born at
Freeport, Maine, in 1809, but was brought to Dayton when he was two years
old. While in his teens he painted signs, carriages, and whatever else he could
find to do with his brush, eventually trying his hand at portrait painting, producing work which attracted so much attention that orders came to him faster

---

[5]Francis C. Sessions, "Ohio Art and Artists," *Magazine of Western History*, vol. IV, 1886,
June, July, August.

than he could execute them. In 1836-'7, he painted portraits of several prominent people in Cincinnati, Cleveland, Columbus and other cities. His associates in the profession universally recognized his excellence in portraits. He lived in New York for a time, until about 1856, later returning to Dayton, where he died in 1869. Two daughters and a son were artists of note: Clara Soule Medlar painted portraits; Octavia Soule Gottschall painted in water color, and on porcelain; Charles Soule, Jr., painted portraits.

John Insco Williams, one of Dayton's most celebrated early painters, was born in 1813. He saved his pennies until he had accumulated enough to pay his way to Philadelphia, where he attended an art school for three years, and where he made the acquaintance of the eminent artist, Thomas Sully. Later, he was a pupil of George Winter, of Lafayette, Indiana. "About this time (1840) the first panorama that had ever been heard of made its appearance, being of an American river.[6] Mr. Williams immediately conceived the idea of painting a panorama of Bible history, as that, he thought, was an exceedingly rich field for such a work. His painting represented sacred history from the creation to the fall of Babylon. This panorama was exhibited in Dayton from about May 30th to June 6, 1849, at the Jefferson Street Baptist Church. It had been previously exhibited at Cincinnati. In 1850, the panorama was destroyed by fire in Independence Hall, Philadelphia. Then Williams went to Cincinnati and began another panorama on a larger scale, this one covering four thousands of yards of canvas. He was very successful with this panorama, exhibiting it in all parts of the United States. This panorama was spoiled in Baltimore by a flood which washed off nearly all the paint; he repainted it, but it was finally destroyed by fire. His fame rests mainly on his portraits. His wife, Mrs. Williams, painted ideal pictures; the best known one is 'Bleeding Kansas,' representing that state in the coils of a serpent, slavery. Two daughters, Eva W. Best, and Luly W. Buchanan, painted creditable work also."[7] The panoramas were also called cycloramas and dioramas; they were much in vogue for a while. The same J. Insco Williams later conducted a successful art school in Cincinnati.

A Quaker lad of Dayton, Edmond Edmondson, self-taught and of retiring disposition, first attracted attention by faithful studies of still life. His maturer vegetable and game pieces were in such demand that he was able to treble his prices on them. Later he took up portrait painting; one of his best studies

---

[6] This refers to Banvard's Panorama of the Mississippi River, described on p. 35 of *Art and Artists of Indiana*, by Mary Q. Burnet, as "Painted on three miles of canvas, exhibiting a vew of country twelve hundred miles in length, extending from the mouth of the Missouri River to the city of New Orleans, and to be by far the largest picture ever executed.

[7] *History of Dayton*, by Henry W. Crew, p. 564.

is that of President Garfield. He went to California for his health and died there.

"One of the most effectual efforts in the way of developing a love for art that was ever made in Dayton, was in 1880, when a few ladies, deeply interested in such work, organized a Decorative Art Society. Teachers were employed in different branches of art, classes were formed, and Professor Broome, of New Jersey, was secured to take charge of the work."[8] An old-fashioned residence, with a large garden, was leased by the Society, and here were held classes in water color, oil, modeling, china painting and other forms of decorative art. Here was made what they called "Miami pottery"; it had a semitransparent body, with a beautiful, hard glaze. Professor Broome converted it into a pottery factory on a commercial basis. The Society continued for six years, and gave a great impetus to the love and study of art, tending significantly toward an improvement in the manner of studying art.

One of the popular portrait painters of central Ohio was Laura C. Birge, of Dayton. She began her art training at home with Clara Soule, and had some art instruction in Cincinnati; later, through the aid of her relatives, the Birge and Payne families of Cleveland, she was enabled to go to Europe and study for three years. She studied with Tiel in Munich, Luminais in Paris, returning by way of England, where she spent some time taking lessons in water-color painting at a guinea (about $5.00) a lesson. She had the distinction of painting the portrait of the Prince of Wales's favorite American girl, Miss Chamberlain, and she received one thousand dollars for the work—not a small sum for that time. In Cincinnati she painted the portraits of Mr. and Mrs. Eugene Zimmerman, parents of the former Duchess of Manchester. There was fine drawing in her portraiture, which was very realistic and beautifully executed, though not distinguished for composition. She was entrusted with the restoration of many beautiful things, and was an excellent art teacher.

SANDUSKY

The Cosmopolitan Art and Literary Association, with offices in Sandusky, was like the Western Art Union of Cincinnati, in that it was an outgrowth of the American Art Union of New York. Mrs. Burnet in *Art and Artists of Indiana,* gives this authentic account of that organization founded in 1854: "Before the end of the year it had a membership of 21,576, the income from subscribers being $64,718. Extra editions of some of the periodicals had to be printed to supply the demand. The Association published two hundred thou-

[8] *History of Dayton,* United Brethren Publishing House, Dayton, p. 586.

sand copies of its illustrated catalogue. The annual drawing, February 28, 1855, was conducted on a real lottery basis: 'The ballots containing the numbers representing the names of the members were then deposited in one wheel, and the ballots containing the names of all the paintings, statuary and statuettes were placed in the other.' The drawing was made under the immediate supervision of inspectors, and each ballot recorded by the secretary."[9] The distributions made at the annual drawings were the finest works of art of the time. For instance, at one drawing, these awards were made: a statuette in bronze of the "Shepherd Boy", by Hiram Powers; two paintings by Frankenstein, "Undercliff Near Gold Spring", and an "Italian Scene", after Vernet. The large membership made the influence of the Association far-reaching. It could not fail to further the cause of art, and it must be recognized as a force contributing, at that time, to the promotion of good taste.

COLUMBUS

One naturally thinks of the capital of a state as the center of its activities in all fields of endeavor, but this is scarcely true of art interests in Ohio. In the matter of art patronage Columbus has been accused, justly, of lagging behind many cities of the same size and advantages. Yet from the earliest decades of the city, when all was rough and uncultivated in its aspect, art had its followers in Columbus, who strove conscientiously to portray beauty in a truthful manner.

Perhaps the first artist in Columbus to achieve more than local fame was William Bambrough, who painted a full-length portrait of George Washington. Before the perfection of photography the demands for perpetuating the features of some one loved or respected seem to explain the development of portrait painting in communities not so well advanced in other phases of art. Bambrough was an Englishman, born at Durham, in 1792, at a time when Washington's name was not pleasant to English ears, so we find some pleasing irony in the coincidence which brought Bambrough to America to paint Washington's portrait. He settled in Columbus in 1819. "This painter was something of a naturalist. He not only surrounded his home with a garden of various flowers, but he became acquainted with Audubon, the great ornithologist, and with him made many tours of the Southern states between the years 1824 and 1832. It is probable that he assisted Audubon in the preparation of those plates which have ever since been the wonder of scientists."[10] Bambrough died in 1860.

---

[9] *Art and Artists of Indiana*, Mary Q. Burnet, p. 82.
[10] *The Ohio State Journal*, October 26, 1911.

The first native painters of any renown were the Walcutt brothers, William, George, and David Broderick, sons of John Macey Walcutt, whose family closely identified its name with the history of Columbus. Tradition says that none of the three brothers had an opportunity for art training until late in life, but that the urge to paint was so strong that they could not resist it. The best known of the three was William, who, in middle life, after he had established himself as a painter, spent seven or eight years in Europe studying with the best painters of the time. There he won the first medal ever awarded an American painter by the French Academy. After he returned to New York he made many portraits. In the latter part of his life he devoted himself to sculpture (see page 139). For several years he was employed by the government as an expert to appraise works of art coming into the port of New York. William Walcutt died in 1882. George Walcutt divided his time between landscapes and portraits, later moving to Kentucky. David Broderick, who set up a studio in St. Louis, made many portraits of Columbus. The Walcutts opened a small museum, the first institution of that kind that Columbus had known.

Chronologically, the next painter of note in Columbus, was John H. Witt, born in Dublin, Wayne County, Indiana, near the Ohio River border, in 1840. When he was eighteen years old he went to Cincinnati to study with J. O. Eaton, who had become renowned for his portrait and figure painting. In 1862, Witt settled in Columbus, and painted his first ambitious picture, "Rebecca at the Well". It was showered with praises, and sold for five hundred dollars, a very good price for that day. It hangs now in the Odd Fellows' Temple, Columbus, and is quite a creditable picture, judged even from modern standards: the color is clear and beautiful, the composition interesting. Many people of Columbus, Zanesville, and central Ohio sat to Witt for their portraits. He is one of the painters most generously represented with portraits on the walls of the State House, thirteen of the fifty-odd portraits of Ohio's governors being attributed to him. 1873 found him in Washington painting portraits of many notables, among them General Sherman, Senator Sherman, Judge Swayne, and Charles Sumner. Mr. Witt took an active part in the life of the capital city, and was a member of a literary club of which James A. Garfield was president. He went to New York in 1878 and became an associate member of the New York Academy of Fine Arts.

Silas Martin was one of the pupils of Witt. He grew to manhood in the quiet village of Westerville, where he began his art career by studying drawing with Mrs. Thompson, who, curiously enough, later was one of his pupils in water color. Mr. Martin enjoyed a wide reputation as a portrait painter.

Probably the best known among his works is his portrait of President McKinley painted while he was governor of Ohio; Mrs. McKinley declared this to be the best portrait ever painted of her husband. During the exposition at St. Louis, it was placed on exhibition in the Ohio Building, and later was removed to New York City, where it is now in the possession of the Ohio Historical Society. In Gray Chapel, at Delaware, are his portraits of Doctor McCabe and Professor Williams; in the Library on the Ohio State University campus at Columbus, is his portrait of Doctor W. O. Thompson, commissioned by the class of 1904; in the State House, Columbus, is his portrait of Governor Thomas Kirker. At the Ohio State University, he was head of the art department from 1898 until his death, in 1906. He was an excellent instructor; among his pupils was George Bellows, who had a deep affection for him, visiting him often during his long, last illness. His later work was landscape and still-life painting. He had a keen perception of color, belonged to the old school, and was never carried away by fads. His friend and fellow artist, Maurice S. Hague, paid him this tribute: "Silas Martin was a producer of the beautiful. His life was spent in searching for it. His work days through the years were given up entirely to honest and sincere efforts to depict it. He has done his part in adding to the world's store of beautiful things."[11]

Another pupil of Witt to attain distinction was Phil Clover, born in Franklin County. He studied in Paris under Durand in 1879, but, it seems, had little other training. When he returned to Columbus he created quite a furor by exhibiting a nude "Fatima" in one of the High Street shop windows. It was displayed with special lighting arrangements, and taken all over the country for exhibition, producing a sensation. Hanging in the Ohio historical exhibit at the World's Fair at Chicago, 1893, was a painting by Phil Clover, called "General Putnam and his Band Landing on the Banks of the Muskingum River, April 7, 1788." The picture has little or nothing to commend it as art, but is interesting historically, and at present hangs in the Ohio State Museum, Columbus. Clover painted landscapes, figures and portraits in oil.

James H. Mosure revealed power as a delineator of negro character. He came to Columbus when ten years old, in 1864, and worked with his father in frescoing, while studying with John H. Witt. He contributed to *Harper's Weekly* and *Leslie's Weekly,* illustrated papers. With headquarters at Atlanta, Georgia, he made the illustrations for the book *Uncle Remus* for D. Appleton & Company. *Harper's Weekly* relates that an allegorical painting, twelve by twenty feet, representing the New South welcoming the nations for the Cotton Exposition, was unveiled and greeted with warm admiration.

---

[11] *The Honey Jar,* October, 1906.

An artist of the greatest promise who did not live to the fullest flowering of his genius was Elis F. Miller, who was born in Canton, but lived nearly all of his life in Columbus. In a highly eulogistic article on Mr. Miller, E. O. Randall writes: "He was widely known as a water-color painter, and in that line he had few, if any, superiors. From choice, rather than confined capabilities, he adhered closely to landscape, and generally chose for his studies bits of simple scenery in which nature posed in her most peaceful, reposeful moods. His drawing was scrupulously accurate and distinct, and his coloring clear and harmonious. He selected the heart of a grove, the bank of a brook, or the base of a hillside, never a long-range nor far-fetched vista of vision. Mr. Miller was more than a water-colorist. His restless abilities drove his deft hand to every variety of work: oil, sepia, water color, crayon, and charcoal."[12] Mr. Miller had three pictures at the annual exhibition of the American Water Color Society, held in 1881, at the Academy of Design, New York City. They received very favorable comment, and two were sold at good prices. New York artists could not understand how a man in Ohio who had never been to Europe nor studied out of Ohio could do such work as Elis F. Miller produced (see page 239).

A painstaking artist who had to work out his own career was John Jay Barber. He was born in Sandusky. After studying law, and being admitted to the bar in 1862, he joined the army. At the close of the war, he returned home in poor health; it was then he became interested in painting, but without any instruction at all. He came to Columbus in 1871 and opened a studio in the wall-paper establishment of E. O. Randall. He was a good draughtsman, his work being rather tight and detailed, with color as nature presented it. His landscapes were beautiful scenes of the Muskingum Valley. Then he began to paint cattle, and so well did he work in this special line that he became recognized for it, his pictures of cattle along the stream with overhanging trees, being honored in nearly all art exhibitions of the East, West, and South. The World's Fair at New Orleans, 1884, awarded him a prize for his cattle "portraits", as they were properly called. Herman C. Baker painted cattle even better than did Barber; unfortunately his promising career was cut short by an early death. George Critchfield was another young man certain to have produced fine work if he had lived only a few years more; most of his work perished in a fire, but some excellent wood carving and very delicate drawings exist. John Tidball must not be omitted, for his work is now historical. Who can again paint the old-time bar with the loafers huddled around a barrel

---

[12] *The Inland Monthly,* February, 1885.

PLATE 41—William McKinley. Albert C. Fauley. State House, Columbus.
(Baker Art Gallery)

stove? The rail fences in his landscapes may soon be a thing of the past, too.

An incident seemingly very insignificant may lead to amazing results. One day in early summer, when Mrs. Virginia Jones, of Circleville, and her daughter, Genevieve, were riding through the country, they saw an oriole's nest hanging from a tree. In an attempt to learn something about it, they found that there was no book dealing with the nests of birds, so they set themselves to the task of making such a work. Neither of them had any art training, and the art schools were closed for the summer. Their only knowledge of the making of lithographs had to be obtained from the encyclopedia. Mrs. Jones's son writes: "Their ability in drawing and coloring is best shown in the sixty-eight plates illustrating *Nests and Eggs of Birds of Ohio*. The drawings were made, free-hand, directly upon lithographic stones. The prints were made upon Whatman's double elephant paper, hot-pressed, and were colored by hand. The work ranks supreme among ornithological publications. The last copy sold brought $1,250.00."[13] Miss Eliza Shulze, Circleville, and Miss Josephine Klippart, Columbus, collaborated with Mrs. Jones and her daughter in making the colored plates for this work, which was intended to serve as a companion to Audubon's bird book. These women worked upon the colored plates for six years, completing their illustrations in 1886, the date of publication. Miss Klippart has done much excellent work in water color. She says that her most important work was the illustration of the *First Ohio Fish Report*. She will be remembered as the founder of the Ohio Water Color Society.

The Columbus artists who were best known beyond their home city were Mr. and Mrs. Albert C. Fauley, who were exceedingly popular at the height of their careers. Mr. Fauley was born at Fultonham, near Zanesville, studied at Philadelphia, then with Benjamin Constant, Bouguereau, and Blanc at Paris. He made many trips abroad, painting pictures of Holland scenes and Venetian waterways. Usually he overworked his canvases, resulting in a woolly technique. He was the leading portraitist of the time in Columbus, and is represented in the State House with portraits of Governors Campbell, McKinley, and Bushnell, and Chief Justices Swan and Williams. The McKinley portrait is a three-quarter-length figure, and is well known through reproductions, as it is probably the most admired of all the McKinley portraits. It hangs in the governor's office in the State House, Columbus (Plate 41).

Mr. and Mrs. Fauley exerted a remarkable influence on the creative fine arts and their appreciation in Columbus. They were active members of the Columbus Art League, and their home was a center for artist groups. They spent sev-

[13] Letter from Dr. Howard Jones, Circleville, Ohio, April 7, 1930.

PLATE 42—Fig. 1, Dogs Afield. Edmund H. Osthaus. Fig. 2, Along the Maumee.
Thomas S. Parkhurst. (Toledo Museum of Art)

eral summers in Massachusetts. Mrs. Fauley received many prizes for her pictures painted around Provincetown and Gloucester. Critics said that Mrs. Fauley (Lucy Stanberry Fauley) was the better painter of the two. She used a full brush with a broad and direct style which showed the influence of Twachtman on the painting of the time. Her landscapes and portraits alike are of high quality. She obtained remarkably good effects through her manner of heavily-laid-on paints. Picturesque characteristics of Italian scenes, the green Michigan woods, or Massachusetts harbor studies, she made into decorative compositions.

The presence of an art school in Columbus doubtless was instrumental in having some art instruction put into the public schools, as we find this account in an article written by Mr. Francis Sessions: "In July, 1883, at a meeting of the National Education Association in Saratoga, New York, a committee was appointed to inquire into methods of art study throughout the country and report upon a course of drawing in public schools. Columbus was reported as one of four cities that had a fully developed course for all grades; the other three cities were in Massachusetts, but the course of study adopted was the one in use in Columbus."[14]

The Paint and Clay Club enrolled as members all the leading artists of the time in Columbus. It had a high standard of requirements for membership, but gradually dwindled down and became extinct.

The Pen and Pencil Club, founded in 1897, must be recognized as an important art influence in Columbus. Many artists, now well known, have been on its membership list at some time; Columbus, never having been an art center, was not able to hold them long, and they moved on to more attractive locations. George Bellows had his studio in the Club rooms; Russell Legge and Sid Walton, were later very active in the Scarab Club, Detroit; Ben Warden was one of the guiding hands in this fine association; Fred Collins has held the torch aloft for many years. The Pen and Pencil Club has carried on all these years without any endowment.

The Columbus artists gained much of their inspiration by visiting the Cincinnati exhibits, the best in the West, as the art exhibits that had been shown in the East during the winter were brought to Cincinnati in the summer.

TOLEDO

The birth of art in Toledo began with the organization of the Draconian Club, about 1875. When it was an infant organization it brought the first

---

[14] *Magazine of Western History*, vol. IV, 1886, June, July, August. "Art and Artists of Ohio," Francis C. Sessions.

PLATE 43—Spirit of '76. A. M. Willard. (City Hall, Cleveland)

art exhibit to Toledo; the exhibit was one of paintings by foreign artists. The chief promoter and sponsor for the exhibit was David R. Locke, otherwise known as Petroleum V. Nasby, whose letters in *The Toledo Blade* entertained the whole country. Mr. Locke was a genuine lover of the beautiful. The success of the first exhibit prompted the Club to arrange for another one two years later. Again Mr. Locke was its chief support, and through *The Blade* he invited artists of Northwest Ohio and all art collectors to send something for the exhibit. The result was truly gratifying, and a wonderfully valuable and interesting exhibit was held.

A man who, for years, was the dean of Toledo painters, Thomas Shrewsbury Parkhurst, was then a very young man. He assisted Mr. Locke with the exhibit, that being the first time Mr. Parkhurst displayed any of his marine paintings. The third exhibit was truly an ambitious one; it attracted thousands of people in comparison to the hundreds who had visited the exhibits formerly. The next stepping-stone in the Toledo art world was the organization by Mr. Parkhurst, of the Toledo Tile Club, in 1893. A quotation from Mr. Parkhurst's fascinating account of it will do more here than volumes could to describe the situation:

"In 1900, the club had its first exhibit in my store in Superior Street, and out of that event grew the movement that resulted in the establishment of the magnificent Toledo Museum of Art. Among exhibitors were George W. Stevens, charter member of the club, then connected with *The Blade* as reporter, David L. Stine, architect of the Lucas County Court House, Edmund H. Osthaus, celebrated painter of dogs, and Harry Brownley, well-known architect.

"After the exhibit, so enthused were we with its success and so fired with the idea of establishing a permanent home for art in Toledo, that a number of us got together and, in connection with Mr. Stevens as leader, talked art museum almost day and night for weeks. Robinson Locke, worthy son of an illustrious sire, became interested and did much through *The Blade* to further the project. Finally Mr. Stevens, in an inspired moment, elicited the coöperation of Edward Drummond Libbey, who gave us the use of an old building in Madison Avenue for museum purposes, but we lacked means to take any particular advantage of his generosity. Finally George Stevens either filched or bought a chair (I have never been able to learn which), and Graff M. Achlin donated one small, framed landscape, which was the first treasure ever owned by the Museum. George would place that picture on the floor in front of the chair and then he would go out scouting for prospective contributors to the Museum fund. One by one he brought Toledo's wealthy residents in, sat them on that old chair in front of the landscape and then eloquently dilated on art and the terrible fate that would surely befall Toledo unless it had an art museum second to none in the United States. Many a thousand-dollar contribution he obtained in that manner. Then, in turn, came hundred-dollar, fifty-dollar, ten-dollar and five-dollar contributions, hundreds of them, until the Museum was assured."[15]

T. S. Parkhurst was a marine painter (Fig. 2, Plate 42), practically self-taught, who was able to put upon canvas the brilliant colors he found in nature. He painted the coves, waves, pools, and trees of the Atlantic coast from Labrador to the Gulf, in all their moods. There is little sky in his pictures, as his view of the sea shore is always from a high point, thus realizing a more brilliant, airy quality. For forty-seven years he lived in Toledo; then in 1916 he went to Carmel-by-the-Sea, California, where he might be near the sea he loved so well. That he was able to get the spiritual quality of the sea, is proved by his poem, "Waves", which he wrote after reading Joyce Kilmer's inspiring lyric, "Trees".

Many of the pictures by Parkhurst have all the elements of earth, sky, land, water, and trees. He painted in a modern manner, using the scheme of three planes: background, middle distance, and foreground. The idea of distance as determined by the three planes is clearly evident in his tree pictures. Simplicity, naturalness, and liquidity, are characteristics of his work. He bathes a sparkling expanse of the sea in the glory of color and movement. Lines depict the force of the waves—there is action everywhere. The color of an emerald-hued pool is enchanting in contrast and gorgeousness.

Mr. Edmund Osthaus was long considered one of the most distinguished representatives in the world of art of Toledo. He was said to be among the world's foremost painters of dogs, though he was equally facile in the painting of landscapes and figures. His early life was full of adventure; he was born at Hildesheim, Germany; went to Mexico with his father and the Emperor Maximilian; then the family fled to America after the execution of Maximilian, and settled in Toledo. He was principal of the Art School of Toledo until 1886, when he decided to devote all his time to painting. Many examples of his work are in Toledo, hanging in the Valentine Theater, Chamber of Commerce lounge, Secor Hotel, Toledo Club, Museum of Art (Fig. 1, Plate 42), and in several Toledo homes. He understood dogs, was very fond of the hunt, and was technically equipped to paint dogs well, since for many years he was a judge in various national field tests for dogs.

The work of Mr. Osthaus is summed up in a masterly way in the following

---

[15] *The Toledo Blade*, September 30, 1922.

account: "Today the specialist has a recognized position which gives him credit
within limits, and possibly causes him to be looked at as narrow from the
broader viewpoint of general work. It is a pleasure, therefore, to find a man,
a painter, who, while restricting his subject matter to a limited field, is nevertheless master of the technique of his craft. Edmund H. Osthaus is not only
a good dog painter—he is a good painter who paints dogs. His drawing is admirable, and his ability to execute a particularly vivid portrait of an animal is
something that always attracts the trained craftsman who knows from experience that this kind of work, unusual as it is, calls for a very special kind of mastery of the different points of art. The best man in any work is apt to be the one
who brings to it the greatest amount of personal interest. Mr. Osthaus does
his dog work from love of that part of the game, and he is fortunate in being
so able in its portrayal. His personal friends have seen many landscapes by
him that are admirable in composition and color. For this reason they are an-
noyed sometimes that he restricts himself to but one public field—that of painting dogs. Sometimes, however, they are pleased, for the lucky one who has an
'Osthaus' of his favorite animal is not only qualified to rank among sportsmen
'who know', but has a constant reminder of how that dog really looked and
was. That is good portraiture, and would be, were the subjects gods or men
or little red apples. Mr. Osthaus's work as a painter of dogs has been, for all
dog men, the perpetuation of the real type of excellence in each breed as he
paints it."[16]

That Toledo is the art center it is today, may be credited largely to the vision
and the patient persistence of these three friends and art pioneers of Toledo:
George W. Stevens, Thomas S. Parkhurst, and Edmund H. Osthaus.

CLEVELAND

The Western Reserve section of Ohio, in many ways, seemed like a bit of
New England set down in the Middle West. This is especially true as to art,
for the few early portrait painters who painted there continued the colonial
traditions of portraiture. A few struggling painters, one or two wood carvers,
and two or three clever stone cutters, constituted the art colony in Cleveland
until a period a little more than fifty years ago.

"A definite art atmosphere began in Cleveland with the work of a little group
of ambitious young men who started a life class in the studio of A. M. Willard."[17] As their names will show, they were the sons of German immigrants

---

[16]*Memoirs of Lucas County,* vol. II, p. 473.
[17]*Art and Archæology,* November, 1923. "Art and Artists of Cleveland," I. T. Frary.

PLATE 44—The Edge of the Woods. John Semon. (Cleveland Museum of Art)

or immigrants themselves, and all of them poor men working hard for a living and an education. These young men were George Grossman, F. C. Gottwald, John Semon, Adam Lehr, Louis Loeb, Herman Herkomer, O. V. Schubert, Daniel Wehrschmidt, Emil Wehrschmidt, Otto Bacher, Arthur Schneider, Max Bohm, and Hubert Herkomer. This brave, enthusiastic thirteen came to be known as the Old Bohemians. Other artists joined the original Bohemians, and in 1882 at the invitation of the city fathers occupied the top floor of the old City Hall, which was the meeting place of the Cleveland Art Club which they had formed in 1876.

The leader, Archibald M. Willard, had the rugged, indomitable spirit of his Vermont family, but little art training except many years of hard work and a few weeks' study in the studio of J. O. Eaton, in New York. However, he had won national recognition from that vital expression of American patriotism, "The Spirit of '76". It was painted on the eve of the Centennial celebration at Philadelphia in 1876, and was originally called "Yankee Doodle". After it had been exhibited at the Centennial, Boston, Washington and other places, the name was changed to "The Spirit of '76" (Plate 43).

Mr. Willard's description of it follows: "The old man in the center was my father, Rev. Daniel Willard, who was born in Vermont, in 1801, which was near enough to '76 to have his mind and sentiment stirred by the stories of that time, especially as he was of Revolutionary stock. He was strong-faced, vigorous, six feet and one inch tall, and was seventy-four years of age when he came up from Wellington to pose for me. By nature he was genial, but when aroused looked as though ready to charge the enemy across the ramparts. The fifer was Hugh Mosier, who lived in a small town to the west of Cleveland. They declined to take him as a soldier of the Civil War because of his age, but he thrust himself and his fife into it. No Fourth of July celebration in the country could get along without him."[18] He was the best fifer in Northern Ohio.

The drummer boy was Henry K. Devereux, "selected from a group of boys attending Brooks Military School, Cleveland. His father, a railroad president, bought the picture and presented it to his native town, Marblehead, Massachusetts, where it now hangs in Abbot Hall. Mr. Willard painted his second 'Spirit of '76' when he was seventy-six years old; on the occasion when it was accepted by the city he was introduced as 'our grand old young man'."[19] He was one of the staunchest figures in pioneer Cleveland art, and a greatly loved leader.

---

[18] *Everybody's,* July, 1917.
[19] *The Spirit of '76,* by Henry K. Devereux.

PLATE 45—Jessica. Louis Loeb. (Cleveland Museum of Art)

Some of the founders of the Cleveland Art Club achieved international reputations. The cousins, Hubert and Herman Herkomer, were probably the most widely known. Hubert Herkomer accumulated one hundred thousand dollars in six months in New York making portraits at three thousand dollars each. Then he went to England, built a fine studio, and was the head of the artists' colony and the famous school at Bushy-Hertz near London. At twenty-six years of age he won a gold medal at the Paris Salon for a picture of some old pensioners of the Crimean War gathered together in a chapel watching one of their number entering his last sleep; it had unusual lighting effects and was called, "The Last Muster." Two medals were awarded to each country; Millais was the English artist who shared the honors with Herkomer, each receiving a medal.

Hubert Herkomer contributed to the early numbers of the London *Graphic* drawings which helped to make his reputation. He made portraits of many members of the royal family and other notables; his water-color portrait of John Ruskin is mentioned by the London *Times* of May 2, 1881, as one of the best of his portraits. Mezzotint engraving was revived by him, and he became the father of modern mezzotint. In fact, he was as versatile as the Italian renaissance masters: a marvelous draughtsman, silversmith, worker in iron, maker of etchings and mezzotints, painter in oil or water color, singer, and actor. For his many achievements he was knighted by the English government.

John Herkomer, the father of Herman Herkomer was a wood carver and modeler. He trained his son to draw at the early age of four. Herman's cousin Hubert was very fond of him, and contributed to his training from childhood to be an artist. In 1880 he was studying at the Art Students' League of New York; he studied for some time in Munich, and later found his cousin in England. There he painted a portrait of Hubert Herkomer in his Oxford robes; it was exhibited at the Royal Academy show, and divided honors with Sargent. His work is largely portraits, with obvious Spanish tendencies. Herman Herkomer returned to Cleveland before 1912, continued westward to California, and has been highly honored there.

Emil and Daniel Wehrschmidt belonged to the Herkomer colony in England. Daniel was a teacher in the Art School and still exhibits in the Royal Academy; Emil has an enviable reputation for making fine copies of old masters. Arthur Schneider found his forte in North Africa, where he was court painter to the Sultan of Morocco, and painted brilliant water-color pictures full of interest and artistic feeling, and the glorious color of that country. George Grossman became an excellent landscape painter, as did John Semon, who excelled in woodland interiors (Plate 44).

PLATE 46—Evening Meal. Max Bohm. (Metropolitan Museum of Art)

Louis Loeb was a remarkable genius, showing a simplicity of character and an independence of spirit. He was a poor boy, but helped himself by teaching others the art which he was learning. When he was only thirteen years old he was apprenticed to a lithographer, and before he was twenty-five he was a well-known worker in that field. He went to Paris to study under Gérôme and obtained a medal at the French Salon. On his return to America he devoted all his time to magazine illustration, in which he attained distinction and was one of the best-paid men. He regarded the business of the illustrator very seriously, giving a thoughtful and beautiful interpretation to every scene he chose. He will be remembered for his illustrations of Mark Twain's *Pudd'n-head Wilson* beginning in *Century,* of November, 1893; for *A Cumberland Vendetta* by John Fox, June, 1894; and the *Via Crucis* of Marion Crawford, 1898-'99; and for many other series.

As a painter Loeb was notable, first of all, in the domain of portraiture, the master of rich, mellow tones, drawn with certainty, and showing ability in construction (Plate 45). His landscapes were marked by a certain likeness to the Barbizon school, but always bore the stamp of independent power. Loeb acquainted himself with imaginative writings to enlarge his spirit in the pursuit of his art; his greatest strength lay in his allegory. One is always conscious of the mysterious in everything allegorical he did, for example, "The Temple of the Winds", which won him a medal at the Pan-American Exposition, Buffalo, 1901. Loeb never put his work before the public until he believed he had put into it the best thought and execution of which he was capable. All his work was done with superior technical skill; there never was a haphazard production. He had an intense desire to help his own people—the Jews, and early became identified with the Zionist movement.

An artist who took for his motto, "produce, not reproduce", was Max Bohm. He believed that an artist should create something, or say nothing. In studying the art of the ages, one attribute is noticeable in the masterpieces that have stood the test of time: the artist had some idea to express and was successful in conveying the idea to the observer. Everything Max Bohm painted had an individual style and dignity, and an idea to present. He was so thoroughly familiar with the fundamental principles of art, that he was not hindered with technical matters and could let his emotion have full freedom. One always finds a broad vision and vital thought in his pictures.

Bohm made his living by his art all his life; as a boy he earned money by drawing and painting, and designing lithographs in Cleveland. When he was nineteen years old (in 1887) he and an aunt, also an artist, went to Paris to study at the Louvre and the Julian Academy. He was only twenty-seven when his first notable success was achieved with the canvas, "En Mer", which was given a place of honor at the Paris Salon. Then he became a sailor, for he believed that an artist should have a well-rounded background, and should know more than one phase of life. So his first period of painting was devoted to pictures of the sea: ships, boats, sailors, and fisherfolk. His sailors are powerful men, who seem to glory in the dangers of their hard life; he himself was a big man, physically, and akin to them in sturdiness. "Crossing the Bar", is one of his interesting sea subjects: an old sailor with sharp features and far-seeing eye, is rowing a boat; beside him sits a small boy thrilled with the experience. The dark tones of the sail and the boat contrast with the whitecaps of the waves. "Bohm painted many canvases with subjects relative to seafaring life, yet with no thought of being considered purely marine paintings in the ordinary sense of carefully computed wave structure, surf and rocks. Material reality was never his goal, rather the existence of unseen force expressed in dramatic terms, at times almost violent, as in the painting known as 'The English Channel', shown in the National Academy."[20]

In the second period or style of Max Bohm, he gave attention to figure painting, especially to women and children, and the joys and loves of motherhood. The French government bought "The Family" for the Luxembourg; people were so enraptured with it that it was necessary to put a railing in front of it to prevent injury to the picture. In the Metropolitan Museum is "The Evening Meal" (Plate 46), a picture which exhibits his breadth of style and optimistic spirit. It has a compact composition, showing an intimate domestic scene of a mother holding a baby upon her arm as she stoops before the hearth where she cooks supper under the attentive eyes of two older children. The group is lighted by the glow from the fire. Bohm painted figures with the simplicity of the classic tradition, yet they were very modern in spirit. "At the moment in the world when figure painting is in danger of becoming absurd when it is not vulgar, Max Bohm's work compels cultivated attention."[21]

Bohm returned to America to make it his permanent home in 1915, and then he began his third and last style of work—mural painting. In the Law Library of the Cuyahoga County Court House, Cleveland, is his historical mural, "The New England Town Meeting". The elders, seated on benches under large trees, are casting their votes in a hat. In the background are New England farmhouses and a blockhouse. Simple masses of dark red, in foliage and cos-

---

[20] Quoted from Milch Galleries catalogue.
[21] Elliott Daingerfield, in catalogue of Grand Central Art Gallery Memorial Exhibition of Works of Bohm.

tumes, are outlined against a grey sky; shadows are deep and soft. An Indian, a soldier in armor, and the men in picturesque high-crowned hats and white collars, make the mural full of interest. The beautiful home of John Munro Longyear, at Brookline, Massachusetts, has in its music room, decorations by Bohm that are said to be among the finest murals in the country. In this series of four panels he uses figures to express the forms and rhythms of music. They leave no doubt of his talent as a mural painter, and attest his ability in making a composition. He lectured for twelve years in Paris and London on the theory and practice of picture composition.

In this early period of the art pioneers there were other able men who helped to pave the way for the future of art in Cleveland: John Kavanaugh, Frank H. Tompkins, Charles Nelan, F. W. Simmons, Joseph De Camp, Kenyon Cox and many more who might well be mentioned. "The ideals of those men were without doubt responsible in large measure for the standards which are maintained by the artistic profession of Cleveland today."[22]

The Cleveland School of Art rendered a large service to the community. Incorporated in 1882 by Mrs. S. H. Kimball, it was a department of Western Reserve University, from 1888 to 1891. Much of the credit for the helpfulness of the Cleveland School of Art during the early years was due to Miss Georgia Leighton Norton, who served as its head from 1890 until 1922, when poor health required her retirement.

Other clubs followed the Cleveland Art Club, some destined to enjoy a short life, while others still exert an active influence for art. A Camera Club sprang into existence in the nineties, presenting some remarkable exhibitions of photographic art, with the work of Carl Semon, nephew of John Semon, the landscape painter, reaching the peak. The year 1893 found the Brush and Palette Club flourishing, and a year later the Water Color Society was formed. The joint exhibition of these three art organizations kept the public aware of what was taking place in the field of art in their city.

"Speaking of exhibitions reminds one of the great Art Loan Exhibition in 1893, in the Garfield Building. The times were bad then, and the rich people of Cleveland felt it their duty to do something for the alleviation of the general suffering. Someone proposed an art exhibit, one worthy of the name. The possessors of paintings all over the land were appealed to. The response was generous, and in a short time several hundreds of worthy paintings could be hung. The success of the enterprise was gratifying in the extreme. A large sum was realized and turned over to the poor funds. Professor Charles Olney,

---

[22] *Art and Archæology,* November, 1923, p. 196.

Mr. Charles F. Brush and Mr. W. J. White, all of Cleveland, and all possessors of fine paintings, had most willingly robbed their walls of their treasures in order to insure the success of the exhibition. The following year a second exhibition of the same nature was arranged . . . . . Since then we have seen some things of great artistic value, but at very rare occasions. At times there were on exhibition in the Olney Art Gallery, Michael Munkacsy's 'Christ Before Pilate', and 'The Last Moments of Mozart', both paintings of world fame. Gérôme's 'Crucifixion' and 'The King of the Desert', were also in this gallery."[23]

*   *   *   *   *

There is a tendency today to fall down and worship false gods, and to think that all paintings executed by a former generation is worthless. Even a slight acquaintance with the early art in Ohio will prove that quite the contrary is true. The artists, as a rule, were conscientious, and, considering the training some of them experienced, the critic will agree that their work is creditable in color, drawing, composition, and the idea expressed. Much of the work of the early artists has been lost, as no effort was made to preserve it. There should be a corner in the museums for a retrospective exhibit, a memorial and historical exhibition showing the advancement of art in Ohio. It might afford a valuable lesson in humility to many of the younger painters.

---

[23] "Art Life in Cleveland," by Carl Lorenz, *Ohio Architect,* June, 1908.

CHAPTER VI

Early Sculptors

WHEN we consider that sculpture was a late development in the United States, we realize that sculptural history began early in the history of Ohio.

Northern peoples, throughout the course of their history, have not been prone to express themselves in sculpture. Their great sculptors may be counted on the fingers of one hand: Thorwaldsen, Flaxman and a few others. Despite the weight of tradition, Scandinavians are at present in the front rank of sculptors. Sculpture in the past has seemed to be a medium more adapted to the people of such southern climes as Egypt, Greece, and Italy. The early settlers in America not only fell heir to this deterring influence of the Anglo-Saxon neglect or indifference to sculpture, but they brought with them the Puritan's overwhelming prejudice against the nude. Besides, the American marble beds of Vermont, Colorado, and Georgia were long undiscovered, so good marble had to be imported from Italy at great expense and with much delay. Nor were there any examples of sculpture here to inspire the creative artist of colonial times to express their ideas in stone.

In spite of these handicaps, we find in Cincinnati as early as 1825 a Vermont lad, Hiram Powers, trying his skill modeling in wax. A German artist, Frederick Eckstein, had a studio there and had won some renown making busts of several prominent Cincinnati citizens. Powers made friends with him and spent all the time he could working with Eckstein, who was able to secure for the young man a position as manager of Letton's Museum of wax figures, which we read of as a very popular place of entertainment. This work was quite to the taste of Powers; he lost no opportunity to model in the medium at hand, making portraits and dramatic tableaux in this fragile material. The advanced step of working in stone soon followed. Among his first marble busts was one of Judge Burnet (Plate 47), now in the Cincinnati Museum. It is still considered matchless in its fidelity of likeness, and continues to be a model for portrait busts.

In 1835 Powers went to Washington, D. C., and attracted much attention there by the busts he made of such distinguished people as General Jackson, Daniel Webster, John C. Calhoun, and Chief Justice Marshall, all very rare types of American character. Nicholas Longworth, of Cincinnati, that good Mæcenas always ready to assist struggling artists, recognized the genius of the

134

PLATE 47—Portrait Bust of Judge Burnet. Hiram Powers. (Cincinnati Museum of Art)

young sculptor and generously contributed the funds so that Powers could go to Europe to study. Italy was then the only place for our ambitious sculptors to receive the training and inspiration necessary to develop their art. His work in Florence soon achieved a considerable reputation. He was one of the first professional sculptors America had produced. Ohio can well claim the honor of sending out the sculptor who first made known to Europe the genius of our country in the art of sculpture; Greenough and Crawford had preceded Powers to Italy, but they had made no reputation for themselves.

Florence continued to be the home of Hiram Powers until his death. Francis Sessions, of Columbus, wrote of visiting him there: "We visited his studio in Florence several times, and were delighted with an exquisitely carved hand of an infant daughter of Powers; although small and simple, it is one of the most touching and artistic of all Powers' productions."[1] Another friend of art, Tuckerman, relates that: "Thorwaldsen visited his (Powers') studio and pronounced his bust of Webster the best work of the kind executed in modern times."[2]

The fame of Hiram Powers rests mainly upon "The Greek Slave", finished in 1843. The subject occurred to him while reading accounts of the sale of beautiful Circassian girls as slaves to the Turks. When Cincinnati received a copy of "The Greek Slave" in 1847, consternation reigned; finally a committee of clergymen was appointed to decide whether it was proper to exhibit a nude figure to the people, and after very careful deliberation it was considered permissible to show the statue. Wherever it was exhibited it created a sensation, and was heralded as one of the greatest works in sculpture. An attempt to say anything new about it would be futile. We can do no better than to turn to Lorado Taft for a description of "The Greek Slave": "She stands stripped and manacled, offered perhaps for sale in a public place. Her right hand resting upon a convenient pillar supports her weary frame; the left repeats the gesture of the 'Venus de Medici'. The head is turned abruptly to the left and bowed. The face is tinged with sadness . . . The artist's ideal, conceived with dignified moderation, was wrought out with infinite pains. Ignorant and unskillful in the modeling of the body, Powers turned with zest to the things he felt he could do well. The fringe and the embroidery on the mantle, with the chain, are very prominent features. The latter is a marvel of patient detail, like the chains which boys whittle out of a single stick . . . If the effect expended upon these accessories had been intelligently applied to the figure itself, the

[1] *Magazine of Western History,* June, July, August, 1886. "Art and Artists," Francis Sessions.
[2] *Book of the Artists,* Tuckerman, p. 278.

PLATE 48—Evangeline. Hiram Powers. (Cincinnati Museum of Art)

result might have been more pleasing to the cultivated taste of today; but it was admirable for its time, and wins our respect even now."[3] Powers made six or eight replicas of the figure; the Cincinnati Museum owns one of them, the Corcoran Gallery of Art another, and the others are said to be in Europe.

According to Goss, "The most beautiful specimens of Powers's work now in Cincinnati are two marble angels on the altar of the cathedral of Saint Peter. There is an interesting story in regard to these angels which states that when Archbishop Purcell was contemplating ordering such sculptures he wrote to Powers asking him about his fee for two angels 'of the usual size'. The reply of Powers was that angels varied so much in size, some being large, some small, that he could not judge what was meant by 'the usual size'. The Archbishop replied, 'Take two of the prettiest girls in Florence and put wings on them.' The sculptor took the hint, and the result of his work may be seen in the two angelic figures of the Italian type of femine loveliness."[4]

"Evangeline", in the Cincinnati Museum, is one of those pretty but sugary and uninspiring busts that Powers made. Similar ones are "Genevra", "Psyche", and "Proserpine"; in most instances a circle of leaves forms a nest or base for these busts. Fashions alter in sculpture as well as in other fields; today that well-smoothed flesh is still lovely, but it is lacking in the vigor and vitality we look for in creations of present-day sculptors (Plate 48).

Nearly every American museum boasts of one or more portrait busts by Powers. Powers never did better work than these. His portrait busts of men are excellent, for instance: of Webster, now in Chicago; Wm. J. Stone, in the Corcoran Gallery of Art; Franklin and Jefferson in the Capitol at Washington. Hiram Powers had a charming personality, which served as a big factor in the surplus of admiration given to him and to everything he chiseled. The fact that his genius budded in Ohio and was developed through the generosity of an Ohio citizen, gives the state a legitimate claim upon him.

An untimely death cut short the career of one promising young Ohio sculptor. The stonecutter's yard has been the cradle of sculpture in all ages. While chiseling out the usually rude memorials to the dead, a dream of beauty has come to many young carvers in stone; it is the primeval origin of the craft of sculpture. In this way, Shubael Clevenger, a Butler County boy, attracted the attention of E. S. Thomas, editor of the *Cincinnati Evening Post,* who sat for a bust so life-like as to give the youth instant recognition. This was said to be the first bust executed in the West. Its carver continued his career in Boston

---

[3] *History of American Sculpture,* Lorado Taft, p. 61.
[4] *Cincinnati, Queen City,* Rev. C. F. Goss, vol. II, p. 439.

by making busts of Henry Clay, Daniel Webster and other prominent men; then he went to Rome where it is said he made a statue called "The North American Indian", that caused considerable comment. He died at sea on the return voyage to the United States.

An interesting phase of early sculpture in Ohio was the pursuit of wood carving by a group of men in Cincinnati. These wood carvers came from Westphalia. They made life-sized statues from linden wood for church altars, and developed a thriving business in ecclesiastical sculpture, having two branches for the work, one in Cincinnati, and another in Covington, Kentucky. At first, there were three men, Mr. Kloster, Joseph Sibbell, and Mr. Allard, the latter removing to Columbus a little later. Then came Joseph and Henry Schroeder, who were followed by Oswald Terlinden, a man who had more artistic feeling in his work than the others. Terlinden did the major part of his work in Cincinnati. This group of Germans made a valuable contribution to Ohio sculpture which must not be overlooked.

A Frenchman, Charles Bullet, worked in Cincinnati from about 1850 to 1860. He was well known to the artist fraternity and became recognized for his sculpture. He is represented in the Cincinnati Museum by the very excellent marble bust of Mrs. Sarah Worthington King Peter, the revered patroness of art in Cincinnati during the fifties. It is a pity we do not have more of Bullet's work, if all of it possessed the merit of the bust of Mrs. Peter. There are also extant in Ohio a number of beautiful low-relief medallions made by M. Bullet; one is owned by the Ohio State Museum, Columbus.

William Walcutt, a native of Columbus, was the sculptor of the Perry statue unveiled in Cleveland, September 10, 1860, on the forty-seventh anniversary of Perry's victory. It was the first work of monumental art undertaken by the citizens of Cleveland. The city made its unveiling an event of éclat and renown; George Bancroft, the historian, was the speaker for the occasion. The sculptor himself unveiled the statue of Italian marble, which represents the naval hero of 1812, whose story has been told to the children for more than a hundred years. It was indeed apposite to have this monument to Perry placed in Cleveland, so near to the scene of the victory, at a spot where the reverberations of the cannon shots had been heard and where the first shouts went up on land for Perry's victory. The statue originally stood in the Public Square, but in 1894 it was removed to Wade Park, and was finally given a more fitting site in Gordon Park on the shore of Lake Erie. To commemorate the achievements of their illustrious men has been ever the custom of nations, and to do so is the justifiable pride of a people. A portrait statue by William Walcutt of

Dr. Samuel M. Smith, stands in front of Saint Francis Hospital, Columbus; it has been the butt of jokes for years, but no doubt was looked upon with admiration at the time of its execution.

One of the dramatic figures in central Ohio art circles was Thomas D. Jones, commonly called, Tom Jones. His long hair and piercing eyes, overshadowed by the famous brigand hat, and an old Roman toga thrown picturesquely over the left shoulder, made him an outstanding figure. He was of Welsh parentage, his family coming from Wales to New York state, thence to Ohio, and settling near Granville in 1837. His education was no more than what the common schools of the time afforded. He was a man of positive talent and originality, but always showed the lack of education. For three or four years he worked on the Ohio canals as a stonemason. In 1841, he went to Cincinnati and became a marble cutter; following that experience, without any special instruction, he began to execute portrait busts, first in wood, then in stone, and shortly in marble. He made such rapid strides, that in 1842 he began work as a real sculptor and continued in that profession for thirty-three years. For about fifteen years he had his studio in Cincinnati; afterward, he established his workroom in the State House, Columbus; then he removed to New York, Boston, Nashville, Detroit, and other parts of the country where his work called him.

The Lincoln Monument in the Capitol, Columbus, is Jones's best-known work. It consists of a large monument surmounted by a heroic-size bust of Lincoln, which preserves with striking faithfulness the well-known features of the martyred president. On one side of the monument is an inscription; on the other is a bas-relief representing the Surrender of Vicksburg taking place under the branches of a large oak tree, from which hangs Spanish moss. General Grant stands well poised, cool-tempered, and stolid, as he receives from General Pemberton a scroll containing the roll of his army. The sculptor has characterized General Sherman well, representing him intensely interested and attentive. The most artistic figure in the group is a graceful, lithe-limbed orderly, on the extreme right, who holds the bridle of a horse.[5] It is said that Grant himself viewed this work and was much pleased with it. It seems fitting that the Capitol, Columbus, should contain a memorial to Lincoln, since he delivered an address from the steps of that building on September 16, 1859, and his body lay in state there on the way to its final resting place, Springfield, Illinois. The monument was unveiled with appropriate ceremonies on January 19, 1871. Jones received less than ten thousand dollars for it, while the records

---

[5] The bust of Lincoln is now on a high pedestal at the top of a stairway in the Capitol, with the inscription and the bas-relief placed on the walls on either side.

show that it cost him more than eleven thousand dollars — an example of the poor business methods usually attributed, though not justly so, to artists.

Tom Jones made portrait busts of Thomas Ewing, Henry Clay, Thomas Corwin, Salmon P. Chase, General William Henry Harrison, and General Zachary Taylor, and he loved to relate anecdotes of the noted characters whom he had modeled. The original plaster models of these portraits have found a fit resting place in the Ohio State Museum, Columbus. Jones was an amusing, interesting talker, quoted Shakespeare fluently, and often said that Tom Corwin was the greatest man he ever knew. He was very improvident, and had no faculty for providing for his old age; during his last years he was cared for by the mercy or charity of friends and relatives. He was buried in the Welsh Hills Cemetery, near Granville, and a granite boulder, his own device, marks the spot.

A name always connected with accounts of art in Cincinnati is that of Moses Ezekiel. While his contact with Cincinnati was brief, yet he should be considered at this point, because, as a man with a background of German training, he contributed a definite German influence in the formative period of our sculpture. Mr. Ezekiel was born in Richmond, Virginia. He received a military education from the Virginia Military Academy at Lexington, and studied anatomy at the Virginia Medical College. He came to Cincinnati in 1868 to enter the art school of J. Insco Williams, also to study modeling with T. D. Jones. The next year he studied at the Royal Art Academy, Berlin, winning in 1873, the Michelbeer prize of Rome for a relief, "The Awakening of Lazarus". Many of Ezekiel's works were sent to this country; the first piece of importance to come to America was "Religious Freedom", a group of several figures shown at the Philadelphia Centennial and later placed permanently in Fairmont Park, Philadelphia.

During his productive years Ezekiel lived in Rome, where he kept a magnificent studio in the ruins of the Baths of Diocletian. He was a picturesque figure who gathered society, artists, and dilettantes around him in his studio for unusual social affairs. The king created him Chevalier of the Crown of Italy with the title, "Sir"; many other distinctions conferred upon him indicate his social and professional standing abroad and at home. Franz Liszt was among the noted people whom he modeled; when the Liszt bust was exhibited in 1866, it was said, "the likeness is truly speaking, and it is modeled in a very masterly way, full of strength and bold in the extreme."[6]

In his early work, his carving was skillful and exquisite, with the German

---

[6] *The Cincinnati Enquirer,* May 18, 1930.

tendency to emphasize realistic detail. After his residence in Rome, his sculpture was characterized by careful surface modeling, though still bearing his earlier meticulous attention to detail. Cincinnati Museum owns his "Eve Hearing the Voice", which was exhibited at the St. Louis Exposition, 1904, and was awarded a silver medal and certificate of honor as being one of the best works by an American sculptor. There is also a "Head of Christ" by Ezekiel in the Cincinnati Museum.

Mr. Taft tells us that "the most important work which Mr. Ezekiel sent to this country was his monument to Thomas Jefferson, at Louisville, Kentucky. In this somewhat whimsical conception the sculptor has placed the author of the Declaration of Independence upon the Liberty Bell, or at least has made use of a bell-shaped pedestal of bronze, surrounded by dainty decorative figures. The idea is novel and interesting, though too fanciful to be impressive. There is much beauty of modeling in various parts of the work, particularly in the subordinate figures."[7]

A very pretentious memorial in the Public Square at Cleveland is the Cuyahoga County Soldiers' Monument, by Levi T. Scofield. It was erected at a cost of $280,000, a figure that would be tremendous even in this year of our Lord, 1932! It was dedicated July 4, 1894; and in spite of frequently recurring protests and efforts to have it removed, it still faces the beholder in the Public Square, Cleveland. A better known work by Mr. Scofield is the one called, "Ohio's Jewels", which was unveiled on Ohio Day at the Chicago World's Fair, September 14, 1893. It was suggested that a group of statuary representing Ohio's most honored citizens be placed in front of the Ohio Building. It was further suggested that a figure symbolizing Cornelia, the mother of the Gracchi, should surmount a pedestal, and that she should seem to say, "These are my jewels", as her outspread hands indicated the noted Ohioans arranged around the shaft below her.

The idea met with approval, and the legislature appropriated $25,000 to carry out the suggestion. After the close of the Exposition at Chicago, some public-spirited citizens of Columbus subscribed the funds to have it brought to Columbus and placed in the State House yard. As a work of art, perhaps the less said about the group, the better. The Roman matron, Cornelia, is much too large in proportion to the rest of the monument; the favorite sons are precariously placed on a narrow ledge from which only a slight shove would displace them. The citizens point to it with pride, largely on account of the senti-

[7] *History of American Sculpture,* Lorado Taft, p. 263.

ment attached to it. The Ohioans placed around the shaft are Grant, Sherman, Sheridan, Stanton, Garfield, Hayes, and Chase.

Mention should be made here of Louis T. Rebisso, the first instructor in modeling at the Cincinnati Art Academy, who made several equestrian statues. The commission for the equestrian statue of General McPherson in Washington was first given to T. D. Jones, but Rebisso was employed to finish it. General Grant, in Lincoln Park, Chicago, and President Harrison, Cincinnati, are his other equestrians, but the three have equally "wooden" horses and inartistic figures. His contribution as a teacher, however, was valuable. He allied himself with another sculptor, Oscar Mundhenck, and to this partnership was added a Mr. Hoffman; the three of them started a bronze foundry in Cincinnati.

James Wilson Alexander McDonald was born at Steubenville, near the house in which Edwin M. Stanton was born. The first work of art he ever saw was a picture which William Walcutt had painted on a silk banner in his studio at Columbus. This was in 1839 or 1840. The boy began to model and soon presented a bust of Henry Clay to the county officials; this stood in the yard of the Jefferson County Court House for several years. He went to St. Louis as an agent of the Wheeler Sewing Machine Company, but kept on modeling, and left some creditable work there, notably a bust of Thomas Benton, Esq. His masterpiece is the statue at West Point to the memory of the gallant General Custer, which earned for him much celebrity and national praise. Its unveiling on August 30, 1879, was made a celebrated occasion. It still stands on the grounds of the West Point Military Academy, but the statue of Custer that surmounted the monument has met an unknown fate; in its place is an obelisk-like shaft. On each side of the base is the original bronze relief; one side pictures General Custer with drawn saber on his horse; other sides show a buffalo head, tomahawks, bow and arrows, the Indians, Sitting Bull, and Jeronimo. McDonald was long a picturesque figure in American monumental art. He delivered lectures on the pyramids, the mound builders and other subjects.

New Orleans possesses four statues by Alexander Doyle, a Steubenville man, who made something of a specialty of military figures. The Margaret statue of white marble has the distinction of being the first monument erected in America to honor a woman. The fund for it was raised by popular subscriptions limited to ten cents. Seated in a chair, a shawl thrown around her shoulders and one arm embracing a child standing beside her, is the matronly figure of Margaret Haughery. She was known as The Orphans' Friend, because of her generosity in giving them bread. She could neither read nor write, but acquired a considerable fortune, which she bequeathed to the various orphan asylums in New Orleans. Doyle later made a bronze statue of Robert E. Lee, to surmount a monument to that general in the Crescent City. At that time (1883) it was the largest bronze statue that had been cast in New York; it is sixteen and one-half feet high and weighs seven thousand pounds. It represents Lee with folded arms surveying the field of battle; the figure stands on a hollow pillar, one hundred feet high, a stairway giving access to the top. General Beauregard and Jefferson Davis are the other monuments by Doyle in New Orleans.

There is no doubt that the taste for sculpture which Doyle evinced so early in life can be accounted for by the fact that his father was in the marble monument business in Steubenville. His father sent him to Italy to study, and to superintend their interests in the Ferrara marble quarries. He was fortunate in getting many commissions when he returned. Busts for individuals were soon followed by the statues of Liberty (in bronze) and John Howard Payne, at Washington. These, with the Margaret, were all done before he was twenty-six years old.

The Garfield monument, Cleveland, dedicated May 30, 1890, is an architectural structure of the Romanesque order. The shape, for the most part, is that of a tower, fifty feet in diameter. A Romanesque porch flanks the tower; below the railing at the top of the porch, is a frieze of historical character, showing in its five panels, scenes from Garfield's life. The deep-shadowed doors open into a vestibule, vaulted in stone and paved with mosaic. Opening from this vestibule is the chamber where stands the Garfield statue by Alexander Doyle. It depicts Garfield speaking in the House of Representatives. Over the statue is a dome, supported by granite columns, which is decorated with a beautiful frieze of Venetian glass showing an allegorical funeral procession of figures lamenting the dead president.

We take an unusual pride in considering, next, and last, Ohio's greatest early sculptor; but to say that is not to award to him a just estimate, nor does it indicate the high place he deserves in American sculpture, because there have been few greater sculptors in the whole nation than J. Q. A. Ward. He was the "sculptor laureate of his day"; today his work steadily gathers about it the lustre of immortality.

Urbana, Champaign County, Ohio, was laid out and named by a man of hardy English stock from Virginia, the father of John Quincy Adams Ward, who was born there in 1830. According to the traditions usually current in regard to great sculptors, when he was a little boy, he got his fingers into some good pottery clay found on his father's six-hundred-acre farm. He made a caricature head of an old negro of that community, and was immediately heralded as a promising sculptor. John Ogden, a learned lawyer of Urbana, gave him his first instruction in modeling. John H. James of Urbana, owned a terra cotta head of Apollo by Hiram Powers, and that was the first work of art that Ward had ever seen. Soon he visited Cincinnati to see the then much-discussed and questionable "Greek Slave", and was greatly thrilled by it.

As young Ward's health was in such a state as to give his family some concern, he was sent to Brooklyn, where it was hoped his health would improve while visiting his sister there. She learned that the most earnest desire of the youth was to study art; so she prevailed upon her friend, Henry Kirke Brown, to give her brother a trial in his studio. Brown asked the boy to model something for him; with much effort he lugged a bag of clay for two miles to his home and made a copy of the "Venus de Medici". Mr. Brown became interested in him at once. Ward could not have found a more thorough teacher, as Brown instructed him in every step of the process of making a piece of sculpture. Brown was an independent sculptor with the courage to denounce the ideals of Canova; and he passed his spirit of self-reliance on to Ward. We are told that the first money Ward earned was the ten dollars Mr. Brown paid him for a wolf's head he modeled for a fountain in Mexico.

At the time Ward was working in Brown's studio, the older sculptor was engaged on the great equestrian statue of Washington, which stands in Union Square, New York City. It was the second equestrian to be made in this country; the first one, of Andrew Jackson, had been made just the year previous (1852) by Clark Mills. The bronze-casters of Europe would not share the secrets of their craft with Americans, so we were dependent upon them for such work. The Frenchmen who had been employed to assist in the expert mechanical work in the erection of the statue went on a strike; then Ward told Brown to discharge the whole lot, as he and Brown could complete the statue themselves. American casters went through many failures and experiments before they became proficient in bronze-casting, and we must give them much credit for their ingenuity. Mr. Ward often said that he passed more days in the belly of the horse than Jonah did in the belly of the whale. He entered Mr. Brown's studio in 1849 and continued working with him for nearly seven years.

A high-relief in the Capitol, Albany, gives us an idea of the simplicity of composition Ward displayed even in his student work. It represents an episode in the voyage of Hendrik Hudson. A young Indian is breaking his arrows as a "Pledge of Peace on the Hudson River." It predicates the noble simplicity which is the special characteristic of his mature and greater works. He always avoided the picturesque and painter-like treatment, preferring to present his subject simply and directly, as the fifth-century Greek sculptor was wont to do.

There was a tendency away from the Roman studios then, and the type of works produced by Hiram Powers was losing caste. We are tempted to quote from Mr. Sheldon, who gives an account of an interview with Mr. Ward, making him say: "There is a cursed atmosphere about that place (Rome) which somehow kills every artist who goes there. The magnetism of the antique statues is so strong that it draws a sculptor's manhood out of him. From the days of Thorwaldsen, the works produced there are namby-pamby when compared with those glorious models. A modern man has modern themes to deal with; and if art is a living thing, fresh from a man's soul, he must live in that of which he treats. Besides, we shall never have good art at home until our best artists reside here."[8] Ward never remained abroad more than a few months at a time, and he lived to see, to his satisfaction, much of the neoclassic sculpture fall into disfavor.

The greater part of 1857-'58 Ward spent in Washington, modeling portrait busts of the leading men of the time. During the year 1860, he was in Ohio. At Columbus, he executed a bust of Governor William Dennison; and one of Doctor Lincoln Goodale, a heroic bust now in Goodale Park, Columbus, which carries the subject's personal characteristics with dignity and conviction. Ward returned to New York and opened a studio in 1861.

The whole country at that period was filled with the emotion that brought on the Civil War; that Ward was stirred too and was a part of the time in which he lived, is proved by his statuette, the "Freedman", now in the Cincinnati Museum (Plate 49). It evidences his sympathy for the slave, but is treated without sentimentality. An account of American sculpture may be said to run parallel with its wars, since the political history of the nation is reflected accurately in its sculpture. Mr. Sturgis tersely states: "His first ideal work, the 'Freedman', a piece never produced larger than a statuette, is curiously characteristic of the man and his whole future way of work; for while expressing the idea of the slave who has broken his fetters, it represents simply a negro in an entirely natural and everyday pose, a man who has just put forth his strength and is looking very quietly at the results; while at the same time the peculiar characteristics of the race, as distinguished from the white man or the red

---

[8] "An American Sculptor," by G. W. Sheldon, *Harper's Magazine*, vol. 57, p. 62.

PLATE 49—The Emancipated Slave. J. Q. A. Ward. (Cincinnati Museum of Art)

Indian, are made prominent, and form a chief subject of interest. In like manner the very slight dress which was called for is treated with reserve."[9]

In order to study the American Indian, Mr. Ward visited the West in 1863. He had in mind a statue for which he needed first-hand study of the form and the movements of the Indian. In Central Park, New York City, we see the result of this concentrated interest in the red man, "The Indian Hunter", which was an enormous success from the first. Perhaps there never was a monument more happily placed than this one to obtain the best effects; we would expect to see the Indian among the trees, in a setting provided by nature. The racial characteristics of the Indian are vividly realized; the piercing, searching eyes of the hunter, the eagerness of the dog to plunge forward, the keenness and alertness of both man and dog, the restraint exerted to hold the dog back, the tense muscles of the Indian's body and his poised figure — are all features that actually startle one upon reaching the statue suddenly. That an artist has a favorite work, as a mother has a favorite child, is beyond question. Later in life Mr. Ward was kept so busy making portrait statues that he could not create ideal pieces of sculpture, but to show his preference for his sculptural masterpiece, a bronze replica of the "Indian Hunter" was placed at his grave in the cemetery in Urbana (Plate 50).

Central Park has among its numerous statues three others by Ward: the "Shakespeare", the "Pilgrim", and the "Private of the Seventh Regiment". Mr. Lorado Taft points out that: "'Shakespeare' is not a great statue, but it is a good one, and must have seemed exceptional for its day."[10] An interesting comparison of the "Pilgrim" may be made with Saint-Gaudens' "Puritan", which was produced only two years after Ward's "Pilgrim", each sculptor interpreting those staunch, hardy, early Americans in a different way. "The Seventh Regiment Soldier" deserves more than the casual notice ordinarily given to our nondescript soldier monuments; we seldom think of them as other than mediocre.

The years Ward spent in making portrait statues were not by any means fallow years; they gave him the experience by which he rose to higher efforts in depicting character. The Horace Greeley statue in the mælstrom of New York traffic, where it receives scarcely a passing glance, is very impressive. It was difficult for the artist to give a sculpturesque quality to such a figure. He placed the founder of the *New York Tribune* in a low armchair, put a paper in his hand, directed his gaze over it as if to show him deliberating upon its

---

[9] "The work of J. Q. A. Ward," by Russell Sturgis, *Scribner's Magazine,* vol. 32, p. 385.
[10] *History of American Sculpture,* Lorado Taft, p. 222.

PLATE 50—The Indian Hunter. J. Q. A. Ward. Central Park, New York City.
(Art Commission of City of New York)

contents, slightly drooped his head and shoulders, and added the characteristic fringe of beard surrounding his face. It is an unusual character portrayal, composed with consummate mastery.

Mr. Ward excelled in fitting the clothing to the person he modeled. He insisted on a perfect anatomical structure under the clothes; this habit of the artist is especially noticeable in the ideal portrait statue of LaFayette, at Burlington, Vermont. The tight-fitting costume of the period when Lafayette visited this country in 1824-'25, not only reveals but accentuates the figure beneath it. It is a statue of the highest merit. This skill of fitting clothes to the form is exemplified also in the Washington statue, standing on the steps of the Sub-Treasury in New York City. Adeline Adams compares the Ward Washington and the Houdon Washington, much to the advantage of the Ward statue: "Ward's statue, appearing almost a century later, owes something to Houdon; every portrait statue of Washington, if worth much, will owe something to Houdon. But what we especially note is, that in this virile presentment of Washington, Ward has chosen the better part of both realism and classicism. The work has something of the serenity of synthesis and elimination of detail that we love in the Parthenon masterpieces, yet it has enough of modern individualism and modern insistence upon expression and emotion to satisfy the longings of the everyday American spectator . . . Here we see this sculptor as he himself would wish to be seen; a sculptor of mankind at its most heroic, for mankind at its daily average."[11]

President Lincoln sent Henry Ward Beecher to England in 1863, hoping to convert that nation to our great national cause through Beecher's convincing oratory. Ward's statue of Beecher, the most striking of all his portrait statues, and the one many critics call his masterpiece, represents the orator on that mission. The massiveness of the figure is increased by a great coat; the intellectual head is set squarely on the shoulders; every feature contributes to the effect of a dominating personality, one that "clears the atmosphere." Ornamentation is not characteristic of Ward's work, but the Beecher pedestal is adorned with figures of simple charm. On one side is a woman who places a palm leaf at his feet; on the other side, a boy supports a little girl who is reaching to place a wreath of leaves on the monument.

The "Garfield", in the Capitol grounds, Washington, is another instance of Ward's enrichment of a statue by the use of allegorical figures. They give him here an opportunity to render the nude. To show that he could treat the form with knowledge, we need only cite these figures of the "Student", the "States-

---

[11] *The Spirit of American Sculpture,* Adeline Adams, p. 63.

man", and the "Warrior", adorning the base of the Garfield monument, erected in 1887 by the Army of the Cumberland. The figures symbolize three eventful phases of Garfield's life. Surrounding the cupola of the state capitol, Hartford, are symbolical figures which Ward made earlier, in 1878; though of great merit, they are placed too high to allow the beholder to obtain a comprehensive view of them. They represent, "Agriculture", "Law", "Science", "Commerce", "Music", and "Equity".

Washington City is embellished by the presence of Ward's statue of General Thomas, of which Lorado Taft speaks in greatest praise: "'General Thomas' is an equestrian statue of the highest value. It is not enough to say that it is the finest work of the kind in Washington; it has few rivals in the country at large."[12] Naturally, the horse predominates in an equestrian statue, but, in common with most equestrian monuments, this one is placed too high to be observed carefully; some one has said that we must look at the horse's belly in all equestrian groups. Ward was an admirer of horses and understood them. The pose of the high-spirited horse and its easy rider is simple, quiet, and commanding. One can see that the dignity of character of the sculptor himself has been put into this work; there was neither bombast nor pretense in his make-up.

Mr. Ward allowed his fancy freedom to roam when he modeled the great quadriga to crown the naval arch erected in New York for the occasion of welcome to Admiral Dewey. It was a group, admirably composed, of sea horses drawing a boat; a "Victory", adapted from the Nike of Samothrace, stood on the prow; the boat rested on churning waves, and Tritons struggled in the water. It was a wonderfully decorative group of sculpture, of a kind seldom produced in America before. One regrets that a conception of such beauty was not executed in enduring marble rather than transitory plaster.

One of Mr. Ward's last works was the pediment for the New York Stock Exchange. It shows clearly that there was no lessening of force throughout his long career. Paul Wayland Bartlett assisted him in modeling the figures, but the design was by Ward. He harmonized five principal groups into a design that is especially successful in mass, and fits most appropriately into the architectural scheme of the building. It was declared to be "the most formidable piece of sculpture yet undertaken in America." The triangular pediment is more than one hundred feet long at the base; a figure representing "Integrity" stands with outstretched hands in the center; on each side of her are two groups of figures, a farmer and a maid, a mechanic and his assistant,

---

[12]*History of American Sculpture,* Lorado Taft, p. 228.

a band of mining prospectors, and a designer trying to fit some plan into the difficult space at the sharp angle of the pediment.

Mr. Ward spent his very last days finishing the bronze equestrian statue of General Hancock, which graces Fairmount Park, Philadelphia. Ward, then very ill, said he was "content to go", after his friend, Herbert Adams, whom he had called in to pass judgment upon the Hancock, pronounced it well done. Some time after the artist's death, when Herbert Adams was delivering an eulogy to Ward, he declared that the General Hancock "will stand as one of the very finest examples of his achievement. Its large monumental impressiveness has seldom been surpassed . . . His life-long habit of doing his best was upon him."[13]

When the National Sculpture Society was founded in 1893, Mr. Ward was one of the prime moving spirits in its organization, and upon its incorporation in 1896, he was made president, in which capacity he served until his death. That record alone would make his life full of service. He also served the National Academy of Design as president, his election being the only instance when a sculptor was selected for the presidency.

Russell Sturgis very aptly summarizes the life work of Ward: "None of the older sculptors are to be compared with him in achievement. In the case of the very few able men of that early generation there is the immense advantage, the delight of the student, of finding work done without academic teaching and in surroundings extremely unfavorable. There is no art quite so pure nor so instructive as that."[14]

The tribute of Adeline Adams is not only a fitting conclusion to a discussion of J. Q. A. Ward, but will serve as a summary to our survey of early Ohio sculpture: "No other American sculptor ever worked more manfully than he to encourage in his own country the various technical processes upon which sculpture depends for its truthful presentation. Further, no other ever anchored his hope so firmly as he, in the value of the American idea, the American standpoint, the American basis — bias, if you will, for the noblest development of our nation's art. No other ever surpassed him in sheer virility of purpose and act. But over and above and beyond these things, few artists of any period have been so gifted as he, in greatness of vision, in passion for truth, in feeling for proportion, not only in the daily matters of his art, but in the larger business of the relation of that art to human life."[15]

---

[13] From address delivered at the Ward Memorial meeting of the Century Club. *John Quincy Adams Ward, An Appreciation,* Adeline Adams, p. 49.
[14] *Scribner's Magazine,* vol. 32, p. 385.
[15] *John Quincy Adams Ward, An Appreciation,* Adeline Adams, p. 20.

CHAPTER VII

Ceramics

OHIO stands supreme in ceramics. It holds first rank in the United States in the value of its clay products, which in 1928 was $81,848,000. The pottery industry is widely distributed in Ohio, and represents a large source of activity and wealth.

The preëminence of Ohio in the manufacture of pottery is due to the presence in many sections of the state of clays particularly well adapted to the art of ceramics, and to the coming of potters into the state very early in its history. Eastern and southeastern Ohio had coal formations that yielded a supply of buff-burning clays suitable for stoneware and yellow-and-brown mottled ware called the American Rockingham from its similarity to the English Rockingham. Other parts of the state had abundant red-burning glacial and alluvial clays that were easily obtained and made into simple earthenware articles of household use: milk pans, jars, jugs, pitchers, platters, plates, and so on.

The homely earthen crocks and jars used in the early days suggest delicious kitchen smells, such as apple butter, pickles, spiced peaches, lard and butter. Many collectors have passed by the common old stoneware as too humble and crude to be sought. In its human interest it probably surpasses the products of many of the crafts. It might be called a folk art, since it was made of clay near at hand for consumption in the immediate neighborhood, and has the touch of the individual craftsman upon it.

The early earthenware is usually divided into three types: stoneware, glazed redware, and unglazed redware. Stoneware is made of a clay that will survive extremely high temperatures in the firing kiln. It receives its glaze in a very simple manner. Near the end of the firing period, when the pieces are white hot, a quantity of white salt is shoveled into the kiln. The salt is vaporized by the intense heat; tiny drops collect on the surface of the clay objects and combine with the hot clay to form a granular surface and an infinitely fine glaze over it. Stoneware is usually gray, gray-brown, or brown. Decoration was confined mostly to cobalt-blue designs of scrolls, eagles, and lettering, achieved by making an incised decoration and dusting cobalt into the incisions. Red earthenware is merely clay, shaped to requirement and baked. If such ware, refined perhaps, were covered with a thin slip or glaze before being fired, the result was glazed redware. There were superb greens and a rich, brilliant black in the glazed redware. In general, lead was an important constituent of transparent glaze, and that metal gave the second distinct division of the early pottery, which included salt-glazed stoneware and lead-glazed pottery (Plate 51).

Muskingum County offered a fertile field for the pottery maker. In Putnam, which is now part of Zanesville, was a valuable formation known as Putnam Hill limestone. The records show that Zanesville had a pottery in 1808 making useful articles of red earthenware with red slip. Good stoneware was made there from 1814 to 1840. After that, pottery reached a high development in Zanesville because experienced potters, hearing of the superior clay deposit there, came from Staffordshire, England, and erected a kiln.

The pottery demand in the Ohio and Mississippi Valleys, as far south as New Orleans, was supplied with stoneware from the Zanesville district. The itinerant potters and the small-farm potters brought their ware to Zanesville, which was the head of navigation on the Muskingum River. Every winter they constructed flatboats or barges, loaded them with corn, bacon, stoneware, and flour ground at the falls of the Muskingum and Licking Rivers. In the summer these barges were floated to New Orleans by way of the Muskingum, Ohio, and Mississippi Rivers, and there the cargoes were disposed of; the timber barges were sawed into lumber and sold, and the crew walked back to Zanesville during the winter months to prepare another barge for the next summer's business. Most of the potteries were very small buildings of logs or planks, with a kiln from ten to fifteen feet in diameter, and were operated by farmers with the aid of from one to four hands.

The Rockingham ware was first produced in Ohio, at East Liverpool, in 1841, and that city continues to be an important ceramic center. Rockingham differs from stoneware in that the glaze is fixed by a second firing to a body of the same composition, but of a more porous texture. James Bennett, who emigrated to America from Derbyshire, England, in 1834, founded this branch of ceramics at East Liverpool. It was only by chance that he learned of the advantage in settling there through the remarks of a casual acquaintance on the steamboat who told him he ought to investigate the resources for pottery making in that vicinity. It determined the industrial history of southeastern Ohio. Examples of that early Rockingham ware are sought with avidity and highly prized by the antiquarians.

A vast expanse is spanned between the simple Rockingham ware of 1840 and the art pottery of today which makes Ohio the Mecca for the person seeking beautiful pottery. Certainly much of the progress of Ohio in the clay industries is due to the fact that the state early realized its valuable resources in clay and took definite steps to develop them in a scientific way. "Ohio estab-

PLATE 51—Early Ohio Stoneware. Five-gallon jar, salt-glazed, decorated with large conventionalized flower design in blue slip. Reverse has name of potter, J. C. Smith, Mogadore. (Rhea Mansfield Knittle)

lished at the Ohio State University, Columbus, the first school of ceramics in the United States. Provision was made by the Legislature in 1894 for a course of practical and scientific instruction in the art of clay working and ceramics. Further, the sum of five thousand dollars was appropriated to establish and maintain it the first year and twenty-five hundred dollars to support it the second year. Edward Orton, Jr., who had wide knowledge of the geology and qualities of Ohio clays, and had practical acquaintance with the various branches of clay working, was chosen director. Through his untiring energy and able teaching the work was made a success."[1]

The catalogue of the University for 1894-'5 announced a two-year course of study which was designed to give those who were engaged, or who expected to be engaged, in the manufacture of clay products an opportunity to learn in the shortest time the rudiments of the sciences which were most likely to be useful to them in their work. The ceramic laboratory work in the second year of the course taught students to apply the knowledge gained from these studies, and thus opened the way towards the creation of a class of trained observers in the practical problems of the industry. The Ceramic School has gained a wide reputation and enrolled students from nearly every state and many foreign countries. Workers of recognized authority and leaders in artistic and mechanical progress have received their training at this school.

The impression has long existed in the public mind that art and the factory have nothing in common. This is not an unreasonable point of view, because the trend of industry has been toward the solution of difficult technical and economic problems. A public appreciation of painting and the other fine arts has been developed definitely apart from an appreciation of the useful arts. Art, in connection with pottery making, should not be confused with mere surface decoration. It is the result of the creative genius of the designer, and envolves a product that can be appreciated by the senses. In ceramics, art satisfies every expectation in form, proportion, color, texture, and interest in the glaze that has been produced by the fire. A survey of the failures and successes of art pottery in Ohio is full of interest. There have been the patience and persistence of the Egyptians, Assyrians, and Saracens in perfecting wonderful colored glazes; there has been evident the enthusiasm of Bernard Palissy, who tore up his cottage floor, after having burned all his furniture to feed his furnace; there have been conceptions as original as in a pair of Chinese pots of the Sung period; but still colored glazes and bodies are by no means developed to their highest possibilities.

---

[1]"History of the Clay Industry in Ohio," by Wilbur Stout, Geological Survey of Ohio, Bulletin 26, p. 101.

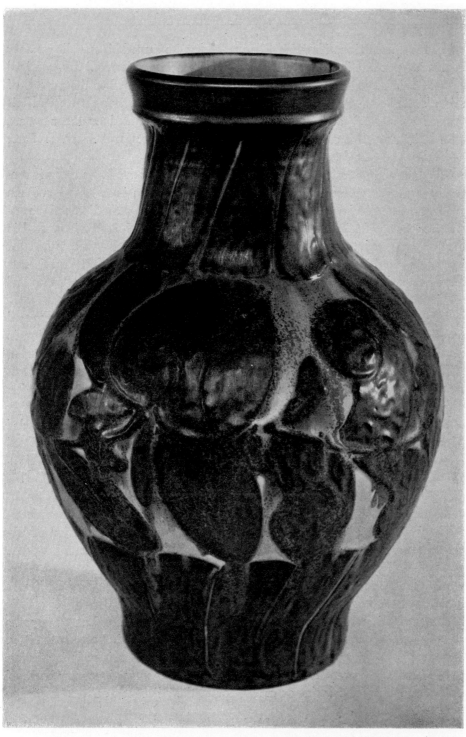

PLATE 52—Rookwood Vase. Terra Verte and Brown-black mat glaze.
(The Rookwood Pottery Company)

"In 1873, a Cincinnati boy, Karl Langenbeck, who earned his spending money by making pen-and-ink drawings on card and writing-table requisites, received a set of china colors from an uncle in Frankfort and turned to the pursuit of this fascinating decoration. His neighbors, Mrs. Maria Longworth Nichols (later Mrs. Storer) and Mrs. Learner Harrison, captivated by the new art, joined him, using his color until they could import some for themselves. Later he became the first ceramic chemist in the country.

"Decorative pottery, which has made Cincinnati celebrated as a ceramic center, however, may be said to have had its real inception in 1875, when Benn Pitman, of the Cincinnati School of Design, procured from the East some overglaze colors and invited a few of the ladies of the city, who were interested in the subject, to meet at his office to talk over the matter of forming a class for instruction in china painting. It was in these rooms that the first experiments in porcelain decoration were made under the direction of Miss Eggers, who had previously acquired some knowledge of the art in Dresden."[2]

About the same time, Miss M. Louise McLaughlin, of Cincinnati, discovered the difficult process of underglaze painting. At the Centennial Exposition in Philadelphia she was much impressed with the display of the Limoges faïence, and determined to discover the method of its decoration. She procured colors from Paris and began her experiments in 1877. She was very successful: her ware has been called the "Cincinnati faïence", and at the Paris Exposition her work attracted so much attention that the jury on ceramic productions awarded her honorable mention for her reproductions of the brilliant, heavily painted Limoges faïence. In April, 1879, Miss McLaughlin, brought together a number of interested women and formed the Pottery Club, which was probably the first club of women organized for that purpose in the United States. This organization later became an important factor in the development of ceramic art in Cincinnati. In the Cincinnati Art Museum may be seen a collection of historical pottery which includes much splendid work of these pioneer women potters of Cincinnati.

The first art pottery in Ohio, the Rookwood Pottery of Cincinnati, was founded in 1880 by Mrs. Maria Longworth Storer, one of the very enthusiastic members of this group of women composing the Pottery Club. The pottery was started in an abandoned schoolhouse given by Mr. Joseph Longworth, Mrs. Storer's father, for the enterprise, which he sustained financially in its earliest years. The pottery was called Rookwood from the Longworth country home of that name, where the rooks, or crows, found the adjacent woods a hospitable

---

[2]"History of the Clay Industry in Ohio," by Wilbur Stout, Geological Survey of Ohio, Bulletin 26, p. 90.

abiding place. Mr. Longworth was fond of saying that the pottery furnished employment to the "idle rich"; and the remark contained more truth than fiction, because it was then very fashionable for women to decorate pieces and have them fired at the pottery. The enthusiasm of these amateurs subsided, as the difficulties of the art were great, yet their influence helped later to sustain the enterprise when it needed encouragement.

William Watts Taylor became the partner of Mrs. Storer and assumed active direction of the pottery in 1883. For several years the enterprise barely maintained itself. The total technical equipment of the pottery consisted of the jealously-guarded knowledge of the craft of an old Staffordshire potter, Joseph Bailey, who was superintendent of the plant.

The old English potters still regarded their industry as a secret — indeed a "black art", as it dealt with fire, so these early craftsmen were not capable of making use of new information or breaking from old traditions. The losses of the pottery were constant and growing, until a friend suggested to Mr. Taylor that he employ a chemist — a startling thing to do. He engaged Karl Langenbeck, who was able to do analytical work; and after months of experience with practical methods he was made superintendent of the pottery. By 1890 the business was on its feet; then Mrs. Storer retired from it, transferring all her interest to Mr. Taylor, who formed the present company and remained its controlling influence until his death in 1913. Under Mr. Taylor's direction as president, the present buildings were erected in 1892, and extended in 1899 and 1904. They crown the summit of Mt. Adams, one of the Cincinnati hills, and command a beautiful view of the surrounding country.

The management of the pottery is directed on lines opposite to the prevailing factory system, as the purpose is to attain a higher art rather than cheaper processes. Absolutely no printing patterns are used, nor are any duplicates made. The clays used for all purposes are American, taken largely from the Ohio Valley. One Japanese artist is employed in the pottery; with that exception the decorators are all Americans, most of them having been trained in the Cincinnati Art Academy. Certainly one may call Rookwood ware an American product.

"The fundamental character of the ware in the earliest period was essentially the same as today. The decoration was then spoken of as the Limoges style, though really of a much earlier origin, and consists in the application to wet clay-pieces of metallic oxides mixed with clay and water, or what is technically known as 'slip'. The process surpasses all others as expression of the potter's art, because it is the most thorough and comprehensive use of the material. The

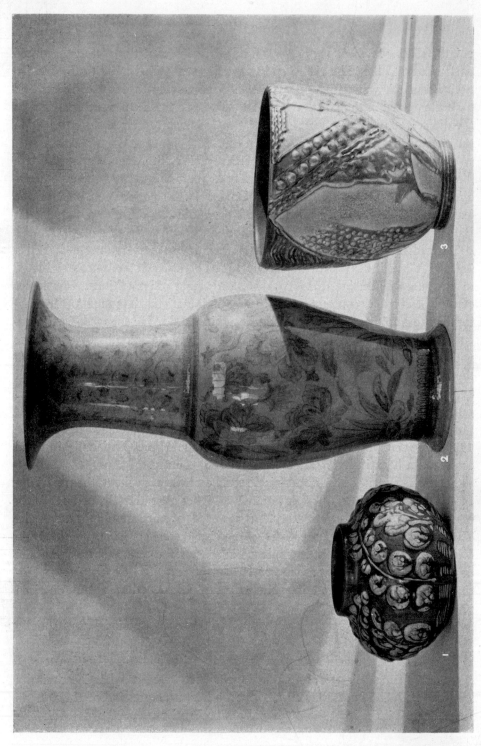

PLATE 53.—Rookwood Pottery. Fig. 1, Wax-mat glaze. Terra Verte lined with orange. Fig. 2, Decorated porcelain, blue on apricot. Fig. 3, Wax-mat glaze, burnt orange on ivory. (The Rookwood Pottery Company)

modeling tool is brought into play quite as much as the brush. Not only are the decorative possibilities of clay revealed through the use of both these instruments, but the colors become the very substance and fibre of the piece, indestructible and themselves of a certain plastic value by their intimate union with the plastic forms. It is well to lay emphasis upon this method and upon its artistic capabilities, not only as characteristic of nearly all of Rookwood's productions, but because practical considerations forbid its common use. Commercial wares must be produced at low cost, and to attain this all risks possible must be eliminated. In Rookwood, seventy-five per cent of its cost is in the vase of dry mud, as it strictly is, before the fire touches it at all."[3]

The famous Tiger Eye was first made at Rookwood in 1884. "This is the very first of the class known as crystalline glazes, since so extensively developed at Sèvres, Copenhagen, and Berlin. In all these, however, the crystals appear on the outer surface of the glaze. In Rookwood alone, entirely unlike these European types, the crystalline formation lies deep in the substance of the glaze in luminous sheets of extraordinary beauty. Still another variety are the mat glazes first made at Rookwood in 1896, and now among the most admired of its productions. In these the special quality is beauty of texture, though the range and variation of color is very great. To many pieces decoration is applied of flowers or other subjects broadly modeled; of motives derived from American Indian designs and of other conventional ornaments in relief or incised.

"The variation of the mat-glaze type, known as 'Vellum' ware, was first shown at St. Louis in 1904, and pronounced by expert judges the only ceramic novelty of the Exposition. Its name indicates the peculiar charm of the glaze texture, and it presents for the first time the extraordinary achievement of a transparent mat glaze developed in the fire and not by acid or other after-treatment. Vellum is the connecting link between the bright and the dull glazes, and as a technical achievement has brought high honors to its inventor, Mr. Stanley Burt, the chemist of the pottery. The 'Ombroso' type of mat glaze was brought out in 1910. The colors are usually in quiet tones of gray and brown, with occasional accents of other colors, and the decorations, if any, of relief modeling or incised designs. The effects cannot be described easily, but it will be found that in 'Ombroso' there has been added to the mat glazes of Rookwood another variation of marked beauty and distinction.

"At Easter, in 1915, the thirty-fifth year of Rookwood was marked by the

---

[3] "The Rookwood Pottery," by William Watts Taylor, p. 5. Reprinted from the *Forensic Quarterly,* September, 1910.

public appearance of Rookwood Soft Porcelain. It represents, as usual, years of chemical research and kiln trials, and the study of old porcelains, particularly certain varieties of old Chinese, which have been found to be of the soft-paste type with the rich, heavy, single color glazes so familiar to collectors. Like these Chinese varieties, the new Rookwood is a soft porcelain with a rich glaze flowing over forms perfectly plain or enriched with subtle low-relief modeling, or sometimes design flatly painted on the clay body."[4]

The Rookwood Pottery has received numerous honors, medals, and prizes at expositions in Europe and America, and its pottery is to be seen in all the world's great museums. The development of the marks used on Rookwood is interesting. At first the name was impressed in the clay; since 1886 a monogram made of R and P has been used. Added at the top is a flame for each year, the year 1900 showing fourteen flames; a Roman numeral indicates the year after 1900. In addition, the decorators have always cut their initials in the clay on the bottom of the pieces painted by them.

Fifty years of investigation and creative effort on the part of the chemist and artist have achieved at Rookwood the finest pottery since the Chinese era. Three new glazes that have caused much excitement are the lovely, soft, "butter-fat" glaze; a beautiful celadon glaze of rich green; and a wax-mat glaze that is similar to the "butter-fat" glaze, but different in effect and quality, having a soft, waxy surface and at times a curdled effect. The wax-mat glaze is the result of the combined experiments of Mr. Burt and John Dee Wareham, the head of the decorators, who got the idea of this new glaze while visiting an exhibit of pottery in Paris. Beginning with the formulas that are common property of all potters, Stanley Burt has improved and developed new combinations until Rookwood glazes are the envy and despair of all craftsmen. No reds, greens, blues, or yellows exceed in intensity and richness of color.

The forms of the vases and bowls are individual and spirited, many of them being reminiscent of the Han period in Chinese art; low, squat bowls, crater-shaped bowls, high-necked jugs, wide-mouthed jars, and other shapes suggest the finest proportions of the work of the Greek potter (Plates 52, 53, 54, 55). Inventiveness in design, personal style and technique, originality in treatment are qualities of their master decorators, among whom are such well-known artists as Matt A. Daly, E. T. Hurley, W. P. McDonald, Lorinda Epply, W. E. Hentschel, Charles S. Todd, Louise Abel and many others.

The Rookwood Pottery, in recent years, has turned its attention to the decoration of the interior and exterior of buildings; panels, figures, and fountains

[4] Booklet issued by Rookwood Pottery, Cincinnati.

PLATE 54—Rookwood Vase. Ivory and black, butter-fat glaze.
(The Rookwood Pottery Company)

are brought safely through the hazards of the kiln, and these are found embellishing hotel lobbies, theaters, and department stores in the large cities. John Dee Wareham has designed all the large panels and lunettes; the first product of his art is the decoration of the Seelback Rathskeller in Louisville, where in the eighteen panels he has used a conventional treatment of castles and medieval motifs. Later came the decorating of the Fort Pitt Hotel in Pittsburgh, and the designing not only of the wall panels but of the dishes and furniture as well.

The sculptors, Clement J. Barnhorn and Ernest Bruce Haswell (see chapter XV, *post*), have supplied the beauty of sculptured form to Rookwood faïence. Not since the days of Della Robbia have glazes been applied to such beautifully modeled surfaces. The Lord & Taylor fountain in New York, and the "Dolphin and Boy" in the Prince George Hotel, New York, best represent this phase of the work. The steady growth of the pottery has been in great part due to the ideals of its founder, Mrs. Storer; both the conservative and the radical speak with the utmost respect for its work.

"The work and influence of Miss M. Louise McLaughlin in the development of art pottery in Cincinnati deserves more than passing mention. She began experimenting in 1877 at the P. L. Coultry Pottery, and produced the first decorative underglaze work in Cincinnati, if not in the country . . . During the period from 1877 to 1895, when her work in underglaze faïence terminated, she produced many beautiful and artistic pieces now treasured in art museums and private collections. Later at her residence at Mt. Auburn she erected a small pottery and a kiln and developed a ware called 'Losanti', which she made from 1898 to 1905. This ware is very translucent, and more closely resembles the oriental porcelain than any other so far produced in this country. She also followed the old Chinese practice of having but one firing of body and glaze. Her work is artistic and original, and has been an inspiration to others."[5]

Mrs. C. A. Plimpton, Cincinnati, led the way into another field of decorative work, which, while not entirely original in its nature, was most interesting as showing the practical and ornamental uses to which the fine, varied, and abundant native clays of Ohio could be put. Her work was mostly in red and yellow clays; the process of decorating consisted in the building-up of the design upon the partly dried, unburnt piece of pottery, in damp clays of different or the same colors, which, through the process of firing, retain their relative color values. After firing, the glaze was added and a final firing given. Her finished product

---

[5] "History of the Clay Industry in Ohio," by Wilbur Stout, Geological Survey of Ohio, Bulletin 26, p. 96.

PLATE 55—Rookwood Vase. Midnight blue, dull texture, lined with orange.
(The Rookwood Pottery Company)

will worthily sustain comparison with the work of the French at Sèvres, and the English at Stokes-upon-Trent, who have shown the beauty of porcelain clays in the *pâte sur pâté* process, in results which rival in costliness and beauty the work of the cameo cutter.

The S. A. Weller Pottery, at Zanesville, about 1894, began the manufacture of an art ware styled Louwelsa. It was in beautiful shades of brown, almost golden, and was hand-turned and hand-decorated by artists. It was very popular for a time, until the market was flooded by cheaper ware made by other factories in imitation of it. Jacques Sicard of France, and his assistant, Henri Gellie, came to America in 1901, to introduce metallic luster pottery, and, learning of the Weller factory, came to Zanesville. They were employed by Mr. Weller and produced the well-known Sicardo ware of beautiful lusters with suggestions of designs under the luster; it was the finest ware ever put out by the Weller Pottery.

As Cincinnati has gained no small measure of fame as the home of Rookwood, so Cleveland is known as the home of the Cowan pottery made in Rocky River adjacent to Cleveland. Much attention has been centered on this pottery, not from the volume of its productions, but from the rare beauty and artistry of the work done there. It was the work from the Cowan studio which first caused the art authorities to recognize ceramic sculpture as a true form of artistic expression; a precedent of long standing was broken when the Pennsylvania Academy of Fine Arts, in 1928, invited an exhibition of Cowan pottery. Up to this time pottery and figures made of clay had occupied a secondary position in relation to the works of sculptors, whose media are marble or bronze.

Guy Cowan, the founder, came from a family of potters that for generations have lived and worked in East Liverpool, a section that is almost as famous a potting district as Staffordshire in England. So he grew up in a ceramic atmosphere, and was a practical potter long before he finished high school. In order to obtain a sound knowledge of all ceramic problems, he attended the New York State School of Ceramics at Alfred, New York. Professor Charles Binns was the leading spirit of that school, and his influence is seen in the pottery of Cowan. After graduation from that school, Cowan began teaching classes in pottery in the Cleveland schools.

The idea of an art pottery grew and grew with Mr. Cowan until, in 1913, he finally opened a studio, with much hesitation and without any sanguine feeling of success. Instead of going back to East Liverpool, where clay and workmen of high skill were available, he preferred to remain in Cleveland, where he could be in close contact with the Cleveland School of Art and through

PLATE 56—Cowan Pottery. Torso by Waylande Gregory. (The Cowan Potters, Inc.)

PLATE 57—Figure and Bowl. (The Cowan Potters, Inc.)

it obtain artists of recognized ability. The situation looked desperate for a long time. The first official recognition of Cowan pottery came in 1917, at the Chicago Art Institute, when it was awarded the first prize for pottery. The activities of the Cowan studio ceased during the war, but resumed the making of pottery in 1920 at Rocky River. Since then many honors and awards have come to Mr. Cowan in recognition of his pottery, perhaps the most notable one being the Mr. and Mrs. Frank A. Logan medal awarded at the annual Arts and Crafts Exhibit at the Chicago Art Institute in 1927; this was in competition with all forms of decorative and applied art.

Impressed by the future possibilities of Cowan pottery as an enterprise worthy of encouragement, a number of generous men and women have taken over the organization and endowed it with ample capital to work out the plans which it has in project. The name of the new company is Cowan Potters, Incorporated, and Mr. Guy Cowan is the president. Mr. Howard P. Eells, Jr., is chairman of the board.

All the clay used in Cowan pottery is imported from England. There are American clays equally well adapted to the making of such pottery, but the extreme care which the British give to its preparation makes it preferable, though more costly. The graceful contour of the vases made by Cowan craftsmen give them a steady popularity; they are finished in ivory or a variety of glazes, in an interesting crackle glaze and mottled crystalline glazes. Beauty and taste are so obviously present in these pieces that it is not saying too much to declare that they have done a great deal in the education of public taste.

It is in ceramic sculpture that we find the most distinctive output of the Cowan Potters. The molds are of plaster of Paris, and made directly from the sculptor's original work, which usually is executed in a patent clay mixed with oil to prevent its drying. The making of the mold is a most delicate and difficult operation, involving cutting the mold into many intricate sectional divisions in order that the cast may not be broken as it is removed. Frequently these molds, which fit together like a puzzle, will contain as many as a dozen sections. A great many examples from the Cowan studio are made only in limited numbers. After the predetermined lot has been successfully cast and fired, the mold is destroyed, just as an etcher will destroy his plate after a limited output has been produced.

The men who perform the many operations in the Cowan Pottery are truly artists in their particular work. The personal work of Mr. Cowan as a sculptor has brought him as much recognition as his achievement as a craftsman. His figures are distinguished by delightful delicacy and a strong sense of the deco-

rative. His "Adam and Eve", a pair of charming figures, are akin to the sculpture of Paul Manship in positions and archaistic tendencies. He is a modernist in his sympathies and execution, yet a fine restraint keeps his work from degenerating into the grotesque. There is a freshness and refinement of taste in everything he does. The Cowan pottery is attracting such artists as Alexander Blazys, Waylande Gregory, Margaret Postgate, Thelma Frazier, Paul Bogatay, and A. D. Jacobson (Plates 56, 57, 58, 59).

Besides the extensive line of decorative pottery made at the Cowan works, their product includes tiles, fountains, and architectural sculpture of unusual beauty. Amplification of their manufacture in this phase can be seen in the interior tile work of the Cleveland Art Museum, as well as in churches and homes in Cleveland and other cities.

The Roseville Pottery Company, Zanesville, makes an interesting art pottery, attractive in design and harmonious in color-blending. The Zane Pottery, Zanesville, makes a pottery with free brush underglaze decoration resembling the Italian ware, also large pieces of effective garden pottery, urns, vases, pedestals, sundials, and bird baths. There are several small potteries organized for the production of art ware, and many pieces of artistic pottery produced in Ohio by factories engaged in other lines of work. Indescribably lovely in form and coloring are the creations of these individual potters: Louise Kitchen and Hazel Clarke Witchner of Toledo, and Victor Schreckengost of Cleveland. The Coptic jars and other pottery designed by the sculptress, May Cook of Columbus, are exceedingly interesting in shape.

It is no longer necessary for Americans to go abroad for exquisite table service. American manufacturers of earthenware have been severely criticized for lack of initiative and originality in design. Some of the criticism has been just; as proof one needs only to note the relative space given to American and imported wares in the best stores. Until quite recently such a position as art director was almost unknown in American tableware factories, except in the Lenox plant and some makers of hotel china. Conditions are changing rapidly; attractive domestic ware is becoming more and more popular. There is an almost universal effort shown by the manufacturers to strike out along new lines in shape, color, and types of decoration. The principal and ever-present danger is an attempt to make cheap ware that can be sold at a popular price, rather than perfecting a very high-grade tableware.

The most distinctive work in recent Ohio tableware manufacture has been done by the Leigh Potters, Incorporated, of Alliance (Charles Leigh Sebring, president). They have caught the significance of what is called modernism in

PLATE 58—Cowan Pottery Vase. (The Cowan Potters, Inc.)

the radical departure in design found in the famous "Green Wheat" pattern which they produce. It is charming, with a beauty that is entirely new and wholly American in spirit. The main appeal of their ware is through its body rather than its applied decoration, although the latter is very good.

Ohio has two firms (the Coxon Belleek China Company, Wooster, and the Morgan China, Incorporated, Canton) which make dinner ware, service plates and specialties that are exquisite. The body of their wares is a rich ivory color, soft and lovely, having some of the characteristic qualities of the famous ware made at Belleek, Ireland. The decoration of the Coxon ware is obviously decalcomania (i.e. produced by transfer from specially prepared paper), but filled in and retouched. The gold used is excellent. The Carnegie Art Institute, Pittsburgh, displays a large collection of Morgan china. The Pope-Gosser China Company, Coshocton, makes a high-grade dinner ware that compares well with foreign ware both in body and design.

Leaders in the ceramic industry had long kept in mind the idea of a collegiate course in ceramic art. This dream came true with the establishment in 1928 of the Ceramic Art School in the Fine Arts Department of Ohio State University, Columbus. The curriculum of the Ceramic Art School leads to the college degree of Bachelor of Fine Arts. To begin the work, the University spent fifteen thousand dollars for equipment, and in the future will build and equip to meet increasing requirements. Professor Arthur E. Baggs, an artist and ceramist, was put in charge of the school. He is well known to the ceramic world as the man who developed the pottery at Marblehead, Massachusetts. The outstanding originality of his work, his mastery of the technical problems in ceramics, and his unusual qualifications as a teacher, have brought him a nationwide recognition that resulted in his selection to lead the new venture. His pupils are already taking places of leadership in ceramic research. The ceramic artist trained at Ohio State University will be able to assist the manufacturers of all clay, glass, and vitreous enamel products. He will be a man who will have the technical and artistic ability to create new ware, to appreciate and fill the technical and artistic requirements wanted by the trade. Market demands, like styles, change rapidly. Purchasers are demanding a finer quality, texture, color and form, as well as qualities to withstand specific usage.

The American Ceramic Society has been contributing for thirty years to the growth of the ceramic industry. This society fully realized that the art development had not kept pace with the technical development. It found that to build up artistic standards in ceramics there must be coöperation between the schools of design and the industrial executives. With this end in view, the

American Ceramic Society interested the General Education Board of the Rockefeller Foundation in the matter, and the board granted four thousand dollars per annum to Ohio State University, Columbus, for a period of two years, beginning July 1, 1930, for the creation of a scholarship in ceramic design applied to tableware, together with the provision for research as to technical and market requirements. Mr. Paul Bogatay, the first recipient of the scholarship, began his work in October, 1930. Surely one must favor the spirit behind the effort which is to discover how our factories and schools may best contribute to the improvement in design of American tableware.

Decorative tiling is another phase of art pottery deserving consideration. The production of this class of ware began in 1874 at Zanesville, where there are now three large factories. The pioneers in this industry had many trials and disappointments: kiln after kiln were failures. Devices were invented to overcome many of the difficulties, and the American Encaustic Tiling Company, Limited, was organized in 1879. Encaustic tile — that is, floor tile with decorative designs inlaid with plastic clays into their surfaces — were made by the company in the manner of those made by the Mintons of England for the Capitol at Washington. Such tile could never be burned as true to surface as our public demanded.

"It became the problem to inlay the designs with clay dust in a clay matrix, without distorting the various colored patterns in the subsequent compression. Through the collaboration of the artist-mechanic and chemist, the necessary appliances were invented and made, and the factory again given the lead in perfected encaustic tile. They were known as 'Alhambra'. The business grew so rapidly that a new plant was necessary to accommodate the trade. The immense works, the largest of the kind in the United States, were completed and ready for use in April, 1892, and has been in active operation since that date."[6]

The American Encaustic Tiling Company, Limited, no longer uses the encaustic process, but retains the name. Their present output consists of dust-pressed and hand-made faïence, glazed and unglazed vitreous and semi-vitreous ware, and glazed, unglazed, and cut mosaics. The indestructible nature of such tiles, designed to stand exceptional physical strain and constant exposure, makes them practical for use in the boldest engineering projects, for example, the Hudson vehicular tunnel and the Philadelphia subway station.

The decorative possibilities in ceramic tiles are unlimited (Plate 60). The American Encaustic Tiling Company, Limited, has an art department responsible for beautiful designs, inspired largely by motifs adapted from the tiles

---

[6]"History of the Clay Industry in Ohio," by Wilbur Stout, Geological Survey of Ohio, Bulletin 26, p. 28.

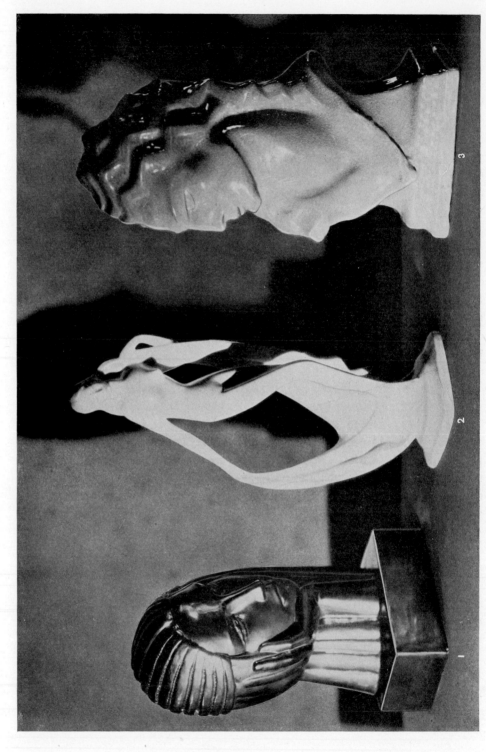

PLATE 59—Cowan Pottery. Fig. 1, *La Revense* head in black, designed by A. D. Jacobson. Fig. 2, Persephone, ivory figure, designed by Waylande Gregory. Fig. 3, Colonial head, terra cotta, designed by Waylande Gregory. (The Cowan Potters, Inc.)

of Spain, Holland, and Tunis. American artists do most of their work, but some German and French ones contribute as well, and all of them are alive to modern decorative requirements. The company makes an unglazed tile which retains all those pleasing irregularities of shade, shape, and texture peculiar to the old tiles of the medieval craftsmen. In the mosaic tiles are developed highly conventionalized animal and flower designs; on a glazed ivory tile are found quaint little early American motifs of ships, weeping willows, birds, and wreaths; silver luster and black or red form the basis of several modern decorative schemes; Mayan motifs feature others; these are only a few of the unprecedented types.

The Mosaic Tile Company came into existence in 1894. The Columbian Exposition in Chicago in 1893 brought a large display of mosaic tiling from foreign countries, which showed the extent it was used abroad and the promise of a rich market here. The polychrome decoration of the Transportation Building on the Exposition grounds awakened such admiration that prominent architects believed imminent the use of ceramic, climate-resisting color for the exterior of buildings. The public was too conservative, however, to take up this idea.

"Aided by the interests of the best architects, the Mosaic Tile Company did some notable work in the line in which it was best equipped, such as the floor of the courthouse in Fort Wayne, Indiana, and the exterior frieze of the Roebling residence in Trenton. But grasping significance of the cross current of popular taste, it turned quickly to the manufacture of tesselated ceramic mosaic as its principal product, for marble mosaic proved insufficiently durable for northern traffic and not impervious enough for sanitary floors, as the management foresaw. Thus diverted from its original purpose, but equal to the emergency, the company met the new issue and became the second in size, though the largest of the larger tile factories to be founded."[7] The Mosaic Tile Company produces a very fine glaze. Their ware is similar to that of the American Encaustic Tiling Company.

A decorative tile company that had a brief but memorable existence, is the Unitile Company of Urichsville. Ex-governor Donahey and his brother, James Donahey, the newspaper artist, started this tile company. The tiles were decorated by inlaying various colored clays to form the designs; when they came from the kiln the surface was smooth and the pattern remained sharp and clear. Subjects such as "Little Red Riding Hood" were carried out in a series of tiles that gave the whole story. The plant burned and was not rebuilt.

---

[7] "History of the Clay Industry in Ohio," by Wilbur Stout, Geological Survey of Ohio, Bulletin 26, p. 29.

PLATE 60—Main Lounge, Stanley Theatre, Jersey City, N. J. (The American Encaustic Tiling Company, Zanesville)

Americans are beginning to realize the wonderful possibilities of decorative ceramic tiles in building interiors, the beautiful qualities of surface and color that can be achieved; their permanence, and the freedom of spontaneous design they encourage. In Spain there is an old proverb used to thrust at the spendthrift, "My son, you will never have a house of tiles!" The best that could come to one in the way of worldly possessions was summed up in that phrase — "a house of tiles". One realizes the truth of the adage when beholding the historic and luxurious House of El Greco at Toledo, Spain. From the tombs of the kings of six thousand years ago may be seen today undamaged Egyptian tiles whose colors are as fresh and brilliant as if they had been fired yesterday. Since then, through every century and nearly every civilization, ceramic tiles have had a glorious artistic history. From Persia and India the Saracens brought the art of beautiful tilemaking to Spain, and thence it spread to Italy, Holland, England, and Mexico. The modern art of tilemaking has indeed a rich heritage!

An industry closely allied to ceramics that has made marked progress, even more than pottery, along artistic lines in recent years, is glassmaking. The Heisey Glass Company, Newark, stands supreme in this country as makers of blown and pressed glass in the plainer styles. Their glass product is excellent in finish, produced under formulas for rare and beautiful colors; they make charming etched decorations, and an interesting output of their factory is the clever reproduction of early American pressed glass from the old Sandwich glass pattern molds.

The Cambridge Glass Company, Cambridge, makes good pressed glass, in clear and colors, with gold encrustations and etched decorations. Ebony and gold Krystol are two of their special colors. The Lotus Glass Company, Barnesville, has been very successful with gold decorations on glass. The Sterling Glass Company, Cincinnati, does the finest of cutwork on imported blanks; it is considered equal to the imported cut rock crystal. The Earl W. Newton Company, Bowling Green, effects good cut rock crystal on American blanks.

The Von Gerichten Studios is one of the oldest and largest concerns in the country producing stained-glass windows. It has been established in Columbus since 1893, and its glass has added the crowning beauty to hundreds of ecclesiastical edifices. The methods of glass painting remain as they were in the medieval period; however, the present craftsmen in stained glass have the privilege of studying the old examples and have a wider range of beautiful translucent colors at their command. This firm maintains the large stock of imported glass necessary to select from, as the best artist will be handicapped by an insufficient variation. To make the most of these colors the designer must be a master of his trade. The Von Gerichten Studios employ the best artists for this work, and for years have been a big factor in training Columbus artists, as they held to the old German plan of having apprentices. A branch shop at Munich, Germany, is under their management. They are endeavoring to create stained-glass windows which equal, or even surpass, the windows of former centuries in merit and beauty, and indeed, many a successful effort is displayed in their studios.

The American Ceramic Society has made a study of the rôle of design as a merchandising factor in the glassware industry. Design is not the obviously simple thing it passes for, and it becomes less simple every day. The most essential point of view is a realization of what design is and its possibilities. The two most important functions of pattern for glass are to emphasize the glassy nature of the medium by accent or contrast (relief, cutting, etching, sandblast, etc.) and to break up a plain area into interesting spaces. Colored glass has possibilities untouched. A real designer should thrill to the beauty of the material itself in order to capitalize the qualities peculiar to it. He should understand that, primarily, an object is built for use. The sincerest kind of design is based on function. The source of the modern spirit is in industry and science, dynamic rhythm of machinery, sweeping elimination of waste, stark function, character. Equally, the industrial world has come to realize that as it puts art into its product, it gets dollars and cents in return. Through the coöperation of the artist and the manufacturer, industry in this country has greatly improved the art qualities of its products during the last few years.

CHAPTER VIII

Ohio-Born Painters With Careers Outside the State

"SOME men are born great, some achieve greatness, and some are born in Ohio," is a saying that has been current in Ohio for many years. It is a very trite statement, one must admit, but it evinces a state pride that Ohioans consider justifiable. One might say that perhaps the men considered in this chapter became great because they had the good judgment to leave the state; be that as it may, there is no denying that Ohio has a galaxy of great men to its credit. Ohio is loath to relinquish claim upon any of its illustrious sons and daughters. While fortune stole these jewels from Ohio's crown to shine in another setting, yet no matter how distantly the attachments of art have carried them, they still belong to Ohio. None can question the legitimate claim of the state upon the important artists discussed in this chapter, and they are presented here with no small pride and gratification.

WORTHINGTON WHITTREDGE

It has already been mentioned (Chap. V, *ante*) that Thomas Cole, the first painter, and usually regarded as the founder of the Hudson River school, found his inspiration in the Ohio River landscapes. It is singular, then, that the last painter of that group should be an Ohioan, Worthington Whittredge, born in Springfield, Ohio, in 1820.

Lacking the traditional classic and historical themes of the European countries, the American painter turned to nature for his inspiration and found it in full measure in the great vistas which our country unfolded to his view. The Hudson River school developed near the middle of the nineteenth century. The school included men of varying attainments, all sharing, however, an eager desire to put the landscape of the New World on canvas. It was their mission to make people see our vast mountains and plains, or rocky seacoasts, forests, and rivers; they preferred perspective and great expanse, expressed with a far horizon. This school of landscape had a very humble beginning, the landscape painters not being so well equipped, technically, as the early portrait painters. The group took its name from the locality where it first painted; though later, when its artists went west to paint the more spectacular scenery of the Rockies and the name Hudson River still clung to them, it might be said that

179

the Hudson River school came to stand for a state of mind — a romantic, grandiose way of looking at nature. Most of these artists were engravers; and their only knowledge of art came from the theatrical landscapes of Turner and other English artists which they saw in engravings. From these engravings they learned to look at nature with that Old World feeling for design. It was this pattern which, being reproduced in England and Düsseldorf, influenced our painters in portraying American landscape.

With cosmopolitanism setting its ideal of freedom before the present-day artist, it is not likely that any group will again follow any particular influence; perhaps that is as it should be. Kenyon Cox tells us, in *Painters and Sculptors*: "The modern student knows too much of the art of all times and countries to choose a single master and docilely follow his teaching. It is doubtful if modern conditions have not rendered forever impossible anything like a local school of painting."[1]

Worthington Whittredge used to recall often the names of his old friends of the Hudson River school: Thomas Doughty, Asher B. Durand, Thomas Cole, F. E. Church, John F. Kensett, Albert Bierstadt, and Thomas Moran, and then he would add, "They are all dead!" He liked to reminisce of those early days of painting, of his student days at Düsseldorf, and of his acquaintance with Lord Leighton in Rome. It is a pleasure to think of Worthington Whittredge as he has been pictured by John W. Alexander, with striking vitality, in the portrait of him which hangs in the National Academy of Design. A man of exceptionally strong physique, he had the lifelong habit of kindness and generosity; his last days were filled with a bountiful harvest of affection and respect by reason of his lovable qualities. Mr. Whittredge stood as the model for Washington, and wore Washington's uniform in Leutze's well-known picture of the hero crossing the Delaware.

At Düsseldorf, Whittredge produced "The Poachers", a work since frequently lithographed. He delineated faithfully an opening into the woods, with sunlight coming through the foliage. He was familiar with all kinds of American landscape and transcribed them lovingly, with a special fondness for bunches of shrubbery, banks of streams, deep-shadowed hollows in the woods, and reaches of grassy plains where cattle grazed (Plate 61). His "Trout Brook in the Catskills," in the Corcoran Gallery of Art, Washington, is an example of his skill in depicting sunlight and shadow in the woods, painted according to his accurate vision. Many years ago Mr. Frank Mather said of this landscape that "as an account of a Catskill brook it is letter-perfect. So easy sandstone ledges lie

---

[1] *Painters and Sculptors,* by Kenyon Cox, p. 9.

PLATE 61—Landscape. Worthington Whittredge. (Cincinnati Museum of Art)

up in nature, so dark water slips over, and trees overhang them; so the sun strikes fitfully through unperceived rifts in the leaf canopy."

As president of the National Academy of Design, in 1875, Whittredge devoted himself to the artist's point of view; he was a picturesque figure, far removed from any commercial interest or sordid ambitions. This painter of the old school lived a long, energetic, and fruitful life. These painters of the Hudson River school were the pioneers of American landscape painting, and their conformity to European formulas united artistic America to European traditions.

ALEXANDER H. WYANT

Alexander H. Wyant was born in Evans Creek, Tuscarawas County, Ohio. There was little in that small town to suggest to the boy what pictures meant, but he had the picture-making faculty, the keen eye of the artist, and the desire to translate the forms of things into line and color. His family was of the wandering type, and soon left Evans Creek to live in or near Defiance, where the lad went to the village school. Interesting tales are told of his lying on the floor in front of the fireplace, with a bit of charcoal making sketches of landscapes on the rough boards of the floor. He was apprenticed to a harnessmaker as soon as he was old enough to be set at a trade, but he preferred to do something with a brush, and so employed his leisure hours at sign painting.

Cincinnati, even in the fifties, acted as a magnet to everyone interested in art. Wyant was attracted thither, where for the first time he learned what painted pictures were like. With a rare instinct for so inexperienced a young man, he early came to admire the work of Inness. He conceived the idea of going to Perth Amboy, New Jersey, to consult with Inness as to whether he should hope to become an artist. The master received him kindly, commented favorably upon his sketches, and Wyant returned to Cincinnati resolved to become a painter.

Nicholas Longworth made it possible for Wyant to go to New York, where he saw a large exhibition of pictures of the Düsseldorf school. The sight of them fired his ambition to study in Europe. A mountain and waterfall landscape by a Norwegian, Hans Gude, especially stirred him; so that when Wyant visited Düsseldorf in 1865, he proceeded at once to Carlsruhe and put himself under the instruction of Hans Gude.

The style of landscape Gude painted was of the grand panoramic scope of high mountains and a great expanse of view, with a blazing sun in the sky. He insisted that Wyant follow his particular manner, but Wyant's independence asserted itself, and he left for England and studied the masters in the

PLATE 62—An Adirondack Brook. Alexander Wyant. (Cincinnati Museum of Art)

National Gallery. Wyant in America had been under the spell of the spectacular Hudson River school of painters; the Düsseldorf idea had enlarged
that conception; and Turner had also aided it, but in London, Constable, whose
work was not of the Düsseldorf type, became his favorite. The influence of
Constable made Wyant abandon his earlier manner. He went to Ireland and
painted pictures with a broad, realistic look unlike the output of any painter
or any school he knew. The Metropolitan Museum, New York, has one of
these paintings, "View of County Kerry, Ireland", painted with a broad, flat
brush and simply massed.

Returning to New York, he painted "View of the Susquehanna", which
brought him associate membership in the National Academy in 1868; one year
later he became a full member. In 1873 he joined a government expedition to
Arizona, where he thought his impaired health might be restored. The hardships
were more than he was able to endure. Stricken with paralysis, he was sent back
East, on a train that passed through his home town, Defiance, where his mother
could have cared for him. But he allowed himself to be carried on to New
York. He argued that to be taken off at a near-West station was to be estranged
from the painter's life on which his determination was still fixed. His right
hand and arm were paralyzed, but nothing thwarted him in training his left
hand to paint.

John C. Van Dyke speaks beautifully of Wyant in his book, *American Painting and Its Tradition:* "The wonder of Wyant's success is greater than that of
Inness, for his boyhood surroundings, if anything, were less stimulating and his
pictorial education far more restricted. Besides, Inness lived on to seventy
years, but Wyant died at fifty-six, having endured ill health, and for the last
ten years of his life — his best working years — been paralyzed in his right
arm and hand. Living much to himself, something of a hermit in his mountain
home, weighed down by misfortunes and disappointments, the wonder grows
that he not only kept up and improved his technique to the end, but that he
preserved his serenity of mood and purity of outlook through it all. He must
have been a man with fortitude of soul beyond the average. It is not every
painter that can turn stumblingblocks into stepping-stones."[2]

He never mingled freely with his fellow men. Mrs. Squires, of Defiance,
speaking of her interview with him, says: "He met us, a tall, spare man, holding the palette in his right hand. He kept his position at the easel after greet-
ing us and we glanced eagerly at the half-finished landscape. We left him conscious of his strength, his reserve — amounting almost to timidity, and that he

---

[2]*American Painting and Its Tradition,* John C. Van Dyke, p. 45.

possessed few of the social gentilities of Chase. His dress was not really untidy, neither was it meticulous, but that of an absorbed workman."

For many years he made his summer home in the Adirondacks, which gave him the theme for many of his paintings. He was a great admirer of Rousseau, and never got away from the wide valley view between the mountains. Fearing that he was getting into a groove in his way of seeing nature, he transferred his studio to the Catskills. From his porch he could command a sweeping outlook of the mountains with their woods, rocks, rivulets, and valleys. No landscape pleased him better than the American one (Plate 62).

Wyant had so much that he longed to do; he also knew that with his late-trained left hand, the years left to do his work were few. It was only by constant application that he could realize some part of his ideal. This concentration of effort affected his outlook, limiting the range of moods of nature that he strove to represent. Such versatility as that of Inness, his alacrity of impression to changing phases of nature, was impossible to Wyant's temperament and circumstances.

The "Broad, Silent Valley" in the Metropolitan Museum is one of the best examples of Wyant's work. It is straightforward painting of a masterful kind. The shadows are not gloomy but are kept transparent; the lights are put in with opaque pigments; all the force is concentrated on the color mass. He could gather the sunlight into a golden mass, as could Diaz, who influenced him greatly. There was never any human interest in his landscapes; not the slightest figure to be seen. He saw the hidden spiritual side of nature, and his painting has been justly compared to Wordsworth's poetry. The phrase "tender lyricism" and other poetic terms have been applied to the qualities to be found in his pictures. He felt the meaning of the mountain woodlands and tried to bring their appeal home to our everyday lives.

"The Mohawk Valley" (Metropolitan Museum) remains as a masterpiece of his early topographical period, wherein the influence of the Düsseldorf school predominates. His more mature and complete expression as a great tonalist is shown in his wood interiors and Irish landscapes. "View in County Kerry, Ireland" (Metropolitan Museum) has a rainy-day atmospheric effect enveloping the low hills and plains beyond; the far-away mountains lift their peaks into a clearing sky where fleecy clouds move slowly. Closely hugging a rocky ledge is a small cabin on the right, a path in the foreground leading to it; a large pool of water with encircling green occupies the center of the canvas.

Prices of his canvases have reached inflated values, though only his best work was put upon the market. After his death, his widow, with regard for his honor, destroyed the pictures that never attained to his intention. Knowing his end was near, he would exclaim: "Had I but five years more in which to paint, even one year, I think I could do the thing I long to do." It is not amiss to call him, in the phrase of the poet Shelley, one of the "inheritors of unfulfilled renown."

KENYON COX

So many talents endowed Kenyon Cox that it is puzzling to determine which one to speak of first. What would not be expected of a man favored with such extraordinary ancestors! If ever a man had a good heritage, Kenyon Cox had. His mother was the daughter of the noted evangelist, Doctor Finney, who was the first president of Oberlin College. His father filled a long list of important government positions; he was a Civil War major-general, and wrote one of the best histories of the war; he was governor of the state of Ohio, also its senator and congressman; he was Secretary of the Interior under President Grant; besides, he was president of the Wabash Railway, and president of the University of Cincinnati; a reputable lawyer, scientist, book reviewer, and an authority on cathedral architecture. With such a father, Kenyon Cox should belong to the *intelligentsia*.

Kenyon Cox was born at Warren, Ohio, in 1856. *The History of Trumbull County* states that, "he studied just enough to keep from being punished, and spent the rest of his time drawing pictures for the amusement of those who sat near him."[3] His fondness for drawing was apparent at an early age. Illness interfered with his going to school; he was under the surgeon's knife several times, and was bedridden from his ninth to his thirteenth year. It may well be supposed, however, that a home education with his family was much more than an ordinary advantage. When he was fourteen years old he was given instruction in drawing; perhaps this early foundation was responsible for his saying that a "thorough mastery of drawing cannot be too much insisted upon".

In 1877, Cox went to Paris to study with Carolus Duran, the popular teacher of the time, and then with the more severe master, Gérôme. He was engrossed with the study of the nude. Upon his return to New York, he was elected to the Society of American Artists, and was one of a group of young men trained in Antwerp, Munich, or Paris, who agitated various changes and finally controlled the old National Academy. He painted nudes for many years, but New York patrons refused to buy them; strange to say, they preferred the nudes painted by French artists. There is no accounting for the taste of the buying public.

---

[3] *The History of Trumbull County,* Harriet Taylor Upton, p. 295.

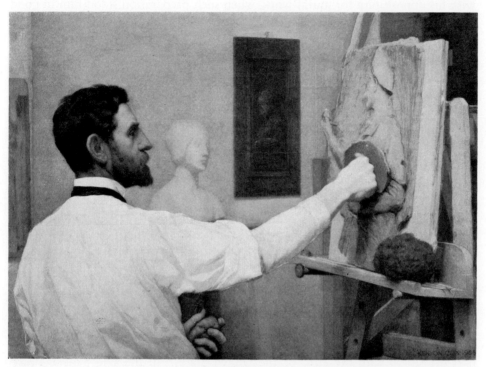

PLATE 63—Saint-Gaudens in His Studio. Kenyon Cox. (Metropolitan Museum of Art)

The reward for such faithful and untiring study of the nude came to Cox with his opportunity for mural work, when such preparation stood him in good stead. There was a growing demand for the decoration of public buildings by murals, and Cox received many commissions. Here is a partial list of them: "Venice", Bowdoin College, Brunswick, Maine; "Art and Science", Library of Congress; "The Reign of Law", Appellate Court, New York City; "Contemplative Spirit of the Law", Minnesota State Capitol; "The Progress of Civilization", Iowa State Capitol; "The Beneficence of the Law", Essex County Court House, Newark, New Jersey; "The Judicial Virtues", Luzerne County Court House, Wilkesbarre, Pennsylvania; "Passing Commerce Pays Tribute to the Port of Cleveland", Federal Building, Cleveland; "The Sources of Wealth", Citizens Building, Cleveland; "The Marriage of the Atlantic and Pacific", and four mosaics in the Wisconsin State Capitol. "The Light of Learning", in the Public Library, Winona, Minnesota, has most beautifully calculated rhythms, with lines and masses balanced perfectly, as in Italian High Renaissance art.

Of the Wisconsin State House murals, representing "The Marriage of the Atlantic and Pacific", here is the artist's own interpretation: "The three panels are to be taken as one picture, symbolizing the opening of the Panama Canal. In the center, America enthroned, blesses the union of the two oceans. The Atlantic, typified by the figure of Neptune, places a ring on the finger of a goddess with a steering oar, who represents the Pacific. Below, two children support the shield with the arms of the United States. In the side panels, Peace and Commerce welcome the nations of the world to the ceremony. To the right, behind the Atlantic, Peace welcomes France with the palette of art, Germany with the book of science, and Great Britain. A muscular boatman drags at the barge with gilded figurehead. In the opposite panel, Commerce, with the attributes of Mercury, beckons to Japan and China, behind whom is a figure symbolizing the Semitic races. Seated in the prow of the boat is the garlanded figure of Polynesia. A water nymph of the local stream plays beside the barge."[4] One can visualize the wealth of symbolism these panels contain. While the paintings are strong in color, they were studied to be placed between the freestanding marble columns, and admirably accomplish their decorative purpose, adding markedly to the beauty and dignity of the Senate Chamber.

"The color he had learned in the Paris schools and the habit of representing the model rather literally had to be foregone in favor of colors and forms suitable for intricate compositions and large wall spaces. . . . From the year 1900 Cox's style of decoration assumed more success of design while his color grew

[4]Official Guide to the Wisconsin Capitol.

richer and more unified. . . . Every mural design was finer than the last, there was a painstaking and gradual development like Dürer's. . . . The public edifices of America owe much to the decorative movement he contributed greatly to energizing, and the influence of his calm and firm example, rooted in the classical traditions, will be a steady force against running off after the bizarre and the eccentric."[5]

The best known of the easel pictures of Kenyon Cox is the "Portrait of Saint-Gaudens in His Studio", in the Metropolitan Museum, New York (Plate 63). The original portrait, painted in 1887, was destroyed in the fire that burned Saint-Gaudens' studio at Windsor, Vermont, in 1904. Mr. Cox painted this replica in 1908, a year after the sculptor's death, from the studies he still had in his studio. The portrait has a threefold interest for us: first in Cox, second in Saint-Gaudens, and third in their mutual friend, William M. Chase, who is the figure in the bas-relief that Saint-Gaudens is represented as working upon. The portrait of Saint-Gaudens is superb; the studio wall is ornamented with some of his sculpture, notably the relief of his son, Homer, as a little boy in his high chair. There is also a cast of the "Unknown Woman" of the Louvre, which Cox and Saint-Gaudens both greatly admired. In fact, Cox was so fond of that bust that he wrote the following poem:

THE UNKNOWN WOMAN

She lived in Florence centuries ago,
    That lady smiling there;
What was her name or rank I do not know,
    I know that she was fair.

For some great man — his name like hers, forgot
    And faded from men's sight—
Loved her — he must have loved her — and has wrought
    This bust for our delight.

Whether he gained her love or had her scorn,
    Full happy was his fate.
He saw her, heard her speak; he was not born
    Four hundred years too late.

The palace throngs in every room but this—
    Here I am left alone.
Love, there is none to see — I press a kiss
    Upon thy lips of stone.

---

[5] *Scribner's Magazine,* vol. 65, "Kenyon Cox," by Frank Jewett Mather, Jr., p. 765.

Another interesting portrait is that of the veteran Cincinnati wood carver, Henry L. Fry, in the Cincinnati Museum. The little old Englishman, wearing a long overcoat, stands before a curtain. The long-bearded face, calm and powerful, with the close-knit brows of a thinker, and the very expressive hand, are as vigorously done as any work of Cox. As a sculptor, Kenyon Cox achieved some renown; his statue of "Greek Science" is shown in the Brooklyn Museum.

Mr. Cox was an art critic for twenty-five years. He began writing as a reviewer for *The Nation*. People whom he met were his staunch friends or his bitter enemies, as he was a strong personality, a natural leader, and a fighter for his convictions. Likewise, his criticisms were straightforward, fearless, clear, and emphatic, with no avoidance of disagreeable paths. "On the all-pervasive Impressionism, the success of which within its proper limits Cox generously acknowledged, he wrote: 'Impressionism which makes light its only subject, and ruthlessly sacrifices clarity and structure in the interest of illusion, is acceptable in inverse proportion to the essential beauty and interest of the objects represented.' For the rest he felt that the handling of the Impressionists was often brutal and ugly, and hindered the obtaining of a modern technique. His intense perceptions of general principles sometimes colored unhappily his particular judgments. He was so resolute in condemning what seemed to him subversive theory that he sometimes swept into the indictment rather notable works. Thus he did scant justice to Rodin's real greatness, it seems to me, largely because Rodin had unwittingly demoralized the young generation of sculpture. The bulk of his writing is sound, hearty, and permanent."[6]

Beginning in 1905, he collected his essays, lectures, and criticisms into book form, giving us such unusual volumes as *Old Masters and New, Painters and Sculptors, The Classic Point of View, Artist and Public,* and *Concerning Painters.* On Whistler, Burne-Jones, and Winslow Homer, no one has written with clearer judgment; he always enriched whatever subject he touched. He gives us his idea of the necessary qualifications for a good critic, when he speaks of the painter Fromentin, in his *Painters and Sculptors:* "When to clear intellect, catholicity of judgment, and special technical knowledge, is added unusual literary power, you have the ideal critic — the man born to interpret the artist to the public."[7]

Kenyon Cox was a teacher, too, and like his friend, William M. Chase, exerted a strong influence upon art education in New York. Many honors came to him, among them doctorates from Oberlin and Dartmouth Colleges. His

---

[6] *Scribner's Magazine,* vol. 65, "Kenyon Cox," by Frank Jewett Mather, Jr., p. 765.
[7] *Painters and Sculptors,* by Kenyon Cox, p. xviii.

wife and son were also very capable artists. *The New York Tribune* said of him at his death, "The American art world suffers a great loss."

WILLIAM HENRY HOWE

An Ohio man who traveled far indeed, and won prizes for his pictures in many lands, was William Henry Howe, born at Ravenna, Ohio, in 1846. This painter received gold, silver, and bronze medals, and all the honors that could then be showered on an artist.

He was of a good old New England family, whose homestead still stands in Concord, Massachusetts. Like so many youths of the time of the Civil War, he answered the call of his country, a service which a grateful country afterwards recognized by the award of a pension that Mr. Howe enjoyed for a number of years. After the war, he drifted to St. Louis and entered the employ of a leading firm of wholesale dry goods merchants, Dodd, Brown & Company, where his advancement was rapid, as he was gifted with a keen commercial sense. So far, his history was that of many of our youth, in no wise exceptional: he gave satisfaction to his employer and lived the life of a southwestern commercial town, save that he had the habit of amusing himself by painting in an amateurish way on Sundays and holidays, at every moment he could wrest from his vocation.

From his avocation there came about a change. When an alert and efficient business man, apparently fixed in a lucrative position in commercial life, makes such a decided change as to embark on the concededly hazardous career of art, he at once becomes exceptional. Our art schools today are crowded with young men and women who "have adopted the art of Raphael from the notion of ease", as Stevenson wittingly writes. Mr. Howe knew that the task before him was not easy, but he knew that in art, as in any profession, there is always room at the top, and he resolutely determined to get there. At first he studied at Düsseldorf for two years, then became the private pupil of Otto von Thoren, and afterwards of Vuillefroy, in Paris, two excellent painters of animals. While Mr. Howe specialized first in landscape painting, he very soon found that this was to serve but as a background for his animal paintings, which have placed him in the foremost rank of cattle painters of his time.

We may well pause for a moment to picture the Paris of the eighties and nineties of the last century in its relation to art. Artists of all nations were gathered there or sent their productions from their native lands to the Salon, for final approval in establishing their reputations. The Salon was (as it is today) the annual exhibition of sculpture and painting housed in a palatial

building in a choice position in the center of the city. Showing literally four or
five thousand examples of various arts, an exhibition was opened each year
with due ceremony by the president of the republic. The "Varnishing Day" of
the Salon vies with the races at Auteuil or any other fashionable affair as pre-
eminently an occasion for all Paris to flock to the exhibit and pay its devotion
to art. It was there, in this whirl of international competition, that Howe won
his spurs as an artist.

In 1883, Mr. Howe's "Uplands of Normandy" was hung in the Paris Salon.
Every year thereafter, until his return to America in 1893, he was honorably
represented in the annual exhibition of the French Academy. For his "Norman
Bull", classed as one of the most attractive pictures in the Salon of 1886, hon-
orable mention was awarded, and in 1887 the Salon saw his "Return of the
Herd", for which a medal was awarded at the Universal Exhibition of 1889.
In 1888, Mr. Howe sent to the Salon "An Early Start to Market", a realistic
painting, showing a Dutchman on a gray horse driving four cows along a
sloppy road. For this he received a first-class medal at the Universal Exhibition.
His "Truants", Salon picture for 1890, showing a group of heifers lost on a
Dutch heath, made him outstanding, and "Vagabonds", was exhibited in Paris,
1893. After gaining fame in France and Holland, Mr. Howe returned to this
country, and in a short time his "Norman Bull", found a permanent home in the
St. Louis Museum. Two of his most famous works, "My Day at Home", and
"Monarch of the Farm", hang in the National Gallery at Washington, D. C.

As one stands before the superb canvas picturing the "Monarch of the Farm"
one suspects (no, one knows) that it is a very great piece of painting. Drawn
absolutely faithful to the last detail, without ever descending to the mere photographic, this figure of the recumbent bull is surrounded by a certain quality of
lambent atmosphere which Howe always acquired in his work. An eminent
critic, F. W. Ruckstuhl, pays very high tribute to the genius of Howe when he
speaks of his painting "Vagabonds": "William Henry Howe is undoubtedly
the most powerful cattle painter this country has produced during the last
generation from the standpoint of feeling for life, true cattle nature, originality
and force of composition and of the expression of vagabonding by the 'bunch'
of cattle. For solidity of drawing and rendering in color, the forms, and the
textures of hides, it has never been surpassed."[8] "The Truants" shows the good
sense of composition in which Mr. Howe excelled; the group of ten yearlings
has been distributed with skill, and while each one remains individual, yet the
herd forms a single mass. He has caught the half-wild movement of the young

---

[8] *The Bronxville Review,* June 2, 1926.

PLATE 64—Cattle. William H. Howe. (Horace Kelley Art Foundation)

animals, before they have confidence in men, and before they assume the stolid gait of the adult (Plate 64).

During his thirteen-year sojourn abroad, he had wisely contributed to the home exhibitions so that his reputation was firmly established here, and the National Academy of Design enrolled him as a member, upon his return. One day, in 1898, he was summoned to the French consulate in New York to receive the cross of the Legion of Honor; it was the crowning honor that came to him from France, the greatest honor which is in the power of the French government to bestow. Mr. and Mrs. Howe decided to make their permanent home in Bronxville, New York, and in so doing they founded what is now the well-known art colony. Other artists soon followed, and before long that particular section was humorously alluded to as "the Latin Quarter". In the summers, the season most appropriate for his work, he was attracted to Old Lyme, Connecticut, where, one of the earliest, he aided the founding of the distinctive artists' colony there. Old Lyme became one of his favorite haunts, for there he found about him the majestic trees and beautiful pastures that appear so often in his paintings.

Cattle and sheep seem to enjoy an unfailing support from those who buy pictures; no one can deny their interesting quality in a landscape. The restfulness of the lowing herd, or the browsing flock of sheep, is reflected upon the observer. One may well say that the painter, too, is apt to gain from the humble animals, and is likely to be an agreeable, cheerful soul. To select only two conspicuous masters of painting from the past centuries, one might call to witness the Dutch painter, Paul Potter, and Troyon, the greatest of French cattle painters, who became famous through persistence in one line of work. The mantle of geniality that wrapped these two old masters descended upon William Henry Howe, an American and an Ohioan. In the early days of Bronxville there was not a man, woman, or child whom he did not know — and was interested in; his was an interest that was returned in kind, as his good fellowship and kindly approach were always welcomed. Mr. Howe died at his home in Bronxville in 1929, a veteran painter, rich in years and honors.

CULLEN YATES

Cullen Yates, born in Bryan, Ohio, is one of America's foremost landscape and marine painters. Descended from a family of valiant pioneers who endured many hardships in settling the Middle West, he spent his boyhood in the country, where he closely observed the trees, and hills, and rivers, during the changing seasons, and learned the language and characters of the birds and the flowers in the open wood. The love of nature instilled in him in his youth, has always been his dominant theme. The voice of the tree and the wave have called to him with never-failing charm.

Interesting stories of his precocious school days, when he began to draw and arrange flowers into good compositions, and to manipulate color harmoniously, are told by the citizens of his boyhood home, where he was considered a genius and where his career was watched hopefully. Similar accounts are related of early artistic efforts of a legion of painters, but this case is extraordinary because the boy had no teacher but nature, and he formed a class of pupils and taught for several years, with no other background than his own self-training. However, Yates had plenty of thorough instruction later, with William M. Chase and Leonard Ochtman, in New York. Then his parents took him to Paris, where he was a pupil of Jean Paul Laurens and Benjamin Constant at the École des Beaux Arts. They sensed Yates's rare ability and gave him every encouragement. Returning to America, he found no ready purchasers for his pictures, so taught art in a Cleveland school for some time. Eventually, he made his way back to New York and opened a studio.

The art of Cullen Yates is peculiarly original and progressive. In every canvas, whether landscape or marine, the sky line is placed very high, almost at the top of the picture. There is an enveloping atmospheric effect that is lovely. His colors are gorgeous in his autumn scenes; for example, "Autumn Gold" is full of amber yellows, golden browns and deep reds; "The Incoming Tide" is a well-known marine in which he has beggared his palette of all colors: red, purple, orange, and yellow play upon the rocks, while the water reflects unusual contrasts in deep blue and greens. Spring scenes, which he seems especially to prefer, have yellow-green grass full of flowers and delicate green fringy foliage; the same delicacy of color is noticeable in "The First Snow"; "The Village Church", showing a chapel nestled at the foot of a hill, has an interesting composition and more human interest than most of his canvases, for seldom is there a figure of any sort either in his landscapes or marines. In his work there is always a feeling of the change taking place in nature, the unseen power and force constantly at work.

Mrs. Bryant, in her indispensable book, *American Pictures and Their Painters,* thus describes "The Rock-Bound Coast", by Cullen Yates, in the National Gallery, Washington: "He certainly put the very spirit of desolateness in it. Stern, uncompromising, immovable, are the attributes written on every line of the projecting rock, and yet the restless, uneasy, persistent wash of the waters is doing its work. Centuries may come and centuries may go, and these two opposing forces will continue to harass each other, always with the odds in favor of the dynamic power. Mr. Yates deals with the fundamentals of life, and how he makes us feel the elemental forces in his strong, straightforward lines! His frank, simple, brush strokes tell the story of the rock-bound coast with the naïveté of a child. It is the work of one whose art speaks the truth and is understood by sage and rustic alike. Even to those who have never seen a rock-bound coast, this picture will bring a message of the ceaseless strife going on between land and water."[9]

Mr. Yates leaves his New York studio early in the spring for his summer home at Shawnee-on-the-Delaware, and there in Pennsylvania he has produced many fine paintings of American landscape, picturesque hills, and peaceful valleys. Spring, summer, autumn, winter; morning, noon, night — every hour nature presents to him a new program in such a country. His marines are painted on the coast of Maine in the fall, and they contain the same mystery and poetry of nature as his landscapes. Has he followed the advice of Rossetti?

> "Listen alone beside the sea—
> Listen alone among the woods."

DeWitt Lockman, in his portait of Cullen Yates, represents him as a man of poise, comfortably seated, hat and cane in hand, and his overcoat on, as if ready to start on a walk, observing nature with keen eyes. Nature is a supreme pleasure to those whose eyes and ears are open, whose minds are alert and sensitive to beauty in light and shade, form and color. Mr. Yates reports that pleasure to us that we may share his joy (Plate 65).

A man's paintings may be interpreted with more interest and enjoyment if we are aware of something of his personality. "It is a well-known fact that an artist's character may be reconstructed from his work, for whatever he is, is recorded with undying truth in his canvas. This to a certain extent explains the subtle charm in the art of Cullen Yates, which, while it expresses the firmness of ideals, yet ever reflects his characteristic gentleness of spirit and helpful attitude toward others, as well as his gift of imagination, poetic vision, and sincere love for all that is really true and beautiful."[10]

ELIZABETH NOURSE

Since 1887 Elizabeth Nourse has lived in Paris. Some three hundred years ago the old Huguenot family of Nourse came to Massachusetts, where one of

---

[9] *American Pictures and Their Painters,* by Mrs. Bryant, p. 244.
[10] *Country Life,* June, 1920.

PLATE 65—Delaware Water Gap. Cullen Yates. (National Academy of Design)

them, Rebecca Nourse, was dragged from her home and put to death on Gallows Hill in Salem for witchcraft. Miss Nourse was born in Cincinnati, a descendant of this family.

As a very young girl she showed much talent for painting, and her parents permitted her to enter the Cincinnati Art Academy. After the death of her parents, she refused a good position as teacher because it would interfere with her coveted ambition to continue her studies in Paris. But to study art in Paris meant that one must have an income, which she did not have. So she and her sister began to earn and save money; when they had accumulated enough to keep them several years in Paris, they set out for France.

Miss Nourse began studying at the Julian Academy. The French are quick to recognize genius and to encourage ability by aiding its development in every way. Some of the best French artists advised her to have her own studio and develop herself independently of masters; they feared the loss of her marked individuality from too constant academic training. In deference to their wishes she began to paint alone, going to Carolus-Duran and Henner for criticism. In 1888 she made her first contribution to the Salon and received the unusual honor of having her picture hung on the line. She was the first American woman on whom was conferred the honor of membership in the Société Nationale des Beaux Arts, founded by Puvis de Chavannes, Dagnan-Bouveret, Rodin, and a number of the younger artists. They admired her work and rejoiced in giving her talent the recognition it deserved. For years she was one of the most able American woman painters in Paris. The French government purchased her "Closed Shutters" for the Luxembourg Museum. The Royal Academies of London, Berlin, and Copenhagen have exhibited her works, and they have been reproduced in the leading art journals of the world.

Elizabeth Nourse paints mothers and nurses, and children, following much the same theme as Mary Cassatt. While she has painted many fine landscapes of Brittany, and bits of the old forest of Rambouillet, scenes of Tunis, and a number of portraits, yet it is in her representations of mother-love that she shows her supreme ability. Her pictures belong to the realistic school, though it is realism that pulls the heartstrings. She has learned to love the peasants, and by living among them she has come to understand their point of view; she reproduces their lovely lives with a beautiful naïveté that is remarkable. With strong, clear strokes she interprets the life of the poor and the humble.

One of the early pictures made in Paris by Miss Nourse was "Le Goûter" (Plate 66); it is now owned by the Chicago Art Institute, and they have always called it "Mother and Children". She gives an interesting account of the

PLATE 66—Le Goûter. Elizabeth Nourse. (The Art Institute of Chicago)

models for that picture: "The children and the mother were Italians. The mother was famous for her beauty when younger; she posed for many artists as a Madonna, and one of the most celebrated artists was Dagnan-Bouveret. She was my model for many years, and all her children took their turn to pose for me. The family were very poor. I used to climb their rickety stairs in a poor, tumble-down house full of Italian models from the Sabine Mountains near Rome. I always said a prayer that I would not catch anything, either bug or disease. When little Bepina came to pose with her mother and the baby, I used to give her a cup of milk, and that is how I found the lovely pose. She used to drink it with lightning speed, to my bewilderment: how could I keep the cup filled? how could I keep her posed? So between the poses I gave her a slice of bread and butter thickly spread with currant jelly."[11] Her pictures are types of human character, not just portraits of her models.

The impress of deep thought is upon every picture she makes. She finds the great truths of life in very common, everyday occurrences; her genius lies in seeing the poetry and beauty in the simplest action. A hurt, grief-stricken child finds comfort in its mother's arms; the father of a small family ready to eat their frugal evening meal, enjoys peace in his humble home as he rests from the toil of the day; a baby sister is mothered in the lap of an older sister; happiness radiates from a group of mothers and children strolling along the dyke; the solemn, religious procession wends its way through a Breton village; a mother's joy in her children fills many happy hours — such, indeed, are the human interest stories which Miss Nourse pictures with lavish tenderness.

The painting of Miss Nourse is no less excellent in technical perfection than in its universal appeal. She exacts much of herself, is most critical of her own work, and is never satisfied until she feels she has interpreted her message correctly. She has the friendship of many French masters, but is not influenced by them, and her work remains her own. Her composition is decorative and balanced; her color is luminous, the lights beautifully handled; the brush work is firm, and the large lines sweeping and beautiful. "The work of a true artist reveals his ideals, the richness or the poverty of his nature. In that of Miss Nourse is shown the broad human sympathy of a strong woman, who believes in art not for art's sake, but also for the sake of a humanity which it can uplift and spiritualize."[12]

ROBERT HENRI

"The man who has honesty, integrity, the love of inquiry, the desire to see beyond, is ready to appreciate good art. He needs no one to give him an art

---

[11] *The Literary Digest,* vol. 89, June 12, 1926. Reproduction used for cover.
[12] *International Studio,* vol. 27, p. 254.

education; he is already qualified. He needs but to see pictures with his active mind, look into them for the things that belong to him, and he will find soon enough in himself an art connoisseur and an art lover of the first order."[13]

In even a brief discussion of Robert Henri, one must state at the beginning that he was an independent person. In practising what he preached, he stood firmly on his own opinions, whether any one agreed with him or not, to the point that he was dubbed a revolutionary.

Robert Henri was born in Cincinnati, Ohio, in 1865, and went to school there. At first he thought he was intended to be a writer, but soon found a stronger attraction in painting. He traveled throughout the West, and then began studying at the Pennsylvania Academy of Fine Arts in Philadelphia, with Thomas Anshutz, one of the greatest art teachers America has had. Leaving that institution in 1886, Henri pursued his studies further with Fleury and Bouguereau at the Julian Academy in Paris. However, he was too independent, even then, to abide by the dogmas of technique taught there; like Rodin, he insisted on breaking all established conventions. So he started out, with his eyes open, to study the galleries of France, Spain, and Italy; he was impressed with the rugged painting of Velasquez, and the pictures of the people of the streets, the sincerity of the peasant and laboring types, made the greatest appeal to him. Courbet, Manet, and Whistler each exerted an influence upon him later, though these were only temporary influences, and emerged from them just himself, supreme in his own right.

"The young man sealed a vow with himself to interpret those things alone in life which appealed to him vitally, whether the subjects were considered paintable or not by the schools. He would make his paintings stand as the history of his own spiritual and esthetic development, and if the world was willing to accept them on these terms, well and good, but if not, then he was resigned to be misunderstood."[14]

Robert Henri was not taken seriously in this country until the French government purchased his picture, "La Neige", from the Paris Salon of 1899, and placed it in the Luxembourg; only a half-dozen Americans had been so honored at that time. He was made a member of the National Academy of Design in 1906, when the Society of American Artists was merged with the Academy, and in a short time he was elected to the jury of selection. He had many differences with the jury; there were no halfway places with Henri — he was either for or against, irrevocably. He stood for the recognition of the painters

---

[13] *The Art Spirit*, by Robert Henri, p. 60.
[14] *The Independent*, "Robert Henri," C. W. Barrell, vol. 64, p. 1427.

who gave evidences of fresh and original points of view. He saw George Luks, Everett Shinn, William Glackens, Arthur Davies, and many others turned down in spite of his protests. Many times he had canvases recalled for further consideration, but the jury each time would decide that they could not be hung. At one time when three of his own pictures had been accepted, one unanimously, and the other painters, so-called revolutionaries, had their works of power and originality refused, he asked and received permission to withdraw two of his paintings, preferring to cast his lot with the rejected. Commenting upon his stand, Henri said: "The fact of a National Academy should mean an organization for the advancement of the art of those who have new ideas to express. That there are such men is the encouraging sign for the future of art in this country, and they should be brought forward and sustained instead of rebuffed in their efforts for recognition."

Henri chose his subjects from all walks of life, ranging from the elegant madame, to the poorest colored urchin on the street. His "Portrait of Mrs. Robert Henri" was exhibited in most of our large cities and awarded many prizes. His wife, too, was a talented painter; in this portrait of her by her husband Mrs. Henri's personality emanates from the canvas. Her graceful, standing figure is against a dark background; the face, flooded with light, has a keen expression, as if giving warning that she is ready to speak at any moment. One of Henri's best-known and most-admired canvases is the "Young Woman in Black", in the Chicago Art Institute. When it was exhibited at the St. Louis Exposition, in 1904, Henri was awarded a silver medal by the International Jury on Art. It is a full-length study of a young American beauty, an exquisite human document. Henri adores to paint children, either of the white, yellow, or dark-skinned races. "Willie Gee", in the Corcoran Gallery, is a Virginia negro boy, shown at the exhibition of the Society of American Artists in 1905. Look into the engaging boy face at the right distance, and those searching eyes are as deep and dark as sea water. "Chow Choy" and "Tam Gan" are very paintable Oriental maids. Demure "Chow Choy" in blue against an apricot-colored background, makes a colorfully fresh impression which is nailed down with all of Henri's characteristic broad, dashing handling. He saw racial characteristics with an unerring eye. "The Dancer in the Yellow Shawl" is a stunning color combination, painted with his fearlessness of stroke that electrifies the observer. In every instance, he disdains details; nothing superfluous is put in, yet there is never any possibility of mistaking the soul of the subject (Plate 67).

When asked how he came to choose such unusual people for his subjects,

PLATE 67—Beatrice. Robert Henri. (Cincinnati Museum of Art)

Henri replied: "The people I like to paint are 'my people', whoever they may be, wherever they may exist, the people through whom dignity of life is manifest, that is, who are in some way expressing themselves naturally along the lines nature intended for them. My people may be old or young, rich or poor, I may speak their language or I may communicate with them only by gestures. But wherever I find them, the Indian at work in the white man's way, the Spanish gypsy moving back to the freedom of the hills, the little boy, quiet and reticent before the stranger, my interest is awakened and my impulse immediately is to tell about them through my own langauge — drawing and painting in color."[15]

Henri's color is usually sober, but strong and luminous, with often a dash of brilliant color, never a Watteau delicacy. Nathaniel Pousette-Dart sums up his art in a concise fashion: "He has painted many children, but each one of them has been brushed into life in a different way. This varied technique is shown also in his color. Always he is an experimenter, mixing brains and paint. His portraits of laboring men are astonishing. One feels that he has fairly cut them out of paint with understanding and feeling. In some of them the paint seems to have been driven onto the canvas with terrific force. His portraits have an air of unstudied alertness, because, in every instance he has done his thinking beforehand. Before he touches brush to canvas, his picture is painted For it is the vision back of his eyes that he paints, and not the image in front of them. This particular quality is very noticeable in his portraits of 'Himself', and 'Herself', in the Chicago Art Institute. There is no seemingly laborious execution, but this does not mean that they have been done with ease. Each canvas is a new adventure, and sometimes the peaks are hard to climb."[16]

Few equaled Robert Henri as a successful teacher. At the New York School of Art he found the possibilities and the potentialities in each student and strove to help the beginner develop himself by inspiring him to think independently and solve his own problems in his own way. Rockwell Kent and George Bellows are two of his students who produced outstanding results; their works are sufficient evidence of Henri's ability to train his students to transfer their own personality to canvas and to keep out of traditional ruts.

For years, some critics complained that we had no American art, national in character. There are no further grounds for that complaint. While Henri understood the old masters and the fundamentals of their art, his art is American to the core. His contribution to American art is immense chiefly because he was

---

[15] *The Craftsman*, February, 1915, p. 459.
[16] *Robert Henri*. by Nathaniel Pousette-Dart, p. x.

a revolutionary and directed art efforts along new channels. We cannot mis-understand his point of view when he says: "Although our artists must be individual, they must also be students, men who think a great deal about life, who read, study — men of the widest possible attainments, and who are con-stantly engaged in finding the special means of expression best suited to the thing they have to say."[17]

The Metropolitan Museum of Art honored Henri with a memorial exhibition of his work in 1931.

GEORGE WESLEY BELLOWS

It is thrilling to think of what George Wesley Bellows might have accom-plished if the gods had favored him with a long life; as it is, his claim on American art annals cannot be denied. He was so interesting as a man that one becomes absorbed in his personality as much as in his art. He was born in Columbus, Ohio, the son of an architect of English descent, who built the Chittenden Hotel, the County Court House, the Central High School, and sev-eral other buildings in that city. As a boy, George Bellows was a star baseball player at Central High School; and when his father sent him, in due time, to Ohio State University, most of that high-school team was there with him, and they scored many victories. He always will be held dear in the memory and hearts of Ohio State University alumni as the most wonderful shortstop the University ever had; a star basketball forward; a member of the Glee Club; and one of the finest all-around athletes and good fellows Ohio State ever boasted. From his well-known "dry" proclivities, his comrades gave him the sobriquet, "Ho" Bellows, making the symbols H_2O into that nickname. During his student days his pencil was busy making sketches, and fortunately many of them have been preserved and are in the possession of his fraternity, Theta Beta Pi.

Bellows was offered a position as shortstop on the Indianapolis baseball team, but refused it and went East to study art. At that time he was twenty-one years old. His father did not approve of his determination, and refused to give him financial aid for the project. The young man was put upon his own resources to earn his way; he was able to turn his baseball experience into cash by sign-ing up with a semi-professional team, called The Howards, of Brooklyn. The pay given to a shortstop was six dollars, to a catcher ten dollars; so, forced by the need of all the extra dollars he could earn, and at the risk of ruining those

---

[17] *The Craftsman,* February, 1908.

valuable hands, he accepted the catcher's job. All the world knows that George Bellows was a great artist, but probably only people in the community where he spent his youth know that his being a good baseball player had a very great deal to do with his becoming a great artist. In connection with this, William A. Ireland says: "He moved into his art career with an extraordinary natural gift of artistic ability, plus the same joy of life and enthusiasm that had made him so keen at second base. I believe it was this 'plus' that lifted him so rapidly to his great success. George Bellows, the baseball player, and George Bellows the international artist, were one and the same."[18]

Bellows's rise in the field of painting was meteoric. Within a few years after going to New York, he became a man to reckon with in his chosen field. Within a short time, he met Robert Henri, who became his teacher, urging him to express his individuality and trust to his esthetic reactions. Until his death Henri was a great aid to him, as instructor, philosopher, champion, and friend; and after Bellows's death, when Henri himself was in his last illness, he sat up in bed to write an introductory note for the book *The Paintings of George Bellows,* which brings together more than one hundred and forty reproductions of his work.

Bellows began exhibiting in 1906, with three portraits. In 1908, he exhibited his first landscape in the National Academy of Design; it was awarded the second Hallgarten prize. From that time on, awards and prizes were coming to him constantly, until the list of them was a long one. He never studied in Europe, nor even traveled there, and remained impervious to the modernistic tendencies of European painters. He was no imitator. He paid no attention to what was fashionable. He saw the development of Matisse, Picasso, Derain, and Cezanne, but while he respected them, their work did not alter his self-directed course. He remained purely American throughout his career.

He chose his subjects from American life: stirring phases of life with high emotional content. He believed it his duty to essay a record of any activity he witnessed. Consequently his range of subjects is a large one; some are gay, others tragic, or satirical, or humorous; he depicted prize fights, agitations of city streets, serious portraits, nudes, landscapes, and what not. His greatest appeal, no doubt, to the layman, was in his pictures of the world of sports. The six fine oils devoted to prize fighting brought him immediate and widespread popularity. He occupied a ringside seat at the Dempsey-Firpo fight, which is the subject of one of the paintings; the others are, "A Stag at Sharkey's", "Club Night", "Ringside Seats", "Introducing John L. Sullivan", and "Both

---

[18] *The Columbus Dispatch,* October 19, 1930.

PLATE 68—Eleanor, Jean and Anna. George Bellows. © (Reproduced by permission
of the Buffalo Fine Arts Academy)

Members of the Club". Bellows was an expert in catching and recording the feeling of life and motion in a crowd, and he could sense the character of an entire class of people; he may be said to resemble a historian in accurately bringing out the essential characteristics of a group. Some of his critics spoke of his subjects as "brutal", or "common", but no critic could complain of his technical quality nor of his faithful transference of what he saw to his canvas.

Bellows offered a very amusing burlesque on a serious subject, in "The Sawdust Trail", where he pictured the Reverend "Billy" Sunday conducting a revival meeting. The large choir forms the background; in the foreground, men are supporting or carrying out women who have swooned in religious fervor. It is an entertaining canvas full of observation and clever painting.

The tragic theme, "The Murder of Edith Cavell", is given a poetic treatment by Bellows. It is night, in a prison. Deep shadows are in all the corners; lanterns make bright spots here and there; the full light from one falls upon Edith Cavell, "enveloping her in an unearthly loveliness" as she descends a stairway. Some guards are sleeping, others hold the lanterns. Everything seems weird and mysterious; one is reminded strongly of Rembrandt's masterly chiaroscuros. The original painting was intended to be a pattern for posters during the World War. An interesting incident is told concerning this picture and Joseph Pennell, who was delivering a lecture on the making of lithographs to a group of artists. Discussion waxed warm during the evening. Mr. Pennell's dictum was that no artist could paint or draw beyond the thing which he himself saw with his own eyes, and he said: "If Mr. Bellows had been himself present at the execution of Edith Cavell, and had seen the whole thing with his own eyes, he would have painted a far more authentic picture than the one he made up out of his head." This gave Mr. Bellows a chance to reply: "No, I was not present at the murder of Edith Cavell, neither, so far as I have been able to learn, was Leonardo present at the Last Supper."

By this time (1918) Bellows was applying that theory of proportion, the dynamic symmetry of Jay Hambidge, to his canvases, and it had improved the structural composition of his pictures. Subsequently he made much use of it in his portrait groups and other paintings. Bellows's family life inspired some of his best canvases, whether of his mother, father, aunt, wife, or children. His good friend, Joseph R. Taylor, gives an interesting analysis of the making of the picture, "Eleanor, Jean and Anna", a group portrait of his mother, aunt, and little daughter (Plate 68). "I think of this painting, together with the 'Emma and Her Family', as his greatest work; it exists of itself, it seems to me as inevitable, as fatal beauty, as any in that select little company scattered about the galleries, in London, in the Louvre, in the Uffizi, of a great and jealous legend, born in the purple. The labor in this case was sure and swift and successful from the beginning, without one experiment or wasted motion; but labor all the greater. Our friend must have had the image ready, long matured in his mind; but the actual work began with his models, the two old ladies and the little girl between them, posed while he made a very careful and detailed pencil drawing of them. Then he attacked the big, blank canvas with a T square and triangle, with an intense architectural planning that fixed mathematically the points of focus and their relation to each other; upon this plot of lines, and of course to this greater scale, he transferred his pencil pose, the faces and the hands falling accurately upon the right line-crossings of his scheme. All this before a touch of the brush, several days of hard and concentrated work. Then he painted the background, the enveloping dusk of the house interior, leaving the three figures silhouetted in white canvas; and then the costumes, calling the wearers in turn for short poses, leaving still blank the hands and faces; and then the hands, wonderful old hands, and then the faces, wonderful old faces, of his aunt on the left and his mother on the right; and last and hardest of all, his little daughter in the middle. With her portrait finished, and without one other additional touch or backward look, the painting was all at once simultaneously finished. No wonder it looks so easy."[19]

Two of his famous portraits are, "My Father", and "Doctor William Oxley Thompson". The former, painted in three hours, shows a strength of individualism, softened by the peace of advancing years. His representation of Doctor Thompson is a bold and impressive figure, at once dignified and compelling, and is a portrait of character rather than a physical likeness. Its merit was recognized when it was hung in the spring exhibit of the National Academy of Design in New York, 1914, and was awarded the portrait prize.

The Metropolitan Museum of New York had accorded only nine native Americans the honor of a memorial exhibition before the one of Bellows's works, in 1925. They were Whistler, Homer, Chase, Thomas Eakins, Ryder, Abbot Thayer, George Fuller, F. E. Church, and Alden Weir — all men who had twenty-five to thirty years' more time to accomplish their labors than Bellows had. The world would not have known Homer at all if he had died at the age of forty-two, for it was not until he was forty-four that he turned his attention to the sea. This is the estimation of George Bellows by Frank Crowninshield in the introduction to the catalogue for the George Bellows Memorial Exhibition held in the Metropolitan Museum in 1925, shortly after his death:

---

[19] *Ohio State Monthly,* vol. 16, 1924.

"His death was nothing short of a tragedy. But it may console his friends to remember that, during his entire career he worked with enthusiasm and heart; that the lyrical quality which we detect as an undertone in so much of his work was born directly of the happiness which he felt in creating it; and that success came to him, at last, on his own terms, without yielding to the demands of public taste and with no thought to monetary gain."

James R. Hopkins adds his tribute to the honor of this Ohio artist, and gives a true analysis of his art. "'The Sawdust Trail', 'The Prize Fight', 'The Death of Edith Cavell', and the vigorous, subtle portraits of his family were some of the innovations indicative of his wide interests. Varied as they are in subject and in technique, his pictures have in common a quality essential to every work of art. This quality lies in their design, the strong contrast in vigorous spots of dark and light masses, which break up the picture shape into a pattern of surpassing completeness. It is this pattern which distinguishes the worth-while art of any age, and when time has weeded out the lesser paintings of our generation, the pictures of George Bellows will remain preëminent and will take a place in the history of the world's art which has been reached by the work of very few Americans."[20]

[20]*Ohio State Monthly,* vol. 16, 1924.

CHAPTER IX

The Rise of Ohio Museums

A GRATIFYING sign that idealism in America is keeping pace with the growth of material prosperity and scientific development is the increasing interest of Americans in art. American appreciation of art is evident chiefly from the fact that Americans of all classes and in great numbers go to the galleries. Our people quite rapidly are becoming art-conscious, or museum-minded. The public is realizing what unusual collections are shown in the museums.

In a single year, approximately a million people visit the Metropolitan Museum of Art in New York City; and a like number visit the Art Institute of Chicago. In London, in 1930, more than ten thousand persons attended the opening of the Italian exhibition at Burlington House. In New York City, crowds were so large at the first modern museum exhibit as to cause entangling traffic jams. The interest is proportionate in other communities. Popular interest in America is not confined to political campaigns, waves of prosperity or depression; in our appreciation of art we are really forging to the fore.

CINCINNATI MUSEUM OF ART

For more than a hundred years there have been among the leaders in public affairs in Ohio, farsighted men and women who realized the contribution made to the public interest by the devotees of culture, and of art particularly. It was natural that in Cincinnati, Ohio's leading center for a large part of the nineteenth century, these ideas first crystallized. Even there progress was made at a slow rate. The review of a few significant dates will help to show the steps by which the art museum and art academy developed as an outgrowth of community life rather than as a standardized institution. The successive efforts to focus art interests may be roughly classified as follows:

Efforts of artists on behalf of painting and sculpture—
    1828—Frank's Gallery of Fine Arts.
    1835—Academy of Fine Arts, Godfrey Frankenstein, president.
    1838—Cincinnati Academy of Fine Arts, John L. Whetstone, president.
    1866—Associated Artists, C. T. Webber, president.

Efforts of patrons on behalf of painting and sculpture—
    1847—Western Art Union, Charles Stetson, president.

211

1854—Ladies' Gallery of Fine Arts, Mrs. Peter, president.
1868—Cincinnati Academy of Fine Arts, W. S. Groesbeck, president.
1869—McMicken School of Design.
1874—Women's Centennial Committee, Mrs. Peter and others.
1876—Women's Room at Centennial Exposition.

Interest in art industries added to that in painting and sculpture—
1877—Women's Art Museum Association, Mrs. Aaron F. Perry, president.
1878—Loan Exhibition in Connover House.
1881—Cincinnati Museum Association, Incorporated.
1884—McMicken School of Design was transferred to Cincinnati Museum Association and became the Art Academy of Cincinnati.

The result of these cumulative efforts, one after another, was the Cincinnati Art Museum. More immediately, perhaps, it was the outcome of the Centennial Exhibition at Philadelphia in 1876. That exhibition first taught great numbers of Americans the practical value of the arts, broadly speaking, not especially painting and sculpture. The people of Cincinnati were in just the right mood for a museum. Mr. A. T. Goshorn, who had been president of one of the successful industrial expositions of Cincinnati, was made director-general of the Centennial of 1876. Close personal relations with Sir Phillip Cunliffe Owen, director of the South Kensington Museum of London (then visiting the exhibition in Philadelphia as one of the British Commission), impressed upon General Goshorn and his associates the value of the South Kensington organization. The Cincinnati Museum was thus founded upon a like basis of service to the people of Cincinnati in all respects in which a museum could be of use. The art industries — ceramics, metal work, and textiles — were accepted upon an equal footing with painting and sculpture.

Prominent in the group of men, who in founding the Cincinnati Art Museum and Art Academy, made stable and permanent the persistent efforts of earlier workers, were Joseph Longworth, Julius Dexter, Melville E. Ingalls, Charles W. West, David Sinton, Reuben Springer, George Hoadly, Elliott Pendleton and others. Mr. Goshorn was the first director; his assistant, J. H. Gest, succeeded him at his death. The city granted to the museum association the right to use twenty acres in Eden Park as a building site, and no more beautiful location could have been selected, as it commands a fine view of the Ohio River and the city with its surrounding hills. The museum receives no support from taxation, but is endowed by private bequests. The original building is of rough, native limestone, designed by J. W. McLaughlin in the Romanesque style under

PLATE 69—Cincinnati Museum of Art. Fig. 1, Entrance Hall.
Fig. 2, Sculpture Court in Schmidlapp wing.

the influence of Richardson. In the Schmidlapp addition to the museum, the
architect, David Burnham, went over to the classic style, which makes a wonderfully appropriate setting for the plaster casts of Greek and Roman sculpture
owned by the museum (Plate 69).

Three new wings have been added recently through the generosity of Mrs.
Mary M. Emery, Miss Mary Hanna, and Mr. Herbert Greer French. The old
building was completely remodeled to meet the needs of a modern museum,
and the entire building was rededicated, January 16, 1930. Mr. Walter H.
Siple is the present director; he comes from the East with progressive methods
of museum work in all its activities. The Museum collections embrace every
phase of art. It is not our intention to catalogue them here. We can only mention some of the most valuable American paintings which the founders bought
early, and thus acquired many of great interest and value: the works of Frank
Duveneck; the Longworth shawls; the O'Conner silver; the Omwake display
of playing cards; the Emery collection containing many English masterpieces;
the Hanna collection of splendid paintings; the Rookwood historical ceramic
collection; musical instruments from all countries; arms and armor. The Museum also contains an art reference library that is unsurpassed.

The articles of incorporation of the Cincinnati Museum of Art makes its
agreement with the city to involve a broad program, not only embracing every
phase of art, but history and natural science as well. They have felt their re-
sponsibility to the workers in the arts — both the artists and artisans. The impulse to create objects of art to suit a present day has seemed of more vital
concern than to cultivate an appreciation only of the art of the past, though the
tastes of the connoisseur and the antiquary have never been neglected. In
maintaining relationships of mutual helpfulness with the art industries of the
city — the Rookwood Pottery, the great color-printing establishments, and
metal working of various kinds — the Museum has kept in close contact with
the many-sided life of the city.

The unique position which the Cincinnati Museum occupies may be thus
briefly stated: "The art museums elsewhere in Ohio have a shorter history, have
been less subject to the conditions which formed the Cincinnati Museum. They
belong to a new period under the influence of a largely increased class of connoisseurs, and they reflect those interests rather more than those of the professional artists and artisans — the workers."[1]

The director of the Cincinnati Museum of Art is also the director of the
Taft Art Gallery, located in almost the center of the city. On May 21, 1927,

---

[1] *The Christian Science Monitor,* October 22, 1925, J. H. Gest.

Mr. and Mrs. Charles P. Taft made a deed of gift of their home and their entire art collection, with a permanent endowment of one million dollars, to the city of Cincinnati. The deed was made subject to the retention of a life estate, "during our lifetime", as it read. The deed conveyed the Taft residence at 316 Pike Street, Cincinnati, a house built by Bartin Baum before 1831, and occupied subsequently by Nicholas Longworth, and by David Sinton, the father of Mrs. Taft. The donors wished the art collection to be kept intact in its present setting.

The collection in embryo, dates back to 1902, when Mr. and Mrs. Taft, during a visit to New York City, took the first step toward acquiring their present art possessions. They chose ten pictures and bore them off in triumph, and with set purpose, to their dignified and peaceful home in Cincinnati. By 1911 their undertaking had been substantially carried through, with a catholicity of taste, excellent and careful selections. The collection includes porcelain, Limoges ware, faïence, bric-a-brac, a dozen or more most carefully chosen Turner water colors, many oil paintings from the Dutch school, a number of *chefs d'œuvre* from English portrait painters, French landscapes of the Barbizon school, and some work of Flemish, Spanish, and American painters. The art collection cannot be valued except to say that it is priceless. It could not be duplicated.

One fact pointed out in the letter from Mr. and Mrs. Taft accompanying the deed of gift is, that a city does not gain its fame from commercial ventures and achievements alone, but that quite frequently cities which have fostered the arts outstrip much larger centers of fame and prestige. These philanthropic Cincinnatians will be revered throughout all time for their wonderful gift to their city and to mankind.

COLUMBUS GALLERY OF FINE ARTS

The Columbus Gallery of Fine Arts, for its inception, goes back to a small club of women who were reading Winkelmann's *History of Art*. The struggles and discouragements encountered in the efforts to have a gallery in Columbus are almost too disheartening to relate, but "it's a long lane that has no turning", and we are happy to continue our chapter with an account of the handsome new Gallery of Fine Arts in Columbus, dedicated in 1931 (Plate 70). The Columbus Art Association had its christening party at the home of Mrs. Alfred Kelley, October 19, 1878. The first assets of the association were books upon art, ranging from standard authorities treating history and ornament to practical handbooks; they later acquired a few fine casts. The first money in the

PLATE 70—Columbus Gallery of Fine Arts.

treasury, $212.00, accrued from the result of a course of lectures given by Mr. French, then director of the Chicago Art Institute. Mr. Francis Sessions generously offered the one thing needful — a room; and here was opened on January 6, 1879, the Columbus Art School, which cannot be considered, in this case, apart from the Gallery of Fine Arts, as the two began and developed together.

Professor W. S. Goodenough, of Massachusetts, who was superintendent of drawing in the Columbus public schools, offered his services gratis as director of the Art School, and his experience was of incalculable value. Teachers were found to whom a percentage of the class receipts was satisfactory compensation for the good cause. Among them was Mrs. Merrill, then Miss Rath, who became an authority in art needlework and ecclesiastical embroidery, recognized not only in this country, but in the schools of Kensington and Paris. The heroic and self-sacrificing work of Miss Dora Norton, who taught nearly all the classes for six or eight years, must be given due credit. The second director was Mr. John E. Hussey, who grew up with the school and continued as director for twenty-five years. The school made much progress under his management; he moved it three times, each time to a better location, until it was finally located in the property now owned by the Columbus Gallery of Fine Arts. Mr. Hussey never was able to take time from his supervision of the school to develop his own painting as he wished, but he contributed much to the art activities of the city, being one of the founders, in 1897, of the Pen and Pencil Club, which is still an active art influence, and the short-lived Paint and Clay Club.

During all these years the hope burned that the struggle for the art school would end by the realization of the bequest made by Mrs. Louise Deshler, who devised for an art gallery her home on Broad street, adding fifty-five thousand dollars — in all about eighty-five thousand dollars. The will was contested, and after five hearings the case was decided adversely to the art interests of the city. At the time of this bequest, an organization called the Columbus Gallery of Fine Arts was incorporated under the laws of Ohio, but the adverse decision in the Deshler will case left the Columbus Gallery of Fine Arts a legal organization without an occupation. As the relations of the Columbus Art Association and the Columbus Gallery of Fine Arts had been intended to be interdependent, a fusion of the two organizations was decided upon in 1887; the gallery assumed control of all the property, and the Association took its place as the working branch.

Through the generosity of Mrs. Bliss, a fund of fifteen thousand dollars came to the gallery for the uses of the school; Mr. P. W. Huntington added one thousand dollars to this, and the interest from these bequests was the only regular endowment for a long time. In 1923, the Columbus Art Association became extinct and its holdings, merged with those of the gallery and the school, is now controlled by the trustees of the gallery. The intentions of Mr. Francis Sessions when he directed the terms of his will were most generous toward the gallery, but, owing to circumstances and the requirements of the law, a delay of many years elapsed before the gallery came into full title of the property he bequeathed to it, which is now the site of the new six-hundred-thousand-dollar gallery, made possible through the gifts of a group of public-spirited citizens of Columbus. Throughout the history of the development of the gallery project, Mr. O. A. Miller has been its constant and enthusiastic supporter, and to him its consummation is largely due. Mr. Franz Huntington, president of the gallery for many years, was another man devoted to the best interests of the gallery.

The one great gift of one hundred thousand dollars, that made the gallery realizable, came unsolicited from Mr. Ferdinand Howald, one of the trustees. As an art connoisseur and patron of contemporary art, Mr. Howald assembled one of the finest single groups of modern paintings in the United States, and it was with a view to having a home for this collection that Mr. Howald made his generous contribution to the building fund. As a collector Mr. Howald showed excellent judgment. In a general survey of his pictures one finds a predominating interest in the impressionistic landscapes of Ernest Lawson, the crowds of Maurice Prendergast, portraits by Douglas Volk, Leon Kroll, and Eugene Speicher, Rockwell Kent's bold landscapes, the marked rhythms of Charles DeMuth, and etchings by Zorn; a large collection of Rhodian plates forms another part of his treasures. Mr. Howald, when asked what particular interest guided his choice of paintings, replied, "Nothing particular, except when I saw a picture that was real art, I wanted it." The pictures which he brought together at an immense cost, the public is privileged to view in the gallery.

The gallery contains a George Bellows Memorial Room, the Frank L. Packard Memorial Library in a room specially prepared for it, the Loan collection of old masters owned by Frederick Schumacher, and many special exhibits.

Because of the beneficent gift of sixty thousand dollars from Mr. Ralph H. Beaton, one of the trustees of the gallery, the art students are enabled to study in a beautiful, new building. The interesting old doorway of the Sessions home, so long used for a gallery, has been preserved and happily incorporated into the new school as an entrance-way.

TOLEDO MUSEUM OF ART

The Toledo Museum of Art was organized in 1901, by a group of prominent Toledo business men headed by Edward Drummond Libbey. For a time it functioned by holding temporary exhibitions in rented quarters in a downtown building. In 1903, George W. Stevens became the first director of the institution, at that time an organization without collections, funds, a building, or any means of permanent support.

In his first annual report, President Edward Drummond Libbey proclaimed a policy of education for the Toledo Museum. With Mr. Stevens's assumption of the directorship, this policy was put into effect. Mr. Libbey and Mr. Stevens believed that a museum could be and should be just as important as a university, a college, or even the public schools. Classes were organized and talks given in the factories, stores, and schools, bringing to the people the message that art is a necessary ingredient in their lives, and that the museum and its facili- were open at all times to those interested.

At the time of the inauguration of the educational activities of the Toledo Museum, some museums of the country had made it a practice to exhibit placards containing information that children were not admitted unless accompanied by adults. The Toledo Museum recognized that it is possible to make the child what we will, and children were therefore made welcome. Since the opening of the museum, thousands of Toledo young people have been taught the history of art, its applications, the fundamentals of good color and of good design, so that when they go into the world as makers or users, they should have the ability to work properly and appreciate all that is good, and to separate it from the bad.

The response to this educational policy was so great that the museum quarters were soon outgrown. President Libbey offered to give a substantial sum for the erection of a museum building, provided the people of Toledo would subscribe an equal amount. This offer was met so readily that President and Mrs. Libbey gave, in addition, the site for the new building, so that the entire fund which had been raised might be used for actual construction. In January, 1912, the new building was opened to the public with a magnificent inaugural exhibition.

Within a short time the development of the museum had reached the limits of its original space; the collections had grown to such an extent that the building was no longer adequate, and plans were made for an addition to increase its size by more than double. The addition was the gift of President Libbey, and was opened in January, 1926. Additional gifts to the museum, through

PLATE 71—Toledo Museum of Art.

Mr. Libbey's will, were a million dollars to erect an auditorium or music hall, another sum for the construction of a school of art, both in connection with the museum, and a fund for the acquisition of works of art and the maintenance of the museum. It now has a tract of land of approximately ten acres almost at the geographical center of the city of Toledo; it is believed to be the largest tract of land owned and occupied by any museum in America.

The building is of white marble, with a frontage of two hundred feet,[2] the style being Greek Ionic of the Periclean period (Plate 71). The collections of the Toledo Museum comprise paintings, prints, books and manuscripts, sculpture, glass, ceramics, Egyptian and classical antiquities, and Oriental art. Among the paintings is a group of old masters, the gift of Mr. Libbey, which include such notable works as the "Man With the Wine Glass," by Velasquez; portrait of Catherine Howard by Holbein, called the finest Holbein in America; the "Flute Player," by Frans Hals, and works by Rembrandt, Cranach, Zurbaran, and other early painters; portraits by Gainsborough, Raeburn, Reynolds, Hoppner; and fine canvases by Constable, Turner, and a number of nineteenth-century Dutch artists.

One collection shows the development of painting in America. In 1922, Mr. Arthur J. Secor presented to the museum a fine group of Barbizon, Dutch, and American paintings, among which are outstanding canvases by Millet, Corot, Rousseau, and Diaz. Since that time there have been added to the Secor collection a number of fine portraits of the English, Dutch, and French schools, including works by Sir Thomas Lawrence, Sir David Wilkie, Nicholas Maes, Ferdinand Bol, and Jacques Louis David. The print collection includes the masterpieces of Albrecht Dürer, both in wood engraving and copper engraving, and a comprehensive group of etchings by Rembrandt, Whistler, and Charles Meryon.

The George W. Stevens Gallery of Books and Manuscripts is perhaps the best exposition of writing and printing in the country. Outstanding pieces of sculpture are works by Paul Manship, Rodin's "Thinker", and a bronze by Bourdelle. The glass collection is regarded as one of the finest in the world, and includes more than three thousand examples of the art of glassmaking, from the fourteenth century B.C. in Egypt to the nineteenth century. Some of the outstanding exhibits are these: a vase of the first century; the Worringen beaker, an important piece of engraved glass of the third century; the Toledo flagon, a fine example of the enameled Arabic glass of the fourteenth century;

---

[2] The completed museum building, with new wings now being erected, will have a frontage of six hundred and fifty feet.

a fine group of Venetian glass; and early American glass, including Stiegel and other types.

Coöperating with the University of Michigan, the Toledo Museum of Art, in 1927, organized a Mesopotamian expedition. As a culmination of the work already done, hundreds of items are at present exhibited in the museum; figurines, coins, lamps, tablets, bits of sarcophagi, bricks, glass, and semi-precious stones show the range of material of historical significance. Excavation there, pursued to its conclusions, should yield much for the enrichment of the museum, and perhaps will furnish valuable information on the beginnings of Indo-European culture.

The most tangible and definite evidence of interest in any museum is its attendance, and attendance for the year 1930 at the Toledo Museum was 215,456. The children are no longer sent to the museum — they go of their own accord. The educational plans maintain close contact with the public schools; and the museum, by means of talks offered to the art, history, and language departments of the high schools, correlates the museum's resources with their studies. There are many classes for younger children on Saturday mornings and Sunday afternoons. While the museum has always been interested primarily in developing educational activities for children, the adult has not been neglected. There are important programs for adults, Sunday concerts, and courses in art appreciation, art history, Oriental art, talks on current exhibitions, and many classes in design, for which credit is given in the University of the City of Toledo. Mr. Blake-More Godwin is the present director. The Toledo Museum has given back to the city manifold returns for its support of the gallery. It has reached an enviable point in public service. It shapes its activities not for the benefit of any group, but for the enjoyment, education, and inspiration of every group within its community life.

ALLEN ART MUSEUM, OBERLIN

One of the first college museums west of the Alleghenies was the Allen Art Museum, at Oberlin, founded in 1908. It came into existence through the interest and encouragement of some of the faculty members, and an unexpected bequest from Mr. and Mrs. Charles P. Olney of their entire collection, with a fund of ten thousand dollars for its maintenance. The collection remained in Cleveland for some time, as there was no suitable place in Oberlin to exhibit it.

Mrs. F. F. Prentiss was the good angel who, in 1917, erected the beautiful museum building, itself an object lesson in art, in memory of her husband, Dr. Dudley Peter Allen. It was erected for the preservation and exhibition of

PLATE 72—Allen Art Museum, Oberlin. Etching by Julia Severance.

works of art, and to provide quarters for the Department of Fine Arts of Oberlin College. Except for the ten thousand dollars from Mr. and Mrs. Olney, it is supported entirely from college funds. It serves as a laboratory for the Department of Fine Arts, the various collections proving of great value to the students. Its activities provide for the guidance of visitors, including school children; and for the supervision of all art instruction in the Oberlin public schools in courses given by art-major students trained in public school art.

The outstanding collections of the Allen Museum include the following *objets d'art*: the Hall collection of Oriental rugs, a carefully chosen group of examples from Asia Minor, Turkestan, Persia, China, Bergamo, and seventeenth-century Ghiordes prayer rugs; a collection of Chinese and Japanese paintings from Mr. Charles F. Freer; the Olney collection, representing many fields of art from America, Europe, and the Orient; the A. Augustus Healy collection of paintings by such artists as George Michel, Joseph Israels, Anton Mauve, Daubigny, Fantin-Latour, and Emma Ciarde. Aside from the extensive use made of the museum by students and the Oberlin public, it has many visitors from all parts of the country; this popularity is partly due to the fact that the museum is located on one of the great national highways. The building is very simple and classic (Plate 72). A small colonnade across the front has its vault covered with gold-and-blue mosaics which are very appropriate. In the rear is a tastefully arranged garden of flowers and pools of water.

BUTLER ART INSTITUTE, YOUNGSTOWN

Internationally known for its steel industries, Youngstown has an esthetic aspect not so well known, but no less important, which puts it in the class of other cities with noteworthy artistic centers and temples of art. Joseph G. Butler, Jr., was one of the first men of Youngstown to realize that the city needed art as well as industry. The idea materialized with his gift to the city of the Butler Art Institute, with a generous endowment for its upkeep (Plate 73). It is always a happy instance when a donor can enjoy, as did Mr. Butler, the pleasure of giving during his lifetime, and witness the joy of the people who profit by his generosity. For years Mr. Butler had been a collector of fine paintings. His permanent collection of eighty paintings, all by American artists, was placed in the Butler Art Institute. His interest was primarily in the art of his own country; it has been said that the only place that exhibited pictures glorifying the American workingman was the Butler Art Institute. His Indian collection is of great historical value and one of the finest in the country. The Institute also contains a collection of miniatures by A. J. Rowell, which includes every president of the United States from Washington to Wilson. This collection was originally intended for the Metropolitan Museum of New York, but after the death of the artist, Mr. Butler purchased the miniatures already painted and finished the collection with a miniature of President Harding, by A. M. Archambault.

Mr. Butler died in 1927. He rose to power in industrial, railroad, and financial circles. The William McKinley Memorial, at Niles, Ohio, is largely the result of his efforts, as he was the originator and president of the association which built this three-hundred-thousand-dollar memorial.

DAYTON ART INSTITUTE

An organized movement for art in Dayton, the Gem City, began when the Montgomery Art Association was formed at a meeting held Friday, June 21, 1912. The very laudable aims and objectives of this organization included the following:

1. By holding meetings to enable those interested in art to coöperate intelligently;

2. To spread art knowledge by exhibiting all works of art and by lectures on art subjects;

3. To promote art development in Dayton and Montgomery County, and to coöperate with art organizations in the United States.

This movement has been practically continuous from the year 1912 to the present time, with patrons as well as producers taking part in it. Mrs. Henry Stoddard was the first president of the active group; she performed a great service in the cause of beauty. In the spring of 1913 the organization held its first exhibition of paintings in the basement of Memorial Hall; the disastrous flood, that had no respect for anything, destroyed all the paintings, though the insurance carried enabled every artist to receive full price for his pictures.

Minutes of the annual meeting in January, 1915, show that among the subjects discussed were city planning, an art commission for Dayton, and the necessity of preserving the old courthouse. In 1917, the association bought its first picture, "Country Scene", by Chauncey F. Rider, at a cost of two hundred dollars. This is the story of the humble beginning of the Dayton Art Institute, but since its incorporation in 1919, a magic wand has produced marvelous changes. From the small, corner property in the business section of the city, the museum has been transferred to a superb building that stands on a little acropolis of its own.

PLATE 73—Butler Art Institute. Youngstown.

Mrs. Harrie Gardner Carnell was the fairy who waved the wand. She presented to the city of Dayton a beautiful building for the Dayton Art Institute. It is dramatically situated on a hill overlooking the curving river and the city. The architect, Edwin B. Green, who planned the Albright Gallery in Buffalo and the Toledo Museum, has used as his inspiration for this edifice a villa built by Vignola for the Farnese family near Viterbo. It is a significant example of Renaissance design. The form is an elongated hollow octagon across whose center reaches an auditorium, leaving between the ends two courts with cloistered sides, supported by columns and capitals from thirteenth-century Italian buildings. A monumental outside stairway, broken by landings and fountains, makes an approach reminiscent of its Italian derivation. The building will serve as an inspiration for bringing together collections of a calibre worthy of being housed in it (Plate 74).

One feature which the Dayton Art Institute has carried on since 1922 is the circulating gallery of portable pictures. This plan has been very successful and has given untold pleasure to many private homes in Dayton and neighboring towns by allowing them for a stated time a painting to hang in their own homes. One can go to the Art Institute and select what he wants from the growing collection of circulating pictures.

Among the collections owned by the Dayton Art Institute, and serving as a *milieu* for the Chinese collection is a Ming temple built in 1430 and still in excellent preservation. The façade of red lacquer doors and windows of intricately wrought pattern includes on each side two massive stone bas-reliefs of waves where dragons are joined in combat. Foremost among the things of interest is the "Peep Show" by Lorado Taft. It reproduces in miniature Donatello's studio in Florence; Ghiberti, Fra Angelico, Masaccio, Paolo Uccello, and Brunelleschi are grouped around, while the great patron of the arts, Cosimo De Medici, stands in the doorway observing the works of Donatello. The "Peep Show" helps us to visualize the art life during the High Renaissance. The director of the Dayton Art Institute is Siegfried Weng, a graduate of the University of Chicago, and one time student and *protégé* of Lorado Taft. The Dayton Art School, modern in every feature, is in the same building and under the same direction as the Art Institute.

OHIO STATE MUSEUM, COLUMBUS

The Ohio State Museum, Columbus is an outgrowth of the Ohio Archæological and Historical Society, organized March 12, 1885, for the purpose of promoting the knowledge of archæology and history of Ohio, by establishing and maintaining a museum and library. In the winters of 1888 and 1889, the society was given space for the museum and library in a room on the third floor of the State House, where the books and relics were arranged as well as possible in cases and shelves. Up to this time they had had merely desk room in one of the alcoves of the State Library.

The society made an extensive exhibit of archæological and historical material at the Chicago Columbian Exposition in 1893. It proved to be one of the distinguishing features of the exposition, attracting wide attention and eliciting complimentary articles in the newspapers throughout the country. Another exhibit was made at the Pan-American Exposition at Buffalo, 1901; another at the Ohio Centennial Celebration at Chillicothe, 1903; also at the Louisiana Purchase Exposition, 1904; and at the Jamestown Exposition, 1907. These exhibits brought the society into wide repute for its original research in Ohio archæology, especially in the work of the mound builders.

The present building was dedicated May 30, 1914. It was made possible through an appropriation of one hundred thousand dollars by the General Assembly, and the gift of the site by the Ohio State University, whose authorities granted the museum the choicest site upon the entire campus. The University architect, Professor J. N. Bradford, designed the beautiful classic structure, which is most appropriate to its uses (Plate 75).

Through coöperation with the public schools, the Ohio State Museum effects one of the most important features of public education, namely, the inculcation in the youth of a knowledge of the past; a study of history and archæology enables them to know something of the early history of the human race, and that is no small acquisition. At the museum is stationed a teacher, thoroughly acquainted with the museum exhibits, who instructs the classes that come daily from the schools. The enthusiastic interest of the children is a revelation to the observer. There is a close coöperation between the various departments of the university and the museum; the fine arts students make extensive use of the collections for purposes of research, and the design classes avail themselves of the primitive motifs to be found there among the mound-builder artifacts and adapt them to modern uses.

The library contains publications of nearly all the historical societies of the country; and, with the addition of the Hayes library at Fremont, may claim to possess the most extensive private collection of Americana in the country, beside being second to none in historical bibliography. The newspaper files are the most complete in the state.

PLATE 74—Dayton Art Institute. Fountain: Joy of the Waters, by Harriet Frismuth
in the South Italian Renaissance Cloister.

CLEVELAND MUSEUM OF ART

Incorporated only in 1913, the growth of the Cleveland Museum is one of the marvels of museum development. The leaven for the museum had been stirring in the community for some time when John Huntington, Horace Kelley, and Hinman B. Hurlbut each provided by will for the establishment of a museum of art in Cleveland. The story of difficulties encountered in working out plans and overcoming legal complications need not be entered into here. The gift of a beautiful lot by Mr. and Mrs. J. Homer Wade solved most satisfactorily the question of location. The Cleveland firm of architects, Hubbell & Benes, prepared the plans for the classic-styled building of Georgia marble (Plate 76). Three years before its completion, Frederic Allen Whiting was appointed director, and through the wisdom of his administration the Cleveland Museum of Art came into being as a working organization. The museum was opened on June 6, 1916.

The task of acquiring collections has been done with the utmost care, the policy of the museum being to accept no works of art with restrictions upon them. Valuable acquisitions came to the museum early. To mention only a few of them: important collections already acquired through the John Huntington trust; the Holden collection of Italian paintings; the Severance collection of arms and armor; and the set of tapestries presented in memory of Doctor Dudley P. Allen. The collections comprise art from ancient Egypt down to contemporary Cleveland, and there are also three galleries of Oriental art. The museum is especially rich in its medieval art. The Garden Court, where is shown architectural sculpture amidst growing ferns and palms, is a delightful place to rest and "feast one's mind." Music, it was felt, had its place in a museum with the other arts, and through the P. J. McMyler endowment fund, a department of musical arts was established. A great pipe organ was installed in the Garden Court, where organ recitals are given.

A constantly developing educational program, local and extensional, is carried on. "The extensional activities include the circulation of exhibits of art objects through the public libraries and branch libraries of the city and its suburbs. These exhibits show materials and processes employed in the production of historic objects of beauty, such as textiles, utensils, armor, jewelry, details of furniture, prints, dolls, and other things. They go also to children's hospitals and public and private schools, where adequate exhibition cases are installed. A member of the museum staff has personal supervision of the installation of these exhibits, and frequently gives interpretative and introductory

PLATE 75—Ohio State Museum, Columbus. View of central hall,
gallery and dome. (Author)

talks to insure intelligent appreciation of them. Wherever an exhibit is installed, the libraries issue reading lists bearing upon the subject."[3]

The local work includes a far-reaching program with the children of the schools, as a result of an arrangement with the Board of Education. All classes above the fourth grade are taken to the museum at least once a year. Museum lessons are planned which correlate with studies taken up in school at the time; armor is considered by those groups studying medieval history; the classical collection is brought to the attention of those studying the Greeks, and so on. Close observation of these children makes possible the segregation of the most promising pupils. At the Saturday morning classes, the children are provided pencil, paper, and crayon, and encouraged to know the museum objects through drawing as well as seeing them. Lecture courses in art appreciation, and special lectures by speakers of established reputation on painting, architecture, sculpture, handicrafts, and other subjects, are features for the adults. William M. Milliken is the present director of the museum.

Too much praise cannot be given the people of Cleveland for their generous support of the museum and its ambitious program of forming notable collections and using them educationally. The museum has been supported from the first largely by income from the Huntington and Kelley foundations; several years ago, however, its activities outgrew this source of income, and a general endowment fund was created to produce an income for general expenses. Other endowments are available for the purchase of art objects, and membership dues form another source of income. "Each year there is a broadening of policies and an increase of activities which keep pace with the growth of the collections and the demands for service made by the public."[4]

AKRON ART INSTITUTE

Apparently most of the art interest in Akron has been due to the art department of Buchtel College, now in the University of Akron, and to the artists connected with that school as teachers. As nearly as can be ascertained, the first artist to be identified with Buchtel College was A. T. Van Laer. He was followed in 1891 by Miss Minnie Fuller, who reorganized the school on the scheme of the Art Students' League of New York City, of which she had been a pupil and later a member. Miss Fuller was succeeded by Mrs. May Sanford Hunt, now of Independence, Ohio. Mrs. Jane Barnhardt, a woman of fine training and much ability as an art educator, is the present head of the Art School of the University of Akron.

[3]*Art and Archæology,* November, 1923, p. 134. Henry Turner Bailey.
[4]*Art and Archæology,* November, 1923, p. 194. Frederic Allen Whiting.

The Akron Art Institute developed, as most organizations of this kind do, out of various preliminary attempts which took the form of art clubs, exhibitions, and associations at various times and places. The present organization was effected in 1922, and was established in rooms in the Public Library, where the institute still maintains its exhibitions. It has the beginnings of a permanent collection, and displays about thirty transient exhibitions each year. A small grant from municipal funds, special contributions, and membership dues from five hundred members constitute its support. Akron has been so absorbed in the phenomenal development of its rubber industry, that art interests have not kept pace with the industrial activities. The director of the Akron Art Institute is a capable, aggressive man, Mr. Theodore H. Pond, who will be able to give the institute its proper place in the community. During the year 1929, eighteen thousand visitors were recorded; weekly lectures for members were given, and Saturday morning classes for children were well attended. Akron can boast of an art connoisseur and collector, Mr. Edwin C. Shaw, whose large collection of paintings and etchings are of sufficient merit to grace any city.

ACADEMY OF FINE ARTS, CANTON

The infant among Ohio museums is the Academy of Fine Arts, at Canton, presented to the city in January, 1928, by F. E. Case. Before 1900, Mr. Case built a magnificent stone residence of the Romanesque order, on the top of a hill, far from the busy hum of the city's life, in the midst of an orchard of apple trees where the bees hummed lazily. When he started to build the house, he had the idea of giving it to the city some day as a museum of fine arts. Now his vision has materialized.

Mr. Case has made his gift perpetual. To effect its everlastingness he has endowed it so generously that so long as Canton continues, the museum will stand as the center of the cultural world of that part of the state. Following out his idea of making it a museum some day, he began collecting rare paintings. He went to the art centers of Europe to find treasures, nor did he neglect the young painters just coming into recognition in this country. Mr. Case's collection is cosmopolitan indeed. Hanging side by side are masterpieces of famous Dutch, French, and German artists, and the best works of American artists. No particular school of art has been followed. The modern is there; the old school, too. Mr. Case is quoted as saying, "I want the spirit of the old masters who have painted the masterpieces of the world to hover over this house, to inspire and to breathe encouragement, to help the struggling young artists over whatever stumblingblocks they may encounter." Surrounding the

PLATE 76—Cleveland Museum of Art.

house are seven acres of ground, set with fine old evergreens, shrubs and vines. With lovely flowers and trees and birds out-of-doors, and exquisite works of art indoors, the Case mansion, now the Academy of Fine Arts, is a wonderful heritage for Canton.

Among the best of the pictures to be seen there is the lovely "Coming Storm.", by Pierre Auguste Cot, the picture which antedates by a few years the large replica by the same artist that hangs now in the Metropolitan Museum. There is an Inness, a Francis Murphy, a Bloomers, some of the finest work of Ridgeway Knight, Thomas Moran, Schreyer, Schenck, William Henry Howe, Lucian Powell, Edward Koenig, Rudolph Koenig, and Warshawsky. Pictures worth thousands of dollars are there, and among them are some good ones painted by Mrs. Case, together with a number of canvases executed by Mr. Case, who began painting very late in life.

*   *   *   *   *

With the organization of historical societies in many counties of the state there have developed a corresponding number of small museums that exhibit much valuable historic material of local interest. They are playing a large part in the pride and interest in county and community history. A small museum of more than local interest is the Johnson-Humrickhouse Museum, opened in 1931 at Coshocton, in that it contains an extraordinary collection of Oriental art, reputed to be one of the finest outside of the very large art centers in America.

Ohio stands among the first states in the Union in the number of its museums. It not only has a great number, but they are all "dusted off" and being used by every class of people, manufacturers, designers, salesmen, students, clubs, schools, merchants and others who can apply the lessons of art to their daily problems. The American mind is called a practical mind, and it is because of this characteristic that the aspiration for beauty expresses itself in forms that will give practical benefits to special groups and individuals, and the whole mass of a community. Each Ohio museum has a real *raison d'être*. In other words, progressive communities build museums that will endure and serve not only this generation but many generations to come. The value of the museum cannot be measured; it is felt in every phase of the life of a community.

ART EDUCATION

Upon the remarkable progress made in art education in Ohio depends the high place the state occupies in the art world today, and its great promise for the future. Education has always been a serious business in Ohio. A prominent historian, in calling attention to the importance of Ohio and Ohio men in the affairs of the nation, traced it back to the lead that Ohio took in the very beginning to the establishment of the public schools, by the provision setting apart one section of land (number sixteen) in each township for the support of the schools.

Once it was thought that the more schooling a man had, the better educated he became, and to complete a college course was to complete his education. But that concept has long since vanished. Now, no boundary separates a man's education from the rest of his life; in fact, his education is his life. A hundred years ago, education was a means of preserving the knowledge of the past; today it is more concerned with improving the future. Most educators define education as anything that helps to shape the human being; hence, the training that enables a man to respond to beauty, to search for truth, to realize his ignorance, and to adapt himself to the situations in which he finds himself, may be called education. Art education is assuredly a vital aid in reaching that goal.

When the McMicken School of Design was founded in Cincinnati, in 1869, it was probably the only school in the state offering instruction in art. After that school became the Cincinnati Art Academy in 1884, it continued for many years to be the most important art school in Ohio. At that time that school was considered as giving only a preliminary training, and the great ambition of the students was to get far enough along in their study to be able to study in a school in the East or in Paris.

In 1893, a small group of art educators that gathered in the Educational Building at the Columbian Exposition, Chicago, decided to organize a society for the advancement of art education. They were enthusiastic over the benefits derived from viewing the art exhibits there, and from the interchange of ideas with art educators from all over the world. The name of the organization was then the Western Drawing-Teachers' Association, but it was changed in 1919 to the Western Arts Association. Meeting in convention each year (excepting one during the War), the association has accomplished an outstanding piece of work. The school exhibits made each year and the addresses delivered at the conventions have aided the advancement of education along the lines of the various arts. The association has a membership of more than twelve hundred of the progressive teachers, supervisors, and directors of fine arts connected with public and private schools. The Western Arts Association is recognized as an organization that has inspired literally thousands of teachers to strive for greater efficiency in the teaching of the arts, not only in Ohio, but in the middle-western states generally.

It should be a matter of pride that no citizen of Ohio need now travel beyond his own state in search of an art school, as there are thirteen universities and colleges with art departments well equipped for teaching every phase of art, and seven schools devoted exclusively to art (see Appendix), besides numerous private schools and instructors. Artists, young or old, will always need to travel, but many students after attending Eastern or Parisian schools are glad to come back to Ohio for study. Such progress in art education is due in large measure to the work and influence of Duveneck, Meakin, Nowottny and other artists mentioned previously (see Chaps. IV, V, *ante*).

There is still one striking deficiency in art education. In the city schools the pupils have the advantage of good art training, but very few village or rural schools have any instruction in art. For eight years there have been concerted and persistent efforts to secure a state supervisor of art, but that has yet to materialize. Every child has the inalienable right to the inspiration that arises from a knowledge of the fundamental experiences which serve as a basis for art appreciation. The child must learn to apply to the problems of life those eternal principles of art — simplicity, balance, harmony, and unity. There are two aims in art teaching: one is to teach the student to draw and to make designs; the other is to train his taste so that he will become a more discriminating observer. Universal art education for the sake of developing good taste will probably follow automatically when it has been proved to the people how to make art a part of their everyday life. Compared with the progress made in the teaching of other subjects, art education has gone as far and accomplished as much or more, and this in a comparatively short time and in the face of the sentiment that art is one of the "frills" foisted upon the schools.

CHAPTER X

The Graphic Arts

THE graphic arts generally have felt the significant and almost revolutionary changes that have taken place in the objects and methods of modern art. Etching, wood engraving, lithography, and the sister arts had been considered stable and conservative, but they have been adapted to the modern needs of expression and have taken on new vitality. Modern art insists upon the function and significance of line, so it is not surprising that the linear arts have such a present popularity, for they offer a complete contrast to the impressionistic art in which line is almost entirely submerged in the interest of luminosity and atmospheric effect. The narrowing of the aims of art was bound to exhaust itself, and line and form were again certain to assume their proper place in the attainment of the ends of art.

Etching, the fascinating form of artistic expression of which Dürer was one of the earliest, and Rembrandt, Whistler, and Meryon the greatest masters, has reasserted itself. Today the world is rich in etchers.

In Ohio, etching may be said to begin with a great artist, Otto Bacher. He began his studies in his native city, Cleveland, with De Scott Evans. Possessed of brilliant faculties and unbounded ambitions, he found a way to go to Europe in 1878 with Willis S. Adams and Sion Wenban. He was one of the first, if not the first, Clevelander who went abroad to study. After some study in Munich he became one of the class of artists instructed by Duveneck in Venice. There he met Whistler, under whose influence he attained high rank as an etcher. He was called the pet pupil of Whistler; it is certain that a very wholesome fellowship existed between them. Bacher, in *With Whistler in Venice,* recounts many fascinating stories of Whistler, who was his lifelong friend. That volume is illustrated with Bacher's inimitable etchings of Venice (Plates 77,78). One group of illustrations shows the changes made on the plate by Bacher, for these different states: the first state shows the original; to the second he added boats in the foreground in dry-point; the fourth state shows further additions in dry-point; and in the seventh and final state he substituted for the boats some entirely new vessels by etching.

As an etcher, Bacher was accorded an equal place with his contemporaries Whistler and Hayden—and this is saying much for a young man. His work with the brush is equal to that with the etching needle. When he returned to America, he established himself in New York and made illustrations for some of the leading publishers.

Elis F. Miller, Columbus, was etching at the same time as Bacher. Mr. Miller was eminently successful, and at his death was becoming recognized in all art centers as an etcher of outstanding ability. He was represented in a handsome portfolio, "Twenty Original American Etchings", put out by a New York publisher in 1885. Rare beauty and extreme delicacy characterize his work.

Frank Duveneck became interested in etching through his pupil, Otto Bacher. Duveneck made many etchings of Venice that were entirely different in viewpoint and handling from those of Bacher or Whistler. Duveneck and Whistler both etched the Riva, and other streets of Venice, but very differently. When Whistler saw the etching of the Riva by Duveneck in the latter's studio — they lived close together in Venice — he said, "Whistler must do the Riva, also," and he did. Duveneck's Venice is swarming with life and is full of maritime splendor, and these were the etchings of Venice that were sent to be displayed at the Painter-Etchers Society, London (Plate 79).

Whistler tells in his extremely characteristic, spicy way, in *The Gentle Art of Making Enemies,* how a number of etchings signed "Frank Duveneck", and exhibited in the Hanover Gallery, London, in 1881, stirred up an amusing squabble. Seymour Hayden and other etching connoisseurs thought they were really Whistler's etchings signed with an assumed name. Mr. Whistler heard of their blunder and challenged Dr. Hayden for an explanation of some remarks that had been made reflecting upon his reputation. Dr. Hayden denied intending any derogatory statements, and wrote: "We know all about Mr. Frank Duveneck, and are delighted to have his etchings." Hayden had arranged for the purchase of the etchings. A long controversy, which seems stupid and malicious, ensued.

Duveneck and Whistler were never especially good friends — they were too far apart in every way. But Duveneck had many friends among the noted Americans in Venice at that time, the Brownings and Henry James among them, and Joseph Pennell, who makes several references to Duveneck in *The Graphic Arts.* "He will live in the future when some of our high-priced geniuses are forgotten," Pennell says.[1]

Ernest Bruce Haswell informs us that the Duveneck etchings of Venice were printed on some very remarkable paper that an old butter-woman in the market had been using for wrapping her wares. One of Duveneck's "boys" in producing a trial print had made the discovery, and after that the etchers who knew bought their paper in the butter market. "While Dueveneck's paintings

---

[1] *The Graphic Arts,* Joseph Pennell, p. 167.

PLATE 77—Entrance to the Grand Canal, Venice. Etching by Otto Bacher. (Cleveland Museum of Art)

may at times suggest other painters and other schools, his etchings are a definite expression of the man. They are brusque and honest, sometimes naïve. A few critics there are who object to the obvious influence of Rembrandt, Hals, and later Velasquez so evident in some of his canvases. . . . Original power Duveneck did possess, and what he did was creative. What he did not do is of small importance against the unique place he does occupy in American art, however foreign the influence."[2]

Twachtman made many etchings during the late eighties, after Whistler had awakened a keen interest in that art and its possibilities. His understanding of space relations and the importance of line gave Twachtman a valuable equipment for etching. He etched twenty-six plates, in size about eight by twelve inches; many of them are reminiscent of a summer spent at Honfleur, Normandy, where he enjoyed the companionship of Homer Martin. While he lived at Bridgeport, Connecticut, he produced some beautiful etchings in his mature style.

Robert Blum began his artistic career as a lithographer; it was not until 1879 that he took up etching. He made an etching of his friend William M. Chase at work. The self-portrait of Blum is held by experts to be a masterpiece of the medium; so was "The Hag", but both plates are lost, and only a few prints exist. Etching carries the personality, the characteristics, of the producer probably more than any other graphic art can reveal them. If the etcher prints his own proofs as Blum did, there is conveyed an intimate and vital attraction. No matter how great a genius may be, if he has not the practical experience of a craftsman, he can do nothing of consequence in etching or the other graphic arts. It requires endless practice to make a satisfactory print. The strength of etching lies in the selection of line, the wise economy and reticence of the drawing. Blum was a consummate master of drawing, and made every line to count for something. He knew what he wanted to express before he began, and put every line there to stay. His extraordinary quality of line may be found in many wonderful illustrations of the old *Century, Scribner's,* and *Harper's* magazines back in the eighties.

Much interest was centered upon lithography in Cleveland about 1880. This was due in great measure to the firm of W. J. Morgan & Company, that transacted a large business in making lithographs and employed talented Cleveland artists for their work. One of the treasured mementoes of early art in Cleveland is *The Sketch Book,* published by the Morgan Company in 1883. The following artists contributed to this volume: Louis Ritter, J. W. Bell, R. Way

[2] Manuscript by Ernest Bruce Haswell.

Smith, A. Bandlow, R. Turner, G. P. Bradley, DeScott Evans, Adam Lehr, George C. Groll, George Grossman, George A. Hopkins, John O. Anderson, E. W. Palmer, Amelia Dueringer, W. H. Eckman, and Will E. Lewis. The original drawings were made on paper, and then were reproduced on stone by what was in that day a new process in this country; the half-tone and zinc processes were not yet developed. *The Sketch Book* was a rare and unique example of American bookmaking. Several Cleveland artists achieved national renown for their lithographs; among them were Daniel Wehrschmidt, A. Bandlow who thus earned five hundred dollars a week, O. V. Schubert, Louis Loeb whom Harper's Publishing Company paid fifteen thousand dollars a year for his lithographs, and George Groll, one of the cleverest of all lithographers.

The potentialities of lithography include reproduction side by side of both fine, delicate lines and tints, and deep, strong, black lines and shadows. Thus the artist may run a complete scale and indulge at the same time both in tonal subtleties and strong contrasts. Pennell gives this brief and comprehensive description of the medium of lithography: "That is surface printing, in which there is no relief or depression, but the work is done by chemical affinity. The design is made on a plate or stone with greasy ink. The surface of the plate or stone is dampened with water. Then ink is rolled on it, which will adhere to the design only or to those parts which are not dampened, because water repels the ink, which is grease, from the undrawn spaces and the ink is attracted to the greasy drawing. When a piece of paper is placed on the plate the inked design comes off on the paper. Lithography is the most abused of all the graphic arts and is the most wonderful."[3]

The cartoonist, W. A. Rogers (see page 276), excels also in making lithographs. He holds that lithography is the most direct of all the mediums for graphic expression, and cites the fact that drawings now may be made on zinc plates instead of stone, the technical difficulties being much lessened by this method. His drawings, in every instance, are made directly on the zinc plate from which they are printed; thus they preserve the entire freshness and spontaneity of the original. Mr. Rogers's recent lithographs picture old and picturesque Washington city houses, typical streets, and alley scenes. Perhaps the artist's chief contribution to the layman is to show him the beauty in commonplace things that he passes unseen. Among the most interesting prints Mr. Rogers has made are those of old houses of Georgetown, which indicate his sensitiveness to beauty and his interest in architectural design. By way of indulging his fine sense of humor he makes skillful character studies of groups of negroes playing games in front of their homes.

---

[3] *The Graphic Arts,* by Joseph Pennell, p. 15.

PLATE 78—Three Ships. Etching by Otto Bacher. (Cleveland Museum of Art)

PLATE 79—Palazzo ca d'Oro. Etching by Frank Duveneck. (Cincinnati Museum of Art)

The war posters issued for Liberty Loans were nearly all done in lithography, but most of them by artists without Mr. Rogers's training in this process. After much experimentation and many disappointments, due to lack of this knowledge, the art schools began to teach lithography, so that many American artists are now very proficient in the medium.

George Bellows did much for the promotion of lithography. From his biography in the catalogue of the Memorial Exhibition of his work, we learn: "He did not take up lithography until the year 1916, ten years after he had begun exhibiting paintings in oil. Although he had less than nine years in which to work at lithography, he yet managed to achieve a total of one hundred and seventy subjects in this medium. Bellows was fortunate in meeting Mr. Bolton Brown, an artist who had long given attention to lithography, and who knew everything there was to know about the technical side of it. In 1921, five years after he began lithography, the artist induced Brown to assist him and to take charge of the actual printing of the lithographs which he had drawn on stone. Four years this partnership continued. His lithographs are being sought out as if they bore the name of Daumier."

Pennell and Bellows long argued the matter of the drawing of a lithograph on paper first; Bellows was opposed to this method, as he felt a true lithograph began on stone. Bellows is one of the few lithographers who has been able to obtain the rich velvety black and the beautiful silvery grays to be found in his exquisite print, "In the Park". There are two states of this, the difference being in the treatment of the background foliage: the first is more open, and details are more carefully drawn. There is an extreme contrast in light and dark. Out of the stone, under his handling, came veritable "songs of strength" on stone.

Lithographs that rank high among the output of this art are those of Charles Locke, who was born at Norwood, Ohio. Their excellence has not been dimmed even when his studies are exhibited in large collections of the most marvelous French lithographs. Certain qualities — plasticity of form and design, and the silvery gray tones he secures — set his work apart from others and bring him success. He is well equipped for the art of lithography, both in color and in black and white. As in all other graphic arts, a lithographer must know how to draw, and that knowledge Mr. Locke possesses to an eminent degree. Besides that, he does all his own printing, which is an immense factor in final results. An account of Mr. Locke's extraordinary training will partially explain his success. He studied painting at the Cincinnati Art Academy with Mr. James R. Hopkins, Mr. Herman Wessel, and Mr. John Weis. He began experimenting with lithography at the Ohio Mechanics Institute, Cincinnati, with

PLATE 80—Sargent Room, Tate Gallery, London, England. Dry point by Walter Tittle. Awarded Arts Committee Prize, National Arts Club, New York City.

Mr. Paul Ashbrook, Mr. Lyons, and Mr. Webb. Then he was invited to work for a time at the Louis C. Tiffany foundation at Oyster Bay, Long Island. In 1922 he was asked to go to New York and become an assistant to Joseph Pennell in his graphic arts class at the Art Students' League. Two years later he was made instructor of lithography at the league, and has been there ever since. In 1927 he was sent to Paris to study and collect lithographs. There he worked under the guidance of that excellent printer, M. Desjobert, who printed all his beautiful French lithographs. Mr. Locke looks at the life of cosmopolitan New York and mirrors it in his art. His fellow passengers on the ferry, or the train, in the subway, men on the street or at the club, society at the academy or the concert, furnish an endless supply of material for his lithographs. He delineates the city and its types and characters as he sees them. His character drawings are blocky patterns of soft woolly grays in different values. There are no insignificant lines, but significant traits are exaggerated.

The announcement of an exhibit of the work of Walter Tittle (who hails from Springfield) always causes a great deal of interest among art lovers and critics. His work holds the interest of the most reserved members of the art world. His artistic career started with the making of illustrations for the best magazines in America, and some European ones, but he abandoned that type of work for the making of etchings, dry points, and lithographs. From his earliest work, Mr. Tittle has excelled in portraits; pen and pencil portraits of personalities appeared serially in *Scribner's* and *Century* magazines, and the London *Strand*. They were published in book form later.

During the Conference on the Limitation of Armaments in Washington, 1921, Mr. Tittle executed dry-point portraits, from life, of the twenty-five leading statesmen of that important conclave. Twenty-five complete sets were autographed personally by the men who sat for them. Some of the eminent sitters were President Harding, David Lloyd George, Aristide Briand, Charles Evans Hughes, Earl Balfour, Elihu Root, Baron Kato, and Prince Tokugawa. The completed collection constitutes the Arms Conference Memorial Portfolio. A set of the portraits was purchased by the American government for the collection in the Library of Congress. The exhibition of the set in London resulted in its purchase by the British government for the British Museum, and a second one for the South Kensington Museum. The English critics wrote enthusiastic articles on the merits of the work.

Not many years ago, before the revival of the graphic arts, it was customary to precede any discussion of etching with an explanation of the process. Even now, the difference between dry point and etching should be pointed out. What

PLATE 81—The Covered Bridge. Etching by E. T. Hurley. (Artist)

is called dry point is produced when the artist makes furrows with the needle in the bare copper plate, leaving the upturned metal standing. These upturned ridges hold the ink and give added richness to the print. Etching, on the other hand, is done by first coating the plate with an acid-resisting ground, and then exposing the plate by drawing with the needle on this ground. After needling the plate is immersed in an acid bath which attacks the exposed lines, different depths of line being obtained by the length of time they are left in the acid.

Perhaps the best known oil paintings of Mr. Tittle are the two each of Joseph Conrad and Bernard Shaw that he made in his London studio in 1924. They have been widely shown and reproduced. He works and exhibits abroad a great deal, having completed thirty portraits in lithograph of leading literary men in Britain. His dry points exhibit as fine an economy of line as an Ingres drawing, and as remarkable composition in light and shade as a Rembrandt etching. The portrait of Jean Louis Forain, to mention one in particular, is a marvelous dry point (Plate 80).

Edward Timothy Hurley is the etcher laureate of Cincinnati; he began his art training with Frank Duveneck. He does not seek for picturesque vistas in Brittany or Spain, but digs for treasure in his own domain. He has given immortality to some of the most delightful haunts of his beloved city in seven books on Cincinnati, containing reproductions of some three hundred of his etchings. Collectively, they give to Cincinnatians a precious storehouse for all time, recording glimpses of places they frequent every day, of beauty which they fail to interpret. Mr. Hurley pictures the romantic side of familiar things, idealizes, and glorifies them. "Fountain Square", a representation of the landmark by which every traveler knows Cincinnati, shows the fountain in one dark mass silhouetted against the brilliantly lighted buildings of the square. Others in the Cincinnati series show streets and spires of the city; market scenes revealing busy housewives and venders in their everyday costumes; public buildings and residences; the Eighth Street viaduct with Mt. Adams in the background; and Garfield Park covered with a mantle of snow. These etchings have been a labor of love, made through years of study and in spare moments from his art work of another sort at the Rookwood pottery. All of them are delightful, but the eye lingers especially over several lace-like snow scenes.

For other scenes, Mr. Hurley has wandered up the Little Miami Valley and caught the kaleidoscopic beauty of the river views. He has studied the characteristics of the landscape along the Ohio River and the streams of the neighborhood. In two series, "Old Mills and Covered Bridges" (Plate 81), and "Highways and Byways", he has etched charming old places, such as a well sweep of the days gone by, a little waterfall in its grandest moments, a small farmyard where a woodpile awaits attention, or a shed door near which sits a man feeding the chickens around him. "Tecumseh", one of the vanished race of wooden Indians that sentineled the tobacco shops years ago, is made the subject of a beautiful etching. In another he has taken an old rail fence for his theme; again, the "Apple Orchard" is full of poetic feeling. His innumerable etchings of "The Town of the Beautiful River", "The Queen City of the West", and the region surrounding are the most noteworthy output of his studio, and have given him a wide recognition. In clear, unimpeded line he can express much insight and character. He has a command of the whole plate, showing everywhere intelligent massing and a sound composition in light and shade. Mr. Hurley has made beautiful colored etchings, and splendid paintings in oil; one of them, "Midnight Mass", is owned by the Museum of Art, Cincinnati.

Etching is only one phase of Mr. Hurley's art activities. Some of his most notable work has been in designs for Rookwood pottery; many specimens of his decoration on that ware are in the large European museums. The invention of the Hurley pastel crayons, and the creation of the Hurley bronzes are other evidences of his many-sided talent.

Paul Ashbrook, Cincinnati, has earned national recognition for his dry-point character delineations. He is at his best when he makes a picture of some person whose ability to do a certain work leaves its impress upon his character. "The Spanish Smuggler" is a typical example, in which the head and shoulders are thrust forward in striking relief, the pose vividly suggesting expressive action. The deep-shadowed eyes pierce the distant sea for enemies; the small section of ship's rigging visible beyond the smuggler's shoulders suggests the dramatic situation. The large hat with rolled brim makes a rich, dark background for the intriguing face. Mr. Ashbrook has a sympathetic understanding of the artistic possibilities of personal traits and gestures, and one is brought to realize that it is his sharp analysis of types that makes him such a wonderful portrait etcher.

Whether Mr. Ashbrook selects types from Spain, Mexico, or at home, they are all done in the same masterly way. "The Old Fiddler" conveys the sound, if that is possible, of the tuning of the fiddle in preparation to put forth strains of "Turkey in the Straw", or "Money Musk", perhaps. The fondest, happiest smile spreads over the old man's face as his hands lovingly touch the fiddle. One knows at once his adorable personality, and the artist leaves no doubt as to his character. The lines, delicate, yet direct and telling, impart no superfluous information.

PLATE 82—Swans. Dry point and aquatint by LeRoy Sauer. (Artist)

A lovely young Spanish peasant girl making lace — "Terese" — has her character beautifully rendered in the scantest possible number of lines; few artists could do as well as Mr. Ashbrook without adding many details, and in that very subordination of details lies his success as a dry-point etcher. The subject of this picture requires a simplicity of pose and treatment, the decisive character of dark and light masses in which he excels. "The Ship Builder" is one of his very popular dry points, one that has made him well known to print collectors, and helped to place him in the front rank of interpreters of national types, because in it he displays an intuitive grasp of personality. Mr. Ashbrook is a painter, also, of Mexican and Spanish incidents and scenes with the unmistakable *milieu* of the country represented. These canvases have a lavish richness and depth of color.

With the laudable object of stimulating an appreciation of prints in the community, and to inspire more artists to cultivate the art, the Dayton Society of Etchers was formed in 1920. Its annual exhibit, strictly limited to the fourteen members of the society, is anticipated with great pride and eagerness by the Daytonians. The society may claim to be unique in this respect, that its members must reside within a short radius of Dayton. However, its influence is much more than local, because it has sponsored for four years an autumn exhibition of the work of the Ohio Print Makers, that has circulated through most of the museums of the state. It has created a wonderful opportunity for the print makers of the state to display their work; the results are immeasurable. LeRoy D. Sauer, president of the society, has been the leading spirit, untiring in his efforts to promote the organization. Etchings and wood blocks, of architectural subjects mainly, constitute a large part of his work. In his wood blocks there is a bold, crisp handling that shows a fine grasp of the essentials of block cutting, and a sincerity and directness that are refreshing. "The Old Courthouse", "Old Perrine House", and "Main Street Bridge" are some of the most pleasing of the local representations he has made; they have a saneness and clearness of idea that show his proficiency (Plate 82). He has exhibited some interesting French doorways in dry point that show a feeling of structure and proportion with no lessening in vigor of line. Another member of the society is Oliver Beacham, whose landscapes in lithograph and etching evidence a genuine love for out-of-doors. The poetic feeling of his landscapes is recognized in charming winter scenes; the unaffected simplicity of the man himself is reflected in such pastoral scenes as "A Bit of Holt Creek", with its properly massed background. Among other members of the society, Daniel Blau, Harold Harlan, and Ferdinand Bordewisch have made many notable dry-point por-

PLATE 83—Back of Firemen's Hall. Etching by Orville E. Peets.
(Cleveland Museum of Art)

traits. Robert Whitmore etches river valley scenes with individuality. These men, with the other talented members of the society, have banded themselves together for earnest work, and as etchers they have proved themselves worthy of attention. The print types — etchings, dry points, soft grounds, lithographs, and wood blocks—are all represented in their exhibits. What cannot be accomplished by such a group of men with artistic tastes and a love for the unusual? The Dayton Society of Etchers promises great things.

Miss Julia Severance, of Oberlin, is another good etcher whose work deserves special mention (Plate 72), though she is probably better known by her portrait sculpture in bas-relief.

In Toledo, the graphic arts have been fostered by J. Ernest Dean. Most of the members of the Toledo Print Club, numbering about twenty in all, have used his studio, opened about 1918, for a place of instruction, and have made it their headquarters; they have used his press for their work.

Mr. and Mrs. Dean (see page 334) were interested in etching as early as 1900, being members then of a Cleveland etching club, one of the first in the state. Mrs. Dean has an excellent plate done in the class of Arthur Dow, Ipswich, Massachusetts, in 1901. Mr. and Mrs. Dean went to Munich in 1910, and there Mr. Dean entered the graphic arts school of John Brockhoff, happy in the opportunity to study processes he had longed to know — mezzotints, aquatints, wood and linoleum block cutting, and lithography. "We were in Munich four years, returning June, 1914. We tried to stir up some interest in prints in the two years we were in Cleveland and vicinity, and did, somewhat, but it took the war, driving home to the United States many students with prints to show, to get the print business going."[4]

All the Toledo print makers turn to him for technical guidance, since he has at his fingers' tips the methods for making the whole family of prints. He likes to work out the same subject in various media to get the variety of tonal effects. Some of his most interesting prints have been evolved from sketches made in Germany and Italy; a notable one is of Venice, called "Chimney Pots and Cathedrals."

Mrs. Dean has taught graphic art for several summers at Miss Cornell's School, South Bristol, Maine. She has made quite a number of carefully designed linoleum block prints in color, rather poster-like than pictorial. It is a way of her own different from the black block craze, so much in vogue at present. Color in prints seems to inoculate the moderns with some "mad" disease.

Of the members of the Toledo Print Club who have done good work, most

---

[4] Quotation from a letter from J. Ernest Dean.

PLATE 84—On the Zattere, Venice. Etching by Hugh Seaver (Cleveland Museum of Art)

have some training, but others have succeeded simply by persistent trials. The prints of John Swalley have been shown several times in the Ohio Print Makers' exhibit and in the Brooklyn Society of Etchers and other shows, receiving a number of prizes. His best work is in aquatint and mezzotint rather than in line, as he has worked more with the brush. Many of his subjects have been selected with the idea of preserving the memory of a few of the picturesque places near Toledo; an old church at Lakeside, a barn along the Maumee, and the old hand bridge at Waterville have afforded him pictures where others might not have seen the promise in the subjects. However, there is no sameness of subject nor of medium in his work. In oil and water color, he loves color, using it in the manner of the impressionists or in great flat surfaces.

Among other members of the club, Florence Cooper has produced good line-work in dry point, etching, and aquatints, which she has exhibited at the Brooklyn, Philadelphia, and National Arts shows. Lulu Snell, a painter of children's portraits in water color, has done some sensitive and delightful children's heads in dry point. I. A. King, who renders architectural drawings, is a master pen draughtsman of the older school, making good etchings. Catherine Lauer does quite vigorous work of a modern type, so daring in line that it compels admiration. Other names that should not be omitted are Mrs. Frank Maxwell, Bertha Richardson, Julia Peters, and Caroline Morgan. The women are more interested in color than in black-and-white drawing.

One year the work of five members of the Toledo Print Club was placed in the Brooklyn Etchers (American Etchers) exhibit. Lavish praise is due Mr. Dean, who has started some notables in his studio, for whose artistic success he is largely responsible. He makes them do their own work, printing and everything, as soon as they can. Graphic art has its own natural troubles, losing a large number of clever artists, many of whom working in black-and-white go into commercial art, and others go into the field of color painting.

To a long list of capabilities, Henry G. Keller (see page 344), of Cleveland, adds another form of art, etching. He has many plates to his credit, all treating the subjects realistically. In lithographs he is noted for his portrayal of animals; his "Horses", "Pig Composition", and "Muleteer", are true to the best traditions of the lithograph. Frank Wilcox (see page 350), another Cleveland master of painting, is bold and forceful in his etchings. Ferdinand Burgdorff expresses his love for the West and his intimate acquaintance with it in such etchings as "The Grand Canyon, Arizona". The vast spaces below and the cathedral-like rock formations are very impressive. He silhouettes a branch or tree in the foreground, thus creating an artistic composition. His individual

PLATE 85—I Hear a Voice in the Wilderness. Wood-block print
by Benjamin Miller. (Artist)

technique displays wonderful values, gradations of shadows, and marvelous detail of still life. Orville H. Peets is another Clevelander renowned for etchings (Plate 83).

The followers of Izaak Walton rejoice in the fishing subjects of Hugh Seaver. He etched his first plate, "Brook Trout No. 1", in 1925. He was trained as an architect, and one would naturally expect his studies to portray architecture rather than angling. The success of his first plate made him follow it with a series including "The Snag", "Trout No. 3", "Youth and Experience", "The Abstract Twins", and "The Black Bass". The last-mentioned plate is considered one of the finest he ever executed. The rhythmic motion of the flowing lines, the floating lily pads above, the sinuous movements of the fish, the simplicity of the pattern and the spacing — all suggest the feeling of the Japanese prints. "The Fisherman", showing a man with bent rod attempting to net a trout, is convincing in subject and opulent in values. His subjects vary, however, and include the study of nudes, Parisian and Venentian scenes (Plate 84), and such local subjects as "The Terminal Tower", "Ore Boats Off Cleveland", and "The Chagrin Valley Hunt Club."

Rudolph Stanley-Brown, an architect by training, is in architectural work with his uncle, Mr. Abram Garfield, and is head of the design department of the Cleveland School of Architecture of Western Reserve University. Consideration is confined here to his work as a graphic artist. During 1919 he exhibited a series of war pictures, some forty-four in all, at the Cleveland Museum of Art; they attracted special attention.

In a charming series of etchings, dry-points, water colors, and colored pencil drawings, Mr. Stanley-Brown has made records of many of the old houses and taverns in the Western Reserve; these should be treasured as much for their historical value as for their artistic interest. It is fortunate that such artists have interested themselves in painting these fine old landmarks while they still exist. His drawing is very satisfying, not too much detailed, yet delicately realistic. By means of the figures in the costumes of the days when these buildings were young, he has succeeded in endowing his pictures with a strong suggestion of that placid and deliberate life of those early days (Plate 20). Many scenes of the Old World are well portrayed in his etchings. There abound in them a fine feeling and a love for the old French cathedral sculpture and sunny market places. Mr. Stanley-Brown's etchings have been exhibited in all the big shows, in those sponsored by the Brooklyn Society, the Pennsylvania Academy of Fine Arts, the National Academy, the Los Angeles Print Club, and others. He has an enthusiastic love for the beauty and bright colors of Venice, which he transcribes in water colors.

PLATE 86—Flowers. Wood-block print by Edna Boies Hopkins. (Artist)

As an illustrator, Mr. Stanley-Brown is listed among the notables. He has illustrated four books, all published by the Harper Publishing Company; two of them, *The Song Book of the American Spirit*, and *The Young Architects*, are by his wife, Katherine Stanley-Brown. They have also produced a new book, *The Story of Printed Pictures*, describing thirty-five graphic processes, with many pictures of the tools to be used, and other illustrations that make it an invaluable asset to the worker in the graphic arts.

Paul B. Travis began exhibiting etchings about 1920, winning several medals at the Cleveland Museum of Art. A group of four etchings, "Rue Grande, Le Mans", "Chartres Cathedral", "The Ohio River at Empire, Ohio", and "Our Hill from Dumstown", won first prize at the 1922 May show at the Cleveland Museum. Later, in 1925, he became interested in lithographs. The Cleveland Print Club purchased his lithograph, "Bass and Minnows", for its publication; a copy of this is in the New York Library, and he has prints in other well-known collections. The Cleveland Museum of Art has his "Head of a Young Man". For a time Mr. Travis turned his attention to painting (see page 356). Now he is occupied with graphic work exclusively, and is making etchings and lithographs of Africa.

The graphic arts in Cleveland took a long stride forward with the formation (in 1930) of the society of the Cleveland Print Makers, in the organization of which Kalman Kubinyi was the prime factor. Through its annual exhibitions of the works of its members (who are all creative artists, meeting once a week to work on plates), the services of this society will forge a close link between the artists and the public. Its members carried off all the prizes at the seventh annual exhibit (in 1930) of the Print Makers of Ohio. The organization of the Cleveland Print Makers is not to be confused with the Print Club, which is a society of Cleveland connoisseurs. Mr. Kubinyi has a working knowledge of all the graphic processes, which he learned from his uncle, a print maker of distinction in Hungary. He is known as a prize winner in etchings. One has only to examine the beautiful book, *The Goldsmith of Florence*, to learn of the excellent work he can do in the way of illustration; in it he has caught the medieval attitude toward black-and-white. Mr. Kubinyi always gets more than the external quality. One feels his strong response to spiritual forces, combined with technical excellence (see page 358).

The Cleveland May show of 1931 exhibited an amazing number of good prints. There were three which tied for first prize, all aquatints, by Joseph Suto, Clarence Carter, and Kalman Kubinyi. The exceptionally high quality of the prints made it necessary to award honorable mention to seven, those of Ivy Ed-

Scheme for a Mountain

PLATE 87—Book illustration. W. A. Dwiggins. (Artist)

mondson, William Gisch, J. J. King, Meade A. Spencer, Carl Binder, Manuel Silberger, and James Lentine. There are in Cleveland many other makers of splendid prints, but lack of space unfortunately prevents more than a passing mention of their respective performances: John Csosz has a charming "Old Street, Paris", and other noteworthy etchings; Carl F. Binder has made many lithographs, "The Toilers", "Athlete", "Returning from the Field", being among the best; Harold G. Griffith's "Water Front", and "Cleveland Skyline", are worthy of note. Many honors have been bestowed upon members of the Print Club.

The woodcut is attracting an increasing attention. Benjamin Miller was one of the first of Ohio artists to revive the ancient art of making wood-block prints, which is said to be the grandfather of the graphic arts, tracing its origin back to the sixth century in China. However, Mr. Miller makes woodcuts of a modern conception, yet bearing some Byzantine and even Gothic suggestions. His subjects are taken, almost exclusively, from the Bible. The intense emotion of its dramatic stories seems to be well expressed in the strong medium of the woodcut.

To illustrate "Is There Anything Left of Religion?" the *Forum* made a wise choice of Miller's woodcuts.[5] The first one, "Adam Naming the Animals", humorously pictures Adam as a very human fellow who has just awakened from a Rip Van Winkle sleep and scratches his head as he looks at the queer animals assembled in front of him. "Samson Destroying the Temple", has the strength and action one expects to find in that subject. "The Voice of One Crying in the Wilderness", is a powerful black-and-white. Saint John, in a flood of light, stands in the desert where thorny cacti grow; he wears the traditional garment, and is accompanied with the scriptural symbols (Plate 85). It is surprising that so few square inches can carry so much feeling: most of the woodcuts are no larger than six or eight, by nine or ten inches. "Christ Entering Jerusalem" has a singular clarity of design and a simplicity that properly goes with the medium. "Saint John in Prison" displays a marvelous, deep, velvety black; the severity of the light and dark heightens the tragedy. In these Mr. Miller has put the woodcut to the medieval function of preaching a sermon. In every instance the clear-cut lines speak eloquently of the tool; often the grain of the wood is used with telling effect. Mr. Miller is equally at ease working either with black-on-white or white-on-black.

There is a note of mysticism in all his work. Mr. Miller has a fertile, inventive mind with plenty of ideas to present. His "Salome" series is now cele-

---

[5] *The Forum*, September, 1929.

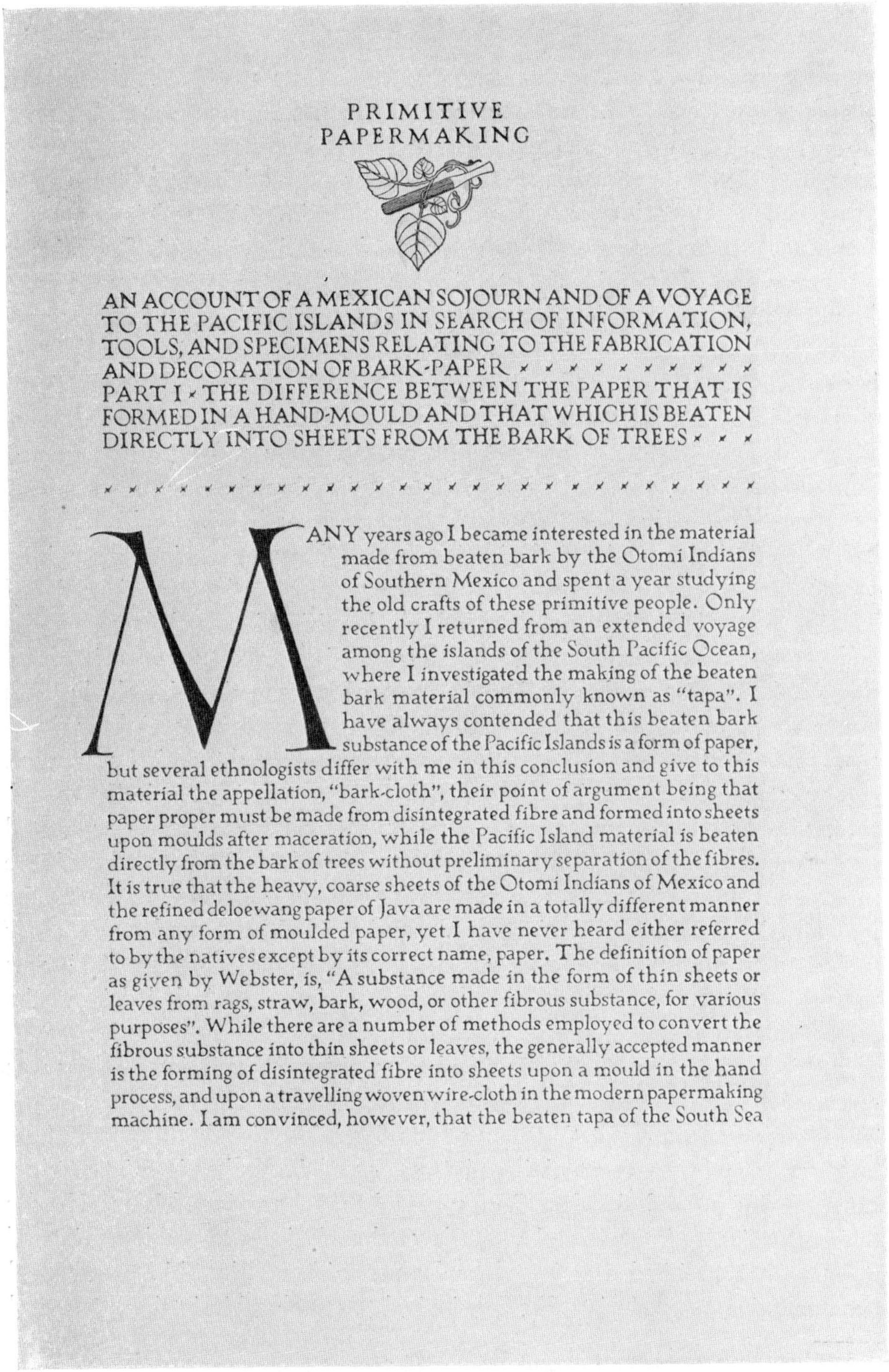

PRIMITIVE
PAPERMAKING

AN ACCOUNT OF A MEXICAN SOJOURN AND OF A VOYAGE
TO THE PACIFIC ISLANDS IN SEARCH OF INFORMATION,
TOOLS, AND SPECIMENS RELATING TO THE FABRICATION
AND DECORATION OF BARK-PAPER ⨯ ⨯ ⨯ ⨯ ⨯ ⨯ ⨯ ⨯ ⨯
PART I ⨯ THE DIFFERENCE BETWEEN THE PAPER THAT IS
FORMED IN A HAND-MOULD AND THAT WHICH IS BEATEN
DIRECTLY INTO SHEETS FROM THE BARK OF TREES ⨯ ⨯ ⨯

⨯ ⨯

MANY years ago I became interested in the material made from beaten bark by the Otomi Indians of Southern Mexico and spent a year studying the old crafts of these primitive people. Only recently I returned from an extended voyage among the islands of the South Pacific Ocean, where I investigated the making of the beaten bark material commonly known as "tapa". I have always contended that this beaten bark substance of the Pacific Islands is a form of paper, but several ethnologists differ with me in this conclusion and give to this material the appellation, "bark-cloth", their point of argument being that paper proper must be made from disintegrated fibre and formed into sheets upon moulds after maceration, while the Pacific Island material is beaten directly from the bark of trees without preliminary separation of the fibres. It is true that the heavy, coarse sheets of the Otomi Indians of Mexico and the refined deloewang paper of Java are made in a totally different manner from any form of moulded paper, yet I have never heard either referred to by the natives except by its correct name, paper. The definition of paper as given by Webster, is, "A substance made in the form of thin sheets or leaves from rags, straw, bark, wood, or other fibrous substance, for various purposes". While there are a number of methods employed to convert the fibrous substance into thin sheets or leaves, the generally accepted manner is the forming of disintegrated fibre into sheets upon a mould in the hand process, and upon a travelling woven wire-cloth in the modern papermaking machine. I am convinced, however, that the beaten tapa of the South Sea

PLATE 88—Book page. Dard Hunter. (Artist)

brated. Two of his prints well known to enthusiasts are "Edgar Allan Poe" and "Aubrey Beardsley". The background of the latter is made by taking selections from Beardsley's designs and weaving them into a beautiful pattern; the elongated features and mystic eyes of Beardsley are reminiscent of the manner of El Greco. Mr. Miller exercises much freedom in design and in the actual woodcut. He was a painter for twenty years before he made his first print in 1924; now he gives entire time to woodcuts. His early work reflected some influence of Japanese prints, of which he was very fond, and of German engraving; his present style, however, is purely individual. M. C. Salaman in his book, *The New Woodcut,* describes one of Miller's works as follows: "A design of intense contemporary significance is 'The City', by Mr. Benjamin Miller. It is a scathing satire on the fatuous frivolity and extravagance supposed to be rife in New York and presumably in other cities, regardless of the needs of the suffering poor, a crowd of inane faces of men and women of every description, laughing and giggling, even a figure in evening dress with a grinning death's head, surrounded by leering women of the town, is gathered in front of a garish background of lights, advertising jazz and dance, movies and sex, while in the center, towering above all, is a tall, gaunt, emaciated figure wearing a halo, and revealing the form of a cross, though nobody takes any note of him."[6] It is a striking example of the grimness and weird mysticism that one finds in his work, beside being a model of his usual technical excellence.

The making of color prints from wood blocks was developed in Europe after the introduction of prints by the Japanese, but the European artists created an entirely new interpretation with the Japanese method. In fact, although the process of printing flat masses of color by hand was borrowed from Japan, the individuality and the rare insight of the artists of Europe produced a really occidental art which had few reminders of its original parentage. This was soon recognized, and sections devoted to color prints were included in all the salons. Museums and collectors added an impetus to the growing interest.

In this atmosphere of enthusiasm and competition, Edna Boies Hopkins was able to produce a new and much-appreciated note with her prints of flowers. These were first shown at the salon of the Société Nationale des Beaux Arts, and Mrs. Hopkins at once took her place as one of the leaders in print making. Museums in England, Sweden, Germany, and France purchased her works for their collections. After several years devoted exclusively to making prints of flowers, she published a series of landscapes with people which augmented her reputation as a colorist. She was invited to membership in the salons and

---

[6] The special spring number (1930) of *Creative Arts.*

print societies of Paris, and her contributions to their exhibitions were eagerly sought.

During her residence in Cincinnati, Mrs. Hopkins spent several summers in Provincetown, where she conducted a class in print making and inspired many of the artists who have since made the Provincetown prints so well known. The making of prints is a responsible undertaking — it permits of no false touch. Mrs. Hopkins has complete mastery of that delicate craft, which requires experience as well as theory. Her prints are not the products of chance. She is very sensitive to color and design, and naturally has been influenced by the modern French art, having lived in Paris many years. Her unusual flower arrangements are soft and lovely in color, with an absolute freedom in handling and no annoying hard edges. Color gradation is a beautiful feature of her prints; in some of them she has used the grain of the wood to advantage in the background. She does not overlook the slightest detail that will make for the success of the print. The charm of her work can be appreciated only by a comparison with that of other flower painters (Plate 86).

Probably the foremost book designer in America is W. A. Dwiggins, born at Martinsville, Ohio. His work is typographic design (with the Mergenthaler Linotype Company, of Brooklyn) and book illustration (Plate 87). He plans the complete format of a book, determines the size, designs the type and title-page, and makes the illustrations. Some artistically executed books he has made recently are *Poe's Tales,* R. R. Donnelley & Sons Co., Chicago; *Dr. Jekyll and Mr. Hyde,* Random House, New York, and *Tartarin of Tarascon,* The Limited Editions Club, New York; all are of limited editions. He says that he has made "acres of lettering and advertisements." When he was nineteen years old he became a student in Frank Holme's School of Illustration, Chicago; he later went to Boston in 1904, and as a free-lance artist served a rigorous apprenticeship in advertising. Since 1928 his time has been given entirely to the fine book designs which have won many medals for him. He has done a considerable amount of writing, too: particularly clear essays and a book, *Layout in Advertising*. He is an indefatigable creator, working on an eighteen-hour schedule, which leaves little time for publicity interviews; consequently he has received few write-ups.

Dard Hunter, of Chillicothe, Ohio, makes books that will rank among the world's most noted publications. He is the first worker in the whole history of the art of typography who makes the paper, designs and makes the type, writes and illustrates his books, and is also the book designer, compositor and publisher (Plate 88). He has achieved distinction in each of these steps in book-

PLATE 89—Bookplates. Professor Thomas E. French. (Artist)

making. An entire book is the result of his labors alone. There is an individuality in every part of his work which carries one back to the days of Aldus, Jenson, and Caxton, reviving the individualism in the work of the ancient master printers. After many years of travel, study, and research, Hunter concluded that to arrive at the excellence of the old masters he must work with their methods; he must have his own handmade paper mill and type foundry. His materials for book production are not paper and type, but linen and cotton rags, bar steel, copper, lead, tin, and antimony. The hand moulds on which the paper for his first two books was made, the letter-punches, matrices, type, and tools that were used in their production are now in the Smithsonian Institution; copies of the books are also in the case, which bears this label: "In the entire history of printing these are the first books to have been made in their entirety by the labor of one man."

Mr. Hunter's particular interest in paper making led him into an investigation that has enriched the world's knowledge on that subject. *Handmade Paper and its Watermarks, Papermaking Through Eighteen Centuries,* and his six other books relating to paper making are extraordinary examples of craftsmanship. The third volume from the private press of Dard Hunter, *Old Papermaking,* represents fifteen years' research in the art of the old paper makers, and was over one year in the press. It is one of the most unique editions ever produced. His paper is really remarkable. His type is artistic and distinctive; it is bolder and without the machine-made exactness of regularity to which we are accustomed. His books are printed in the limited editions. It is seldom that one of them gets on the market, but when there is one available it commands a considerable premium, usually eight or ten times as great as the original price.

From the woodcut down to the modern photomechanical process, every method employed in the illustration of books is used for bookplates also. The name label pasted on the inside of the front cover of a book to indicate its ownership is called a bookplate, or an *ex libris*. There should be some personal or private feature in a bookplate that will make it different from any other. Artistic bookplates are infrequent because the owner usually insists upon the artist inserting all sorts of personal fancies. The greatest danger in making bookplates is in overcrowding the plate. The design should be simple, dignified, and appropriate to the medium. The copper or steel engraving is considered by many designers as best adapted to the formal, stately, and dignified style, and has been employed from the time of Paul Revere, who was one of the first bookplate designers in America.

Thomas E. French, of the department of engineering drawing, at Ohio State University, is not only one of the world's authorities today on bookplates, but is also a designer of *ex libris*. Several times he has been awarded the American Bookplate Society prizes. He has originated the seals, arms, and bookplates for a number of American colleges. Looking over some of the plates of Professor French, one will be impressed with his versatility both in design and execution. The charm of the plate he designed for the Phi Gamma Delta Club of New York is due to its symmetry and balance. Around the fraternity coat-of-arms is a beautiful rendering of acanthus ornament. The lettering is part and parcel of the design. There will also be noted the remarque, an old sailing ship, head on, with a lighthouse for the crest. For the Library of the Ohio State University, Professor French designed a bookplate which contains a view of the library and the seal of the university, surrounded by a border of buckeye leaves. His bookplate for the William Raimond Baird Library of American College Fraternity Literature has a portrait of Mr. Baird and a tiny medallion with a view of the Acropolis in it, and a true Greek akroterion at the top. The Julius Stone bookplate gives an intimate, cozy view of his fireplace; while for the archæologist, William C. Mills, he made an unusual plate with the mound-builder artifacts used as motifs. He is happy, too, in the difficult field of designing feminine bookplates; the one for his daughter Janet French has a softness of tone, and a dainty composition of a delicate landscape with a lake.

Whatever Professor French designs is technically correct and artistic (Plate 89). He is an unrivalled authority on everything that has to do with prints, and his keen judgment is sought on every form of art. He has had much to do with the development of an art spirit in Ohio. Students who come in contact with him are enriched by an appreciative point of view which continues throughout their lives, and many artists received their first impetus in his encouraging and inspiring talks. His interest and support has been given as wholeheartedly to the fine arts department as to the pursuit of engineering drawing.

There is much interest now in *ex libris,* and many books have appeared on the subject. There is quite a fad for collecting them. Libraries, museums, colleges, and learned societies vie with each other in the size and variety of their collections. Cleveland has some notable collections: The Rowfant Club collection, the collection of Paul Lemperly, and of John J. Wood. The Rowfant Club, a discriminating book club, has beautiful plates executed by Will Low and Sidney Smith, and a number of bookplates are owned by its different members. Cleveland designers of bookplates include Jessie Harrows Jones, Mrs. James Carson Barron, Lillian W. Hunter, Helen Andrews, Otto Hoffman,

Florence Post, George Adomeit, and Florence Estelle Little. The designer of a bookplate shows what a very big thing a little plate can be; he brings to its miniature face the task of interpreting beauty, and its size has nothing to do with its real magnitude. The time is approaching when no real book lover can deny himself a work of art to link himself with his books forever. A happy future is in store for these fine things.

CHAPTER XI

Newspaper Artists

CARICATURE has the patent of a most respectable antiquity. Its traditions are quite distinguished. When the history of the American cartoon is investigated and written, it will doubtless lead back through devious ways to the satirical verse of the Greeks and the Romans, to the first painters of *genre* subjects in Holland, including the great Peter Breughel, and then on down to to the great satirists of England and France. In this line of succession William Hogarth will fill an important place with his brilliant and humorous comment on the life of his time. Individual work in political caricature made its appearance in America at the time of the Stamp Act and the War of the Revolution. Before the end of the Civil War it passed into the hands of the weeklies, with *Harper's* always in the lead.

Every great daily newspaper now considers the cartoonist an essential member of its staff. Public opinion may be guided by a good cartoon, serving as a valuable asset to the carrying out of the policy of a paper; or its purpose may be to reflect public opinion. Most of the work included under the heading of cartoons contains an element of humorous exaggeration, frequently unsparing sarcasm, and shrewd delineation of character. A caricature that makes an extremely gross or unnatural exaggeration of personal features has little or no consideration as a work of art; one rejoices that the day of the picture lampoon is past. However, if the exaggeration of the peculiar characteristics of the subject are within reasonable limits, even more than a slight emphasis upon a peculiarity of figure or feature, it may be approved by the rules of art generally recognized. The most important phase of caricature is without doubt its educational value.

The cartoonist must be a versatile man; no one deserves greater respect than he! His first qualification is a technical one, that of drawing, in which he must be sure and skillful. In addition he must have a keen sense of humor, the ability to see the ridiculous side of a situation. He needs a background of history and an understanding of affairs. He must be a shrewd observer and an original thinker with an idea which he can express with telling effect; his apt turn of a bit of humor is bound to influence one more than any mere prosaic presentation of an idea. When it comes to the application of the pictorial method to the explanation of a policy, or a principle, to the defense of an issue, to the enforcement of a right, or to the exposure of a wrong, the cartoonist has no superior, possibly no equal.

270

The first real appearance of the colored comic supplement was a part of the Sunday *New York World,* November 18, 1894. The pictures were of a clown off on a picnic with a wolf hound. After a hearty meal the two fell asleep and were visited by an anaconda which ate the wolf hound. The clown awakened to find that the snake was taking a siesta while it digested the dog, so he performed a nice little operation on the snake's side and pulled out the dog's feet; and then the impish clown led away the famous anaconda-dog. This mythical animal was called "The Origin of a New Species", and was the creation of Richard Fenton Outcault, born at Lancaster, Ohio.

Mr. Outcault had been trained as a draughtsman, and had been in the employ of Edison, who sent him to Paris to do some work. Before starting to make comics he was employed by the *Electrical World,* but to stick to such exacting work as the drawing of parts of dynamos was very displeasing to him, so he transferred his activities to the colored comic supplement. His great success came with the "Yellow Kid", in 1896. Here is its story: "Edward Harrigan's play was running successfully in New York. In it occurred a song, 'Maggie Murphy's Home', which began with the words, 'Down in Hogan's Alley'. Outcault had laid the scene of a little series of comics in Hogan's Alley, and found that the pictures were acceptable to *Truth.* After some months on the *World* it occurred to him that he might continue the interrupted series in the comic supplement, and he forthwith carried out the idea. Topics that held public attention were burlesqued by the dwellers in Hogan's Alley. The wedding of Miss Vanderbilt and the Duke of Marlborough was the first subject treated; the Klondike was discovered there. The 'Kid' came on the scene first simply as one of the chorus to help fill in the picture, and took no prominent part. By a happy inspiration the man who laid out the color scheme gave a glaring yellow to the gown (really, night shirt) in which Mr. Outcault had clothed him. Mr. Outcault emphasized the ears of the brat; promoted him to a speaking part by inscribing some legend on his gown. A 'Yellow Kid' epidemic ravaged the land. The 'Kid' appeared on buttons, cracker tins, fans show cards, cigarette packages, and was finally dramatized. He had arrived!"[1]

There was a sharp rivalry between the *New York World* and the *New York Journal.* "By that time the *Journal* had a color press as well as the *World,* so Mr. Outcault was hired away from the *World* at some fabulous sum, and took his pencil and his 'Kid' over to the newer paper. The *World* then secured George Luks to draw 'Yellow Kids'. There were lawsuits for breaking of contracts and for infringement of copyright brought by both papers, and the comic art-

[1] *Everybody's Magazine,* vol. 12, pp. 768-9, Roy E. McCardell.

ists profited. The rivalry between the *World* and the *Journal* caused papers, without the attraction of Mr. Outcault's and Mr. Luks's work, to describe those papers as 'Yellow Kid' journals, and then by dropping the monosyllable to call them simply 'yellow journals'. So from Mr. Outcault's creation has come the term 'yellow journalism' with all that it implies for good or evil."[2]

In 1901, Outcault created "Pore Lil Mose", and in 1902, "Buster Brown"; both were produced in the *New York Herald*. The original of "Buster Brown", his greatest triumph, was his son, Richard F., Jr.; "Buster Brown's Mamma" was Mrs. Outcault as her husband saw her. "Buster Brown and Tige" were syndicated and put into book form. Belts, suits, collars, stockings, and so on and on, bore the popular name of "Buster Brown."

Even though he was not the original comic supplement artist, the dean of cartoonists, both by age and reputation, is Frederick Burr Opper, born at Madison, Lake County, Ohio. For thirty years his drawings have appeared in the Hearst newspapers. He was certain that the public wanted action and a continuation of effort on the part of their favorite comic characters. The original "Yellow Kid" had no action. Opper's characters are all energetic and full of life. "Maud", the mule, was always obstreperous; "Alphonse and Gaston" were always trying to outdo each other; "Happy Hooligan" with his tomato-can hat (Plate 90), and his brothers, "Gloomy Gus" and "Montmorency", could not be accused of passivity.

Mr. Opper considers "The Great Republican Circus" one of his most effective political cartoons. It represents the G. O. P. elephant carefully stepping over, without injuring, the fat-bellied trusts that lie in the ring. The common people being outwitted by the trusts was the theme he used most about 1895, and he made good play against the magnate and the trusts. "Mr. Opper's purpose seems to be first of all, to excite your mirth, and consequently he never fails to produce a certain effect. When you take up one of his cartoons in which the various stout, sturdy, and well-fed gentlemen typifying the different trusts are engaged in some pleasant game the object of which is the robbing, or abusing of the pitiable, dwarfish figure representative of the common people, your first impulse is a desire to laugh at the ludicrous contrast. It is only afterwards that you begin to think seriously how badly the abject little victim is being treated, and what a claim he has upon your sympathy and indignation. In those series designed along party lines, such as 'Willie and His Papa', this method is even more effective, since it begins by disarming party opposition."[3]

---

[2] *Everybody's Magazine,* vol. 12, pp. 768-9, Roy E. McCardell.
[3] *History of the Nineteenth Century in Caricature,* Maurice, p. 362.

PLATE 90—Drawing of Happy Hooligan. Frederick Opper. (Artist)

The forceful series, "Willie and His Papa", appeared in the *New York Journal*. For pure and simple fun, as well as for powerful influence, they were perhaps the best cartoons of the presidential campaign of 1900. They pictured President McKinley as the child of the trusts; the head of McKinley was placed on the body of a little boy wearing a Little Lord Fauntleroy collar. "Papa" was a corpulent, diamond-studded character representing the trusts; Mark Hanna was the "Nursie". It is said that the series created something like two million laughs a day, until it was abruptly discontinued after McKinley's assassination.

Mr. Opper made another side-splitting series in which he put President Roosevelt through a number of perilous hunting adventures. The president greatly enjoyed these friendly sallies, and wrote the artist a letter of appreciation.

From the time Mr. Opper left the village school, he cherished the determination to become an artist. He had the courage to go to New York and begin work at the bottom of the ladder, making window advertising cards. At the age of twenty-three he was artist for *Puck,* and much of the success of that magazine is due to his conscientious labor. "The Suburban Resident", the caricature of a gentleman loaded with parcels and bundles, rushing frantically for a train, was made for *Puck* and created much merriment; "The County Fair Orator", made for *Puck* in 1888, was full of human interest. Mr. Opper can finish a drawing smoothly — though a caricature too meticulously drawn may lose its humor. With a skilled pen or brush — almost inspired, it seems, to the layman — he makes a stroke here, and one there, and behold, a "speaking" figure is produced.

During the presidential campaign of McKinley, the cartoonist who did valiant service for him was Grant E. Hamilton. Mr. Hamilton was born at Youngstown, Ohio, near the birthplace of McKinley, and knew him from boyhood. This noted cartoonist never studied at an art school, but loved to draw everything, and while still a mere youth he sold his sketches to *Harper's, Puck,* and the *New York Daily Graphic*. So many of his drawings were used by the *Graphic,* that they finally sent for him to join their staff, and engaged him to give his entire time to that paper. That started him on his successful career. In a reminiscent mood, he thus spoke of his days with the *Graphic:* "He [Hamilton] says that it was the greatest school for artists, and mentions some of its graduates: B. Gilliam, DeThulstrup, E. Kemble, C. S. Reinhart, E. A. Abbey, A. B. Frost, and C. J. Taylor. These men were his art associates on that paper, which had eight pages of illustrations."[4]

He left the *Graphic* to join the staff of *Judge,* where he became a fixture.

---

[4] *The Bookman,* vol. XI, p. 339, June, 1900.

PLATE 91—Cartoon: Partner Wanted in the Show Business. W. A. Rogers. (Artist)

Added to his keen power of observation, Hamilton had another faculty which cannot be overestimated in a cartoonist — a wonderful memory. He could remember even the complicated construction of all kinds of machinery. The cartoonist seldom uses a model or has a chance to draw from life, so his memory has to be his storehouse from which to draw. Hamilton had, too, the necessary insight into affairs to be able to anticipate results accurately; his cartoon announcing the result of McKinley's election was prepared and in press two weeks before that event.

Hamilton's cartoons of the Spanish-American War show how a cartoon may bring home the issues involved and strengthen faith in the justice of a cause; they show, too, to what lengths a nation may go when unbalanced by the bitterness of war. "The Spanish Brute Adds Mutilation to Murder", is the title of a bloodcurdling cartoon by Hamilton. Spain is represented by a hideous, monster-like man; his hands are dripping with blood, one hand smears up a tombstone erected to the sailors of the *Maine,* the other clutches a terrible knife. His victims lie on the ground around him; his face has a vicious expression of national prejudice. There is no great amount of detail to be studied in order to have a complete understanding of the cartoon, for its very simplicity explains it.

When Bryan appealed to the farmer in 1896 with his "16 to 1" free silver idea, Hamilton took it off in an exceedingly powerful cartoon, called "The Temptation". Bryan in the form of a great angel of darkness, has led the farmer to a mountain top where he can gaze down upon the riches of the world. Before his eyes stretch, far and away, oceans and rivers and mountains of silver. It is grim and tragic, almost beyond the ethics of present-day cartoons.

Men of all shades of political belief enjoyed the cartoon of Roosevelt by Hamilton. During the campaign of 1904, the Democrats charged Roosevelt with having ambitions to become a Cæsar, so Hamilton pictured him looking into a millinery shop window and admiring an imported hat in the shape of an imperial crown of the European style.

William A. Rogers, who was born in Springfield, Ohio, is well-known as a cartoonist and illustrator. He spent the greater part of his life in New York, going there to illustrate for *Harper's Weekly* in 1877. Within recent years he has taken up his residence in Washington, D. C. In a letter he writes: "Got my art training as I went along, was associated at *Harper's* with Edwin A. Abbey and Charles Stanley Reinhart under the supervision of Charles Parsons. About as good a school as could have been had." His drawing is always beyond question. Even Joseph Pennell, who bemoaned the taste of the American public

PLATE 92—Drawing of Abe Martin. Kin Hubbard. (Artist)

for the cartoons and comic drawings of the newspapers, says, "though W. A. Rogers is very good indeed."[5]

During the Hancock campaign Mr. Rogers began making a series of political cartoons, but continued to illustrate books and magazines. In 1879, he went to Leadville, Colorado, to picture the great mining boom for *Harper's Magazine*. In this series of pictures the human interest prevails, as it does in all of his work: a shepherd starting off for the range with his sheep; a lone miner on a donkey; a curious collection of miners' cottages in Hungry Gulch; a rear view of a big overland vehicle, several guns and a jug in sight, a tar bucket hanging below; the broad-brimmed hats, high boots, western costumes and customs— all furnish pictorial descriptions of that lively place, Leadville.

Mr. Rogers joined the staff of the *New York Herald* as cartoonist in 1901, continuing there during the lifetime of James Gordon Bennet and until after the close of the war. His cartoons of the war, in the New York and Paris editions of the *Herald,* attracted world-wide attention; and his posters, such as "Paid in Full" and others now in the Smithsonian Institution, were extraordinarily effective and significant. He was a member and one of the founders of the division of Pictorial Publicity, which furnished designs for war posters and illustrations to the government, entirely without pay of any kind.

After the war, Mr. Rogers, together with other members of the Society of Illustrators, opened their school for wounded soldiers, of which he was the head for three years. He undertook reconstruction work for the veterans, conducting a class in illustrating and cartooning for those who had been disabled and who hoped through this medium to secure a means of future livelihood, and a restoration of health. In recognition of his service, both during and after the war, France decorated him with the cross of the Legion of Honor.

Several books have been written by Mr. Rogers. One is a book full of delightful reminiscences of art and artists in New York in the last fifty years, called *A World Worth While.* He has also written and illustrated three juveniles: *Danny's Partner, The Miracle Man,* and *The Lost Caravan.* The Cartoonists of America gave a dinner in New York City, in 1929, to honor F. B. Opper, Charles Dana Gibson, and W. A. Rogers. Mayor Walker presided, and over one thousand guests were assembled for the occasion. Mr. Rogers and Mr. Opper are the oldest cartoonists in the country in age, and in years of service (Plate 91).

Lest we forget, the service the artists rendered during the World War must be mentioned. The work of creating and stimulating patriotic feeling through

---

[5] *The Graphic Arts,* Joseph Pennell, p. 104.

THE WESTERN RESERVE PIONEER.

They pull up by the side of the smooth macadam, over there is an old log cabin, once a home of a pioneer family.

"Think of the courage our forefathers had, those who toiled, suffered and starved at times and struggled through it all, cheerfully helping to build a nation, and now, when things don't seem to go just right for us, I wonder if we wouldn't be better off, if we had a little of that same indomitable courage."

PLATE 93—Cartoon: The Western Reserve Pioneer. J. Hal Donahey. (Artist)

posters and cartoons cannot be measured. Camouflage was another department in which the training of the artist proved of enormous value. The range-
finding pictures had a corresponding value. A less conspicuous field was that
of relief maps made by the sculptors as an aid to the soldier in understanding
map reading and the topography of a region. The sculptor, the painter, and
the draughtsman simplified the difficult lessons the soldier had to learn. It is
just another angle to the old, old truth that art is an universal language. It is
the opening through which big and important things may be visualized. One
trained to perceive, needs nothing more than a Greek marble to grasp the spirit
of the fifth-century Greeks, nor more than a glance at the high-pointed Gothic
arches to understand the intense religious fervor of the Middle Ages.

Bellefontaine claims the honor of being the birthplace of Frank McKinney
Hubbard, who was known to the world as Kin Hubbard. "My first art work
was done on the *Indianapolis News*, where I began as a caricaturist, not cartoonist. Later I evolved the character Abe Martin, a column-wide feature composed of an illustration of the character and a paragraphic comment on the
news of the day, or about almost anything. During the last ten years my only
work in the way of art has been confined to illustrations for my Abe Martin
feature and a weekly two-column-wide essay called 'Short Furrows'. . . . I have
drawn a new picture of Abe Martin every day for over eighteen years. Abe
Martin has been syndicated for years in an average of one hundred and seventy
daily papers in this country and abroad." So he wrote in a letter just a few
weeks before his death on Christmas Day, 1930.

"Abe Martin" was a homely, long-legged, baggy-trousered figure, with wisps
of hair sticking out from under his shapeless hat. He usually leaned against
a post, a tree, or a store front (Plate 92). He was a mythical personage whose
habitat was the hills of Brown County, Indiana. His philosophy was chiefly
that of the corner grocery or the livery stable of a small town. He was created
after Mr. Hubbard had made a trip through Indiana during one of the presidential campaigns of William Jennings Bryan. In his autobiography he describes "Abe": "I drew a character which I called Abe Martin, and for several
days I wrote two unrelated sentences bearing on politics and things in general
and published them beneath the picture. Very often I had things to say that
Abe Martin would not be likely to say, so, from time to time, I quoted various
neighbors of his: Constable Newt Plum, Miss Tawney Apple, ticket-seller of a
nickel theater, Squire Marsh Swallow, Tilford Moots, Lafe Bud, Miss Fawn
Lippincot, Stew Nugent, Rev. Wiley Tanger, Dr. Mopps, Pinkey Kerr and
other familiar country-town characters." Never more than one person appeared
in the sketch.

PLATE 96—Cartoon: Losing Time by Waiting. Ray Evans. (Artist)

ered twenty national political conventions, a record which few newspaper men
can reach. He presented the originals of his unusual collection of cartoons of
Roosevelt, covering a long period of years, to the Roosevelt Memorial Association in New York. Before the originals left Cleveland, they were photographed
by the Educational Museum of the Cleveland public schools, and lantern slides
were made. From these negatives the enlargements were made which Mr.
Harold T. Clark presented to the Cleveland Public Library and to the Ohio
State Museum. This successful effort to preserve Mr. Donahey's original
drawings proves their inestimable historical value. The cartoons are rich as
the personal narrative of a man — alert, sensitive, and sympathetic. The "big
stick", prominent teeth, fierce eyes, square jaw, and other characteristics of
Roosevelt were unmistakable features that were kept before the public; they
seemed to offer a standing challenge to the cartoonist.

Coincident with a sojourn in Tucson and southern Arizona, Mr. Donahey
put forth a series of cleverly written articles accompanied by even cleverer cartoons for *The Cleveland Plain Dealer*. He absorbed the scenery and climate of
Tucson in its desert-mountain setting; grubbed among the ancient ruins of
pueblos in the San Pedro River Valley; breathed the atmosphere of dude ranches
and poked a little fun at the dudes themselves. Donahey wrote up and pictured
the rodeo with a captivating detail given to the various feats of western range
prowess, and finally told his paper's readers of his thrilling experience while
on a wild-horse round-up.

Other cartoon series for his paper have included these subjects: "In Egypt",
"Down Presidential Valley", "See America First", "May Days in Ohio",
"Mayaland in Yucatan", and "Arizona Pueblos" (Plate 93).

For his recreation, Mr. Donahey is concerned in the digging of fossils, relics,
and the exploration of old ruins. It is an avocation which takes him to the far
corners of the earth, and Egypt, South America, and Mexico all have their lure.
He mixes the making of modern political cartoons with writing about the history of a civilization four thousand years old. He has executed a number of
travel sketches and stories, mostly in Egypt, Yucatan, and Arizona. Although
an artist by profession, Mr. Donahey is also a business man, and gives one
that impression at once. He deals frankly with everyday problems, derives
much pleasure from his daily work, and lives a life without show, pretense, or
bombast.

In a recent interview, William A. Ireland gave this account of himself. He
was born in Chillicothe, but came to Columbus when he was eighteen or nineteen years old. After considering offers from Cleveland and Columbus papers,

PLATE 97—Cartoon: The Demon Chaperon. Don Wootton. (Artist)

he chose Columbus because of its being nearer to his home and parents. He says that luck put him into a really fine position, as the audience he reaches through the *Columbus Dispatch* is one of the finest in America. Not the least of a cartoonist's difficulties is the very mixed character of his public. Men and women of many nationalities, of varied professions and occupations, and of many grades of educational attainments must be pleased. The Columbus people are home-loving folk who think conservatively; they are, in a large per cent, "Buckeyes", or Ohio-born men and women who have been drawn to the capital city; and the population of Columbus is almost entirely American-born. Offers received by Mr. Ireland, from newspapers from coast to coast, have never lured him from the *Columbus Dispatch,* where he is charmed with his work.

The definition of Mr. Ireland for a cartoon is that it is a visualized editorial, with symbols used to express an opinion on some topic of the day. While he makes some political cartoons, he gets away from hackneyed political subjects, and pictures everyday life, or touches the most important subjects of the day's news. He never puts out a commonplace cartoon (Plates 94, 95). His execution is clever, and a sly, winning humor permeates all his work. The idea is the main thing, however. It is a privileged community that can have the advantage, day after day, of the ideas such an original thinker puts forth. He always lends his influence to every worthy civic project, and his cartoons have been a powerful factor in the success of such enterprises. In home and family scenes his drawings are exceptional. Mr. Ireland was a pioneer in the lighter way of handling political issues, avoiding the bitterness of the older satirical type of cartoon.

"The Passing Show", the colored page of the Sunday *Columbus Dispatch,* is a well-known institution in central Ohio. People will say to one another, "Did you see so-and-so in the 'Passing Show'?" It is one of Mr. Ireland's happy creations that is universal in its appeal. The page is made up of several colored drawings, mostly humorous, bearing upon incidents of travel, championing some worthy charitable project, emphasizing some bit of news, or giving praise where it is due; no subject is too trivial or serious to receive delineation on this page which he signs with a shamrock encircled by a scroll.

The *Columbus Dispatch* is fortunate in having another fine artist, Ray O. Evans, on its staff. That his work is excellent goes without saying. There are so few positions open to cartoonists that only the best can survive. Mr. Evans's cartoons show rare acumen and insight. He is gifted with a remarkable "cartoon sense", and succeeds in putting the real gist of a public question in pic-

PLATE 98—Cartoon: Headed for Oblivion? Claude Shafer. (Artist)

ture form. He treats the humorous as well as the serious subject (Plate 96). One notable phase of Mr. Evans's work is in portraiture; while attending a convention he, with a few telling strokes, makes portraits of all the prominent leaders there. They cannot be called caricatures, as the characteristics of each person are only noted, not exaggerated. These portraits may have more than ephemeral value, for they are so striking that he who rushes from page to page of the newspaper will pause for a moment to consider them. The artist must adjust himself to the feverish hurry that prevails, and the aversion of the average person to contemplate anything leisurely.

For two years, Mr. Evans was with Frank Munsey as special staff artist on the *Baltimore News* and the *Baltimore American.* He made political cartoons for *Puck* during the Wilson campaign, and executed many telling posters during the World War. Then for eight years he made a daily editorial cartoon for the *Baltimore American.* However, he says, with touching tribute of the regard of one cartoonist for another, that his most important training has been his work with Mr. Ireland on the *Dispatch.* Both of these artists frequently have their work reproduced in *The Literary Digest.* Mr. Evans serves as a member of the advisory staff to the Federal Board of Cartooning.

A third artist on the *Columbus Dispatch* is Dudley T. Fisher, Jr. He has developed a new series of rhymes and pictures that has received many favorable comments and is appearing through a syndicate in several papers. His "Annabelle and Flo" page presents topics pertaining to the daily activities of the home in a unique way. House cleaning, making garden, putting up the screens, mowing the lawn, shoveling the snow, and washing the car are typical tasks that these modern girls discuss in jingles.

In addition to having the qualification of good draughtsmanship required for cartoon making, Mr. Fisher is one of the few newspaper artists who can paint. Painting, with all that it implies in the study of picture qualities, has given him an unusual sense of decorative possibilities and has undoubtedly had much to do with the success of his work. The outstanding originality of his pages and their technical qualities stamp him as an exceptional newspaper artist. That there are three good artists connected with a single newspaper is unusual and gives the appearance of favoritism in the consideration of newspaper artists, but such is not the case.

The art director of the *Cleveland Press,* Don Wootton, achieved a reputation for his caricatures of famous people that appeared daily for some time in *The Cleveland Plain Dealer.* Prominent men in business, politics, banking, law, and other professions were drawn alternately with leaders of the sporting world and well-known characters about town. Likenesses of prominent actors at the theaters and occasionally sketches from the screen at a motion-picture house, made a popular series for the playgoing public. An endeavor was made to please all the groups for which a big daily newspaper is published (Plate 97).

Mr. Wootton writes entertainingly of how he makes his caricatures. "The best place to pick up sketches of prominent men is at their favorite restaurants during the lunch hour. I have often made rough sketches of some well-known man while seated a few tables away from my victim. When unconscious that he is being sketched, his expression is entirely natural and at such moments the best likeness can be secured. I depend a good deal upon memory to get the form of features of each individual. Sometimes I do not make a sketch at all, but draw my impression of the face when I return to the office. At first I worked for caricature of the face only. Now I include every peculiarity of his person and even his most characteristic postures. I believe that these things are as truly characteristic of him as his features, and are as easily recognized."

The work of Mr. Wootton is carried by many papers throughout the country, as it is syndicated by the Newspaper Enterprise Association. His editorial cartoons, snappy in technique, and fresh in ideas, have come out in the Cleveland papers, *The Literary Digest, Review of Reviews, Cosmopolitan,* and other papers and magazines.

Claude Shafer is the political cartoonist on *The Cincinnati Times-Star.* The reproduction of many of his cartoons in the *Review of Reviews, Manchester Guardian, The Literary Digest,* and Mark Sullivan's book, *Our Times,* is proof of the esteem in which he is held for getting at the kernel of a political issue or situation. Mr. Shafer made a reputation for himself during the World War. He made sketches and stories of many of the soldier training camps in the United States; then was sent overseas by the Scripps-Howard papers and the Young Men's Christian Association. For the papers he made sketches and did correspondent work; for the "Y" he entertained the soldiers in the front-line trenches in France with chalk talks. He experienced many phases of the war, even to the thrilling one of being on submarine chasers with Admirals Sims and Wilson.

"Old Man Grump", a cartoon character made by Mr. Shafer, has been popular for more than ten years, as has "Dopey Dan", "Tillie Tinkle", "Jasper", and others of his creating. His cartoon feature for the children, "The Doodle-bugs", has been syndicated by the George Matthew Adams Service for several years, appearing in twenty or more weekly papers, and reaching an ever-enthusiastic and appreciative audience of youngsters (Plate 98).

Almost every Ohio newspaper of any consequence has its favorite cartoonist. Many of the best pictorial wits have been developed in this fertile field before being lured to New York. Such a one is Robert M. Brinkerhoff, of Toledo, who now maintains a studio in New York. He has a flair for travel, and for looking up and knowing quaint characters whom he can picture in his cartoons and illustrated stories. For four months of the year he lives in the heart of the Maine woods, where his observant eyes can find much of interest to record in his drawings. In order to keep his imagination fertile, every cartoonist has to stimulate it by keeping his eyes and ears open at all times for new material.

Mr. Brinkerhoff won an unusual prize, a thousand-dollar gold bar awarded him for a story about Colorado which appeared in the *Toledo Blade*. His stories and illustrations entitled "Dear Mon", which came out in *The Country Gentleman,* made him well known. *Little Mary Mixup in Fairyland* is one of the successful books for children he has written and illustrated. His cartoons are fresh and bright, compellingly funny, capitalizing the fads and activities of the moment. Mr. Brinkerhoff succeeds in recording the variations in the pulse beat of public opinion from day to day. It is an exacting sort of work, but he carries it on with a full knowledge of all the technical rules and practices of the profession. A long list of periodicals have used his work: *Toledo Blade, Cleveland Leader, Cincinnati Post, New York Mail, New York Evening World, The Saturday Evening Post.*

A cartoonist with a wide reputation is E. A. Bushnell, who was for fifteen years or more on the *Cincinnati Post. The Cincinnati Times-Star* published his cartoons for a year or two, until his work was distributed through a Cleveland syndicate. Florida claimed him next, and now he is retired to free-lancing in Cincinnati. He is a very wonderful draughtsman; his cartoons sparkle with originality and brilliancy. Another Cincinnati cartoonist is James A. Whiteford, now on the *Cincinnati Enquirer.* He is layout man, a sketch assignment man, and maker of sport cartoons. His work is noteworthy.

DeVoss Woodward Driscoll, who died in 1916, was a well-known cartoonist and newspaper man of Dayton. He became an expert advertising writer and was head of the advertising department at the National Cash Register Company.

The only well-known woman in the country who executes her ideas in cartoons and comic strips is Edwina Dumm. She began newspaper work in Columbus by making cartoons through the Wilson-Hughes campaign and the declaration of war with Germany for the *Monitor,* a Republican party organ started by Governor Willis, but discontinued after a brief existence. Now she has her studio in New York, and her work is syndicated by the George Matthew Adams

Service. One hundred and fifty papers publish her comic strip called "Cap Stubbs", in which the characters are a boy, and his grandmother, and his dog, "Tippy". The boy is a Tom Sawyer type, a husky high-powered American boy, whom everybody likes — no Little Lord Fauntleroy ties and collars for him! "Tippy" is the outcast dog of the street, just a common little woolly nondescript dog who shares the stage with "Cap" in their many troubles and adventures.

Miss Dumm specializes in picturing dogs. There are women etchers and painters who have won success by drawing dogs, but in nearly every case the dogs have been aristocrats of one breed or another. Miss Dumm chooses dogs that would not win a blue ribbon in any show, but the kind that would be a boy's steadfast pal. For *Life,* she makes a weekly page of a dog called "Sinbad". He is a lively, mischievous fellow who is always just escaping with his life from some escapade. He is a terror, a distress to the boys, to the other dogs, and to all adults; everyone is expecting trouble when "Sinbad" appears. The drawings are well done, the humor is certain to produce many laughs, and the situations are cleverly planned. The "Sinbad" series has been put into book form. A *Book Without Words* would be an appropriate title for it, just as there are songs without words; for words are unnecessary when a story is as realistically and graphically conceived as are Miss Dumm's productions. *Life* uses many of her drawings for cover pages. She illustrated the book, *Two Gentlemen and a Lady,* by Alexander Woollcott, the dramatic critic and great lover of dogs. Personally, Miss Dumm is small, demure, and much interested in athletics. She was born in Upper Sandusky, Ohio. In the field of comic illustration and cartoon making, men are still almost scot-free from feminine competition, as there are very few women in the profession.

The Newspaper Enterprise Association of Cleveland has an eye for rising young talent to add to their comic-art staff. The comic strips they syndicate have the requisite of humor dealing with familiar subjects, and an air of vital, breezy optimism. One of their artists, Gene Ahern of Cleveland, won fame with the "Major Hoople" boarding house series: "Egad" sets everyone thinking of "Major Hoople." "Out Our Way", by Jim Williams of Alliance, made an instant hit. George Clark, author of "Side Glances", entered a contest with seventy-two other artists to draw a poster for the annual Cleveland Community Fund drive. Clark's poster won first prize, five hundred dollars, and was selected for use in similar drives in forty-two American cities. Merrill Blosser, who was once sports cartoonist for *The Cleveland Plain Dealer,* now finds expression in "Freckles and His Friends." Edgar E. Martin, in "Boots and Her

Buddies", makes the most truly feminine character in any comic strip in America; "Boots" marches across the newspaper pages of the nation.

Alfred J. Frueh, born at Lima, Ohio, is one of the most notable caricaturists in New York City; some of his enthusiastic admirers claim that he is America's greatest caricaturist. Noted actors and concert singers have been the subjects of his most remarkable caricatures.

Other Ohioans of note in the cartoon world include the following: Harry Bressler, on *The Dayton News;* Bill Klinger, *The Cleveland Plain Dealer;* Noel Sickles, *The Ohio State Journal;* Web Brown, *The Akron Beacon Journal;* Paton Edwards, *Akron Times-Press;* Jesse Cargill, *Central Press Associated News Syndicate, Cleveland;* Harry Westerman, *The Ohio State Journal;* and H. J. Keys, *Columbus Citizen.*

Many papers have added to their staffs a sports cartoonist who produces a daily drawing about some prominent figure in wrestling, prize fighting, golf, swimming, racing, or other sport. The field is rich in fun and humor. The sketch artist may glorify the victor or reveal some incident of the sport that will have a general appeal.

Much artistic interest has been shifted to the advertising pages of the magazines and newspapers. Advertising is as serious as any other form of art. It is a hopeful sign when big business demands advertisements well designed in every way, spacing, arrangement of printing, and good illutrations to carry the story. The designer of advertising cuts is subjected to severe criticism and keen competition that spurs him on to find new esthetic suggestions in the interpretation of great business undertakings.

American newspaper art has developed in a spirit distinctively native to the soil, though the brevity and seriousness of the French caricature left its influence upon it, and the British tradition of vigorous pen draughtsmanship has been retained. The names of newspaper artists mentioned here do not exhaust the list of Ohioans who have made names for themselves in this kind of work. Young men are coming on all the time who produce work that influences thinking men and women, and the men who have made cartoons for ten or twenty years are still creating them and giving the people the advantage of their mature thought and original thinking. Would a serious, solemn lecture have half as much influence as one of their clever drawings? It may be recalled that Benjamin Franklin was the man who introduced the element of burlesque into American journalism, and that *Poor Richard* was the great comic almanac of the country for many years. Franklin wrote: "Pieces of pleasantry and mirth have a secret charm in them to allay the heats and tumults of our spirit, and to make a man forget his restless resentments. They have a strange power in them to hush disorders of the soul and reduce us to a serene and placid state of mind."[7]

There is every indication that in the future the influence of the cartoon will steadily increase. The newspaper realizes that its cartoons may reflect its policy more powerfully than any staid editorial column. The public, the average everyday man and woman, enjoys the wit, the sarcasm, if any, and the logic that is found so clearly, concisely, and cleverly expressed in the work of the newspaper artists.

---

[7] Quoted in *Caricature and Comic Art,* Parton, p. 303.

CHAPTER XII

Some Prominent Ohio Painters, 1900 to 1930

WHAT would one not give to have a glance, fifty years hence, of the art of today? What will be said of it after it has been in a museum fifty years? There will doubtless be some important changes in the valuation of the art of 1932! There are kaleidoscopic changes in life, and with them comes the change in our views of art. At least a fresh outlook relieves the monotony and weariness of many art shows, where there is no such thing as originality. The final task of judging modern work must be left to the future, which "pronounces lastly on each deed." In the development of a new style there are always mistakes and folly and ugliness, but time will weed them out. Many people worry unnecessarily about the product that will in years to come represent the art in America today. There is no cause for worry at all; only the best will survive. Works made to be the last word may be ignored in a few years.

There is no attempt here to analyze, piecemeal, each picture that is mentioned. The work of the critic is beyond these boundaries. Whistler, in *The Gentle Art of Making Enemies,* says: "No! Let there be no critics! They are not a necessary evil! But an evil quite unnecessary, though an evil certainly. Harm they do, and not good. Furnished as they are with the means of furthering their foolishness, they spread prejudice abroad; and through the papers, at their service, thousands are warned against the work they have yet to look upon. . . . Eloquence alone shall guide them and the readiest writer or wordiest talker is perforce their professor."[1]

CINCINNATI[2]

John H. Sharp, like another Cincinnati painter, Farny, has made a specialty of the American Indian. Mr. Sharp is now a veteran painter and is still exhibiting virile work. He has a foundation of thorough art training, received in American and European centers, lastly with Duveneck in Spain.

He paints the American Indian with historical correctness as few other men

---

[1] *The Gentle Art of Making Enemies,* Whistler, p. 31.

[2] It is always worth while to keep in touch with the art of Cincinnati, and note its progress from year to year. Through the interesting letters of Mary L. Alexander, published weekly in the *Cincinnati Enquirer,* it is easy to follow the activities of artists there. Her letters have been a storehouse of information from which have been drawn many of the facts concerning the Cincinnati artists dealt with in this chapter.

have painted him (Plate 99). He spends his winters near the Custer battlefield on the Crow Reservation of Montana, where the United States Government built and maintains a studio for him. Becoming interested in the Southwest, he allied himself with the the Taos colony of painters, and there one finds him in the summers. In 1900, twelve of his portraits of famous Indians and a number of landscapes were purchased for the Smithsonian Institution in Washington. Mrs. Phœbe Hearst bought eighty of his Indian pictures for the University of California and gave him a commission for many more. Mr. Sharp's pictorial record of the Indian is invaluable.

Now that Taos is on the route of so many tourists, his studio there is one of the show places. It is built in the old-style Mexican architecture, with one window that overlooks the Taos Valley, and it is from this window that he paints many of the far-reaching views that one sees in his paintings. Here he has painted the moonlight and firelight pictures so familiarly known among his works. Mr. Sharp is a sincere painter, endeavoring to translate the effects that exist in nature; thus his work is convincing in its appeal.

Among the great artists of the country, there is no hesitation in naming Edward Henry Potthast, who was born in Cincinnati and received his training in that city. He was one of a small coterie of artists (including Sharp and others) forming a life class that later merged into the Art Club, and was taken over by Duveneck, who gave them criticisms on Sunday mornings. He loved to paint sunlight, and children playing at the seashore; these subjects formed his most usual themes. They were expressed in extremely popular pictures, especially the one called, "A Holiday", which hangs in the Chicago Art Institute. It is full of sunlight, shining on the children's faces, their yellow hair, and their light summer dresses. The waves roll in and dash up in whitecaps; the colored shadows dance and ripple on the water. The wide sea meets the sky almost at the top of the canvas. Ten little children are having a fine time playing in the sand, and the canvas is exuberant of life and fun. No wonder that the children love this picture.

Potthast painted landscapes that were solid and realistic, always with a broad, sincere presentation of nature. He pictured the Grand Canyon with all its supreme gorgeousness of color. The color quality of his pictures makes the strongest appeal. "In Gloucester Harbor", has the same gay spirit of his seaside groups, but it is not an ordinary subject for him. Whatever he painted—"Dutch Interior", hazy day, the sea, or the myriad effects of sunlight—it had great power expressed through an apparently easy effort.

The art of Charles S. Kaelin takes one back to Duveneck, and one recalls

PLATE 99—Indian Chief. J. H. Sharp. (Cincinnati Museum of Art)

the great friendship of the two artists and their work together for many summers in Massachusetts. Duveneck's influence is apparent in some of the painting Kaelin did there, especially a large picture in lively color of sea, sky, and rocks entitled "The Granite Shore at Gloucester."

Lithography was the profession Kaelin originally followed, and he was an expert in that field, following the teachings of his Swiss father. The art of painting appealed to him first through the medium of pastel, and then it became his whole vocation. He did nothing by halves. He seemed to be a full-fledged painter from the start. About twenty-five of his beautiful pastels were exhibited in Cincinnati and won him recognition at once. Duveneck saw the great merit in these pastels and recommended them to the general chairman of the Panama-Pacific Exposition, Mr. J. E. D. Trask, who immediately invited Mr. Kaelin to exhibit them at the exposition. He did so, and the pastels were awarded a silver medal there. After that event a few of his pictures sold, but he was never a promoter of the sale of his work. He loved to paint, but when a picture was finished, he was through with it. It was through his friends, always, that his pictures were framed and exhibited. He lived in the most meager circumstances, actually in need and often suffering privation.

After a time, Mr. Kaelin abandoned pastel painting and began the use of oil. He established his studio in a little fisherman's shanty at Rockport, and lived there twenty years. Most of his views of the sea and Rockport harbor were painted from the little window of that shanty. His life at Rockport reminds one of Winslow Homer, in that each lived the life of a recluse and was called a hermit painter.

Kaelin was satisfied to paint the same view over and over again with only slight variations; possibly he was lacking in initiative, but the quality of his work was never questioned. Nature moved him deeply; his response was genuine and truthful in color, mass, and atmosphere. Petty details he avoided; each object was given the value it had in nature. His aim was to paint sincerely, and the artists agree that he reached his goal. Mr. Kaelin entered the painting class that Twachtman taught when he came back from Munich, and was one who continued the subtle painting of Twachtman's style. It is noticeable in many of the Rockport pictures: "Rocks and Coast Woods", for example, "is Twachtmanesque[3] in its mood and delicacy; the lavenders, blues, and greens of a coastal wood, fairly bloom with light."[4]

Mr. Kaelin's later canvases were in the nature of wood interiors, with such

---

[3] See Chapter IV, *ante.*
[4] The *Cincinnati Enquirer,* February 16, 1930, Mary L. Alexander.

descriptive titles as "Magic Frost," "Fall Tapestry," "Spring Snow in the Woods," "Mystery," "December Woods," and "Winter Abstraction." These studies represent a change in his technique, showing the tapestry effects of the impressionists. Rich color-spots characterize this phase of his work; light and shade play among the thick foliage of the trees, and there is an instinctive feeling for pattern. These pictures are excellent delineations of forests that few painters have equalled. He commanded the greatest respect and admiration from the artist fraternity for the true paint-quality of his work.

Edward C. Volkert is one of the earlier pupils of Duveneck[5] and reflects much credit upon that powerfully influential painter of Cincinnati. He has made a name for himself as a cattle painter, and is undoubtedly one of the best in the country. Pure landscapes and snow scenes interest him, but his favorite portrayal is of cattle grazing quietly on a hill, by the sea, or in a rough pasture land. He seldom pictures cattle in their stalls or sheds. When they are in a landscape, it is brought up to the same standard of excellence with which the cattle are painted; where there is a tree, it is done carefully, and is made to add a decorative quality. Volkert's feeling for landscapes is thus closely joined with his cattle themes. The appearance of the herds in the early morning, when the shifting lights give charm and many changing colors to the background is the setting that gives him his fondest inspiration. He uses small dots of pure broken color, one juxtaposed against the other, to give the vivid effect of high sunlight. His brush work is facile, his draughtsmanship faultless.

"New England Pastures," by Mr. Volkert, was purchased for the Hughes High School, Cincinnati. The movement to hang original paintings in the schools ought to be commended and encouraged, and it is fortunate that such a fine painting was selected for the purpose in this instance. This canvas has a freshness, a wholesomeness, and a fine out-of-door feeling that will influence the children to cultivate a greater love of nature, and it will develop in them a finer appreciation of good paintings. Such daily contacts will make children intolerant of inferior painting. Many of Mr. Volkert's pictures suggest the skies and cattle of Holland, but they are truly American. This scene of New England has an expanse of sky patterned with clouds fascinating to the eye. "The Wood Pasture," is one of his interesting studies of sunlight; as the glow comes through the leaves, the shadows make a pattern of lace on the cow's body. "Pastures by the Sea." is another New England setting in which a herd of cattle is shown grazing peacefully along the shore.

The studio of Mr. Volkert is at Old Lyme, Connecticut, in the rural scenery

---

[5] See Chapter IV, *ante*.

PLATE 100—Day Dreams. H. H. Wessel. Owned by Dr. Albert Freiberg. (Artist)

he has presented in his paintings. The art center at Old Lyme is an ideal place for him to paint. Henry W. Ranger was among the first painters to discover Old Lyme, and he gathered a group of enthusiastic coworkers around him. Miss Florence Griswold gave these artists a home under her hospitable roof and encouraged them in every way. The visitor today may see on the paneled walls of her home the work of such noted American artists as Childe Hassam, Bruce Crane, William H. Howe, Willard Metcalf, and several others. Old Lyme held its first exhibition in 1902 in the public library; in 1922 it built its own gallery on land adjoining Miss Griswold's home. The town has become famous as a painting field. Visitors go there by the thousands from all parts of the country when the annual exhibition opens with great festivities early in August. Ohio is proud to be represented in that distinguished colony by such an able artist as Mr. Volkert.

Out-of-door painting fascinates Paul Ashbrook. His paintings in oil of Spain and Majorca have a strong racial flavor, and exhibit a daringly vivid coloring. Mexico offered him many paintable subjects — bridges, mountains, street corners — which he caught with much enthusiasm and fidelity. The same mastery that one finds in his etchings is exhibited in his paintings.

The prominence of Herman H. Wessel as a painter has been rightly earned by his fine pictorial design, his use of color, and well-balanced composition. His striking canvases both in oil and water color prove him a superb painter, and link his name with that of his master, Duveneck. As to subject, Wessel's field is extensive. Landscapes with rich color flashing through them, he paints in an easy technique, which reveals his ability to enliven their inherent beauty into even gayer scenes that abound in pleasure. Clean-cut portraits devoid of shadows, modeled against dark blue backgrounds, emphasize the modern note. In decorative figure painting, he uses for the main motif a partially nude figure painted against soft green-and-old-rose foliage background (Plate 100). The term *distingué* can be applied appropriately to his colors, which he plays together as an orchestration.

A number of landscapes painted by Mr. Wessel in Brittany, Spain, the Balearic Islands, and Bavaria, give such a delightful general impression at first glance, that one must stop to analyze their art values and grasp the fine points in their technical creation. Color is brilliantly handled, and creates the mood in most instances. The South of France and St. Tropez furnish subjects for many of his pictures that are revels in the Mediterranean blue. "The Docks at St. Tropez" and "Fountain at St. Tropez" are two of his finest landscapes in oil; both are impressionistic and luminous. "The Paris Bookstalls" brings charming reminisences of those age-old rows of miniature shops along the Seine. The river is treated with atmospheric effect, and the trees along the bank add much to the pattern; the quaint characters thumbing the old books and prints are painted with authority and vividness. Paris streets and unfrequented corners Mr. Wessel has used as favorite expressions of sojourns there.

Recent European contacts have brought some change in his work. Entangling alliances of motifs in his painting entitled "Music," are quite confusing and laugh-provoking. "It is very amusing, and is a color impression of a Parisian brass band, and we have reason to believe that his European experience has given him a new outlook on the principles of modern art."[6] Mrs. (Bessie Hoover) Wessel is a painter, also, and one of her fine decorative portraits recently exhibited shows that she, too, has fallen under the spell of the Parisian modern trends.

The entire range of painting executed by Mr. Wessel is wholesome and exhilarating. One feels that he has mixed his paint with some of the pleasure he experienced in painting, and thus he has imparted a very personal note to his canvases. As instructor at the Cincinnati Art Academy, Mr. Wessel has been of inestimable value to art education.

Dixie Selden speaks beautifully of her master, Frank Duveneck, and her output speaks eloquently of him, too. She attacks her work with a directness that is born from Duveneck's teaching. Her technique is fluent, her stroke is fresh, vigorous, and dexterous, whether she is painting a portrait or a flower composition. Her portrait of Duveneck won much favorable comment at the Pennsylvania Academy of Fine Arts in 1919, and was reproduced as an illustration for the exhibit catalogue. Part of the attention given it was naturally from interest in the subject, but none the less because of Miss Selden's success in achieving a wonderful likeness of Duveneck (Plate 101). She does not stop at recording the correct physiognomy and characteristic pose; she always makes one feel the spirit and personality of the sitter. She is sympathetic, and sensitive to the emotional qualities, and has the necessary command of technique to put her interpretation of a character upon canvas with sureness. In many of her portraits the sitter has a direct glance that conveys an immediate contact with the observer. She has painted portraits of many notables of her home city and elsewhere; of Doctor Charles Frederick Hicks, president of the University of Cincinnati from 1900 to 1927; of Elizabeth Gutman Kaye, the celebrated singer of Hungarian and Russian folk songs; and of many others.

Of Brittany, Miss Selden made many accurate and interesting studies. "The

---

[6] The *Cincinnati Enquirer,* November 2, 1930, Mary L. Alexander.

Blue Net, Concarneau", is a gay and brilliantly colored composition of sardine boats anchored in the bay while their sails are drying. Calm, dignified Breton peasants in colorful costumes depicted with all the fidelity of her portraits, are redolent of the very spirit and environment of that charming land. In Spain, Portugal, and Morocco, she painted canvases which reflect the enthusiasm of first impressions. She obtained the effects of brilliant colors under the semi-tropical sun in canvases that possess a highly decorative value. "The Garden of the Royal Washington Irving Hotel, Granada", is delightful in an all-over interest made by the orange umbrellas over the tables, bright sunlight flickering in between yellow-green foliage, and the black suits of the waiters enhancing the colors — the whole composed into a beautiful pattern. A landscape with the very characteristic mountains and distance of Spain is seen in "The Alhambra," one of her finest works, spontaneous in effect, and showing frank brushwork. She paints flower studies such as "Dahlias", and "Petunias", in the same distinctive flowing manner, rich in marvelous color harmonies.

More recent work of Miss Selden has been done in Mexico. Dark-skinned Mexicans wearing huge sombreros furnished picturesque subjects for her brush to chronicle in her usual masterly fashion. In several pictures the landscape background reaches into far vistas. The pure landscapes without incidents in the foreground found an interest for her in Mexico. In one glorious sky picture, "Clouds," there is great beauty in the movement of the clouds and the carefully modeled earth forms. "The Outskirts of Taxco" presents a church spire in the middle distance where the street lines converge; blue mountains extend into a wide background giving a feeling of great space. The color pattern is vivid but delightful with painted sunshine on the road, the houses, and the orange-red roofs.

Miss Dixie Selden is one of the most loved personages in Cincinnati. Of her Mrs. Alexander writes this happy encomium: "We always owe a debt of gratitude for her paintings. They jog us out of the monotony of dullness of everyday life into a joyous mood. There is something so very deft and gracious about them that it casts a glamour over all."

Brilliant effects in that subtle medium, water color, have brought fame to Emma Mendenhall, another pupil of Duveneck. A just estimate of her art is obtained only by considering the tonal values in her skillful handling of free-wash. Her workmanship compels admiration. Careful plans for her pictures insure the correct pigment at the first touch, and prepare the right contact of brush and paper for transparency and fluid brilliancy. Sometimes she uses opaque water color. Her pure water-color pictures are very beautiful.

PLATE 101—Portrait of Frank Duveneck. Dixie Selden. (Cincinnati Museum of Art)

Miss Mendenhall loved to paint the market scenes in small villages of Normandy and Brittany, recording their characteristic peasant costumes and color. A much higher pitch of color, naturally demanded by the character of the country, comes in her paintings made more recently in Spain and Morocco. Water color is the exact medium with which to capture the emotional delight in Spanish gardens, of which she made a pictorial series. The Arab garden is a captive garden, enclosed in patios where time itself seems to linger. Graceful archways, walls where the fragrant jasmine climbs, quivering rows of cypresses, delicate clustering myrtles, yews and laurels, and the heavenly blue tiles — all these, and more, with water that rushes and splashes in channels and fountains, are found in her paintings of the Generalife and Alhambra gardens. "The Gate of Justice", and "The Gypsy Caves", though opposite in dignity and grandeur, are beautiful in color and in their truthful interpretation of Spain.

Rapid changes of light, color, and movement characterize the painting of Miss Mendenhall in Mexico, where as in Spain, she gets all the glory of a tropical country. It is not surprising that the fields most alluring to the modern painter are northern Africa and Mexico. She happily selects the most typical Mexican scenes; slow-moving, lazy peons with no thought of tomorrow, sleepy little towns for the moment alive with venders, heavily loaded burros trudging along, or landscapes with an abundance of cacti. From the crevice of an old wall, a Bougainvillæa vine gives an esthetic note of purple to a common fountain square where the people do their family washing. None of Miss Mendenhall's paintings are more individual than her sketch-pad records of Mexico. Used swiftly, for notes or sketches, water color becomes as autobiographical as handwriting. It lends itself to those lighter moods in which the artist pictures the gayety of a passing scene, or comments with humor or satire on the drama enacted before him.

Miss Mendenhall executes portraits in the fascinating medium, pastel. Her genius asserts itself in the use of colored crayons, their flower-like color being especially suited to women's portraits. In making a portrait she grasps the psychology of the sitter, virtually drawing him out of himself. Her portraits think and speak, lifting her art above that of the mere technician; she possesses the ability to comprehend the whole nature of the subject. Pastel has a soft, ethereal quality that makes it an admirable medium for treating subjects with poetical feeling.

The achievements of John E. Weis are noteworthy, both in portraits and in landscape. It is interesting to review exhibits of his work and note his remarkable progress. Among his early portraits is a small, red-headed boy, whom he

PLATE 102—Portrait of Miss Hake. John E. Weis. (Artist)

dubbed "Carrots"; character is realized with every brush stroke, and the plain little fellow speaks for himself. It is done with splendid color and craftsmanship. A fine character drawing is the portrait of Rabbi David Philipson, of the Rockdale Avenue Temple, Cincinnati. The eyes are keen and sharp, the bearing that of an aristocrat — calm and stately. The spots of light made by the hands and face are contrasted with the dark to make an interesting balance. The portrait is not cluttered with unnecessary details, masses being the dominant factors. Mr. Weis succeeds in the structure of heads and forms, giving the essentials of anatomy that carry the suggestion of a real figure (Plate 102).

In the portrait of Doctor Augustus Ravogli, Mr. Weis has given a free interpretation of the man who has rendered such valuable service to the State Medical Association and to the University of Cincinnati. A keen observation of facial details and an acute sensitiveness to personality are traits that this painter possesses. A remarkable quality in this picture is the characteristic posture which the sitter exhibits: Doctor Ravogli sits in his office chair, with shoulders slightly raised from resting his arms on the high arms of the chair— no doubt his most frequent attitude.

Weis paints some portraits in the bold manner of Robert Henri. Of George Dent Crabbs, he made an outdoor portrait — an ensemble which is very difficult to paint because of the conflicting lights. The whole setting is a happy one. Mr. Crabb sits in a wicker chair on the porch, with much color, and light and shade playing an important part in the picture, and intensifying the alert character of the man.

In many fine landscapes and figure paintings one is impressed with the versatility of Weis, and always remarks his strong, vigorous brushwork. Among his landscapes are a number of spirited snow scenes inspired for the nonce by the influence of Gardner Symonds. Mr. Weis has painted many views of Gloucester, Massachusetts. Docks, wharves, rickety old houses, a mackerel sky, sunny rocks, a fine old tree, or an expanse of blue sea with weight and movement — all of these he painted in his virile way. "New Paint", is a boat at the dock; he has made one feel the huge bulk and weight of the vessel so realistically, that it almost plunges out of the picture. He responds quickly and determines to reproduce his reactions to a selected scene. He makes one feel the atmospheric quality of the setting. "Charm" is the word to be used in thinking of his old New England houses. He makes effective designs of the spots of sunlight forming delicate tracery on the dazzling white houses. Light and air play a frolic around them. These canvases are treated in a decorative manner, the color making handsome tapestries. He inspires the feel of age-old charm in these houses.

PLATE 103—Ohio River, Cincinnati. Frank H. Myers. Owned by Dr. Mislin. (Artist)

One cannot fail to be enthusiastic about the painting of Mr. Weis, whether in portraits or landscape; he builds up a perfect ensemble with all the parts in harmony. The quality of his work may be explained in a measure by the background of his sound training with Duveneck, Meakin, Hopkins, and Wessel at the Cincinnati Art Academy.

John Rettig painted excellent pictures of Holland and Venice. He was a master poet of the brush for these countries with a hazy air and a peculiarly soft gray light. The picturesque costumes of the Isle of Marken, and the Dutch windmills have attracted scores and scores of artists. Mr. Rettig gave one unusual intimate bits of Dutch interiors, and again produced general panoramas of the low country with its countless herds of cattle and rank green salt grass being cut for hay. Can an inlander like an Ohioan imagine hay being pitched onto a boat instead of a wagon? This painter took one to the fish market, visited an old Dutch Reformed church, or gave a picture of the dyke; yet they were all landscapes of the simplest kind, but beautifully painted ,with emphasis only upon the vital things that give significance to the picture. "The Knitter", is an adorable Dutch figure, directly lighted, in an indoor setting. His subjects were chosen to represent characteristics of the Dutch, of Volendam particularly, that he was so fond of painting.

Cincinnati has other fine artists trained by Duveneck who are carrying on his traditions in a way that reflects credit to their master and to themselves; among them are Martin Rettig (considered an expert in identifying Duveneck paintings), Effie Corwin Trader, Frances Wiley Faig, and Alma Knauber, whose major interest has always been painting landscape in water color.

Stephen and Elizabeth Heil Alke find their themes in the landscape of the Ohio River Valley; whether they are portraying harvest time, a crisp fall morning, blooming spring or snow-bound winter, there is loveliness everywhere in their canvases. Mr. and Mrs. Alke have a similarity of style, both enter into full sympathy with the moods of nature. There is no human interest in their canvases. "Their compositions are determined by the slope of a hill, the sweep of a meadow, the winding of a brook and the aspect of the environing nature—nature which to them seems to bring calm contentment and happiness because they are in accord with it; they are pupils of nature."[7] Mrs. Alke paints beautiful studies of flowers and still life — begonias, peonies, and other flowers grown at their farm in the valley where they paint those peaceful scenes so much admired.

Annette Covington is doing remarkable work in pencil portrait drawings, as

---

[7] The *Cincinnati Enquirer,* November 2, 1930, Mary L. Alexander.

well as in other kinds of creative expression. Miss Covington, through her activity in the Cincinnati Women's Art Club, is an invaluable aid to the cause of art in Cincinnati.

Frank H. Myers is an artist who received his training largely from Mr. Wessel. He displays an extraordinary sense of design in his decorative paintings, though his work includes portraits, still-life studies, and landscapes. In his earlier landscapes, he painted nature just as it is in the Cincinnati environment of Mt. Adams and Burnet Woods, or as he found it in the scenes depicted in his "Sycamores" in Michigan, or on the "California Coast", or in "The Spanish Port". These canvases are all fine transcriptions of nature, but present little of the creative imagination of his later work. Children enjoying the sport of sledding down the Cincinnati hills are represented in a winter landscape that reminds one of Peter Breughel in the way the bare trees and little figures are scattered over the canvas. It is called, "Old Man Winter." Still life he paints for the sheer joy of form and color; his gifts are diversified (Plate 103).

The portraits executed by Mr. Myers must be given consideration. There is an unusual informality in the portrait of John Bunker, smoking. The artist knows the value of a hand in a portrait, introducing it holding the pipe in a characteristic posture. In the elegant and refined portrait of Miss Bertha Bauer, of the Cincinnati Conservatory of Music, is exemplified the direct grasp of character in which this artist excels. It is handsomely painted in a competent style. The portraits of John Sage and Augustus Palm are other notable products of his brush.

Interesting as Mr. Myers is in landscape and portrait, his forte is in decorative painting, which he has made the basis of experimentation for several years. No doubt a style of art is a habit of thought. He has worked to make his pattern fill the space and suggest a satisfied completion. "The Burden" admirably reaches that goal, and recalls a Japanese print in its design of a stooped figure carrying a great load on its back. "The Son of the Soil", solves a design problem with no trepidation, and organizes the rich color and interesting shapes to form a combination exhibiting a pleasing unity. A farmer with his white plowhorses are the principal parts of the design, but the sky and the undulating hills also function in it.

"Mr. Myers has been more somber in the use of color in 'The Woman and the Broom'; the color is just as rich though not as brilliant, and it is an even more solidly-built-up structural design. Depth is obtained by structural units, which are houses and roads that impel the eye to travel back into the far field of the vision. This is called by some modernists 'the design of recession in

PLATE 104—A Cumberland Silhouette. James R. Hopkins. (Artist)

painting', and it is the new means of obtaining perspective."[8] The future of decorative painting as developed by Mr. Myers will be worth taking into account. A pupil of the Cincinnati Art Academy, under Frank Myers, is Leah Verity Hook of Middletown, who is attaining distinction as a painter of portraits and Arizona landscapes.

The art critics have given unstinted recognition to Marie Rauchfuss (Macpherson). She studied with Frank Duveneck at the Cincinnati Art Academy, and with Harry Stickroth at the Chicago Art Institute. It is not far from the mark to say that training practically guarantees work that bears the stamp of quality, when the student has the ability of Marie Rauchfuss. Her paintings have been exhibited at the Carnegie International, the National Academy of Design, the Architectural League of New York, the Chicago Art Institute, not to mention many lesser exhibitions, and have received a great number of awards. The Hoosier Salon, held in Chicago in 1930, awarded her a special prize for the outstanding picture by a woman artist. The flower pictures she paints are exquisite.

From sea to sea, Julie Morrow De Forest draws material for her impressionistic landscapes. Looking over her pictures will carry one from New England cottages, and Provincetown motifs, through the Ohio River Valley, on to the Pacific Coast. Whatever site she selects reveals luminous transcription with a subjective aspect that evidences the painter's emotional reaction to the beautiful color and the sensitive moods of nature. Among her successful large paintings inspired by Cincinnati scenes are some interesting old houses seen through a sparkling effect of sun and foliage, similar to pictures painted at Old Lyme, Connecticut, by members of that colony. An appreciation of early American houses is seen in other architectural themes — "Marblehead Doorway", "Sunlit Gables", and "A Rose Arbor" — painted with all their inherent charm and quaintness and made into decorative landscapes skillfully handled. Mrs. De-Forest's paintings are enveloped in light and atmosphere, with plenty of freedom in color and a cheerfulness that is contagious.

Louis Endres paints in oil and water color particularly brilliant Moroccan landscapes and figures. The interesting natives, the clear sunlight and contrasting shadows of that region have a certain fascination for him. In his pictures there is an insistence on pattern, conscientious draughtsmanship in every line and form, a broad and vivid rendering, pure color and fine harmonies. The Atlas Mountains, the heart of the desert, the shopping districts radiant with hanging textiles, a succession of fine old Moorish arches, or architectural

---

[8] The *Cincinnati Enquirer,* October 19, 1930, Mary L. Alexander.

interiors he renders with greatest sympathy, adding the picturesque figures of camels and their drivers, a group of Moroccans squatting on the street, or a girl reclining on a rug, to make the environment complete. He has gone farther into Africa and painted fields that few artists have reached.

Reginald Grooms secures a great variety in his work, from the more conventional mode of treating a subject to painting in the modern idiom. He can turn to a sensitive treatment of light and air when the subject is appropriate. In his New England scenes he stresses the design in nature, using rich color and adhering to a realistic treatment of a simple composition. With a restricted palette, this water-color painter can do more than indicate form and pattern; he makes a unity of the two, and even with the limited colors gives his color tones more strength. Imagination is not lacking in his modern manner, the quality of fantasy and emotion being very noticeable. His painting, "Noon", was hung at the June, 1931, Cincinnati Art Museum exhibit. Arthur Helwig, like Mr. Grooms, is a product of the Cincinnati Art Academy, who is attracting considerable attention and much favorable comment. Myer Abel, too, paints with modern feeling; it will be interesting to watch the development of these younger men.

A partial list of Cincinnati murals follows: The University of Cincinnati boasts murals by H. H. Wessel, L. H. Meakin, Frances Wiley Faig, and others; the Woodward High School has decorations by E. C. Volkert; the Westwood High School murals are by Harland J. Johnson and Francis W. Swain; Evanston School shows murals by Norbert Heermann; the Hughes High School murals are by H. H. Wessel and John E. Weis; and there are murals by Ernest F. Tyler in the Union Central Life building.[9]

Cincinnati has developed a definite center for batik dying, with Charles Stewart Todd leading in this craft. To create beautiful and appropriate designs is indeed an art, and here Mr. Todd has given time and thought to specific problems of interior decorations. Outstanding examples of his work are the French Gothic panels which he made for the entrance hall of the home of Mr. and Mrs. Otto Luedeking, of Cincinnati. William Hentschel holds a

---

[9] Ohio has many fine mural paintings in the public buildings of its larger cities, and even in some smaller county seat towns. How many have seen the delightful mural in Coshocton? In its county courthouse is "Bouquet's Expedition," by Arthur Woelfle; there is another mural by him in the Mahoning County courthouse at Youngstown. Edwin H. Blashfield was awarded the gold medal of the New York Architectural League in 1911 for a series of murals decorating the dome of the Mahoning County courthouse. The series is considered among the best of the artist's work, and depicts four periods of law: the Mosaic Law; the Roman Law; the Ecclesiastical Law; and the Common Law of England. Banks in many smaller cities have notable murals, one of the largest being in the Old National City Bank at Lima. There are interesting murals to be found in many clubs, hotels and theatres throughout the State, but they suffer from the usual neglect on the part of the public, because attention is not called to them through adequate publicity.

PLATE 105—Figure. James R. Hopkins. (Artist)

unique place as a decorative artist of creative ability; his designs take novel forms and his color-organizations are amazingly beautiful. Dolly Ernst, Henrietta Fischer, Lucy Radtke, and Anita Fenton are other Cincinnatians specializing in the field of batiks.

The artists of Cincinnati win renown for impressive technical accomplishments. The spirit of art that dominated that city in the nineties continues to manifest itself, and the beauty of the past is alive and dynamic as it comes into harmony with the esthetics of the present.

COLUMBUS

The spell of the Cumberland Mountains invited James R. Hopkins to explore the artistic possibilities of that singularly picturesque region. He was the first painter to discover the appeal of the Kentucky mountaineers of the Cumberland Gap, famous from the days when Daniel Boone trailed it, and at the time of the Civil War known as one of the strategic gateways to the South. Its mountain caves, dense woods and turbulent brooks, its deep valleys and moonshine stills, and above all, its taciturn mountaineers, suggested to Mr. Hopkins ideal pictures with something crudely romantic about them.

These primitive Kentuckians had furnished themes for song and story; had been the subjects for exhaustive sociological research, were beneficiaries of the Rockefeller Foundation; and yet they furnished a virgin field to the painter. Mr. Hopkins has proved that the Indian is not the only picturesque figure in America. His very studies of the mountaineers have an important place in the folk annals of America. The typical long-legged, awkward mountaineers he painted truthfully not only in physique, but in expression. Much praise has been given him for painting these types exactly as he saw them. In 1919, when "A Mountain Courtship", was exhibited, it created a furor as one of the most interesting canvases painted in America in many years. The picture shows two lovers, hand in hand, walking along the banks of the Cumberland. The purple haze of a late afternoon falls over the river and the wooded hillside beyond. The lovelorn swain is a weak-minded youth in appearance, the girl is fresh and wistful, while the girl's mother, who stalks in front of them a short distance, is grim and severe. The painter has expressed true sentiment in the picture, a bit of heartfelt mood, and it is plausible that its message has touched many hearts. Several of the museums very quickly acquired the canvases representing other aspects of this individual theme of his (Plate 104).

One of the most extraordinary mountaineer characters that Mr. Hopkins painted was "Andy", the local preacher. First he pictured him with an ax in

PLATE 106—Kitty Anne Cockley. Alice Schille. (Artist)

hand, standing beside the whitewashed woodshed. Later was painted "The Circuit Rider", showing "Andy" as a preacher, dressed in a black-and-white striped shirt, open at the neck, with his Bible under his arm, and seated on a white, somnolent mule. The lean, wiry, figure, with haggard Spanish-like face, is endowed with rugged strength; the mountain winds and rains have tanned his skin. His corded hands hold the reins; under the saddle is a brightly colored patchwork quilt or pad. The ensemble is a splendid piece of work. On week days "Andy" came to town to sell vegetables and poultry from his farm. Another canvas shows him in that vocation, a chicken under each arm, standing before a background of bold foliage. Dramatic in the fullest sense of the word is "The Moonshiner." Just inside the entrance to a cave sits the outlaw, holding a gun in his hand; a strong light plays on his tense face. Some of the admirers of Mr. Hopkins's painting of the mountaineers have called him the Millet of the Cumberland. In his interest in these people, he never forgets the pattern he sets out to make, nor loses sight of their artistic qualities.

At the present, Mr. Hopkins is engaged in decorative figure painting, the type of work he did before painting in Kentucky. After a thorough academic training with Duveneck in Cincinnati, and with other masters in Paris, he went to Japan, the source of inspiration for so many American artists. With Mrs. Hopkins (see page 264) he made a tour of the world, studying in Japan, China, Ceylon, and Egypt. "The Bamboo Screen" is a reflection of that Oriental influence. A woman dressed in a Japanese kimono, her back to the observer, stands looking through a bamboo screen. Both subject and treatment suggest the Japanese print, Whistleresque perhaps. The design is beautiful, due to Mr. Hopkins's wonderful grasp of spacing and arrangement.

Dreamy figures against colored backgrounds (Plate 105) Mr. Hopkins executes with consummate mastery of pigment. His work is sane, and his compositions are attacked with amazing sureness. "Each stroke is premeditated, whether the spaces and harmonies of color are to resolve themselves into the form of a nude or a preacher."[10]

Many strongly characterized portraits are the product of his brush, among them the portraits of General Edward Orton, Jr., Dr. W. O. Thompson, and Mrs. Nicholas Longworth; each displays a fine sympathy and insight into the character of the particular person. There is always a breadth and expansiveness to this artist's work, the result of an active mind working directly and simply, without need of resorting to tricks or accessories. He commands the respect of the critics and the admiration of the public. Mr. Hopkins is the only asso-

---

[10] *International Studio,* February, 1918, E. B. Haswell.

ciate member of the National Academy residing in Ohio.[11] Many honors have been awarded him at home and abroad. Art education has a serious interest for him. After the death of his master, Frank Duveneck, he took his place on the faculty of the Cincinnati Art Academy. He is now chairman and professor of the department of fine arts at Ohio State University. A legion of fine artists owe their training to his sound instruction.

Alice Schille is probably the foremost woman painter in Ohio. She is not "without honor in her own country", for Columbus appreciates her artistic achievements and is justly proud of the many honors that have been conferred upon her. She has endeared herself to her home city. Her paintings in oil have a permanent interest, because they are not of any particular time, locality or environment. They are beautiful interpretations of life in many phases: in little children, in old folks, in the trees, flowers and sunshine.

In making portraits of children, Miss Schille has produced work worthy of a true artist. Such engaging child-life pictures are the spontaneous output of one who knows children as they are, and loves them with an understanding that can not be counterfeited. "Miss Nancy", "Anne and Beau", and "Kitty Anne Cockley" (Plate 106) are a few of the captivating children she has portrayed; their expressions are animated, and their faces have a winning brightness.

"The Little Nurse", won the prize at the Women's Art Club of New York in 1908. It depicts the head and shoulders of an invalid, perhaps the mother, who lies in bed; a little Dutch maid, wearing a quaint cap and black gown, is perched on the side of the bed. The eyes of the mother are turned lovingly toward the little nurse, who is the center of interest in the picture. Every detail of the maiden — from the coquettish tilt of her head bent over the knitting in her hands, to the peeping forth of her wooden shoes on the stool where they rest — endears her to the critic and disarms objection if there could be any. The rare quality of this picture lies in its power to take one into the atmosphere of tender solicitude and loving understanding that makes one feel not

---

[11] The part Ohioans have played in the history of the National Academy of Design is of great interest and a matter for congratulation. To be elected to membership in that organization is the greatest American honor that can come to a native artist. This association of artists was founded in 1825; it has maintained a free school for art students since its organization, and yearly holds two exhibitions of the current art of the country. In the more than one hundred years of its existence, it has had sixteen presidents, and of them three were Ohioans: J. Q. A. Ward, who served 1873-'74, Worthington Whittredge serving from 1874 to 1877, and Cass Gilbert, from 1926 to the present. In the list of deceased academicians are twenty-four men from Ohio; present members from Ohio number six, and associate members three, as follows: Ernest L. Blumenschein, N.A.; Charles C. Curran, N.A.; Cullen Yates, N.A.; Evelyn B. Longman (Batchelder), N.A.; Charles H. Neihaus, N.A.; Cass Gilbert, N.A.; John Ward Dunsmore, A.N.A.; James R. Hopkins, A.N.A., and Edward C. Volkert, A.N.A. Many of the prizes awarded annually by the academy have been bestowed upon the artists of Ohio.

the poverty of the peasants, but rather the wealth of love that enriches their lives. Miss Schille is keenly sensitive to the spirit, mood, or temper of her subject, and adds that honesty and completeness of her own which make a painting a work of art.

Splendid bits of impressionism are Miss Schille's brilliant water-color pictures of many countries. In "The Melon Market" one feels the life and movement of the crowd, which is diversified in a fine manner. She paints poetry and loveliness into the most commonplace subjects, giving a new and beautiful vision to the matter-of-fact eyes. In all her pictures of crowds, the little figures are put in with an alert and suggestive touch. "The Grey Market" and "Idlers from the Market" are two charming market scenes attesting the facility with which she paints in water color. "The Pig Market", is particularly vibrant in color and truthful in values. "Brittany Horse Fair" and "Stormy Day in Amsterdam Market" have a refinement and unusually fine color sense and general excellence of selection and treatment, rarely to be found.

"Life in Corsica", which was shown recently in the Philadelphia Water Color Club exhibit, and reproduced in the catalogue, indicates the crisp quality, the luminosity, and the sense of true values characteristic of her work. Miss Schille is delightfully diverting when she uses water color for her notes on the passing scenes in the countries she visits in the summer. The gay or the serious. often the humorous, incident is chosen. At times she paints in water color with the freedom one associates with oil on a large canvas, using dashing sweeps of the brush. Her work as a whole is done with vigor, refuting the accepted idea that women painters always reveal a sweet, feminine quality in their pictures. Her manner of execution is masterfully masculine.

The students of the Columbus Art School, where she teaches during the winter, are fortunate in having her instruction in the handling of water color, and in the painting of oil portraits. In addition to these responsibilities, she maintains a steady production of beautiful pictures.

Pictures of dogs trace their lineage back to historic precedents. The mosaic, "Beware the Dog", Pompeii, is the one attraction which visitors to the buried city are certain to seek. Landseer gave the dog almost human attributes and endeared it to the public as man's best friend in life or death. A few years ago there appeared on the covers of sporting magazines and humorous weeklies a kind of dog portraiture that was new and compelling. These dog portraits created a furor; the first one appeared on *The Country Gentleman,* and soon one national magazine after another began to use them.

When Mrs. P. T. O'Connor wanted portraits of her pets for her book, *Dog*

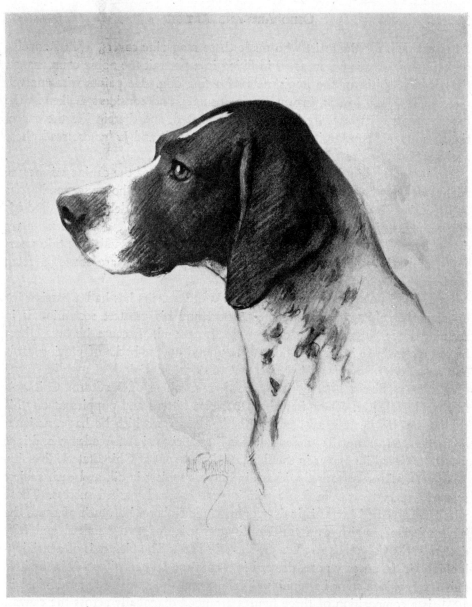

PLATE 107—Sam. Will Rannells. (Artist)

Stars, she sent for the artist who made these magazine covers, Will Rannells, of Columbus. He is unsurpassed in fixing in a portrait the noble countenance, the glowing spirit, or the impishness of a fine dog. He paints with marvelously delicate brushwork, in water color usually, and considers a likeness the first requisite. His drawing is alive and animated, and therein lies the exceptional value of his portraits of dogs. Wherever *Life* and *Judge* are read, there also are his dog covers known (Plate 107).

Mr. Rannells is in demand as a painter of portraits of the canine aristocrats. Many fine dogs have sat for their portraits to this artist who understands dogs and painting so well that invariably the proud owner is delighted to find his dog's characteristic expression fixed on canvas. "Mack", a beautiful setter owned by J. Walter Jeffrey, of Columbus, is one of Mr. Rannells's best dog portraits, and others of famous dogs of famous personages are scattered from New York City to the West.

From his childhood days in Zanesville, Will Rannells has had a passion for dogs; he has always been their benefactor, and his greatest recreation is in rescuing some "just common dog" from the pound. Because he loves them he can make those irresistible dogs to be found on the backs of playing cards and on magazine covers. At the request of Mrs. Frederic McLaughlin (Irene Castle) he made the 1930 Christmas card for Orphans of the Storm, Chicago's famous dog shelter. There have been cats and kittens and puppies among his studies, but his heart is avowedly with the dogs for which he has a national reputation. Mr. Rannells graduated from the Cincinnati Art Academy, and is at present a valued instructor in the fine arts department at Ohio State University.

Yeteve Smith has worked with a diversity of subject in oil, and each subject seems to be her forte. In figure painting she has had marked success. Those who have watched her artistic development remember with much pleasure the "Intermission", which won the Huntington prize of two hundred and fifty dollars at the Columbus Art League show in 1926. The picture is of a striking-looking girl in an easy pose, dressed in a costume that manifests Miss Smith's flair for exquisite color harmonies. "Wings of Faith", which she exhibited in 1931, is a composition of three figures arranged diagonally across the canvas. The central figure is an old colored woman with square shoulders and solidly built form. There is no doubt of her piety and seriousness; she pins her faith to the Book, which is spread open in her lap; her hands are laid flat upon its pages. The day she posed she had attended a funeral, and remarked to the artist that she could not help "frettin' with the mourners". A little colored newsboy rests his chin in his hand and leans against her in simple faith; a younger woman turns trustingly towards the older woman. While interest is focused upon the old woman, the other figures are just as carefully executed, and taken altogether it is a powerful group.

Among Miss Smith's portraits, the one of William Williams Mather, first state geologist, is unusual in that it successfully carries likeness and character from an old daguerreotype to a fine canvas. Doctor John A. Bownocker is the subject of another portrait by Miss Smith, in which she drives immediately for the personality and cuts down detail to the necessary minimum. Perhaps the portrait that has brought her most renown is the one of Doctor John W. Hoffman, president of Ohio Wesleyan University, Delaware. It vividly presents a grandeur not usually found in portrait effects. The technique is bold and direct. "The portrait is one of the most valued of all the art possessions of the university."[12]

Intimate glimpses of the Maine woods and shore, the Patuxent River and Chesapeake Bay region, Miss Smith has made into beautiful landscapes. "St. Petersburg" is a colorful bit depicting the blue waters of the bay fronting that Florida city; "Tampa Bay", is a charming study of blues and yellow-green. In industrial subjects, she has painted "Stone Quarry", where labor and construction are arranged into a blocky pattern executed in the most delicate gradations of gray. Even animal painting has received its share of attention; "Winners", shows the Ohio State queen cow, Maud Ormsby, and a milkmaid placed against a background of apple blossoms. Miss Smith paints still life with the same interesting composition, well-built forms, and strong, virile color, that she reveals in all her other subjects. There is always a breadth and bigness to her work.

Robert O. Chadeayne chooses to express himself in the field of landscape painting. During the school year he teaches life painting and drawing at the Columbus Art School. In the summers he maintains a studio at Cornwall-on-the-Hudson, or lives alone on the Delaware River, intensely studying landscape in all its moods and phases. Summer vacation never descends into boredom for him. His "Winter", a back-yard scene, glorious in crystal-clear atmosphere, was mentioned by Forbes Watson as one among twelve oustanding pictures of the annual exhibition at the Pennsylvania Academy of Fine Arts. It is cleancut, with brilliant sunshine on the snow cast against deep mystic shadows. He interprets street scenes similar to Burchfield's. "Street Scene, Hancock, N. Y.," was one of the one hundred and fifty out of three thousand paintings chosen for the 1930 Corcoran Biennial show at Washington, which was said to be the finest group of contemporary American art ever brought together.

---

[12] The Delaware *Journal-Herald,* June 18, 1929.

PLATE 108 — 1930. Guy Brown Wiser. (Columbus Gallery of Fine Arts)

"Point Mountain", is a beautiful landscape composed of a stream leading back between mountains mirrored in the water, with hazy, distant hills for the background. His choice of color is amazing, the values are correct, and the proper relation of sky to hills and foreground is skillfully maintained. The hills are painted flat with little modeling, and above all, the landscape is kept simple, giving a peaceful and serene effect. Mr. Chadeayne paints nature in a virile, spontaneous way, modern of course, but not extremely so, as he does not go into abstractions. "Two Calla Lillies" represents his most modernistic manner. He is alive to the beauties of nature, and has great zest for catching them on the canvas. Henry McBride, now editor of *Creative Art,* when he was art critic for the *New York Herald,* said of him: "Mr. Chadeayne openly avows a penchant for the Hudson River. The Hudson River school has vanished so effectively and so completely into the museums, that most of the odium that used to attach to that phrase has vanished too. Mr. Chadeayne need have no fear of that. He may, if he wishes, start a perfectly new Hudson River school, and perhaps with better success than the last one. He paints directly and with considerable feeling, and very often his compositions have a pleasing unexpectedness."

Unusual and well-deserved honors have been awarded Mabel DeBra King for her paintings. She received the Joseph Lewis Meyrich prize for pure water color, awarded by the Baltimore Water Color Society at its 1931 exhibit, held at the Baltimore Museum of Art. Her award was the only one given by the society that year. The prize-winning picture was "Nuremberg's Marketplace"; it was particularly liked by all observers. Many of her pictures are of European places, such as "Cologne Cathedral", "Obersee", and "Berchtesgaden Churchyard". She was also represented in the Corcoran Biennial of 1930; her paintings add excellence in no small measure to any exhibit. "Norway Fjords" illustrates her bold, sure way of handling the brush; this picture was chosen by the National Association of Women Painters and Sculptors to be sent to England for the thirtieth exhibition of the Women's International Art Club at the Gallery of the Royal Society of British Artists. She has had a thorough training, receiving diplomas from Ohio State University, Yale University, and Pratt Institute.

After graduating as an architect from Cornell University, Guy Brown Wiser served two years in the air service in France during the war. Upon returning to the United States, he found that there was little activity in building operations, so he entered the painting field and discovered that was where he really belonged. In 1924 he attended the American School of Art at Fontainebleau, and there he got the idea that he must paint portraits. Such progress, almost phenomenal, has resulted from his work, that any follower of the local and national exhibitions is familiar with the wide range and the exceptional quality of his paintings.

Mr. Wiser's creative effort is not confined within the limits of any particular school or style of painting. He is esteemed by some art lovers as a conservative, while to others he is known as a modernist. In reality, he is a young man whose work is yet formative. He is never satisfied with his work, but is always experimenting, and that is a sign of artistic health. His work bears the impact of an individual and personal point of view, whether it is his excellently painted straightforward portraits, or his more daring abstractions.

The portrait of an "Old Lady", Mr. Wiser considers one of his best. It won the Walter Lippincott prize at the Pennsylvania Academy of Fine Arts in 1927. The Colonel George T. Buckingham prize was awarded him at the Hoosier Salon, Chicago, in 1929 and 1930. A quick, direct and satisfactory portrait is the one of Judge Abernathy. A one-hour sketch of George Trautman, done with a big, wide brush, has a sparkle of freshness that some more meticulously finished portraits lack. "Doctor Montgomery", a study of the president of Muskingum College, "Nancy Studebaker", and "Colonel Carlisle" are other masterly portraits by his hand.

The outstanding work of Mr. Wiser has been in figure painting. "The Card Players", or "Faculty Club No. 1", was one of the first to attract attention. Next appeared "The Chess Players", or "Faculty Club No. 2", a group of two players and a spectator silhouetted against a window. This was the winner of the Harry G. Nye prize for two hundred dollars at the 1931 Hoosier Salon. The Nye prize is based upon artist-member vote only. The climax of Mr. Wiser's figure painting, up to date, is reached in "1930", a gripping presentation of unemployment. Four figures, resigned and very despondent, are placed against the radiance of a serene day. A dramatic or stagelike effect has been avoided, yet the tragedy in the grim faces and dispirited attitudes of the four men is unmistakable. From the standpoint of composition, "1930" (Plate 108) is excellent. It is built upon a simple dark-and-light pattern. The powerful design of the figures arranged in a triangle, with the standing figure at the right of the center as its apex, is counterbalanced by the pyramidal shape of the light area on the left of the center. The few horizontal lines of the clouds strengthen by contrast the vertical lines of the figures. The light areas made by the hands and faces are placed with extreme care.

In the few abstractions Mr. Wiser has painted, he has experimented with areas and lines. "Torso", one of the best of them, was exhibited at the 1930 Corcoran Biennial. He is a young man who will be heard from in the future, and whose career will be watched with keen interest.

To see one of the rhythmical arrangements of flowers and vines by Mark Russell is to know that he is one of the finest designers in the entire country. The exacting duties of assistant professor in the fine arts department at Ohio State University have prevented Alice Robinson from painting as many of her charming landscapes as one would wish. Harriet Kirkpatrick, painter of Provincetown scenes, developed the art exhibit at the Ohio State Fair into a real art show, that is a credit to the state. David Snodgrass, in colorful interpretations of North Africa, has made an enviable reputation for himself. The list might be extended much further, as there are many others in Columbus distinguished in the practice of art.

CHAPTER XIII

Prominent Ohio Painters, 1900 to 1930

(Continued)

TOLEDO

THE dean of Toledo painters is Wilder M. Darling. His studio, now closed, has been a haven for some of the most discriminating art patrons, as well as for the distinguished spirit who called it home, and he has exercised a potent influence in the art activities of Toledo. Mr. Darling began studying art when he was only fourteen years old, with Henry Mosler of Cincinnati; later he worked under Duveneck in Munich, and Laurens in Paris. From the instructors he chose, one would know that he was most interested in figure painting. He had a passion for Dutch and Breton subjects, and much of his best work was done in Holland.

Many friends of art who know Mr. Darling tell of the startling prices attached to his canvases. No matter what were the demands for bread and butter, he absolutely refused to lower the figures beneath what he thought a picture was worth, believing that purchasers of the future would be willing to pay the price. He never sold a picture just for the sake of making a sale.

Luther Emerson Van Gorder was internationally known as a painter of busy corners and street scenes of Paris; one of his characteristic canvases hangs in the permanent collection of the Toledo Museum of Art. Except for a brief period of work on a Toledo newspaper, he dedicated his entire life to painting, exhibiting in New York, and at the Paris Salon for many years.

Kate Brainard Lamb has exhibited her landscape paintings at the National Academy, the Chicago Art Institute, and the Pennsylvania Academy of Fine Arts, in addition to showing her work in many Ohio exhibitions of art. "A Glimpse of the Sound, Long Island", is an example of her delightful landscape.

A young Toledoan of unusual promise was Harry I. Stickroth. He had been awarded the Prix de Rome, and with the advantage of three years' study at the American Academy at Rome, was just reaching the maturity of his powers at the time of his death, which occurred when he was only thirty-one years old. His drawings were exquisite. Probably no living draughtsman made more perfect drawings. The quality of his paintings was such as to put him in the forefront of the American decorative school. He was associated with Barry Faulkner in the mural decorations for the Cunard Building in New York. His un-

PLATE 109—The Old Mill, Zoar. Benjamin Cratz. (Artist)

timely death was a great loss to the mural-painting profession. Just before his death he was also enjoying marked success as an instructor at the Chicago Art Institute.

Benjamin Cratz, the well-known colorist of Toledo, began his art studies with Edmund Osthaus, the painter of dogs. Later studies were made with George Elmer Browne in Europe. Mr. Cratz studied also in Provincetown, the source of inspiration to so many of the best American landscape and *genre* painters. The quaint architecture of France and Spain has given him his happiest subjects. Of his work, the late George W. Stevens, director of the Toledo Museum, said: "He has a strong feeling for pleasing composition and an unerring sense of the picturesque, which qualities, with his habit of good color, combine to adequately record the charm of the romantic byways in which he has found inspiration."

"Afternoon–Tangier", is a canvas representative of the most felicitous mood and style of Mr. Cratz. Effective in treatment of soft shadows and sunlight, it is rich in poetic feeling; splendid coloring lends vividness to the canvas. Wide, upspringing arches, which he used again and again in his paintings, form the architectural motif. He keeps his architectural passages solid and alive, with sufficient foliation to make agreeable contrast. Figures are introduced for accent and human interest. "Tangier Harbor", is another canvas reminiscent of the luminous sky of Morocco. He plays his color easily through the various buildings on the hillside forming the background. The harbor is filled with boats. The lateen sails, dyed in crimson, make singing curves of color athwart the canvas.

There is a personal appeal in all of the work of Mr. Cratz. "Cottages in Picardy", is boldly handled; the tree forms flicker with broken light and shade —all done in stipple effect that gives a scintillating aspect. It is a decorative canvas, and his choice of romantic subject, as usual, adds greatly to its success. "Sardine Boats, Brittany", is a vivid, imaginative and well-unified seaport ensemble. Many market scenes in French villages are all interesting in theme and treatment, with the large groups of people showing skillful massing and coloration.

Mr. Cratz paints in and about Toledo, in Canada and Massachusetts, and abroad. He does not neglect the picturesque subjects to be found at home (Plate 109). "Chateau Frontenac, Quebec", is a fine handling of architecture, trees, river, and distant mountains. At first glance one would say that it is an Old World setting. In spite of all the lure of history and the associations connected with European subjects, Mr. Cratz finds his most complete expression in a simple midsummer American landscape of fresh greens and gold light.

PLATE 110—On the Maumee. Anna Thorne. (Artist)

Forty years ago, when Toledo was the clover-seed market of the entire country, the father of Benjamin Cratz was a shrewd trader in seeds, and held ambitions that his son Benjamin would be a merchant in seeds like himself. But the plan of the father went astray, when the boy definitely cast his lot with the fraternity of artists. The seed business probably lost a valuable member, but art gained a good landscape painter and a true devotee.

Anna L. Thorne is among the strongest exponents of modernism in painting in Toledo. She too, was a pupil of Edmund Osthaus. He taught her to paint the veins in every leaf, and she spent a long time unlearning his tight technique. Her present impressionistic painting reflects none of it (Plate 110).

In New Orleans, Miss Thorne painted the old Rue Royale. She pictured bright sunlight and purple shadows on those mellow walls that have a pattern distinctively their own in the patches of broken plaster. Then she went to Paris, receiving there the honor of having her paintings "hung on the line" at the Salon.

It was in North Africa that Miss Thorne found her joy supreme! In her water-color street scenes the picturesque Moroccan is found in characteristic pursuits. Beautiful young native women in orange and deep-green dresses are arranged into charming compositions. Miss Thorne became a friend of the nomads, and thus was able to do more than simply draw their figures and paint their costumes: she could share their emotions and express the spirit of those people sympathetically. Miss Thorne has a taste for the unusual little villages in Sardinia and other Mediterranean spots.

In the neighborhood of Toledo, the cliffs of Catawba, the beach at Marblehead, the fishing shacks at Sandusky, and the bluffs up the Maumee, have all been delineated by her brush in impressionistic fashion. Her figures and heads in oil have received marked recognition. Miss Thorne gives the following good advice to one contemplating the purchase of a picture: "Buy a picture because you love it and for no other reason. . . . Buy a picture because the figures are arranged in a way that seems harmonious, and because the color strikes you as being right, and because it arouses a pleasant emotion in you just to have it around. That's the essence of art appreciation, anyway."[1]

A quotation from a letter from Helen Niles will show that her education in art was exceptional: "I studied with many different people; the great Robert Henri, my friend and master, was the one from whom I got all that was vital in my studies. I worked with him in New York, and went abroad with him four times—twice with a class, and twice just as a friend. I also went abroad

---

[1] *The Toledo Sunday Times,* May 5, 1929.

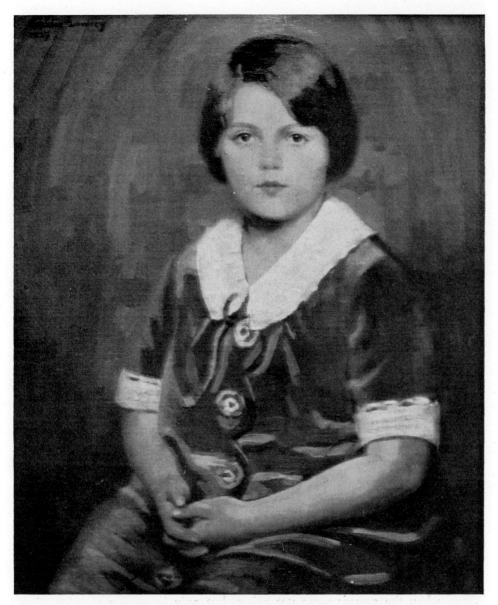

PLATE 111—Elise Biechler. Rosalie Lowery. (Artist)

with Mr. Chase." She has been considered the leading woman portrait painter in Toledo.

Her portrait technique is bold, vivid and very colorful; her delineation is subtle. Many of her subjects are picturesque foreign types; others owe their interest entirely to the forceful way in which they are drawn. Her technique resembles that of Henri, as one would expect. One of the best of her canvases is a "Portrait of a Young Girl", showing a young woman garbed in a cream-colored gown and a large black hat that accentuates the coloring of the face and eyes. Miss Niles paints exquisite flower studies.

"I really think my own history as an artist would be rather interesting, for after many years, I have the feeling maybe it's just beginning after all."[2] Such enthusiasm for her work makes Grace Rhodes Dean a fine artist. Her program of creative work consists of water colors and prints (see page 254). From 1917 to 1925, Mrs. Dean taught painting, drawing, and composition at the Toledo Museum of Art, and during that time she became interested in water color. She is president of the Ohio Water Color Society. Her paintings have been exhibited at the Ohio and Michigan museums, at Omaha, Nebraska, Charleston, South Carolina, and at the International Exhibition of Water Colors at Chicago.

A beautiful patterning of line, a fine feeling for texture, a skillful use of close values, and an elimination of petty details, are characteristics of her technique. In landscape, she has depicted the cottonwoods of Nebraska; she has shown the picturesque lines of High Bridge, New York, with its charming arches in the distance and a foreground of trees and foliage; other products of her brush include many compositions of willow and poplar trees, bridges and houses around Ipswich, Massachusetts, medieval castles of Germany, and beautiful gardens and villas of Italian towns. Her charcoal drawings of Siena, Assisi, and Spoleto, have a delightful play of light and shade, with a pleasing color note where the drawing has been washed with flat tones of water colors, producing brilliant effects. In pure water color, she makes exquisite flower studies; "Flowers in the Window", won honorable mention at the 1931 Toledo show, when the awards were not prizes, but only honorable mention. Portraits and figures in oil claim a share of her talent.

As an art teacher at Scott High School, Caroline Morgan has given the inspiration for many an artistic career, and not a few of her pupils reflect credit upon her instruction. She paints landscape in the summer at Carmel-by-the-Sea, California, or some other art colony.

---

[2] Letter from Mrs. Dean.

PLATE 112—The Umbrian Valley. Frederick C. Gottwald. (Cleveland Museum of Art)

Louis U. Bruyere paints landscapes in water color. "Vermont Hills", "Brook", and "Red Barn", were pictures with claim to distinction, exhibited in the Toledo annual exhibit, 1931. "Vermont Hills", won honorable mention.

Morris Henry Hobbs reproduces landscapes in oil or water color. He chooses picturesque scenes in France, New England, or Ohio. "Hill Country", exhibited at the 1931 Toledo annual, was a charming landscape; "Brittany Boats" was equally fascinating.

Kenneth Bradley Loomis puts forth strikingly modernistic canvases. "Sea Gulls", is a powerfully vigorous and decorative painting; in portraits he expresses the same vitality. His mural decorations have been used by some of the best architects of New York City, and he has been very successful in designing stained-glass windows. Fritz Boehmer paints exquisitely delicate and lovely miniature portraits on china and ivory.

No Ohio city has more promise for the future of art than Toledo, with its magnificent museum space of literally acres, and the intense interest in art of its citizens. The artistic background that has been given the school children is beginning to yield a harvest.

DAYTON

Dayton has always been a beautiful city, from the time when Daniel Cooper planned its wide streets in 1795, and when John W. VanCleve planted the hundreds of elms (about 1850) that lend shade and grace to those streets, down to the present day. One would expect many artists of renown to live in a city having such a secure foundation of beauty.

The work and teaching of the early painters (see Chapter V, *ante*) left a lasting impression and influence. Later, a Daytonian, Walter (Otto) Beck, the painter of the wonderful series of "The Life of Christ", in the Brooklyn Museum, continued a guidance and teaching that is bearing fruit today. Art was added to the curriculum of Steele High School, Dayton, in 1906, with Miss Annie Campbell as the teacher, and many pupils took advantage of the opportunity to study with her, whose influence has been a powerful factor in the growth of art in Dayton. Her painting shows an independence and originality in design.

Ernest L. Blumenschein is another artist who figured in the record of Dayton art. "Dayton, Ohio, gave me the foundation for my work," he writes, replying to an enquiry about his connection with Ohio. His artistic training was received at the Cincinnati Art Academy. Combined with excellent draughtsmanship, he had a highly developed imagination, and these qualifications made him one of the best American illustrators during a large part of his life. It was not until he was forty-three years old that he was able to abandon commercial art and devote himself entirely to painting, an ambition that had always been before him.

There were no painters living in New Mexico when Mr. Blumenschein first visited Taos in 1898. He discovered the wealth of artistic material in the landscapes of New Mexico, and in the life of the Indians there. It was not long after these discoveries that other artists settled in Taos, and the names of Walter Ufer, O. E. Berninghaus, Victor Higgins, Irving Couse, and several others brought renown to that remote little village. Blumenschein finds expression in the form and color of the actual surroundings and scenes of Taos, the valleys, the mountains, the clouds, an Indian face, or an Indian dance—sometimes a little church. There is much variety in his composition and subject matter, though the one ever-present theme is the life of the Pueblo Indian and the New Mexican landscape. The Indian as he is today is the interest found in most of Mr. Blumenschein's pictures, though he has reconstructed Indian battle scenes and given symbolic interpretations of Indian beliefs and legends.

Mr. Blumenschein makes his permanent home in the beautiful valley near the Indian pueblo in the northern part of New Mexico. His paintings are in many of the prominent museums, Brooklyn, Cincinnati, Toronto, and many others, and have done much to spread the fame of the so-called Taos school. The words that might best characterize his work are these: decorative, colorful, brilliant, imaginative. The painting of the strong light of the Southwest is full of pitfalls for the unwary, but not for Mr. Blumenschein; he paints light dramatically, charges it with rich color and makes one feel the glowing warmth of the sun.

Artists who are active in Dayton today are numerous; a brief account of them follows: Abby Lytle Wuichet began her training with Laura Birge, continuing it with Frank Duveneck, W. M. Chase, and Kenyon Cox. Her compositions of flowers and still life are carefully planned; she also has to her credit many strong portraits and charming landscapes. Juliet Burdoin, of Canadian birth and Parisian training, has exhibited her oil and water-color landscapes and flower studies in important Eastern shows, and has painted portraits of several notable women.

Mrs. Jess Brown Aull makes pictures, stunning in color, of French towns frequented by the artists. "Boats of Concarneau", is a beautiful example of her oil paintings, in which a bright-colored sail is the dominant note. She has a mastery of technique seldom encountered. In portraits she displays the same

PLATE 113—Under the Dune. Ora Coltman. (Cleveland Museum of Art)

strong manner of painting. "The Old New England House", and "The Red Book", are canvases showing her unusual ability. John W. King is a former student of H. H. Wessel and John Weis at the Cincinnati Art Academy. His paintings have received notable awards. He was the winner of the Colonel George T. Buckingham prize at the Hoosier Salon, Chicago, 1927, and the winner of the Eugene Buffington award at the Hoosier Salon, Chicago, 1930. He is a painter of portraits and *genre* and still-life subjects; his three-quarter-length portrait of "Peg" is well composed and well executed. Mr. King is an instructor at the Dayton Art Institute during the school year, and teaches at the Cincinnati Art Academy during the summer school.

Rosalie Lowery paints flower studies and remarkably fine portraits of youth and adults. Children have inspired some of her finest portraits (Plate 111). Because of her vigorous and competent style, the demand for her work has been great; she was called to California to paint a number of portraits. She obtains, in a portrait, in addition to a splendid likeness, a fine arrangement of lights and darks; for example, her portrait of Jane Reece is exceptional.[3] In this particular case it was one Dayton artist lovingly portraying another one, as Jane Reece does some of the finest photographic work in the country. Miss Lowery, with an excellent art training, constantly improves her technique; she has recently been studying with Cecelia Beaux.

Martha K. Schauer is a water-colorist who has been honored in exhibitions of work of internationally known painters. In 1929, six of her pictures were hung in the International Show of Water Color Artists at the Brooklyn Museum. The names of these pictures indicate her type of work: "Nasturtiums", "Garden Flowers", "A Bowl of Flowers", "The Last of the Garden", "Yellow Chrysanthemums", and "Autumn Flowers". Her technique is crisp and sparkling, and shows a confidence and proficiency in her handling of the medium of water color. Her work always brings forth much praise at the annual shows of the Ohio Water Color Society. Miss Schauer is art instructor at Stivers High School, Dayton.

Theodore H. Pond, former director of the Dayton Art School, was responsible for the development of metal work and other crafts in that school, and

---

[3] The activity in pictorial art is so multifaceted that photography as a fine art deserves much more mention than the limitations of space allow. It is with profound pleasure that the progress of photography is noted here. The first All-Ohio Salon of Pictorial Photography was held in Columbus, November, 1931. The collection of one hundred and fifty-one prints exhibited contained work as good as that shown at any of the great international salons. In artistic knowledge, especially chiaroscuro, and technical skill the selected prints were outstanding. Awards were given to Nicholas Bori of Cincinnati, Jane Reece of Dayton, Katherine Anderson of Chillicothe, Axel Bahnsen of Yellow Springs, I. W. Gottshall of Toledo, H. P. Herron of Akron, and Ray Lee Jackson of Columbus.

PLATE 114—Returning from the Feria. Henry G. Keller. (Cleveland Museum of Art)

this fact accounts largely for the many good craftsmen in Dayton; exceptional ones are Bernice E. Buyer and Walter Pfeiffer, creating most exquisite jewelry and metal work, and B. B. Thresher who executes wood and ivory carvings.

A city like Dayton, that stimulates its people to bring beauty out of the commonplace, is truly no mean city. With the inspiration accruing from a beautiful new Art Institute and the continued public enthusiasm for art, the artists of Dayton will reach the greatest heights in their endeavors.

CLEVELAND

In pursuance of the policy of the Cleveland Museum of Art to promote creative efforts in the future, it sponsors an annual exhibit of the work of Cleveland artists, besides collecting and exhibiting the fine arts of the past. The first exhibit was in the spring of 1919, and it has been held every spring since in the month of May, until it has come to be known as the May Show. In twelve years it has brought about an amazing development in Cleveland art, so that the whole country has become conscious of Cleveland's position as a forward-looking art center. The museum has brought the artists and the public together. Cleveland now has faith in her artists, and the artists have gained confidence in themselves. Art has never flourished in any age without patrons, and patronage has always played an immensely important part in the growth of the great schools of the past. The sales of Cleveland art products have increased each year, and unquestionably have been an encouragement to the artist who feels that he can live and find recognition in Cleveland. The artists have unanimously backed up the museum's efforts and have given of their best. They have been urged to interpret Cleveland and its environs, to make use of the picturesque material at hand and reveal its beauty to the people of the city. Art-loving citizens have been the donors of many prizes that have stimulated the high quality of the work submitted. Cleveland is changing the familiar adage to be read thus: "An artist is not without honor in his own city — in Cleveland."

After forty-one years of continuous service as teacher of life-drawing and painting at the Cleveland School of Art, Frederick Carl Gottwald retired in June, 1926. The announcement by the trustees of the school, of his retirement at his own request, states: "The influence of Mr. Gottwald in the development of Cleveland as an art center is simply immeasurable. There is hardly an artist or craftsman of reputation in the city that has not at one time or another studied with him in day or evening classes at the art school or at the John Huntington Polytechnic Institute. He leaves his teaching at the very height of his powers, to devote himself to landscape painting."

PLATE 115—The Bonbon Box. William J. Edmondson. (Artist)

Since the founding of the first art organization in the city, in 1876, Mr. Gottwald has been a quiet, but ever powerful force in developing art appreciation. He was only a boy when his friend, Otto Bacher, persuaded him to join the drawing class taught by A. M. Willard. Mr. Gottwald was among the first to follow the urge to go to Europe to study, remaining four years at the Royal Academy at Munich. Then he worked with William M. Chase in New York, and eventually returned to his home city, Cleveland, to devote his life to teaching the principles of art.

In spite of Mr. Gottwald's busy life spent in teaching night classes as well as day sessions of the school, he kept up his own painting, first making himself famous by Dutch interiors. Later, until the outbreak of the war, he went to Italy in the summers and brought back landscapes of delicate and subtle color, contrasting strangely with the rugged character of his earlier Dutch work. The Cleveland Museum of Art owns one of these beautiful Italian landscapes. It is a distant view of a long stretch across the Umbrian Valley (Plate 112). A tiny river meanders through the valley; in the foreground are tall Lombardy poplars, whose vertical lines contrast with the wide horizontal line of the broad valley; a hillside town with its church and campanile add human features to the view.

One of the outstanding canvases by Mr. Gottwald, "The Dreamer", a portrait for which he received the Penton Medal at the 1919 May Show at the Cleveland Museum, was purchased in 1930 by the Cleveland Society of Artists as a nucleus of a permanent collection of paintings by Cleveland artists. Every member of the society considered Mr. Gottwald as deserving to be the first artist to receive the honor. During his long art career, fads and fancies in theories have come and gone, but he has remained sane and true to the fundamental principles of art. In the art history of Cleveland he has, by his patient and intelligent efforts, been an important part in its progress and development, contributing more than any other individual artist.

Ora Coltman has made a steady contribution to the art life of Cleveland. When his "Portygee Neighborhood" was exhibited in the 1925 annual show, it was considered one of the most effective pictures in the whole exhibition, being remarkable for its striking pattern. The traditional Provincetown streets and quaint houses have furnished themes for many of his oils; the "Red House" received much favorable comment at the 1928 Pennsylvania Academy of Fine Arts show. In 1929, "On Felicity Street", a delightful New Orleans scene, won honorable mention at the annual show. Mr. Coltman excels in exquisite colored prints of groups of houses (Plate 113).

At the annual May Shows of the work of Cleveland artists, Henry G. Keller has won more awards in the past than any other artist. He is the only Clevelander who has been invited to exhibit at the Annual International Exhibition at Carnegie Institute, Pittsburgh. His honors have been well deserved. He is a modest, tireless artist and teacher. Ever since he finished his training at European art centers, he has spent his life giving to his pupils and to the public his interpretation of creative beauty. He has spent his vacations in various parts of the world, from New Mexico and Porto Rico to Spain, always hunting, recording, and creating. Mr. Keller's aim is to express his deepest impressions in the most vigorous and harmonious art at his command.

At the 1926 annual exhibition in Cleveland he won the exceptional special prize for the single finest picture in the exhibition. He truly affixed on this canvas the poetry and enchantment of southern Spain, and called it "Memories of Andalusia." There is the ever-present mountainous background of Spain; beside a road are some peasants in characteristic costumes and pursuits, selling water and fruits, leisurely surveying the landscape; a few donkeys lead the eye across the canvas as they move along in an interesting rhythm. There is a mellowness of color and a breadth of treatment that remind one of the Old Masters, yet the work is entirely individual.

A special prize for maintained excellence was awarded Mr. Keller at the May Show of 1923 for an entire group of ten paintings in oil and water color, representing some of his work in Spain. The sparkle of the intensely brilliant sunlight, the gorgeous color, and the striking tonal contrasts of that romantic country dominate the pictures. In the water color, "The Impressions of a Bull Fight", is evolved a powerful pattern of line and color out of a tense, dramatic moment when the bull gores the picador's horse. Again, an interesting pattern is seen in a pyramid of fruit piled high in a basket. "Returning from the Feria" (Plate 114). "Evening at the Escorial", "Fishermen of Vigo", are other especially fine pictures among the ten.

In 1925, Mr. Keller was awarded first prize for a group of three miscellaneous oil paintings. Two of them were still-life subjects, "The Madonna of Ivory", and "Three Periods of Art", showing modern tendencies in form, rhythm, and arrangement. The third was another charming interpretation of Spain, in which he secured the inner reality and atmosphere of the country— some peasants with donkeys and a goat along a road by the sea. The patient donkey, the Spanish beast of burden, Mr. Keller individualizes with genuine art. For the last few years his works have been entered in the annual shows, "not in competition"; but his oils and water colors have added much importance to the classes in which they appear.

PLATE 116—Landscape. George G. Adomeit. (Artist)

In draughtsmanship, composition, and color, Mr. Keller exhibits surpassing artistry, regardless of theme. His numerous studies of the Pacific Coast bring out the great rocky formations with extraordinary effectiveness. "Rocks and Cormorants", is a strong colorful rendition of the sea; one feels the power of the wind on the surging waves and the rush of the water that sways and swells. One is conscious at first only of the spirit of the sea, but soon realizes the remarkable skill exerted to convey it. Birds are frequently found in Mr. Keller's decorative water scenes. He can make his technique express feathers in sleekness, in color, and in velvety texture. The birds are usually introduced in the Japanese conventional manner — all done in gradations of grays suffused with light. He makes them express rhythm and movement with brilliant decorative qualities.

In 1928, Mr. Keller received first prize in a national contest at San Antonio, Texas, for "Ranch Life, Western Texas". His canvas was one of twenty-eight considered. It pictured cowboys driving a herd of cattle along a stream, a range of hills lying just beyond. It had all the power and excellence one associates with the work of Mr. Keller. He brings to his art an intensity of thought and sincerity.

William J. Edmondson has developed a style peculiarly his own. He is not subservient to any school of art, nor does he follow the modern academic rules; neither is he bound by old traditions in expressing his individuality, which strongly characterizes his work. He paints portraits of women that are equally satisfactory both as pictures and as portraits (Plate 115). A unique decorative effect is produced in "The Blue Feather", owned by the Cleveland Museum of Art. A beautiful girl with golden hair, dressed in a blue kimono, trimming a hat tinted in blue and gold, makes a splendid color harmony, heightened by the effect of a strong ray of light. The exquisite profile and the hands are executed with utmost care. The contours are considered well, and the light and dark in the pattern make it pictorially successful.

A canvas similar in composition and treatment, "The Egyptian Beads", is one of Mr. Edmondson's charming portrait studies. In this canvas brilliant blacks strike a rich keynote. A lovely blond girl is the subject, her beauty enhanced by a sleeveless black velvet jacket. She sits beside a table covered with a richly embroidered black cover, on which stands a high-luster-black Chinese vase. She lifts a string of bright-hued beads from a bowl. His lavish use of color gives a first impression of a leaning toward the ultramodernistic style, but upon second glance it is found to be finely balanced and harmonized delightfully. He gets an effect of extreme boldness through his unusual use of color.

PLATE 117—Trailing Fog. Frank N. Wilcox. (Cleveland Museum of Art)

A figure painting somewhat on the same order is "The Beginner", which created so much comment at the Chicago Art Institute when it was on exhibit there for six weeks in 1917. It is a figure of a dreamy young girl learning to knit for the soldiers, perhaps for the youth of her visions. The picture possesses a simple beauty of outline and an unusual charm. The color scheme is strong, but not too striking. Her blouse is pale green and yellow, shadowy, transparent, while the drapery behind her has a blue ground with orange-yellow patches, and her black beads lend a distinctive touch.

Mr. Edmondson has established a reputation for portraits — of men as well as of women. Among the most virile of his portraits are those of David C. Wills, E. L. Whittemore, H. H. Johnson, Professor F. H. Herrick, Reverend J. G. Frazier, and Doctor Burton. Children, too, he has portrayed; for example "Lewis Baldwin" is a joy! His big eyes are fixed, it seems, upon the painter who worked upon his portrait. Mr. Edmondson paints not only all ages, but all conditions, and the Irishman "Pat" receives as masterly attention as more dignified sitters.

The painting of landscape by Mr. Edmondson has always stood slightly in the shadow of his accomplished portraiture. He paints landscape with the eye of the portraitist. His out-of-door studies are not painted, however, with photographic hardness; though the places are recognizable, they are interpreted to give one the atmosphere and feeling of a region. His landscapes are fresh and free from commonplace color harmonies; in fact, rather daring dissonances give a particular interest to them. California and the West, a mountain rising from a misty plain, white adobe houses with red tile roofs, swaying trees in a raging storm — these scenes are painted freely and directly. Here is a versatile artist who paints both quiet, resposeful portrait figures, and the gorgeous colorful breadth of landscape in beautifully composed subtle patterns.

A successful business career usually leaves no time nor inclination for anything else. However, George G. Adomeit has followed an artistic career in addition to a genuine business; his experience in art is one of the rare exceptions where painting is an avocation. He carried on his art training under the direction of Mr. Gottwald in the evening classes and during the summer vacations. Many friends have watched the steady growth of power in his painting. Every year, in the May Show at the Museum, he has exhibited, and he has been honored with many awards there.

Industrial enterprises have been the subjects of many of Mr. Adomeit's pictures. In his canvas "The High Level Bridge", he made and solved an interesting design-problem of the teeming activities around that section of Cleveland.

PLATE 118—Washerwomen at Goyen. Abel Warshawsky. (Cleveland Museum of Art)

Symbols of new Cleveland — the Terminal Tower, and the Ohio Bell Telephone Building — are seen behind the old cemetery in a canvas he calls, "Memorials", that is especially interesting. "Symbols of Industry", is another stunning industrial picture with the Terminal Tower in the distance. The industrial life of Cleveland affords many possibilities, and it is not surprising that Mr. Adomeit undertakes subjects that are at hand in such profusion.

In landscape, Mr. Adomeit knows how to paint the broad spaces of the hills of Ohio (Plate 116). First prize in landscape was awarded him in the 1923 show for "Autumn Hills", painted in Pownal, Vermont; in this the mellow autumn sunlight is diffused over the Green Mountains that stretch away to the horizon; the bright clouds scattered over a large expanse of sky bring the scene into a harmonious whole. "The First Snow", was exhibited in the 1930 Carnegie International Exhibition in Pittsburgh. It is a back-yard view of some city houses, in which ash barrels, garbage cans, and other unsightly objects are transformed by a covering of fresh, white, beautiful snow. It is a fine picture. Picturesque Breton fishing villages and the rock coasts of Maine have interested him enough to be transferred to canvas by his brush. His work always displays a particularly rich use of color and a fine sense of design.

The ability of Mr. Adomeit as a draughtsman gave him a chance to work in a lithographic plant when he was a very young man. He was one of the founders of the Caxton Company, one of Cleveland's foremost engraving and publishing houses in which he is still active as director of art.

Frank N. Wilcox paints landscapes in oil and water color with a sureness that distinguishes the master. He knows how to interpret rocks and mountains, islands and lakes, with the world that belongs to them. He is not interested in rocks and mountains simply as such, but in the struggle of human life with nature. One always feels signs of life, cattle or people, somewhere in his landscapes. Mr. Wilcox believes that all art is an emotional experience. He believes further that the forms in nature must be interpreted rather than copied. It is said of him that he gets the atmosphere of a scene without a great mass of unnecessary detail, picking out salient points only (Plate 117).

Mr. Wilcox has had a sound art training. His prize-winning feats began with a prize for drawing, earned when he was only thirteen, and have become regular annual experiences. Landscapes of many countries, on both sides of the Atlantic, have been his subjects. Surpassing achievements resulted from a year's study in France. He received an exceptional award, special commendation, for an entire group of five oils and five water colors, at the 1926 Cleveland Annual Exhibition. These were scenes of the Luxembourg gardens, views of St. Malo, and the Tours section of the Loire. He made many intimate French studies that are vivid impressions rather than meticulously finished landscapes. Dramatic cloudy skies help to give many of them the feeling of force, characteristic of his work.

The beauty of Ohio landscape has not been neglected by Mr. Wilcox. The May exhibit of Cleveland artists held in 1923 contained his "June Evening", which was awarded first prize in water color. It is a typical Ohio rural scene, showing a farmer with his team working in the fields; the cottage, trees, and clouds have been organized into a beautifully decorative pattern. "The Gravel Pit", is done in broad strokes, typifying the vigorous natural setting; it contains the expected note of human interest — horses hitched to a wagon which some men are loading with gravel. Another interesting canvas is the "Blacksmith Shop", representing the now infrequent sight of a smith shoeing a horse. This study reveals a splendid arrangement of light and dark values. The two latter oil paintings were prize winners at the Cleveland Art Annual in 1922.

Canada has become the source of Mr. Wilcox's enthusiasm for the last few summers. "Bonaventure Island", is a mature, successful production, as are many other paintings of Gaspe County, Canada. Majestic hills, shadowy deep glens, colorful French inhabitants, eccentric local characters, cliff-nesting little sea parrots — these are some of the interesting things he finds to paint in Canada. He does nothing superficially, but carries on a research problem in whatever field he may find need of information. One whole summer he studied clouds; another summer he devoted to the anatomy of the horse. The practical knowledge which he gains, combined with his unusual talent for design, and his sensitiveness to beauty, plus constant tireless working, produces the fine art of Frank N. Wilcox.

Two Clevelanders, the Warshawsky brothers, Abel and Xander, spend most of their time abroad painting favorite haunts. In Europe, scenes of pictorial interest are at hand without searching for them. The real name of Xander is Alexander. "Both brothers are incorrigible exhibitors in the salons; but the French, who are always messing up foreign names in print, used to put them both down in the salon catalogue as A. Warshawsky, so that nobody could tell which was which or even that there were two of them. So Aleck said waggishly that he would adopt Prohibition and drop the Ale out of his name; and ever since he has been Xander, or as the salon catalogue has it, X."[4]

Abel is an outdoor painter *par excellence;* atmospheric, impressionistic effects of rain and snow on Paris streets and bridges are his favorite themes.

---

[4] *Paris on Parade,* R. F. Wilson, p. 228.

PLATE 119—Eze, Côte d'Azur. William J. Eastman. (Cleveland Museum of Art)

Notre Dame has inspired many of his best canvases; the Gothic feeling, the richness of the stained-glass interior, he records with certainty and the ability to see the best in a subject. *Paris on Parade* is enhanced by reproductions of many of Abel's paintings as illustrations. "Winter on the Avenue de l'Opéra", "The Madeleine Flower Market", "Boulevard des Italiens in Spring" are some of his typical pictures, in which one finds a masterly handling of light and shade. The color quality belonging only to Venice — fishing boats from Chioggia, and the canals — furnishes vital subjects for him; few artists paint water better than he does. His training experience in the Latin Quarter gave him a foundation broad enough to paint either figure or landscape. He renders the Breton peasant in quaint costume with the same freedom that abounds in his landscape (Plate 118).

Xander Warshawsky searches for quiet little villages and unusual peasant types to paint. His painting is more in the modern manner, more like that of Cezanne than Abel's work, but he does not carry it to such an extreme that the layman fails to understand it or to see its beauty. Paintings by the Warshawsky brothers hang in many American galleries, as well as in the Luxembourg.

It would be difficult for any one to be unimpressed with the flood of color in the paintings of William J. Eastman. From his earliest paintings of landscapes, he has shown his original ideas on the subject of color. He believed that when a landscape was built upon the principles of pure design, gold, silver, black, and white could be used without breaking the color harmony. An interesting example is "The Lost Romance", in which he has painted the sky a silver, like the shimmer of an early evening light, and has given an air of mystery in the dark woods that suggests the mood of a fairy tale. It is a pleasant, but whimiscal interpretation of nature.

In 1917, Mr. Eastman made a series of decorative panels for the store of William Taylor, Son & Company, representing a review of French historical costumes from the picturesque dress of 1650 down to 1912, when Paul Poiret made history in modern dress. These are more than mere decorative panels; they evidence his genius for the placing of color masses, and are interesting in line and composition. He had the courage to express himself in brilliant colors, put together with regard for harmony, though in combinations out of the ordinary. The Penton Medal for excellence and first prize for water-color landscape were awarded him at the 1919 Cleveland show for "Shore Acres in Winter", a delicate snow scene of subtle gradations in tone.

Recent years have brought greater strength and vitality to Mr. Eastman's work. His distinctive feeling for color and decorative qualities is more deeply

PLATE 120—St. George, Bermuda. Carl W. Broemel. (Cleveland Museum of Art)

impressed than ever. In the Balearic Islands and the Mediterranean region, where the modern artist is flooded with the color he loves, Mr. Eastman has painted canvases of great beauty (Plate 119). He catches and records the traveler's first impression and intense feeling for new scenes; and, with his extreme sensitiveness to color values and pattern, he conveys the romantic character of whatever he chooses to paint. "After the Service", painted in the cathedral at Valencia is tremendously effective in the contrast afforded by the dark reaches of the building with the gold and red streaming through the stained glass, and the candle-glow from a ceremonial procession. An interior of the cathedral of Chartres is another of his finest paintings. "Houses in Capri at Night" shows more than the sentimental attitude most artists have for that mountainous island, for he pictures the rugged rocks and stucco walls with a sculpturesque solidity and power. From travel in the Scandinavian countries, Mr. Eastman absorbed the expressionistic use of color by the artists there, and through that he has obtained a weird and mysterious effect in his "Paris by Night". Mr. Eastman is a fine, sound artist. Whatever he paints, still life or landscape, in oil or water color, it is always startling in tone and shade.

Since 1924 the race in water-color painting in Cleveland has been fast and furious, until it has become the most important feature of the annual May Show at the museum. In the past, Boston was the foremost water-color center. The water-colorists of Cleveland have achieved an enviable reputation in the country at large, making that city now the leading city in this medium in America. The stampede in water color was started by the work of Carl Broemel, whose pictures in that medium won first prize in 1924 and again in 1925. He used pure water color; other talent had been working in semi-opaque and opaque water color. Bermuda has furnished most of the themes for Broemel's clear and brilliant air-and-sunshine effects (Plate 120). "Touch of Spring in the Air", "After the Shower", "Golden Sunlight", and "Dancing Light of Morning", are typical titles of pictures that sparkle with the brilliance of tropical sunlight. These canvases show his marked ability in handling Southern subjects. Using thin, transparent washes for the most part, he captures a fine quality of freshness, warmth and vigor. One feels the freedom of the open air. Mr. Broemel can find beauty in local settings, too, so often overlooked by the artist; a "Rocky River Landscape" may be mentioned as an example. Canada and the West have also been delineated by his brush. He paints in oil, having exhibited an oil painting at the Pennsylvania Academy of Fine Arts show in 1931, but his greatest renown comes from pure water color.

Clarence H. Carter, William Sommer, Edwin G. Sommer, and Stanley Clough are foremost among the group of water-colorists. Antimo Beneduce had an exhibit of his bold, striking water colors at the Corcoran Gallery in 1929. Carl F. Binder and Sandor Vago are not only fine water-colorists, but do equally excellent work in oil. They are both foreign born; Mr. Binder received his art training at Düsseldorf, Germany, and came to the United States when he was nineteen years old; Sandor Vago is a native of Budapest, Hungary, where he studied at the Royal Academy. Antonio di Nardo, Joseph Boersig and John Csosz are others eminent in water-color painting.

Grace V. Kelly serves the cause of art well in Cleveland by her writings for *The Plain Dealer*. Her reviews and criticisms are just, and arrived at with knowledge of the craft, as she is an artist of ability herself (Plate 121). Miss Kelly has painted many odd corners and old shacks along the river in Cleveland, perpetuating street scenes that probably will not exist many years. One called "Ugly as Sin" has a stark telephone pole in the foreground, and a row of small stores with false fronts along a narrow street; another is a line of buildings showing through an envelope of smoke and steam, named "For to Admire and For to See" — the title taken from Kipling; other pictures of unsightly houses are "Under the Hill", and "Fishing Boats". The last two were hung in the Paris Salon in the Spring of 1927. At the May Show, in 1924, she won second prize for "The Farm House", a subject interpreted with much humor, and again in 1925, for "The Farmer's Wife."

In 1930, Miss Kelly exhibited a number of water colors painted in Ireland, rendered with an appreciation of the beauties of that unique island. There is a bleakness in the landscape, and yet a softness of vegetation and atmosphere found nowhere else than in Ireland. Her paintings are characterized by sureness and directness, with impressions of changing clouds and mist and quick shifting of tones and colors. One entrancing picture is of a cottage nestling under a group of trees, with an old mill near by to give its tone of romance to the setting. Sheep browse peacefully in the foreground while a rainstorm passes over the distant valley. There is a sculptural quality of form in all her paintings, but it is particularly noticeable in a group of Irish fishwives, chatting together on a street corner in the swirling mist and fog; here are no details — merely broad masses reveal their pudgy forms.

Artist and explorer! Paul B. Travis experienced this unusual combination of vocations during a year spent in Africa. A continent that has not even begun to be explored and pictured by artists was a wonderful, beautiful place to Mr. Travis, who thinks Paris is decadent and unwholesome as a Mecca for art students. He loves Africa. To see the pygmies he walked two hundred and

PLATE 121—Provincetown Having Its Morning Fog. Grace V. Kelly.
(Cleveland Museum of Art)

seventy miles to get to their villages in the geographical center of the continent, one thousand miles from any railroad.

The boyhood of Mr. Travis was signalized by two major interests, love for the out-of-doors, and a passion for Africa, the country of Stanley's adventures. Spending a year in his beloved country collecting primitive African art was made possible by the Gilpin Players, and a number of colored citizens of Cleveland called the African Art Sponsors. These two groups jointly raised fifteen hundred dollars for the project. Mr. Travis brought back many rare objects of African art for the Cleveland Museum of Art, the Museum of Natural History, and the Playhouse Settlement. The collection includes many magnificent spears, a buffalo-hide shield, an ostrich-feather headdress, African implements, weapons, musical instruments, and wearing apparel. Many hazardous experiences were undergone in obtaining rare birds for the Museum of Natural History.

Mr. Travis went to Africa primarily for picture inspiration, and he succeeded in recording many amazingly vivid and astonishing impressions of the equatorial region. "Rain in the Belgian Congo", is a powerful presentation of wind and weather; this received honorable mention in the Cleveland show of 1929. The same year he won first prize in oil landscape for "Mt. Kilimanjaro, Evening", in which exotic trees of peculiar shape create an air of mystery; the color and tone of the canvas are rich. The breadth and strength of his technique succeed in giving reality to the majesty of Africa. "Pygmy Hunters in the Congo Forest", is a study of individual personalities arranged in interesting form rhythms, with a subdued rich color, and the intense quality of life avidly sought by the modern artist (Plate 122). There is a something about these African canvases that awes and impresses one; perhaps it is the impression of vastness, of melancholy serenity, and primitive quality that puts a person in tune with nature. The Brooklyn Museum owns Mr. Travis's water color, "Crater Lake, Ruanda."

The following very touching tribute to his instructor is written by Mr. Travis: "I owe all my training to Mr. Keller, who is, I think, one of the very best artists Ohio has produced." The subjects of Mr. Travis range through figure studies, still life, and landscape. He is equally at home with oil, water color, the etcher's needle, and the lithographer's crayon (see page 260).

At the 1930 show, Kalman Kubinyi was awarded premier honor in the class of oil portraits for a fine portrait of an elderly couple, "Matyas Smayda and His Wife." The artist has caught the pair in a moment of repose after a day's hard toil that has left its story in their resigned expressions, bent shoulders,

PLATE 122—Pygmy Hunters, Congo Forest. Paul Bough Travis.
(Cleveland Museum of Art)

stolid forms, and horny hands (Plate 123). As is usual with Kubinyi, he obtains in this picture the psychological force which gives striking sincerity to his creations. The cool, silvery tonality is harmonious with the subject and the design (see page 260).

Charles Burchfield is the first American artist to see the artistic possibilities of the "Main Street" of small towns, a subject that some writers have attacked so clamorously. He pictures the store buildings with their walls extending up into false fronts, and makes them as stark and drab as they really are. He has been hailed as a great genius in his remarkable presentation of these subjects, which he carries out with the same earnestness in woodcuts (Plate 124) as in water color. In the Eleventh International Water Color Show, at Chicago, May, 1931, was "Civic Improvement" — the ironic title of a canvas depicting an event common enough in modern America. Two woodmen are chopping down the trees along the street, thus robbing it of its only possible claim to beauty, as the residences are of the ugliest type. The picture preaches a sermon and deserves a big ovation from tree lovers.

Mr. Burchfield makes another type of picture — decorative tree-and-flower patterns — with much modernistic feeling. Moods are reflected in his pictures, and thus they must be judged by those who feel rather than by persons demanding a camera-like exactness. Henry G. Keller says of his work: "It is the art of a man who wanders alone amid a world of never-ceasing wonders, Shelley-like in his sensitiveness. His art is expressionism in the best sense of the word. It is founded on keen feeling, reflective organization, bringing every sense into the play."[5]

The Cleveland Museum instituted a class of industrial painting for the May Show, hoping to inspire the artists to recreate upon canvas the industrial forces at work in the valley of the Cuyahoga. There have been extraordinary results from this innovation. Carl F. Gaertner for three successive years took first prize in this class: "Up the River at Upson's", won first prize in 1923; "The Shops", in 1924; and "Snow and Steel", in 1925. In 1926 Gaertner won first place with a group of three industrial subjects — "Four o'Clock", "The Allegheny", and "The Pie Wagon". Again in 1928 he won first prize in that class with "Emma Furnace". They are dramatic interpretations of modern industry in vital, artistic pictures. The second prize in oil painting, 1931, was awarded to Gaertner's "The Popcorn Man". It is a night scene of mystery and poetic feeling; the little popcorn wagon is a glow of light on the street; with the spots of lamplight the artist has sustained the strong color through the very

[5] *Cleveland Topics,* November 24, 1917.

PLATE 123—Matyas Smayda and Wife. Kalman Kubinyi. (Cleveland Museum of Art)

dark masses. It was a problem which he solved successfully, and is reminiscent of some of the work of George Bellows.

Cleveland still has a certain claim on Louise B. Maloney, though her residence abroad has been extended. Her art finds keen admirers, as all of it is endowed with her own vitality and indomitable character. In the obscure Italian village of Anticoli in the Abruzzi Mountains, she has painted portraits of the peasants with a charming simplicity. In subtlety of character analysis and solid structural quality her canvases are able performances. Her restrained and distinguished color sense and feeling for form have made her oil portraits winners of first prizes for four years — 1924, '26, '27, '28. Here are a few typical names of the subjects: "Francesca", "Bianca", "Caterina", and "Antonia". These portraits are small, but very sensitive, showing the Italian types beautifully individualized. "Francesca" has a dreamy, wistful expression; all of her peasant studies are distinguished by a confident originality. Her still-life groups of flowers and vegetables are rich in color and have the same individuality of approach that characterizes her portraits. First place was given to her "Zinnias and Asters", and "Eggplant and Onions", in 1930.

Cora M. Holden has won prizes for her portraits, which have solid workmanlike qualities, and well merit the awards. She was very successful in her murals for the Medical Library, Cleveland. Rolf Stoll has shown unusual talent in mural and decorative designs. Hugh Seaver paints as well as he etches (see page 258), which is praise extraordinary. Norris Rahming can organize a landscape into a decorative pattern of great strength; examples of his work are "Mediterranean Fishing Village", "Carcassone", and "St. Martin du Canigou." Mary Susan Collins is a versatile artist carrying off prizes in oil landscape and still life, also in the crafts (batiks, etc.). Emery Gellert makes charming portraits in that too-often-neglected medium, pastel. Walter Brough paints portraits in pastels that are notable for a delicate sensitiveness of color; he also does portraits in oil having a fine distinction of color and character-delineation. Landscapes and murals he executes in a masterly manner. Paul Shively has won success in a series of water color New England scenes in which there is a remarkable feeling for light and intensity. "Boats and Piers", "A Wash Line", "Rockport Street", and "Incoming Tide", are a few of the many interesting ones in the series. Groups of them won honors and prizes in the 1925, '26, '27, '29 annual shows. Other Cleveland artists who are claimants for honors, are Max Bachofen, Gordon Barrick, Willard Combes, Glenn Moore Shaw, Elsa Vick Shaw, and August Biehle.

One of the finest features of the annual May Show of the work of Cleve-

PLATE 124—A Carolina Village. Wood block designed by Charles Burchfield
and cut by J. J. Lankes. (Cleveland Museum of Art)

land artists is that it includes the work of the craftsmen. William Morris brought the arts and crafts to full fruition in the last years of the nineteenth century. Now almost every art exhibition is spiced with a variety of *objects d'art* in which versatility is strikingly demonstrated. The displays of pottery, glass, tapestry, and metal work are effectively stimulating a keener appreciation of beauty in all things. Strictly speaking, there is no such thing as a minor art. There should be no distinction between the fine and so-called minor or allied arts, for if there is art at all in the channels of industry and the crafts, the art displayed there is just as fine as it is anywhere; for the observer the paramount need is to see and realize art in whatever form it may appear.

The jewelry art at present is at its highest development. Horace Potter, of the Potter-Bentley Studios, Cleveland, had a Boston training in the crafts, and produces beautiful enamels, silverware and jewelry. It is work like his which helps to convince the public of the difference between handmade and machine work, individual and mass production, and at the same time places the craftsman in the artist class with the painter, sculptor, and architect. John Burton and Frederick Wade Hitchings are other Cleveland jewelry makers who are winning prizes for their work. In the 1931 annual show the craft entries were especially numerous. In photography, Ethel Standiford-Mehling carried off the honors with a delightful study entitled "The Printer". Donna M. Hall is one of several votaries of the fascinating craft of block printing in textiles, and Helen Bolly exhibited some fine examples of batik dyeing. Furniture, embroidery, and metal work in silver, brass, iron and pewter, greatly enhanced the crafts exhibit.

Cleveland has some exceptional murals in the county courthouse; a large lunette of the "Magna Charta", by Frank Brangwyn, and on the opposite wall is Violet Oakley's "Constitutional Convention" — both are magnificent paintings. "The Town Meeting in New England", by Max Bohm, in the Law Library has been described (see page 131). In the Federal Building are murals by Frank D. Millet, Will H. Low, Crowninshield, Kenyon Cox and Blashfield. The bank buildings of the Cleveland Trust Company, and the Union Trust Company contain some fine murals. In the latter building Kenyon Cox has depicted the sources of wealth, and Blashfield has described the uses of wealth.

In a *résumé* of the art of a city it is inevitable that many fine artists should pass unmentioned. It could not be otherwise when there are so many artists producing work of high quality. Cleveland art is marching forward, and the city may be justly proud of its artists.

CHAPTER XIV

Contemporary Tendencies in Architecture

IT is the intention in this chapter to try to show in what direction Ohio architecture is going, and to inquire if it has distinctive characteristics of its own. Is there anything more difficult to do than this? There is much in a bird's-eye view of modern building construction that is encouraging. The great factor in architecture at the present is the experimentation that is taking place. There is need for the architect who is able to see his problem in relation to the present, who sees it intelligently, and who can apply his knowledge to the limits of the time. Social, political, industrial, and economical conditions are all important practical factors in architectural design. The discovery and use of new materials have made rapid and radical changes in structural forms, with attendant innovations more or less satisfying. It is always a questionable process to strive for originality merely for the sake of being original. Whatever is truthful of function, is appropriate to the surroundings; and whatever can lay claim to beauty, is legitimate and logical in architecture.

The tendencies in Ohio architecture of today may be roughly classified something like this: first, the skyscrapers, the most characteristic type of American architecture, favor the modernistic mass effects, as do many large commercial buildings; second, the public buildings such as museums, libraries, banks, and railway stations, adhere to the classic inspiration; third, the churches are largely of Gothic tendency; fourth, the schools and colleges reflect generally Tudor or Elizabethan variants; fifth, the residences, in a great variety of styles, exhibit Gothic, classic, English derivations. A wave of eclecticism, choosing from many styles, is spreading over the country.

SKYSCRAPERS

In the building of great commercial and public buildings, new problems and methods have arisen, due to the development of great industries; due also to the fact that the architect now works in conjunction with mechanical, electrical, heating, and structural engineers, and not alone as formerly; and to the fact that there is a new type of construction with which to deal. Steel-cage construction is only about thirty-five years old, and in that short time, with the increasing use of concrete and glass, it has entirely revolutionized building processes. Such immense strides have been taken in the last few years that it is not easy to believe that the first skyscraper was erected only in the closing

365

years of the nineteenth century. The graphic word, skyscraper, came out of some fertile mind when the Masonic Temple in Chicago took the skyward race up to twenty-two stories.

Somewhat previous to this time the floors of large buildings were carried on wrought-iron beams, resting on cast-iron columns. The next step, logically, was to use an iron skeleton for the walls, finally covering them with masonry. The use of skeleton construction throughout quickly followed; then steel took the place of iron, and building mounted higher and higher. Steel construction was badly bungled at first. Although the buildings were supported by steel, they were made to look like stone-supported buildings; the idea prevailed that the building should be in three parts like a column with a base, a shaft, and a heavy cornice as a capital. Because it was a vertical architecture, there was a feeling that it should have Gothic ornaments; pinnacles, and towers with imitation buttresses.

When Louis Sullivan built the Prudential (Guaranty) Building in Buffalo, he brought an original idea into steel-skeleton building. His idea was that the form should be dictated by the function, and that architects should be freed from the arbitrary conventions of form so as to permit of a creative use of them. Masonry construction, as far as tall buildings were concerned, had to be forgotten. The old idea of imposing one column above another had to give way to a continuity of vertical lines. Sullivan believed that loftiness is the chief appeal of a tall building. Ornament for the Prudential Building was entirely original with Sullivan. The tall piers terminate in arches; the attic windows repeat the lines of the curved arches; the cornice is very light. Thus the tall building was emancipated from crippling conventions, horizontal bands of emphasis were bidden adieu, and cornices were ruled out.

The Woolworth Building, of New York City, built in 1911-'13, represents the conquest of the perpendicular motif over the horizontal tradition in the skyscraper. The structural framework is emphasized completely in the design, and while the ornament is foreign to it, yet it is used intelligently and not beyond its function as ornament. T. E. Tallmadge pronounces upon it this verdict: "Undoubtedly it is one of the great monuments of the world."[1] No excuses are given in this chapter for quoting this bit of praise of the Woolworth Building, since the architect was an Ohioan, Cass Gilbert, born at Zanesville. When making a list of America's recent notable achievements, the poet Christopher Morley remarked that, "America's most effective poets, the architects and builders, continue to do the incredible." To the layman, such a structure

---

[1] *The Story of American Architecture,* T. E. Tallmadge, p. 257.

PLATE 125—American Insurance Union Citadel, Columbus.

as the Woolworth Building and the many even higher ones that have been erected later, do seem like incredible marvels.

One has not far to go in seeking examples of skyscrapers in Ohio. The capital city has the American Insurance Union Building, whose tower dominates the horizon from whatever point one views Columbus. Its construction marks a milestone in the growth of the city. In New York a tower more or less would make little difference, but in Columbus it signalizes the transition from a large, overgrown country town to a city. It stands out against the sky line so sharply that it cannot be ignored. A few statistics regarding the Citadel or the A.I.U., as it is commonly called, will be of interest. It was designed by C. Howard Crane of Detroit. It was built in three years, 1924-1927, by a force of six hundred and fifty workmen. The height is 555.5 feet, the base being one hundred and eighty-eight feet square. In addition to office-suites and storerooms, the Citadel embraces a luxurious theater of four thousand seating capacity, and six hundred rooms used as an annex to the Deshler-Wallick Hotel. It was the first building in Ohio to be erected on a caisson foundation; each of the forty-four giant concrete pillars penetrates the earth to a depth of one hundred and twelve feet.

The tera cotta surface prompted Roger L. Waring, architectural superintendent, to say: "It is beautiful to look upon. It radiates warmth and sunshine. As the waters of the lake reflect in their depth each new mood in nature, so every hour in the day changes its appearance as the light strikes it from each new angle. Wind, rain and storm will only serve to mellow and enrich its dignity." In its beauty and sturdiness it reminds one of mighty trees. As the king of trees gives majesty to the forest, so this finest of surfaces gives majesty to the Citadel. Cherubs on the top of the tower form an appropriate crown for this king of buildings; below the crown, ornamenting the parapet, are six gigantic eagles. Sculptured groups contribute added decoration to the building, but there is nothing to interrupt the sweeping vertical lines. Dudley Crafts Watson, of Chicago Art Institute, declared the A.I.U. of Columbus to be the most beautiful building between New York and Chicago (Plate 125).

The designer of the fifty-two story Terminal Tower at Cleveland was not worried with Old World traditions concerning a railway station. The Tower with its two accompanying office buildings now forms Cleveland's transportation center in Public Square. "It functions not only as a station for through and local trains, but it is the first attempt, so far as known, that has ever been made in this country to unify a city's transportation system under one roof. Trains and taxicabs there are of course. There are also street cars and rapid-transit interurban lines. Heretofore the lowly street car has been obliged to stay out in the street, there to discharge its customers in all sorts of weather."[2]

Here are some interesting figures of the Terminal Tower of fifty-two stories. It is seven hundred and eight feet high. Adjoining the Tower are two eighteen-story buildings containing the Builder's Exchange, the Medical Arts Building, and nine floors of garage space. In the Terminal is the Cleveland Hotel, the Midland Bank, and a department store. The terminal area proper covers thirty-five acres; fourteen hundred buildings were torn down to make way for it. The cost was in the neighborhood of two hundred million dollars. The Tower exhibits an entire emphasis on the vertical; the round shaft recedes from a square base and rises with alternating plain and colonnaded stories until it reaches the summit. "Highest ever" records are soon eclipsed by these swiftly growing steel skeletons that in a short time transform the whole sky line of a city.

The idea of the Cleveland Terminal came from O. P. and M. J. Van Sweringen, Cleveland real estate dealers, who needed a downtown terminus for the rapid-transit line serving their ten-thousand acre development in Shaker Heights village. The New York Central and Big Four Railroads were the guarantors of the project to build this giant terminal and its great tower. The engineers made their plans large enough to care for the Erie, Baltimore and Ohio, and Pennsylvania Railroads, as it is thought that they will eventually use the terminal. The terminal group of buildings seems likely to check the rapid growth from the Public Square eastward on Euclid Avenue, and stage a comeback for the Public Square, which many people thought had seen its best day.

Architects have now turned their attention to building blocks, and have treated whole squares as a single unit. The idea opens up a vista of possibilities for enhancing the beauty of American cities. The unity of design (many examples in cities of the Old World may be cited) obtained by one building covering a whole block is infinitely more pleasing to the eye than a heterogeneous collection of fifteen or twenty different styles of architecture strung along the side of a block. Economy of building construction and the pooling of resources are other advantages of the block plan. Cincinnati leads off in this development with the Carew Tower, which is located in the chief business section of the city. It is designed with the unique idea of supplying under one roof nearly all the needs of its tenants. In this forty-six story structure is an office building, a seven-hundred-room hotel, two department stores, a car-parking garage, and a number of specialty shops; the ensemble thus performs many

[2] Albert Sidney Gregg, *World's Work*, February, 1930, p. 54.

PLATE 126—McClain High School, Greenfield. (Board of Education, Greenfield)

housing functions and solves snarly parking and traffic problems. The mass of the building presents a most interesting outline, as the new setbacks begin at the eighth floor, much lower than on most of the skyscrapers. W. W. Ahlschlager, architect, is to be congratulated upon this notable building achievement; associated with him in the work were Messrs. Delano and Aldrich.

Toledo has a successful setback type of skyscraper in the New Ohio Savings Bank. In height it affords a sharp contrast with the old Nasby Building, now called the Security Bank Building, whose tower (patterned after the Giralda Tower, in Seville, Spain) was considered, when it was built, the last word in high buildings in Toledo.

In the large commercial building class, the modernistic style makes an inning in the Cincinnati and suburban Bell Telephone Building, designed by Harry Hake, architect. The Union Central Building, of Cincinnati, is another fine building in the commercial class, but of the renaissance style; Cass Gilbert, and Garber & Woodward were the architects. The Hanna Building, Cleveland, is a notable structure of which Charles A. Platt was the architect. There are several other buildings of the large commercial class in the smaller cities of the state; they show the modernistic trend and have the qualifications of good architecture.

GOVERNMENT BUILDINGS

The horizontal type of building is exemplified in government buildings, museums, libraries, banks, and railway stations, where classic ideas usually prevail.

The cities of the Middle West have grown so rapidly that mistakes have been made because architects did not have time to consider the best possible arrangements. About thirty years ago Cleveland discovered that most of its public buildings had to be replaced, and it was therefore decided to make a plan to bring these buildings into some relation with each other. A so-called group plan was worked out, which involved a rearrangement of considerable magnitude. The plan of the grouping consisted of a large esplanade and plaza in the form of a Latin cross, the main axis running from near the center of the city north to the lake. Entrance to the Mall, as it is popularly known, is from Superior Avenue with the Federal Building at the left and the Public Library at the right. At the north are the Court House at the left and the City Hall at the right, on a bluff overlooking the lake. Other buildings in the plan are the Public Auditorium and the Education Building.

The first building to be erected in the civic center was the Federal Building, which in its architectural design determined to a great extent the character of the architecture and the selection of the material for the succeeding buildings. For the Federal Building a Corinthian order was selected, for the Cuyahoga County Court House a composite order was the choice (both orders with fluted columns) and a simple Doric order with no flutings was used for the City Hall. The material in the City Hall is granite. The Doric order was used in the grand lobby which extends through three stories; a barrel-vaulted ceiling, with lunettes at each end, admits light to the lobby. The cost of the City Hall was three million dollars.

The development of the Cleveland civic center was one of the first of importance among such undertakings taking place over the country. The buildings have been executed with the utmost simplicity and with but little ornamentation other than a few sculptured groups. People of the Middle West believe that they like plain buildings, but perhaps it is nearer the truth to say that there are not a great many designers who know how to use ornament well. This successful group plan in Cleveland has encouraged other centers of growth in the same city. Euclid Avenue is the principal business street; new office buildings, banks, and stores are so effective that one is justified in describing it as a fine street. The buildings are generally light-colored; some are of stone, and many are of terra cotta in imitation of stone or granite. Superior Avenue has a fine group of public and commercial buildings. A notable structure among these is the Federal Reserve Bank of Cleveland; many authorities rate it among the very finest buildings in the country. Walker & Weeks were the architects.

Postoffices, or Federal buildings, in county-seat towns are, as a rule, so much more pretentious than their surroundings that they exert little architectural influence upon a community. The State Office Building now being constructed in Columbus was designed by Harry Hake, an able architect of Cincinnati. The architect's sketch gives graphic testimony that it will be an interesting building carrying the effect of mass that distinguishes the modern idiom. There is a singular beauty in all the elements of line that add charm to the bulk and strength of the edifice; the material, Georgia marble, gives it a permanent and monumental aspect. It is a fourteen-story structure with the setback beginning almost at the top, with the thirteenth story. The building is one more unit in a civic group plan to beautify the Scioto River front in Columbus's downtown district.

EDUCATIONAL INSTITUTIONS

The centralized school buildings in the rural districts are yet a long way from giving any marked esthetic reaction; most of them are ugly box-like

PLATE 127—Fig. 1, Wise Center, Cincinnati. (Fechheimer and Ihorst, Architects.)
Fig. 2, Ohio State University Library, Columbus. (Author)

structures, with no excuse for being so. Beauty is no more expensive than ugliness. Just as the generation of the past is judged by the houses they built, so will this generation be open to criticism for what is being done by its architects and taxpayers.

City high schools are beautiful, for they follow English lines to a great extent. The importance of housing children in good buildings during their school years has not been overlooked, and school buildings have been improved constantly. They are substantial, adapted to meet the needs, and not too elaborate. In scientific arrangement they have been evolved to near perfection. Light, safety and sanitation have been considered as the first requisites.

A few outstanding school buildings in the state are the following: Withrow High School, Cincinnati, Garber & Woodward, architects; Oakwood Schools, Dayton, Schenck & Williams, architects; Cleveland Heights High School, Cleveland, W. R. McCornack, architect; East High School, Columbus, Howell & Thomas, architects; West High School, Columbus, Howard Dwight Smith, architect; and the McClain Schools, Greenfield, W. B. Ittner, architect. The latter has received more publicity than the others, having been erected by private funds, but it does not surpass the others architecturally (Plate 126).

As it was a city's vision only a few years ago, so it is now a city's pride—the new University of the City of Toledo. It is easily one of the finest municipal universities in the country. President Henry J. Doermann was the leader in the movement for this temple of learning in Toledo. The high, square tower of University Hall dominates the entire countryside. The building is in Tudor Gothic style, frequently referred to in this country as Collegiate Gothic; with much of the strength of line and majesty of the original Gothic, it separates from the Old World models in abandoning the flying buttresses, and substituting rectangular window openings for the Gothic arches. With the exception of Gothic arches and decoration on the great tower, it exhibits more simple and severe contours than its European ancestors. The roof lines are sharply sloping.

The Toledo University structure is the creation of Mills, Rhines, Bellman & Nordhoff, of Toledo, and is one of their finest achievements. The building is made up of six distinct units, connected by covered hallways. The exterior of rough Lannon stone, has an interesting color symphony of gray-white mottled with rust-brown. The main entrance, directly beneath the tower, is a huge open archway. This leads into the tower porch, which has a high arched ceiling modeled after Daneway Hall, a famous English manse of the sixteenth century. The tower rises two hundred and five feet above the street. A massive field house, a theater, shops, laboratories, classrooms, and all other needs

PLATE 128—St. Monica Church, Cleveland. (Crowe and Schulte, Architects)

are anticipated and provided for in this beautiful and practical gift of Toledo to its youth. The edifice has a beautiful setting in a campus of gently rolling ground enhanced by towering elms. Through the one hundred and fourteen acres of the university grounds, the tiny Ottawa River winds slowly and quietly about in wooded ravines.

SOCIAL AND COMMUNITY BUILDINGS

Claude Bragdon in *Architecture and Democracy,* describes at length the Community House at Camp Sherman, Chillicothe (destroyed by fire March 5, 1920), which illustrated the ideal relation of the work of the architect and the engineer. The exterior of this building (constructed at a cost of $170,000.00), which occupied an acre of ground, had no particular distinction. The interior however, was entitled to consideration. It had the form of a cross, symbolic of its dedication to the use of the Red Cross of the State of Ohio. "It stands in symbolic relation to the times; it represents what may be called the architecture of service; it is among the first of the new temples of the new democracy, dedicated to the uses of simple, rational, social life. . . . The cross is divided into side aisles, nave and crossing, with galleries and mezzanines so arranged as to shorten the arms of the cross in its upper stages, leaving the clerestory surrounding the crossing unimpeded and well defined. The light comes for the most part from high windows, filtering down in tempered brightness to the floor. The bones of the structure are everywhere in evidence, and an element of its beauty, by reason of its admirably direct and logical arrangement of posts and trusses. . . . The building attained its final synthesis through the collaboration of a Cleveland architect and a national army captain of engineers."[3]

"Dreams long dwelt on amount to prayers, and prayers wrought in faith come true." This quotation from the "Rosebush of a Thousand Thorns", by Mabel Wagnalls Jones, was the idea promoting the construction of the Wagnalls Memorial at Lithopolis, a building in which the name of the late Adam Wagnalls, cofounder of the Funk and Wagnalls Company, publishers of *The Literary Digest,* and the Standard Dictionary, will be perpetuated forever. Mrs. Jones conceived the memorial to her father and mother, and dedicated it to the community where they spent their early lives. It was built in 1925. The project with its endowment represents an outlay of half a million dollars.

The building, a beautiful structure of Tudor Gothic architecture, was designed by Ray Sims, a Columbus architect. The lines of the heavy stone edifice are low; the stone was quarried by hand from the ancient limestone quarries at

---

[3]*Architecture and Democracy,* Claude Bragdon, p. 31.

Lithopolis. A square tower with crenelated top is a feature of the building. Expert craftsmen were used in every phase of the construction; hand-carved woodwork, stone and bronze tablets, and stained glass are all unique throughout in design. Mrs. Jones has given to this tiny village and to Bloom Township, Fairfield County, this permanent legacy consisting of the building, its equipment, and its endowment. The memorial contains a library which includes the entire Wagnalls collection of original manuscripts and rare volumes; an auditorium with a fine pipe organ; a community center equipped with kitchen, tables, and all requirements for social gatherings; and special rooms for the original works of Edwin Markham, and the paintings of John Ward Dunsmore, a painter of historical subjects. The auditorium walls are hung with many original sketches for *The Literary Digest* cover pages. Such a memorial is a "living" one. To contribute to the advancement of the people of Bloom Township and to give them, free of charge, the best in art and literature is the service performed by this eminently useful memorial.

Wise Center, Cincinnati, an adjunct to a synagogue, is a community building of unusual interest (Fig. 1, Plate 127). It is of a modified Romanesque character with the ashlar work of split-faced Weymouth granite in colors varying from deep golden brown to grayish yellow. The trimmings are of Bedford stone. In mass it suggests the modernistic rather than the Romanesque. The building includes an auditorium seating seven hundred and fifty people, a stage equipped for giving dramatic performances, concerts, and entertainments, and dining room and kitchen facilities that will provide for five hundred people. The building is used also as a Sunday school, containing classrooms and kindergarten rooms, a men's clubroom, the Rabbi's study and library. Fechheimer & Ihorst were the architects of this commodious and serviceable structure.

CHURCHES

Nowhere has the development of good architecture been more astounding than in the realm of ecclesiastical buildings. The leavening that made Gothic church building rise to splendid achievement in America was the work and personality of Bertram Goodhue, of the firm of Cram, Goodhue & Ferguson. At his death, only a few years ago, he was paid the most sincere and glowing tributes by his friends in the architectural profession, and he was said to have wielded an influence in extent second only to that of Richardson.

"Thanks to the influence of this firm (Cram, Goodhue & Ferguson), American churches during the past twenty-five years have with few exceptions adopted the Gothic style. The Evangelical Church has occasionally reverted

PLATE 129—The Temple, Cleveland. (Cleveland Museum of Art)

to the colonial type, the Roman Catholic to the basilica. The Christian Science Church has generally preferred the Roman dome and portico. But the Gothic has been, and still is, the style most generally approved; and those modern Gothic chapels and cathedrals, which 'have all the virtues of the originals except originality', are unquestionably an improvement upon the debased classical and Romanesque forms of the churches built during the late nineteenth century."[4]

The Church of the Covenant, Cleveland, by Cram, Goodhue & Ferguson, exemplifies that firm's work in which Mr. Goodhue expressed medieval Gothic with a magic hand. It resembles English Gothic rather than the French. The Westminster Church, Dayton, is another fine example of Gothic building; Schenck & Williams, architects, had as associate architects Cram & Ferguson. The St. Cecilia Church, Oakley, Cincinnati (Crowe & Schulte, architects) was awarded the bronze tablet in the ecclesiastical class for 1930; it has a perpendicular Gothic window over the entrance, and an interesting tower with a spire. A notable example of Gothic architecture in Cleveland is the Church of Our Saviour.

Columbus has an example of modified Gothic in the First Congregational Church, of which John Russell Pope, New York, was the architect. The style is simple, unadorned early Gothic, in which the beauty is expressed by lines and proportions, and the obvious function of every part of the structural design. The material is dark-gray stone, with some brown shading, and a trim of buff Indiana limestone at the tops of the buttresses and around the entrances and windows. The sloping roof is of copper, as is also the *flèche,* the little arrow-like spire that rises from the center of the structure. Over the main entrance is a beautiful rose window enlaced with delicate stone tracery. The interior has a minimum of decoration, keeping an air of simple religious dignity. The complete cost of the church approached a million dollars.

The new Toledo cathedral, Our Lady Queen of the Holy Rosary, is a distinctive building in the purely Spanish plateresque style of architecture. That style was chosen for the reason that it was so closely associated with Toledo in Spain, where the Santa Cruz Hospital was built in plateresque style for Cardinal Mendoza. The Spaniards who invented the style were Gothic architects, who changed their style as opportunity presented itself and who became ornamentalists instead of builders. The name, plateresque, is derived from this Spanish effort to build after the Italian Renaissance style, and implies a resemblance to the work of the silversmith, or *platero,* in scale and delicacy of execution.

---

[4]*Art in America,* by Suzanne LaFollette, p. 27.

The Toledo cathedral follows the Gothic in its structural members, but gives the details in refined Renaissance treatment. William R. Perry, Pittsburgh, was the architect who conceived its beauty. The entire front elevation, from the steps to the tops of the pair of great towers, is rich in historical and symbolical details. The large rose window is perhaps the most outstanding decoration of the façade. The huge entrance is set in an archway, containing a number of small panels representing various details relative to the symbolism of the church. The great length of the cathedral is supported by a series of buttresses along each side and at the back. Each of these is topped with a pinnacle. Between the buttresses are double rows of Gothic windows. In all parts of the edifice there is a wealth of beautiful carvings and statuary including statues of the patron saints of the many nationalities represented in Toledo.

St. Monica Church, Cincinnati, designed by Crowe & Schulte, is a fine piece of ecclesiastical architecture (Plate 128). Located on one of the Queen City hills, its tower rises proudly and gracefully to glorify the mother of St. Augustine. It breathes the modern spirit and frankness of expression, yet it is indebted to the Romanesque and Byzantine styles, though the old forms are sensibly adapted. The traditional orientation of having the chancel at the east end is observed, but the tower is at the south instead of the west. Rising in a bold mass, the church is dominated by its tower, which rises from a simple, strong base to an open and beautiful yet restrained summit. The church is crowned with a red tile roof.

Looking at the church from the west, we see the long narthex with its superimposed balcony, and the rose window. On the central axis is a semicircular baptistry surmounted by a sculptured crucifixion group by Clement J. Barnhorn, and high above — over the rose window — is a slender statue of Saint Monica (see page 398). Buttresses expressing the termination of the side aisles form the rich central composition. The side aisles are kept low and are subordinated, thus placing the accent on the bold mass of the nave. On the north side there is a delightful transept chapel marked by a small tower reproducing the form of the large tower on the south. A wealth of symbolism is incorporated into the decoration and structure of the church; the numerous symbols both of the interior and the exterior furnish that element of interest that is so fascinating a part of the medieval cathedrals. The cost of the church was $432,000.

The Temple Tifereth Israel, Cleveland, is among the largest and most costly synagogues of the country (Plate 129). It seats two thousand people, and cost $2,250,000. Its architect was Charles R. Greco, Boston. The form of the

PLATE 130—The Perry Monument, Put-in-Bay. (Webster P. Huntington)

main temple is circular, as that form is best adapted to the seating of a congregation, but the entire building takes the shape of a seven-sided polygon to fit the lot on which it stands. The exterior is of Indiana limestone, laid in wide and narrow courses alternately, which after a brief weathering will give a slightly banded effect similar to that of Santa Sophia and other buildings in the Near East. The main dome and the smaller domes are of a special yellow-buff tile; over the entrance arches are inlays of colored marbles. Two tones of wall tile are used on the interior; the impression of color in the material and the lighting is beautifully soft, rich, and mellow. Each of the seven interior faces has a great arch, enclosing smaller blind arches, with a broad band of arabesque spanning it. The great arch over the Ark (the focal point of the interior) and choir gallery, recedes in the form of a barrel ceiling. The ensemble of the Temple is oriental, more nearly resembling Byzantine than any other style. The church of St. Agnes, Cleveland, may be mentioned, finally, as a fine example of Romanesque.

MEMORIALS

One of the largest architectural competitions ever held in America or Europe was for the Perry's Victory Memorial at Put-in-Bay. The National Fine Arts Commission appointed by President Taft in 1911 chose the winning design.

The architectural scheme of the memorial presents a composition of a great Doric column placed on a broad plaza elevated, as compared with its height, only slightly above the grounds, so that the entire memorial appears to arise from the sea. This effect is further enhanced by its reflection in Lake Erie on both sides, as the isthmus on which it stands is but a few feet removed from either shore. The Doric order, treated without ornament of any kind, seemed to the architect, Joseph H. Freelander, of New York City, best adapted to convey the impression of grandeur and simplicity which the memorial is intended to suggest. The stone selected for the entire work was pink Milford granite.

The column is 352 feet high, with a diameter of forty-five feet at the base, and thirty-five and a half feet at the neck. "It is the highest monument in the world, excepting the Washington Monument, the greatest battle monument in the world, and the most massive column ever attempted by ancients or moderns."[5] It has a physical setting of great beauty, for the scene disclosed from the top gallery is unrivaled. One can look across to West Sister Island, the scene of Perry's victory, from whence Commodore Perry sent his famous mes-

---

[5] *Official Souvenir,* the Perry's Victory Memorial.

sage to General Harrison, "We have met the enemy and they are ours." Rising above the gallery is the great tripod, monumental in itself, which supports a massive bowl designed for illumination purposes; its two hundred lamps afford a soft glow that penetrates the heavens at night. As a work of art, the memorial is satisfying (Plate 130). It not only commemorates the victory of Commodore Perry, September 10, 1813, but also is dedicated to the principle of international peace by arbitration.

The Harding Memorial at Marion is a tomb of unique design. A few historical observations may explain it: a circular temple with a court in the center was common in ancient Greece; the Romans planted trees on the steps of their pyramidal tombs; and one of the glories of the Middle Ages was the Gothic cloister, with its charming garden and surrounding arcade. Thus the Harding Memorial, embodying these ideas, is circular in plan. It contains a circular cloister, open to the air, and has vines planted on the roof of the interior colonnade. Where it differs from the monuments of the past is that it has no doorway. It may be aptly described as a garden crypt.

Forty-eight massive white Georgia marble columns, symbolizing the forty-eight states, support the circular roof. As the visitor approaches the memorial he beholds an attractive sunlit interior. The entire conception has nothing of the usual oppressive feeling generally experienced upon entering a tomb. It is in no way forbidding. The landscaping plan of the ten-acre plot is that of a Latin cross, with the tomb placed at the intersection of the arms of the cross. When the elm trees planted along the arms of the cross, and willow tree of the interior have reached their growth, the memorial will be beautiful indeed. No tomb like this has ever been constructed. The bodies of President and Mrs. Harding were placed in the tomb, December 21, 1927. The building is two hundred and fifty feet in circumference, eighty feet in diameter, fifty feet in height, and cost eight hundred thousand dollars. The architects were Pittsburgh men, Henry Hornbostel and associate, Eric Fisher Wood.

MISCELLANEOUS BUILDINGS

Libraries, especially the Carnegie buildings, follow the classic idea of exhibiting columns, architrave, and pediment. Reposeful, horizontal lines predominate, but characteristic features are frequently exaggerated, for example, the entasis on columns, which easily loses all subtlety and becomes too obvious. One of the finest libraries in the state is the Ohio State University Library, Columbus, which is a true example of the Renaissance form (Fig. 2, Plate 127). The perfectly chaste and beautiful Library of the University of Cincinnati

(Harry Hake, architect) was awarded in the year 1930 the bronze tablet in the educational building class. The Cleveland Public Library is a beautiful building, well adapted to its use; it is a noteworthy case where utility and beauty go hand in hand.

Banks in large number reflect "the glory that was Greece" in their architecture; there is still a large following after the old tradition that a treasure house must be like a Greek temple. Many banks have taken on the character of big business buildings, the first floor being occupied with the bank proper, the other floors arranged as office suites.

There is a long list of hotels in Ohio cities acknowledged to be architecturally good. The Deshler-Wallick Hotel, Columbus, of Pompeian design, with its many griffins and other Pompeian decorative features, is one of the most attractive hostelries. The Netherland Plaza in the Carew Tower, Cincinnati, is a palatial hotel equal in every way to the metropolitan hotels of the East. The appointments are in keeping with the impressive beauty of the terraced, upward-sweeping walls of that building whose ramparts seem to reach the sky.

The modern movement in architecture is by no means confined to the skyscraper; there are many architects following Sullivan's idea. Modernism has had every opportunity in the factory building. Pressed by the demands of the material, of economy and function, the architects have been forced to cast aside all architectural formulas. The modern factory becomes an original expression of American architecture, because the needs dictate geometrical forms.

The architecture of the buildings housing the National Cash Register Company, Dayton, is largely the work of F. M. Andrews, although there are two buildings — the garage and the schoolhouse — designed by McKim, Mead & White. The outstanding features of the plant (for example, buildings with wall areas consisting of eighty per cent of glass, beautiful grounds, and the face-brick sides of the buildings) were conceived by Mr. John H. Patterson, founder of the business, and were carried out as early as 1888 against the most severe criticism. These features are today the very essentials of a modern factory. "Our plant consists of twenty-four buildings containing fifty-four acres of floor space. The buildings are widely separated by beautiful lawns, shrubbery, and drives, and all communication from building to building is carried on through underground tunnels or overhead bridges, thus preserving a park-like atmosphere which enhances the value of the surrounding residence district instead of depreciating it, as so often is done when an industrial plant is near a residence district."[6]

---

[6] Excerpt from a letter from Mr. Wm. Hartman, superintendent of the National Cash Register Company.

The architect, Norman Bel Geddes, has made plans for the Toledo Scale Company's new plant, which is to be modernistic and the last word in factory building, it is said, though its construction has not yet been undertaken.

The stadium! The very word conjures up visions of a wildly enthusiastic crowd of football fans, cheering vociferously one moment, waiting in tense breathless expectancy the next, as they watch the progress of the battle on the field. Ohio State University boasts a vast pile of concrete and steel resembling the amphitheaters built by the ancient Romans for their sports. The horseshoe-shaped stadium at Columbus was designed by Howard Dwight Smith, to seat the sixty-three thousand fans that attend the great football games. Over the main entrance is a half-dome, and flanking it on each side are towers, one hundred and nine feet high; there are also two towers at the open end of the horseshoe. When bright-colored pennants float from the towers and the tall flagpoles all around the horseshoe, and the gaily dressed crowd fills the seats, the ensemble makes a glorious, colorful picture, unequalled in any other sort of gathering place but a stadium. The Ohio State University stadium was built in 1922 at a cost of nearly two millions of dollars. It covers a ground area of ten acres.

Cleveland has erected on the lake front a new municipal stadium which was provided for in 1928 by a bond issue of $2,500,000. Architecturally, the structure has a pleasing appearance, its mottled-gray brick wall surface and terra cotta trim being in complete harmony. It is of reinforced concrete and structural steel, carried on composite piles of wood and concrete. In dimensions, this great egg-shaped building is eight hundred feet long over all, extending from east to west, and seven hundred and twenty feet wide from north to south. One of the predominating architectural features of the stadium is the use of sheet aluminum for the upper exterior walls, which enclose the entire structure. This structural use of aluminum represents the largest (and one of the first) examples in the country. The weight of this material is approximately one-third the weight of steel; thus it is advantageous for use in the ventilated superstructure of the stadium. The seating capacity of the building is eighty thousand, but with the installation of seats in the field proper, on a slight incline, a total of one hundred and twenty-five thousand may be seated in comfort. It is claimed to be the only stadium constructed to accommodate every type of athletic contest and outdoor spectacle, and represents the newest idea in stadium design.

For sheer bigness, the municipal airport hangar at Akron exceeds everything. It is not only one of the largest buildings in the world, but it is the largest building in the world without pillars or posts to support it. Its shape is that of an elongated archway, twelve hundred feet long, three hundred and sixty feet wide, and two hundred feet high. It is said to have an unequalled, unobstructed floor area — three hundred and eighty-nine thousand square feet. This immense hangar is used by the Goodyear-Zeppelin Corporation for the construction of the gigantic airships of the United States Navy. The cost was two and a half million dollars. The plans of the aviation department are full of interest to the architectural profession.

RESIDENCES

It is in his own home that the average person comes into most intimate contact with architecture. What has it done for him? It has given him a beautiful and convenient modern home. The attractive home magazines are largely responsible for the all-absorbing interest in the modern home and its decoration; the praise of such periodicals should be sung unceasingly! The many better-homes contests that have been sponsored by different organizations have also aided the movement in favor of better living conditions in the home. Plans and suggestions for domestic architecture have been presented in a fascinating way.

Most works on architecture consider the homes of the wealthy and well-to-do and take little account of the homes of the working and middle-classes. That even the small suburban home can be delightfully individual and interesting has been demonstrated by ingenious architects. It can be something more than just "one of a row of houses."

There are many types of residences. During the first decade of the twentieth century the bungalow type was immensely popular. It developed from the Dutch Colonial and is characterized by low lines that fit into the ground, exhibiting gambrel roofs and dormer windows, and is usually not more than a story and a half in height. New trends in small-house designs suggest the Early American, Scottish, and Norman cottages, while larger houses are reminiscent of the English manor houses and Tudor castles. There are many kinds of building material that can be adapted to the style of architecture.

The Early American cottage lends itself to the purpose of the builder who, with a limited budget, sets out to create a lovely home. It reflects the harmony and purposefulness of home life. It is generally a one-and-a-half storied structure covered with broad-lapped siding, having a central entrance, a chimney at the gable end, and shutters at the windows. An honest interior provides large rooms, low ceilings and large fireplaces. With modern requirements of living, there is need of many refinements in the original Early American plan; but if these are honestly expressed and all so-called stunts omitted, there may be additions that will add to the comfort of living, in no way taking the house out of character: for example, heating plants, as many bathrooms as one can afford, and a garage for the family cars in lieu of the stable of olden days.

The interest taken by architects in the steep-pitched roofs, pointed gables, and white walls of Normandy is quite comprehensible; perhaps the charm of the house is mingled with that of the country. Picturesqueness is a great asset of the Norman house. The walls may be of rough hand-finished plaster, random stone, or half-timber; usually a heavy oak entrance-way is a prominent feature. Numerous groups of leaded windows add attractiveness. Particular care has been given to kitchen arrangement in the modern house, and very properly, too, for economy of time and steps must be figured carefully by the modern housewife.

The architecture of England, which covers many periods, seems especially well adapted to Ohio use, where climatic conditions approximate those of England. The flexibility and suitability of the English Elizabethan and Tudor of the Gothic period have in recent years made them very desirable models. Although the population of Ohio is made up of people from all nations, it is probable that as a whole they have the nearest affinity to the English, in temperament and ideals.

So we find the architect turning to the past for his designs in residences, as in churches, and confining his new experiments to the new types of buildings such as skyscrapers, business blocks, and factories. However, a disciple of Louis Sullivan, Frank Lloyd Wright, designed a type of house for the Middle West that harmonized with the landscapes and was very successful; it was a house of "gently sloping roofs, low proportions, quiet sky lines, suppressed, heavy chimneys, and sheltering overhangs, low terraces, and outreaching walls sequestering private gardens."

A few outstanding examples of such residences may be mentioned. The residence of Mr. Ward W. Canaday, Toledo, is an interesting Norman manor located in the Ottawa Hills section of the city. The designer, Frank J. Forster, shows a sympathetic understanding of the medieval builders. The dwelling is a rambling whitewashed structure of stone, stucco, and timber; the variety of materials is used with much skill. Norman towers and leaded windows enhance the design. A thatched roof is suggested by the use of green and purple slate laid irregularly. There is an interesting arrangement of little French dormers, and windows at the roof line. The interior finish is of Tudor panel-

PLATE 131—Residence of Julius Fleischmann, Cincinnati. (Stanley Matthews, Architect)

ling. A verbal description is scarcely adequate to convey a sense of its success. Berea is proud of the residence of William Spang, designed by the Cleveland architects, Bohnard & Parsson. Norman roof, windows, and chimneys, lapped siding, an entrance with classic details in its modillions, and curved pediment, are some of its features.

At Indian Hill, near Cincinnati, is the country place of Mr. and Mrs. Julius Fleischmann (Plate 131). It is an elegant home, but so modest and well-mannered that it has none of the swagger of a show place about it. The style is derived from no particular historic period, though Norman influence is seen in the roof, chimney, and tower. Stanley Matthews and C. W. Short were the architects. This dwelling has the atmosphere of sincerity, permanence, sturdiness, and charm that accompanies the North European style.

An adaptation of the English Tudor style is the residence of Mr. Ralph Hoyer, Columbus. Ray Sims was the architect. The walls of local limestone laid up in random rubble fashion find their contrast of material in ornamental stucco and some half-timber work. The rugged appearance of the roof is obtained by slate varying in color, size and thickness. Tudor spirit is shown in the many-gabled roof line and in the chimney. Three Cleveland residences of English ancestry are those of Mrs. H. P. Eells, Warren Bicknell, and M. A. Bradley; all of them were designed by Frank B. Meade and James M. Hamilton. The traditional English house is outdone in the features of many more bathrooms and much more glass surface in steel-casement leaded windows.

APARTMENT HOUSES

The concentration of huge numbers of people in a few cities has vitally affected architecture. The Buckeye state in 1930 attained a population division of 67.8 per cent urban and 32.2 per cent rural. This means that two out of every three persons in Ohio now live in urban areas. This situation has caused the decline of the one-family house because of cost of lots and building material; thus it has furthered the building of the apartment house. Statistics reveal that even the two-family house is receding in favor of the apartment house. The intelligent coöperation of the builder of the one-family house has stimulated the architect to do his best; but in the case of the apartment house, all the builder demands, as a rule, is that it be a revenue producer, and that demand has been fatal to the architectural aspect of the apartment house. The inevitable result is that with few exceptions, they are very ugly. However, there are hopeful signs of improvement, as in the last few years a few good-looking apartment houses have been erected in Ohio cities. The architect should recognize the crowded conditions of living in an apartment and plan to meet the needs of the occupants. Entrances and stairways should be enlarged and improved; there should be a play space for children and a separate entrance for them and their velocipedes and whatnots. There is no reason why art and utility cannot be combined.

The grouping of small houses in beyond-the-corporation additions is often baneful, as the luxury of artistic design is usually the first thing to be abandoned in the curtailing of building expense. The life of an ordinary dwelling is estimated from thirty to fifty years. May it not be forecast, with confidence, that the next generation will demand that the place where it lives shall be a beautiful place? One would like to hope so. The balance is clearly on the side of improvement.

After all, what is the one quality above all others that makes good architecture? Scale, taste, charm, distinction, personality, and proportion are words commonly used, but they are too hackneyed; something more vital is needed. Roger H. Bullard says that the "essence of architecture is solid geometrical form." People are prone to think of architecture as decorative features, but the important thing is the underlying solid form which serves as the background for the decoration.

The new and unique expression in architecture is now generally accepted. "Every phase of life is consciously or unconsciously experiencing new expressions. We are living in a tremendous, vital, conscious age. The architect of today is indeed fortunate. Is it possible to visualize the architectural possibilities of the future — the magnitude, the scope of its development? After many years of quiet traditionalism, architecture has again become a dynamic, living art. Our contemporary architecture will establish itself permanently, if the architect is guided by honesty and sincerity in his interpretations. Thus conceived and thus developed, the present generation of architects will give to the world, due to the catholicity of modern culture, the first international or universal architecture. Only such examples of architecture that have been sincere and honest expressions of their physical elements have continued to merit a place in the realm of the arts."[7]

LANDSCAPE ARCHITECTURE

Closely allied to architecture is the art that enhances and embellishes it with the proper surroundings — landscape architecture. "Its most important function is to create and preserve beauty in the surroundings of human habitation and in the broader natural scenery of the country."

---

[7] *The Architect,* October, 1930, L. G. Scherer.

PLATE 132—Fine Arts Garden, Cleveland. (Cleveland Museum of Art)

The average family has come to realize that a beautiful home is the most profitable investment for the enjoyment of life. Here, again, credit in large measure is due the home-and-garden magazines for the service they have rendered in guiding and helping the people to feel the need of beautification, in assisting them to create beauty around their homes. The garden clubs, too, in nearly every city, have through rivalry and competition, brought the interest in gardens to white heat. Even the tiniest city lot has its quota of flowers and shrubs. Who knows—Ohio gardens may yet rival the perfection and gorgeousness of the English gardens. The home owner has been awakened to the fact that home extends to the property line, and that it is not just the house itself. A home is reduced to a mere house — a picture without a frame — unless there are small evergreens or shrubs planted close to the house to soften the lines and make the house "belong" and seem a part of the whole scheme.

As one motors through Ohio he may see beautiful gardens in the smallest villages. Rock gardens, tremendously in vogue at present, have made it possible to beautify the most unpromising spots. Strange to say, the farmhouses in many instances are barren and uninviting, and entirely lacking in landscape beautification; but the Agricultural Extension Department is offering helpful suggestions along this line to farmers, and conditions are favorable for improvement. Where country homes have been built among the trees, the natural beauties of the site have been preserved and used to the best advantage.

Good examples of landscape architecture of a pretentious sort are becoming very numerous around the larger cities of Ohio. To catalogue or list them would be a delight, but it would go far beyond the space allotted here. Some striking features enlivening these properties include the following: entrance terraces carefully planted; formal pools with aquatic plants; beautiful vistas; axes accented by fountains, or a bit of garden architecture or shelter; sundials, bird baths, garden sculpture; inviting walks and seats; masses of bright-colored flowers; swimming pools; and vine-clad high-walled enclosures. There are gardens devoted to planting special flowers, for example, iris, peonies, dahlias, wild flowers and the like. Most of these plots are in American style, but there are excellent examples of foreign landscape style successfully transplanted and adapted to Ohio. Many new home acres are not yet old enough to show the result of the careful and intelligent planning and planting bestowed upon them. Some new suburban developments are under severe restrictions for the promotion of landscape beauty.

There have been community efforts in landscape architecture where keen interest has been aroused in such projects. A beacon light is Cleveland's Fine

Arts Garden, to mention no more than one example of what may be accomplished in the crystallization of ideals of dignity and beauty. The Garden Club of Cleveland took the initiative in improving the portion of Wade Park between Euclid Avenue and the Art Museum. The city agreed to provide the water and drainage, and to do the grading and planting according to the specifications of the architects, Olmstead Brothers. The Garden Club provided the architectural and sculptural features. It represents five years' work and a half million dollars expenditure; it is one of the most beautiful features of the Cleveland park system, and its beauty is visible to the multitudes who pass daily on Euclid Avenue, the city's busiest street. It gives a worthy approach to the Art Museum, in front of which are balustraded marble terraces that lead down to an oval garden, where there is a beautiful fountain of white Georgia marble. A natural hollow contains a small lake (Plate 132); balustrades make the changed levels and separate the features of the scheme. The dedication of the Fine Arts Garden was made a memorable occasion.

Landscape architecture is playing a most important part in making Ohio a state of beautiful homes. Who dare say that industrialism and commercial activity are all-absorbing? The industry, business, and agriculture of the state were long ago stabilized, so that art may bloom in its gardens now. "The higher attributes and amenities now have their place in the intellectual development of the state. They are, after all, the things which make life worth living."

CHAPTER XV

Outstanding Sculptors of Today

IT is as difficult to evaluate modern sculpture as it is to pass judgment upon modern painting. In twenty-five years our opinions may be discounted more than fifty per cent. Estimates vary exceedingly with the years, but, even conscious of that danger, we propose here to undertake a brief survey of the activities of Ohio sculptors in the last thirty or thirty-five years.

There is a growing interest in sculpture, particularly that used for architectural decoration, but it is still an artistic luxury and far from being a part of our daily lives as it was with the Greeks. The World War occasioned an increased demand for sculpture for monuments and buildings. Fortunately it has been a much better sculpture than that which followed the Civil War, which was scarcely deserving the name, as the horrible memorials that deface many of our towns and villages sufficiently testify. Bronze soldiers that were sold at so much per pound are traditional figures, devoid of personal style or character.

The tendency in contemporary sculpture is a carefully-thought-out arrangement of masses; instead of a confusion of detail, the sculptor's feeling for shape and mass is very evident. There is a striving to make stone interpret, to make it symbolic or expressive of the ideas of the time; consequently, we see in the present-day sculpture much of the so-called modernistic note that permeates other phases of art and life. With such an illustrious forerunner as J. Q. A. Ward, it is not surprising to find the established sculptors of Ohio sharing the honors of their profession with the sculptors of Europe and earning awards and distinctions in the Old World not second to those received by its native sculptors.

The many artists trained in Cincinnati are sufficient proof of the successful effort of the citizens to create during the nineties an environment of esthetic influences, in which young artists could develop their ideas. Among the number is the sculptor Clement J. Barnhorn, who is still an active force in the world of sculpture.

Mr. Barnhorn received his academic training at Saint Xavier's College. Then followed a period of toil and denial, of laborious carving in wood and marble, under the direction of the veteran English wood carver, Henry L. Fry, and with the instruction of the Italian, Rebisso, in modeling. For eleven years he worked, developing a remarkable craftsmanship. It is not uncommon to

394

hear some painter deride the crafts, but he is the last person who should do so, as art and craft are inseparable: they must go hand in hand in order to complete a successful work. The Cincinnati Art Academy realized that Barnhorn had more than ordinary skill in execution, that he had a talent of great promise. Consequently it was arranged that he should go to Europe to study and develop his native ability. For five years, in Paris, he modeled with Puech and Mercié, and studied drawing at the Julian Academy; he finished his European stay by spending six months in Italy.

The benefits of such study are admittedly enormous, though usually more or less intangible; in this instance Barnhorn had a concrete evidence in the "Magdalen", which won an honorable mention at the Salon of 1895, and later earned a bronze medal at the Paris Exposition of 1900 (Plate 133). The triteness of the subject would seem to preclude, from the first, any originality in representing it; but this recumbent, nude figure speaks to us in terms of unmistakable anguish, and the harmony and grace of the lines create a definite esthetic reaction. At the same exposition he received another medal, the *Art Nouveau*, for a piece of decorative domestic design, a carved wood piano case. The forms of two trees, conventionalized, make the legs of the piano; boughs extend from each side along the lower part of the keyboard, then go up on the sides and spread across the top, forming a setting for a figure in the center. The ensemble demonstrates his proficiency in wood carving; and the design suggests the material, but the criticism has been made, perhaps justly, that, "The feature which may seem unsatisfactory is that the ornament composes the structure instead of growing upon it."[1]

One of his pupils, Ernest Bruce Haswell, pays him this loving tribute: "Not many sculptors come back from Paris having achieved so much, and when Rebisso died, the pupil filled the place of his old master at the Cincinnati Art Academy. Here he has taught ever since, a teacher as capable of imparting his knowledge as of demonstrating his theory. He may be less of a sculptor than some, but none have surpassed him in ideality of aim and seriousness of purpose; a master of technique that is not conventional, that cares not for effect, his work stands out boldly in an age when technique has ceased to be a means and has become an end."[2]

The commissions Mr. Barnhorn has received for public memorials have been numerous. One of the finest memorials erected in America since the war is his "Fountain", at Hughes High School, Cincinnati; another "Fountain" is at

[1] Charles H. Caffin, *International Studio,* vol. 20, p. cxli.
[2] Ernest Bruce Haswell, *International Studio,* vol. 55, p. xliii.

PLATE 133—Magdalen. Clement J. Barnhorn. (Sculptor)

Shortridge High School, Indianapolis; both are beautiful works, wonderfully executed. For the Queen City Club, Cincinnati, he made a mantel decoration in bronze, "Mænads", which represents lithe, spirited, and graceful Greek dancers in a most interesting rhythmic movement. An even greater success is in the beautiful spirit that he has shown in his mural tablets, bearing ideal figures instead of portraits; this is very noticeable in the design for the Poland memorial, which shows an angel holding a scroll. The "Madonna of the Lilies" is an exquisite low-relief, catching the spirit of the Italian Renaissance in its simplicity, in the subtle difference of planes, and in the refinement of the treatment.

Mr. Barnhorn is especially happy in portraying children. He grasps the child's attitude and understands it so well that among his greatest successes are those figures of joyous, dancing, and exuberant youths. For instance, the boy in the "Dolphin and Boy", is an adorable fellow. A visit to Mr. Barnhorn's studio found him modeling a lovely little girl who was enjoying being teased by him; there was a beautiful feeling of *camaraderie* between them. He was engaged on a group, "Industry Protecting Art and Music". A man wearing a blacksmith's apron represented Industry; beside him was Art symbolized by a boy with a palette; while Music was this little girl seated, holding a mandolin. A talk with Mr. Barnhorn is very stimulating. He is full of energy; he interests one with reminiscences of his work with Duveneck; and, above all, one realizes he has a wholehearted sympathy with all the life about him — and that explains why his sculpture is always of the spirit, the inner life. Of all his fascinating children, with turtles or dolphins or other fountain accessories, perhaps none of them are more attractive than those of the Clara Bauer Memorial Fountain, Cincinnati Conservatory of Music.

Another suggestion from the Renaissance, of which Barnhorn has made good use, is the glazed terra cotta. The "Dolphin and Boy" fountain for the Prince George Hotel, New York; the "Holmes" fountain in Cincinnati; a lunette for the Sailor's Institute, New York; the "Four Seasons" fountain in Pittsburgh, and the Lord and Taylor fountain in New York, are all of Rookwood faïence. These sculptured fountains and decorations made of terra cotta are covered with an opaque glaze, in which the colors are mixed as in enamel.

A different tone, but one just as dominant, is the religious feeling in his "Madonna and Child" for the Covington Cathedral (Plate 134). The divinity of the child is made apparent; and in this piece especially Barnhorn succeeds in making us feel his power. Again, in the Wetterer memorial, we have a Christ that satisfies the most exacting; here the Savior is a grown man holding

PLATE 134—Alma Mater. Clement J. Barnhorn. (Cincinnati Museum of Art)

an open book as a symbol of Christianity, and raising his hand in benediction. Both of these figures are free from affectation and mannerism.

Mr. Barnhorn's ecclesiastical sculpture reaches its peak in "The Crucifixion Group" and "St. Monica" on the façade of the church of St. Monica, Fairview Heights, Cincinnati. The "St. Monica" has a beautiful feeling for architectural lines, and won for him the annual prize of the Samuel B. and Rosa F. Sachs endowment for the most outstanding achievement in the field of art executed during the year 1929. A well-deserved tribute to Mr. Barnhorn is a story by F. A. Thoma in the *Extension Magazine;* he calls him "A Carver of Sermons in Stone". Mr. Thoma gives a vivid description of Barnhorn's intimacy with Duveneck and his devotion to his twin brother, Henry Barnhorn.

It would not be possible to calculate the great influence of Mr. Barnhorn upon the sculpture of the Middle West; he has taught very many of the young men who are producing good work today. He has helped dozens of promising students in music or sculpture over serious financial stumblingblocks, and loaned money to several especially talented beginners to study a year or more in Europe. The world knows nothing of these actions; he always has given cheerfully, without any thought of publicity or reaction to his credit.

Charles Henry Niehaus, one of the many Cincinnati artists of German ancestry, began his study of modeling at the McMicken School of Design. After a deadly lethargy overtook sculpture in the studios of Americans studying and working in Rome and Florence, Paris became the accepted center of instruction for aspiring American sculptors. Niehaus, however, went to Munich for his training; his group, "Fleeting Time", won a medal, a first prize, and a diploma for him at the Royal Academy of Munich.

He came back to America in 1881, just at the moment when interest was running high in the glorification of President Garfield, whose assassination had been a recent event. The State of Ohio had appropriated funds for a statue to be placed in the Capitol at Washington; and through popular subscription another one was to be erected in Cincinnati. The young Ohio sculptor received both commissions. The consensus of opinion in art circles is that the Cincinnati "Garfield" is Niehaus's best work, though his record of achievement can be brought down to the present day.

The Washington "Garfield" was modeled in Cincinnati, but executed in Rome; the Cincinnati "Garfield" was both modeled and executed in Rome (Plate 135). Both are dramatic, immortalizing Garfield's oratorical gifts. The gesture of the hands and arms of the Cincinnati statue indicate his eloquence; the head is superb, and is carried well over the square shoulders and broad chest. Mr. Barnhorn, who was a coworker of Niehaus in a marble shop in Cincinnati when they were both young, stated with much enthusiasm to the writer that: "There never was a finer head made than that of Niehaus's Garfield". Lorado Taft characterizes this head as "delightful in its plastic freedom".

Another commission came to Niehaus from Ohio, a statue of William Allen to be placed in Statuary Hall of the Capitol, Washington. These three statues were substantial successes. His direct method of going straight to the character of his subject shows the influence of realism obtained from the Munich school.

Then he set out for Rome, established a studio near the Villa Borghese, and centered his efforts entirely upon the study of the nude. As a result of this stay in Italy, we find in his subsequent work a more subtle movement of figure, with a more refined feeling in arrangement and texture of drapery, and a perfect knowledge of form. Out of this period in Rome, came the "Scraper", representing an athlete scraping the oil from his body with a strigil. It is a splendidly modeled Greek athlete, and it received the strongest praise at the Columbian Exposition, Chicago, 1893. It is considered one of the few good nudes in American sculpture. The American sculptor seldom has an opportunity to use the nude, except in a decorative sense. "Cæstus", and "Silenus", are other examples of Niehaus's rendering of the antique subjects, but he has always introduced realism into them. They are never the wholly ideal classic figure.

We are indebted to Mr. Charles H. Caffin for this information: "So Niehaus had to wait many years before he could use frankly the results of his studies at Rome. The opportunity came with the erection of a monument to the memory of Colonel Edwin L. Drake, who sunk the first oil well in Pennsylvania, in 1859. The donor, who preserved his incognito, but who is supposed to have been one of the officials of the Standard Oil Company, demanded an architectural structure with planes on which the story of Drake's life and achievements might be inscribed, and instead of a representation of himself a figure typical of his work. Thus arose occasion for 'The Driller'. . . . 'The Driller', therefore, was an unusual opportunity for Niehaus, of which he made characteristic use. That is to say, the realism of the figure as it kneels with hammer uplifted to drive the drill into the ground, is admirably true, while the figure has a classic dignity of composition; and its expression of control, as well as the putting forth of force, brings it within the domain of ideal beauty."[3]

The intense love Niehaus possessed for the mythological and classical subjects again guided him when he selected the theme for the national monument

[3]Charles H. Caffin, *American Masters of Sculpture*, p. 123.

PLATE 135—Head of Statue of President Garfield, Cincinnati.
Charles Henry Niehaus. (Sculptor)

to the author of the "Star Spangled Banner", Francis Scott Key, at Fort Mc-Henry, Baltimore, where the thrilling song was written. The award was given to him by the National Art Commission over a large number of competitors. By the happy choice of a symbolical figure, Orpheus, he was able to honor the art of music, as well as to pay tribute to the writer of the poem. The colossal statue, twenty-five feet high, is very beautiful. Orpheus has a lithe, graceful figure like that of a young Olympian victor, with a poise indicating a swift forward movement. From the top of the fine head and face, to the toe of the sandal, every line is a subtle curve of exquisite charm. The lyre is made according to legend, of tortoise shell and goat's horns. Upon the front of the pedestal, profusely decorated with classic moldings, is a medallion portrait of Key, flanked by patriotic emblems. Most people feel that this is the masterpiece of Niehaus; in it he approaches the excellence of the great classic masterpieces of antiquity.

A committee of the National Sculpture Society, awarded to Niehaus, out of a large number of designs offered in competition, the first prize and the commission for the Washington statue of Samuel Hahnemann, the founder of homeopathy. The great physician, with elbows resting comfortably on the arms of a chair, leans his head ponderingly on his right hand. The statue has the repose that one always hopes to find in monumental art; the pose, the dignity, and the esthetic appeal reflect Niehaus's mastery of the antique; every fold in the long drapery has been given careful attention for its value in line to the ensemble as viewed from every direction. This portrait statue has an exedra setting, which is ornamented by four bronze reliefs illustrating events in the life of Doctor Hahnemann. The principal inscription, "Hahnemann", is near the top of the center of the back of the exedra.

The most successful bas-reliefs of Niehaus are the two historical panels of the Astor memorial doors for Trinity Church, New York City. This commission was another one awarded to him from competition of designs. He represented these scenes from religious history in a realistic manner; the foreground figures, being sharply undercut, stand out nearly wholly detached; the vacant spaces of the composition have been estimated carefully in relation to the decorated spaces. A commission for the equestrian statue of Robert E. Lee, Richmond, Virginia, is still another outcome of Niehaus's success over many competitors.

Three statues of Lincoln have been executed by Niehaus. One is a seated figure of heroic size in bronze, owned by the Historical Society of Buffalo, New York; the second is almost a replica of the first, except for a slight difference in the chair, and it is one of the chief ornaments of Muskegon, Michigan; the third is a bust of purest Crestele marble, translucent to an unusual degree. The latter reaches the high-water mark of Niehaus's portrait busts. Lincoln wears a soft, rolling collar and a flat, bow tie somewhat askew, and the hair is treated with the same idea of carelessness. We hear it said that Lincoln's face was the "saddest face ever seen"; but Niehaus makes him sober and grave rather than sad, with eyes that look directly at the beholder.

In his portrait bust of John Quincy Adams Ward, Niehaus achieved the difficult task of attempting to show the hands as well as the face of the person portrayed. He probably borrowed the idea from the early Florentine sculptors, and it is carried out exceedingly well. Ward, with his strong, interesting face, is shown wearing his working smock, and holding his mallet and chisel in his hands. Niehaus's bust of Beethoven, in the Cincinnati Museum, gives us an instance of his ability to make a splendid decorative effect out of a portrait bust; it is somewhat idealized, but charming, showing the artistic feeling both of the subject and the sculptor. In the Library of Congress are his "Moses", and "Gibbon"; the former is quite impressive and is sometimes compared to the Moses of Michelangelo. Niehaus is at his best when he is portraying character. He is able to show us the dominant traits of his subject, and combine the whole into a creditable monumental work. The portrait statue of McKinley in front of the mausoleum at Canton, Ohio, is the work of Niehaus.

An American sculptor whose attention has been devoted almost wholly to modeling animals, is Eli Harvey, born at Ogden, Ohio. He was another pupil of Rebisso in Cincinnati. Animals of the cat tribe, the lion, jaguar, and leopard, are the ones he chooses to delineate in clay; their suppleness of body, sinuous grace, and stealthy movement, catch his imagination. His observation of animals is confined to those in captivity; he has never hunted in the wilds for his subjects. His studies were made in private menageries at Neuilly and Asnières, and at the Jardin des Plantes in Paris. His work is quite apropos to the adornment of public parks, as his statues of animals have the qualities of good sculpture and are very true to life, since by a patient and scrupulous observation of animal life he taught himself to crystallize swift action itself. A sculptured group representing a lioness fondling her cub, "The Maternal Caress", in the Metropolitan Museum of Art, New York City, is a superb example of the serene repose he can give to animals (Plate 136).

Mr. Harvey has used the lion motif to good advantage for architectural decoration in a pediment for the New York Zoological Society lion house. At the Salon of 1898 was exhibited his "Rampant Jaguar"; his "Lion Roaring",

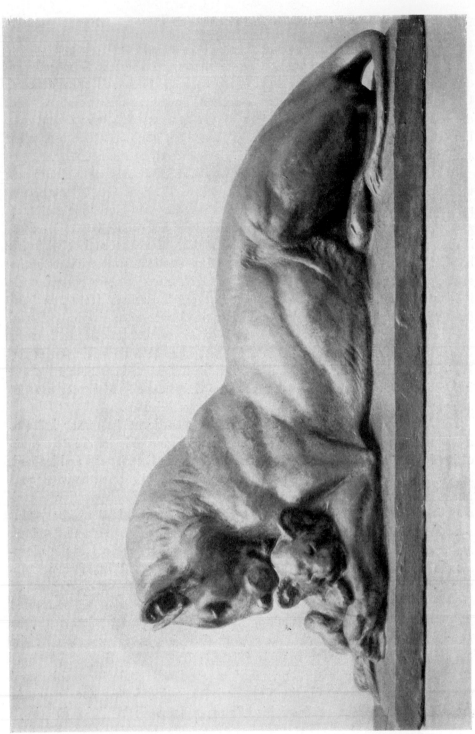

PLATE 136—Lioness and Cub: "The Maternal Caress." Eli Harvey. (Metropolitan Museum of Art)

"Lion Cubs", and bas-reliefs were exhibited at the Pan-American Exposition, 1901. His studio in New York is filled with animal studies. There the visitor may see "America's Aristocrat", the name he has given to a proud, defiant elk that is just ready to leap away into space; the forest king, a splendid lion, lies couchant after the fashion of the lions of Landseer on Nelson's monument; in London some beautiful greyhounds are modeled with the light grace characteristic of them.

An interesting account of how Mr. Harvey began to sculpture animals is told by Jessie Lamont: "The summer of 1898 found Mr. Harvey in the Forest of Fontainebleau, in a certain wild spot that at close of day commands a wide sweep over purpling hills and a view of a stretch of country that seems to extend vastly under the sweeping shadows. This spot is reached by an ascent through the pine trees, and during the twilight hours was sought by the artist and his comrade, the little woman who has been both inspiration and helpmate through many years.

"These two and a young Italian, who posed as model, wended their way through the silent woods at sunset each evening. A canvas was set up; the model reclined on the hilly slope; several lion skins were spread to give the tawny note to the picture, and thus was conceived and executed the painting of 'Orpheus Charming the Animals'. This picture with its purple twilight tones, the gold-haired young demigod with his lyre stretched on the rocky bank, and the lions and tigers grouped about in charmed attention, was hung on the line in the Paris Salon of 1899, and the following year was again exhibited and won the gold medal at the Paris-Provence Exposition.

"The animals in this picture absorbed the interest of the painter to an extent that caused him to take up animal study thereafter and devote himself exclusively to this phase of art in its sculptural form."[4]

Herman N. Matzen, the Cleveland sculptor, a veteran from point of service as instructor, has made himself famous by a long career of artistic activities and creations. He is a native of Denmark, and has all the strength, with the grace and balance, of the great northern artists. A letter from Mrs. Matzen tells of the memorial erected over the resting place of the Collinwood fire victims: "The Collinwood fire memorial is a bas-relief, not large, and in its mitigation of a horror by beauty shows the mission of art. On a field of poppies is a central kneeling figure, the mother of great tenderness, while about her hover confidingly a number of little children whom she is trying to shelter with her wings. There is a beauty in the lines and grouping as a whole, as

---

[4] *International Studio,* vol. 51, p. cvi.

well as in the expression of the individual figures. The group seems to typify universal mother love, which in the end receives the children of the earth." The circular lines of the composition lead the eye to the center and suggest the old masterpiece, the "Madonna of the Chair" by Raphael, but the theme and the beautiful interpretation are the sculptor's own, every line manifesting the clearness, simplicity, and strength which are characteristic of his work.

It is claimed that the Cleveland Court House rivals in sculptural decorations any other structure of the kind in the United States. This rating is based on the eminence of the five sculptors entrusted with the work; they were Karl Bitter, Isador Konti, Daniel C. French, Herbert Adams, and Herman N. Matzen. Placed above the cornice on the north and the south are ten heroic-sized marble statues representing the sources of our law and its development. Mr. Matzen's contributions are the "Moses", and "Pope Gregory IX". Moses, as the giver of the decalog to the Hebrew nation, has been chosen to typify the moral code or Biblical law. Mr. Matzen shows us a bearded Moses, standing, with the tablets in his hands. He represents the great leader of the Exodus as a strong commanding figure, possessing not only wisdom and justice, but the fiery impulse which moved him to hurl the tablets from him in anger. Pope Gregory IX represents canon law, since his tireless efforts went far to establish a thirteenth-century code of laws for the Church of Rome. Mr. Matzen portrays this medieval legate and crusader, who collected papal decretals with the same energy that he used in persecuting heretics, as he is shown in a mosaic portrait in one of the oldest churches in Rome. The statue is a seated figure of strong intellect and dominating character.

When Mr. Matzen modeled the head of Richard Wagner for the Wagner Monument in Edgewater Park, Cleveland, he followed the bust which his old teacher, Schapper of the Berlin Academy, modeled from life about 1880, and which Siegfrid Wagner, son of the composer of the music dramas, preferred to any other. The figure shows Wagner as he looked at rehearsal, baton in the right hand, score in the left, and coat flung open; the familiar cap in which Lenbach painted him, is given the hasty Wagnerian tilt above his bushy hair. Every line suggests energy; the face is of one who listens and dreams. The pedestal plays an unusually important part. "Just a rose on my grave if you will — that is enough", Richard Wagner is said to have replied when some one asked his wishes in regard to a monument. Remembering this, the sculptor has modeled a rose tree, "straight and flat and German", at each corner of the pedestal, which has been most carefully proportioned to the figure. At the base of the statue are unfinished masses of stone, and above them branches of oak,

PLATE 137—Nymph and Faun. Fountain figure in the garden of Mr. E. W. Edwards,
Cincinnati. Ernest Bruce Haswell, Sculptor. (Sculptor)

whose leaves Germany uses in place of the classic laurel when she crowns her sons of genius.

Mr. Matzen's "Schiller", in Detroit represents the poet in the latest invalid stages of his life, when he wrote his best thoughts in the Weimar garden. It is a satisfying, sympathetic interpretation of Schiller. "Finis", the Haserot memorial, Cleveland, is impressive and simple. Seated in the center of a circular seat, is a winged figure holding a turned-down torch, which typifies the end of life. The wings represent the flight of the spirit, and add a decorative feature which relieves the severity of the architectural design. If Mr. Matzen had never done another work, his popular reputation could rest on the two colossal symbolic groups, "War" and "Peace", for the Soldiers' and Sailors' Monument, Indianapolis. They are so large that colossal does not seem an adequate word in describing them. It is claimed they are the two largest groups that have ever been cut out of stone. Mr. Matzen's resignation as an instructor in the Cleveland School of Art, 1926, ended many years of service there.

As Millet glorified in paint the peasant worker in the fields of France, so Max Kalish glorifies in bronze the American laborer of today. Mr. Kalish was born in Poland, but has adopted Ohio as his home, and Ohio has taken him as her adopted son. His sculpture has stirred more than a little comment during the last four or five years. The New York critics have adulated him to the skies, and on the other hand, have torn him to bits, according to the impulse of the conservative or radical opinion. All admit his striking craftsmanship. The more conservative say that his work is much too close to Rodin in style, but one's acceptance of that depends, again, upon whether or not he likes Rodin.

Mr. Kalish has spent most of his life among the laborers in the shops of Cleveland. His attitude toward the workman is not that of benevolence; instead, he confers dignity, nobility, and triumph upon him. "Why I take the worker for a model" is a point he discusses in *The Survey*: "Were I a sculptor of the Greek period, I should go to the games and watch the athletes, or to the baths, and create the beauty to be found there. Had I lived during the Middle Ages or the Renaissance, I should have created the beautiful and spiritual of that period. But inasmuch as I live at the present time, I desire to create those subjects with which I am most familiar, mainly those people who live and work about me, those whom I can observe in the flesh. I seek to perpetuate the beauty and grace of action of the people of today, particularly the workmen of America. It is my honest opinion that only by interpreting our own time, the Industrial Age, can we ever hope to produce a real epoch in art."[5]

[5] *The Survey,* vol. 59, p. 691.

"The Steel Worker", "The Woodcutter", "The Boat-Puller", "The Laborer", "The Farmer", "The Riveter", "The Locomotive Engineer", are all fine masculine figures, each showing the bulging muscles and the straining torso of a physically vigorous man exhibiting his power. In the catalogue issued by the Ferargil Galleries when the sculpture of Kalish was exhibited there, Henry Turner Bailey is quoted as saying: "His laborers are of the efficient type, their powers concentrated on the act of the moment, which becomes a typical act, the result of habitual state of mind. Their athletic figures, whether resting or working, have that innate natural grace good workmen always have when not self-conscious. His American laborer is what an American workman should be, not a dull peasant, not a helpless clod, like the "Man with the Hoe", but an alert, thoughtful, ambitious person, not content with things as they are, but having convictions and ideals — a robust, optimistic person consciously on the way to something better."

Ernest Bruce Haswell, of Cincinnati, is a sculptor equally at ease, whether working in relief or in the round. An outstanding example of his work is the memorial feature of the Nippert Memorial Stadium at Cincinnati University. In bas-relief, a ten-foot figure of a football player on the five-yard line, is shown running with the ball. The principal lines are diagonal ones to accent the swift movement of the figure, in which the sculptor has caught the intense, vital struggle of football. The modeling is crisp, exquisite, simply and directly done. Carved above the figure are the words: "Five more yards to go — and then drop." These were the last words of Jimmy Nippert, the football star of Cincinnati University who died on Christmas, 1923, from injuries received in the Thanksgiving Day game; the stadium is built in his memory. It is a choice of subject that will go far in developing an art that is American in spirit.

Among the best monuments of 1919, is listed the Northcott memorial at Springfield, Illinois, by Mr. Haswell. It is an interesting memorial in the form of a bench and drinking fountain, and "one of the finest symbolic expressions in low-relief sculpture that has been executed as a cemetery memorial." The harmony of lines, the curves, and the delicacy of the work contribute to furnish a unique esthetic appeal. The design of the Northcott memorial symbolizes life and death, by means of two life-size figures in bas-relief on the high back of the bench. Life is represented as the central figure, with outspread wings that form a beautifully curved line at the top of the back. She kneels and with one hand places a garland of poppies on an urn; the other hand, extended, offers a cup to a seated figure. Above the figure is carved in proper relation the line from Edwin Markham's poem on Lincoln: "He was as friendly as a way-

PLATE 138—Mother and Child. Erwin F. Frey. (Sculptor)

side well", a quotation which those who knew William A. Northcott, claim best typifies the man to whom the memorial is dedicated.

Mr. Haswell has made many lovely fountain groups for Cincinnati gardens. As a designer he knows how to put his ideas into sculpturesque forms which are decorative yet not too ornate. He is especially happy in his mass composition, in groups that hold together, and are enriched by small decorative motifs taken from nature. The "Nymph and Faun" fountain which enhances the gardens of E. W. Edwards, Cincinnati, is full of charm and witchery; besides, the sculptor's feeling for shape and mass is very evident (Plate 137). A fountain which shows his imagination is the duck fountain, situated in the garden of Frank M. Andrews, Fort Thomas. Water spouts from the bills of two chunky, solid ducks, that sit on two low pedestals at each side of the pool. These are clever birds, conventionalized, of course, with their heads drawn down into a simple outline. They are cast in pewter. A frog and a turtle repose in the water. A background for the pool is a decorative mosaic made by Richard Grant, the landscape artist. It accentuates the blue-grays of the pewter, and makes an exceedingly satisfactory completion of the fountain. The increasing demand for garden sculpture is a most gratifying and wholesome omen that people are developing appreciation of beauty in their surroundings. Something is wrong with folk who exclaim over a single isolated beautiful garden —we should be so accustomed to them that they would seem a part of our lives and not a thing apart from us. Mr. Haswell is a versatile artist, whose achievements are splendid and numerous; he is a man with a background of more than art training alone, being a writer and lecturer as well as a sculptor. Some of the finest products of the Rookwood Pottery have been executed from designs made by Mr. Haswell.

The fame of Erwin Frey in the Middle West has been greatly augmented by his latest work, an heroic portrait statue in bronze of Doctor William Oxley Thompson, who was president of Ohio State University from 1899 to 1925. The statue is eleven feet in height. Dr. Thompson is represented in a simple, straight posture, wearing the academic gown, as most students visualize him. The classes of '23, '25, '26, and '28 were the donors of the monument. It is one of the few instances of a statue being erected to a man who is still living. Dr. Thompson, thoroughly deserving of the honor, was present, and took part in the unveiling ceremonies in Columbus, June, 1930.

Mr. Frey was fortunate in having the subject himself pose for the statue, enabling him to obtain and present the salient characteristics of the man— dignity of character, ease and self-possession of pose. One finds a careful parallelism of lines in the folds of the robe; this feature gives the statue an architectural character appropriate for its setting in front of the University Library, which is designed in Italian Renaissance style. The sculptor has shown supreme skill in formalizing the drapery and making its lines significant. He has suggested the bulk and weight of the figure in a way that reminds one of Egyptian solidity; and above all, he has kept it a monumental portrait unencumbered by details.

In his "Madonna", which received honorable mention at the Chicago Art Institute in 1925, Mr. Frey has grasped the essence of French medieval art. The forms are handled with decision and power, giving concrete evidence of his vitality (Plate 138). In architectural sculpture he has been especially successful; an example is the relief of an Indian head, designed for the entrance to the Indianola High School, Columbus. The arrangement of the feathers of the encircling headdress, the long braids of hair that hang down on each side of the face, the angular Indian features — all are made to accentuate the architectural lines in a happy manner. In some terra cotta heads he presents a modern note that is far removed from the effete artificiality and studied estheticism so frequently seen; there is an undoubted sincerity in all his work. He has created portrait busts, basketball trophies, and other excellent sculpture; Mr. Frey is a true artist. He received honorable mention in the Paris Salon, 1923. His training, which began with Clement J. Barnhorn of Cincinnati, has been unusual and more varied than that of most sculptors. He has worked in ceramics and as a medalist, and assisted in the erection of the gigantic sculptures at the Panama-Pacific Exposition at San Francisco in 1915. Knowing every phase of technicality in sculpture, he has not been bound by method, and has been able to execute freely and develop a marked individuality in his sculpture.

The friends of Cleveland sculpture presented to the Museum of Art in the lake city, a heroic-size bronze by Alexander Blazys, a Cleveland sculptor. It depicts "City Fettering Nature" (Plate 139), with the city represented by a remarkably muscular, herculean figure, towering over and binding with ropes the also virile but conquered figure of Nature. The twisting, writhing muscles and torsos suggest the power and treatment of Michelangelo; Mr. Blazys has made them veritable Titans, full of fury. He has made other large decorative groups; a notable one is "The Girl and the Elephant", in which the dominant lines have a very beautiful rhythm, and the mass of the composition is satisfactory in its ensemble. It is a unique piece of sculpture; one is induced to walk all around it to follow the lines and see just how the girl is placed on

PLATE 139—City Fettering Nature. At north entrance of Cleveland Museum of Art.
Alexander Blazys. (Sculptor)

top of the elephant. The group reflects, to a marked degree, the unusual power and artistic personality of Mr. Blazys.

This Russian sculptor, who has adopted Ohio as his permanent home, believes that the ideal of artists should be unity in composition, resulting from unity of conception. The whole composition should be tied up in one piece, and in his large decorative groups mentioned that is a noticeable quality. He feels greater freedom for the expression of his ideas in the large things, always remembering that the composition must carry successfully from every point of view.

The fact that Mr. Blazys has worked in wood, copper, clay, and marble bears witness to the versatility of his genius. "The Russian Dancers", a pair of small figures, exhibit rhythmic movement and simplicity of modeling; "The Volga Boat Song", is virile and poetic; "The Blacksmith", showing the workman ready to strike the anvil, holds an arrested rhythmical pose; these pieces were awarded first prize at the 1926 May Show in Cleveland. Mr. Blazys is particularly happy, too, in portraiture. He carved in wood a portrait of the great artist, Henry G. Keller, while Mr. Keller painted his portrait; thus neither of these indefatigable artists lost a moment of time. Of Archie Bell, he made a portrait full of the sitter's personality, an almost speaking likeness. Mr. Blazys receives remarkable praise from his contemporaries for his technical skill, his originality, and his individuality. His sculpture is a distinct contribution to art exhibitions. Through the sympathetic coöperation of Mr. Blazys and the Cowan Pottery, some ceramic sculpture of a highly artistic character has been produced; for example, the figure of Moses, represented in a blue glaze, and several striking peasant figures are noteworthy productions of their combined efforts.

Of the more than two hundred sculptors mentioned in Lorado Taft's *History of American Sculpture,* published in 1917, less than twenty-five are women sculptors. There are many more women following the profession of sculpture now. The art of modeling in clay and cutting in stone seems too sturdy a process to be connected with feminine attainments; yet Ohio has several women who have attained more than ordinary renown in the field of sculpture, and some of the younger women give greater promise than the men of their own years.

A woman sculptor with the inspiration and technique necessary to carry out her visions, is Annetta J. St. Gaudens, who won her first scholarship by modeling animals on a central Ohio farm. She is a well-trained sculptor, having worked for years in the studio of her brother-in-law, Augustus Saint-Gaudens. That fact alone gives her the stamp of quality, because Saint-Gaudens made

PLATE 140—Madonna of the Farm. Annetta J. St. Gaudens. (Sculptor)

no mistakes in selecting his assistants; they were all gifted. Annetta J. St. Gaudens was an invaluable aid to her talented husband, Louis St. Gaudens, in working with him on his figures for the Washington Union Station.

The child, in varying moods, is her favorite motif. Her "Bedtime Madonna" won honorable mention at San Francisco; the mother appeal is so strong that every one loves the tranquil, maternal figure, and the tired, sleepy little children embraced in her arms (Plate 140). One of her best-known works, however, is a bronze bird bath, made to commemorate Percy Mackaye's "Bird Masque", given in the spring of 1913 at Meriden, New Hampshire, at the time when Cornish, just below, was the summer capital of President Wilson. The President himself attended the play; Margaret Wilson sang, and Eleanor Wilson (Mrs. McAdoo) danced in the rôle of the "Bird Spirit", at the festival. The masque was so well received that it was given all over the country. Helen Foster Barnett was instrumental in having the bird bath made. The frieze around the heavy pedestal supporting the bowl of the bath consists of the many interesting people who took part in the masque; among them were Stephen Parrish, father of Maxfield Parrish, Percy Mackaye, the author, the daughter of Kenyon Cox, Witter Bynner, Erwin Frey, and Helen Foster Barnett. The sharp, bird beaks projecting from the foreheads add to the stateliness of the procession; the beautiful dignity of it all is very impressive. A border of conventionalized foliage ornaments the top. Several terra cotta copies of the bath were made.

Collaborating with her son Paul, who is a potter, Mrs. St. Gaudens is making some delightfully individual pieces of sculptured pottery. Vases, bowls, and candlesticks are some of their beautiful products. She makes flower-holders formed of rings of adorable, laughing children with their heads thrown back roguishly. Alice Van Leer Carrick speaks beautifully of one of Annetta J. St. Gaudens's bowls: "Her 'Brotherhood Bowl' appeals to the spirit as well as to the eye. It is round, globular in shape, the top has a band of flowers, the little children of all lands clasping hands in love and friendliness, and circling the earth with brotherhood and understanding."[6]

The work of Frances Grimes is little known to the general public because most of her portrait-reliefs are kept in private collections. After graduating from Pratt Institute, where she modeled with Herbert Adams, she became his assistant, helping him in his studio and giving criticism in his classes. She remained with Mr. Adams from 1894 to 1900. From 1901 to 1907, she assisted Saint-Gaudens in his studio at Cornish, New Hampshire. Saint-Gaudens se-

---

[6] *Country Life,* January, 1926, "The Orchard Potteries," by Alice Van Leer Carrick.

lected her to model the head of Christ for the Phillips Brooks Memorial, Boston; and she was one of his loyal, valued helpers who was with him until the last. For several years she has devoted her time to making bronze and marble portrait-busts and reliefs. She is particularly felicitous in children's portraits; she succeeds in getting the quality of the child's flesh, as well as the very subtle planes and the expression (Plate 141). Of special merit are her portraits of Master Harold Clement, and Carolyn and Patricia Clement. Her low-reliefs show the delicacy that we would expect from a student of Herbert Adams. Especially beautiful are two medallions, with graceful, rhythmic dancing figures, which were exhibited at San Francisco, 1929. One of her strongest portraits is of Bishop Potter in Grace Church, New York.

Adeline Adams makes this comment on her work: "After the mechanical roughing-out of the pointing machine is over, Miss Grimes herself finishes all her marbles, whether created in the round or in relief . . . and because her designs for marble are from the first rude beginnings in the clay imagined with a full realization of their final possibilities in marble, they naturally have an integrity not always attained in the work of sculptors unfamiliar with the chisel."[7] To no one is Vasari's dictum more applicable, that a sculptor sees in his block of marble the form that has already grown in his mind.

Few among our modern sculptors know much about the actual execution of a statue in marble. Their work is usually the conception and modeling of their statue in clay, wax, or other plastic material. The actual chiseling in marble is left to skillful artisans who copy the model blindly, often with serious faults in workmanship. Miss Grimes is not a sculptor of this class. She is one whose genius and skill are at ease either with the chisel or modeling tool.

Mary L. Alexander occupies a unique place in the art world, being so versatile in her accomplishments that it is difficult to classify her. Her contributions on art to the *Cincinnati Enquirer* show a keen power of analysis and much insight as a critic, but first praise should be given to Mrs. Alexander as a sculptor; her child portraiture, both in the round and in relief is regarded as especially felicitous. A memorial tablet in low-relief to her instructor, Vincent Nowottny, is very beautiful in its delicate gradations of planes and in composition (Plate 142). It is placed in the Cincinnati Art Academy where Nowottny's teaching guided pupils for so many years. A statue that received the praise of both critic and layman is her "Doughboy", a monument to the gold-star boys; it stands before the Wyoming Club House, Wyoming, Ohio.

Louise Abel, a well-known Cincinnati sculptor, combines ceramics with

---

[7] *The Spirit of American Sculpture,* Adeline Adams, p. 151.

modeling. Her first training with Barnhorn gave her a thorough sculptural background, that, together with her experience gained from working at the Rookwood Pottery, makes her eminently well fitted for her practice of art. She has made some exceedingly interesting statuettes, forms that eliminate all obvious details and give us only the ones contributing to the design. Two other very promising young women students of Mr. Barnhorn are Miss Clotilde Zanetta, a Chilean, and Mrs. Gladys Huling Theis. Mrs. Theis made a bust of Barnhorn which stresses the decisive character of her instructor; the forms are truly plastic, but firm, are closely studied and produce a satisfactory likeness and an interesting study of character.

The Ohio woman sculptor who has achieved perhaps the greatest renown is Evelyn B. Longman. The story of her life and achievements reads like a page from a fabulous storybook; but one must read between the lines to understand the pluck, endurance, and ambition that made her unusual career materialize. She was one of a large family that possessed little of this world's goods; and at the early age of fourteen she was forced to earn her own living by performing such tasks as a young girl could do in a large wholesale establishment in Chicago.

She had a keen sense of beauty in all things, and an innate love of refinement which instinctively led her to spend her evenings studying at the Chicago Art Institute. By dint of small savings at every corner, she enabled herself to attend Olivet College, Michigan. There she studied drawing and painting; and it was there she first essayed, without instruction, attempts at modeling. She soon realized that it was sculpture that should have all her attention. With that in mind she returned to Chicago to study seriously at the Art Institute, managing to pay her expenses by working in the Library at night. She proved such an apt pupil under the tutelage of Lorado Taft, that after a year she began teaching drawing and anatomy; and upon her graduation she assumed control of the summer school of modeling at Chicago Art Institute.

Then came a bold step — she went to New York and worked in the studios of Herman A. MacNeil and Isidore Konti, assisting them with the decorations for the Pan-American Exposition, 1901, at Buffalo. Promotions came rapidly now. She became assistant to Daniel Chester French, dividing her time between his studio and her own which she had opened.

The first important work upon which she displayed her skill was the figure of "Victory", designed for the Varied Industries Building at the St. Louis Exposition, 1904; but placed, instead, upon Festival Hall, the central building of the exposition; thus her figure became the crowning piece of sculpture of the

PLATE 141—Child's Portrait in Low-relief. Frances Grimes. (Sculptor)

PLATE 142—The Nowottny Tablet. Mary Alexander. (Cincinnati Museum of Art)

whole exposition. Contrary to the old Greek tradition that a female figure should always represent victory, she was independent enough to use a strong male figure, though it is characterized by the subtle grace and refinement found in all her work. For this colossal, virile figure she was awarded a silver medal. When the exposition was ended, the original plaster model was given a place in the Chicago Art Institute. The Union League Club of Chicago obtained a small replica in bronze graceful enough to adorn their reception hall.

Evelyn Longman, now Mrs. Batchelder, has received recognition in every competition for commissions where she has entered her work. One award that would have delighted any artist was the commission for the great bronze doors of the Memorial Chapel at the Naval Academy, Annapolis. Thirty-three of the greatest sculptors of the country were represented in this notable, open and anonymous competition for a twenty-thousand-dollar commission. The bronze doors are composed of a few, somewhat over life-size, figures in low-relief, expressing in beauty and rhythm as lofty ideals and sentiments as it is possible for sculpture to represent. The outside dimensions of the doors and transoms are ten by twenty-two feet. The transom subject is "Peace and Prosperity Honoring the Ashes of the Dead". The main panel of the door at the left represents "Science and Invention"; the other represents "Warlike Patriotism". They were a gift from Colonel Robert W. Thompson as a memorial to his class of 1868. Another remarkable pair of doors made by Mrs. Batchelder are the ones for the Library at Wellesley College.

Two notable memorials from her mallet and chisel, which she actually uses herself, are the groups for the Foster mausoleum at Middleborough, New York, and the Wells memorial at Lowell, Massachusetts. The former consists of three figures, Faith, Hope, and Charity, arranged in a close, interesting composition; the latter shows an angel and a grief-stricken woman covered with most delicate draperies, beneath which are revealed the living bodies, modeled with precision and exactness. She selects and makes use of ornament in a masterful way equalled by few sculptors.

In her portrait busts, Mrs. Batchelder aims first at fidelity of character and concentration upon the most significant trait of the person. When J. Q. A. Ward offered a prize to American sculptors for the best portrait bust, Mrs. Batchelder's representation of Kate Parsenow, the German actress, won second place in the competition. At the San Francisco Exposition, 1915, she exhibited the largest piece by a woman sculptor; it was "The Fountain of Ceres", a beautiful figure representing the goddess of harvest. Also at the San Francisco Exposition was her "Peggy" or "Bacchante", a laughing, vivacious face full of *joie de vivre,* that is most refreshing. "Consecration", too, was shown there; it is one of the most beautiful conceptions of all times. Two nude figures form the composition — the man stoops slightly to kiss the forehead of the woman. A memorial plaque to the pioneer railroad builder, General William Jackson Palmer, "The Prophet of Colorado's Greatness", was recently unveiled at Colorado Springs. It was designed by Mrs. Batchelder. A virile portrait of the "Prophet", seated with a newspaper on his knee, and his faithful dog beside him, makes up the composition; mountains form the background. Mrs. Batchelder was the first woman sculptor to be elected a full academician of the National Academy of Design, New York City.

Any attempt to classify modern sculptors must appear arbitrary, since Ohio sculptors are very numerous and produce many different grades of work. The work of the sculptors discussed here proves that foreign study is no longer necessary. Today, even the work done in the American Academy at Rome is done under American artists; though what is done there is bound to possess a classic flavor. The sculptors mentioned were chosen because their work is most representative of the time and seems to constitute an American art.

CHAPTER XVI
Summary

AS we bring to a close the survey of artistic accomplishments in Ohio, we may well ask: what are the distinctive contributions of the state to art? How has the life of the people of the state been enhanced by such achievements? May the future of art in Ohio be conceived or gauged by the far-reaching influence of the men of vision who laid the artistic background?

It is clear that the art of the mound builder is the beginning of our heritage. Though their culture developed under primitive conditions which have been long since overcome by the toil and genius of later generations, these early people wrote the first chapter in the history of the art of Ohio; consequently we have an intense human interest in all of the activities of these "first" Ohioans, a profound gratitude for their creative leisure spared from the duties of an arduous life, and an amazement and quickening of the imagination when we analyze the beauty of their artifacts. The pots of clay and metal, the objects cut and made from flint, when put together tell the outlines of the story of these people. That is one of the human services of art. That is how art measures civilization.

The mounds of the Ohio area are among the most noted of all the tumuli in the world, and they have yielded from exploration the greatest wealth of artifacts. Is there another mound so unique as the Great Serpent Mound? Have there ever been more conjectures about any ancient structure, its use and purpose? The mounds indicate beyond a doubt the existence of a vanished race of more than ordinary attainments. From the time of the early years of the settlement at Marietta, when C. R. Sullivan painted a picture (see page 104) of the prehistoric earthworks there, to the present, it has been recognized that Ohio was the scene of great activity for the mound builder, and the mounds he built in the state, with the relics they contain, are a definite contribution to the art of the state.

In the art of the pioneer, there are plenty of opportunities to form definite impressions, for which thanks are due the enthusiastic antiquarian for preserving the specimens of the handiwork of earlier days. Ohio has many collectors of products of the early crafts who assemble articles of beauty or of historic value and preserve them, eventually passing them on to museums of art where they are conserved for the common good. Old furniture, books, prints, manuscripts, glass bottles and dishes, early stoneware, pewter, coverlets, and samplers are among the great variety of things which have been the specific objects of the enthusiasm of the collectors of Ohio. The most searching investigation

423

would fail to reveal the vast extent of these collections; almost every family has a coverlet, a sampler, or some other prized possession of this kind, made by its ancestors. Collecting gives great impetus to the development of taste and a knowledge of the handiwork of the pioneers. There is no need for speculation as to this definite contribution to Ohio art, since after all the pioneer's achievements are not far removed in time. The sturdiness, sincerity, and simplicity that dominated the early crafts have been carried down through the years as a prime requisite for all Ohio art. It would not be possible to estimate the honest esthetic influence of the pioneer crafts upon later developments. We revere the memory of these first civilized artists and artisans of Ohio.

Architecture is perhaps the maturest expression of Ohio art. After the advancement of the prosperity of the state, there was a corresponding development in taste and discrimination, and buildings took on a character that was remarkable for a new state "out West". The architectural movements in the East were taken up and echoed by the Middle West; the Colonial and post-Colonial styles appear in all their beauty in the Western Reserve section of the state; the Georgian style, in all its dignity, it to be found in the south-central part. Ohio has as many (possibly more) fine examples of the Greek Revival style of architecture as any other state; Cincinnati, Columbus, Zanesville, Lancaster, Granville, Mt. Vernon and many other Ohio cities are graced with such buildings. The state is also rich in the Victorian Gothic architecture used for colleges and institutions, as at the time of the popularity of that form (*circa* 1870) there were many state institutions and small colleges being built in the state. The numerous examples of the Richardsonian style in homes, churches, and public buildings attest how that style actually ran riot in Ohio (see Chap. III, *ante*). Everyone is interested in architecture, as it is an art expression of broad social value, and the state can boast of many worth-while buildings. The aims and purposes of Ohio architects have been many and manifold: the creation of city and village buildings designed to promote the health and character of families; of dignified schools and museums to advance the education of the children; of safe and beautiful theaters; of government buildings impressive in scale and grandeur; of offices and factories that are convenient and sanitary, and not lacking in beauty; and of homes that are beautiful and commodious, contributing to the home-loving qualities by which the people of the state are characterized.

The artistic impulse of the early painters has become so strong that it is not easy to conceive the beginning of their timid efforts, but without these men

Ohio would not have her present place in art. The impulse gained momentum, until in the nineties there was in Cincinnati the group of masters in painting, headed by Duveneck, that laid the artistic foundation of the entire state. The people of Ohio have had the courage and imagination to build upon this foundation an art that is serving its citizens today, and will be for the happiness and betterment of all the generations to come. That group of Cincinnati artists made a very definite contribution to the art of Ohio and to the art of the nation. Their influence was far-reaching. They studied in Europe and brought back the tendencies of the art teaching of Munich, Paris, and Italy, but adapted these foreign ideals to the needs of their art and at the same time retained its native individuality. So it has been with all the art movements transferred from the East to Ohio, at different times, from the influence of the early Hudson River school of landscape painting down to the extreme modernistic movement. New Yorkers at present consider art in Ohio very conservative, but it simply is a matter of Ohioans adapting the abstractions of the ultramoderns to their needs and not adopting them *in toto* in imitative fashion. The soundness of the early art teaching in Ohio insures a safe and sane art.

The preëminence of Ohio in ceramics is unquestioned. The whole nation is indebted to the state for its contribution to that phase of art. Steubenville and Zanesville have, almost from the date of their settlement, furnished clay products of enormous value. The Rookwood Pottery holds a unique place in the art pottery of the world, with representative exhibits of its ware in the great European museums. From late developments in Ohio ceramics, wonderful new glazes, and the teaching of ceramic art in the Ohio State University, it is safe to anticipate for this art a brilliant future that will surpass all past records. Who could keep silence of all this? One is justified in making such forecasts. Aside from our immediate consideration, it is to be repeated that the value of the output of Ohio potteries runs into amazing figures.

The slight urge toward sculpture in the early history of the state developed into the remarkable expressions of J. Q. A. Ward, who gave an incalculable impetus to the rise of American sculpture to the high position it occupies at present among the sculpture of the world. Too much emphasis cannot be placed on that phase of art in Ohio. Hiram Powers began his training in Cincinnati; he was the first sculptor to make known to Europe the fact that America had men of genius in sculpture. While the classic influence of Rome dominated in the early sculpture, with the development of sculpture by J. Q. A. Ward it became a vigorous native art and has remained so. The world today must acknowledge such Ohio sculptors as Erwin Frey, Ernest Bruce Haswell, and Alexander Blazys.

What has Ohio contributed to the cultural history of the nation? It would not be possible to measure the extent of the influence exerted by Ohio artists. As a sculptor, J. Q. A. Ward should be placed second only to Augustus Saint-Gaudens or Daniel Chester French in national significance, as he was predominantly instrumental in shaping American sculpture with a definite American characteristic. In the realm of painting, Frank Duveneck's teaching developed many of the most noted painters of the nation. A cross section of the art of any part of the United States will reveal the names of prominent Ohio artists. New York City and Washington have long enjoyed the fame accruing from such Ohio painters as Worthington Whittredge, Alexander Wyant, E. F. Andrews, Max Bohm, Cullen Yates, Robert Henri and George Bellows. Ohio art has never been local or provincial, but has always been an integral part of the artistic development of the nation.

A standard of excellence in the graphic arts in Ohio was set by Otto Bacher. There has been no lowering of that standard. Benjamin Miller, E. T. Hurley, and other graphic artists of Cincinnati, the members of the Dayton Society of Etchers, of the Toledo Print Club, and of the Cleveland Print Makers, are exhibiting work that takes its place of honor in the national print shows. The pioneers of newspaper art, the Ohioans Frederick Opper, W. A. Rogers, and Richard Outcault, have given the state a distinctive place which it has continued to hold in that field, and the eastern metropolitan papers have formed the habit of looking to Ohio for their artists.

The many museums in Ohio have helped to democratize art and bring it to the people, rather than to limit the understanding of it to the talented or privileged few who enjoyed it before the days of so many museums. Aside from the public museums there are almost countless private collections of *objets d'art* in the state. Rare paintings, bronzes, carved ivory, laces, bookplates, books, prints, and Indian relics are a few of the kinds of objects that have received attention from the enthusiastic art connoisseurs and patrons of art in Ohio. These collections are evidence of the taste and culture in the state. The public schools in many cities are acquiring original paintings and sculpture to ornament their buildings and to familiarize the children with original works of art. The Ohio museums and collections have played an important part in art education.

It is not necessary to review the changes that have taken place in the teaching of art. It has been to the advantage of art that in a practical age it has vindicated its claims and proved its merit as a vital educational force. The average business man no longer needs to be convinced that art consists in design and color; the public is sympathetic and demands further education in beauty. A cultural balance to the material prosperity of the state is assured.

With the superb training the artist can obtain in the state, what may we not hope for from him? Has there ever been a time when so many painters and artists, of all sorts, were experimenting with so many different effects? Some adhere to the conservative traditions, others conform objects to angles, or go into painted abstractions; still others like the linear patterns of the Japanese, or the flat painting of the Persians. Modern art is a welding together of ideas that make for growth and progress. The painting of today needs a continual reëvaluation, but of one thing we are certain: the art that survives will be good. We who live between the past and the future know that the high ideals of the state will be maintained. A century of machinery and the World War changed the world for everyone. A different tempo marks the rhythm of life and accomplishes things with a sharp accent. The public, with a newly awakened art consciousness, is making honest attempts to discover the merits in contemporary art movements, and that is a healthy omen for the future.

Even considering the great achievements of art already counted in the state, one can predict with confidence that the story of Ohio art is just begun. Today Ohio painters, sculptors, architects, craftsmen, and other artists are hard at work, accomplishing, progressing far beyond past imagination. The Ohio artist acknowledges the artistic appeal of the state, from the shores of Lake Erie, through the fertile plains and wheat fields of the central section, to the hills skirting the Ohio River on the South. The artist's America is no longer confined to New York City and the East, but stretches across the continent from East to West and recognizes the distinctive place Ohio holds as an inspiration for the painter.

The material resources of Ohio are secure, substantial and abundant; with every essential industry of the state forging ahead, it is certain that art will not be a slacker. With such nationally known artists as Henry G. Keller, Frank Wilcox, James R. Hopkins, Herman H. Wessel and John Weis holding high the quality of Ohio art production, and infusing that standard through their teaching and encouragement into the present and future painters, there is no limit to the possibilities in art achievements in the state. One is stirred with enthusiasm when contemplating the wonderful future of art in Ohio.

APPENDIX A

Art Sales Galleries

It is fitting that recognition should be given here to the contribution made by the sales galleries in many of the cities of the state. They have exhibited and promoted the sale of the work of many artists, thus encouraging them materially and spiritually. The service which the sales galleries have performed has been invaluable to the cause of art. An essentially complete list follows:

Cincinnati:

A. B. Closson, Jr. & Co., 112 West 4th St.
Traxel Art Co., 132 West 4th St.
The Art Center, 15 East 8th St.
Mary L. Alexander's Studio, 1767 East McMillan St.
Charles Stewart Todd's Park Avenue Studio.

Cleveland:

The Gage Galleries, 2258 Euclid Ave.
Korner & Wood Company, 1512 Euclid Ave.
Riddles Galleries, 3230 Euclid Ave.
Leamon Galleries, Union Trust Building.
Potter Bentley Studios, Inc., 10405 Carnegie Ave.
Vixseboxse Art Gallery, 6539 Euclid Ave.
Linder's Little Gallery.

Columbus:

Sifrit's, 184 South High Street.

Toledo:

Mohr Art Galleries, 915 Madison Ave.

APPENDIX B

Art Organizations in Ohio

OHIO STATE ASSOCIATION OF ARCHITECTS, Walter R. McCornack, 10006 Carnegie Ave., Cleveland, President; Galen F. Oman, 2569 N. High St., Columbus, Secretary. Organized 1915. Membership, 319.

AKRON ART INSTITUTE, Public Library Building, Akron. David W. Stevenson, President. Founded 1921. Membership, 500.

EXHIBIT BY "OHIO BORN WOMEN ARTISTS," Charlotte M. Hoff, Chairman of Art Division, Akron and Summit County Federation of Women's Clubs, and Director, Akron Art Institute. Organized 1926. Membership, 35.

OLD SETTLERS' ART CLUB, 355 West North Street, Akron. William T. Perry, Secretary. Founded 1914; reorganized 1924.

UNIVERSITY ART CLUB, University of Akron, Akron. Leona M. Knabe, President. Organized 1926. Membership, 32.

CANTON WOMAN'S CLUB, 821 Market Ave., North Canton. Mrs. C. H. Corbett, President. Organized 1920. Membership, 760.

CINCINNATI ARCHITECTURAL CLUB, 527 East Third Street, Cincinnati. George Franz, President. Organized 1911. Membership, 98.

CINCINNATI ART CLUB, 527 E. Third St., Cincinnati. Theodore C. Dorl, President; Chas. Schlapp, Secretary. Organized 1892. Membership, 200.

CINCINNATI CHAPTER AMERICAN INSTITUTE OF ARCHITECTS, Ernest Pickerington, University of Cincinnati, President; Russell Potter, 1304 American Bldg., Secretary.

CINCINNATI MUSEUM ASSOCIATION, Eden Park, Cincinnati. C. J. Livingood, President. Incorporated 1881. Membership, 246.

CRAFTERS COMPANY, Cincinnati. (Elizabeth R. Kellog, Secretary, Hotel Alms), Cincinnati. Organized 1911. Membership, 500. Mrs. Rudolph Wurlitzer, President.

DUVENECK SOCIETY OF PAINTERS AND SCULPTORS, Art Academy, Cincinnati. John E. Weis, Pres.-Treas. Organized 1915. Membership is limited to 20.

MACDOWELL SOCIETY OF CINCINNATI, William G. Werner, President, 3838 Middleton Ave., Cincinnati. Organized 1913. Membership, 150.

MUNICIPAL ART SOCIETY OF CINCINNATI (Frederick H. Chatfield, Secretary, c/o Chatfield & Woods, 3rd and Plum), Cincinnati. John Dee Wareham, President. Organized 1894. Membership, 50.

THREE ARTS CLUB, Marion. Mrs. Dale Lawrence, President, Smeltzer Road, R. R. 5. Mrs. Fred Isler, Secretary, Prospect.

WOMAN'S ART CLUB OF CINCINNATI, Cincinnati. Mrs. Marie MacPherson, President. Margaret S. Tinne, Secretary. Organized 1892. Membership, 300.

BUSINESS MEN'S ART CLUB OF CLEVELAND (Ernest F. Crummel, Sec.-Treas., 1512 Euclid Avenue), Cleveland. William T. Higbee, President. Organized 1928. Membership, 50.

CITY PLAN COMMISSION OF CLEVELAND, City Hall, Cleveland. William M. Murphy, Executive Secretary. Organized 1915. Composed of the city manager and ten civilians.

CLEVELAND ART ASSOCIATION, 3018 Kingsley Road, Shaker Heights, Cleveland. Mrs. F. H. Westlake, President. Organized 1915. Membership, 200.

THE CLEVELAND ART CENTER, 1224 Huron Road, Cleveland. Lewis P. Wilson, President. Founded 1928. Membership, 221.

CLEVELAND CHAPTER AMERICAN INSTITUTE OF ARCHITECTS (James Duthie, Secretary, Terminal Tower Building), Cleveland. P. L. Small, President. Organized 1890. Membership: Regular members 99; associate, 31.

CLEVELAND MUSEUM OF ART, East Boulevard, Wade Park, Cleveland. John L. Severance, President. Incorporated 1913. Membership, over 6,453.

CLEVELAND SCHOOL OF ART, 11441 Juniper Road, Cleveland. Mrs. Stevenson Burke, President. Founded 1882.

ALUMNI ASSOCIATION CLEVELAND SCHOOL OF ART, Juniper Road, Cleveland. Albert C. Young, President. Organized 1911. Membership, 500.

CLEVELAND SOCIETY OF ARTISTS, 2022 East 88th St., Cleveland. Carl W. Broemel, President. Organized 1913. Membership, 125.

KOKOON ARTS CLUB, 2109 East 40th Street, Cleveland. Clarence G. Wing, President. Organized 1911. Membership, 70. H. S. Roof, Secretary.

PRINT CLUB, Box 2081, Station E., Cleveland. Charles B. Gleason, President. Organized 1919. Membership, 221.

THE CLEVELAND PRINT MAKERS, 2341 Carnegie Ave. Organized 1930. John Huntington Polytechnical School. Mrs. Raymond, Secretary. Kalman Kubinyi, President.

THE HORACE KELLEY ART FOUNDATION, 1968 Union Trust Building, Cleveland. Alfred Kelley, Pres.-Treas. Organized 1899. Membership, 8.

WOMAN'S ART CLUB OF CLEVELAND (Helen E. Hewes, Cor.-Sec., 1528 Westwood Ave., Lakewood, Ohio). Grace Walsh, President. Organized 1912. Membership, 83.

COLUMBUS ART LEAGUE (Miss Betty Walker, Sec.-Treas., 141 E. Woodruff Ave.), Columbus. Hoyt Sherman, President. Organized 1909 as Art Students' League. Membership, 205.

ART HISTORY CLUB, Columbus. Mrs. Robt. Seeds, President, 1262 Fair Ave., Columbus. Membership, 35.

COLUMBUS CHAPTER AMERICAN INSTITUTE OF ARCHITECTS (R. C. Kempton, Secretary, 1694 N. High Street), Columbus. W. C. Ronan, President. Organized 1913. Membership, 36.

COLUMBUS GALLERY OF FINE ARTS, 478 East Broad Street, Columbus. O. A. Miller, President. Founded 1878. Membership, 300.

OHIO WATER COLOR SOCIETY, President, Grace Rhodes Dean, Toledo. Organized 1925. Membership, 50.

PEN AND PENCIL CLUB, 393 Library Park, South, Columbus. Sterling Wyrick, President. Organized 1897. Membership, 75.

DAYTON ART INSTITUTE (Formerly Dayton Museum of Arts), Monument Avenue and St. Clair Street, Dayton. Robert Patterson, President. Reorganized in 1919. Annual attendance, 30,000.

DAYTON CHAPTER AMERICAN INSTITUTE OF ARCHITECTS, Ellasson Smith, Secretary, Dayton. Edwin Simpson, President. Organized 1899. Membership, 23.

DAYTON SOCIETY OF ETCHERS, Dayton Art Institute, Dayton. LeRoy D. Sauer, President. Organized 1921. Membership limited to 10.

ART STUDY CLUB OF CENTRAL HIGH SCHOOL, Central High School, Lima. Debbert Drake, President. Organized 1919. Membership, 15.

ART STUDY CLUB (Mrs. C. E. Schell, Secretary, 445 South Woodlawn), Lima. Mrs. Peter M. Hulsken, President. Organized 1919. Membership, 33.

MARION ART CLUB (Mrs. Edward Cowan, Cor.-Sec., 665 Garard Avenue), Marion. Mrs. James Crawmer, President. Organized 1921. Membership, 40.

OBERLIN ART ASSOCIATION, Allen Memorial Art Museum, Oberlin College, Oberlin. Clarence Ward, President. Organized 1912.

DUDLEY PETER ALLEN MEMORIAL ART MUSEUM, Oberlin College, Oberlin. Mrs. Hazel B. King, Curator. Building dedicated 1917.

PAINESVILLE ART ASSOCIATION (Mrs. K. D. Park, Secretary, 374 Avery Place), Painesville. Mrs. B. B. Ruttenbur, President. Organized 1921. Membership, 55.

ART STUDY CLUB (Mrs. DeWitt Owen, Secretary, 332 Hancock St.), Sandusky. Mrs. L. D. Morton, President. Organized 1901. Membership, 20.

THE BUSINESS WOMEN'S CLUB (Elize Kranhulic, Secretary, Huran Ave.), Sandusky. Wilma K. Link, President. Organized 1913; incorporated 1926. Membership, 610.

TIFFIN WOMAN'S CLUB, Frost Parkway, Tiffin. Mrs. R. D. Niles, President. Federated 1920. Membership, 500. Mrs. S. J. Diamond, Secretary.

ARTKLAN–TOLEDO, 401 Meredith Building, Jefferson and Michigan Streets, Toledo. J. DeViney, President. Organized 1913. Membership, 50. Men Artists.

TOLEDO CHAPTER AMERICAN INSTITUTE OF ARCHITECTS (Louis U. Bruyere, Secretary, Board of Education), Toledo. Chester B. Lee, President. Organized 1914. Membership, 22.

TOLEDO FEDERATION OF ART SOCIETIES, Toledo Museum of Art, Toledo. I. W. Gotshall, President.

TOLEDO MUSEUM OF ART, Monroe Street at Scottwood Avenue, Toledo. Arthur J. Secor, President. Incorporated 1901. Membership, 2,100.

THE TOLEDO WOMEN ARTISTS, President, Mrs. Frank Maxwell, 2111 Sherwood Road.

THE TOLEDO ART LEAGUE WOMEN ARTISTS, President, Mrs. Byron Gardner, 2208 Central Grove Ave.

THE ART ALLIANCE (Helena Hastings, Cor.-Sec., 526 Parmelee Ave.), Youngstown. President, Mrs. Paul Weber. Organized 1929. Membership, 60.

BUTLER ART INSTITUTE, 524 Wick Avenue, Youngstown. Henry A. Butler, President. Established 1919.

MAHONING SOCIETY OF PAINTERS (Mrs. Anna S. Davis, Secretary, 309 Arlington St.), Youngstown. Charles Hoover, President. Organized 1920. Membership, 50.

EASTERN OHIO CHAPTER AMERICAN INSTITUTE OF ARCHITECTS, Youngstown. Barton E. Brooke, President. Walter J. Canfield, Secretary.

WESTERN ARTS ASSOCIATION, Harry E. Wood, Sec.-Treas., 5215 College Ave., Indianapolis, Ind. Organized 1893. Over 1,300 members.

WYANT ART CLUB, Defiance.

OHIO FEDERATION OF WOMEN'S CLUBS, Art Division Chairman, Mrs. S. J. Podlewski, 317 North Street, Steubenville, Ohio.

YOUNGSTOWN SOCIETY OF WOMEN ARTISTS, Mrs. Howard Sutton, President, 14 East Midlothian Boulevard.

THE BUCKEYE CLUB, Youngstown. James L. Wick, President, Belle Vista and Price Road.

APPENDIX C

Art Schools of Ohio

AKRON

UNIVERSITY OF AKRON, *Art Department.*

Jane S. Barnhardt, head of department; three instructors. Department founded 1922. Elements and history of art, applied design, costume design, interor decoration, commercial art. Municipal University free to city students; tuition, $180 for outside students. Term, ten months. Enrollment, 262.

ATHENS

OHIO UNIVERSITY, *Art Department, College of Education.*

Edna M. Way, head of department; six instructors. Founded 1905. Reorganized 1914. Four-year art supervisors' and teachers' course, giving B.S. in Education for Art teachers. Courses in art education, applied design, costume design, in poster advertising, in interior decoration, house decoration, pottery, illustration, practical art, art appreciation, bookbinding. Day classes; evening extension classes. Tuition, $70 a year. Thirty-eight weeks' course. Total enrollment, over 500.

Summer. Frances Laughlin, acting head of art department; four instructors. Supervision and teaching of art. Tuition, $15, plus course fees. Term of nine weeks. Enrollment, 230.

CINCINNATI

ART ACADEMY, Eden Park.

Walter H. Siple, director; fifteen instructors. Founded 1869. Drawing, painting, modeling, design, applied art, handicraft design, china painting, metal work, leather work, bookbinding. Thirty scholarships. Day and evening classes. Tuition, $100 for eight months; evening, $15. Enrollment, 541.

Summer: Walter H. Siple, director. Six instructors. Drawing, painting, modeling, design. Tuition, $40 for eight weeks. Enrollment, 85.

OHIO MECHANICS INSTITUTE, *Department of Applied Arts,* Central Parkway
and Walnut Streets.

John T. Faig, president; eighteen instructors. Founded 1828; art department 1856. Architectural and mechanical drawing, industrial design, graphic arts, lithography; several scholarships in lithography. Tuition, $90 and $100 day classes, for nine months; $20 to $40 evening classes, for six months. Enrollment, about 200 students in art, including evening class.

Summer. One instructor. Comprehensive art, commercial art. Tuition, $12.50 to $20 for six weeks. Enrollment, about 40.

CLEVELAND

CLEVELAND SCHOOL OF ARCHITECTURE, 11015 Euclid Avenue.

Francis R. Bacon, director; twenty-one instructors. Course established 1921; school incorporated 1924. Full collegiate course in architecture. Tuition, $300 for eight and one-half months. Enrollment, 100.

433

Cleveland School of Art, 11441 Juniper Road.
Henry Hunt Clark, director; forty-five instructors. Founded 1882. Portraiture, landscape, teacher training, advertising, art, sculpture, illustrating, crafts, decorative design. Graduate school, individual special courses under supervision. Scholarships and prizes. Frequent special exhibitions. Tuition, $300 for eight and one-half months; evening courses, $30 for eight months. Children's and Summer courses. Enrollment, 1,540.

College for Women of Western Reserve University.
Helen M. Smith, dean; one instructor. Founded 1888. Two courses each in the history of ancient and the history of modern art. Tuition, $300 for nine months. Enrollment, 7.

John Huntington Polytechnic Institute, 2341 Carnegie Avenue.
Alfred J. Mewett, acting director; nineteen instructors. Founded 1918. Architectural design, architectural rendering, bookbinding, building construction, patent procedure, lettering, commercial life drawing, advertising, engineering salesmanship, human figure in decoration, architectural and modern building construction, designing for foundry practice, forming of metals, contract law, art in printing, graphic and commercial life drawing. Evening classes with privilege of working during the day. Tuition free. Term of eight and a half months. Enrollment, 1,000.

COLUMBUS

Art School of the Columbus Gallery of Fine Arts, 492 East Broad Street.
Karl S. Bolander, director; six instructors. Founded 1879, by the Columbus Art Association. Drawing, painting, illustrative advertising, design. Day, evening, and Saturday classes. Tuition: $125, day; $50, evening; $30, Saturday. Term of eight months. Diploma Course for four years. Enrollment, 150.

Ohio State University, *Department of Fine Arts.*
James R. Hopkins, head of department; twenty-two instructors. Founded 1898. Drawing, painting, modeling, design, teacher training, ceramic art, landscape architecture, history of art. Tuition, $45 for eight months. Enrollment, 2,600; four quarters. *Summer course.*

Ohio State University, *Department of Architecture.*
Charles St. J. Chubb, chairman; seven instructors. Department founded 1900. Architecture and architectural engineering. Tuition: $60 for Ohio residents, $105 for non-residents, for eight and one-half months. Enrollment, 220.

DAYTON

Dayton Art Institute, Monument Avenue and St. Clair Street.
Six instructors. Founded 1919. Graphic, plastic, commercial art, industrial design, industrial arts, interior decoration, art appreciation, art history. Saturday classes for children. Tuition: day, $100 for eight months; evening, $30; Saturday, $16. Enrollment, 236.
Summer. Founded 1927. Three instructors. Design, moleding, water color, special class for children. Tuition, $10 per course for five weeks. Enrollment, 85.

DELAWARE

Ohio Wesleyan University, School of Fine Arts.
Sallie Thomson Humphreys, director; six instructors. Founded 1864. Drawing, painting, and design in both theory and practice; crafts, normal art, home decoration, his-

tory and appreciation of art and historic ornament, porcelain decoration. Tuition, $250 for nine months. Enrollment, 257.

OBERLIN

OBERLIN COLLEGE, *Department of Fine Arts.*
Clarence Ward, head of department; ten instructors. Founded 1917. Theory and practice of ancient, medieval and modern architecture, painting and sculpture. Art course included in college tuition $300. Term of nine months. Enrollment, about 400.

OXFORD

MIAMI UNIVERSITY, School of Education, *Art Department.*
Amy M. Swisher, head of department; four instructors. Founded 1909. Elementary and advanced drawing design, technical problems in design and craft, free-hand sketching and painting. Tuition, $75. Ten months' term. Enrollment, 425. Special art supervisors' course, 42.

MIAMI UNIVERSITY, School of Fine Arts.
Dean Theodore Kratt, head. Five instructors. Architecture, design, painting, history of art. Tuition, $75. Ten months' term. Enrollment, 250.

WESTERN COLLEGE FOR WOMEN.
Miss Merle Ackerman, head of art department; one instructor. Founded 1855. Painting, drawing, design, interior decoration, history of art, crafts. Studio fee, $5. Term of nine months. Enrollment, 112.

PAINESVILLE

LAKE ERIE COLLEGE.
Marie Riggins, A.M., Professor; and Jane G. Gale, B.S., Assistant Professor in charge. Founded 1880. History of art, drawing, painting, applied art, design, interior decoration, appreciation of art, lettering, poster work. Tuition, included in college fee. Enrollment, 80.

TOLEDO

SCHOOL OF THE TOLEDO MUSEUM OF ART, Monroe Street and Scottwood Avenue.
Mrs. George W. Stevens, director; Mrs. Blake-More Godwin, dean; three instructors. Color and design, figure drawing, home furnishing, special courses for commercial and industrial groups, fashion drawing, lettering, poster. Free instruction to select pupils from Toledo grade schools, high school and university students and adults. Day and evening classes. Term of eight and one-half months. Enrollment, 1,138.

WESTERVILLE

OTTERBEIN UNIVERSITY, *Fine Arts Department.*
Miss Delphine Dunn, director; one instructor. Founded 1847. Fine and normal arts, applied design. Tuition, $100 for term of nine months. Enrollment, about 50.

WOOSTER

COLLEGE OF WOOSTER, *Art Department.*
John B. Kelso, head of department. Two instructors. Founded 1870. Greek art, architecture, Italian art, survey. Day and evening classes. Tuition included in that of college. Term of nine months. Enrollment, 80.

YELLOW SPRINGS

ANTIOCH COLLEGE, *Art Department.*
Irving Cannon, head of department; three instructors. Applied esthetics, introduction to art, free-hand drawing and painting, modeling, art through the ages. Tuition, $300. Term of ten months. Enrollment, 61.

YOUNGSTOWN

SCHOOL OF THE BUTLER ART INSTITUTE, 542 Wick Avenue.
Margaret Evans, director; one instructor. Founded 1921. Drawing from casts, still life, landscape, color. Annual exhibition. Tuition free. Term of nine months. Enrollment, 212.

APPENDIX D

Biographical List of Ohio Artists

(In conformity with the *American Art Annual,* the same abbreviations are used here. Architects, except a few deceased ones, are not listed, because the *Annuary* of the American Institute of Architects publishes a complete list.)

ABBREVIATIONS

Arch.—Architect.
B.—Block Printer.
C.—Craftsman.
D.—Designer.
E.—Etcher.
Engr.—Engraver.
I.—Illustrator.
L.—Lecturer.
Ldscp. Arch.—Landscape Architect.
Ldscp. P.—Landscape Painter.
Lith.—Lithographer.
Min. P.—Miniature Painter.
Mural P.—Mural Painter.
News A.—Newspaper Artist.
P.—Painter.
Port. P.—Portrait Painter.
S.—Sculptor.
T.—Teacher.
W.—Writer.
*—Deceased.

SOCIETIES

AA—Art Association (preceded by name of city).
AC—Art Club (preceded by name of city).
AFA—American Federation of Arts.
AFAS—American Fine Arts Society, New York.
AIA—American Institute of Architects.
AIC—Art Institute of Chicago.
AI Graphic A—American Institute of Graphic Arts.
Alliance—Art Alliance of America.
Allied AA—Allied Artists of America.
Am. Acad. AL—American Academy of Arts and Letters.
Am. APL—American Artists Professional League.
ANA—Associate of National Academy of Design.
ASL of NY—Art Students' League of New York.
AS Min. P—American Society of Miniature Painters, New York.

AWCS—American Water Color Society.
CAL—Columbus Art League.
Cin. AA—Cincinnati Art Academy.
Cin. WAC—Cincinnati Woman's Art Club.
Cleve. MA—Cleveland Museum of Art.
CPM—Cleveland Print Makers.
Day. SE—Dayton Society of Etchers.
FAIA—Fellow American Institute of Architects.
GFLA—Guild of Free Lance Artists.
HS—Hoosier Salon.
Inter. Soc. AL—International Society of Arts and Letters.
Inter. Soc. SPG—International Society of Sculptors, Painters, Gravers.
Mural P—National Society of Mural Painters
NA—National Academy of Design (Academicians) New York.
NAC—National Arts Club.
NAD—National Academy of Design (Used chiefly for the school).
Nat. Inst. AL—National Institute of Arts and Letters.
NA Women PS—National Association of Women Painters and Sculptors.
NSS—National Sculpture Society.
NY Arch. L—New York Architectural League.
NYWCC—New York Water Color Club.
Ohio-Born WP—Ohio-Born Women Painters.
Ohio WCS—Ohio Water Color Society.
PAFA—Pennsylvania Academy of Fine Arts.
PBC—Pen and Brush Club, New York.
PPC—Pen and Pencil Club, Columbus.
Port. P.—National Association of Portrait Painters.
PS—Painters and Sculptors.
Salma. C.—Salmagundi Club, New York.
SAA—Society of American Artists.
SAC—Society of Arts and Crafts.
SI—Society of Illustrators.
S Indp. A—Society of Independent Artists.
SSAL—Southern States Art League.
SWA—Society of Western Artists.
WAA—Western Arts Association.

ABEL, LOUISE, Rookwood Pottery, Cincinnati, Ohio (S. C.) b. Mt. Healthy, Ohio, 1894. Studied Cin. AA with Barnhorn, Meakin, Wessel. Figures in pottery. Member: Cin. AC.

ABEL, MYER, 2238 Gilbert Ave., Cincinnati, Ohio (P. E. T.) Studied Cin. AA; Julian Academy; Académie Moderne, Paris. Work: Cincinnati, New York, San Francisco, Chicago.

ACHERT, FRED, 10 E. 3rd St., Cincinnati, Ohio (P.) Member: Cin AC.

ADAM, WILBUR G., Malabry Court, 675 North Michigan Avenue, Chicago, Ill. (P. I.) b. Cincinnati, Ohio, July 23, 1898. Pupil of Duveneck, L. H. Meakin, James R. Hopkins, H. H. Wessel, C. A. Lord. Member: Tiffany Foundation; Cin. AC. Award: Augustus S. Peabody prize, AIC, 1925. Painted Glacier Park. Portraits of Ambassador Dawes' family.

ADNEY, EDWIN TAPPEN* (News A.) b. Athens, Ohio, July 13, 1868; d. *circa* 1923. Studied ASL of NY for three years. Artist and special correspondent for *Harper's Weekly* and *London Chronicle* at Klondike, 1897-98. Special correspondent for *Collier's Weekly* at Cape Nome, 1900. Painter and writer on outdoor subjects. Lecturer, Am. Soc. Prevention Cruelty to Animals, 1902-04. Lt. Canadian Engineers, CEF, 1916. Author, "The Klondike Stampede," 1899. Joint author of *Harper's Outdoor Book for Boys,* 1908.

ADOMEIT, GEORGE GUSTAV, Caxton Bldg.; h. 2054 East 102nd St., Cleveland, Ohio (P.) b. Germany, Jan. 15, 1879. Pupil of F. C. Gottwald. Member: Cleveland SA; AI Graphic A; Cleveland Print C; AFA. Awards: Prize, Ohio State Fair, 1922; Prize, Cleveland Museum of Art, 1923; 1927.

ALDRICH, FRANK HANDY, care of Toledo Museum of Art, Toledo, Ohio (P. I. C. L. T.) b. Wauseon, O., Mar. 29, 1866. Pupil of Twachtman, Metcalf, Knaufft. Member: Toledo Artklan, Custodian of Ancient Books and Manuscripts, Toledo Museum of Art. Owner of bookplates.

ALEXANDER, MARY LOUISE, 28 Alexandra Bldg.; h. 2238 Gilbert Ave., Cincinnati, Ohio. (S. W. T.) Pupil of Meakin, Duveneck, Barnhorn, Grafly, Nowottny. Member: Cin. Woman's AC; MacDowell Soc., Cincinnati; PBC. Work: Vincent Nowottny tablet, Cincinnati Art Academy.

ALKE, ELIZABETH HEIL (MRS. STEPHEN), R.F.D. 2, New Richmond, Ohio (P.) Work: decorative landscape. Member: Western AC; NA Women PS; Cin. WAC. Exhibits many places, East and Chicago.

ALKE, STEPHEN, R.F.D. 2, New Richmond, Ohio (P.) Portraits and Landscapes.

ALLEN, ANNE HUNTINGTON (MRS. THOMAS W.), 418 9th St., Santa Monica, Calif. (P.) Member: Cin. Woman's AC.

ALLEN, MARY COLEMAN, 22 West Franklin St., Troy, Ohio (Min. P.) b. Troy, O., Aug. 9, 1888. Pupil of Duveneck, Alice Beckington of ASL of NY. Member: Am. Soc. Min. P.; Calif. Soc. Min. P.; N.A. Women PS.

ALLIS, C. HARRY, care of National Arts Club, Gramercy Park, New York City (P.) b. Dayton, Ohio. Studied at Detroit Museum of Art School, and Bay View Academy. Member: Allied AA; Scarab C; NAC; Salma. C; Imperial AL of London; Munich S. Amer. P; Paris AAA; SWA. Represented in the Ackerman collection, San Francisco; "Pig'n Whistle" collection, Los Angeles; Univ. of Oregon, Eugene; Ateneo, San Juan, Porto Rico; "The Covered Bridge," Detroit Institute of Art.

AMANN, C. R., Philadelphia, Pa. (News A.) b. Nov. 24, 1877, Columbus, Ohio. Head of color printing at Curtis Publishing Co., Philadelphia. Member: PPC.

AMES, MAY, 9315 Miles Avenue, Cleveland, Ohio (T. P. L.) b. Cleveland. Cleveland Art Club training; also Cleveland School of Art; Rhode Island School of Design; Europe. Work: oil landscapes placed in homes of Chile, S.A.; Philippines; Chicago; Buffalo; New York. Awards: one year scholarship; $25 on oil still life. Member: Woman's AC, Cleveland; Buffalo Soc. of A; Ohio-Born Women Artists; NA Women PS. Instructor Cleveland School of Art, eighteen years. Lecturer on Art History.

ANDERSON, KARL, Westport, Conn. (P. I.) b. Oxford, Ohio, Jan. 13, 1874. Pupil of AIC; Colarossi Academy in Paris; studied in Holland, Italy, Madrid. Member: ANA, 1913; NA, 1923; Am. PS; SI; Salma. C.; NAC; Contemporary; Allied AA. Awards: silver medal C.I. Pittsburgh, 1910; Lippincott prize, PAFA, 1916; Altman prize ($500), NAD, 1917; French gold medal, AIC, 1919; gold medal, NAC, 1920. Work: "The Idlers," Art Institute of Chicago; "Sisters," City Art Museum, St. Louis; "Apple Gatherers," Cleveland Museum; "The Heirloom," Pennsylvania Academy, Philadelphia; "Her Ladyship's Attendants," Harrison Gallery, Los Angeles Museum.

ANDERSON, GEORGE* (Arch.) b. 1869, Cincinnati; d. Oct. 4, 1916, Cincinnati. Son of Larz Anderson. Educated at Columbia Univ., N. Y.; École des Beaux Arts, Paris. Entered office of Samuel Hannaford & Sons of Cincinnati, later associated with A. O. Elzner. President of Cin. Chapter of AIA at his death.

ANDREWS, ELIPHALET FRAZER* (Port. P.) b. Steubenville, Ohio, June 11, 1835; d. Mar. 19, 1915, Washington, D. C. Studied Düsseldorf; Paris. Founded Corcoran School of Art, Washington, D. C., and was its director 1887 to 1902. Represented: portraits of Jefferson, Martha Washington, Dolly Madison in Washington; Governors Foster and Hoadley in State House, Columbus; Garfield in Steubenville, City Building; Baron von Steuben, and other portraits in Carnegie Library, Steubenville.

ANKENEY, JOHN SITES, 3703 Hall St., Dallas, Texas (P.T.) b. Xenia, Ohio, Apr. 21, 1870. Pupil of Twachtman, Chase, Du Mond, Saint-Gaudens and Ross in U. S.; Lefebvre, Aman-Jean, and Menard in Europe. Member: Am. Art Asso., Paris; St. Louis AG; NAC; Salma. C; Columbia AA. Represented in Univ. of Missouri; Bethany College, Lindsborg, Kan.; Lindenwood College, St. Charles, Mo.; Christian College, Columbia, Mo.; Director of Dallas Public Art Gallery, Dallas Texas.

ARMBRUSTER, A. E., 3102 North High Street, Columbus, Ohio (P.) b. Zanesville, Oct. 22, 1867. Proprietor of Armbruster Studio where many artists have worked. Member: PPC.

ARMBRUSTER, OTTO HERMAN* (I. Scene Painter.) b. Ohio, Aug. 28, 1865; d. Aug. 15, 1908, N. Y. Pupil of M. Armbruster. Member: Salma. C; Kit-Kat C in N. Y.

ARMSTRONG, BARBARA, Ogunquit, Maine (P.) b. Bellaire, Ohio, 1896. Pupil of Hamilton E. Field.

ARTER, J. CHARLES* (P.) b. Hanoverton, Ohio; d. Alliance, Ohio, Dec. 29, 1923. Worked in Cin., then Paris. Had studios in Venice, London, N. Y. Painted portraits of many famous personages. Decorated by King and Queen of Italy for portraits he made of them. Specialty of flowers, Venetian and Japanese scenes. Two paintings in Paris Salon, 1890.

ASHBROOK, PAUL, 3 Hedgerow Lane, Cincinnati, Ohio; summer, care of American Express Co., Paris (P. I. E. T.) b. New York City, Jan. 3, 1867. Pupil of ASL of NY; Duveneck. Member: Cincinnati AC; Duveneck Soc.

AULL, JESS BROWN, Dayton, Ohio (P.) Studied with Gottwald, Cleveland Art School; Saugatuck; Paris at Colarossi Acad.; Lucien Simon; Charles Hawthorne. Member: Ohio-Born Women Artists. Landscapes, flowers, portraits.

AULT, GEO. C., 11 Charles St., New York, N. Y. (P.) b. Cleveland, 1891. Member: Soc. Indp. A.

BACHER, OTTO HENRY* (P.E.I.) b. Cleveland, Ohio, Mar. 31, 1856; d. Bronxville, N.Y., Aug. 16, 1909. Pupil of Duveneck, Cincinnati; Carolus Duran, Boulager, Lefebvre in Paris; Whistler in Venice. His book *Whistler in Venice*, published 1908. Member: ANA, 1906; SAA; SI. Awards: Hon. men., Buffalo, 1901; silver medal, St. Louis, 1904.

BACHOFEN, MAX, 11418 Euclid Ave., Cleveland, Ohio; Castroville, Texas (P.) b. New Brannen, Canton, Zurich, Switzerland, Aug. 25, 1903. Cleveland School of Art training. Work: landscape, still life in oil and water color. Many landscapes placed in private collections, Cleveland. Awards: hon. men., Cleveland Mus., 1927, 1929; first prize, Cleveland Mus., 1928, 1931, for oil landscape. Came to America in 1910.

BAER, WILLIAM JACOB, 226 W. 59th St., New York City; h. 174 Walnut St., East Orange, New Jersey (Min. P.) b. Cincinnati, Ohio, Jan. 29, 1860. Pupil of McMicken School of Design, Cincinnati; Royal Academy, Munich. Member: ANA; Amer. Soc. Min. P.; Pa. Soc. Min. P. (hon. life) ; Calif. Soc. Min. P. (hon.). Awards, bronze medal, Paris Exp., 1900, bronze medal, Pan. Amer. Exp., Buffalo, 1901; silver medal, Charleston Exp., 1902; hors concours, St. Louis Exp., 1904 (Jury of Awards) ; gold medal, P.-P. Exp., San. F., 1915. Work: "Aurora" and "Nymph," "Phoebe," Walters' Gallery, Baltimore; "Lady in Pink," Jaffe Collection, Hamburg; "Daphne," and portraits in oil, Brooklyn Institute Museum; "Murray Marvin," Montclair, N. J. Museum.

BAGGS, ARTHUR E., Ohio State University, Columbus, Ohio (C. T.) b. Oct. 27, 1886, Alfred, N. Y. Studied: College of Ceramics, Alfred, N. Y.; ASL of NY; Harvard Univ. Member: Am. Ceramic S.; Boston S. of Arts and Crafts; Nat'l Soc. Craftsmen. Awards: Armour prize for pottery, Chicago, 1915; Boston Soc. of Arts and Crafts, 1925; Charles F. Binns medal, 1928; first prize, Cleveland, 1928. Director of Marblehead Potteries, 1908-15; associate ceramist Cowan pottery, 1925-28; Professor Ceramic art, Ohio State Univ.

BAILEY, HENRY TURNER* (I. C. T. W. L.) b. North Scituate, Mass., Dec. 9, 1865; d. Chicago, Nov. 26, 1931. Pupil of Mass. Normal Art School in Boston. Member Cleve. AA; College AA; Cleve. SA; Cleve. AIA; AFA. Director, Chautauqua Summer School of Arts and Crafts, 1906-1916; dean Cleveland School of Art, 1917-30, and John Huntington Polytechnic Institute, Cleveland, 1919-30. Represented in Vanderpoel AA Collection, Chicago.

BAKER, CATHERINE ISABELLE, 2590 Glenmour Ave., Columbus, Ohio (P. T.) b. Columbus. Pupil of Alice Schille. Member: CAL. Award: hon. men., CAL, 1928.

BAKER, CONN, 40 East Norwich Avenue, Columbus, Ohio (P.) b. Jan. 31, 1872, Toledo. Work: oil landscape. Member: PPC.

BAKER, DON, 241 Franklin St., Westerville, Ohio (P.) Studied with Barnitz, Urbana, Ohio. Silas Martin, Ohio State Univ.; N. Y. School of Art; Robert Henri's School, N. Y. Member: CAL. Work: portrait and landscape; "The Hay Field," first prize, Ohio State Fair, 1912; "Nelsonville," first prize, Ohio State Fair, 1917; "October Stream," "The Pool," "The Silver Cloud," exhibited N. Y., 1921, Society of Ind. Artists; "Hilda," Calif. prize, 1921. Member: PPC.

BAKER, ELIZABETH GOWDY* (Port. P.) b. Xenia, Ohio, 1860; d. Oct. 11, 1927, New York City. Pupil of ASL of NY; Cooper Union; Pa. Acad. of FA; Cowles Art School, Boston; Frederick Freer; Rome; Florence; Paris. Member: Nat'l Art C.; Aquarellists; NAWPS. Represented: Xenia Theological Seminary, St. Louis; Engineer's Club, 8th Regiment, 75th Regiment Armories, N. Y.; Collins College, Winter Park, Fla.; Phillips Andover Acad., Andover, Mass.; Iowa His. Soc., State Capitol, Des Moines; Springfield Art Mus., Springfield, Mass.; Univ. of Chicago Library. "Edwin Markham." Specialty of water color portraits; invented table and easel for water to run either way. Medal, Cooper Union. Also portrait in oil.

BAKER, HERMAN C.* (P.) b. Toledo, Ohio, Sept. 13, 1873; d. July 2, 1902, Columbus. Studied with Richard Pauli, New York, who gave him the Barbizon influence. Work: cattle pictures especially, landscape. Paintings placed in many homes over the country and in Columbus.

BALL, L. CLARENCE* (P. T. I.) b. Mt. Vernon, Ohio, July 4, 1858; d. South Bend, Ind., Oct. 9, 1915. Self-taught; pupil NA. Member: Chicago SA; Cliff Dwellers, Chicago. Represented: Library, South Bend, Ind. Specialty, landscapes with cattle and sheep. Exhibited SWA; Exhibited Indiana Art Circuit.

BAMBROUGH, WILLIAM* (P.) b. Durham, England, 1792. Came to Columbus, 1819.

BANDLOW, A., Lithographer, Cleveland, Ohio (I.)

BARBER, JOHN JAY* (P.) b. Sandusky, Ohio, Apr. 21, 1840. Studio in Columbus, 1871. No instruction in painting. Work: landscapes of Muskingum Valley; cattle pictures: "Elysium of the Herd," "Pride of Eastwood Jerseys," "A Thirsty Party," "In Pastures Green," "Cool Retreat." Prize at World's Fair, New Orleans, 1884.

BARNEY, MRS. ALICE PIKE, Studio House, Sheridan Circle, Washington, D. C. (P. W.) b. Cincinnati, Ohio, Jan. 14, 1860. Pupil of Carolus Duran: Whistler, Henner. Member: AFA. Work: portrait of Whistler for Conrad's book of *Noted Men;* also used in other books on Whistler; Portrait of Natalie Barney, owned by the French government; Portrait of Hon. Calhoun, State Dept., Washington, D. C. Producer of original plays.

BARNHARDT (MRS.) JANE SARGENT, 283 Buchtel Ave., Akron, Ohio (P. T.) b. Rochester, N. Y. Studied: Boston School of Design; Cleveland School of Art; ASL of NY; Columbia University; Raymond F. Ensign; James Barton Haney; Otto W. Beck; Horace Potter; Nina V. Waldeck; Europe. Member: Western Arts Asso.; College Arts Asso.; Ohio Art Teachers Asso. (twice president of latter). Work: Head of Art Dept. University of Akron.

BARNHORN, CLEMENT JOHN, Art Museum; h. 409 Broadway, Cincinnati, Ohio (S.) b. Cincinnati, 1857. Pupil of Rebisso, in Cincinnati; Bougereau, Peuch, Mercié, Ferrier and Julian Academy in Paris. Member: NSS, 1899; Cincinnati, AC. Awards: Hon. mention, Paris Salon,1895; bronze medal, Paris Exp., 1900; Hon. mention, Pan-Amer. Expo., Buffalo, 1901; silver medal, St. Louis Expo., 1904. Work: "Theodore Thomas," Cincinnati Music Club; "Fountain," Shortridge High School, Indianapolis; Fountain figure, Prince George Hotel, New York; "Fountain," Hughes High School, Cincinnati; "Magdalen," Cincinnati Art Museum; "Portrait Bust," Public Library, Cincinnati; "Madonna and Child," Cathedral Façade, Covington, Ky.; "Fountain," Conservatory of Music, Cincinnati; eleven panels in Cincinnati Court House; Portrait of Major C. R. Holmes, Cincinnati General Hospital; Dr. P. S. Connor, relief, Good Samaritan Hospital, Cincinnati.

BARRIE, ERWIN S., 1188 Arbury Ave., Hubbard Woods, Ill. (P.) b. Canton, Ohio, 1886. Pupil AIC. Member: Chicago AC; Business Men's AC of Chicago.

BATTLES, D. BLAKE, Art and Color Section, General Motors Corporation. Detroit, Mich. (P. C. T.) b. Wellington, Ohio, Dec. 25, 1887. Pupil of Henry Keller, F. C. Gottwald, Herman Matzen. Member: Cleveland SA.

BEACHAM, OLIVER CONLEY, 215 Oakwood Ave., Dayton, Ohio (P. E.) b. Xenia, Ohio, Oct. 4, 1862. Member: Dayton SE; Am. APL; Sketch Club. Work: landscape in oil; WC and copperplate etching.

BEACHEY, MARGARET, Evansville, Ind. (P. T.) b. Lebanon, Ohio. Pupil Cin. AA; ASL of NY; Teachers' College, Columbia Univ. of N. Y. Member: Arts and Crafts Society of Evansville, Ind. Supervisor of drawing in public schools of Evansville.

BEARD, ADELINE BELLE (P. T. I.) b. Painesville, Ohio. Studied: portraits with Wyatt Eaton and W. M. Chase; Cooper Union, and ASL of NY.

BEARD, ALICE, 350½ West 24th St., New York City; summer, Bearsville, Ulster Co., N. Y. (P. I.) b. Cincinnati, Ohio. Member: NA Women PS. Award: prize, NAC, 1925.

BEARD, DANIEL CARTER ("DAN BEARD"), Suffern, N. Y. (P. I.) b. Cincinnati, Ohio, June 21, 1850; 4th son of James Henry Beard, NA. Pupil of Sartain and Beckwith at ASL of NY. Member: SI; Ind. SS; ASL of NY (hon.) Specialty, animals and illustrating books on outdoor life; cartoonist, historical Americana. Illustrated for *Cosmopolitan, Harper's, Century, Scribner's, Life, Puck, Judge,* and works of Mark Twain.

BEARD, FRANK,* 3rd son of James H. Beard. With *Harper's* during Civil War. Professor of Fine Arts, Syracuse Univ. b. Cin., 1842; d. Chicago, 1905.

BEARD, GEORGE,* flourished Cincinnati, 1840. (Min. P.)

BEARD, HENRY* (P.) Second son of J. H. Beard. Painted *genre*. Made designs for Prang's publications.

BEARD, JAMES CARTER,* (P. I.) b. Cincinnati, O., June 6, 1837; d. New Orleans, Nov. 15, 1913. Brother of Daniel C. Beard of Brooklyn. Specialty: delineating animals, "Billy Possum," etc.

BEARD, JAMES H.* (P.) b. Buffalo, N. Y., 1814; in Cincinnati, 1834-'76; d. 1893. Animal subjects. Portraits: Gen. Taylor, Gen. Harrison, Chas. Hammond. "The Poor Relation," "The Emigrants," "The Last Victim of the Deluge." Elected NA, 1872.

BEARD, LINA, Flushing, L. I., N. Y. (I.) b. Cincinnati, O. Sister of Daniel C. Beard. Pupil of Cooper Union and ASL of NY. Author and illustrator with her sister, Adelia, of *Little Folks Handy Book*.

BEARD, WILLIAM H.* (P.) b. Painesville, Ohio; left there *c.* 1840; d. Feb. 20, 1900. Bears and other animals were his subjects. Elected NA 1862. Published textbook "Action in Art." Brother of James H. Beard.

BECK, GEORGE JACOB* (P.) In Cincinnati *c.* 1800. Decorated barge of Gen. Wilkinson.

BECK, WALTER, Innisfree, Millbrook, N. Y. (P.) b. Dayton, Ohio, Mar. 11, 1864. Pupil of Issac Broome, of Trenton; Munich Academy under Gysis and Loefftz; sculpture under Rumann. Member: N.Y. Arch. Lg., 1902; NAC (life); Wash. AC; Painters and Sculptors Gal. Asso.; AFA. Awards: first prize, National competition for mural decorations of the City Hall, Cincinnati, 1897; silver medal, Sesquicentennial Expo., Phila., 1926. Work: "The Life of Christ" (20 pictures), and "Portrait of a Lady," Brooklyn Institute Museum; two paintings illustrating the "Life of Christ," and ten pictures comprising eighty portraits, illustrating the Civil War, National Gallery, Washington, D. C. Author of two books on photography.

BELL, CLARA LOUISE, 52 West 57th St., New York City (P.) b. Newton Falls, Ohio. Pupil of Cleveland School of Art; ASL of NY; Edith Stevenson Wright; Henry G. Keller. Member: A. S. Min. P.; NA Women PS; NYWCC; Studio C. Awards: Penton medal for excellence with first prize for miniature, Cleveland Museum of Art, 1919; first prize for miniature, Cleveland Museum of Art, 1923, 1925, 1926; first prize for miniature Studio Club, New York, 1926; first prize for water color, Studio Club, New York, 1929. Work: "Andrew Lawton, Esq.," Masonic Temple, Youngstown, Ohio.

BELL, JOHN W.* (P.) Warren, Ohio. Flourished *c.* 1870. Charter member Cleveland AC. Studied New York. Work: autumn landscapes, privately owned.

BELLOWS, GEORGE WESLEY* (P.) b. Columbus, Ohio, Aug. 12, 1882; d. N. Y., Jan. 8, 1925. Pupil of Maratta, Jay Hambidge, Henri, in N. Y. ANA, 1908; NA, 1913. Member: Am. Painters; Nat'l Arts C; S. Indp. A.; Los Angeles Modern Art S.; Nat'l Inst. Arts and Letters; New S. of Painters; Lg. of Am. A.; Honorary Member, Boston AC. Work: "Up Hudson," Metro. Mus.; "North River," Pa. Acad. of FA; "Polo at Lakewood," Columbus Gallery; "Blackwell's Bridge," Toledo Mus.; "Love of Winter," Chicago AI; "A Day in June," Detroit Mus.; "Stag at Sharkey's," St. Louis Mus.; "Eleanor, Jean and Anna," Albright Gallery, Buffalo; "Emma and Her Children," Boston Mus. Awards: gold medal, Pan. Pac. Expo., 1915; Maynard prize, NAD, 1914; Isador medal, NAD, 1916; Temple medal, Pa. Acad. of FA; Beck gold medal, Pa. Acad. of FA, 1921; first Clark prize, and Corcoran gold medal, Corcoran Gallery, 1924; and many others.

BENEDUCE, ANTIMO, 1893 East 84th St., Cleveland, Ohio (P.) b. St. Antimo, Naples, Italy, Mar. 28, 1900. Studied: Cleveland Sch. of Art; NAD; Chas. Hawthorne's Summer School. Hon. men., water color, 1925, Cleveland annual show. Member: Cleveland Soc. of A.; Ohio WCP; North Shore AA, Gloucester; Gloucester Soc. of A. Work exhibited in important museums of country.

BENTZ, JOHN, 171 Lakeview Avenue, Leonia, N. J. (Min. P., E. T.) b. Columbus, Ohio, Pupil of Robert Blum; Kenyon Cox; W. M. Chase. Member: ASL of NY; Pa. Soc. Min. P.; Am. S. Min. P.

BERGER, MARCIA, 218 Hosea Ave., Clifton, Cincinnati, Ohio (P.) Water-color still life, and flowers. Shared first prize, 1930, WAC. Member: Cin. WAC.

BETTMAN, LILLIAN W. (MRS. ALFRED), Stanley and Kroger Ave., Cincinnati, Ohio (P.) Studied with Emma Mendenhall. Awarded Cin. Woman's AC prizes, 1930. Work: still life, flowers, portraits. Promoted flower culture. Member: Cin. WAC.

BIESTER, ANTHONY* (P.) b. Cleves, Germany, 1837; d. Madisonville, Ohio, Mar. 26, 1917. Studied: Germany, Holland, Belgium, France. Member: Cin. AC; Gold Medal Indiana State Fair. Work: portrait, landscape, "Archbishop Purcell," "Bishop Henni," decorations in St. John's Church, Lewisburg, Ky.

BINDER, CARL F., 1378 Vandemar St., Cleveland Heights, Ohio (P.) b. Bisingen Hohen-zollern, Germany, Feb. 10, 1887, came over when 19 yrs. old. Training received at Düsseldorf, Germany. Work: oil, water color, lithography. Represented PAFA; Pittsburgh International Exhibit. Awards: second prize for decorative oil painting; first prize for lithographs; second prize for figure composition. Member: Kokoon Arts Club, Cleveland.

BIRGE, LAURA C.* (Port. P.) b. Seneca Falls, N. Y.; resident, Dayton, c. 1876; d. c. 1928. Studied with Prof. Rimmer, N. Y.; Munich; Paris. Represented: "Governor Vance," State House, Columbus; many portraits in Cleveland.

BLACK, MRS. KATE ELEANOR* (P. C.) b. London, 1855; came to Cincinnati, 1899; d. Dec. 14, 1924. Pupil of Cin. AA. Member: Cin. WAC. Awards: bronze medal, Provincial Exhibition, New Westminster, B. C., Canada.

BLACKMAN, CARRIE HORTON (MRS. GEORGE BLACKMAN), 17 Southmoor Avenue, St. Louis, Mo. (P.W.) b. Cincinnati, Ohio. Pupil of St. Louis School of Fine Arts; Chaplin in Paris. Member: St. Louis AG. Specialty, children's portraits.

BLAKE, JAMES EDWARD* (Ldscp. P.) b. Peru, Ind., June 8, 1864; d. Cincinnati, Ohio, Feb. 11, 1912. Pupil of Meakin, Clark, Sharp, Nowottny, Duveneck. Member, Cin. AC.

BLAU, DANIEL, Dayton Art. Inst.; h. 27 Yale Ave., Dayton, Ohio (P. E. T.) b. Dayton, O., Feb. 2, 1894. Pupil of Art Academy of Cincinnati; Dayton Art Inst. Member: Dayton SE.

BLAZEY, LAWRENCE E., Carnegie Hall, 1221 Huron Rd.; h. 2017 Bunts Rd., Cleveland, Ohio (P. T.) b. Cleveland, April 6, 1902. Member: Cleveland SA.

BLAZYS, ALEXANDER, Cleveland School of Art; 9601 Talbot Street, Cleveland, Ohio. (S. T.) b. Lithuania, Feb. 16, 1894. Pupil of S. Volnuchin. Awards: first prize for sculpture, Cleveland Museum of Art, 1926, 1927, 1928. Work: "Russian Dancers," Cleveland Museum of Art.

BLESCH, CLARA, 2370 Brentwood Road, Columbus, Ohio (P.) b. Columbus. Studied: Columbus, Detroit. Member: Columbus AL; Ohio-Born Women Artists; Ohio WCS. Work: water-color landscapes. Exhibited Buffalo, Cincinnati, Washington, D. C.

BLUM, ALEX. A., 1520 Chestnut St., Philadelphia, Pa. (P. E.) b. Cincinnati Ohio, Feb. 7, 1889. Pupil of Duveneck in Cincinnati; Mielatz in New York. Member: Phila. Sketch C.; Phila. Alliance. Work: Four etchings in Congressional Library, Washington; etchings in Museum of Fine Arts, Boston.

BLUM, ROBERT FREDERICK* (P. E. Mural P.) b. Cincinnati, July 9, 1857; d. N. Y., June 8, 1903. Student: McMicken School of Design; N. Y.; Europe. Member: NAD. Represented: "Venetian Lace Makers," "Swallows," Cin. Mus.; murals, Mendelssohn

Hall, N. Y.; pastel, geisha girls of Japan; illustrations of book on Japan. "Ameya," Metropolitan Mus., N. Y. Elected NA, 1893.

BLUMENSCHEIN, ERNEST LEONARD, Taos, New Mexico (P. I.) b. Pittsburgh, Pa., May 26, 1874. Pupil: Cin. AA; ASL of NY; Constant Laurens, Collin, Paris. Member: ANA, 1910; NA, 1926; Salma C.; SI, 1901; AWCS; Paris AAA; New Mexican Painters; Taos Society. Work: Cincinnati Museum; Dayton Art Inst.; Wichita Mus.; Kansas City Library; Harrison Collection, Los Angeles; Milwaukee Art Inst.; Pratt Inst., Brooklyn; Fort Worth Mus.; Nat'l Mus., Washington; 5 Murals, Missouri Capitol, Jefferson City, Mo. Awards: Beck prize, Phila. WCC, 1909; Isidor portrait prize, Salma. C., 1910, 1911; Isidor medal, NAD, 1912; first Altman prize ($1,000), NAD, 1921; silver medal, Sesqui-Cen., 1916; Ranger Purchase prize, NAD, 1923, 1929.

BOEBINGER, CHARLES WILLIAM, Walnut and Central Parkway, Cincinnati, Ohio; h. R. R. 13 West Adams Rd., Mt. Healthy, Ohio. (P. L. C. T.) b. Cincinnati, June 17, 1876. Pupil of Cincinnati Art Academy; ASL of NY; John F. Carlson, Walter Crane in England. Member: Western Drawing and Manual Teachers Assoc.; 3rd International Art Congress at London, 4th Congress at Dresden. Instructor of art, Ohio Mechanics Institute.

BOEHMER, FRITZ, 918 Baker Street, Toledo, Ohio (P.) Haida, Czechoslovakia, June 4, 1875. Studied Dresden, Germany. Work: miniature paintings. Member: Artklan, Toledo.

BOERSIG, JOSEPH A., 4260 West 49th St., Cleveland, Ohio (P.) b. Parma, Ohio, May 8, 1896. Studied Cleveland Sch. of Art. Work: water color, oil. Member: Kokoon AC.

BOGER, FRED, 931 Lagonda Ave., Springfield, Ohio (P. I.) b. Baltimore, Md., Oct. 12, 1857. Pupil of Frank Duveneck in Cincinnati. Member: Cincinnati AC. Work: "Judge Alphonso Taft," Alphonso Taft Law College, University of Cincinnati; portraits of George B. Cox and August Herrman at Blaine Club, Cincinnati.

BOGGS, FRANK M.* (P.) b. 1855, Springfield, Ohio; d. Aug. 11, 1926, Meudon, France. Studied: École des Beaux Arts; Gérôme. French Government purchased for the Luxembourg his "Place de la Bastille," and "Isigny" for Museum of Niort.

BOHM, MAX* (L. P.) b. 1868, Cleveland; d. Sept. 19, 1923, Provincetown, Mass. Pupil of Laurens, Guillemet, and Constant in Paris. ANA, 1917; NA, 1920. Member: Salma. C.; Mural Painters; Provincetown AA; Cleveland AC; Lg. AA; Paris Soc. of Am. Painters; Chelsea Arts C., London. Prizes: third-class medal Paris Salon, 1898; silver medal, Paris Expo., 1900; bronze medal, Pan-Am., Buffalo, 1901; silver medal, St. Louis, 1904; gold medal Pan-Pac., 1915; Clark prize, NAD, 1917. Works: mural in Cleveland Courthouse; "Nature and Imagination," Metro. Mus.; portrait of Governor Lind, Capitol, St. Paul, Minn.; Nat'l Gal., Washington; portrait of Rev. Mary Baker Eddy.

BOHNERT, HERBERT, 2258 Euclid Ave., Cleveland, Ohio (P. I.) b. Cleveland, 1888. Pupil Cleveland Art School.

BOLANDER, KARL S., 478 East Broad St., Columbus, Ohio (P. T. L.) b. Marion, Ohio, May 3, 1893. Pupil of Dow, Walter Sargent, Ensign, MacGilvary, Walter Beck, Lemos, Ohio State University, Pratt Inst., Berkshire Summer School of Art, Univ. of Chicago. Member: Columbus AL; Ohio WCS; Eastern AA; Western AA. Director, Columbus Gallery of Fine Arts and Columbus Art School.

BORDEWISCH, FERDINAND F., 4001 East Third St., Dayton, Ohio (E. I.) b. Kettlersville, Ohio, June 2, 1889. Pupil of Bridgman, Fogarty and Mora. Member: Dayton SE; ASL of NY.

BOSWORTH, SALA* (P.) b. Sept. 15, 1805, Halifax, Mass.; came to Marietta, Ohio, 1816; d. Cin., Dec. 22, 1890. Studied Phila. AA, 1827-8. Work: Many portraits of South-

Central Ohio people; "Gen. Rufus Putnam," Marietta College Library; miniatures on ivory; landscapes in water color.

BRADLEY, GEORGE P., 1042 St. Clair, N.W., Cleveland, Ohio (P.) Fine water color. Art-glass worker and landscapist.

BRANNON, WM. P.* (Port. P.) Came to Cincinnati, 1840; d. 1866. Portrait of Dr. Lyman Beecher.

BRESSLER, HARRY, 730 Torrington Place, Dayton, Ohio (News A.) b. Austria, Jan. 7, 1893. Studied: ASL of NY; NAD. Work: editorial cartoonist for *Dayton News, Springfield News, Miami* (Fla.) *News*. Formerly with King Features Syndicate, N. Y.; Democratic Nat'l Committee cartoonist for campaign of 1928. Member: Dayton AI.

BRIDWELL, HARRY L., 287 McCormick Place, Cincinnati, Ohio (P.) b. Leesburg, Ohio, 1861. Member: Cin. AC.

BRIGHAM, CLARA RUST (MRS. W. E. BRIGHAM), 460 Rochambeau Ave., Providence, R. I. (P. C.) b. Cleveland, July 25, 1879. Pupil of Blanche Dillaye, William Brigham. Member: Prov. AC; Needle and Bobbin Club; Handicraft Club, Providence; AFA. Director: Industrial Dept., Federal Hill House.

BRINKERHOFF, ROBERT MOORE, 50 West 67th St., New York, N. Y. (News A. I.) b. Toledo, O., May 4, 1880. Pupil of ASL of NY; Colarossi Academy in Paris. Member: SI, 1912. Illustrations in *Saturday Evening Post, Red Book,* etc. Author of short story series, "Dear Mom," "Little Mary Mixup in Fairyland" (Duffield), 1926. Cartoons in New York *Evening World, Evening Mail,* etc.

BROEMEL, CARL WILLIAM, 849 Hanna Bldg., h. 3471 Warren Road, Cleveland, Ohio (P.) b. Cleveland, Sept. 5, 1891. Pupil of H. G. Keller, Cleveland; Robert Engles in Munich. Member: Cleveland SA. Awards: first prize for water colors, Cleveland Museum of Art, 1924 and 1925; second prize, 1926. Work: "Air and Sunshine" and "St. George, Bermuda," Cleveland Museum of Art; "Royal Palms, Barbados," Brooklyn Museum.

BROOKS, ALDEN FINNEY, 4357 St. Lawrence Ave., Chicago, Ill.; summer, Hilaire Cottage, R.F.D., 2, Fennville, Mich. (P. S.) b. West Williamsfield, Ohio, April 3, 1840. Pupil of Edwin White in Chicago; Carolus-Duran in Paris. Member: Chicago SA. Awards: Yerkes prize, Chicago SA, 1892; Illinois State Fair prize, 1895. Work: "Boys Fishing," Union Club, Chicago; "Gen. George H. Thomas" and "Judge Kirk Hawes," Public Library, Chicago; "Gov. Jno. R. Tanner," Capitol, Springfield, Ill.; "Isaac Elwood" and "James Glidden," State Normal School, De Kalb, Ill.; "Vice-Pres. Sandison," State Normal School, Terre Haute, Ind.; Vanderpoel Art Asso. Collection, Chicago.

BROOKS, ARTHUR D., 11936 Carlton Road, Cleveland, Ohio; summer, Chatham, Mass. (P.) b. Cleveland, May 23, 1877. Pupil of Henry Keller. Member: Cleveland SA. Award: second prize in decoration, Cleveland Museum of Art, 1926.

BROUGH, WALTER, 2341 Carnegie Ave., Cleveland, Ohio (P.) b. Philadelphia, Pa., Sept. 2, 1890. Studied Pa. Acad. Work: portrait, landscape, mural, in Cleveland Public Library, Western Reserve University; Masonic Temple; Allen Memorial Library; Wooster College; St. Paul's Church, Cleveland; First National Bank, Saginaw.

BROWNE, FRANCES E., 11 The Westminster, Walnut Hills, Cincinnati, Ohio (P.) Member: Cin. WAC.

BROWNLEE, ALEXANDER* (P.) d. Cleveland, Ohio, Oct. 24, 1905.

BRUBECK, ELMER J., 1311 Green Road, S. Euclid, Ohio (P.) b. Springfield O., Oct. 23, 1890. Studied Cleveland School of Arts; Paris; Munich. Work: portraiture, oil, water color, in private collections. Awards: first prize, figure composition, 1929; second prize portrait, 1930, Cleveland annual show. Member: Kokoon Arts C.

BRUYERE, LOUIS U., 539 Winthrop St., Toledo, Ohio (P.) b. Newark, N. J., Oct. 18, 1884. Studied Newark, N. J., and Univ. of Pa. Work: water-color landscape, "Vermont Hills." Member: Artklan, Toledo, Ohio. Prizes at Toledo Museum of Art.

BRYANT, EVERETT LLOYD, 243 West Biddle St., Baltimore, Md. (P.) b. Galion, Ohio, Nov. 13, 1864. Pupil of Blanc and Couture in Paris; Herkomer in London; Anshutz, Chase and Breckenridge in Philadelphia. Member: Balto. WCC; Charcoal C. Award: Silver medal, Pan.-Pac. Expo., San. F., 1915. Specialty, mural painting. Work: "Asters," Pa. Acad. of Fine Arts, Phila.; "A Study," St. Paul Institute.

BULLETT, CHARLES* (S.) Frenchman, flourished in Cincinnati, c. 1850. Work: bust of Mrs. S. W. K. Peter, Cin. Mus.; Medallion portraits.

BURCHFIELD, CHARLES E., Box 78, Gardenville, New York (P. D.) b. Ashtabula Harbor, Ohio, April 9, 1893. Pupil of Cleveland School of Art. Member: AFA. Awards: First prize, water color, Cleveland SA, 1921; Penton medal for water color, Cleveland Museum, 1921; Jennie Sesnan gold medal, PAFA, 1929. Works: "February Thaw," Brooklyn Museum of Art; "The False Front," "August Afternoon," Metropolitan Museum of Art; "Mining Village in Winter," "March Wind," Cleveland Museum of Art; "Winter–East Liverpool, Ohio," Albright Gallery, Buffalo, N. Y.

BURDOIN, MRS. JULIET, 515 Grand Ave., Dayton, Ohio (P.) b. Toronto, Canada. Studied Toronto Art School; pupil of J. W. L. Foster; Paris with Bouguereau and Gabriel Ferrier. Member: Woman's Art Asso. of Canada; Gloucester Soc. of A.; Associate Member of North Shore Soc. of A. Work: portrait, landscape, flowers in water color and oil. Exhibited Boston, Cambridge, New York. Portraits: Mrs. Robert Andrews, Mrs. Godfrey Carden.

BURER, ANNA R., 670 June St., Walnut Hills, Cincinnati, Ohio (C.) Work: leather, book bindings, etc. Asso. Member Cin. Woman's AC.

BURGDORFF, FERDINAND, 1813 Rock Rd., Cleveland Heights, Ohio; Bohemian Club, San Francisco, Calif.; summer, Pebble Beach, Monterey, Co., Calif. (P.) b. Cleveland, Nov. 7, 1881. Pupil of Cleveland School of Art. Member: Salma. C.; AFA; Calif. SE. Work: "Old Wharf," Memorial Museum, San Francisco; "Grand Canyon," Cleveland Museum of Art; "Venus," Hotel Del Monte, Del Monte, Calif.

BURR, GEORGE ELBERT, 70 West Lynwood St., Phoenix, Ariz. (P. I. E.) b. near Cleveland, Ohio. Pupil AIC; studied five years in Europe. Member: Chicago SE; Denver AA; Calif. SE; Am. SE; AI Graphic A; Soc. Française aux États Unis; Brooklyn SE; Calif. PM. Made illustrations for catalogue of Heber Bishop Collection of Jades at Metropolitan Museum. Work in Library of Congress, Washington, D.C.; New York Public Library; Museum of Newark, N. J.; City Museum, St. Louis; Brooklyn Museum; Cleveland Museum; Metropolitan Museum; Detroit Institute; Art Institute, Chicago; Denver Art Museum; Colorado State University; Public Library, Santa Barbara, Calif.; Carnegie Institute; Toledo Museum; Los Angeles Museum; California State Library; Luxembourg, Paris; Bibliothéque Nationale, Paris; Victoria and Albert Museum; British Museum, London.

BURROUGHS, ED., Dayton Art Institute, Dayton, Ohio (P. T.) Studied Maryland Art Institute, Baltimore. Instructor in design, Dayton Art Institute. Work: murals, still life and landscapes.

BUSHNELL, E. A., 920 Locust St., Cincinnati, Ohio (News A.) Cartoonist *Cincinnati Post,* 1900-'14; *Times-Star,* 1916; free lance.

CADWALADER, LOUISE, 3120 Eton Ave., Berkeley, Calif. (P. C.) b. Cincinnati, Ohio. Pupil of Carlson; William M. Chase; John Rich Cahill; Winold Reiss; Ralph Johannot; Rudolph Schaeffer; ASL of NY; Cincinnati Art Acad. Member: San Francisco S. Women A.; Boston SAC; Alliance.

CALDER, MRS. JOSEPHINE, 1861 Parkwood Avenue, Toledo, Ohio (P.) Member: NA Women PS.

CALVIN, KATHARINE, 139 N. Forge St., Akron, Ohio (P.) Studied in Europe. Work: portraits and landscapes.

CAMPBELL, ANNIE, 130 East Monument Avenue, Dayton, Ohio (P. T.) Studied with Laura Birge, Otto Dow, Walter Beck, Ralph Johannot. Teacher at Steele High School, Dayton. Represented: landscapes in Steele High School, Dayton. Member: S Indp. A.

CAMPBELL, HARRIET DUNN (MRS. W. D. CAMPBELL), 1780 W. First Ave., Columbus, Ohio; summer, Huron, Ohio (P. S. T.) b. Columbus, Aug. 16, 1873. Pupil of Robert Henri; William M. Chase; Arthur W. Dow; Kenneth Miller; George Bridgman; Charles Hawthorne. Member: Columbus AL; Ohio WCS; Ohio-Born Women Painters. Awards: Hon. mention for oil, 1920, 1921, for water color, 1923, Columbus Art League; hon. mention, Ohio State Fair, 1922; Robert Wolf water color prize, Columbus Art League, 1927.

CANFIELD, BIRTLET KING* (S.) b. Ravenna, Ohio, Dec. 12, 1866; d. Ravenna, Nov. 30, 1912. Studied Cleveland; with Falguière, Paris. Hon. mention, Paris Salon, 1896. Member: Arch Lg. of N. Y.; Salma. C. Work: specialty of dogs and other animals. Death was result of being bitten by a dog.

CANFIELD, WILLIAM PARKER, 284 Lora Ave., Youngstown, Ohio (News A.) b. Youngstown, Oct. 15, 1874. Work: cartoons and commercial. Sec-Treas. of Liberty Engraving Co., Pittsburgh, Pa. Started art career with *Vindicator,* Youngstown; *Pittsburgh Times, Pittsburgh Press, Pittsburgh Post,* have carried his work.

CARABELLI, JOSEPH* (S.) b. Italy, 1850; d. Cleveland, Ohio, Apr. 19, 1911. Member: Ohio Legislature. Work: "Industry," exterior of Federal Bldg., N. Y.

CARGILL, JESSE TAYLOR, 1435 East 12th St., Cleveland, Ohio (News A.) b. Waco, Texas, July 19, 1892. Studied Chicago Academy of Fine Arts. Began with *Kansas City Journal-Post,* 1921. With Central Press Association News Syndicate, Cleveland, Ohio. Member: Cleveland Print Club.

CARLSEN, FLORA BELLE (MRS. HAROLD CARLSEN), 300 East 163rd Street, New York, N. Y. (P. S.) b. Cleveland, Ohio, March 7, 1878. Pupil of F. C. Jones; Du Bois; Matzen; Solon Borglum; Lentelli. Member: NA Women PS.

CARPENTER, NEWTON H.,* b. 1853, Olmstead Falls, Ohio; d. May 27, 1918, Chicago. Business Manager of Chicago AI from its founding, 1881, until his death. President Am. Mus. Asso.; President Mus. Director's Asso.; Treasurer Am. Fed. of A.

CARRELL, HENRY CLAY* (Arch.) b. Cincinnati, Ohio; d. Philadelphia, Oct. 19, 1915. Educated in Cincinnati. Member of firm Gillespie & Carrell, N. Y. Member: FAIA.

CARRINGTON, JAMES BEEBEE* (L. W. Art Editor.) b. Columbus, Ohio; d. July 14, 1929, Ridgefield, Conn. Became Asso. Editor of *Scribner's Magazine,* 1887, and later editor of *Architecture.* Member: Salma. C.

CARROLL, JOHN, Rehn Gallery, New York City (P.) b. Wichita, Kan., Aug. 14, 1892. Connected with Cincinnati art activities. Awards: 1925, first Purchase Prize, Los Angeles; 1924, first Purchase Prize, PAFA; 1927, second prize, Chicago AI; 1924; hon. men., Inter. Pittsburgh; 1928, first prize lithograph, San Francisco; 1929, first prize painting, San Francisco. Work: PAFA; Harrison Gallery, Los Angeles; Detroit AI; Herron AI, Indianapolis.

CARTER, CLARENCE H., 10646 Euclid Ave., Cleveland, Ohio; summer, 454 West Church St., Elmira, N. Y. (P.) b. Portsmouth, Ohio, March 26, 1904. Pupil of Henry G. Keller, William J. Eastman, Paul B. Travis, Hans Hoffman. Member: Cleveland Art Center. Awards: third prize for portrait, ninth annual exhibition of work by Cleveland artists and craftsmen, Cleveland Museum of Art, 1927; first prize for water color, third prize for figure composition, Cleveland Museum of Art, 1928. Work: "The Patient Cow," water color, and "A Woman of the Sabines," oil, Cleveland Museum of Art; water color, "Sommer Bros., Stoves and Hardware," Brooklyn Institute of Arts and Sciences, Brooklyn, N. Y.

CASSIDY, IRA D. GERALD, 922 El Camino del Cañon, Santa Fe, N. M. (P. I.) b. Cincinnati, Ohio. Pupil of Cincinnati Academy; NAD in New York; ASL of NY. Member: NAC; Salma. C; Denver AA. Award: grand prize and gold medal, Panama-Calif. Expo., San Diego, Calif., 1915; prize ($500), Chicago Galleries Assn., 1929. Works: decorations on Indian Arts Bldg., San Diego, Calif.; decorations, "Last of the Indians," Hotel Gramatan, Bronxville, N. Y.; "Reflections," Freer Collection, Detroit, Mich. Represented in San Diego Museum and Museum of New Mexico; Freer Collection, Washington, D. C.; Canton (China) Christian College; El Onate Theatre, Santa Fe.

CASSIDY, LAURA E., 6426 Desmond Ave., Madisonville, Ohio (P.) Member: Cincinnati Woman's AC; Calif. WCS.

CASTONA, GIOVANNI, Highland and Dorchester Avenues; h. 293 Dorchester Avenue, Cincinnati, Ohio (P. S.) b. Italy, Oct. 2, 1896. Pupil of School of Boston Museum of Fine Arts; Philip L. Hale, Lesley P. Thompson, Huger Elliott, F. M. Lamb, Henry James. Member: Soc. AC, Brockton; Boston AC; Cincinnati AC. Awards: hon. men., PAFA, 1918; hon. men., Springfield AA, 1926. Work: "After the Storm," Public Library, Brockton, Mass.; "Threatening," Springfield Art Association; "Painted Stage Settings," Boston Opera House, Boston, Mass.

CAVALLY, FREDERICK L., 19 Gables Apt., Cincinnati, Ohio (C. Art Photographer). Studied Cincinnati and West. Member: AA Denver, Colorado; AA Cincinnati. Work permanently placed throughout East and West.

CAVANARO, MILDRED SNARR (MRS. EMELIE), 2134 Sinton Ave., Walnut Hills, Cincinnat, Ohio (P.) Water-color decorative and modernistic figures. Member: Cin. AC.

CHADEAYNE, ROBERT O., Columbus Gallery of Fine Arts, East Broad St.; h. 207 Marshall Ave., Columbus, Ohio; summer, Cedar Lane, Cornwall, N. Y. (P. T.) b. Cornwall, Dec. 13, 1897. Pupil of C. K. Chatterton, George Lux, John Sloan, George Bridgman. Member: Columbus AL. Awards: John Lambert prize, PAFA, 1919; Norman Wait Harris bronze medal and cash prize, AIC, 1920; first prize, Columbus AI, 1928, 1929. Work: "Back Yards," Lambert Collection, PAFA, Philadelphia, Pa.

CHAMBERLAIN, EMILY H.* (I.) b. Shelby, Ohio; d. New York, Feb. 28, 1916. Studied Pratt Inst.; Paris; London. Specialty of drawing children. Did much work for *Saint Nicholas,* and *Youth's Companion.* Member: Nat'l Arts C.; Art Worker's Club for Women.

CHAPMAN, CARLTON THEODORE* (P. I.) b. 1860, New London, Ohio; d. Feb. 12, 1925, New York. Pupil NAD; ASL of NY; Julian Academy, Paris; ANA, 1900; NA, 1914. Member: SAA, 1892; Century Association; Lotos C; AWCS; Artists' Fund Association; Nat'l Arts C. Awards: silver medal Boston, 1892; medal Chicago, 1893; medal Atlanta, Ga., 1895; bronze medal, Pan.-Amer., 1901; bronze medal, Charleston, Expo., 1902. Works: "A Rocky Coast," Toledo Mus.; "Calm in Gloucester Harbor," Brooklyn Inst. Mus.; "Bonhomme Richard," "Serapis," St. Louis Mus.

CHRISTY, HOWARD CHANDLER, Hotel des Artistes, 1 West 67th St., New York, N. Y.; summer, The Barracks, Duncan Falls, Ohio (I.) b. Morgan Co., Ohio, Jan. 10, 1873. Pupil of NAD, ASL, and Chase, in New York. Member: SI, 1915. Awards: bronze medal, Paris Expo., 1900; hon. men., Pan-Amer. Expo., Buffalo, 1901. Illustrations for all the well-known publishers. One of Roosevelt's "Rough Riders."

CHURCHILL, ALFRED VANCE, Smith College Museum of Art; h. 38 Franklin Street,

Northampton, Mass. (P. T.) b. Oberlin, Ohio, Aug. 14, 1864. Pupil of Julian Academy in Paris. Member: Union Internationale des Beaux Arts; College AA; North Shore AA. Director, Art Dept., Iowa College, 1891-'93; director, Art Dept., Teachers College, Columbia Univ., New York, 1897-1905; lecturer, Johns Hopkins Univ., Baltimore, 1902-'03; University of Chicago, 1914, 1916 and 1917; Professor of the History and Interpretation of Art, Smith College, Northampton, Mass., since 1907; director, Smith College Museum of Art, since 1920; editor, Smith College Art Museum Bulletin.

CLARK, BERGIE C.* (P.) b. Butler Co., Ohio, Dec. 13, 1868; d. Madison, Ind., March 16, 1912. Pupil William McKendree Snyder.

CLAWSON, W. R.* (P.) b. Jan. 16, 1885, Eaton, Ohio; d. 1929, Cincinnati. Member: Cin. AC.

CLEVENGER, SHUBAEL VAIL* (S.) b. Middletown, Ohio, 1812; d. at sea, 1844. Studied Cincinnati, Boston, Italy. Work: "Henry Clay," Metro. Mus. N. Y.; "Washington Allston," Pa. Acad., Phila; Busts of Judge John Davis, Lemuel Perkins, Boston Athenæum; "Webster," "Edward Everett."

CLOUGH, STANLEY THOMAS, R.F.D. 2, Mentor, Ohio (P.) b. Cleveland, May 11, 1905. Studied Cleveland School of Art; John Huntington Polytechnic School. Work: water color landscape. Awards: Cleveland annual, 1928, second prize, decorative panel; 1929, first prize, industrial painting; 1930, third prize, landscape.

CLOVER, PHILIP* (P.) b. Franklin Co., Ohio, 1842; d. spring of 1905. Studied with Durand, Paris. Lived in Columbus, Ohio. Painted landscape and figures. Work: historical scene in Ohio State Museum, Columbus, Ohio; many portraits of Chicago politicians; two sensational pictures, "The Criminal," "Fatima," the latter exhibited all over the country.

CLYMER, EDWIN SWIFT, Lanesville P.O., Gloucester, Mass. (P.) b. Cincinnati, Ohio, 1871. Pupil of PAFA. Member: Phila. Sketch C.; Phila. WCC. Work in Reading, Pa., Museum of Art.

COAST, OSCAR R., 123 East Micheltorena St., Santa Barbara, Calif. (P.) b. Salem, Ohio, 1851. Studied with Yewell, Thomas Hicks, and Failer, in Paris and Rome. Member: Salma. C., 1897; Wash. AC; Santa Barbara AC; AFA. Specialty, landscapes.

COCHRAN, ALLEN D., Woodstock, N. Y. (P.) b. Cincinnati, Ohio, Oct. 23, 1888. Pupil of Kenyon Cox and Birge Harrison. Member: Salma. C.

COLBURN, ELEANOR RUTH (MRS. J. E.)* (P.) b. 1866, Dayton, Ohio; d. 1929, Chicago. Pupil Chicago AI. Awarded Municipal Art Lg. prize, 1908. Member: Chicago Soc. of Artists; Asso. Member Chicago WCC. Work, "An Offshore Wind," Chicago, AI.

COLE, THOMAS* (Ldscp. P.) b. England, 1801; d. in the Catskills, 1848. Lived in Steubenville, Ohio, when a young man; Hudson River School. Studied in Europe, 1829 to 1832. Two series of pictures, "The Voyage of Life," and "The Course of Empire," are the ones by which he will be best remembered.

COLE, VIRGINIA THURMAN, 389 Library Park, South, Columbus, Ohio (P. T.) b. Columbus. Pupil of George Elmer Browne; Alice Schille; Columbus Art School. Member: Ohio WCS; Columbus AL.

COLEMAN, GLENN O.* (P.) b. Springfield, Ohio, July 18, 1887; d. May, 1932. Pupil of Henri. Member: S Indp. A; Whitney Studio C; New Soc. A. Award: third prize, Carnegie Institute, 1928. Work: "Manetta Lane," Luxembourg Museum; "Coenties Slip," Newark Museum, Newark, N. J.

COLLINS, FRED L., 1603 Franklin Ave., Columbus, Ohio; summer, Ancaster, Ontario, Canada (I.) b. Prince Edward Island, Jan. 1, 1876. Pupil of Hamilton Art School; S. J. Ireland. Member: Columbus PPC (Secy.-Treas. since 1903). Manager, Art Dept., Bucher Engraving Co.

COLLINS, MARY SUSAN, 1816 Wellesley Ave., East Cleveland, Ohio (P. C.) b. Bay City, Mich. Studied ASL of NY; Museum of FA, Boston; Columbia Univ. Work: oil landscape, still life, craft work, batik. Represented in Cleveland Museum, "Primrose"; Women's City Club, Cleveland, landscape, "The Climbers"; Public Schools, collection of landscape, "Road to Dorset Hollow." Awards: Penton medal, Cleveland, 1921; first prize, batik, Cleveland, 1921; first prize, landscape, Cleveland, 1924; first prize, still life, 1929, Purchase prize, Chicago Galleries Asso., 1927. Member: Woman's AC of Cleveland; AFA.

COLLINS, WALTER, Lykes Hall, 302 North Boulevard, Tampa, Fla.; h. Seffner, Fla. (P. I. L. T.) b. Dayton, Ohio, Sept. 26, 1870. Pupil of Julian and Colarossi Acad. in Paris; Hyman's School of Illustration, Munich; Martz Weinholdt, Walter Thor, Royal Academy in Munich; Adolf von Menzel in Berlin; Cin. AA. Member: SSAL; Tampa Art Institute.

COLTMAN, ORA, 11415 Mayfield Rd., Cleveland, Ohio (P. S.) b. Shelby, Ohio, 1860. Pupil ASL of NY; Julian Academy in Paris; Magidey Schule, Munich. Member: Cleveland Soc. of Artists.

COMAN, HARRIET* (P.) Teacher in Columbus Art School, c. 1890. Work: still life.

COMSTOCK, FRANCES BASSETT, 178 Highwood Ave., Leonia, N. J. (P.S.I.) b. Elyria, Ohio, Oct. 16, 1881. Pupil of Gari Melchers, Frederick W. Freer, and John Vanderpoel. Member: NYWCC.

CONE, GRACE COTTON (MRS. STEPHEN E.) 194 East McMillan St., Mt. Auburn, Cincinnati, Ohio (Ldscp. A.) Promoted garden clubs. Member: Cin. WAC.

CONES, NANCY FORD (MRS. JAMES), Loveland, Ohio (C.) Artistic photography. Member: Cin. WAC.

CONWAY, JOHN SEVERINUS* (P. S.) b. 1852, Dayton, Ohio; d. Dec. 25, 1925, Tenafly, N. J. Pupil of Conrad Diehl; Jules Lefebvre; Boulanger; Aimé Millet. Member: NY Arch. Lg.; NSS. Works: Mural, Chamber of Commerce, and Soldier's Monument, Milwaukee, Wis.

COOK, MAY ELIZABETH, 1550 Clifton Ave.; h. 1546 Richmond Ave., Columbus, Ohio (S.) b. Chillicothe, Ohio, Dec. 1881. Pupil of Paul Bartlett; École des Beaux Arts and Colarossi Academy in Paris. Member: Columbus Lg. of Artists; Am. Ceramic Soc. (assoc.); Plastic C; NA Women PS; Alliance; Phila. Alliance; Gallery FA, Columbus; AFA; Union Internationale des Beaux Arts des Lettres, Paris. Represented in Carnegie Library, Columbus; Ohio State University, Columbus; National Museum, Washington, D. C.; memorial panels, Colorado Springs; Chillicothe; war work, wax models from life masks for reconstruction work among wounded soldiers.

COOKE, CHARLES H., 6329 Glenwood Ave., Chicago, Ill. (P.) b. Toledo, Ohio, July 31, 1859. Pupil of AIC. Member: Palette and Chisel C; AIC Alumni Asso.; S. Indp. A; Chicago NJSA; Am. APL; Ill. Acad. FA.

COOKMAN, CHARLES E.* (P.) b. 1854, Columbus, Ohio; d. New York, 1913. Work: portrait, marine, and landscape. Professor, Osgood Art Institute, N. Y. Member: Salma. C.

COOPER, ELIZABETH, Stanford, Conn. (S.) b. Dayton, Ohio, 1901. Specialty of animals.

COOPER, FLORENCE A., 1413 Harvard Blvd., Toledo, Ohio (E. T.) b. Galion, Ohio, Feb. 2, 1882. Studied Teachers' College, Columbia Univ. Work: etchings; teaching Fine Arts. Member: Nat'l Fed.; Toledo Women Artists; Print Club. Exhibited Dayton SE; Brooklyn Etchers; Philadelphia Print Club; Cleveland Print Club; Toledo Artists Show.

CORWIN, AARON H.* (Port. P.) In Cincinnati, Ohio, c. 1820; d. London, 1830.

COUROUX, MRS. ALICE MUTH, Paris, France (P.) b. Cincinnati, Ohio. Studied with Zuloaga. Work: painting and batiks. Member: Cin. WAC.

COVINGTON, ANNETTE, 5542 Covington Ave., Madisonville, Ohio (P. W.) Pupil of Barnhorn; ASL of NY; Twachtman; Chase, at Shinnecock Hills, L. I.; Henry Mosler. Teacher at Lake Forest Univ. Ill.; Univ. of Chicago. Work: portrait of Edgar Stillman Kelley, Miami Univ., Oxford, Ohio; Prof. McFarland, O.S. Univ. Library, Columbus, Ohio; numerous pencil portrait drawings; landscape, Hamilton, Ohio, high school; illustrations for monograph on tiger beetles. Prize, Woman's AC. Member: Cin.WAC.

COWAN, R. GUY, care of Cowan Pottery, Rocky River, Ohio; h. 1499 Cohasset Ave., Lakewood, Ohio (S. C.) b. East Liverpool, Ohio, Aug. 1, 1884. Pupil of N.Y.S. School of Ceramics. Member: Am. Ceramic Soc.; Cleveland SA. Awards: first prize for pottery, 1917, and Logan medal for applied design, 1924, Art Inst. of Chicago; first prize for pottery, Cleveland Museum, 1925.

COX, KENYON* (Mural P. S. T. W. L.) b. Warren, Ohio, 1856; d. New York, March 17, 1919. Studied with Carolus Duran, Gérôme, Paris. Member: ANA, 1900;NA, 1903; SAA; NY Arch. Lg.; Nat'l Inst. AL; Am. Acad. AL; Mural P; Lotos C. Awards: second Hallgarten prize, NAD, 1889; two bronze medals, Paris, 1889; Temple silver medal, Pa. Acad. FA, 1891; medal Col. Expo. 1893; gold medal St. Louis, 1904; medal for mural painting, NY Arch. Lg., 1909; Isador medal NAD, 1910. Work: "Harp Player," "Portrait of Saint-Gaudens," Metro. Mus.; "Portrait of Henry L. Fry," Cincinnati Mus.; Murals (see chapter VIII); two lunettes, Memorials to his Father and Mother, Oberlin College; Statue, "Greek Science," Brooklyn Inst.; books (see chapter VIII); "Plenty," National Gallery, Washington.

CRAIG, CHARLES, Colorado Springs, Colo. (P.) b. farm in Morgan Co., Ohio, 1846. Studied PAFA. Painter of Indians, cowboys, plains, and mountains. Represented with Indian paintings in many collections United States and foreign.

CRAMER, MIRIAM E., 8210 Carnegie Ave., Cleveland, Ohio (S. P.) b. Nov. 16, 1885, Hamburg, Germany. Studied Cleveland; N. Y. Awards: Herman Matzen scholarship, and other prizes. Member: Woman's AC, Cleveland. Work: Lima Public Library.

CRANCH, JOHN* (P.) b. Washington D. C., 1807; d. Urbana, Ohio, 1891. ANA, 1853, Student of Sully; Italy. Portraits and original compositions.

CRAPSEY, CHARLES*, (Arch.) b. Cincinnati, Ohio; d. Cincinnati, July 26, 1909. Followed profession of architecture for thirty-four years. Work: many churches, among them the Presbyterian Church of Seattle, Wash. Member: FAIA.

CRATZ, BENJAMIN A., 609 Acklin Ave., Toledo, Ohio; summer, Highland Ave., Headlands, Rockport, Mass. (P.) b. Shanesville, Tuscarawas, Co., Ohio, May 1, 1886. Pupil of George Elmer Browne; Julian in Paris. Member: Toledo Artklan; Provincetown AA; Beachcombers Club; Springfield (Ill.) AA; Salma. C; AFA; Gloucester AA; North Shore AA; Rockport AA.

CRAWFORD, BRENETTA HERMANN (MRS. EARL STETSON CRAWFORD), 41 The Enclosure, Nutley, N. J.; care of Guaranty Trust Co., Paris, France. (P. I. T.) b. Toledo, Ohio, Oct. 27, 1875. Pupil of ASL of NY; Colarossi and Carmen Academies, in Paris. Member: Port. P.; Am. S. Min. P.; NA Women PS.

CRITCHFIELD, GEORGE MANSUR* (P.) b. Columbus, Ohio, June 27, 1870; d. Flint, Ohio, Sept. 23, 1897. Studied ASL of NY; Beaux Arts, Julian Academy, Paris; Chicago. Considered authority on Art History. Work: wood carving, pen and pencil drawings, building decoration for St. Mary's of the Springs School, Columbus; work owned by Mrs. Rossiter Bohannon, Columbus.

CROW, MRS. PHIL, Lima, Ohio (P.) Work: oil still life. Member: Ohio-Born WP.

CULBERTSON, QUEENIE, 4120 Forest Ave., Norwood, Cincinnati, Ohio (P. I.) b. San

Angelo, Texas. Pupil of Frank Duveneck; William DeL.Dodge. Member: Cin. WAC.

CURRAN, CHARLES COURTNEY, 39 West 67th Street, New York City (P.) b. Hartford, Ky., Feb. 13, 1861. Spent early life in Sandusky, Ohio. Pupil of Cincinnati School of Design; ASL and NAD in New York; Julian Academy under Constant, Lefebvre and Doucet in Paris. Member: ANA, 1888; NA, 1904; NYWCC; AWCS; Salma. C.; Lotos Club. Awards: third Hallgarten prize; NAD, 1888; hon. men. Paris Salon, 1890; many others. Represented: "Perfume of the Roses," National Gallery, Washington; "The Breezy Day," Pa. Acad., Philadelphia; "The Golden Hour," Columbus; "The Swimming Pool," Toledo Museum of Art.

CURRIER, CYRUS BATES, 1347 Lucille Ave., Los Angeles, Calif (P. I.) b. Marietta, Ohio, Dec. 13, 1868. Pupil of Julian Academy, Bouguereau, Constant, Mucha, Paris. Member: Salma. C.

CURRIER, E. W.* (P.) b. Oct. 11, 1857, Marietta, Ohio; d. Nov. 15, 1918, San Francisco. Pupil of Chicago Academy of FA; G. L. Clough, N.Y. Member: San Francisco AA. Awards: silver medal for water color, silver medal for oil, Alaska-Yukon Expo., Seattle, 1909.

CSOSZ, JOHN, 14918 Superior Rd., Cleveland, Ohio (P. E.) b. Hungary, Oct. 2, 1897. Pupil of Gottwald and Keller. Member: Cleveland SA. Work: "End of a Perfect Day," Public School Collection; portrait, Dr. Henderson, Memorial Library; mural decorations, Holy Ghost Church, Cleveland; "Atlanta," University Club, Akron.

DAHLING, EDNA M., 2663 Gilbert Ave., Walnut Hills, Cincinnati, Ohio (Min. P. C.) Asso. Member, Cin. AC.

DALRYMPLE, LUCILE STEVENSON, Fine Arts Bldg.; h. 4704 Drexel Blvd., Chicago, Ill.; summer, Marais du Cygne, R.F.D. 1, Port Clinton, Ohio (P.) b. Sandusky, Ohio, Oct. 29, 1882. Pupil of AIC, and J. Francis Smith Acad., Chicago. Member: Cordon C; AIC Alumni; Chicago S. Min. P.; South Side AA; Renaissance Soc. U. of C.; AFA. Work: portraits of Mr. J. T. Gillick, director's room, Union Station, Chicago; I. C. Elston, Elston Bank, Crawfordsville, Ind.; Betsey Gates Mills, Betsey Mills Club, Marietta, Ohio; portraits of Presidents of Wabash College—Dr. J. F. Tuttle, Dr. G. S. Burroughs, Dr. William P. Kane, Dr. George L. Mackintosh, Dr. Charles White, Theodore H. Ristline, in Trustees' Room, Wabash College, Crawfordsville, Ind.; Dr. Alfred Tyler Perry, Marietta College, Marietta, Ohio. Miniature, "Youth," purchased by Ill. AFA, for Permanent Gallery, Springfield, Ill.

DALY, MRS. MATT, 127 Third Street, Norwood, Ohio (P.) Rookwood pottery artist.

DALY, MATT A., Apts. 7 and 9, 127 East Third Street, Norwood, Ohio (P.) b. Cincinnati, Jan. 13, 1860. Pupil of Duveneck, Noble and Lutz. Member: Cincinnati AC; Am. APL. Represented in Cincinnati Art Museum; University of Cincinnati.

DARLING, KATHERINE W.* sister of Wilder M. Darling. b. Sandusky, Ohio; d. from infection—scarlet fever—slums in N.Y. Studied Cooper's Inst. N. Y. under Chase; with Mrs. Frank Scott, flower painter.

DARLING, WILDER M., Cleveland, Ohio, and Holland (P.) b. Sandusky, Ohio. Studied with Henry Mosler, Cincinnati; Duveneck, Munich; Laurens, Paris; Chase, N. Y.; London. Lived many years in Toledo. Work: Dutch and Breton figure painting. Received many honors; medals at Paris Salon.

DARROW, CHARLES K.* (D.) b. Marietta, Ohio; d. Orange, N. J., May 11, 1916. Work: Stuyvesant Studio Bldg. design, Maplewood, N. J.

DAVIS, MRS. CORNELIA CASSADY* (P.) b. Cleves, Ohio, Dec. 18, 1870; d. Cincinnati, Dec. 23, 1920. Pupil of Lutz, Noble, Duveneck, Cin. AA. Member: Cin. AC. Awards: fourth prize Osborne competition, N.Y., 1906; first prize Ohio Suffrage poster, 1912.

Work: portrait of Mrs. McKinley, Westminster Central Hall, London; "The Hopi Indian Snake Ceremony," Eli Tovar Gallery, Grand Canyon, Arizona.

DAWLEY, HERBERT M., Chatham, N. J. (S. W.) b. Chillicothe, Ohio, Mar. 15, 1880. Pupil of ASL of Buffalo, N. Y. Member: Buffalo SA. Award: Fellowship prize, 1915, Buffalo SA.

DEAN (MRS.) GRACE RHOADES, 1064 Oakwood Ave., Toledo, Ohio (E. P.) b. Cleveland, Jan. 15, 1878. Pupil of Cleveland School of Art; Kenyon Cox; Arthur W. Dow; and studied in Munich. Member: NA Women PS; Cleveland Woman's AC; Toledo Athena Soc.; Ohio WCS; AFA; Dayton SE. Awards: prize for etching, Toledo Art Mus., 1918; second prize for landscape decoration, 1920, and first water color prize, 1924, Toledo Federation of Art Societies; prize, Ohio State Fair, 1922.

DEAN, JAMES ERNEST, 1064 Oakwood Ave., Toledo, Ohio (P. E. T.) b. East Smithfield, Pa., Feb. 23, 1871. Pupil of Twachtman, Beckwith, Chase, McCarter; Hayek, Brockhoff, and Groeber in Munich. Member: Toledo Artklan.

DE BENKELAER, MRS. LAURA HOLLIDAY, 1346 College Ave., Topeka, Kan. (S.) b. Cincinnati, Ohio, 1885. Pupil CAA. Member: Cin. WC. Work: State Normal School, Geneseo, N. Y.; Washburn College, Topeka, Kan:

DEBRA, MABEL MASON (MRS. ROBERT M. KING), Department of Fine Arts, Ohio State University; h. 2084 Neil Ave., Columbus, Ohio (P. I. T.) b. Milledgeville, Ohio, Oct. 24, 1899. Pupil of Henry B. Snell, Will S. Taylor, Walter Beck. Member: NYWCC; Wash. WCC; Ohio WCS; Columbus AL. Award: Robert Wolfe water color prize, Columbus Art League, 1929; Joseph Lewis Weyrich memorial prize, Baltimore WCS, 1931.

DECAMP, JOSEPH RODEFER* (P. T.) b. Cincinnati, Ohio, Nov. 5, 1858; d. Feb. 11, 1923, Bocagrande, Fla. Studied McMicken School of Design; Royal Acad. Munich; with Duveneck in Florence. Instructor, PAFA, Philadelphia; Boston Mus. of Fine Arts. Member: "Ten" Am. Painters; Boston Guild of Artists; NIA and Letters. Awards: first prize City Hall decoration competition, Philadelphia; Temple gold medal, PAFA, Phila., 1899; hon. men., Paris Expo., 1900; gold medal, St. Louis Expo., 1904; Wm. A. Clark, and Corcoran silver medal, 1909. Represented: "The Guitar Player," Boston Mus.; "Roosevelt," Harvard Union, Cambridge, Mass.; Portrait of Duveneck, "Girl Drying Her Hair," Cin. Mus.; "The New Gown," Wilstach Gal., Philadelphia; "Sally" and "Daniel Merriman," Worcester Mus., Mass.; "Dr. Howard Furness," and "Little Hotel," PAFA, Philadelphia.

DEHNER, WALTER LEONARD, Whitehouse, Ohio (P. Ldscp. A. T.) b. Buffalo, N. Y.; Aug. 13, 1898. Pupil of ASL of NY, Woodstock, and PAFA. Director of Art, University of Porto Rico.

DEIKE, CLARA L., 1309 West 111th St., Cleveland, Ohio (L. P. T.) b. Detroit, Mich. Pupil of H. G. Keller; F. C. Gottwald; H. H. Breckenridge; Herr Han Hofmann in Munich. Member: Woman's AC, Cleveland; Cor Ardens, Chicago. Awards: second prize, Cleveland Museum, 1922; first prize and first hon. men., Cleveland Museum, 1923; second prize, Cleveland Museum of Art, 1925; third prize, Cleveland Museum, 1926; hon. men., group drawings, 1927, and first prize, Cleveland Museum, 1928. Work: "Italian Fishing Boats, Gloucester, Mass.," and "Through the Trees," Central High School, Cleveland; "Flowers," Public School Art Collection, Cleveland Board of Education. Lecturer on Modern Creative Design.

DEKLYN, CHARLES F., Cleveland, Ohio (P.)

DELLENBAUGH, FREDERICK SAMUEL (P. W.) b. McConnelsville, Ohio, 1853. Pupil of Carolus Duran and Julian Academy. Librarian, Am. Geo. Soc. Many travels—Iceland, Spitzbergen, Norway, S. Am. in 1906. Many trips to S.W. in early days.

DEMING, EDWIN WILLARD, 15 Gramercy Park, New York, N. Y. (P. S. I.) b. Ashland, Ohio, Aug. 26, 1860. Pupil of ASL of NY; Lefebvre and Boulanger in Paris. Member: Mural P.; Wash. AC; (life) NAC. Speciality: Indian and animal subjects. Awards: silver medal, AAS, 1892; bronze medal, St. Louis Expo., 1904; bronze medal for sculpture, Pan.-Pac. Expo., San Francisco, 1915. Work: two mural paintings, Morris High School, New York City; "Braddock's Defeat" and "Discovery of Wisconsin," mural decorations, Wis. Historical Soc., Madison, Wis.; "The Fight," and "Mutual Surprise," two bronzes, Metropolitan Museum, New York; "The Watering Place," "Pueblo Buffalo Dance" and "Sioux War Dance," Art Museum, Montclair, N. J.; "Mourning Brave," National Museum, Washington, D. C.; also represented in American Museum of Natural History, New York, Heye Foundation, Explorers' Club, National Arts Club, and Montifeore Home for Crippled Children.

DENGLER, FRANK (S.) b. Cincinnati, Ohio, 1853. Studied abroad. Teacher at Boston Museum in Modeling. 1877 back to Cincinnati. Work: "Azzo and Melda," ideal head of America.

DENNISON, LUCY, Women's City Club, Wick Ave.; 33 Scott St., Youngstown, Ohio (P.) b. Youngstown, Apr. 3, 1902. Pupil of Butler AI; James R. Hopkins, Daniel Garber. Member: Youngstown S. Women A.; Mahoning SP.

DENNY, MILO B., 901 Chateau Avenue, Cincinnati, Ohio; summer, Taos, N. M. (P.) b. Waubeek, Iowa, Apr. 21, 1887. Pupil of AIC; N. Y. ASL; Cornell Coll. Sch. of Art.

DESILVER, CARL H.* (Art Collector). b. Cincinnati, Ohio, Jan. 9, 1846; d. Brooklyn, Mar. 10, 1913. President, Brooklyn AA, 1896 to his death.

DESJARDINS, S. E.* (Arch.) d. Cincinnati, Ohio, Nov. 2, 1916. Member firm of Desjardins & Hayward. Member: FAIA.

DEVEREAUX, MARIAN, Hotel Sinton, Cincinnati, Ohio. (W.) *Cincinnati Enquirer.* Asso. member Cin. AC.

DEWEY, CHAS. S., 2708 Lake View Ave., Chicago, Ill. (P.) b. Cadiz, Ohio, 1880. Member: Chicago Soc. of A.

DILL, HOWARD MALCOLM, 405 Realty Bldg., Dayton, Ohio (Ldscp. Arch.) b. Richmond, Ind., Feb. 11, 1899. Studied Harvard Graduate School of Ldscp. Arch. Work: landscape architecture in private grounds, land subdivisions, parks, cemeteries, institutions. Awards: first prize design for small home grounds, Boston, 1921. Member: Amer. Soc. Ldscp. Arch.; Dayton AI.

DODD, JESSIE HART,* (I. P. T. C.) b. Apr. 18, 1868, Cincinnati, Ohio; d. Oct. 16, 1911, Cincinnati. Pupil of PAFA; Howard Pyle at Drexel Inst., Philadelphia.

DONAHEY, JAMES HARRISON, *Plain Dealer,* Cleveland, Ohio; h. Aurora, Ohio (I. C. W. L. Cartoonist). b. West Chester, Ohio, Apr. 8, 1875. Pupil of Cleveland School of Art. Member: Cleveland AA; Amer. Press Humorists Soc.

DONAHEY, WILLIAM, 2331 Cleveland Ave., Chicago, Ill. (News A. I. W.) b. West Chester, Ohio, Oct. 19, 1883. Began as artist on *Cleveland Plain Dealer,* 1903. Writer and illustrator for children's features in newspapers, magazines, books. Author: *The Teenie Weenie* books. Wife, Mary Dickerson, writer of children's stories, "The Wonderful Wishes of Jackey and Jean," "Down Spider Web Lane."

DOUGLAS, WALTER, 264 West 19th St., New York, N. Y.; summer, Block Island, R. I. (P.) b. Cincinnati, Ohio, Jan. 14, 1868. Pupil of Chase, NAD and ASL of N. Y. Member: AWCS; Salma. C., 1904; Art Center of the Oranges. Work: "In the Shade," Dallas (Texas) AA. Specialty: poultry.

DOW, PETER* (C.) b. 1822; d. Mar. 9, 1919, Toledo, Ohio. Photographer, authority on photography; written much on the subject.

DOYLE, ALEXANDER* (S.) b. Steubenville, Ohio, Jan. 28, 1858; d. Dec. 21, 1922, Boston. Studied in Italy. Represented: "Margaret Statue," "Gen. Robert E. Lee," "Gen. Beauregard," "Jefferson Davis," in New Orleans; "John Howard Payne," in Washington, D. C.; "Francis Scott Key," Frederick, Md.; eight colossal allegorical marble statues in rotunda of Capitol, Indianapolis; "Garfield," Cleveland; "Gen. James B. Steedman," Toledo.

DRISCOLL, DEVOSS WOODWARD* (News A.) b. Sidney, Ohio, 1873; d. Dayton, Ohio, Nov. 22, 1916. Cartoonist, *Dayton News.*

DRURY, HERBERT R., Drury Lane, Willoughby, Ohio (P.) b. Cleveland, Aug. 21, 1873. Pupil of Carlson and Du Mond. Member: Cleveland SA.

DULIN, JAMES H., 2476 Lawrence Ave., Toledo, Ohio (P. E.) b. Kansas City, Mo., Oct. 24, 1888. Studied Chicago AI; Colarossi and Julian Academies, Paris. Exhibited, Paris Salon, 1926-'27-'28-'29. Lived in Paris 1918-'30.

DUMLER, MARTIN GEORGE, 127 East Third Street; h. 1607 Dexter Ave., Cincinnati, Ohio (P.) b. Cincinnati, Dec. 22, 1868. Pupil of Edward H. Potthast, M. Rettig, and R. Busebaum. Member: Salma. C; Cincinnati AC.

DUMM, EDWINA, Talmadge Hill, New Canaan, Conn. (News A.) b. Upper Sandusky, Ohio, 1893. Studied Columbus Art School; ASL of NY. Work: cartoons and comic strips, "Cap and Stubbs" syndicated by George Matthews Adams Service Co.; cover pages, and weekly page, "Sinbad," for *Life.*

DUNCANSON, R. S.* (P.) (Negro). Began work in Cincinnati in 1843; d. in Europe, 1871. Anti-slavery League sent him to Edinburgh to study. Work: portraits of Summer and Birney; landscapes, fruits and flowers; "The Lotus Eaters," Windsor Castle, England; "The Water Nymphs," "Trial of Shakespeare," "Shylock and Jessica."

DUNLAP, ZOE FLEMING* (Min. P. W. Woodcarver). b. 1872, Cincinnati, Ohio; d. May 26, 1927, Cincinnati. Pupil of Cin. AA under Nowottny; Paris. Member: NAC; Cin. WAC.

DUNN, DELPHINE, 58 College Ave., Westerville, Ohio (P. T.) b. Glenwood, Ind. Pupil of Artus Van Briggle, Daniel Garber, H. Breckenridge, L. Soutter in Paris. Member: CAL; AFA; Gloucester SA. Exhibited Hoosier Salon, 1930. Art director of Otterbein College, Westerville, Ohio.

DUNN, MRS. LOUISE M., 1541 Crawford Road, Cleveland, Ohio (P.) b. East Liverpool, Ohio, 1875. Pupil of H. G. Keller. Member: Cleveland SA; AFA. Award: second prize for water color, Cleveland Museum, 1923.

DUNSMORE, JOHN WARD, 96 Fifth Ave., New York, N. Y. (P.) b. near Cincinnati, Ohio, Feb. 29, 1856. Pupil of Cincinnati Art Academy; Couture in Paris. Member: ANA; N. Y. Arch. Lg., 1903; Salma. C., 1903; Boston AC, 1881; AWCS; A Fund S; Cincinnati AC; AFA. Award: medal, Mass. Charitable Mechanics' Assoc., Boston, 1881; Evans prize, Salma. C., 1914. Director, Detroit Museum of Art, 1888-'90; Detroit School of Arts, 1890-'94. Work: "Macbeth," Ohio Mechanics' Institute, Cincinnati; "All's Fair in Love and War," Lassell Seminary, Auburndale, Mass. Represented in Salma. Club and NAD, New York; Cincinnati Art Museum; Wagnalls Memorial, Lithopolis. Specialties: historical subjects and portraits.

DUSTIN, SILAS S., Bryson Bldg., 2nd and Spring Sts., Los Angeles, Calif. (Ldscp. P.) b. Richfield, Ohio. Pupil of NAD and William M. Chase. Member: A. Fund S.; Salma. C.; Laguna Beach AA; Calif. AC. Represented in Seattle Museum of Art; Portland, Ore., Museum of Art; Berkshire Athenæum and Museum, Pittsfield, Mass.

DUVENECK, FRANK* (P. T. S.) b. Covington, Ky., 1848; d. Cincinnati, Ohio, Jan. 3, 1919. Studied at Munich under Wilhelm Dietz, 1870-'73. Won studio prize at Munich; medal at Columbian Expo., Chicago, 1893; special gold medal of honor for thirty paintings at Pan.-Pac. Expo., at San Francisco, 1915. Member: NA, 1906; Am. Inst. of Art and Letters. Represented: 100 paintings, sculpture, etchings, Cin. Mus.; murals, St. Mary's Cathedral, Covington, Ky.; sculptured memorial to wife, Florence, Italy; statue of Emerson, Emerson Hall, Harvard Univ.

DWIGGINS, WILLIAM ADDISON, 30 Ipswich St., Boston, Mass.; h. Hingham Center, Mass. (I. W.) b. Martinsville, Ohio, June 19, 1880. Work: Typographic design. Studied Holmes Sch. of Ill., Chicago. Awarded many medals. Illustrated many books.

DWIGHT, MABEL, 34 Grove St., New York, N. Y. (P. Lith.) b. Cincinnati, Ohio, Jan. 29, 1876. Pupil of Arthur Mathews. Work: lithographs in Metropolitan Museum; Museum of Fine Arts, Boston; Cleveland Museum of Art; Art Institute of Chicago; Victoria and Albert Museum, London; Bibliothéque Nationale, Paris.

DWIGHT, MRS. ROSLYN VAIL, 1019 Redway Ave., Avondale, Cincinnati, Ohio (P.) Pastel portraits. Member: Cin. WAC.

EARHART, JOHN FRANKLIN, Fernbank, Cincinnati, Ohio (Ldscp. P.) b. Ohio, Mar. 12, 1853. Member: Cin. AC. Award: landscape prize ($100), Cin. AC, 1903. Teacher, University of Cincinnati.

EASTMAN, WILLIAM J., 1868 East 82nd Street, Cleveland, Ohio (P. C. W. T.) b. Nov. 14, 1888. Member: Cleveland SA; Cleveland AA. Award: first prize, Penton medal, Cleveland Museum of Art, 1919.

EATON, JOSEPH ORVILLE* (P.) b. Newark, Ohio, Feb. 8, 1829; d. Yonkers, N. Y., Feb. 7, 1875. Studied with Jacob Cox, Indianapolis. Painted landscapes and figures. Taught in Cincinnati. Work: "View on the Hudson," "Greek Water-Carrier," "Lady Godiva," portraits in Cincinnati, New York, London. Elected ANA, 1866.

ECHERT, FLORENCE, The Valencia, 276 St. George St., Augustine, Fla.; summer, Little Chalet, Intervale, White Mountains, N. H. (P.C.) b. Cincinnati, Ohio. Pupil of Cincinnati AA; ASL of N. Y.; W. M. Chase. Member: Cin. WAC.

ECKSTEIN, FREDERICK* (P. S.) In Cincinnati, 1826. Wax figures.

EDGAR, ISABEL* (P.) Worked in Dayton, Ohio. Studied with Frederick Freer and Chase. Water color. Portraits of children especially.

EDMONDSON, EDMOND* (P.) b. Dayton, Ohio; flourished c. 1875; d. in California. Still life and portraits. Represented: "President Garfield," Odd Fellow's Hall, Dayton.

EDMONDSON, WILLIAM J., 2362 Euclid Ave., Cleveland, Ohio; h. 2812 Scarborough Rd., Cleveland Heights, Ohio (P.) b. Norwalk, Ohio, Aug. 22, 1868. Pupil of Academy of the Fine Arts, Philadelphia, under Vonnoh and Chase; Julian Academy, Paris, under Lefebvre; Aman-Jean Academy, Paris. Member: Fellowship PAFA; Cleveland SA; Cleveland AA. Awards: second Toppan prize, PAFA; European traveling scholarship, PAFA; first prize, figure painting; popular vote prize, and Penton medal, Cleveland Museum of Art, 1919; first prize for decorative and mural painting, Cleveland Museum, 1923. Work in: Delgado Art Museum, New Orleans; Cleveland Museum; Western Reserve University; Society for Savings, Cleveland; Fellowship PAFA, Philadelphia; State House, Columbus, Ohio; Municipal Collection, Cleveland.

EGAN, JOSEPH BYRON, 3285 Silsby Road, Cleveland Heights, Ohio (I.) b. Apr. 22, 1906, Cleveland, Ohio. Work: illustration, water color, lithographs. Awards: first prize, 1929, first prize, 1931, Cleveland Museum, on illustration. "Monday," owned by Cleveland Museum. Member: Cleveland Print Makers.

EICHELBERGER, ROBERT A.* (P.) b. May 20, 1861, Fletcher, Miami Co., Ohio; d. 1890. Educated Urbana. Studied Munich, 1880; Paris; New York. Work: marines.

EISENLOHR, E. G., 324 Eads Ave., Station A, Dallas, Texas (P. L. I.) b. Cincinnati, Ohio, Nov. 9, 1872. Pupil of R. J. Onderdonk and F. Reaugh in Texas; Academy Karlsruhe, Germany, under G. Schoenleber. Member: Salma. C.; AFA. Work: "The Sentinel of the Canyon," Dallas Public Art Gallery; Elizabeth Ney Mus., Austin, Texas. Author of "Study and Enjoyment of Pictures"; "Tendencies in Art and Their Significance"; "Landscape Painters."

EMERSON, EDITH, Lower Cogslea, St. George's Road, Mt. Airy, Philadelphia, Pa. (P.) b. Oxford, Ohio. Pupil of AIC; PAFA and Violet Oakley. Member: Fellowship PAFA; Phila. Print C; Phila. Alliance; Mural P.; Phila. WCC; Alumni AIC. Work: mural decorations in the Little Theatre, Philadelphia; Roosevelt memorial window, Temple Keneseth Israel, Philadelphia, Pa.; Moorestown Trust Co., Moorestown, N. J. Represented in the Pennsylvania Academy of the Fine Arts; Vanderpoel AA. Collection, Chicago; illustrations in *Asia* and *The Century Magazine.*

ENDRES, LOUIS J., Oakley, Cincinnati, Ohio (P. L.) Work: mural, "Harvesting Scene," Withrow High School, Cincinnati; mural, Oakley, Cin.; Algerian Chiefs painted in North Africa.

ENNEKING, JOHN JOSEPH* (Ldscp. P.) b. Oct. 4, 1841, Minster, Ohio; d. Nov. 16, 1916, Boston, Mass. Son of farmer. Enlisted in Civil War on Union side, severely wounded. 1868 studied lithography in Boston; 1873 Munich under Lehr; Venice; Paris under Bonnat and Daubigny. Awards: four gold, four silver medals, Mass. Charitable Mechanics' Asso., Boston; hon. men. Paris, 1900; silver medal Buffalo, 1901; gold medal Pan.-Pac., 1915. Member: Guild of Boston Artists; Boston AC; Rotary Paint and Clay C. Work: "Autumn in New England," Worcester Mus.; "Hillside," Boston Mus.

ELZNER, A. O., 227 Greendale Ave., Cincinnati, Ohio (Arch. P.) Studied with Thos. Noble, McMicken School of Design; Ohio Mechanics' Inst.; Life with C. T. Webber, Frank Duveneck. Member: Cin. AC.

EPPLY, LORINDA, 45 Alexandria Apts., Gilbert Ave. and Locust, Cincinnati, Ohio (P. E.) Studied with E. T. Hurley. Member: Cin. AC.

ERDMANN, RICHARD FREDERICK, 405 South Cornell St., Albuquerque, N. M. (P.) b. Chillicothe, Ohio, Feb. 12, 1894. Pupil of L. H. Meakin, James Hopkins, Herman Wessel, Paul Jones, Charles Curran, Frank Durmond, George Luks, Frank Duveneck.

ERNST, DOLLY M. (MRS. G. O.), 6128 Fairway Drive, Pleasant Ridge, Cincinnati, Ohio (C.) Studied with Mr. Hentschel, Cin. AA. Member: Cin AC. Work: batiks; illuminated pages in book presented to J. M. Thomssen, Cin.

ERNST, RICHARD, Cleveland, Ohio (S.) His life work has been making excellent reproductions of ornamental sculpture in plaster.

ERVIN, GLADYS DEE, 709 Terrace Ave., Dayton, Ky. (P.) Member: Cin. WAC.

ESTE, FLORENCE* (Ldscp. P., Engr.) b. 1860, Cincinnati, Ohio; d. Apr. 25, 1926, Paris. Pupil of Pa. Acad. of Fine Arts, Philadelphia; Alexander Noyal, Paris. Hon. member, Phila. WCC; Asso. member, Société Nationale des Beaux Arts. Work: "Pasture Land," "Brittany Pines," PAFA, Philadelphia; "Landscape," purchased by French Government, Luxembourg.

EVANS, DeSCOTT* (P. T.) b. Wayne Co., Ind., Mar. 28, 1847; d. 1898 on ill-fated *La Bourgoyne.* Instructor in Cleveland *c.* 1874. Portraits: "The First Snow Storm," "Day Before the Wedding."

EVANS, JESSIE BENTON, 1517 East 61st Street, Chicago, Ill.; winter, Scottsdale, Ariz. (P. E. T.) b. Akron, Ohio, Mar. 24, 1866. Pupil of AIC and William Chase in Chicago; Zanetti Zilla in Venice; Salvator Rosa, Naples. Member: Chicago SA; Chicago AC; Phoenix AC; AFA. Awards: first prize, landscape, 1913 and 1923, and second portrait prize, 1923, Arizonia State Fair. Work: "On the Way to McDowell," Municipal coll.; "Morning," Country Club, Phoenix, Ariz.; "On the Verde River." and "Gray Day," Arizonia Club. Represented in the College Club, Chicago; Public

School Art Societies, Chicago; Phoenix and Mesa, Ariz.; Vanderpoel AA Collection, Chicago; Art Institute, Akron, Ohio.

EVANS, MARGARET, care Butler Art Institute; h. 810 Glenwood Ave., Youngstown, Ohio (P. C. L. T.) b. Youngstown. Pupil of Birge Harrison and John Carlson at the ASL of NY., Woodstock; Columbia Univ.; Arthur Dow; special course in Europe. Director of the Butler Art Institute.

EVANS, RAY O., 137 Crestview Road, Columbus, Ohio (News A.) b. Dec. 1, 1887, Columbus. Studied Ohio State University. Began as advertising artist with *Columbus Dispatch,* 1910; cartoonist *Dayton News,* 1912-'13; *Baltimore American,* 1913-'20; *Columbus Dispatch* since 1922. Creator of special features, "Maryland Movies," "Snapshots at Annapolis," "Pertinent Portraits," "Kindly Caricatures," illustrations for *Solomon Spiffledink* by Louis Ludlow. Member: advisory staff Federal Board of Cartooning.

EVATT, HARRIET, R.F.D. 1, Worthington, Ohio (P.) b. Knoxville, Tenn., June 24, 1896. Studied Columbus School of Fine Arts. Work: portrait and landscape in oil and water color. Member: CAL; Ohio WCS. Daughter of John McCullough Torrey, mural painter, born in Ohio.

EVERETT, ELIZABETH RINEHART, 602 36th Ave., North, Seattle, Wash. (P. S. I. E. C.) b. Toledo, Ohio. Pupil of Walter Isaacs. Awards: sweepstake prize, 1926; first prize, 1927, 1928, Western Washington Fair.

EZEKIEL, SIR MOSES* (S.) b. Richmond, Va., 1844; d. Rome, Mar. 27, 1917. Studied with Insco Williams and T. B. Jones, Cincinnati; Berlin. Awards: Michelbeer prize Royal Art Academy, Berlin, 1873; Crosses for Merit and Art from Emperor of Germany; created Chevalier of the Crown of Italy by the King. Work: "Religious Freedom," Fairmount Park, Philadelphia.; "Faith," Cemetery, Rome; "Thomas Jefferson," Louisville, Ky.; 200 monuments, statues, portraits, and reliefs.

FAIG, FRANCES WILEY (MRS. JOHN L.), 3345 Whitfield Ave., Clifton, Cincinnati, Ohio. (P.) Pupil of Duveneck, Grover, and Hawthorne. Member: MacD. C. of Cincinnati; Cin. WAC. Work: mural decorations in Engineering Library, University of Cincinnati; landscape, figure and portrait.

FANNING, RALPH, Dept. of Fine Arts, Ohio State Univ., Columbus; summer, Riverhead, L. I., New York (P. W. L. T.) b. New York, Nov. 29, 1889. Pupil of Cornell and Univ. of Ill. Member: Ohio Soc. WCP; Columbus A. Lg. Lecturer for Bureau of University Travel. Professor of History of the Fine Arts, Ohio State University.

FARIS, BEN H., The Primrose Bldg., Cincinnati, Ohio (I.) b. St. Clairsville, 1862. Pupil Cin. AC.

FARNY, HENRY F.* (P.) b. Ribeauville, France, 1847. Came to Cincinnati, 1853; d. Dec. 24, 1916, Cincinnati. Studied Munich. Awarded bronze medal for "Peace" at St. Louis Expo., 1904. Represented: "In the Valley of Shadow," "Toilers of the Plain," Cin. Art Mus.; "The Song of the Talking Wire," "The Hill Behind the School House," "The Apaches Are Out," Taft collection, Cincinnati; large collection owned by Mrs. Larz Anderson, Cincinnati. Member: International Jury of Awards, Chicago Expo., 1893.

FARROW, WILLIAM MCKNIGHT, Art Institute of Chicago; h. 6038 South Racine Ave., Chicago, Ill. (P. E. W. L. T.) b. Dayton, Ohio, April 13, 1885. Pupil of AIC. Member Alumni AIC; All-Illinois SFA; Chicago AL. Awards: Eames MacVeagh prize for etching, Chicago Art League, 1928; Charles S. Peterson prize, Chicago Art League, 1929. Work: "Christmas Eve," Woman's Club, Western Springs, Ill.; "Mother Nature's Mirror," Phillips Junior High School, Chicago; portrait of Abraham Lincoln, Stuart Community House, Gary, Ind.

FAULEY, ALBERT C.* (P.) b. Fultonham, Ohio, 1858; d. Columbus, Ohio, Dec. 15, 1919. Pupil of Bouguereau, Constant and Blanc, Paris. Portraits and landscapes. Member: SWA; CAL; PPC. Represented: Col. Gal. F. Arts, "Venice." McKinley portrait. Prize, $150 CAL.

FAULEY, LUCY S.* (MRS. ALBERT C. FAULEY). (P.) b. Fultonham, Ohio; d. March 20, 1926, Columbus, Ohio. Work: landscape, portrait.

FAY, AGNES PRIZER (MRS. W. E.), 3515 Kroger Ave., Cincinnati, Ohio. (P.) Studied Cin. AA. Water-color painter. Member: Cin AC.

FENTON, ANITA, Cincinnati, Ohio (C.) Work: batiks, screens.

FENTON, MARY LOUISE, Highland and Kinsey Ave., Mt. Auburn, Cincinnati, Ohio (C.) Asso. member Cin. AC.

FIELD, THOMAS V., 1654 Pratt Blvd., Chicago, Ill. (Ldscp. P.) b. Cincinnati, Ohio, Dec. 1866. Member: Business Men's AC, Chicago; AAAC. Exhibited: AIC, 1928; HS, 1929.

FISCHER, HENRIETTA, 3460 Oxford Terrace, Clifton, Cincinnati, Ohio (C. T.) Work: batiks, jewelry, etc.; teacher at Hughes' High School, Cin. Member: Cin. AC.

FISCHER, MARTIN, College of Medicine, Eden Ave.; 2236 Auburn Ave., Cincinnati, Ohio (P. W. L.) b. Kiel, Germany, Nov. 10, 1879. Member: Duveneck Soc. of Painters; Cin. AC. Work: murals, Physiological Laboratory, College of Medicine and Assembly Hall, College of Pharmacy, Cincinnati. Wrote book on color. Assembled exhibition of paintings by physicians and surgeons of Cincinnati. Painted in Japan and Honolulu.

FISHER, ALICE R. (MRS. CLARENCE A.) 804 22nd Street, N.E., Canton, Ohio. (P.) b. Owosso, Mich., Mar. 18, 1882. Studied: Cleveland School of Art; Paris; Rome; Munich. Work: landscape, still life, permanently placed Owosso, Mich. Library. Award: second prize, still life, Cleveland show, 1929. Member: Cleveland WAC; AFA. Exhibited: Corcoran Gallery, 1924; Los Angeles Mus.; Brooks Memorial Gallery, Memphis, Tenn.; Columbus, Ohio; through the West.

FISHER, DUDLEY T., JR., 2205 Fairfax Road, Columbus, Ohio (News A.) b. April 27, 1890, Columbus. Artist with *The Columbus Dispatch*. Member: PPC; CAL.

FISHER, IRMA, 7621 Star Ave., Cleveland, Ohio. Exhibits: PAFA, 1925.

FISHER, MRS. LILY FRY, Loveland, Ohio (P.) Member: Cin. WAC.

FISHER, MARTIN* (Arch.) b. 1851; d. Jan. 4, 1929, Cincinnati, Ohio. Specialized in factory buildings. Drew plans for some of the most beautiful homes in Cincinnati.

FITZGERALD, PITT LOOFBOURROW, 515 Grove Ave., Columbus, Ohio (P. I.) b. Washington C. H., Ohio, October 3, 1893. Pupil of PAFA and N. C. Wyeth. Member: Columbus PPC; Columbus AL.

FINKLE, MELIK, New York City (S.) b. Roumania. Asst. to Barnhorn, Cincinnati, 1910-'20. Work: modernistic; raised work on china.

FLISHER, EDITH E., 167 Eighth Avenue, North; h. 8 West End Apartments, Nashville, Tenn. (P. C. T.) b. Cleveland, Ohio, Sept. 26, 1890. Pupil of PAFA. Member: Nashville AA; Nashville Des. Club. Work: portrait of Gov. Tom Rye, State Capitol, Nashville; portrait of Dr. J. A. Crook, Union Univ., Jackson, Tenn.

FOLAWN, THOMAS JEFFERSON, 1805 Marine St., Boulder, Colo.; summer, Santa Fe, N. M. (P.) b. Youngstown, Ohio. Pupil of C. S. Niles, Colorado School of Fine Arts; van Waeyenberge in Paris; J. M. Waloft in N. Y. Member: Denver Art Asso.; Brush and Pencil Club, St. Louis; S. Indp. A.; Boulder AA; AAPL; Boulder AG. Award: hon. men. oil painting, Springville, Utah, AA.

FOWLER, EVANGELINE, Binkley Hall, Kidd Key College, Sherman, Texas (P. W. L. T.) b. Kingsville, Ohio. Pupil of ASL of NY; PAFA; Delaye and Carl in France. Member: Dallas AA. Awards: gold medal, Cotton Centennial, New Orleans, 1885; Saint-Gaudens bronze medal, World's Columbian Exposition, Chicago, 1893.

FORRER, MRS. MARY PIERCE* (P.) In Dayton, Ohio, about 1870. Work: water color, oil, china, modeling, and wood carving. Teacher, Cooper Acad.

FORSYTH, WILLIAM, 15 South Emerson Ave., Irvington, Ind. (P. T.) b. Hamilton Co., Ohio. Pupil of Royal Academy in Munich, under Loefftz, Benczur, Gysis and Lietzenmeyer. Member: Art Assoc. of Indianapolis; AWCS. Instructor, Herron Art Institute. Awards: medal, Munich, 1885; silver medal for water color, and bronze medal for oil, St. Louis Expo., 1904; bronze medal, Buenos Aires Expo., 1910; Fine Arts Bldg. prize ($500), SWA, 1910; bronze medal for oil, and silver medal for water colors, Pan.-Pac. Expo., San Francisco, 1915; Foulke prize, Richmond, Ind., 1923; Holcomb prize, 1924, and Landon prize, 1925, Indianapolis AA. Work: "Autumn at Vernon," "The Constitutional Elm-Corydon," "Close of a Summer Day," "Still Life," "Old Market Woman" and "In October," Art Association, Indianapolis; "Autumn Roadside," and "The Smoker," Public Library, Richmond, Ind.; flower piece, Brooklyn Museum; Vanderpoel AA Collection, Chicago.

FOX, MILTON S., 2587 Nottingham Lane, Cleveland, Ohio (P. W.) b. New York City, March 29, 1904. Studied Cleveland School of Art; Julian Academy, Paris. Work: all phases of painting and graphic arts; lithographs in Cleveland Mus. Awards: hon. men. portraits and water color, and third prize lithograph, Cleveland Mus. Art critic Cleveland Sunday News. Specialty of portraits of people and horses.

FOY, EDITH GELLENBECK (MRS. E. A., JR.), 6322 Grandvista Ave., Cincinnati, Ohio (P.) b. Cincinnati, Oct. 9, 1893. Pupil of Wessel, Meakin, Hopkins, Weis. Member: Cincinnati WAC. Esthetic dancing and journalism.

FRANCISCO, J. BOND, 1401 Albany St., Los Angeles, Calif. (P.) b. Cincinnati, Ohio, Dec. 14, 1863. Pupil of Fechner in Berlin; Nauen Schule in Munich; Bouguereau, Robert-Fleury and Courtois, in Paris. Member: Laguna Beach Asso.; S. Calif. AC; Los Angeles P and SC.

FRANK, WALTER BENJAMIN OLIVER, 503 Wilson Ave., Columbus, Ohio (P.) b. Jan. 18, 1883. Work: oil, water color, commercial artist. Studied with Robert Henri. Member: PPC, CAL.

FRANKENSTEIN, GODFREY N.* (P.) b. Sept. 8, 1820, Germany; d. New York, Feb. 24, 1873. Resided Springfield, Ohio, most of his life. Self-taught. Work: panorama of Niagara Falls; many small paintings of Niagara Falls; views of the Alps; portraits of J. Q. Adams, Wm. C. Bryant.

FRANKENSTEIN, JOHN* (S. P.) b. c. 1817, Germany; lived Cincinnati and Springfield, Ohio; d. New York. Work: "Christ Mocked in the Prætorium," "Isaiah and the Infant Saviour," portraits, busts.

FRANZ, EUGENE JOSEPH A. M. (P.) b. Aug. 21, 1866, Canton, Ohio. Pupil of his father, Jos. Franz; Cleveland Art School, 1891-'92; associated in landscape painting with Wm. T. Mathews, N. Y. Academy for twenty-six years; also with Jeanette Agnew, Pittsburgh Art School; Thomas S. Moran, Phila. Acad.; Geo. Parsons, Royal Acad. England. Work: low-keyed Barbizon-like landscapes, owned in private collections, and in Soper collection in Toronto, Canada; water-color designs for gold and enamel jewelry, winning gold medal in 1890 for jewelry design in competition open to United States and Canada.

FRENCH, THOMAS E., Ohio State University, Columbus, Ohio (E.) b. Mansfield, Ohio. Studied with Nettleton and Shinn, Dayton, Ohio. Award: Am. Bookplate Soc., 1916, 1921. Work: etchings; bookplates in Ohio State University Library; libraries of Franklin College, Western Reserve Historical Soc.; Denison University; Coshocton Carnegie

Library; N. Y. Public Library; Phi Gamma Delta Club, N. Y. Member: Asso. Belge des Collectionneurs et Dessinateurs d'Ex Libris; CAL.

FREY, ERWIN F., Hayes Hall, Ohio State University; h. 4837 Olentangy Blvd., Beechwold, Columbus, Ohio (S. T.) b. Lima, Ohio, Apr. 21, 1892. Pupil of C. J. Barnhorn, James Fraser, Henri Bouchard, Paul Landowski. Member: NSS; Columbus AL. Awards: hon. men. Paris Salon, 1923; hon. men. AIC, 1925. Work: Beatty Memorial, Springfield, Ohio; "Madonna and Child," Lamme Engineering Medal, Ohio State University; General Custer; Doctor W. O. Thompson.

FRIES, CHARLES ARTHUR, 2843 E Street; h. 2876 F Street, San Diego, Calif. (P. I. T.) b. Hillsboro, Ohio, Aug. 14, 1854. Studied at Cin. AA. Member: San Diego AG; Laguna Beach AA; La Jolla AA; Calif. AC. Awards: silver medal, Seattle FAS., 1911; silver medal, Pan.-Pac. Expo., 1915. Represented in San Diego Fine Arts Gallery.

FRUEH, ALFRED J., 34 Perry St., New York City (News A.) b. Lima, Ohio, Sept. 2, 1880. Training: Paris. Caricaturist with St. Louis *Post Dispatch,* five years; N. Y. *World,* twenty-three years. Caricatured famous actors, concert singers, and men connected with the Teapot Dome oil scandal. Work: Print Room, Met. Mus.

FROEHLICH, HUGO B.* (T.) b. 1872, Dayton, Ohio; d. June 10, 1925, Newark, N. J. Studied Pratt Inst. N. Y. Director, Fawcett School of Industrial Arts, Newark, N. J., twelve years; director of manual arts in public schools, Newark, N. J.

FRY, HENRY L.* (C.) b. England; came to Cincinnati *c.* 1845. Wood carver.

FRY, LAURA A., R.F.D. 4, Loveland, Ohio (P. T. C.) b. Cincinnati, Ohio. Pupil of Noble, Rebisso; ASL of NY; Studied in France and England. Awards: two medals Columbian Expo., 1893; three prizes in wood carving, Cincinnati. Member: Cincinnati Pottery Club; Lafayette Woman's Art Club; Lafayette Art Asso.; Cin. WAC. Head of Art Dept., Purdue University. Paints individualistic, still life; good feeling for color.

FRY, WILLIAM H.* (C.) b. Bath, England, Feb. 5, 1830; d. Cincinnati, Ohio, Dec. 26, 1929. Wood carver. Panels, Music Hall Organ, Cincinnati. Collection of his wood carving owned by daughter, Laura Fry, Cincinnati.

FRYE, CARL R., 203 East Broad St., Columbus, Ohio (Ldscp. Arch.) b. South Hadley, Mass., June 28, 1892. Studied Mass. State College under Frank A. Waugh.

FULLER, MINNIE, Cotter Ave., Akron, Ohio (Port P., T.) Studied ASL of NY. Taught at Buchtel College, Akron.

GAERTNER, CARL F., 401 Prospect-Fourth Bldg., Cleveland, Ohio; h. 3325 Greenway Rd., Shaker Village, Ohio (P. I. E. T.) b. Cleveland, Apr. 18, 1898. Pupil of Cleveland School of Art; F. N. Wilcox and H. G. Keller. Member: Cleveland SA. Awards: second prize, 1922, first prize, 1923, and first prize, 1924, Cleveland Museum of Art. Work: "The Ripsaw," Cleveland Museum of Art; "The Furnace," Midday Club of Cleveland, and mural war memorial in Kenyon College.

GALE, CHARLES F.* (P.) b. Columbus, Ohio, July 3, 1874; d. Columbus, Aug. 2, 1917. Studied at Columbus AS. Work: water colors in Columbus homes. Member: PPC; CAL.

GANDOLA, PAUL MARIO, 12208-10 Euclid Ave.; care the Cleveland Society of Artists. 2022 East 88th St., Cleveland, Ohio (S. A. C.) b. Besano, Italy, Aug. 15, 1889. Pupil of Milan Academy of Fine Art. Member: Cleveland SA; Cleveland Sculptors Society.

GANO, KATHARINE V., 2411 Upland Place, Walnut Hills, Cincinnati, Ohio (I.) b. Cincinnati, 1884. Pupil of Duveneck. Member: Cin. WAC.

GARDNER, DONALD, 12 Park Ave., North, Bronxville, N. Y. (I.) b. Akron, Ohio. Member: SI; GFLA.

GARRETSON, DELLA, Dexter, Mich.; summer, Ogunquit, Me. (P.) b. Logan, Ohio, Apr. 12, 1860. Pupil of Detroit Art Museum; NAD; ASL of NY.

GARRISON, JOHN LOUIS, 179 Clinton Place Ave., Columbus, Ohio (P. I.) b. Cincinnati, June 14, 1867. Pupil of Nowottny and Goltz. Member: Columbus PPC.

GASCHE, CHARLES* (P.) b. Wooster, Ohio, 1846; d. Wooster, 1886. Studied with Reinhart in N. Y. Work: portrait, landscape, figure, interior decoration of churches and Masonic halls in many Ohio towns; Court House at Wooster, Ohio. Exhibited Chicago.

GEBHART, PAUL, 1101 Citizens Bldg., Cleveland, Ohio; h. 41 Sagamore Rd., R.F.D. 4, Willoughby, Ohio (News A.) b. Greenville, Pa., Jan. 2, 1890. Pupil, Cleveland SA. Member: Cleveland SA.

GELLERT, EMERY, 3920 Euclid Ave., Cleveland, Ohio (P.) b. Budapest, Hungary, July 24, 1889. Pupil of Papp, Kriesch, Ignace and Geza Udvary. Member: "Feszek," Hungarian AC. Award: prize, Cleveland Museum, 1925. Work: "The Life of Joseph," The Temple, Cleveland; "Heart of Jesus," St. Margaret's Church, Cleveland; "Christ's Resurrection," and "Moses Receives the Ten Commandments," Greek-Cathedral Church, Detroit, Mich.

GENIN, SYLVESTER* (P.) b. Ohio, 1822; d. 1850. Little training; historical painter.

GEST, JOSEPH HENRY, Art Museum, Eden Park; h. 2144 Grandin Road, Cincinnati, Ohio (P.) b. Cincinnati, 1859. Member: NAC; Cin. Municipal AC. Director Emeritus, Cincinnati Museum; President, Rookwood Pottery. Member: Nat. Gallery of Art Comm.

GILBERT, CASS, New York City (Arch.) b. Zanesville, Ohio, 1859. Studied Mass. Inst. of Technology. One of founders of Arch. Lg. of America, and president; twice president of Am. Inst. of Arch.; Nat'l Inst of Arts and Letters, president; 1926 president of NAD. Work: Woolworth Building, N. Y.; libraries of Detroit, St. Louis; Customhouse, N. Y.; Art Museum, St. Louis; State Capitols of Minn., Ark., and West Va.

GILLESPIE, JOHN, 54 South Garfield Ave., Columbus, Ohio; summer, McConnellsville, Ohio (P.) b. Malta, Ohio, May 15, 1901. Pupil of School of the Columbus Gallery of FA. Member: Columbus A. Lg.; Ohio WCS. Award: Walter A. Jones water-color prize, 1924, at Columbus Art League. Superv. of Art, Columbus Junior Acad., and Columbus Acad.

GILLETTE, LESTER A., 717 Fillmore St., Topeka, Kans. (P. T.) b. Columbus, Ohio, Oct. 5, 1855. Pupil of Hill, Williams, Chase, Jacobs, Carlson, and AIC. Member: Topeka AG; Miami AA; Gloucester SA; AFA.

GISCH, WILLIAM S., 3346 Bosworth Rd., Cleveland, Ohio (P. E.) b. Cleveland, July 3, 1906. Studied Cleveland School of Art; John Huntington Polytechnical School. Work: oil, etching, design. Awards: first prize, Cleveland, 1926, free-hand drawing; second prize, 1930, lithograph. Member: Kokoon Arts C.

GLASS, SARAH KRAMER, 107 Mt. Pleasant Ave., East Gloucester, Mass. (P.) b. Troy, Ohio, Nov. 7, 1885. Pupil of Bertha Menzler Peyton; ASL of NY; Grand Central School of Art. Member: NA Women PS; North Shore AA; Gloucester SA.

GOODMAN, ARTHUR JULE* (Port. P.) b. Hartford, Conn.; d. Cleveland, Ohio, Oct. 3, 1926. Painted many notables, including "Buffalo Bill" Cody, whose portrait was made for King Edward VII, and hangs in Buckingham Palace, London.

GOTTHOLD, FLORENCE WOLF (MRS. FREDERICK GOTTHOLD), 67 West 52nd St., New York, N. Y.; summer, Wilton, Conn. (P. C.) b. Uhrichsville, Ohio, Oct. 3, 1858. Pupil of B. R. Fitz, H. Siddons Mowbray and H. G. Dearth. Member: N. Y. Pen and Brush C.; MacD. C.; Greenwich SA; NA Women PS; Silvermine GA; Gld. of Book Workers; Wilton SA.

GOTTWALD, FREDERICK CARL, 1890 East 97th Street, Cleveland, Ohio (P. T.) b. in 1860. Pupil of ASL of NY; Royal Academy, Munich. Member: Cleveland SA. Work:

"The Umbrian Valley, Italy," Cleveland Museum. Instructor in Cleveland School of Art for forty-one years.

GRANT, LAWRENCE W., Provincetown, Mass. (P.) b. Cleveland, Ohio, June 10, 1886. Pupil of Chase in New York; Laurens and Lefebvre in Paris. Member: Salma. C.

GRAY, ABBY, 1545 Blair Ave., Walnut Hills, Cincinnati, Ohio (C.) Leather, jewelry, etc. Member: Cin. WAC.

GRAY, A. DONALD, 6709 Euclid Ave., Cleveland, Ohio (Ldscp. Arch.) b. Tyrone, Pa., Feb. 24, 1891. Studied: Bucknell Univ.; Harvard Landscape School. Work: landscape architecture.

GREGORY, WAYLANDE DE SANTIOS, Cowan Potters, Inc., Rocky River, Ohio (S. C.) b. Baxter Springs, Kan. Studied: Kansas State Teachers' College; Art Inst. of Kansas City; Lorado Taft, Chicago; Florence, Italy. Work: bronze, "Asa Turner Memorial," Chicago Univ.; fountain, Univ. of Chic; "Antelope," Gorham Co., "Dolores Del Rio," portrait; ceramics, "Rhine Maidens"; Luedeking residence, Cincinnati; panel, Goldfarb roof, N. Y.; "Nautch Dancer," Cleveland Mus. Awards: ceramics, "Nymph and Two Fauns," Cleveland Mus., first prize, 1929; Chicago exhibit, 1930; exhibited PAFA; N. Y. Arch. L.

GREENAMYER, MRS. LEAH J., 117 East Warren Ave., Youngstown, Ohio (P.C.W.L.T.) b. Ashtabula, Ohio, Apr. 17, 1891. Pupil of Cora B. Austin, George S. Krispinsky, Grace Williamson, John Lloyd, Butler Art Institute. Member: Youngstown Art Alliance; Columbus AL; Cleveland Art Center; Mahoning Soc. of Painters; Ohio-Born WP. Art editor of Youngstown *Sunday Vindicator*.

GREENLAND, MRS. BLANCHE, Cincinnati, Ohio (W.) Owner and publisher of *Cincinnati Fine Arts Journal*.

GREVE, CHERRY, 530 Maxwell Ave., Vernonville, Cincinnati, Ohio (P. W.) Art critic *Cincinnati Times Star*. Member: Cin. WAC.

GRIFFITH, HAROLD G., 1932 East 116th St., Cleveland, Ohio (E.) b. Jamestown, N. Y., Jan. 15, 1904. Studied Cleveland School of Art. Awards: second prize and hon. men. Work: etching in Clevelannd Mus.

GRIMES, FRANCES, 229 East 48th St., New York, N. Y. (S.) b. Braceville, Ohio, Jan. 25, 1869. Pupil of Pratt Inst. in Brooklyn. Member: NSS, 1912; NA Women PS; AFA. Awards: silver medal for medals, Pan.-Pac. Expo., San Francisco, 1915; McMillin sculpture prize, NA Women PS, 1916. Work: overmantel, Washington Irving High School, New York City; "Girl by Pool" and "Boy with Duck," Toledo Museum of Art; busts of Charlotte Cushman and Emma Willard, Hall of Fame; many bas-relief portraits of children.

GRISWOLD, CASIMIR CLAYTON* (P.) b. 1834, Delaware, Ohio; d. June 7, 1918, Pough-keepsie, N. Y. Studied engraving in Cincinnati; painting in Rome; ANA, 1866; NA, 1867.

GROLL, GEORGE (I.) Flourished in Cleveland *c.* 1880. Work: lithography.

GROOMS, REGINALD L., Germania Bldg., 31 East 12th St.; h. 2211 Fulton Ave., Cincinnati, Ohio (P. T.) b. Cincinnati, Nov. 15, 1900. Pupil of Cin. Art Acad.; Laurens, Pages and Royer at Julian Academy in Paris. Member: Duveneck SPS; Cin. AC. Work: "The Harbor," Hughes High School, and "The Tuna Fleet," College High School, Cincinnati.

GROSSMAN, GEORGE (P.) Flourished in Cleveland, Ohio, *c.* 1880. Work: landscapes and miniatures. Member: Cleve. AC.

GRUB, ANTON* (P.) Flourished in Cleveland, Ohio, *c.* 1880. Work: landscape painter.

HAGUE, MAURICE STEWART, 1470 Fair Ave., Columbus, Ohio (Ldscp. P.) b. Richmond, Jefferson Co., Ohio, May 12, 1862. Member: S Indp. A. Work in Columbus Gallery of Fine Arts.

HAIGHT, MRS. MARY TRIVETT, Fernbank, Cincinnati, Ohio (P.) Work: murals in Women's Building, World's Fair, Chicago, 1893. Member: Cin. WAC.

HAINES, MARIE BRUNER, College Station, Texas; summer, Taos, N. M. (P.I.C.W.L.T.) b. Cincinnati, Ohio, Nov. 16, 1885. Pupil of Noble, Volk, Francis Jones, Du Mond, Dimitri Romanofsky. Awards: first portrait prize, Southern Artists Exhibition, Atlanta, 1917; first prize, figure painting, Macon, 1920. Represented in Agricultural Mechanical College, College Station, Texas; Museum of New Mexico, Sante Fe, gesso panels; decorations in theatre, Bryan, Texas. Specialty: mural decorations in gesso. Member: Southern SAL; Texas FAA.

HALDEMAN, M. O.* (P.) b. Marion, Ohio; d. Indianapolis, Ind., Sept. 21, 1902. Self-taught. Water-color painter.

HAMILTON, CLARA L. (MRS. V. C.), Kokomo, Ind. (P.) b. Belle Center, Ohio, Apr. 8, 1872. Pupil of Frederick Gottwald, Forsyth, Coats, Cleveland School of Art. Member: AA of Kokomo H. S.

HAMILTON, GRANT E.* (News A.) b. Youngstown, Ohio, Aug. 6, 1862; d. c. 1915. Art editor of *Judge* and *Leslie's Weekly*. Member: Lotos Club.

HAMILTON, WILBUR DEAN, Trinity Court, Dartmouth, St., Boston, Mass. (P. I. C.) b. Somerfield, Ohio, 1864. Pupil of École des Beaux Arts in Paris. Member: Copley S., 1903; Boston GA; St. Botolph C. Awards: Jordan prize in Boston; medal, Atlanta Expo., 1895; gold medal, Pan.-Pac. Expo., San Francisco, 1915. Work: "Beacon Street, Boston," R. I. School of Design, Providence. Represented in Boston Museum, Boston University, American University, John Wesley Memorial Room, Lincoln College, Oxford, England. Instructor at Mass. Normal Art School.

HAMMOND, RICHARD HENRY, 806 Barr St., Cincinnati, Ohio (P.) b. Cincinnati, 1854. Pupil of Weber, Noble, Duveneck. Member: Cin. AC.

HANNAFORD, SAMUEL* (Arch.) b. Devonshire, Eng., April 7, 1835; d. Cincinnati, Ohio, Jan. 7, 1911. Came to United States in 1845; settled on farm near Cincinnati. Training: Farmers' College, Cincinnati; office of John R. Hamilton; in 1857 opened office for himself; firm was Anderson & Hannaford, later, Hannaford & Proctor, 1887 Hannaford & Sons. Work: Music Hall, City Hall, Grand and Palace Hotels, St. Paul Office Bldg., Odd Fellow's Temple, Cin.; Annex to State Capitol, Columbus; court-houses, Greene, Monroe, Washington Counties; Terre Haute, Ind.; many fine residences in Cincinnati. Advocate of manual training and technical education; director of Ohio Mechanics' Institute at his death; once editor of *Western Architect and Builder*. Member: FAIA.

HARLAN, HAROLD COFFMAN, 2905 Salem Ave., at Benton, Dayton, Ohio (I. E. Arch.) b. Dayton, Ohio, April 5, 1890. Pupil of Max Seiffert, Carl Howell. Member: AIA; Dayton SE; Dayton AG; Ohio State A. of Arch.

HARPER, EDITH WALTERS (MRS. GEORGE D.), 2119 Alpine Place, Cincinnati, Ohio (Port. P.) Pupil of Duveneck. Member: Cin. WAC.

HARPER, GEORGE COEBURN, 116 Orchard Drive, Northville, Mich. (E.) b. Leetonia, Ohio, Oct. 23, 1887. Pupil of Cleveland School of Art, ASL of NY. Member: Scarab C. Work: "Christmas Mornin'," Bibliothéque Nationale, Paris; "Mountain Home," Los Angeles Museum of Art, Los Angeles, Calif.

HARVEY, ELI, 130 Champion Place, Alhambra, Calif. (S. P. C.) b. Ogden, Ohio, Sept. 23, 1860. Pupil of Cincinnati Academy under Lutz, Noble and Rebisso; Julian Academy in Paris under Lefebvre, Constant and Doucet; Delacluse Academy under Delance and Callot, and of Fremiet at the Jardin des Plantes. Member: NSS, 1902; N. Y. Arch. Lg., 1903; Paris AAA; Am. Soc. Animal P and S; Allied AA; Nat. des Beaux Arts; Calif. AC; Laguna Beach AA; AFA. Awards: first-class gold medal for painting, Paris-Province Expo., 1900; Wanamaker prize for sculpture, Paris AAA, 1900; bronze medal for sculpture, Pan.-Pac. Expo., Buffalo, 1901; bronze medal, St. Louis Expo., 1904; bronze medal, Pan.-Pac. Expo., San Francisco, 1915. Work: "Maternal Caress," and American bald eagle for honor roll, Metropolitan Museum, New York; sculpture for lion house, New York Zoo; recumbent lions for Eaton Mausoleum; portrait of "Dinah," gorilla, for New York Zoölogical Society; medal commemorating entry of the United States into the war, for American Numismatic Society; Eagles for the Victory Arch, New York; American Elk for BPOE; sculpture for the Evangeline Blashfield Memorial Fountain; Brown Bear Mascot for Brown Univ., Providence; represented in museums of St. Louis, Liverpool, Newark, Cincinnati; American Museum of Natural History, and Metropolitan Museum of Art, New York.

HASWELL, ERNEST BRUCE, 4004 La Crosse Ave., Cincinnati, Ohio (S. W. L. T.) b. Kentucky, July 25, 1887. Pupil of Barnhorn, Meakin, Dubois. Member: Cin. Mac.D. S.; Cin. AC; Crafter's Guild. Work: "Spinoza," bas relief Hebrew Union College and Spinoza House, The Hague; "Northcott Memorial," Springfield, Ill.; Cincinnati Mus.; Rookwood Pottery; Garden Sculpture; St. Coleman's Church, Cleveland; War Memorials; portraits of Generals Greene, St. Clair, Wayne, Greenville, Ohio; Nippert Memorial, Univ. of Cincinnati.

HAUSER, JOHN* (P.) d. Clifton, Ohio, Oct. 6, 1913, aged 55 years. Painted Indian subjects chiefly.

HAYDEN, EDWARD PARKER* (Ldscp. P.) b. Haydenville, Ohio, May 21, 1858; d. Feb. 7, 1921, at Haydenville, Mass. Lived in Columbus most of his life. Studied ASL of NY; Europe. Member: London Art Club, London, Eng.; Salma. C. Exhibited: Royal Acad.; National Acad.; Boston AC; Philadelphia AC. Specialized in New England landscape.

HAY, MRS. GENEVIEVE LEE* (S. T.) b. Cleveland, Ohio, 1881; d. Apr. 7, 1918, Flemington, N. J. Pupil of Henri, Cooper Union, ASL of NY. Member: MacDowell Club.

HAYS, BARTON S.* (P.) b. Greenville, Ohio, Apr. 5, 1826; d. Minneapolis, Minn., Mar. 14, 1914. Painter of portraits, landscapes, and still life.

HEATH, MISS EUGENIA A.* (P. T.) b. Florence, Erie Co., Ohio, 1843. Lived past middle life. Studied Art School of N. Y. Work: portraits, landscapes.

HEIDENREICH, GEORGE, Cleveland, Ohio (S.) Work: architectural and decorative wood carving; bust of Schiller, in Cleveland Public Library.

HELMICH, HOWARD* (P. E. I.) b. Zanesville, Ohio, 1845; d. Georgetown, Washington, D. C., Apr. 28, 1907. Studied Cabanel, Beaux Arts, Paris. Lived in England some years. Member: Royal Society of British Artists; Royal Society of Painters-Etchers. Professor of Art at Georgetown Univ.

HELWIG, ARTHUR L., Cincinnati Art Academy, Cincinnati, Ohio (P.) Studied Cin. AA; Julian Academy, Académie Moderne, Paris. Member: Cin. AC; MacDowell Soc. Awards: Louis C. Tiffany Fellowship; Fleischman Endowment Student Fund.

HENDERSON, DORCAS (MRS. J. R. SHAFFER), 2373 East 70th St., Chicago, Ill. (P.) b. Kenton, Ohio. Studied Cleveland Art School; AIC; with George Elmer Browne in Europe. Exhibited landscapes in oil and water color at Chicago, New York City, and Paris. Member: Three Arts Club, Chicago; Illinois Women's Ath. Club.

HENRI, ROBERT* (P. T.) b. Cincinnati, Ohio, June 24, 1865; d. New York, July 12, 1929. Studied PAFA; Julian Academy, École des Beaux Arts, Paris. Awards: silver medal, Pan-Amer. Expo., Buffalo, 1901; silver medal, St. Louis Expo., 1904; Harris prize, Chicago AI, 1905; gold medal, AC of Phila., 1909; silver medal, Buenos Aires Expo., 1910; silver medal, Pan.-Pac. Expo., 1915; Temple gold medal, PAFA, 1929; many others. Member: SAA; ANA, 1904; NA, 1906; NAC; S Indp. A; Boston AC;

New Soc. of Artists. Work: "La Neige," Luxembourg, Paris; "Young Woman in Black," "Himself," "Herself," AIC; "Dancer in Yellow Shawl," Columbus Gallery; "The Spanish Gypsy," Metro. Mus.; "Girl with Fan," PAFA.

HENRY, CHARLES* (Arch.) b. Vernon, Trumbull Co., Ohio, 1847; d. Akron, Ohio, Nov. 2, 1915.

HERBERT, FRANCIS* (P.) b. 1864, Richmondale, Ohio; d. May, 1918, Columbus, Ohio. Portrait of McKinley best known work.

HERKOMER, HERMAN, Aurora, Calif. (P.) b. Cleveland, 1862. Studied with Willis Adams, Frank Tompkins, Cleveland, 1877; ASL of NY, 1880; Munich three months. Awards: gold medal, 1915, Pan.-Pac. Expo. Work: portraits, Alpine studies.

HERKOMER, JOHN HUBERT (P. E.) In Cleveland c. 1876. Studio and school at Bushy-Hertz, near London, Eng. Work: portraits of John Ruskin, Self, many Englishmen, Queen Victoria, Lord Avebury.

HERSCH, LEE F. (P.) Cleveland artist who worked on range-finding pictures at Taos, N. M., during the war.

HICKS, HERBERT, John's Bldg., 407 Locust St., Philadelphia, Pa.; h. 402 High St., Clarendon, Va. (P. I.) b. Columbus, Ohio, June 26, 1894. Pupil of Messer, Brooks, Wagner, Garber and Harding; Corcoran School of Art; Chester Springs School; PAFA. Member: Wash. WCC.

HILLS, ANNA ALTHEA, Laguna Beach, Calif. (P. L. T.) b. Ravenna, Ohio. Pupil of AIC, Cooper Union; Julian in Paris. Member: Calif. AC; (pres.) Laguna Beach AA; Wash. WCC. Awards: bronze medal, Pan.-Calif. Expo., San Diego, 1915; bronze medal, Calif. State Fair, 1919; landscape prize, Laguna Beach Art Assn., 1922 and 1923; prize, Orange Co. Fair, 1925.

HIRST, CLAUDE R. (MRS.), 65 W. 11th St., New York (P.) b. Cincinnati, Ohio.

HITCHCOCK, ARTHUR E.* (Arch.) b. Perrysburg, Ohio, Dec. 20, 1866; d. Nov. 22, 1902. Graduate of Oberlin College; eight years practical architectural work in Toledo; two years in Philadelphia and Boston. Member of firm Becker & Hitchcock, Toledo; erected many buildings in that city; Newbury School, Messinger Block. Member: FAIA; Boston Arch. C.; Toledo Tile C.

HITCHCOCK, LUCIUS WOLCOTT, Premium Point Park, New Rochelle, N. Y. (P. I.) b. West Williamsfield, Ohio, December 2, 1868. Pupil of ASL of NY; Lefebvre, Constant, Laurens and Colarossi Academy in Paris. Member: SI, 1904; Salma. C., 1907; New Rochelle AA. Awards: silver medal for illustration, Paris, 1900; hon. men., Pan-Amer. Expo., Buffalo, 1901; silver medal for illustration and bronze medal for painting, St. Louis Expo., 1904.

HITE, GEORGE HARRISON* (Min. P.) b. Urbana, Ohio; d. Morrisania, N. Y., 1880. In Cincinnati and all through the South.

HOBBS, MORRIS H., 670 Hinman Ave., Evanstown, Ill. (P. E.) Work: in Toledo. Oil landscape, etching.

HODGIN, MARSTON DEAN, Miami University, Oxford, Ohio (P.) b. Cambridge, Ohio, Dec. 3, 1903. Pupil of F. F. Brown, R. L. Coats, J. R. Hopkins, Charles Hawthorne; Art Dept., Ind. University under R. E. Burke and T. C. Steele; Walter Sargent, Univ. of Chicago. Member: Ind. AC; Richmond AA; Oxford AC. Awards: hon. men., Indiana Painters' Exhibition, 1924-1925; first prize, still life, 1925-1926, first prize, portrait, 1927-1928, first prize, landscape, 1928-1929 at Richmond AA Exhibit. Work: "On Clear Creek," owned by Morton High School, Richmond, Ind. Instructor, Fine Arts, Miami University, Oxford, Ohio.

HOEGLAND, ENID, 2542 Ingleside Ave., Walnut Hills, Cincinnati, Ohio (P.) Studied Cin. AA. Member: Cin. WAC.

HOFF, CHARLOTTE M., 463 W. Market St., Akron, Ohio (P.) Studied: Cleveland School of Art; N. Y. School of Art; Chase, Henri, Parsons. Member: Alumni Three Arts Club, N. Y.; Ohio WCS; Woman's AC, Cleveland. Founder of Ohio-Born Women Artists Exhibit. Work: landscape and portrait, oil and water colors.

HOFFMAN, BELLE, 140 West 57th St., New York, N. Y. (P. I.) b. Garrettsville, Ohio, Apr. 28, 1889. Pupil of Henry Snell; Cleveland School of Art; ASL of NY. Member: NA Women PS; AFA; Cleveland WAC. Award: second landscape prize, Cleveland Museum, 1923.

HOHNHORST, WILL, 3219 Oak Road, Cleveland Heights, Cleveland, Ohio (P.) Member: Cleveland SA.

HOLDEN, CORA MILLET, 2049 Cornell Rd., Cleveland, Ohio (P. T.) b. Alexandria, Va., Feb. 5, 1895. Pupil of Cyrus Dallin; Joseph DeCamp; Mass. School of Art; Cleveland School of Art. Work: mural decorations "Separation" and "Reunion" war memorials at Goodyear Hall, Akron, Ohio; "Steel Production," mural decoration, Federal Reserve Bank, Cleveland; series of four mural decorations, Allen Memorial Medical Library, Cleveland. Specialty, portraits and murals.

HOLLINGSWORTH, CEYLON E., 1322 Florencedale Ave., Youngstown, Ohio (W. P. T. News A.) Studied Chautauqua Art School, under W. M. Chase in N. Y. Work: illustration, landscape, figure, portraits, all mediums. Member: Buckeye Club.

HOLLOWAY, IDA HOLTERHOFF (MRS. GEORGE C. HOLLOWAY), 2523 Ritchie Ave., East W. H., Cincinnati, Ohio (P. I. C.) b. Cincinnati. Pupil of Cincinnati Art Academy under Frank Duveneck; Henry B. Snell, and studied in Europe. Member: Cin. WAC; MacD. C.; The Crafters C., Cincinnati. Work: water color pictures of Brittany and Italy; oil decorative flower pictures.

HOLMES, WM. H. (P.) b. Harrison Co., Ohio, 1846. Self-taught. Awards: first Corcoran prize, Wash. Water Color Club, 1900, Wash. Water Color Club, 1902; Parson prize. Member: Wash. Water Color Club; Soc. of Wash. Artists; Curator Nat'l Gallery of Art, and Archæologist Smithsonian Inst. "Midsummer" at Corcoran, painted in 1907.

HOOK, LEAH VERITY (MRS. CHAS. R.), 7 Alameda Ave., Middletown, Ohio (P.) Portraits, still life. Studied N. Y.; Jane Freeman; Alpheus Cole. Exhibited: Anderson's Gallery, N. Y.; Closson's Gallery, Cin.; Biltmore Hotel, Phoenix, Ariz.; Art Center, Middletown, Ohio.

HOPKINS, EDNA BOIES (MRS. JAMES R. HOPKINS), Ohio State University, Columbus, Ohio; 55 rue de Dantzig, Paris, France (Engr.) b. in Michigan. Member: Société Internationale des Graveurs en Couleurs; Société Internationale des Graveurs sur Bois; Société Nationale des Beaux Arts in Paris. Award: silver medal, Pan. Pac. Expo., San Francisco, 1915. Work in Library of Congress, Washington, D. C.; Walker Art Gallery, Liverpool; National Museum, Stockholm; Kunst Gewerke Museum, Berlin; Bibliothéque d'Art et Archæologie, Paris; Cincinnati Art Museum; Detroit Institute of Arts.

HOPKINS, JAMES R., Ohio State Univ., Columbus; 55 rue de Dantzig, Paris, France (T. P.) b. in Ohio, 1878. Pupil of Cin. AA. Member: ANA; Paris AAA; Associate Société Nationale des Beaux Arts, Paris. Awards: Lippincott prize, PAFA, 1908; bronze medal, Buenos Aires, 1910; gold medal, Pan.-Pac. Expo., San Francisco, 1915; Harris bronze medal and prize ($300), AIC, 1916; Clarke prize, NAD, 1920. Work: "Frivolity," Cincinnati Museum; "A Kentucky Mountaineer," Chicago Art Institute; "Reflections," Atlanta Art Association; portrait of Mrs. Nicholas Longworth.

HOPKINS, C. E., 3525 Trimble Ave., Evanston, Cincinnati, Ohio (P. E.) b. Cincinnati, 1886. Pupil of Nowottny and Barnhorn. Member: Cin. AC.

HOUSTON, GRACE, Indiana State Teachers College, Art Dept., Indiana, Pa.; summer,

Pennsylvania State College, Art Dept., State College, Pa. (P. T.) b. Marysville, Ohio. Pupil of N. Y. School of Applied Design; Provincetown Art Colony. Member: Pittsburgh AA; Alliance. Art Supervisor, Pittsburgh, Pa.

HOWARD, KATHARINE LANE* (I. Poet). b. New York; d. July 5, 1929, Cincinnati, Ohio. Much of the art work in Audubon's bird books was done by her; wrote and illustrated *The Little God,* a child book of verse that has been adopted for use in English schools.

HOWARD, HUGH HUNTINGTON* (P.) b. 1860, Cherry Valley, Ohio; d. July 25, 1927, Cleveland, Ohio. Member: Cleveland Soc. of Artists. Work: Impressionistic landscapes and marines.

HOWE, WILLIAM HENRY* (P.) b. Ravenna, Ohio, 1846; d. New York, Mar. 15, 1929. Studied Düsseldorf, Germany; with Otto von Thoren, animal painter, Paris. Awards: Crystal Palace, London; Boston; New Orleans; California; Atlanta; Pan-Amer. Expo.; Chevalier of Legion of Honor, Paris, 1899. Member: ANA, 1894; NA, 1897; Lotos C; Salma. C.; Nat'l Soc. of Arts and Letters; trustee of National Gallery, Washington. Work: "Uplands of Normandy"; "Norman Bull," St. Louis Mus.; "Return of the Herd." Represented in Carnegie, Cleveland, Detroit, and National Gallery, Wash.

HOWELL, CARL E.* (Arch.) b. Apr. 1, 1897; d. June 20, 1930, Columbus, Ohio. Studied CAS, Philadelphia; France; Spain. Member of firm Howell & Thomas, Columbus, and Cleveland. Work: many buildings in Columbus and Cleveland. Prizes: New York, Philadelphia. Member: PPC; CAL; Nat'l Arch. Lg.; Architects Club, Columbus.

HOWELL, HELEN, 2417 Salutaris Ave., Walnut Hills, Cincinnati, Ohio (P.) Specialty of silhouettes of children. Member: Cin. WAC.

HUBBARD, FRANK MCKINNEY* (News A.) b. Bellefontaine, Ohio; d. Dec. 25, 1930, Indianapolis, Ind. Cartoonist on *Indianapolis News.*

HUBBARD, PLATT, Old Lyme, Conn. (P.) b. Columbus, Ohio, 1889. Pupil of Henri.

HUNT, MRS. MAY SANFORD, Independence, Ohio (P. T.) Studied Cleveland School of Art; New York. Taught Buchtel College, Akron.

HUNT, UNA CLARKE (MRS. ARTHUR P. HUNT), Pasaconaway, N. H. (P. I.) b. Cincinnati, Ohio, Jan. 6, 1876. Pupil of Boston Museum School and Denman W. Ross. Member: Wash. WCC. Work: Reredos in St. Michael's Church, Geneseo, N. Y.

HUNTER, DARD, The Mountain House, Chillicothe, Ohio (I. W.) b. Steubenville, Ohio, Nov. 29, 1883. Studied K. K. Graphische Lehr und Versuchs Anstalt, Vienna; K. K. Kunstgewerbe Schule, Vienna; Technical College, Finsbury, London; Ohio State University. Work: graphic arts placed in museums of America, Europe, and Orient. Awards: gold medal, Amer. Inst. of Graphic Arts, 1931; hon. degree, Doctor of Letters, Lawrence College, Appleton, Wis., 1931. Member: Amer. Inst. of Graphic Arts; Rowfant Club, Cleveland. Author of many books on paper making. Designed over one hundred books since 1900. Art director of Roycroft Shop, East Aurora, New York, 1903-1907.

HUNTINGTON, FRANCIS ROPES (FRANZ)* (P.) b. Columbus, Ohio, Sept. 3, 1875; d. Columbus, Mar. 1, 1928. Studied with Mr. and Mrs. Albert Fauley. Work: oil landscape, impressionistic, pastel. Paintings placed in Huntington Bank, and residences of Columbus. Hon. men. at Carnegie Inst. for picture of "Bridge Construction." President of Columbus Gallery of Fine Arts many years. Banker.

HURLEY, EDWARD TIMOTHY, Rookwood Pottery; h. 2112 St. James Ave., W. H., Cincinnati, Ohio (P. I. E. C.) b. Cincinnati, Oct. 10, 1869. Pupil of Cin. AA under Frank Duveneck. Member: Cincinnati AC; Chicago SE; Richmond AA; Crafters Company of Cincinnati. Awards: gold medal for originality in art workmanship, St. Louis World's Fair, 1904; Logan medal, AIC, 1921; landscape prize, Columbus, 1921. Work: "Midnight Mass," Cincinnati Museum; etchings in Richmond (Ind.) Art

Association; Art Association of Indianapolis; Detroit Institute; Toledo Museum of Art; New York Public Library; Library of Congress, Washington D. C.; Chicago Art Institute; British Museum, London, England. Illustrated with etchings, and published seven books on Cincinnati.

HURLEY, IRENE BISHOP (MRS. E. T.)* (Min. P.) b. Dec. 5, 1881, Colorado Springs, Colo.; d. Mar., 1905, Troy, N. Y. Pupil ASL of NY, under Kenyon Cox; Manbell Fry; Fayette Barnum. Member: NYWCC; Nat'l Asso. WPS. Worked in Cincinnati.

HURST, L. E., Avon, Lorain Co., Ohio (P. I.) b. Avon, Ohio, 1883. Pupil of Cleveland School of Art, under Gottwald & Keller. Specialty: botanical illustrations.

HUSSEY, JOHN E., Columbus, Ohio (P.) Water color landscapes, flowers, and Florida views exhibited Lakeside, Ohio. Member: CAL; PPC. Landscape Gardener, Ohio State University.

HUTTON (MRS. DOROTHY WACKERMAN), 3964 Packard Street, Long Island City, N. Y. (P. D.) b. Cleveland, Ohio, Feb. 9, 1899. Pupil of Minneapolis School of Art; Mary Moulton Cheney; Richard Lahey; Anthony Angarole; André L'hôte. Member: Alliance.

HUMPHREYS, F.* (E.) Capital engraver of portraits and subject plates in mezzotint and line. Employed 1850-'60 by Methodist Book Concern, Cincinnati.

HUMPHREYS, ALBERT, 96 Fifth Ave., New York (P. S.) b. near Cincinnati, Ohio. Pupil Gérôme, Paris. Paintings in Detroit Art Inst.; Boston Library. Sculpture in National Gallery.

HUMPHREYS, SALLIE THOMSON, School of Fine Arts, Ohio Wesleyan University; h. 162 North Sandusky St., Delaware, Ohio (P. D. L. T.) b. Delaware, Ohio. Pupil of Emma Humphreys; Washington, D. C., ASL; N. Y. School of FAA; studied at Colarossi Academy in Paris, and various places in Europe. Member: Coll. AA; Wash. WCC; Wash. AC; AFA. Work: designs for textiles, wall paper, cretonne, cotton and linen materials reproduced by leading firms. Author of lectures on "Design in Its Relation to the Home," "Textile Design," "Interior Decoration," and "The Value of Art Instruction to the College Student." Instructor in Design, Washington Art Students' League, 1897-1904; Baltimore Water Color Club, 1902-1903. Director, School of Fine Arts, Ohio Wesleyan University.

IMFELD, FRED* (P.) d. in Cincinnati, Sept. 5, 1927.

INGRAHAM, GEO. H., 1127 Guardian Building, Cleveland, Ohio (E.) b. New Bedford, Mass., 1870.

IRELAND, WILLIAM ADDISON, *Columbus Evening Dispatch;* h. 264 Woodland Avenue, Columbus, Ohio (News A.) b. Chillicothe, Ohio, Jan. 8, 1880. Member: Columbus PPC.

IVONE, ARTURO, 127 East Third St., Studio Bldg., Cincinnati, Ohio (S.) b. Naples, Italy, May 29, 1894. Pupil of Mossuti, Naples; Ettene Ferrari, Rome; C. J. Barnhorn, Cincinnati. Member: Cin. AC. Work: Stephen C. Foster memorial bronze bust, Music Hall, Cincinnati, Ohio. Commission for statue of Columbus.

JACOBS, WM. LEROY* (I.) b. Cleveland, Ohio, 1869; d. New York, April 8, 1917. Studied Julian's and Colarossi's, Paris. Work: illustrations for *Century, Scribner's,* and other magazines. Member: Society of Illustrators.

JAMES, ALICE A. S. (MRS.) (P. I.) b. Urbana, Ohio, 1870. Exhibited: Philadelphia, Chicago, Washington, and Paris Salon. Illustrated *Harper's* and *Century.*

JAQUES, BERTHA E. (MRS.), 4316 Greenwood Ave., Chicago, Ill. (E.) b. Covington, Ohio. Pupil Chicago AI. Work in New York Public Library, Congressional Library, Washington.

JARVIS, W. FREDERICK, 315 East Quincy St., San Antonio, Texas (P. L. T.) b. Monroe

Co., Ohio. Pupil of Silas Martin, Charles Bullett, Madam Schille. Member: SSAL; S Indp. A. Award: gold medal, Tri-State Fair, 1926.

JEWETT, CHAS. A.* (Engr.) b. Lancaster, Mass., 1816; d. New York, 1878. Good line engraver of subject plates in N. Y., 1838. Cincinnati, 1853, extensive engraving business there. 1860 in N. Y.

JIROUCH, FRANK L., 1445 East 47th St., Cleveland, Ohio (P. S.) b. Cleveland, Mar. 3, 1878. Pupil of Matzen, Ludikie, Grafly, Garber, Pearson, Landowski, Bouchard. Member: NSS; Cleveland SA; Fellowship PAFA. Work: bronze relief in Church of Lady of Lourdes; "Diana of Ephesus," Union National Bank; stone pediment, United Savings and Trust Bank; Chapman Memorial, Cleveland Ball Park; Altar of Sacrifice, Cleveland; Spanish War Monument, Columbus, Ohio; "Day and Night," Wade Park, Cleveland; Maine Memorial Tablet, Havana, Cuba.

JOHNSON, BURT W.* (S. T.) b. 1890, Flint, Ohio; d. Mar. 27, 1927. Pupil of Louis St. Gaudens; J. E. Frazer; Robert Aitken; George Bridgman. Member: Laguna Art Asso.; N. Y. Arch. Lg. Works: "Spanish Music Fountain," "Greek Tablet," Pomona College, Calif.; panel, "Christ," St. Francis Hospital, La Crosse, Wis.; much work in Los Angeles; World War Memorial, College Park, Atlanta, Ga.; Dimick Statue, West Palm Beach, Fla.

JOHNSON, FRANCES GOLDRICK, 2641 Fair Ave., Columbus, Ohio (S.) Exhibited, HS, 1930. Asst. instructor at Ohio State University, Fine Arts Dept.

JOHNSON, JEANNE PAYNE (MRS. LOUIS C. JOHNSON), 39 Remsen St., Brooklyn, New York; summer, Stony Brook, L. I., N. Y. (P.) b. near Danville, Ohio, Apr. 14, 1887. Pupil of ASL of NY; Mme. La Farge, Richard Miller and Lucien Simon in Paris. Member: Brooklyn S. Min. P; NA Women PS.

JONES, GENEVIEVE ESTELLE* (P.) b. Cleveland, Ohio, 1846; d. Circleville, Ohio, 1879. Self-taught. Work: collaborated with Mrs. Virginia Jones in illustrating *Nests and Eggs of the Birds of Ohio*.

JONES, JESSIE BARROWS, 11896 Carlton Road, Cleveland, Ohio; 432 South Beach Street, Daytona Beach, Fla. (P. C.) b. Cleveland, Mar. 15, 1865. Pupil of Twachtman, Chase, Hitchcock. Member: Cleveland AA; Alumni Asso., Cleveland School of Art.

JONES, PAUL, Cincinnati, Ohio (P.) Work: decorative, commercial. Exhibited, Cin. Men's AC.

JONES, THOMAS D.* (S.) b. Onedia Co., New York, Dec. 12, 1812; d. Columbus, Ohio, Feb. 27, 1881. Work: "Lincoln," State House, Columbus; bust of Tom Corwin, Lebanon Public Library; bust of Zachary Taylor, Baton Rouge, La.; medallion of Henry Clay, Washington, D. C. Elected, ANA, 1853.

JONES, VIRGINIA (MRS. N. E.)* (P.) b. New London, Conn., 1826; d. Circleville, Ohio, 1906. Self-taught. Work: illustrating *Nests and Eggs of the Birds of Ohio*.

JOUETT, MATTHEW HENRY* (Port. P.) b. Harrodsburg, Ky., Apr. 22, 1788; d. Lexington, Ky., Aug. 10, 1827. In Cincinnati, c. 1820. Pupil of Gilbert Stuart, Boston. Portraits in many Kentucky homes; "John Grimes," in Metro. N. Y.

JUDAH, HARRIET BRANDON* (P.) b. Piqua, Ohio, July 4, 1808; d. Vincennes, Ind., June, 1884.

KAELIN, CHARLES SALIS* (P.) b. Cincinnati, Ohio, Dec. 19, 1858; d. Rockport, Mass., Mar. 28, 1929. Pupil Cincinnati Art School. Award: silver medal, Pan.-Pac. Expo., San Francisco, 1915. Works: Cincinnati University Club, Queen City Club and Cincinnati Museum. Member: North Shore AA; Rockport AA; Philadelphia AC; Cin. AC.

KAHN, ISAAC, 4609 Eastern Ave.; h. 327 Kemper Lane Apts., Cincinnati, Ohio (P. S.) b. Cincinnati, Aug. 16, 1882. Pupil of Duveneck. Member: Cin. AC; Ceramic Soc.

KALISH, MAX, 37 East 57th St., New York, N. Y.; The Fine Arts Bldg.; h. 3226 Euclid

Ave., Cleveland, Ohio (S.) b. Poland, Mar. 1, 1891. Pupil of Matzen, Adams, Calder, Injalbert. Member: AFA. Awards: First prize for sculpture, Cleveland Museum of Art, 1924 and 1925. Work: "Laborer at Rest," and "Torso," Cleveland Museum of Art; Lincoln Monument, Cleveland.

KAPPES, KARL, 410 Monroe St., Toledo, Ohio; summer, Liberty Center, Ohio (P. T.) b. Zanesville, Ohio, May 28, 1861. Pupil of William M. Chase in New York; Benjamin Constant in Paris; Carl Marr in Munich. Member: Scarab C; AFA.

KARNS, MRS. JACK* (S. T.) d. in Dayton, Ohio, 1929. Studied in Munich. Leader of Art Club, Dayton. Head of Occupational Therapy School at National Soldiers' Home, Dayton, Ohio.

KAUFMAN, EDWIN, 3338 East 135th St., Cleveland, Ohio (P. E.) b. Cleveland, Dec. 6, 1906. Studied Cleveland School of Art; Académie Scandinav, Paris; Hoffman School, Munich. Work placed in Cleveland Mus., Print Club. Awards: Agnes grand prize, $1,000; traveling scholarship; third prize lithograph, Cleveland. Member: Cleveland Print Makers. Work: portraits and etchings.

KAVANAUGH, JOHN* (P.) Flourished Cleveland, 1890. Studied Munich with Loefftz, Paris three years. Exhibited Salon each year. Work: portrait and figure painting; portrait of J. H. Wade; "The Washerwomen," Paris Expo.

KAY, GERTRUDE E., 133 S. Union Ave., Alliance, Ohio (I.W.) b. Alliance, July 8, 1884. Studied: Philadelphia School of Design for women four years; Howard Pyle. Began work in Phila., 1903. Illustrated magazines and her own books. Member: NA Women PS; Plastic Club, Phila.; Author's Lg. of Amer. Author: *When the Sandman Comes,* 1916; *Book of Wishes,* 1917; *The Fairy Who Believed in Human Beings,* 1918; *Us Kids and the Circus,* 1927.

KEHRER, F. A., 150 Sherman Ave., Columbus, Ohio (I.) Member: PPC. Lay-out man with *Ohio State Journal.*

KEISTER, ROY C., 1909 Republic Bldg., Chicago, Ill. (I.) b. Ohio, 1886. Pupil AIC.

KELLER, HENRY GEORGE, 1391 Addison Road, Cleveland, Ohio (P.) b. Cleveland, Apr. 3, 1870. Pupil of Bergman at Düsseldorf; Baische at Karlsruhe; Zugel at Munich. Awards: silver medal, Munich, 1902; special awards for maintained excellence, Cleveland Museum of Art, 1919 and 1922. Work: "In the Sand Pit," Cleveland Museum; also represented in the Phillips Memorial Art Gallery, Washington, D. C. Instructor of composition and design, Cleveland School of Art.

KELLOGG, ELIZABETH, Alms Hotel, McMillan St., Cincinnati, Ohio (W.) Formerly librarian at Cin. Mus.

KELLOGG, MINER K.* (P.) b. Cincinnati, Ohio, *c.* 1828. Pictures of Oriental life. Studio in Paris and Florence. Work: miniatures.

KELLY, GRACE VERONICA, Standard Theatre Bldg., 811 Prospect Ave.; h. 1835 Wadene St., East Cleveland, Ohio (P. I. W. T.) b. Cleveland, Jan. 21, 1884. Pupil of H. G. Keller. Awards: second prize for water color, 1924; second prize for landscape and hon. men. for water color, Cleveland Museum of Art, 1925. Work: "Sunset on the Cuyahoga River," Cleveland Heights Public Schools; "Back Yard Activities," owned by the city of Cleveland. Illustrates for papers and magazines. Art critic for *Cleveland Plain Dealer.*

KEMPER, RUBY WEBB, Milford, Ohio (P. C.) b. Cincinnati, Ohio, Dec. 8, 1883. Pupil of T. E. Noble, L. H. Meakin, W. H. Fry, Frank Duveneck, Anna Riis. Member: Cincinnati Ceramic Club; Cin. WAC; The Crafters Soc. Paints still life.

KENDALL, KATE* (P.) Cleveland, Ohio; d. 1915. Water colors.

KERR, RUTH, Cincinnati, Ohio (S.) Pupil of Barnhorn. Award: prize at Cin. Woman's City Club. Work: portrait sculpture.

KEYES, H. J., *The Citizen,* Columbus, Ohio (News A.) b. May 1, 1886, Alliance, Ohio. Cartoonist with *The Columbus Citizen.*

KIEFER, SAMUEL P.* (P.) b. Portsmouth, Ohio, Oct. 14, 1865; d. Columbus, Ohio, Dec. 21, 1916. Member of firm of Orr, Kiefer Photograph Co., nationally recognized. Work: oil landscape and animals. Member: PPC.

KIESS, GRACE (MRS. SWIGGETT), Washington, D. C. (P. T. C.) Dynamic symmetry applied to still life. Exhibited, Hoosier Salon. Teacher of crafts at Withrow High School, Cincinnati.

KING, JOHN M., Dayton Art Institute, Dayton, Ohio (P. T.) b. Richmond, Ohio. Studied Cin. AA with Wessel. Award: second prize on portrait at Hoosier Salon, 1929. Teacher Dayton Art Institute. Work: landscape, figure, portrait.

KING, MARION PERMELIA, 14 Sherman St., Ashtabula, Ohio (S.) b. Ashtabula, Oct. 7, 1894. Pupil of Charles Grafly. Member: Cleveland School of Art Alumni; Fellowship PAFA; Allied AA; S Indp. A; AFA. Awards: Cresson Traveling Scholarship, PAFA, 1923-1925; Stimson prize, 1925.

KINGSBURY, EDNA A., 1128 East Ohio St., Indianapolis, Ind. (P.) b. Xenia, Ohio, May 5, 1888. Pupil of J. Ottis Adams, Otto Stark, William Forsyth. Member: Springfield AA; S Indp. A. Exhibited: Hoosier Salon, 1925, "Winter Day"; Ind. N. Y., 1928, "Moonrise," "Winter Evening"; 1926, "Winter Day," "Sunset," "Approaching Storm." Work: oil and water color landscapes and portraits.

KINGSLEY, ELBRIDGE* (P. Engr.) b. Sept. 17, 1842, Carthage, Ohio; d. Aug. 28, 1918, Brooklyn. Pupil of Cooper Inst. Member: Ruskin Art C., Calif.; Soc. of Wood Engrs., N. Y. Awards: gold medal, Paris, 1889; medal, Chicago, 1893; gold medal Midwinter Expo., Calif, 1894. Complete collection of his engravings in room devoted to his work, Dwight Art Bldg., Mt. Holyoke, College, S. Hadley, Mass.; many examples in print dept., N. Y. Public Library.

KINSEY, ALBERTA (P. I.) Studied AIC; CAA. Teacher of art, Lebanon Univ., Lebanon, Ohio. Member: Cin. WAC; Art. Asso., and Arts and Crafts Club, New Orleans. Represented: Cin. A. M. and Delgado Mus.

KINSMAN-WATERS, RAY, 1143 Lincoln Rd., Columbus, Ohio (P. C. T.) b. Columbus, July 21, 1887. Pupil of Columbus Art School; Alice Schille. Member: NYWCC; Lg. of Columbus A.; Ohio WCC. Awards: water color prize, Lg. of Columbus A., 1923.

KIRKPATRICK, HARRIET, 1153 Westwood Ave., Columbus, Ohio (P. T.) b. Reynoldsburg, Ohio. Studied Columbus Art School, Josephine Klippart, Chas. Hawthorne, John Carlson, Ernest Thurn. Member: Columbus AL; Ohio WC. Award: Robert Wolf water color prize, 1922. Work: water color landscapes; head of Art Dept., Columbus School for Girls; teacher, Louisiana State Normal; art director, Ohio State Fair, 1921-'27.

KISER, VIRGINIA LEE, 81 Miami Ave., Columbus, Ohio (P. E. C.) b. Virginia. Pupil of William M. Chase, F. Vincent Du Mond, F. Luis Mora, Joseph Pennell. Member: Columbus AL; Pittsburgh AA; AFA; Ohio WCS.

KITCHELL, JOSEPH GRAY, Mountain Lakes, N. J. (P. W.) b. Cincinnati, Ohio, 1862. Photographic editor of *Quarterly Illustrator.* In 1900 he produced the Kitchell "Composite Madonna," a merging of the most important madonnas painted by the great masters during 300 years, which attracted wide attention in America and Europe. In 1915, he invented and patented a new method of reproducing pictures known as "Subchromatic art," examples of which were accepted by the Metro. Mus. NAD., Congr. Lib., Brit. Mus. Bibliothéque Nationale, Paris.

KLASSEN, JOHN P., 339 Jackson St., Bluffton, Ohio (S. T.) b. Russia, April 8, 1888. Studied in Germany, 1909-1914. Served in Russian army, making posters for Red

Cross. Member: Western AA; Society of Medalists. Work: two marble busts, Bluffton College.

KLINGER, KENNETH P. (BILL), 9627 Eureka Parkway, Pauna Heights, Cleveland, Ohio (News A.) b. Greenville, Ohio, 1897. Studied Ohio Univ.; AIC. Work: illustration, *Cleveland Plain Dealer;* illustrated history of Cleveland.

KLIPPART, JOSEPHINE, 275 East Town Street, Columbus, Ohio (Ldscp.) b. Canton, Ohio. Founder of the Ohio Water Color Society, 1923. Member: CAL; Ohio WCS. Illustrated first Ohio fish report.

KNAUBER, ALMA JORDAN, School of Household Administration, The University of Cincinnati; 3331 Arrow Avenue, Cincinnati, Ohio (P. T.) b. Cincinnati, Aug. 24, 1893. Pupil of F. Duveneck, L. H. Meakin, C. J. Barnhorn, Hopkins, Hawthorne, and studied in France and England. Member: Cincinnati WAC; Am. APL; Tau Sigma Delta, Hon. Arch. Frat.; College AA; Columbus AL; Ohio WCS; Western AA.

KOCH, (DR.) BERTHE COUCH, 303 E. Whittier St., Columbus, Ohio (P. T.) b. Columbus, Oct. 1, 1899. Studied Ohio State Univ.; Columbia Univ.; Columbus Art School; Art Colonies at Provincetown, Rockport, Mass.; Gifford Beal, NA; Leon Kroll, NA; Chas. Martin, Chas. F. Kelley, AIC. Work: oil landscape, block printing. Awards: Univ. Scholar in Fine Arts, Univ. Fellow in Fine Arts, Ohio State Univ.; Ph.D. (first one granted in creative painting). Member: CAL; NAWPS; Ohio-Born WP; Rockport AA.

KOCH, HELEN C. 253 Hearne Ave., Cincinnati, Ohio (P. C. T. D.) b. Cincinnati, Mar. 2, 1895. Pupil of L. H. Meakin, James Hopkins, Henry B. Snell. Member: Western AA; Cin. WAC; Crafters.

KOHLER, ROSE, 2 West 88th St., New York City (P.) Work: animal subjects. Member: Cin. WAC.

KRAFFT, CARL R., 416 North Harvey Ave., Oak Park, Ill. (P.) b. Reading, Ohio, Aug. 23, 1884. Pupil of AIC; Chicago FA Academy. Member: Chicago PS; Cliff Dwellers; Society of Ozark Painters; Austin, Oak Park and River Forest Art Lg. Awards: Englewood Woman's Club prize, AIC, 1915; Municipal Art. Lg., purchase prize, 1916; hon. men., Chicago AG, 1916; Fine Arts Bldg. prize, Artists Guild, 1917; first Logan medal and $500, AIC, 1925; Medal of Honor, Allied AA, 1925; Harry Frank prize for figure composition, AIC, 1925. Represented by "Charms of the Ozarks," Municipal Art League Collection, Chicago; "Morning Fog," and "Mill Creek in Winter," City of Chicago; "Day After Christmas," and "Woods in Snow," in Oak Park Art League; "Tree Tapestry," South Shore Country Club, Chicago; "Morning Light," Illinois State Museum; series of murals, First National Bank, Elmhurst, Ill.; "Autumn Spirit," Richmond (Ind.) AA.

KUBINYI, KALMAN, 9522 Parkview Ave., Cleveland, Ohio (P. E. I.) b. Cleveland, July 29, 1906. Studied Cleveland Art School; Munich. Work: oil portraits, etchings in Cleveland Mus.; illustrated *Sokar and the Crocodile, The Goldsmith of Florence* and *The Boy Jesus and His Companions.* Member: Cleveland Print Club; President, Cleveland Print Makers Club. Awards: first prize in oil portrait, second in relief cuts, third in etching, Cleveland May Show. Instructor, John Huntington Polytechnic School.

KUHLMAN, G. EDWARD, 107 West First St., Oil City, Pa. (P. W. L.) b. Woodville, Ohio, Sept. 26, 1882. Pupil of PAFA; AIC. Studied abroad. Represented in Public Museum, Oshkosh, Wis. Specialty: altar paintings for churches, and landscape.

KURTZ, ESTAH F.* (P.) d. 1925, Forest, Hardin Co., Ohio. Studied Ohio Northern University. Work: "Stag at the Bridge."

LACHANCE, GEORGES, Park Lane Hotel, Toledo, Ohio (Port. P., Mural P.) b. Utica, New York, Oct. 13, 1888. Pupil St. Louis School of Fine Arts; George Ichbaum. Member:

SIA. Represented: Toledo Mus.; Ainslee Galleries, N. Y.; DePauw University; mural, Knox Co., Courthouse, Ind.

LAMB, KATE BRAINARD, Toledo, Ohio (P.)

LAUER, CATHERINE GAVIN, 433 Rockingham St., Toledo, Ohio (P.) b. Toledo, June 3, 1907. Studied: Colo. State Teachers' College, Greeley, Colo.; Boothbay Studios, Maine; Teachers' College, Columbia Univ. Member: Toledo Women Artists; Toledo AL; Toledo Print Club. Work exhibited: Art Alliance, Philadelphia; Cleveland International Competitive Ex., 1931; Ohio Print Makers' Ex., 1929-'30; 1930-'31; Toledo exhibits. Work: water color and prints. Second hon. men. water color, Toledo, 1931.

LAWMAN, JASPER HOLMAN* (P.) b. 1825, Cleveland, Ohio; d. April 1, 1906, Pittsburgh. Pa. Pupil of Couture, Paris. Pictures in London and New York. Portraits of leading Western Pennsylvania folks.

LANGSDORF, CLARA M., 3964 Eastern Ave., Cincinnati, Ohio (P.) Member: S Indp. A; Cin. WAC. Work: still life.

LEE, HOMER* (P. E.) b. Mansfield, Ohio, May 18, 1856; d. Jan. 26, 1923. Pupil of John Lee, his father; R. C. Minor; Robert MacIntosh of Toronto; Europe. Founder of Homer Lee Banknote Co., N. Y.. Member: Lotos C.; Salma. C.; Artist's Fund Soc. Awards: hon. men. Paris Expo., 1900; bronze medal, Charleston Expo., 1902.

LEE, SAM* (Ldscp. P.) In Cincinnati c. 1835.

LEHMER, CAROLINE, Beechcrest Lane, East Walnut Hills, Cincinnati, Ohio (P.) Member: Cin. WAC.

LEHR, ADAM* (P.) b. Cleveland, Ohio, Nov. 1, 1853; d. c. 1910. Pupil ASL of NY. Work: landscapes; still life paintings.

LEITNER, LEANDER, 348 East 50 St., New York; summer, Edgemoor, Del. (P. I. C.) b. Delphos, Ohio, Apr. 30, 1873. Pupil of ASL of NY; J. B. Whittaker, Henry Prellwitz, Joseph Boston, and F. V. Dumond. Member: S Indp. A; Alliance.

LEONARD, H. PHILLIPS, 1470 West First Ave., Columbus, Ohio (I.) Billboard artist. Member: PPC.

LENSKI, LOIS (MRS. ARTHUR COVEY), Harwinton, Conn. (P. I.) b. Springfield, Ohio, Oct. 14, 1893. Pupil of Kenneth H. Miller; Walter Bayes in London. Award: Logan medal, AIC, 1923. Author and illustrator of *Skipping Village, A Little Girl of 100* (Stokes), *Jack Horner's Pie, Alphabet People* (Harper's), *The Wonder City,* (Coward-McCawn), and illustrator of numerous other children's books. Work: mural decorations for Children's Orthopedic Hospital, Orange, N. J.; Lord and Taylor's, New York.

LIMBACH, RUSSELL T., 305 Union Trust Co.; h. 10115 Superior Ave., Cleveland, Ohio (P. I. E. T.) b. Massillon, Ohio, Nov. 9, 1904. Awards: first prizes in lithography and illustration, 1926, second prizes, 1927; first prize in lithography, second prize for water color, third prize for illustration, 1928, Cleveland Museum of Art. Work: "Spring Night," Los Angeles Museum of Art, Los Angeles, Calif.; "The Bathers," "Fraternity House," and "The Iron Fence," Cleveland Mueseum of Art.

LIND, FRANK* (P.) b. Columbus, Ohio, July 4, 1865; d. Columbus, Dec. 27, 1927. Work: water color; one placed in Governor's mansion, Columbus. Member: PPC.

LINDSAY, THOMAS C.* (Port. P.) Flourished in Cincinnati c. 1880.

LINES, CHAS. M.* (P.) b. 1862; d. Jan., 1931, Cleveland, Ohio. Twelve years secretary for Cleveland Society of Artists. Member: Ohio WCS. Work: landscape, "Land's End, Rockport, Mass."; "Laguna Beach, Calif."

LIPPERT, LEON, 119 E. Fifth St., Government Sq., Cincinnati, Ohio; h. 658 Nelson P., Newport, Ky. (P.) b. in Bavaria, Mar. 15, 1863. Pupil of Cin. Art Academy, under Nowottny and Duveneck, and studied abroad. Member: Cin. AC.

LLOYD, LUCILE, 1125 East Raleigh St., Glendale, Calif. (Mural P.) b. Cincinnati, Ohio,

Aug. 20, 1894. Pupil of Frank Fairbanks, and Eugene Savage. Member: American Bookplate Soc. Work: "The Madonna of the Covered Wagon," So. Pasadena Jr., H. S., Calif.

LOCKE, CHARLES WHEELER, 78 Columbia Heights, Brooklyn, N. Y.; summer, 3906 Hazel Ave., Norwood, Ohio. (P. I. E. T.) b. Cincinnati, Aug. 31, 1899. Pupil of Joseph Pennell, H. H. Wessel, John E. Weis, etc. Member: Duveneck Soc. Represented in Metropolitan Museum, New York; British Museum, London; Cincinnati Museum.

LOEB, LOUIS* (P.) b. Nov. 7, 1866, Cleveland, Ohio; d. July 12, 1909, Canterbury, N. H. Studied with Gérôme in Paris. Spent most of his life in New York. Awards: hon. men., Salon of 1895; third class medal, Salon, 1897; silver medal for drawing, silver medal for painting, Pan-Amer. Expo., Buffalo, 1901; Hallgarten prize, NAD, 1902; Webb prize, Soc. of Am. Artists, 1903; silver medal, St. Louis, 1904; Carnegie prize Soc. Am. Artists, 1905; first prize, Soc. Wash. Artists, 1906. Member: Soc. Am. Artists; Arch. Lg. N. Y.; Soc. of Illustrators; ANA, 1901; NA, 1906. Work: "Temple of the Winds," Metro. Mus. N. Y.

LONGMAN, EVELYN B. (MRS. N. H. BATCHELDER), Windsor, Conn. (S.) b. Winchester, Ohio, Nov. 21, 1874. Pupil of AIC, under Taft; French in New York. Member: NSS, 1906; ANA, 1909; NA, 1919; Am. Numismatic Soc.; N. Y. Municipal AS; Concord AA; Conn. AFA; AFA. Awards: silver medal, St. Louis Expo., 1904; silver medal, Pan.-Pac. Expo., San Francisco, 1915; Shaw memorial prize, NAD, 1918 and 1926; W.M.R. French gold medal, AIC, 1920; Widener gold medal, PAFA, 1921; Wastrous gold medal, NAD, 1924; Flagg prize, Conn., AFA, 1926. Work: bronze doors of chapel, U. S. Naval Academy, Annapolis; bronze doors of library, Wellesley College, Wellesley, Mass.; Ryle memorial, Public Library, Paterson, N. J.; "Torso," bust of Henry Bacon, and "Victory," Metropolitan Museum, New York; "Victory" and "Electricity," Toledo Museum; Allison Monument, Des Moines, Iowa.; "Electricity," American Telephone and Telegraph Bldg., New York; Centennial Monument, Chicago; Naugatuck War Memorial, Naugatuck, Conn.; Theodore C. Williams Memorial, All Souls' Church, New York; Spanish War Memorial, Hartford, Conn.; also represented in Chicago Art Institute; City Art Museum, St. Louis; Cincinnati Museum of Art; Cleveland Museum; Herron Art Institute, Indianapolis.

LOOMIS, KENNETH BRADLEY, 181 Broadway, Dobbs Ferry, New York; 408 Millard Ave., Toledo, Ohio (P.) b. Steubenville, Ohio, August 25, 1900. Studied: AIC; NAD; ASL of NY; Rome; Florence; Italy. Work: murals, portraits, stained glass. Work placed: Woodward High School, Toledo, Ohio; Peddie School, Hightstown, N. J.; private residences, N. Y. Exhibited various New York galleries.

LOOSE, ALBERT, Dayton, Ohio (I.) Pen and ink similar to Aubrey Beardsley's work.

LORD, CAROLINE A.* (P. T.) b. Cincinnati, Ohio, Mar. 10, 1860; d. 1928. Pupil of ASL of NY; Julian Academy in Paris; CAA. Member: Cin. WAC (hon.) Instructor in CAA. Awards: bronze medal, Columbian Expo., Chicago, 1893; fellowship prize, Buffalo, FAS, 1925. Work: "First Communion" and "Old Woman," Cincinnati Museum; "Professor Lord," O. S. U. Library.

LORENZ, CARL (P.) Cleveland, Ohio, c. 1890. Landscapes, marines, impressionist.

LORRAINE, ALMA ROYER, 1617 California Ave., Seattle, Wash. (P. T.) b. Randolph, Ohio. Pupil of AIC; Alexandra Harrison; Bouguereau in Paris; Molinari in Rome. Award: silver medal, Alaska-Yukon-Pacific Expo., Seattle, 1909. Work: "Aqueducts of Claudius," West Chester Seminary. Specialty: oil portraits and studies of animals.

LOSEE, MARIE, Valejo, Calif. (P. C.) b. Lima, Ohio, 1899. Studied AIC. Work: crafts, china, and leather. Teaches wood carving. Formerly painted in oil.

LOWREY, ROSALIE, 1035 Harvard Blvd., Dayton, Ohio (P. I.) b. Dayton, Ohio, Feb. 27,

1893. Pupil of ASL of NY; Dayton AI; PAFA. Member: Ohio WCS. Work: portrait of Leola Clark, Patterson School, Dayton; portrait of Grace Greene, Dayton Junior Teachers' College, Dayton; illustrated *Our Little Folks* (U. B. Publishing House); portraits of Bishop Matthews and Vera Blum, Bonebreak Seminary, Dayton.

LUCE, LEONARD E., Keith Bldg., Euclid at 17th St.; h. 3291 Yorkshire Road, Cleveland, Ohio (P. I.) b. Ashtabula, Ohio, Sept. 27, 1893. Pupil of Gottwald, Keller and Du Mond. Member: Cleveland SA.

LUNDBERG, AUGUST F.* (Ldscp. P.) b. May, 15, 1878, Copenhagen, Den.; d. Columbus, Ohio, Aug. 17, 1928. Figure and scenic painter. Member: PPC; CAL. Exhibited PAFA.

LUQUIENS, ELIZABETH KOLL, 189 East Rock Road, New Haven, Conn.; summer, Waterville, N. H. (P.) b. Salem, Ohio, Jan. 19, 1878. Pupil of Albert G. Thompson; Delecluse and Mucha in Paris. Member: New Haven Paint and Clay C.; Conn. AFA.

LYNCH, ALMA (MRS. HARRY T.), 10 The Verona, Walnut Hills, Cincinnati, Ohio (C.) Designer of decorative cards and picture panels. Work exhibited nationally. Asso. member Cin. WAC.

LYNCH, G. LESLIE, 300 King Ave., Columbus, Ohio (T. Ldscp. Arch.) b. Villisca, Iowa, Aug. 2, 1896. Member: CAL.

LYND, J. NORMAN, 300 Denton Ave., Lynbrook, L. I., New York (I.) b. Northwood, Logan Co., Ohio, November 15, 1878. Member: SI, 1913; GFLA.

LYMAN, JOSEPH* (P.) b. Ravenna, Ohio, July 17, 1843; d. Wallingford, Conn., Mar. 5, 1913. Educated in Cleveland; spent most of life in N. Y.; studied under Dolph and Samuel Coleman. Award: bronze medal, St. Louis Expo., 1904. Member: Century Asso.; ANA, 1886.

MACAULEY, CHARLES RAYMOND, care *The Brooklyn Eagle,* Brooklyn, N. Y. (News A. W.) b. Canton, Ohio, Mar. 29, 1871. Award: $50 prize *Cleveland Press,* 1891. Work: *Cleveland World; New York Herald; Life; New York World; Collier's; Success;* and other periodicals.

MACEACHEN, J. D.* (News A.) b. Jan. 16, 1878, Shawnee, Ohio; d. May 11, 1911. Cartoonist, oil, and theatre scenes. "Mirror Lake," curtain of Southern Theatre, Columbus. Worked for Cincinnati Eng. Co. Member: PPC.

MACHIN, MRS. GRACE KEELER* (P. W.) b. Ohio, 1841; d. Asbury Park, N. J., Aug. 16, 1917. Served in Art Department of St. Louis Expo., 1904.

MACLEAN, JOHN ARTHUR, Toledo Museum of Art, Toledo, Ohio. b. Winchester, Mass., Sept. 22, 1879. Curator, Cleveland Museum of Art, 1914-'22; assistant director, Chicago Art Inst., 1922-'23; director Art Asso. of Indianapolis, 1923-'26; curator, Oriental Art, Toledo Museum since 1926.

MACPHERSON, MARIE RAUCHFUSS (MRS. JAS. F.), 3625 Marburg Ave., Hyde Park, Cincinnati, Ohio (P.) Studied Cin. AA, under Duveneck; Art Inst., Chicago, under Harry I. Stickroth. Exhibited: Carnegie International; Nat'l Acad. Design, N. Y.; Arch. League, N. Y.; Chicago A. Inst.; Buffalo; Cincinnati. Awards: special prize, 1930, for outstanding work by woman at Hoosier Salon; prize at Cincinnati, 1930, for flower painting. Member: Cin. WAC.

MAIRE, FRANCES* (P.) b. Pennsylvania. Painted in Lima, Ohio.

MAHR, GEORGE, 471 E. Broad St., Columbus, Ohio (S.) b. Frankfort am Main, Germany. Came to Columbus, Oct., 1930. Work: architectural decorations for 40 S. Third St., Columbus; portrait sculpture; Stadelsches Art Institute, Frankfort; Deutches Museum, Dresden; University, Heidelberg. Awards: many prizes in Germany and commissions in competition.

MALONEY, LOUISE B., 100 Amsterdam Centrum, Holland (P.) Cleveland artist. Studied

ASL of NY. Awards: first prize, oil portraits, 1924-'26-'27-'28; first prize, still life, 1930, Annual Cleveland Show.

MARSH, MARY E., 1089½ W. 35th Place, Los Angeles, Calif. (P.) b. Cincinnati, Ohio. Member: Calif. Art Club; Laguna Beach Art Asso.; Assistant Art Curator, Los Angeles, Calif. Pupil of F. Berger, Chicago Acad. of FA; Cin. AA.

MARTIN, SILAS* (P. T.) b. Columbus, Ohio, Nov. 20, 1841; d. Columbus, 1906. Studied with Witt. Work: landscape; still life; portraits of McKinley; Governor Thos. Kirker, State House, Columbus; Shakespeare, Otterbein University; Dr. McCabe, Prof. Williams, O. W. U., Del.; Hon. T. Ewing Miller; Francis Sessions; Jane Coombs, actress; Gen. Chas. Walcutt; Dr. W. O. Thompson; Josiah Smith; Mr. Townsend; Baron von Liebig, Library, O. S. U., Columbus

MASON, MRS. MARY TOWNSEND (MRS. WILLIAM CLARKE MASON), 8233 Seminole Ave., Chestnut Hill, Philadelphia, Pa. b. Zanesville, Ohio, Mar. 21, 1886. Pupil of Chase and Breckenridge at PAFA; Maryland Inst., Baltimore. Member: Fellowship PAFA; Phila. Alliance; Plastic C., 1927; NA Women PS; AFA; SSAL. Awards: Cresson traveling scholarship, PAFA, 1909; gold medal, Plastic C., 1921 and 1924; Mary Smith prize, PAFA, 1922. Work: "Blue and Gold," Fellowship PAFA; "Still Life with Fruit," PAFA.

MATHEWS, WILLIAM T.* (Port. P.) b. Bristol, England, May 7, 1821; lived in Canton, and New Philadelphia, Ohio. Came to United States, 1883; d. Washington, D. C., Jan. 11, 1905. Studied with Chas. Soule, Cincinnati. Member: NAD. Work: portraits of McKinley, Lincoln, Webster, Bryant, Garfield, Gov. Allen and Bishop, State House.

MATZEN, HERMAN N., 5005 Euclid Ave.; h. 2423 Woodmere Drive, Cleveland, Ohio (S. T.) b. Denmark, July 15, 1861. Pupil of Munich and Berlin Academies of Fine Art. Member: NSS; NAD; Cleveland SA. Awards: second medal, Berlin, 1895; first medal, Berlin Expo., 1896. Work: "War" and "Peace," Indianapolis Soldiers' and Sailors' monument; Schiller monument, Detroit; "Law" and "Justice," Akron (Ohio) County Courthouse; Wagner monument, Cleveland; Burke Mausoleum; "Moses" and "Gregory," Cleveland Courthouse; "Cain and Abel," Lake County Courthouse; Tom L. Johnson monument, Cleveland Public Square; Holden Mausoleum; Thomas White memorial, Cleveland; Holden Memorial Tablet, Harvard University, Cambridge; Haserot monument, Cleveland; Hatch Memorial, Western Reserve Univ., Cleveland; Collinwood Fire Memorial, Lakeview Cemetery, Cleveland.

MAXWELL, CORALEE DELONG, 1935 East 93rd St., Cleveland, Ohio (S.) b. in Ohio, Sept. 13, 1878. Pupil of Herman Matzen. Member: Cleveland WAC; Cleveland Art Center; AFA. Awards: hon. men., Cleveland Museum of Art, 1926; first prize, Bernard's Gallery, N. Y., 1928. Work: portrait bust of Pres. Robert Vinson, West. Res. Univ., Cleveland; Dryad fountain.

McBURNEY, JAMES E., 1521 East 61st St., Chicago, Ill. (P. I. L. T.) b. Lore City, Ohio, Nov. 22, 1868. Studied with Arthur W. Dow, Howard Pyle, Charles H. Davis; and in Paris. Member: Calif. AC; Cliff Dwellers, Chicago; Chicago PS; All-Ill. SFA. Award: silver medal, Pan.-Calif. Expo., San Diego, 1915. Work: "The Mission Period" and "The Spanish Period," Southern California Counties' Commission, San Diego; eight panels, Nat. Bank of Woodlawn, Chicago; five historical panels, Federal Bank and Trust Co., Dubuque, Iowa, Madison, Wis.; twenty panels, D. C. Wentworth School, Chicago; twelve industrial panels, State Agricultural Exposition Bldg., Los Angeles; three panels, "Life of George Rogers Clark," Parkside School, Chicago; twelve panels, "Women Through the Ages," Women's League Building, University of Michigan, Ann Arbor. Instructor, College of Fine and Applied Arts, A. E. F. University, Coté d'Or, France, 1919. Lecturer on History of Art, AIC, 1920. Director, School Department, Art Inst. of Peoria, 1925-1926.

MCCARTHY, HELEN K.* (P.) b. Poland, Ohio; d. Nov. 1, 1927. Pupil, Philadelphia School of Design; Daingerfield and Snell. Awards: 1914 gold medal, Plastic Club; 1918, Mary Smith prize; 1919, PAFA, sketch prize; 1926, hon. men. NA Women PS.

MCCORD, WILLIAM A.* (P. I.) b. Cincinnati, Ohio; d. Nov. 8, 1918. Self-taught. Member: CAC.

MCDONALD, JAMES WILSON ALEXANDER* (S.) b. Aug. 25, 1824, Steubenville, Ohio; d. Aug. 14, 1908, Yonkers, N. Y. Work: statues of Gen. Custer, West Point; Washington Irving, Brooklyn; bust, Chas. O'Connor, Appellate Court, N. Y.; Fitz-Greene Halleck, Central Park, N. Y.; Thomas Benton, Esq., St. Louis.

MCDONALD, WILLIAM PURCELL* (P.) b. Cincinnati, Ohio, Sept. 18, 1865; d. 1931. Pupil of Cin. AA, under Duveneck. Member: Cin. AC; Duveneck Soc. PS. On Rookwood Pottery staff since 1882.

MCFALL, JAY VAUGHN* (I.) b. Sandusky, Ohio, 1878; d. Detroit, Mich., Dec. 5, 1912. Studied ASL of NY. Work seen in *Saturday Evening Post.*

MCLAUGHLIN, MARY LOUISE, 4011 Sherwood Ave., Arnsby Place, Cincinnati, Ohio (C. W.) Made porcelain (Losanti) ware, 1898. Exhibited Paris, 1900. Awards: silver medal for decorative work, 1889; hon. men. for china painting, Chicago; gold medal, Atlanta; silver medal, Nashville; bronze medal, Buffalo, 1901. Member: Cin. WAC. Author: *China Painting, Pottery Decoration, Painting in Oil, Suggestions to China Painters.*

MEAKIN, LEWIS HENRY* (Ldscp. P. T.) b. Newcastle, England, July 12, 1850; d. Cincinnati, Ohio, Aug. 14, 1917. Studied McMicken School of Design; Munich, 1882; France, under W. L. Picknell, 1892-'93. Represented: "In British Columbia," Chicago Art Inst.; "Ohio Valley and Kentucky Hills," "Kicking Horse Valley," "Spring Time," Cin Art Mus. Elected ANA, 1913.

MENDENHALL, EMMA, 2629 Moorman Ave., Walnut Hills, Cincinnati, Ohio (P.) b. Cincinnati. Pupil of Cin. AA, under Nowottny and Duveneck; Julian Academy in Paris; summer school under Mrs. Rhoda Holmes Nicholls, Woodbury and Snell. Member: Cin. WAC; AWCS; NA Women PS; Cincinnati MacDowell C.; NYWCC; Wash. WCC. Work: water color market scenes and villages of France; flowers; still life; pastel portraits; scenes of Mexico; Spain.

MENTEL, LILLIAN A., 3429 Zumstein Ave., Hyde Park, Cincinnati, Ohio (P. I. T.) b. Cincinnati, Nov. 2, 1882. Pupil of Cincinnati Art Academy and Pratt Inst. Member: Cin. WAC. Work: batiks.

MERWIN, MRS. ANTOINETTE DE FOREST, Armada Studio, 19064 Armada Drive, Pasadena, Calif. (P. T.) b. Cleveland, Ohio, July 27, 1861. Pupil of ASL of NY; St. Paul School of Fine Arts under Burt Harwood; Merson; Courtois; Collin and James McNeill Whistler. Member: Calif. AC.; Pasadena SA; Pasadena FAS; San Diego AG. Award: hon. men., Paris Salon, 1900. Works: "Fisherfolk, Volendam Noord, Holland," owned by the Boston Art Club; "California Fruit and Flowers," Cuyamaca Club, San Diego, Calif.

MESSICK, T. B., Indianapolis, Ind. (I.) b. Zanesville, Ohio, Jan. 28, 1878. Commercial work for automobile companies. Photography. Member: PPC.

MEURER, CHARLES A., Terrace Park, Ohio (P.) b. Germany, Mar. 15, 1865. Pupil of Julian Academy, Bouguereau, Doucet and Ferrier, in Paris. Member: Cin. AC. Specialty: still life; also sheep and cattle.

MEYENBERG, JOHN C., 127 E. 3rd St., Cincinnati, Ohio (S.) b. Tell City, Ind., 1860. Pupil CAA under Thomas S. Noble; Beaux Art under Jules Thomas. Member: CAC.

Work: Egbert Memorial, Fort Thomas, Ky.; pediment, Covington, Ky. Carnegie Library; Aunt Lou Memorial, Lincoln Grove Cemetery; Benn Pitman Memorial, Cincinnati Library.

MEYER, ENNO, Milford, Ohio (P. S. I. E.) b. Cincinnati, August 16, 1874. Pupil of Duveneck. Member: Cin. AC.

MILLAR, ADDISON THOMAS* (P. E.) b. Warren, Ohio, Oct. 4, 1860; killed in automobile accident, Sept. 8, 1913. Pupil of Chase in N. Y.; Benjamin-Constant, Boldini, Paris. Member: Salma. C.; one of so-called Silvermine group of artists. Work: "Still Life," Rhode Island School of Design, Providence; "Old Streets of Madrid," Detroit Mus.; etchings in N. Y. Public Library; Congressional Library; Detroit Mus.; Bibliothèque Nationale, Paris.

MILLER, BENJAMIN, 131 East 3rd St., Cincinnati, Ohio (P. Xylographer). b. Cincinnati. Pupil of Duveneck. Award: first hon. men., Print Club of Phila., 1929. Represented in Bibliothèque Nationale, Paris; permanent collections Cincinnati Art Museum, and Minneapolis Institute of Fine Arts.

MILLER, ELIS F.* (P. E.) b. Canton, Ohio, 1840; d. Columbus, 1884. Work: water color landscapes, etchings. Represented in Carnegie Library, Columbus; large collection of his work owned by Dr. J. F. Baldwin, Columbus.

MILLER, FRANCIS P.* (P.) b. Columbus, Ohio; d. New York City, 1930. Studied: New York, Paris, Berlin. Most notable painting, "Valley Girl," painted in Columbus about 1886.

MILLER, HARRIETTE G., Whimsy Farm, Arlington, Vt.; 17 rue de la Tour, Paris, France (S.) b. Cleveland, Ohio. Member: Am. Woman's Assn.; NA Women PS; Alliance.

MILLER, IRIS MARIE ANDREWS (MRS. WM. N. MILLER), 1135 Chicago Blvd., Detroit, Mich. (P.) b. Ada, Ohio, Mar. 28, 1881. Pupil of Chase, Henri, Breckenridge, Mora. Member: Detroit S. Women P.; NA Women PS; NAC; AFA. Awards: portrait prize, exhibition by Mich. Artists, 1923; Founders prize, Mich. Artists Ex., 1924; Scarab gold medal, Mich. Artists Ex., 1929.

MILLER, JOHN R., 617 East 25th St., Indianapolis, Ind. (P.) b. Hamilton, Ohio. Pupil of William Forsyth.

MILLER, KATE RENO* (P. T.) b. in Illinois; d. Dec., 1929, Cincinnati, Ohio. Pupil of Cincinnati Art Academy; Duveneck; Hawthorne. Member: Cin. WAC. Instructor, Cincinnati Art Academy. Work: landscape, still life.

MILLER, WILLIAM* (Min. P.) b. Lexington, May 27, 1835; d. Apr. 27, 1907, New York. In Cincinnati c. 1847.

MILLESON, ROYAL HILL, 2336 Osgood St., Chicago, Ill. (Ldscp. A.) b. Batavia, Ohio, 1849. Member: Chicago Soc. of A.; Boston Art Asso. Work: "Mt. Hood, Oregon," Herron Art Inst., Indianapolis. Author: *The Artists Point of View.*"

MITIUS, LOUIS* (Port. P.) d. Cincinnati, Ohio, Dec. 28, 1911, aged 69 years. For nine years assistant superintendent of institution for old men.

MOELLER, ZELLA, Akron, Ohio (P.) Studied Perkins' School.

MORGAN, ALEXANDER CONVERSE, 134 West 73rd St., New York, N. Y. (P.) b. Sandusky, Ohio, July 1, 1849. Member: Artists' Fund S. (Pres.); Century Association; Salma. C.

MORGAN, THEO. J., 456 N St., S.W., Washington, D. C.; Provincetown, Mass. (P.) b. Cincinnati, Ohio, Nov. 1, 1872. Member: Wash. SA; Wash. AC; NAC; NYWCC; Beachcombers; Wash. WCC; San Diego AA; San Antonio AL; San Antonio Palette Association. Awards: first prize, Texas Wild Flower Competition ($1,500), 1928; gold medal, most meritorious painting, Davis Wild Flower Competition, also hon. men. 1929. Represented at University of Indiana, Bloomington, Ind.; Aurora, Ill., Art

Association; Women's Hospital, Cleveland; Museum of Fine Arts, Houston, Texas; Delgado Museum of Art, New Orleans; Witte Memorial Museum, San Antonio, Texas; Girl Scouts of America, Barracks, San Antonio; Women's Building, Harlingen, Texas.

MORLAN, DOROTHY, 6030 Lowell Ave., Indianapolis, Ind. (Ldscp. P.) b. Salem, Ohio. Pupil of Albert Morlan; J. Ottis Adams; William Forsyth; Robert Henri; PAFA. Member: SWA. Exhibited: HS, 1930.

MORROW, JULIE (MRS. CORNELIUS WORTENDYKE DE FOREST), Vernon Manor, Cincinnati, Ohio (P. W. T.) b. New York, N. Y. Pupil of Lie, Carlson and Hawthorne. Member: NA Women PS; Provincetown AA; Marblehead AA; Cincinnati AC; American APL; Laguna Beach AA; AFA. Represented in Wadleigh Library, N. Y.

MOSLER, HENRY* (P.) b. New York, June 6, 1841; d. N. Y., Apr. 21, 1920. In Cincinnati during the 70's. Studied with J. H. Beard, Cin.; Mencke and Kindler, Düsseldorf; Hebert, Paris; Wagner, Munich. During Civil War acted as special artist for *Harper's Weekly*. Represented: "The Biskarian Minstrel," Toledo; "The Rainy Day," PAFA; "The Prodigal's Return," Luxembourg, Paris; "Return of the Shrimp Fishers," Cin. Mus.; "Wedding Feast in Brittany," Metropolitan, N. Y.; "Saying Grace," Corcoran, Washington, D. C. Awards: medal at Royal Acad., Munich, 1874; gold medal, Nice, 1884; gold medal, Paris, 1888; many other honors.

MOSURE, JAMES H.* (P. I.) Came to Columbus in 1864. Studied with Witt. Illustrated *Uncle Remus, Harper's* and *Leslie's Magazines*.

MOTE, ALDEN* (P.) b. West Milton, Ohio, August 27, 1840; d. Jan. 13, 1917, Richmond, Ind. Member: Art Institute of Philadelphia. Lived in Richmond after 1880. Work: portrait of Daniel A. Reid, in Reid Memorial Hospital, Richmond, Ind.

MOTE, MARCUS* (P. I. T.) b. West Milton, Ohio, 1817; d. Richmond, Ind. Maintained an art school in Richmond, Ind., for some years. Made Sunday school and Bible illustrations.

MOTT, SEWARD H., 3866 Carnegie Ave., Cleveland, Ohio (Ldscp. Arch.) b. Bouckville, N. Y., Oct. 11, 1888. Work in office of Wm. Pitkin, Jr., and Seward H. Mott, Inc., since 1912. Studied European gardens, college campus plans and large real estate developments.

MOTTO, JOSEPH C., Hawken School, South Euclid, Ohio; h. 1536 East 41st, Cleveland (S.) b. Cleveland, Mar. 6, 1892. Pupil of Matzen, MacNeal and Heber. Member: Cleveland SA; Cleveland SS. Award: first prize, Cleveland Museum of Art, 1922. Work: Shakespeare bust, City of Cleveland; bust of Prof. Wilson, Western Reserve Univ., Cleveland; Matzen bust, Cleveland School of Art; Lincoln bust, Hawken School, South Elucid.

MUELLER, JOHN CHARLES, 2042 Weyer Ave., Norwood, Ohio (I. C. D. W.) b. Cincinnati, Nov. 3, 1889. Pupil of Nowottny, Duveneck, Meakin, Miller, Cincinnati Art Academy. Member: Cincinnati AC. Awards: hon. men. for book cover, Advertisers Club of the World; first prize for emblem design, Nat. Asso. Advertising Specialty Manufacturers. Designer of the official flag for the city of Norwood, Ohio.

MULLIKIN, MARY AUGUSTA, 397 Elgin Terrace, Tientsin, China (P. L.) b. in Ohio. Pupil of Walter Beck in Cincinnati; Birge Harrison at Woodstock; Whistler in Paris. Member: China Soc. of Science and Arts; AFA. Work: Lasell Seminary, Auburndale, Mass.; Pekin Inst. of Fine Arts; in collection of Ex-Pres. Hsu Shih Chang, of China.

MUNDHENCK, OSCAR* (S.) b. 1848; d. Cincinnati, Ohio, Apr. 1, 1922. For over thirty years conducted art foundry in Cincinnati.

MUNSELL, W. A. O., 416 Stimson Bldg., Los Angeles, Calif. (P.) b. Cold Water, Ohio, 1866.

MUNSON, SAMUEL B.* (Engr.) b. Connecticut, 1806; d. Cincinnati, Ohio, 1880. In 1836 came to Cincinnati. Member of bank-note engraving firm of Doolittle & Munson.

MURDOCK, FLORENCE, 2448 Maplewood Ave., Mt. Auburn, Cincinnati, Ohio (P.) Work: water-color landscapes, gardens and fountains. Member: Cin. WAC.

MUSGRAVE, HELEN GREEN, Truro, Mass. (P. T.) b. Cincinnati, Ohio, Mar. 6, 1890. Pupil of Cincinnati Art Acad.; Julian Academy in Paris; New York School of Fine and Applied Art. Member: Provincetown AA.

MYERS, FRANK HARMON, Art Academy; h. 3625 Tamarack Avenue, Cincinnati, Ohio (P. T.) b. Cleves, Ohio, Feb. 23, 1899. Pupil of Duveneck, Wessel, Weis. Member: Cin. AC; MacDowell Soc.; Duveneck PSS. Work: landscape "Golf By the Sea," Cincinnati Woman's Club; "Circus" decoration, Cincinnati Children's Hospital; four canvases, University of Cincinnati; marine, Hughes High School, Cincinnati; portrait of Miss Bertha Bauer, Cin. Cons. of Music. Instructor in drawing and painting, Art Academy, Cincinnati.

MYERS, MRS. SADIE S., 862 Mitchell Ave., Cincinnati, Ohio (P.) Pupil of Mosler and Duveneck. Work: oil, figures, miniatures. Asso. member Cin. WAC.

NACHTRIEB, MICHAEL STRIEBY* (P.) b. Wooster, Ohio, Aug. 25, 1835; d. Wooster, Dec. 27, 1916. Studied N. Y. Works: decorative painting of cabins in Ohio and Mississippi River boats; landscape; still life; portraits of Lincoln (Corcoran Gallery); Col. Morgan; Edwin Booth; College of Bishops of Episcopal Church, Bishop's Hall, Gambier, Ohio; portraits of founders and early presidents of Wooster College (destroyed by fire, 1901).

NEAGLE, JOHN* (Port. P.) b. Boston. In Cincinnati, 1810. Studied in Philadelphia with Sully. Work: portraits; "Pat Lyon, the Blacksmith."

NELAN, CHARLES* (News A.) b. Akron, Ohio, 1858; d. Cave Springs, Ga., Dec. 7, 1904. On staff of N. Y. *Herald* from 1898. Studied Buchtel College, four years; NAD. Work: Cleveland *Town Topics, Press;* Philadelphia *North American;* N. Y. *Globe,* from 1903.

NETTLETON, JAMES B.* (Arch.) b. 1862, Medina, Ohio; d. Apr. 28, 1927, Detroit. AIA.

NEUBAUER, FREDERICK AUGUST, 22 Hurlbert Block, 6th and Vine Sts., Cincinnati, Ohio (Ldscp. P. I.) b. Cincinnati, 1855. Pupil Cin. AA. Member: Cin. AC.

NEWSON, ALFRED* (P.) b. Steubenville, Ohio. Flourished *c.* 1820. Deaf mute. Greater part of life spent in Philadelphia.

NEWTON, CLARA CHIPMAN, Alexandra Building, Walnut Hills, Cincinnati, Ohio (P.) Work: water-color still life, and flowers. Member: Cin. WAC.

NICKUM, CHAS N.* (P.) b. Dayton, Ohio, Feb. 12, 1844; d. Indianapolis, Ind., Oct. 2, 1913. Painted portrait of Abraham Lincoln.

NICODEMUS, CHESTER, Columbus Art School, Columbus, Ohio (S. T.) b. Barberton, Ohio. Graduated Cleveland School of Art, 1925. Studied with Matzen. Instructor, Col. Art School. Represented: fountains and garden figures in gardens of Robert Patterson and Mrs. Wm. Stroup, Dayton, Ohio. Member: Nat'l Soc. of Medalists.

NIEHAUS, CHARLES HENRY, Eagle Crest Studio, Grantwood, N. J. (S.) b. Cincinnati, Ohio, Jan. 24, 1855. Pupil of McMicken School of Cincinnati; Royal Academy in Munich. Member, ANA, 1902; NA, 1906; NY Arch. L., 1895; NSS, 1893; Salma. C., 1908; Nat. Inst. AL. Awards: gold medal, Pan-Amer. Expo., Buffalo, 1901; gold medal, Charleston, Expo., 1902; gold medal, St. Louis Expo., 1904. Work: "Dr. Hahnemann" and "John Paul Jones," Washington, D. C.; "Garfield," Cincinnati; Astor Memorial doors, Trinity Church, New York; "Cæstus" and "The Scraper," Metropolitan Museum, New York; "Francis Scott Key," Baltimore; Soldiers' and Sailors' monuments, Hoboken, Newark, and Hackensack, N. J.; statues of Clay, Mc-

Dowell, and Allen, Statuary Hall, Capitol, Washington; "The Driller," Titusville, Pa.

NILES, HELEN JAMES, 2249 Parkwood Ave., Toledo, Ohio (P.) b. Toledo. Studied: ASL of NY; with Twachtman; Henri in Spain and Holland; Chase in Europe. Work: portraits and flower studies. Member: ASPS.

NOBLE, THOMAS S.* (P. T.) b. Kentucky. Studied with Couture, Paris, and Munich. Selected by Nicholas Longworth as director of Cin. A. School, served there thirty-five years.

NORRIS, W. J., 56 East 8th Ave., Columbus, Ohio (P. T. I.) b. Chicago, Aug. 20, 1869. Head of Terry Engraving Co. Instructor at Ohio State University sixteen years. Member PPC; CAL.

NORTON, HELEN GAYLORD, Laguna Beach, Calif.; h. 189 Magnolia Ave., Riverside, Calif. (P.) b. Portsmouth, Ohio, Apr. 12, 1882. Pupil of Mills College; Jean Manhaim. Member: Laguna Beach AA; Calif. AC. Awards: second prize, Riverside Co. Fair, 1914; first prize, Southern Calif. Fair, 1920; second prize, 1921; first prize, Southern Calif. Fair, 1922 and 1923. Specialty: landscapes and marines.

NOURSE, ELIZABETH, 80 Rue d'Assas, Paris, France (P.) b. Cincinnati, Ohio, 1860. Pupil of Art Academy in Cincinnati; Lefebvre, Henner and Carolus-Duran in Paris. Member: Soc. Nat. des Beaux Arts, 1901; Paris Woman's AAA; NA Women PS (hon.). Awards: medal, Columbian Expo., Chicago, 1893; third-class medal, Inst. de Carthage, Tunis, 1897; first-class gold medal, Nashville, Expo., 1897; silver medal, Paris Expo., 1900; silver medal, St. Louis Expo., 1904; gold medal, Pan.-Pac. Expo., San Francisco, 1915; Laetare medal, Univ., Notre Dame, So. Bend, Ind., 1921. Work: "Closed Shutters," Luxembourg Museum, Paris; "Peasant Woman of Borst" and "First Communion," Cincinnati Museum; "Twilight," Toledo Museum; "Happy Days," Detroit Institute; "Mother and Children," Art Institute, Chicago; "Fisher Girl of Picardy," National Gallery, Washington; "Under the Trees," Nebraska Museum; "Summer," Museum, Adelaide, Australia; "Summer Hours," Museum, Newark, N. J.

NOWOTTNY, VINCENT* (P. T.) b. Mt. Vernon, Ohio, 1854; killed in runaway accident, Alderson, W. Va., Oct. 21, 1908. Studied at Munich, 1881-'85. Member of CAA faculty many years.

NUNAMAKER, KENNETH R., Center Bridge, Pa. (Ldscp. P.) b. Akron, Ohio. Exhibited, NAD, 1925.

NUSE, ROY CLEVELAND, Rushland, Pa. (P. T.) b. Springfield, Ohio, Feb. 23, 1885. Pupil of Duveneck; Cin. AA; PAFA. Awards: Cresson European scholarship, PAFA, 1918; second Cresson, first Toppan and first Thouron prizes, PAFA, 1918; medal. Phila. Sketch C., 1921. Represented in collection of Beaver College, Pa. Director of Beachwood School of Fine Arts, Jenkintown, Pa.

OAKES, WILBUR L., 1464 Lincoln Ave., Lakewood, Cleveland, Ohio (P.) b. Cleveland, Dec. 1, 1876. Pupil of F. C. Gottwald; A. T. Hibbard at Rockport, Mass; Cleveland School of Art. Member: Cleveland SA.

O'MEARA, JEAN COLLOW (MRS. JOSEPH, JR.), 1915 Clarion Ave., Evanston, Ind. (P.) Studied Cin. AA; Paris. Member: Cin WAC.

ORR, J. E.* (P.) b. Cincinnati, Ohio, Oct. 26, 1867; d. Columbus, Oct. 26, 1921. President PPC for five years. Promoter of art activities. Work: water color.

OSBORNE, CAROLINE MARGARET, 1906 7. 105th St., Cleveland, Ohio (P.) b. Florence, Erie County. Art training in Paris. Work: landscape, Italy, Switzerland, Brittany, United States. Exhibited, Paris Salon. Graduate of Lake Erie College, Painesville.

OSGOOD, ADELAIDE HARRIETT* (China P.) b. Columbus, Ohio, 1842; d. New York, Nov. 26, 1910. Founded Osgood Art School (1878) in New York, first school outside of a factory in which decorative china painting was taught.

OSGOOD, LAURA HOWE, Dayton, Ohio (C.) Ceramist. Pottery with crystal glaze.

OPPER, FREDERICK BURR, 62 Circuit Rd., New Rochelle, N. Y. (News A. W.) b. Madison, Lake Co., Ohio, Jan. 2, 1857. On art staff, *Frank Leslie's,* 3 years; *Puck,* 18 years; *Hearst's* since 1899. Illustrator for Bill Nye, Mark Twain, Hobart (Dinkelspiel), Dunne (Dooley). Author: "The Folks in Funnyville," and other verses. Member: Players' Club.

OSTHAUS, EDMUND* (P.) b. Hildesheim, Germany; d. Jan. 30, 1928, Marianna, Jackson Co., Fla. Home, Toledo, Ohio, and Los Angeles. Educated at Josephinum Gymnasium, Hildesheim; Royal Acad. of Arts, Düsseldorf. Came to Toledo, 1883. Specialty of hunting dogs.

OUTCAULT, RICHARD F.* (News A.) b. Lancaster, Ohio, Jan. 4, 1863; d. Flushing, L. I., N. Y., Sept. 25, 1928. Studied McMicken School of Design. 1895 made "Hogan's Alley" for *N. Y. Sunday World.* "Yellow Kid," "Buster Brown," "Pore Lil Mose," followed.

PACKARD, FRANK L.* (Arch.) FAIA. b. 1866, Delaware, Ohio; d. Oct. 26, 1923, Columbus. Chosen by President Harding as his representative in the purchase of the site, the designing, and construction of the Embassy Bldg., at Rio de Janeiro. Work: Girls' Industrial School, Delaware; Capitol Annex, Charleston, W. Va.; Columbus Savings and Trust Co., Huntington National Bank; Memorial Hall, Elks' Club, Columbus Club, Columbus and Aladdin Clubs, Columbus.

PALMER, E. W., 1905 East 71st St., Cleveland, Ohio (P.) b. Cleveland. Work: black and white, animals, oil, water color. Member: Cleveland Art Club.

PALMER, HATTIE VIRGINIA YOUNG (MRS. C. F. PALMER), 2616 Albany St., Houston, Texas (P. T.) b. Ripley, Ohio. Pupil of the Cincinnati Art Academy. Member: Houston AL; Ind. AA; Ind. State Ceramic C; Texas FAA; Am. APL; SSAL.

PARKHURST, THOMAS SHREWSBURY* (Ldscp. P. I.) b. Aug. 1, 1853, Manchester, Eng.; d. 1923, Carmel-by-the-Sea, Calif. Member: Toledo Tile Club; Salma. C.; Nat'l Arts Club; Lima Art Lg.; Des Moines AC; Oklahoma A. Lg. Works: "October Skies," "The Spirit of the Maumee," Toledo Mus.; "Landscape," Grand Rapids Art Asso.; "Chariot of the Sky," Oakland, Calif. Art Museum.

PATTON, ROY EDWIN, 131 West 18th St., Erie, Pa. (P. E. L. T.) b. Springfield, Ohio, Apr. 7, 1878. Pupil of Catlin, Erickson, Cross. Member: Erie AC; Fine Art Palette C.

PAULDING, JOHN, 1600 Monroe Bldg., 104 South Michigan Ave., Chicago, Ill.; h. Park Ridge, Ill. (S.) b. Darke County, Ohio, Apr. 5, 1883. Pupil of AIC. Member: Alumni AIC; Chicago Gal. A.; Cliff Dwellers; Chicago PS.

PAYANT, FELIX, Fine Arts Dept., Ohio State University, Columbus (D. T.) b. Faribault, Minn., Apr. 10, 1891. Studied Columbia Univ., Pratt Inst., CAA. Work: design, editor of *Design.* Member: CAL.

PAYNE, EMMA LANE, Studio Stop, 14 R.F.D., Euclid, Ohio (P. L. T.) b. Canada, May 5, 1874. Pupil of F. C. Gottwald; Leonard Ochtman. Member: Cleveland WAC; Cleveland SA.

PEETS, ORVILLE HOUGHTON, 683 Lake View Road, Cleveland, Ohio; Woodstock, N. Y. (P. E.) b. Cleveland, Aug. 13, 1884. Pupil of Baschet and Laurens in Paris. Member: Salma. C. Award: hon. men., Paris Salon, 1914. Painting owned by French Government in the Luxembourg, Paris; represented in the Hispanic Museum, New York; and by etchings and woodcuts in Museum of Art, Cleveland.

PEIXOTTO, GEORGE, The Chatlet, Crestwood, Westchester Co., New York; summer, Martha's Vineyard, Mass. (P.) b. Cleveland, Ohio. Pupil of Meissonier and Munkacsy. Member: Société des Artistes Français. Award: silver medal, Royal Academy, Dresden. Represented in Eastnor Castle, Eng.; Corcoran Gallery, Washington, D. C.; Widener

Memorial Library, Harvard University; murals in New Amsterdam Theatre, and Park National Bank, New York.

PEPPARD, MISS LORENA, 449 N. Buckeye St., Wooster, Ohio (P.) Studied Oberlin College; Cin. AA under Nowottny, Meakin, Noble and Duveneck; Boston Museum under Philip Hale. Exhibited Cincinnati WAC, Cincinnati Art Museum, Akron Art Institute, AS Min. P. Work: portraits and miniatures scattered over Ohio, Kentucky, New York, Massachusetts; landscapes; portraits of Wayne County Judges, Courthouse, Wooster, Ohio. Pottery decorations.

PERDUE, W. K., 2915 Tenth St., N.W., Canton, Ohio (P. C. W.) b. Minerva, Ohio, May 17, 1884. Pupil of Dr. Esenwein.

PERIN, GAIL D., 765 Ridgeway Avenue, Avondale, Cincinnati, Ohio (P.) Member: Cin. WAC.

PFEIFFER, PHILIP* (Arch.) b. Germany, 1860; came to Cincinnati, 1885; d. July 4, 1925, Cincinnati, Ohio.

PFENNINGER, ANNA, 11705 Detroit Ave., Cleveland, Ohio (S.) Studied Cleveland Art School. Work: portrait bust of Lincoln, "The Modern David."

PHILBIN, CLARA, 2126 Auburn Ave., Mt. Auburn, Cincinnati, Ohio (S.) Pupil of Barnhorn. Member: Cin. WAC.

PHILLIPS, CLARENCE COLES* (I.) b. 1880, Springfield, Ohio; d. June 12, 1927, New Rochelle, N. Y. Pupil of Chase Art School. Member: New Rochelle AA; GFLA; Author's Lg. of Am. Work: designs for magazine covers, depicting young women of extraordinary beauty. Illustrated: *Saturday Evening Post; Good Housekeeping; Ladies' Home Journal; Life; Liberty; McCall's; Woman's Home Companion.*

PICKARD, THOMAS W., 106 Nelson Road, Columbus, Ohio (P.) b. 1866, Guelph, Ontario. Work: oil landscape. Member: PPC, CAL.

PICKERING, ERNEST, University of Cincinnati, Cincinnati, Ohio (C.) Formerly at University, Urbana, Ill. Work: wook blocks.

PIERSCHE, JOHN J.* (P.) b. Columbus, Ohio, 1861; d. Columbus, 1921. Wood carver. Taught art in North High School, Columbus. Work: pastel and crayon portraits.

PITKIN, WILLIAM, JR., 3866 Carnegie Ave., Cleveland, Ohio (Ldscp. Arch.) b. Rochester, N. Y., June 3, 1884. Studied Cornell Univ.; Gardens of England, France, Italy. Work: campus plans, colleges, Univ. of Michigan, Wooster College, Western Reserve, etc.; country estates, large residential real estate projects.

POND, THEODORE HANFORD, Akron Art Institute, Akron, Ohio (P. C. W. L. T.) b. Beirut, Syria, Sept. 27, 1873. Graduate of Pratt Institute. Member: Boston SAC; Alliance; Am. Assoc. of Museums; Asso. of Art Museum Directors; AFA; College AA. Director, Akron Art Inst.

PORTER, W. T.* (P.) In Cincinnati, Ohio c. 1870. Pupil of Isherwood, scenic painter, N. Y. Work: panorama of "Fairyland." Scenic painter of Pike's Theatre.

POTTHAST, EDWARD HENRY* (Ldscp. P.) b. Cincinnati, Ohio, 1857; d. 1927. Studied Cin. AA; Antwerp, Munich, Paris. Awards: Clark prize, NA, 1899; silver medal, St. Louis, 1904; medal, San Francisco, 1915. Member: NA, 1906; Nat. Inst. AL. Work: "Dutch Interior," Cincinnati Mus.; specialty of seaside pictures; "A Holiday," AIC; "A Day at the Seashore," "Sunlight and Shadow," "Grand Canyon," "A Happy Day," "Gloucester Harbor."

POWELL, ARTHUR J. E., 59 East 59th St., New York, N. Y. (P.) b. Vanwert, Ohio, Dec. 11, 1864. Pupil of San Francisco School of Design; St. Louis School of Fine Arts; Julian Academy, Toulouse and Ferrier in Paris. Member: ANA, 1921; Salma. C., 1904; Paris AAA; A. Fund S.; Allied AA; NAC (life); NYWCC. Awards: Vezin prize ($100), Salma. C., 1913; Ranger Purchase prize, NAD, 1921.

POWELL, WILLIAM H.* (P.) b. New York State. In Cincinnati, Ohio, 1833-'45; d. 1879. Studied with Henry Inman; Paris; Rome. Represented: "De Soto Discovering the Mississippi," Capitol, Washington, D. C.; "The Battle of Lake Erie," Capitol, Columbus, Ohio. Elected, ANA, 1879.

POWERS, HIRAM* (S.) b. July 29, 1805, Woodstock, Vt.; d. Florence, Italy, June 27, 1873. Studied with Eckstein, Cincinnati; Florence; Rome. Work: "The Greek Slave," Corcoran Gallery, Washington, D. C.; "Eve Disconsolate," "Evangeline," Cin. Mus.; "Fisher Boy," "California," Metro. Mus., N. Y.; "Proserpine," Pa. Acad., Philadelphia; "Webster," Boston.

PRASUHN, JOHN G., 1308 Hiatt St., Indianapolis, Ind. (S.) b. Versailles, Ohio, Dec. 25, 1877. Pupil Chicago Art Institute under Lorado Taft and Charles J. Mulligan. Member: Chicago Civic Club; SS of Indiana. Represented: "Classic Music of Time," Music Group on Pavilion, in Lincoln Park, Chicago; "Lions," on the Taft Columbus Memorial Monument, Washington, D. C.

PRICE, MARGARET EVANS, 16304 Clifton Blvd., Cleveland, Ohio (P. I.) b. Chicago, 1888. Pupil of Mass. Normal Art School. Work: illustrates children's books.

PUGH, ELIZABETH WORTHINGTON (MRS. A. H.), 1820 Dexter Ave., Walnut Hills, Cincinnati, Ohio (P. C.) Member: Cin. WAC.

QUINN, JOHN* (Art Patron). b. Tiffin, Ohio, 1870; d. New York, 1924. Conducted campaign which resulted in the removal of all duty on modern works of art brought into this country, and was one of the organizers of the international exhibition of modern art held in 1913. Elected Honorary Fellow for life of the Metropolitan Museum in recognition of his services in the cause of free art.

RACHLE, GEORGE* (S.) d. Cleveland, Ohio, 1909. Work: Centaur fountain, now destroyed, in Wade Park, Cleveland.

RADTKE, LUCY, Anna Louise Inn, Cincinnati, Ohio (P. C.) Studied Cin. AA. Work: batiks, still life. Member: Cin. WAC.

RAHMING, NORRIS, 3226 Euclid Ave., Cleveland, Ohio (P.) b. New York City, May 1, 1886. Studied Cleveland School of Art; New York; Paris. Work: oil and water color landscape; Newark, N. J., Muesum; Cleveland Museum; Midday Club, Cleveland. Prizes received at Cleveland annual show. Exhibited at Toledo, St. Louis, Boston, Newark, N. J., Museums. Member: Cleveland Society of Artists.

RANDOLPH, LEE F., care Calif. School of Fine Arts, San Francisco, Calif. (P. E. Ldscp. Arch.) b. Ravenna, Ohio, June 3, 1880. Pupil of Cin. AA; ASL of NY under Cox; École des Beaux Arts and Julian Academy, in Paris. Member: Chicago SE; Calif. SE; San Francisco AA. Awards: bronze medal for painting, San Francisco AA, 1919. Work in Luxembourg, Paris. Director, California School of Fine Arts.

RANNELLS, WILL, 57 Lexington Ave., Columbus, Ohio (P. L. T.) b. Caldwell, Ohio, July 21, 1892. Pupil of Cin. AA. Member: FGLA. Work: cover designs and illustrations for *Life, Judge, Country Gentleman, Farm and Fireside, McClure's, Outing, Sportsmen's Digest,* and *The People's Home Journal;* calendar designs and backs for Congress playing cards. Illustrated: *Dog Stars.* Specializes in portraits of dogs. Instructor, Dept. of Fine Arts, Ohio State University.

RANSOME, CAROLINE L.* (Port. P.) b. Newark; resided in Cleveland; d. Washington, D. C., 1909. Studied with Durand, N. Y.; Kaulbach, Munich. Work: portrait of Joshua R. Giddings, first work of art, by a woman, purchased by the United States Government, hangs in House of Representatives, Washington; portraits of Governors Brough and Jacob D. Cox, in State House, Columbus. Other portraits: President Garfield, Salmon P. Chase, Alexander Hamilton.

RAPP, GEORGE W.* (Arch.) FAIA. d. Jan. 10, 1918, Cincinnati, Ohio.

RAYMOND, GRACE RUSSELL, 923 Mansfield Street, Winfield, Kan.; Piazza Monte d'Oro 29, Rome, Italy (P. T.) b. Mt. Vernon, Ohio, May 1, 1877. Pupil of AIC; School of Applied Design, New York; Corcoran School, Washington; studied in Paris and Rome. Member: Wash. WCC; AFA. Instructor, drawing and painting, Southwestern College, Winfield, Kan.

REAM, CARDUCIUS P.* (P.) b. Lancaster, Ohio, 1837; d. Chicago, June 20, 1917. Studied in Europe. Represented in AIC.

REASER, WILBUR AARON, 15 Arden Place, Yonkers, N. Y. (P. L.) b. Hickville, Ohio, December 25, 1860. Pupil of Mark Hopkins Inst. in San Francisco; Constant and Lefebvre in Paris. Member: San Francisco AA. Awards: gold and silver medals, Calif. Expo., 1894; first Hallgarten prize, NAD, 1897. Specialty: portraits. Work: "Mother and Daughter," Carnegie Gallery, Pittsburgh; "Old Man and Sleeping Child," Art Gallery, Des Moines, Iowa; portraits of Senator W. B. Allison, U. S. Senate Lobby, Washington; Senator C. S. Page, the Capitol, Montpelier, Vt.; Senator N. B. Scott, the Capitol, Charleston, W. Va.; Bishop Lewis, State Historical Society, Des Moines, Iowa.

REBECK, STEVEN AUGUST, 1028 Roanoke Rd., Cleveland Heights, Ohio (S.) b. Cleveland, May 25, 1891. Pupil of Karl Bitter, Carl Heber, Cleveland School of Art, Herman Matzen. Member: Cleveland Sculpture Soc.; Cleveland SA; NSS (assoc.). Awards: medal for portrait bust, Cleveland Museum of Art, 1922; award for sculpture, Cleveland Museum, 1923. Work: "Shakespeare," Cleveland, Ohio; Soldiers' Memorial, Alliance, Ohio; heroic statue, "Sphinx," Civil Courthouse, St. Louis, Mo.

REBISSO, LOUIS T.* (S. T.) b. Italy, 1837; d. May 3, 1899, Cincinnati, Ohio. Work: "Gen. Grant," Chicago; "Gen. McPherson," Wash.; "Pres. Harrison," Cincinnati. Instructor, Cin. AA.

REDETTE, BOYD M.* (P.) b. Feb. 16, 1885, Fredericksburg, Ohio; d. Oct. 27, 1918, Philadelphia, Pa. Exhibited: Middle-West show, Denver, Colo., received hon. men. Member: PPC of Columbus; NYWCC. Worked on *Columbus Dispatch*.

REEDER, LYDIA MORROW (MRS. C. W.), 412 W. 9th Ave., Columbus, Ohio (P.) b. Martinsville, Ohio, Apr. 14, 1885. Studied Columbus Art School; Ohio State University; AIC; with Alice Schille, Chas. Hawthorne, Jas. R. Hopkins, Leopold Seyffert; M.A. Ohio State University. Member: CAL; Ohio WCS. Work: water color and oil.

REECE, JANE, Dayton, Ohio (C.) Artistic photography. Exhibited all parts of United States and Europe.

REID, THOMAS BUCHANAN* (P.) b. Chester County, Pa., 1822. In Cincinnati, Ohio, 1838. Work: "Longfellow's Children," "Milton Dictating Paradise Lost." Poet, author of "Sheridan's Ride."

REILLY, JOHN, 131 East 3rd Street, Cincinnati, Ohio (P.) Member: Valley of the Moon SP. Coterie sent exhibition to Evanston, Ill.

RETTIG, JOHN* b. 1859, Cincinnati, Ohio; d. May 1, 1932, Cincinnati. Pupil of CAA, Duveneck, Potthast; Collin, Courtois, and Prinet in Paris. Member: Salma. C.; Cincinnati AC (hon.); AFA. Work: "The Sick Doll," "The Sisters," "Old Dutch Kitchen," and many scenes of Holland. Director of pageants.

RETTIG, MARTIN, 127 East 3rd Street; h. 110 Findlay Street, Cincinnati, Ohio (P.) b. Cincinnati. Pupil of Frank Duveneck. Member: Cin. AC. Considered a Duveneck expert.

REYNOLDS, HARRY REUBEN, Utah Agricultural College, Logan, Utah (P. C. L. T.) b. Centerburg, Ohio, Jan. 29, 1898. Pupil of AIC; Lee Randolph, Birger Sandzen. Member: Oakland AL; Alumni AIC; Delta Phi Delta. Award: Harper Brothers' gold medal, AIC, 1923.

REYNOLDS, RICHARD* (P.) b. 1827, England; d. Jan., 1918, Cincinnati, Ohio. Came to America when young man. Descendant of Sir Joshua Reynolds.

RHEAD, LOIS WHITCOMB, 504 College St., E. Liverpool, Ohio; summer, Santa Barbara, Calif. (S. C.) b. Chicago, Ill., Jan. 16, 1897. Pupil of F. H. Rhead; L. V. Solon. Member: NA Women PS; Amer. Ceramic S.

RICHARDSON, JOHN NEWTON* (Arch.) FAIA. b. Perth, Scotland, Feb. 28, 1837; d. Cleveland, Ohio, May 6, 1902. Designed many Cleveland buildings; Masonic Temple, Scottish Rite Cathedral, Jewish Orphan Asylum, St. John's Church.

RITTER, LOUIS* (P.) d. after 1883. Cleveland painter; one of "Duveneck Boys."

ROBINSON, ALICE, 1607 Perry St., Columbus, Ohio (P. T.) b. Congruity, Pa. Studied CAA; ASL of NY; B.S. degree at Columbia Univ.; with Chas. Hawthorne, Frank Swift Chase, Henry Snell. Work: landscape. Member: CAL; Ohio WCS. Associate Professor, Ohio State Univ., Dept. of Fine Arts.

ROBERTSON, MABELLE FISHWICK (MRS. H. G.), Western Ave. and Park, Amer. Univ. Park, N.W., Washington, D. C. (C.) Work: metal, copper. Member: Cin. WAC.

ROCHE, MARTIN* (Arch.) b. 1853, Ohio; d. June 5, 1927, Chicago. Member of firm Holabrook & Roche, who originated the skeleton steel-frame type of skyscraper office building. FAIA, 1889. Work: Soldiers' Field Stadium, Chicago.

ROCKHILL, MRS. CHAS., 2334 Upland Place, Hyde Park, Cincinnati, Ohio (W.) Organized joint exhibitions of men and women's art clubs.

ROGERS, REBECCA* (P.) Resident of Dayton, Ohio, about 1880. Decorative flower studies.

ROGERS, WILLIAM ALLEN, 3331 P St., N.W., Washington, D. C. (I.News A.) b. Springfield, Ohio, May 23, 1854. Illustrator and cartoonist for *Daily Graphic*, N. Y., 1873-77, later for *Harper's Weekly, Harper's Magazine, Life, St. Nicholas, Century*. Decorated Chevalier Legion of Honor of France for war cartoons. Member: SI; Century Asso.

ROSEN, CHARLES, Woodstock, N. Y. (P.) Teacher at Columbus Art School several years. b. Westmoreland Co., Pa., Apr. 28, 1878. Pupil NAD; NY School of Art; Chase, Du Mond, F. C. Jones. Member: ANA, 1912; NA, 1917; Salma. C.; NAC. Awards: third Hallgarten prize, NAD, 1910; first Hallgarten prize, NAD, 1912; Shaw purchase prize, Salma. C., 1914; hon. men., CI, Pittsburgh, 1914; silver medal, San Francisco, 1915; Inness gold medal, NAD, 1916; Altman prize, NAD, 1916; first prize, CAL, 1925; Sesnan gold medal, PAFA, 1926. Work: "Washed-Out Bottom Lands," Minn. S. of FA; "Late Sunlight," Duluth FAA; "Frozen River," Delgado Museum, New Orleans; "Winter Sunlight," Butler AI, Youngstown, Ohio; "North Haven," St. Louis; "Ice-Bound Coast," Univ. of Mich., Ann Arbor.

ROSENTHAL, DAVID, 30 Hurbert Block, Cincinnati, Ohio (P. I.) b. Cincinnati, 1876. Studied in Italy.

RORIMER, LOUIS, 2232 Euclid Ave., Cleveland, Ohio (T. C.) b. Cleveland, Sept. 12, 1872. Studied: Munich; Julian Academy, Paris. Taught design in Cleveland School of Art eighteen years. Interior decorator under firm name of Rorimer-Brooks. Member: Salma. C.; Rowfant Club, Cleveland.

ROSS, DENMAN WALDO, 24 Craigie St., Cambridge, Mass. (P. W. L. T.) b. Cincinnati, Ohio, Jan. 10, 1853. Member: Copley S., 1892; Boston SAC (life); AFA; Boston S. Arch.; Arch. C.; Fellow Am. Acad. AL. Trustee, Museum of Fine Arts, Boston. Lecturer on "Theory of Design," at Harvard Univ.

ROSTAING, AUGUSTUS.* Flourished in Cincinnati, Ohio, *c.* 1835. Cameo cutter.

ROYER, JACOB, Dayton, Ohio (Ldscp. P.) b. Dayton. Self-taught.

RUSSELL, MARK, Columbus Art School, Columbus, Ohio (P. T.) Studied with Barnitz at Wittenburg; with Kenyon Cox and Fawcett, ASL of NY. Member: Columbus AL. Work: with newspaper syndicate; commercial designing; instructor of art in Columbus High School of Commerce; instructor, Columbus Art School.

RUTHRAUFF, FREDERICK G., 2586 Polk Ave., Ogden, Utah (P. W.) b. Findlay, Ohio, Aug. 6, 1878. Pupil of William V. Cahill, William H. Clapp, Henri Morrisett in Paris. Member: Berkeley LFA; Calif. AC; Ogden AS.

RYDEN, HENNING, 47 Fifth Ave., New York, N. Y.; 93 West Duncan St., Columbus, Ohio (S. D. P.) b. in Sweden, Jan. 21, 1869. Pupil of AIC; studied in Berlin and London. Member: Salma. C., 1908; AFA. Award: hon. men., Pan.-Pac. Expo., San Francisco, 1915. Work: American Numismatic Society.

SARGEANT, CLARA McCLEAN, 2258 Euclid Ave., Cleveland, Ohio; 15706 Grovewood Ave., Northeast, Cleveland, Ohio (P.) b. Washington, Iowa, June 24, 1889. Pupil of Cleveland School of Art; ASL of NY; Corcoran School, Washington, D. C. Member: Woman's AC, Cleveland. Awards: third portrait prize, 1922, and hon. men., 1924-1928, Cleveland MA.

SAUER, LeRoy D., Mutual Home Bldg.; h. 506 Volusia Ave., Dayton, Ohio (E. C. T.) b. Dayton, Feb. 17, 1894. Pupil of Peixotto, Hopkins, Meakin, Wessel, Keller, Orr, Lachman. Member: Dayton SE; Dayton GFA.

SAVILLE, BRUCE WILDER, 185 Sixth Ave., New York, N. Y. (S. T.) b. Quincy, Mass., Mar. 16, 1893. Four years in Columbus, Ohio. Pupil of Boston Normal Art School under Dallin; Mr. and Mrs. Kitson. Member: Copley S.; Boston AL; Boston AC; NSS; NY Arch. Lg.; NAC; AFA. Work: World War Memorial, Ravenna, Ohio; Peace Memorial, State House Yard, Columbus; Mack Memorial, Ohio State University, Columbus; Ohio State War Memorial, Columbus; three panels Jeffrey Mfg. Co., office, Columbus; Anthony Wayne Memorial, Toledo; John and John Quincy Adams Memorial, Wollaston, Mass.

SCHAEFER, MARTHA WILBY (MRS. H. FREDERICK), 2145 Luray Ave., Walnut Hills, Cincinnati, Ohio (P.) Work: portraits. Member: Cin. WAC.

SCHAUER, MARTHA K., 356 Kenilworth Ave., Dayton, Ohio (P. W. L. T.) b. Troy, Ohio, Feb. 13, 1889. Pupil of Pratt Inst.; Columbia Univ. Member: Ohio WCS; Ohio-Born WP. Specialty: flower studies and still life in water color. Head of Art Dept., Stivers High School, Dayton.

SCHEIBNER, VIRA McILRATH (MRS.) 20 Aviles Street, St. Augustine, Fla. (P.) b. Cleveland, Ohio, Aug. 12, 1889. Pupil of Robert Spencer; Charles Rosen; Edouard van Waeyenberger in England. Member: Fellowship PAFA; NA Women PS.

SCHELL, C. G., 780 Jager St., Columbus, Ohio (P.) b. Jan. 15, 1877, Stuttgart, Germany. Work: theatre scenes. Member: PPC.

SCHEVILL, WILLIAM V., 319 East 57th St., New York, N. Y. (Port. P.). b. Cincinnati, Ohio, Mar. 2, 1864. Pupil of Loefftz, Lindenscmidtt and Gysis, in Munich. Member: Century Assoc.; Salma. C.; Kuenstler Genossenschaft; St. Louis GA; AFA. Award: bronze medal, St. Louis Expo., 1904. Work: "In Love," Cincinnati Mus.; portrait sketch, Prince Henry of Prussia, Herron Art Institute, Indianapolis: Leipsic Art Museum; portrait of Chancellor Hall, and Judge Hitchcock, Washington University, St. Louis; portrait of Ex-president Taft, War Dept., Washington, D. C., and St. Louis Art Museum.

SCHILLE, ALICE, 1166 Bryden Road, Columbus, Ohio (P.) Pupil of Columbus Art School; ASL of NY, and NY School of Art under Chase and Cox; Prinet, Collin, Courtois and Colarossi Academy in Paris. Member: AWCS (assoc.); NYWCC; Boston WCC; NA Women PS; Chicago WCC; Phila. WCC. Awards: Corcoran prize, Washington WCC, 1908; NY Woman's AC prize, 1908 and 1909; participant Fine Arts Bldg. prize, SWA, 1913; gold medal for water colors, Pan.-Pac. Expo., San Francisco, 1915; Phila. water color prize, PAFA, 1915; first prize ($200), Columbus AL, 1919; Stevens prize, Columbus Art Lg., 1920; Fine Arts prize, NA Women PS, 1929. Work: "The

Melon Market," Herron Art Institute, Indianapolis; "Mother and Child," Philadelphia AC; "The Market Place," Columbus Gallery of Fine Arts.

SCHMIDT, CARL, Silvermine, Norwalk, Conn. (P.) b. Warren, Ohio, May 6, 1889. Pupil of NAD under Carlsen; and in Florence, Italy. Work: "The Mill," Butler Art Inst.; mural, "The Nativity."

SCHMIDT, KATHERINE (MRS. YASUS KUNIYOSHI), 106 Columbia Heights, Brooklyn, N. Y.; summer, Ogunquit, Me. (P.) b. Xenia, Ohio, Aug. 15, 1898. Pupil of K. H. Miller. Member: Salons of America; Brooklyn Soc. Modern Art. Work: modernistic exhibit, Daniel Gallery, N. Y.

SCHNEIDER, ARTHUR* (P.) Flourished in Cleveland, Ohio c. 1880. Work: scenes of North Africa. Member: old Cleveland AC.

SCHREIBER, ANNA SCHILLING, 694 Park St., S., Columbus, Ohio (P.) b. Columbus, Oct. 10, 1877. Studied Columbus Art School; Miss Klippart; Mrs. Obetz; Ohio State Univ. Work: water color, oil, crafts, batiks, advertising, etc. Awards: H. M. CAL. Member: CAL; WAA. Conducts private summer school of art.

SCHUBERT, ORLANDO V.* (P.) d. Dec., 1928, St. Petersburg, Fla., aged 84 yrs. Studied with C. Schwerdt, Cleveland; worked in Cleveland at lithography and painting marines.

SCHWAB, EDITH FISHER (MRS. C.), 310 Prospect St., New Haven, Conn (P.) b. Cincinnati, Ohio, 1862. Member: NA Women PS.

SCHWARTZKOPF, EARL C., care of Willys-Overland Co., Toledo, Ohio (P. I.) b. in Ohio, 1888. Member: Toledo Tile Club.

SCHWILL, WILLIAM* (Port. P.) b. Clifton, Cincinnati, Ohio, c. 1860. Studied with Carl Marr, Munich.

SCHOFIELD, LEVI TUCKER* (S. Arch.) b. Cleveland, Ohio, Nov. 9, 1842; d. Feb. 25, 1917, Cleveland. Studied, Cincinnati. Member: Cleveland Chapter AIA; NY Arch. Lg. Work: "Our Jewels," State House Yard, Columbus; "Soldiers' and Sailors' Monument," Cleveland.

SCOTT, MRS. JOSEPHINE B., Perrysburg, Ohio (P.) Member: Athena Club, Toledo. Exhibited, World's Fair, Chicago, 1893, three pictures, "Buttonwood Island," "Turkeyfoot Rocks," "Fort Meigs," now in Ohio State Museum, Columbus, Ohio.

SEAVER, HUGH, 11409 Glenwood Ave., Cleveland, Ohio (P. E.) b. Nov. 4, 1896, Cleveland. Graduate of Mass. Inst. of Tech. in architecture. Work: landscape and fishing subjects in oil, water color, etching. Work permanently placed in Cleveland Museum. Awards: etching first prize, 1927; third prize, 1928. Member: Cleveland Soc. A.

SELDEN, MISS DIXIE, No. 5, The Deventer Bldg., 1203 East McMillan St., Walnut Hills, Cincinnati, Ohio (Port. and Ldscp. P., I) b. Cincinnati. Pupil of Cincinnati Art Acad., under Duveneck; W. M. Chase; H. B. Snell. Member: Cin. WAC; NA Women PS; Cin. MacD. S.

SEMON, JOHN* (P.) b. Cleveland, Ohio, Feb. 22, 1852; d. Dec. 18, 1917. Painted landscapes and wood interiors. Became blind at height of career. Member: old Cleveland AC. Work: "Edge of Woods," Cleveland Mus.

SENYARD, GEORGE* (P.) d. Olmstead Falls, Ohio, Jan. 18, 1924. Toured the country with Lincoln, sketching him in the debates with Stephen A. Douglas over the slavery issue.

SEVERANCE, JULIA G., 68 South Professor St., Oberlin, Ohio (S. E.) b. Oberlin, Jan. 11, 1877. Studied ASL of NY; Italy. Work: portrait sculpture, round and low relief; "The Leffingwell Tablet," St. Mary's School, Knoxville, Ill.; "George Frederick Wright," "Cobb Memorial Tablet," "Tablet to Mr. and Mrs. Fenelon B. Rice," "James Ralph Severance Tablet," in Oberlin College Buildings. Member: Cleveland WAC. Etching in Print Depart., Library of Congress.

SHACKELTON, CHAS.* (P.) d. 1921, aged 64 years. Cleveland painter of portraits.

SHAFER, CLAUDE, *Cincinnati Times-Star,* Cincinnati, Ohio (News A.) b. Little Hocking, Washington Co., Ohio, Jan. 7, 1878. Studied Cin. AA. Work has appeared *Cincinnati Post, Cincinnati Enquirer,* and many magazines. Creator of "Old Man Grump," "Dopey Dan," "Tillie Tinkle," "Jasper," and others.

SHALER, FREDERICK R.* (P.) b. Findley, Ohio, Dec. 15, 1880; d. Taormina, Italy, Dec. 27, 1916. Studied with Chase and Du Mond, N. Y. Studio in N. Y.

SHARP, JOSEPH HENRY, winter, Crow Agency, Montana; summer, Taos, N. M.; permanent, 1481 Corson St., Pasadena, Calif. (P. I. T.) b. Bridgeport, Ohio, Sept. 27, 1859. Pupil of Royal Academy in Munich, and under Marr; Julian Academy in Paris, under Laurens and Benjamin-Constant; Veriat in Antwerp; Duveneck in Spain. Member: Cin. AC; Calif. AC; Salma. C.; Taos Soc. of Artists; Calif. PM; AFA. Ten years on faculty, Cincinnati Art Acad. Awards: silver medal, Dept. of Ethnology, Pan-Am. Expo., Buffalo, 1901; first portrait prize, Cincinnati AC, 1901; gold medal, Pan.-Calif. Expo., San Diego, 1915 and 1916. Specialty: types of Indians. Work: "Harvest Dance—Pueblo Indians," "Old Dog-Crow Indian Chief," and "Strikes His Enemy Pretty," Cincinnati Mus.; "Chief Flat Iron," Herron Art Inst., Indianapolis; "The Great Sleep," and nearly one hundred portraits of Indians and Indian pictures, University of California; eleven Indian portraits, Smithsonian Institution, Washington; "1920 Ration Day on the Reservation," "A Young Chief's Mission," Butler Museum, Youngstown; "Voice of the Great Spirit," and fifteen Indian *genre* pictures, Smithsonian Institution, Washington; two Indian portraits, Museum of Sante Fe, N. M.

SHAW, BENJAMIN* Steubenville, Ohio. Painted birds.

SHELTON, DR. VIOLETTA, Groton Bldg., 7th and Race Sts., Cincinnati, Ohio (S.) Work: plastic surgery. Assoc. member Cin. WAC.

SHERMAN, HOYT LEON, 1758 N. High St., Columbus, Ohio (P. E. T.) b. Lafayette, Ala., Nov. 7, 1903. Studied Ohio State University and Europe. Work: painting, etching, lithography, teaching. Member: CAL. Award: CAL black and white prize. Interested in stage design.

SHERROD, NELLE, 215 Main St., Lawrenceburg, Ind. (P.) Member: Cin. WAC.

SHINN, VICTOR* (Ldscp. P.) d. Dayton, Ohio, *c.* 1925. Studied with Mr. Broome; Pratt Inst. Worked in charcoal, pen and ink, water color, oil. Teacher in Brooklyn.

SHIVELY, PAUL, American Express Co., Paris, France (P.) Cleveland artist. Work: water color landscape. Awards: 1925-'26-'27-'29 water-color prizes, Cleveland Show.

SHOKLER, HARRY, 99½ W. 3rd St., New York, N. Y. (P.) b. Cincinnati, Ohio, Apr. 27, 1896. Pupil of Herman Wessel, Daniel Garber, Howard Giles.

SCHULZE, ELIZA J.* (P.) Lived in Circleville, Ohio. b. 1847; d. *c.* 1920, Reading, Pa. Work: collaborated with Mrs. Virginia Jones in illustrating *Nests and Eggs of Birds of Ohio.*

SIBBELL, JOSEPH* (S.) b. Germany; d. July 10, 1907, New York. Worked in Cincinnati, Ohio. Best known work is large statue of St. Patrick, in St. Patrick's Cathedral, N. Y. Number of subordinate statues in that cathedral are his work; made death mask of Archbishop Corrigan.

SIEBENTHALER, GEORGE, 3001 Catalpa Drive, Dayton, Ohio (Ldscp. Arch.) b. Dayton, June 2, 1905. Studied Cornell Univ., and European gardens. Award: annual AIA medal for scholastic record. Member: Dayton AI; Engineers' Club, Dayton; Junior Member, Amer. Society Ldscp. Arch.

SIEBERT, ANNIE WARE SABINE, 182 West 10th Ave., Columbus, Ohio (P.) b. Cambridge, Mass. Studied drawing with Edward Barnard, Boston; oil with Chas W. Hawthorne at Provincetown, Mass.; two years with Jas. R. Hopkins at Ohio State Univ.

Work: miniatures, exhibited in New York with Am. SMP; at Philadelphia with Pa. SMP. Oil paintings exhibited in Columbus. Member: CAL.

SIMMONS, F. W.* (P.) Cleveland painter. Work: portrait of Judge Willis Vickery.

SINDELAR, THOS. A., 15 Maiden Lane, New York (I.) b. Cleveland, Ohio, 1867. Studio in New York for years. Pupil, Mucha, Paris.

SINKS, ALOIS E.* (P. Critic). b. Dayton, Ohio, Oct., 1848; d. Indianapolis, 1881.

SINZ, WALTER A., care of The Cleveland School of Art; h. 6013 Olive Court, Cleveland, Ohio (S. T.) b. Cleveland, July 13, 1881. Pupil of Herman N. Matzen; Landowski in Paris. Member: Cleveland SA; Cleveland SS. Awards: Certificate of Merit, Cleveland Museum, 1922 and 1923. Work: Cleveland 125th Anniversary medal; fountain, Y M.C.A., Cleveland; Cleveland Flower Show medal; sculpture group, St. Luke's Hospital, Cleveland. Instructor in sculpture, Cleveland School of Art. Work: chiefly architectural sculpture.

SITZMAN, EDWARD R., Columbia Securities Bldg., Indianapolis, Ind. (Ldscp. P.) b. Cincinnati, Ohio, 1873. Pupil of Duveneck. Member: Indiana AC.

SLOAN, WILHELMINE, Hotel Wentworth, 59 W. 46th St., New York (P.) b. Jackson, Ohio. Studied CAA; NAD; Pa. Acad., at Chester Springs. Awards: hon. men. CAA; Cin. Women's City Club, 1926. Member: Cin. WAC. Work: specialty of children's portraits; mural in Central Life Insurance Building, Cincinnati.

SLOCUM, ANNETTE M., 250 W. 154th St., New York City (S.) b. Cleveland, Ohio. Studied PAFA. Portraiture specialty.

SLUSSER, JEAN PAUL, 1324 Pontiac St., Ann Arbor, Mich. (P. C. W. T.) b. Wauseon, Ohio, Dec. 15, 1886. Pupil of John F. Carlson, Wm. M. Paxton, Philip Hale, Henry L. McFee. Member: Detroit SAC.

SLUTZ, HELEN BEATRICE, 7320 Paxton Ave., Chicago, Ill.; 1546 North Serrano Ave., Hollywood, Calif. (P.) b. Cleveland, Ohio, Apr. 15, 1886. Pupil of Cleveland School of Art. Member: Calif. S. Min. P.; Artland C. of Los Angeles; AFA.

SMITH, ALLEN, JR.* (P.) Early portrait painter of Cleveland.

SMITH, EDWIN B.* (Port. P.) In Cincinnati, c. 1825.

SMITH, ELIZA LLOYD, 3511 Porter St.; 3702 Macomb St., Washington, D. C.; Bluemont, Va. (P.) b. Urbana, Ohio, July 21, 1872. Pupil of Corcoran Art School, Washington, D. C. Member: Wash. WCC.

SMITH, F. CARL, 217 Oakland Ave., Pasadena, Calif.; summer, Laguna Beach, Calif. (Port. P.) b. Cincinnati, Ohio, Sept. 7, 1868. Pupil of Bouguereau, Ferrier and Constant in Paris. Member: S. Wash. A.; Wash. WCC; Paris AAA; California AC; Pasadena Fine Arts C; Laguna Beach AA (life). Awards: hon. men. for water color, AAS, 1902; second figure prize, Southwest Museum, 1921. Work: portraits of Mrs. Charles W. Fairbanks and Mrs. John Ewing Walker, D.A.R., Continental Hall, Washington; former speaker Joseph Cannon, Public Library, Minneapolis; Samuel P. Langley, Allegheny (Pa.) Observatory; Governor Shafroth, the Capitol, Denver; Governor Willis of Ohio in Capitol, Columbus, and Speaker Clark, the Capitol, Washington, D. C.

SMITH, ISABEL E. (MRS. F. CARL SMITH), 217 Oakland Ave., Pasadena, Calif. (Min. P.) b. Smith's Landing, near Cincinnati, Ohio. Pupil of L'hermitte, Delance and Callott in Paris. Member: Paris Woman's AC; Pasadena Fine Arts C.

SMITH, R. WAY* (P.) Cleveland landscape painter c. 1880. Work in many Cleveland homes.

SMITH, YETEVE, 1262 Eastwood Ave., Columbus, Ohio (P.) b. Columbus. Studied in Germany two years; with Alfredo Galli, N. Y.; Washington Art School, Washington, D. C.; with J. R. Hopkins, Ohio State Univ. Awards: Franz Huntington first prize, 1926; Keith-Albee landscape prize, 1929. Work: portrait, figure, landscape. Dr. John

A. Bownocker, Orton Memorial Library, Columbus; William Williams Mather, Orton Memorial Library, Columbus; "Winners," Townsend Hall, O.S.U., Columbus; two landscapes, Ohio Union, O.S.U., Columbus; Dr. John W. Hoffman, Gray Chapel, Delaware, Ohio. Member: Ohio WCS; CAL; Ohio-Born WP; Altrusa.

SNELL, LULU M., 430 Cordova Place, Toledo, Ohio (P.) Work: children's portraits, etchings.

SNODGRASS, DAVID, 1655 Roxbury Road, Columbus, Ohio (P.) b. Kenton, Ohio, June 10, 1902. Training received Art Inst., Chicago; with Castelucho and Baznansha, Paris. Work: portraits; water color pictures of North Africa. Member: Independent Artists, Paris.

SOMMER, EDWIN G., 2121 East 21st St., h. Elderhood Ave., East Cleveland, Ohio; summer, Route 3, Macedonia, Ohio (P. I. E. C.) b. Roseville, N J., June 29, 1899. Pupil of William Sommer. Member: Kokoon AC. Awards: first prize for illustration, second prize for water color, 1923; and second prize for illustration, 1924, Cleveland Museum of Art. "The Shower," "The Return" and "The Castle on the Moon," Cleveland MA; "The Lost Prince," Cleveland Public Schools; mural decoration in the Embassy Club, Cleveland.

SONNTAG, WILLIAM L.* (Ldscp. P.) b. East Liberty, Pa., 1822; d. 1900, Cincinnati, Ohio. Came to Cincinnati, 1842. Self-taught. Member: NA. Work: Hudson River School type landscape. "Morning in the Alleghenies," "Fog Rising Off Mount Adams," "Spirit of Solitude."

SOTTEK, FRANK, 381 South Detroit Ave., Toledo, Ohio (P. I. E. W.) b. Toledo, Oct. 10, 1874. Member: Artklan; Toledo Federation of Art Societies. Award: first prize, Toledo Fed. of Art Societies, 1924.

SOULE, CHARLES, SR.* (Port P.) b. Freeport, Maine, Sept. 2, 1809; d. Dayton, Ohio, Mar. 30, 1869. Subjects were prominent people of Cincinnati and the West.

SPACKMAN, CYRIL SAUNDERS, 29 Blake Road, East Croydon, Surrey, England (P. E. Arch.) b. Cleveland, Ohio, Aug. 15, 1887. Pupil of Henry A. Keller in Cleveland; King's College Architectural Studio, London. Member: R.S.B.A.; R.S. Min. P.; R.S. of Antiquaries of Ireland; F. S. of Antiquaries of Scotland; F.R.S.A.; So. Eastern Soc. Arch.; AFA; Society Graphic A; Cleveland SA; Chicago SE; Faculty of Arts; AIA; Fellow, Member of Council; Art Advisor of the Inc. Association of Architects and Surveyors. Represented in Cleveland Museum; AIC; Print Room of the British Museum; permanent collection of the City of Hull. Designed medal of Masonic Million Memorial. Art Editor of *The Parthenon*.

SPANGLER, F. M., Montgomery, Ala. (News A.) b. Osborn, Ohio, Mar. 15, 1877. Cartoonist on *Montgomery Advertiser*. Worked in Columbus at Bucher Engraving Co. Member: PPC.

SPENCER, LILY MARTIN* (P.) b. 1822, Exeter, England; resided, Marietta, Ohio, many years; d. May 22, 1901, New York City. Studied Cincinnati. Award: gold medal, Philadedphia Centennial, 1876. Work: "Truth Unveiling Falsehood," "Algeria," portraits of Mrs. Elizabeth Cady Stanton, Mrs. Benj. Harrison, Robert Ingersoll, Grant, Sherman, W. C. Bryant.

SPRINGER, CARL, Brevort, Mich. (P.) b. Fultonham, Ohio, Nov. 4, 1874. Member: ASL of NY; PPC. Awards: prize, Scarab C., Detroit, 1916; hon. men., Ohio State Expo., 1920; first prize, Columbus Art League, 1920; second prize, Columbus Art League, 1924; Pitts Flateau prize, Columbus Art League, 1926. Represented in Gallery of Fine Arts, Columbus.

SQUIRE, MAUD HUNT, Vence, Alpes Maritimes, France (I. E. P.) b. Cincinnati, Ohio. Pupil of Cincinnati AA. Member: NYWCC; Chicago SE; Société du Salon d'Automne, Paris. Work: "Concarneau Fisherman" and "At the Well," Herron Art Institute, Indianapolis; South Kensington Museum, London; Corcoran Gallery, Washington, D. C. Wood-block printing.

STAHL, M. LOUISE, Ohio State University, Athens, Ohio (P.) b. Cincinnati. Pupil of Cin. Art Academy under Meakin and Nowottny; ASL of NY, under Volk, Mowbray and Blum; also of Chase in N. Y. and Spain, and Hawthorne and Webster in Provincetown, Mass.; Gaspard at Taos, N. M. Member: Cincinnati WAC; Provincetown AA; AFA.

STANLEY-BROWN, RUDOLPH, 1899 E. 87th St., Cleveland, Ohio (P.I.E.Arch.T.) b. Mentor, Ohio, Apr. 9, 1889. Pupil of Cleveland School of Arch; École des Beaux Arts, Paris. Member: AIA; S. of Beaux Arts Architects; Cleveland Print C. Represented by etchings in Cleveland Museum of Art and Yale University, New Haven, Conn.

STARR, IDA M. H., Hope House, Easton, Md. (P. W.) b. Cincinnati, Ohio, July 11, 1859. Pupil of Myra Edgerly, Lillian Adams, and Howard Schultze. Member: S Indp. A of New York, Chicago, and Buffalo.

STEMLER, OTTO ADOLPH, 5833 Kennedy Ave., Cincinnati, Ohio (P.) b. Cincinnati, Jan. 30, 1872. Studied Cin. AA. With Standard Pub. Co., Cincinnati, since 1906. All work being reproduced by that company. Specializes in large, colored Biblical pictures and illustrations for Sunday schools. Work: "The Transfiguration," "Jesus and the Nations," "Christ by the Sea," "A Living Sacrifice," "Call to the Disciples."

STEVENS, GEORGE W.* d. Oct. 29, 1926, Toledo, Ohio. Director, Toledo Mus., 1903-1926; president, Asso. Mus. Directors; vice-pres., Faculty of Arts, London. Member: Salma. C.

STEWART, ALEXANDER W.* (Arch.) b. 1867; d. August 13, 1928, Cincinnati, Ohio. Graduate of Kenyon College. Designed number of important buildings in Ohio.

ST. GAUDENS, PAUL, Windsor, Vt. (C.) b. Flint, Ohio, 1900. Studied drawing, ceramics, sculpture, in United States and Europe. Member: SAC, Boston; Society of Ceramic Art, N. Y. Work: pottery, ornamental tiles and panels in Mayan design.

ST. GAUDENS, ANNETTA JOHNSON (MRS. LOUIS ST. GAUDENS), Windsor, Vt. (S.) b. Flint, Ohio, Sept. 11, 1869. Pupil of Columbus Art School; ASL of NY under Twachtman and Saint-Gaudens. Member: NA Women PS. Awards: McMillin prize, NA Women PS, 1913; hon. men. and silver medal, Pan.-Calif. Expo., San Diego, 1915. Work: sculptural pottery, bronze bird bath, Meriden, N. H.

STICKROTH, HARRY IVAN* (P. T.) b. Toledo, Ohio, c. 1890; d. Oct. 17, 1922, Chicago. Art training: Fellow, American Acad. of Rome, three years, 1914-'17; studied NAD. Awards: Lazarus scholarship for mural painting, 1914-'17. Exhibited: NAD, 1912-'13; NYWCC, 1913; Arch. Lg. N. Y., 1920; Toledo Mus.; AIC. Work: mural painting, portraits, etc.; mural, Cunard Bldg., N. Y. (with Barry Faulkner). Instructor, AIC.

STIEN* (Port. P.) d. on way to Europe. Flourished c. 1823, in Steubenville, Ohio.

STILSON, ETHEL M., 1962 East 79th St.; 2259 Cedar Ave., Cleveland, Ohio (P.) Member: NA Women PS; Cleveland WAC.

STOHR, JULIA COLLINS (MRS. PETER C. STOHR), Conifer, Lovell, Me. (P.) b. Toledo, Ohio, Sept. 2, 1866. Pupil of Cooper Union and ASL of NY under Beckwith, Chase, J. Alden Weir, Freer, and W. L. Lathrop, and in Paris. Member: Art Workers' Guild of St. Paul; Minnesota State Art Soc.; Chicago WCC; NA Women PS.

STOLL, ROLF, 1851 Hillside Ave., East Cleveland, Ohio (P.I.T.) b. Heidelberg, Germany, Nov. 11, 1892. Pupil of Académie of Fine Arts in Karlsruhe; Académie of Fine Arts in Stuttgart, Germany. Member: Cleveland SA; Kokoon AC. Awards: first prize, Cleve. MA, 1925; first and second prizes, Cleve. MA, 1926; hon. men. Cleve. MA, 1927. Represented by decorative panels in art, 1927; represented by decorative panels in the Public Library, Cleveland; oil painting, Gallery of Fine Arts, Columbus.

STONER, HARRY, 18 West 37th St., New York, N. Y. (Mural P. I.) b. Springfield, Ohio, Jan. 21, 1880. Member: Arch. Lg. of N. Y.; GFLA. Work: design for glass mosaic curtain, executed by Tiffany Studios for the National Theatre, Mexico City.

STOW, MARIE MARTIN (MRS. B. F.)* (P.) b. Dec. 8, 1831; d. Mar. 5, 1920. Work: portraits; "Garfield."

STREATOR, HAROLD A., Box 345, Morristown, N. J. (P.) b. Cleveland, Ohio. Pupil of ASL of NY. Member: Salma. C., Boston, Mass.

STUBBS, MARY HELEN, 4429 Ellis Ave., Chicago, Ill. (P. I. C. T.) b. Greenville, Ohio, Oct. 31, 1867. Pupil of Cincinnati Art Academy; Julian Academy in Paris. Member: Cincinnati WAC; Cincinnati Ceramic C. Award: hon. men. Columbian Expo., Chicago, 1893.

SULLIVAN, CHARLES* (P.) b. Aug. 16, 1794, Frankfort, Pa.; came to Marietta, Ohio, 1833; d. Nov. 26, 1867, Marietta. Studied with Sully, Philadelphia. Work: landscapes of Georgia and Tennessee; portraits of James K. Polk, Mrs. Polk, Major Gordon; historical views of Marietta, "The Mound Builder Earthworks in 1788."

SVENDSEN, CHARLES C., 555 Elberon Ave., Price Hill, Cincinnati, Ohio (P.) b. Cincinnati, Dec. 7, 1871. Pupil of Bouguereau, Ferrier and Colarossi Academy in Paris. Member: Cincinnati AC. Award: bronze medal, St. Louis Expo., 1904. Specialty: figure and pastoral scenes.

SWAIN, FRANCIS WILLIAM, Southern Railway Bldg.; h. 1028 Underwood Place, Cincinnati, Ohio; summer, 2799 Clay St., San Francisco, Calif. (P. E.) b. Oakland, Calif., Mar. 24, 1892. Pupil of Frank Duveneck and F. Van Sloun. Member: Cincinnati AC; Calif. SE. Work: decoration in Westwood School, Cincinnati.

SWALLEY, JOHN F., 1053 Lincoln Ave., Toledo, Ohio (P. E.) b. Toledo, Sept. 5, 1887. Member: Dayton SE; Toledo Artklan.

SYKES, MRS. ANNIE G., 3007 Vernon Place, Vernonville, Cincinnati, Ohio (P.) b. Brookline, Mass. Pupil of Boston Museum School; Cincinnati Art Academy under Duveneck. Member: Cin. WAC; NA Women PS. Work: water-color fishing villages; Bermuda series.

TAIT, JOHN ROBINSON* (Ldscp. P.) b. Cincinnati, Ohio, Jan. 14, 1834; d. Baltimore, Md., July 29, 1909. Studied, Düsseldorf and Munich. Honorary member Charcoal Club, Baltimore. Award: medals, Cin. Ex., 1871-'72.

TAUSZKY, DAVID ANTHONY, 47 Fifth Avenue, New York, N. Y.; 511 Garfield, S. Pasadena, Calif. (Port. P.) b. Cincinnati, Ohio, Sept. 4, 1878. Pupil of ASL of NY, under Blum; Julian Academy in Paris, under Laurens and Constant. Member: Salma. C., 1907; Allied AA; Laguna AA. Awards: Sargent prize, Art Inst., Pasadena, 1928; first prize, Santa Ana, 1928; first hon. men., Allied AA., 1928; sketch prize, Salma. C., 1929. Work: portrait of Emp. Franz Josef I, Criminal Court, Vienna; portrait of George W. Wingate, Wingate School, New York, N. Y.

TAYLOR, MRS. ALMIRA JEWETT, 331 Bryant Ave., Clifton, Cincinnati, Ohio (P.) Member: Cin. WAC.

TAYLOR, HENRY FITCH* (P.) b. 1853, Cincinnati, Ohio; d. Sept. 10, 1925, Plainfield, N. H. Studied Julian Academy. Originated the Taylor system of organized color.

TAYLOR, JAMES E.* (P.) b. Dec. 12, 1839, Cincinnati, Ohio; d. June 22, 1901, New York. Painted panorama of War of the Revolution, exhibited in West. Settled in New York, 1860. Engaged by Frank Leslie as war correspondent and artist. Painted pictures of Indians after 1867. After 1883, painted water color; illustrated magazines.

TEAL, WILLIAM PATCHELL, 129 Laurel St., Milford, Ohio (T. P.) Studied Cin. AA.

Member: Duveneck Society of P., Cincinnati; Cin. AC. Work placed in Hughes High School, Cincinnati; Walnut Hills High School, Cincinnati.

THEIS, GLADYS HULING, Cincinnati, Ohio (S.) Pupil of C. J. Barnhorn. Work: portrait bust of Barnhorn.

THEISS, JOHN WILLIAM, 29 Glenwood Ave., Springfield, Ohio (P.) b. Zelionople, Pa., Sept. 20, 1863. Pupil of Lorenzo P. Latimer. Work: water-color painter.

THEOBALD, ELISABETH STURTEVANT (MRS. SAMUEL THEOBALD, JR.), 40 Crescent Ave., Arrochar, S. I., New York; 430 East 57th St., New York, N. Y. (S. P.) b. Cleveland, Ohio, July 6, 1876. Pupil of Chase, Mora, Hawthorne, F. C. Gottwald, Herman Matzen. Member: NA Women PS; PS.

THORMANN, JOSEPH* (P.) Flourished in Cleveland, Ohio, c. 1880. Animal painter.

THORNE, ANNA LOUISE, 504 Legrange St., Toledo, Ohio (P. E. W. L.) b. Toledo, Dec. 21, 1878. Pupil of AIC; ASL of NY; Delacluse, M. Castolucio and André L'hôte in Paris. Member: Detroit S Women P; Ohio-Born WP; Athena Soc.; Michigan Acad. of Science; Arts and Letters; Am. APL. Work: landscape, still life, paintings of New Orleans, North Africa.

THORP, FREEMAN (Port. P.) b. Geneva, Ashtabula County, Ohio, 1844. Represented: Governor Trimble, John Sherman, Garfield, in State House, Columbus.

THURBER, CAROLINE (MRS. DEXTER THURBER), 320 Tappan St., Brookline, Mass. (Port. P.) b. Oberlin, Ohio. Studied in Italy, Germany, England, and Paris. Work: portraits for Mt. Holyoke College; Western College for Women, Oxford, Ohio; Oberlin College; Boston University; and the Supreme Courts of Iowa and Rhode Island; portraits of Angelo Patri; Robert Andrews Millikan; Margaret Deland; Dallas Lore Sharp; Dorothy George, and other professional people.

TIDBALL, JOHN SATTERLEE* (P.) b. Washington, D. C., Nov. 17, 1859; d. Columbus, Ohio, Oct. 19, 1920. Son of Gen. John C. Tidball. Came to Columbus, c. 1844; spent remainder of life there. Attended Wm. Blake's school for boys, at Gambier, Ohio; graduated Cornell Univ.; studied Cooper Union, N. Y. Work: pastel, oil, sepia, crayon, water color. Pastel portraits a specialty. Sketches of Virginia. Teacher of drawing at O. S. U., Columbus, nine years.

TIBBITT, RALPH S* (P.) b. 1849; d. Mar. 5, 1930, Sandusky, Ohio. Work: portrait and landscape.

TICE, TEMP., 1652 Bellefontaine St., Indianapolis, Ind. (T. P.) b. Batavia, Ohio. Pupil Indiana Art School under Steele, Forsyth, and Adams. Teacher, Herron Art Institute.

TINNE, MARGARET, 291 Southern Ave., Mt. Auburn, Cincinnati, Ohio (P.) Pupil of Emma Mendenhall. Work: water-color flowers and English baronial halls. Member: Cin. WAC.

TITTLE, WALTER ERNEST, 123 E. 77th St., New York, N. Y.; and 135 S. Light Street, Springfield, Ohio (P. E.) b. Springfield, Oct. 9, 1883. Pupil of Chase, Henri and Mora, in New York. Member: Royal Society of Arts, London, England. Author and illustrator, *Colonial Holidays, The First Nantucket Tea Party,* etc. Etchings in Chicago Art Inst.; Cleveland Art Museum; Library of Congress, and National Gallery, Washington; New York Public Library; Brooklyn Museum; California State Library; British Museum; Victoria and Albert Museum, London; Fitzwilliam Museum, Cambridge, England.

TITUS (MR.) ALME BAXTER, 2924 Juniper St., San Diego, Calif. (P. I. T.) b. Cincinnati, Ohio, Apr. 5, 1883. Pupil of ASL of NY, Harrison, Mora, Bridgman, Du Mond, Chase, San Francisco Inst. Award: silver medal, Pan.-Pac. Expo., San Francisco, 1915.

TODD, CHARLES STEWART, 2513 Park Ave., Cincinnati, Ohio (P.) b. Owensboro, Ky.,

Dec. 16, 1885. Pupil of Cincinnati Art Academy; Albert Herter in New York. Member: Cin. AC; Cin. MacDowell Soc.; Boston SAC. Work: batik hangings.

TOMPKINS, FRANK H.* (P.) b. New York State. Studied with Noble, CAA; ASL of NY; Munich; Paris. Made reputation in Boston with landscapes and portraits. Shot himself. Worked in Cleveland, c. 1890.

TOZZER, A. CLARE, 7342 Lower River Road, Fernbank, Cincinnati, Ohio (C.) At mountain schools, Asheville, N. C. Member: Cin. WAC.

TRADER, EFFIE CORWIN, 3000 Vernon Place, Cincinnati, Ohio (Min. P.) b. Xenia, Ohio, Feb. 18, 1874. Pupil of CAA; with Duveneck; T. Dube, in Paris. Member: Cin. WAC; Cin. MacD. C; Pa. S. of Min. P.; AS of Min. P. Work: large portraits in oil; miniatures on ivory.

TRAVIS, PAUL BOUGH, care of the Cleveland School of Art; h. 1634 Belmar Road, Cleveland, Ohio (P. E. T.) b. Wellsville, Ohio, Jan. 2, 1891. Pupil of H. G. Keller. Awards: first prize and Penton medal, 1921; first prize for etching and for portraiture, 1922; hon. men., water color, 1928; first prize landscape, hon. men., figure and water colors, 1929, Cleveland AA. Work: seven etchings, two lithographs, five drawings, two water colors, Cleveland Museum of Art; lithograph, New York Public Library. In 1929, artist member Dr. Geo. W. Crile, Cleveland Museum of Natural History, African expedition.

TREFETHEN, JESSIE B., 35 South Professor St., Oberlin, Ohio; summer, Trefethen, Me. (P. L. T.) b. Peak's Island, Me. Pupil of Henry McCarter; PAFA. Member: Fellowship PAFA.

TRIPP, B. ASHBURTON, 1921 Guarantee Title Bldg., Cleveland, Ohio (Ldscp. Arch.) b. Schenectady, N. Y., Nov. 15, 1887. Training at Harvard Dept. of Fine Arts. Work: landscape architecture, design, pen technique, water color, decorative maps. Award: first prize architectural rendering, Cleveland Museum. Member: Print Club.

TRUMP, RACHAEL BULLEY (MRS. CHARLES C. TRUMP), 503 Baird Road, Merion, Pa. (P.) b. Canton, Ohio, May 3, 1890. Pupil of Syracuse University. Member: NA Women PS; Phila. Alliance; Plastic C. Work: "Judge Knapp," United States Circuit Court of Appeals, Richmond, Va.

TSCHUDY, HERBERT BOLIVAR, Brooklyn Museum, Brooklyn, N. Y. (P. I.) b. Plattsburg, Ohio, Dec. 28, 1874. Pupil of ASL of NY; Member: Brooklyn Society of Modern Artists; Brooklyn WCC; Phila. WCC; AFA. Work: decorative panels, four water colors in Brooklyn Museum; water color, State Museum, Santa Fe, N. M.

TUTTLE, MAY McARTHUR THOMPSON (P.) b. Hillsboro, Ohio, 1847. Portrait and landscape painter; lecturer on color; author of chronological chart of schools of painting. Portrait of mother at St. Louis Expo., 1904; Prof. Tuttle, Cornell Univ.

TWACHTMAN, JOHN H.* (Ldscp. P. E.) b. Cincinnati, Ohio, Aug. 4, 1853; d. Gloucester, Mass., July, 1902. Studied with Duveneck in Cincinnati, Venice and Florence; Prof. Ludwig Loefftz, Munich; Lefebvre, Boulanger, Julian Acad., Paris. Member: "Ten" Am. Artists. Represented: "The Waterfall," Metropolitan, N. Y.; "The Waterfall," "Normandy River," "Springtime," Cincinnati Museum; "Niagara in Winter," "Yellowstone Park," "Gloucester Harbor."

UHL, S. JEROME* (Port. P.) b. Millersburg, Ohio, 1842; d. Apr. 12, 1916, Cincinnati. Studied with Carlous Duran, Puvis de Chavannes. Exhibited: Paris Salon; Berlin; Vienna. Represented: portraits of President Cleveland, Corcoran Gallery, Washington; Governors Foraker and Pattison, in State House, Columbus; Henry Howe, State Library, Columbus. Member: Salma. C.; WA; WWC.

VAGO, SANDOR, 3920 Euclid Ave., Cleveland, Ohio (P.) b. Mezolaborcz, Hungary, Aug. 8, 1887. Studied Royal Academy, Budapest; Munich. Work: figure composition, portraits, flowers. Represented: Nat'l Salon, Public Buildings, Budapest; Museum, Public Buildings, Cleveland; Bluffton College, Ohio. Awards: hon. men., Budapest; second prize, Cleveland, portraits, flowers. Member: hon. life member, Nat'l Salon, Budapest; Cleveland Soc. of A; S Inde. A.

VAILLANT, LOUIS DAVID, 219 East 61st St., New York, N. Y.; summer, Washington, Conn. (Mural P.) b. Cleveland, Ohio, Dec. 14, 1875. Pupil of ASL of NY, under Mowbray. Member: ASL of NY; N. Y. Arch. Lg., 1902; Mural P., N. Y. Municipal AS; Century Assoc.; Salma. C.; AFA. Award: second Hallgarten prize, NAD, 1910. Work: stained glass windows in meeting house, Ethical Culture Society, New York; ceiling decoration, First National Bank, Titusville, Pa.

VALENTIEN, ANNA M. (MRS. A. R. VALENTIEN), 3903 Georgia St., San Diego, Calif. (S. Potter I.) b. Cincinnati, Ohio, Feb. 27, 1862. Pupil of Cincinnati Art Academy, under Rebisso; Rodin, Injalbert and Bourdelle, in Paris. Member: San Diego AG; San Diego FAS; La Jolla AA. Awards: gold medal, Atlanta Expo., 1895; collaborative gold medal, Pan.-Calif. Expo., San Diego, 1915; two gold medals, Pan.-Calif. Expo., San Diego, 1916; highest award and cash prize, Sacramento State Fair, 1919.

VALENTINE, ALBERT R.* (P. Potter) b. May 11, 1862, Cincinnati, Ohio; d. Aug. 5, 1925. Pupil of Noble and Duveneck at Cin. AA. Awards: gold medal for pottery, Paris Expo., 1900; silver medal for painting, Pan.-Pac. Expo., 1915. Work: fifty paintings of wild flowers in State Library of California, at Sacramento.

VALENTINE, DE ALTON, 32 Union Sq.; h. 135 West 16th St., New York, N. Y. (I.) b. Cleveland, Ohio, June 6, 1889. Pupil of Ufer, J. Wellington Reynolds. Member: SI; GFLA; Players.

VAN GORDER, LUTHER EMERSON* (P.) b. Warren, Ohio, 1857; d. Feb. 1, 1931, Toledo, Ohio. Studied with Chase, C. Y. Turner, N. Y.; with Carolus Duran, Paris. Work: Parisian street scenes, "Quai aux Fleurs," Paris; two paintings in Toledo Mus. Member: NYWCC; Am. Asso. of A.; Toledo Tile C.

VAN LEAR, A. T.* (P. T.) Lived in Akron, Ohio, many years; d. New York City c. 1920. Head of Art Dept., of Buchtel College when it started.

VAN SLYCK, LUCILLE, 328 Rockdale Ave., Cincinnati, Ohio (P.) b. Cincinnati, July 8, 1898. Pupil of H. H. Wessel; J. R. Hopkins; J. E. Weis; Hawthorne; I. C. Olinsky. Member: S. Indp. A; Salons of Amer.; Cin. AC.

VARNEY, LUELLA (MADAME SERRAO), 1875 E. 81st St., Cleveland, Ohio; Working, Rome, Italy (S.) b. Angola, N. Y., 1865. Work: portrait statues of Bishop Rappe, St. John's Cathedral, Cleveland; Perkins' Memorial, Lake View Cemetery, Cleveland; busts of Mark Twain, Mr. Brett, Susan B. Anthony, Cleveland Library; Senator Rice, State Capitol, Minn.; Archbishop of Odessa, Odessa, Russia.

VER BECK, FRANK, care of Curtis Brown, Ltd., 6 Henrietta St., Covent Garden, London, England (I.) b. Belmont Co., Ohio, 1858. Illustrator and author of *A Short Little Tale from Bruintown, Timothy Turtle's Great Day, The Donkey Child, The Little Cat Who Journeyed to St. Ives, Ver Beck's Book of Bears, The Elephant Child, The Little Lost Lamb, Piggywiggen, The Little Bear Who Ran Away from Bruintown, Little Black Sambo and the Baby Elephant*, etc. Designer of the Ver Beck earthenware models.

VOLKERT, EDWARD CHARLES, Lyme, Conn. (P.) b. Cincinnati, Ohio, Sept. 19, 1871. Pupil of Frank Duveneck in Cincinnati; ASL of NY. Member: ANA; NYWCC; AWCS; Allied AA; Salma. C.; Union Inter. des Beaux Arts et des Lettres; Cincinnati MacD. S.; Am. Soc. Animal PS; NAC (life); Conn. AFA; AFA. Awards: Hudnut prize, NYWCC, 1919; Cooper prize, Conn. AFA, 1925; Gedney Bunce prize, Conn.

Acad., FA, 1929. Work: decoration, Woodward and Hughes High School, Cincinnati; Hamilton High School, Hamilton, Ohio; Montclair, N. J., Museum. Specialty: cattle.

VUILLEMENOT, FRED A., 2441 West Brook Drive, Toledo, Ohio (P. S. I.) b. Ronchamp, France, Dec. 17, 1890. Pupil of Hector Lemaire, E. Deully, David, Benouard. Member: Alliance; Art Decoratif. Awards: Prix wicart de Lille and Prix du Ministre, France. Work: silver plaquette, Cravereau Museum, France.

WADDELL, MARTHA E., City Club, 505 Wick Ave.; h. 409 Second St., Scienceville, Youngstown, Ohio (P. W. T.) b. Ontario, Canada, Feb. 27, 1904. Pupil of Butler AI. Member: NA Women PS; Cleveland Art Center; Columbus AL; Youngstown Alliance.

WAIT, BLANCHE, 3741 Aylesburo Ave., Hyde Park, Cincinnati, Ohio (P.) Member: Cin. WAC.

WALCUTT, DAVID BRODERICK* (P.) b. Columbus, Ohio, 1825.

WALCUTT, GEORGE* (P.) b. Columbus, Ohio, 1825. Work: landscape and portrait.

WALCUTT, WILLIAM W.* (P. S.) b. Columbus, Ohio, 1819; d. 1882.

WALDECK, NINA V., 2258 Euclid Ave., Cleveland, Ohio; h. 1364 West Clifton Blvd., Lakewood, Ohio; winter, 2607 North Dixie Ave., Orlando, Fla. (P. I. E. T.) b. Cleveland, Jan. 26, 1868. Pupil of Chase; Max Bohm; Julian Academy, in Paris. Member: Orlando AA; Cleveland WAC. Work: portraits of Jane Elliott Snow, Woman's C., Cleveland; Bishop Schram, Ursuline Acad., Cleveland.

WALKER, F. R., 1900 Euclid Ave., Cleveland, Ohio (P.) Member: Cleveland SA.

WALKER, GEORGE W., Euclid Beach Park, Cleveland, Ohio (P.)

WALKER, HAROLD E., Madison Court, Toledo, Ohio (P.) b. Scotch Ridge, Ohio, Nov. 6, 1890. Pupil of Almon Whiting, Karl Kappes, Frederick Trautman, Wilder M. Darling, Ross Moffett. Member: Toledo Artklan; Beachcombers. Awards: first prize, 1922, and hon. men., 1923, Toledo Museum of Art. Work: "Overhauling the Nets," permanent collection, John H. Vanderpoel Art Association, Chicago.

WALTMAN, HARRY FRANKLIN, Dover Plains, N. Y. (P.) b. in Ohio, Apr. 16, 1871. Pupil of Constant and Laurens, in Paris. Member: ANA, 1917; Salma. C., 1897; Allied AA; NAC. Awards: Isidor prize, Salma. C., 1916; prize, NAC, 1927. Work: "Vermont Woods in Winter," Butler Art Institute, Youngstown, Ohio.

WALTON, S. W., Scarab Club, Detroit, Mich (P.) b. Apr. 3, 1878, Fergus, Ontario. Curator Scarab Club, Detroit. Work: scenic billboard painter in Columbus ten years. Member: PPC.

WANDS, ALFRED JAMES, 9337 Amesbury Ave., Cleveland, Ohio (P. I. T.) b. Cleveland, Feb. 19, 1902. Pupil of Cleveland School of Art; F. N. Wilcox; H. G. Keller; John Hunington Inst.; studied in Europe. Member: Cleve. SA; Cleve. A. Center; Ohio WCS; Balto. WCC. Awards: prize for painting, 1923; prize for drawing, 1926, Cleveland Museum; Chaloner prize, New York, 1926; first prize in lithograph, second prize, figure composition, hon. men. in landscape and in drawing, Cleve. MA, 1929. Work: "The Last Load" and "Seated Nude," Cleveland MA; "Alttenha Valley," Cleveland Public Schools.

WARD, EDGAR MELVILLE* (P.) b. Feb. 24, 1839, Urbana, Ohio; d. May 15, 1915, New York City. Brother of J. Q. A. Ward. Studied NAD; Beaux Arts, Cabanel, Paris, eight years. Graduated Miami Univ. *Genre* subjects. Work: "The Coppersmith," Metro. Mus., N. Y.; "The Sabot Maker," received medal, Paris Salon, later purchased by French Government; "The Block Maker," Nat'l Gallery, Washington. ANA, 1875; NA, 1883. Professor of drawing and painting at NAD, 1880-1909. Bronze medal, Buffalo, 1901. Member: Century Asso.

WARD, JOHN QUINCY ADAMS* (S.) b. Urbana, Ohio, June 29, 1830; d. May 1, 1910, New York. Studied with H. K. Browne, N. Y. Member: NA, 1863; president, NA,

1874; founder and president until his death of NSS; Arch. Lg. Work: "Freedman," Cincinnati Mus.; "Indian Hunter," "Private of 7th Regiment," Central Park, N. Y.; statues of Beecher, Greeley, N. Y.; Washington, Garfield, General Thomas, Washington, D. C.; pediment, New York Stock Exchange; "Victory," Dewey Arch; "Dr. Goodale," Columbus; allegorical figures, State House, Hartford, Conn.

WARD, WINIFRED, 2006 Mt. Vernon St., Philadelphia, Pa. (S.) b. Cleveland, 1889. Studied Grafly, PAFA. Member: S Indp. A; NA Women PS.

WARDEN, BENJAMIN WHEELER* (P.) b. Feb. 10, 1877, Athens, Ohio; d. July 6, 1928, Columbus. Studied CAS. Work: oil, water color, modeling, photography, commercial artist Bucher Eng. Co. Paintings in fifty Columbus homes. Many prizes received. Member: PPC; CAL. Served as president of both, Columbus, Ohio.

WAREHAM, JOHN HAMILTON DEE, Rookwood Pottery Co.; h. 3329 Morrison Avenue, Clifton, Cincinnati, Ohio (P. C.) b. Grand Ledge, Mich. Pupil of Duveneck and Meakin. Member: Cincinnati Municipal AS. Award: bronze medal, St. Louis Expo., 1904. Decorations in Fort Pitt Hotel, Pittsburgh; Seelbach Hotel, Louisville; Hotel Sinton, Cincinnati; Poli's Theatre, Washington, D. C.

WARSHAWSKY, A. G., care Foinet, Paris, France; summer, Pointe de Croix, Bretagne, France (P.) b. Sharon, Pa., Dec. 28, 1883. Pupil of Mowbray and Loeb, N. Y.; Winslow Homer. Member: Paris AAA; Salon d'Automne; Cin. AC. Work: mural decoration, "The Dance," Rorimer Brooks Studio, Cleveland; Cleveland Museum; Minneapolis Art Institute.

WARSHAWSKY, XANDER, 16 Villa Seurat, Paris, France (P.) b. Cleveland, Ohio, Mar. 29, 1887. Pupil of NAD. Member: Paris AAA; Group X.Y.Z., Paris. Work: "Overlooking the Mediterranean," Cleveland Museum.

WATERBURY, CHARLES DANN* (Arch.) b. Sandusky, Ohio, 1868; d. Washington, D. C., Oct. 9, 1918. Jan., 1918, made Asst. Chief in draughting room of the Engineering Section of the Construction Division of the Army; May, 1918, commissioned captain. Member: AIA, 1909.

WATSON, ADELE, 20 West 10th St., New York, N. Y.; summer, 283 South Grand Ave., Pasadena, Calif. (P.) b. Toledo, Ohio, Apr. 30, 1873. Pupil of ASL of NY, and Raphael Collin in Paris. Member: PBC; NA Women PS; S Indp. A.

WATKINS, WILLIAM* (Min. P.) b. England or Wales; d. 1850. Flourished in Steubenville, Ohio, c. 1825; Cincinnati later.

WEAVER, MRS. EMMA MATERN, Greencastle, Ind. (P. T.) b. Sandusky, Ohio. Pupil, Adelphi College, Brooklyn; Cin. AA; ASL of NY; Berlin and Paris.

WEBBER, CHAS. T.* (P.) Cincinnati, Ohio. Represented: "Rip Van Winkle," Cin. Art Museum; portraits of Governors Charles Anderson and R. B. Hayes in State House, Columbus.

WEBER, AUGUST JAMES, 131 East Third St., Cincinnati, Ohio; h. 419 Fourth St. Marietta, Ohio (P.) b. Marietta, Oct. 21, 1889. Pupil of Meakin and Duveneck in Cincinnati. Member: Cin. AC; Valley of the Moon SP; Ohio WCS.

WEBSTER, MARY HORTENSE, Midway Studios, 6016 Ellis Ave., Chicago, Ill. (P. S. T.) b. Oberlin, Ohio. Pupil of Cincinnati Art Academy under Barnhorn and Nowottny; Injalbert, Verlet, and Waldmann in Paris; Hitchcock in Holland; Hawthorne in Provincetown; Lorado Taft in Chicago.

WEHRSCHMIDT, DAN (P.) Cleveland painter of Herkomer's School, England. Member: old Cleveland AC.

WEHRSCHMIDT, EMIL (P.) Cleveland painter of Herkomer's School, England. Member: old Cleveland AC.

WEILAND, JAMES, 58 West 57th St., New York, N. Y.; summer, Lyme, Conn. (Port. P.)

b. Toledo, Ohio. Pupil of NAD; Royal Academy in Munich; Delacluse and Colarossi Academy in Paris. Member: Salma. C.; Allied AA; Provincetown AA. Represented in the National Museum, Washington, D. C.

WEIS, JOHN ELLSWORTH, Art Academy, Cincinnati, Ohio; h. 2155 Fulton Ave., W. H., Cincinnati (P. W. T.) b. Higginsport, Ohio, Sept. 11, 1892. Pupil of Duveneck, Meakin, Hopkins, and Wessel. Member: Cin. AC; Cin. MacD. C; Duveneck Soc. of P. and S. Work: landscapes; portrait of Geo. Dent Crabbs, Patron of Art.

WEISBRODT, H. W.* (Engr.) b. 1856; d. Sept. 6, 1927, Cincinnati, Ohio.

WEISS, GERTRUDE MARKS (MRS. H. B.) 721 Avon Fields Lane, Cincinnati, Ohio (P.) Member: Cin. WAC.

WELLA, MRS. EMILY* (P. T.) b. Delaware, Ohio, May 31, 1846; d. Rochester, N. Y., 1925. Member: Rochester AC.

WELDON, CHAS. D., 51 West 10th St., New York City (P. I.) b. Mansfield, Ohio, c. 1855. Pupil of Walter Shirlaw, N. Y.; Munkacsy, Paris; twelve years in Orient. Award: bronze medal, Charleston Expo., 1902. Member: ANA, 1889; NA, 1897; Century Assoc. Work: illustrated for *Harper's Weekly,* Lafoadio Hearn, Julian Ralph's book, *Alone in China.* Several oil and water-color paintings owned by Mr. Reid Carpenter, Mansfield, Ohio. Specialty of restoring and reclaiming old paintings.

WENBAN, SION* (E.) Cleveland artist; flourished c. 1880. Studio in Munich, Germany, many years. Steel engraver.

WENG, SIEGFRIED, Dayton, Ohio (S. C.) Studied Lorado Taft, Chicago Art Institute. Wood cuts. Director of Dayton Art Institute.

WENGER, BYRON F., Columbus, Ohio (S.) b. Canton, Ohio, 1899. Studied with Frey, Ohio State University, Columbus; Paris. Member: Columbus AL. Work: sculpture, lithographs, etchings, painting.

WESSEL, BESSIE HOOVER (MRS. H. H.), 2152 Alpine Place, Cincinnati, Ohio (P.) Studied Cin. AA, with Duveneck. Work: portraits, still life, miniatures of Barnhorn and Duveneck. Member: Cin. WAC.

WESSEL, HERMAN H., Art Museum; h. 2152 Alpine Place, Cincinnati, Ohio (P. E. T.) b. Vincennes, Ind., 1878. Pupil of Frank Duveneck. Awards: Fine Arts prize, SWA, 1915; first portrait prize, Columbus, 1922; first prize, Atlanta, 1920. Represented in Cincinnati Museum; Engineering College, University of Cincinnati; murals in Scioto Co. (Ohio) Courthouse; Federal Reserve Bank Branch, and Holmes Memorial Hospital, Cincinnati.

WESTERMAN, HARRY JAMES, 3500 Riverside Drive, Columbus, Ohio (News A.) b. Parkersburg, W. Va., Aug. 8, 1877. Pupil of Columbus Art School. Member: PPC; CAL; S Indp. A; Lg. Amer. A. Cartoonists, McClure Newspaper Syndicate.

WETMORE, MARY MINERVA, 511 W. Church St., Champaign, Ill. (P. T.) b. Canfield, Ohio. Pupil Cleveland School of Art; ASL of NY; Julian Academy; Colarossi, Paris. Member: Chicago Soc. of Artists; NA Women PS. Instructor at University of Illinois.

WHITE, CARL F.* (Arch.) b. 1881, Cleveland, Ohio; d. Apr. 26, 1915, Cleveland. Graduated in Architecture from Cornell, 1905. Partnership with Henry L. Shupe, Cleveland. Secretary of Cleveland Chapter AIA.

WHITE, CLARENCE H.* (Photographer. T.) b. Carlisle, Ohio, 1871; d. Mexico City, July 8, 1925. Founder of the Photo-secession of America. Member: Vienna Camera Club; Camera Club, N. Y.; Pictorial Photographers of America. Work in leading museums here and abroad. Lecturer, Columbia Univ.; Brooklyn Inst. of Arts and Sciences.

WHITEFORD, JAMES A., *Cincinnati Enquirer,* Cincinnati, Ohio (News A.) Cartoonist, *Times-Star;* free-lance; *Enquirer.*

WHITMORE, ROBERT HOUSTON, R.R. 1, Yellow Springs, Ohio (P. E.) b. Dayton, Ohio,

Feb. 22, 1890. Pupil of AIC; Cincinnati Art Academy; H. M. Walcott, James R. Hopkins. Member: Dayton Society of Etchers; ASL of Chicago. Awards: Goodman prize, ASL of Chicago, 1920; Bryan prize, Calif. PM, 1924. Represented in Dayton Museum; Steel High School; Normal School, Dayton; Los Angeles Museum of History, Science and Art. Asst. Professor of Fine Arts, Antioch College, Yellow Springs.

WHITTEKER, LILLIAN E., Cincinnati, Ohio (P.) Pupil of Hopkins. Work: landscapes, marionettes. Member: Cin. WAC. In Paris, 1930.

WHITTREDGE, THOMAS WORTHINGTON* (Ldscp. P.; Port. P.) b. Springfield, Ohio, 1820; d. Summit, N. J., Feb. 25, 1910. Studied in London, Paris, Antwerp, and Düsseldorf, under Andreas Achenbach. Member: NA, 1861; president of the Academy, 1875-'76; Century Association; Lotos Club. Awards: bronze medal, Centennial Expo., Philadelphia, 1876; hon. men., Paris Expo., 1889; silver medal, Pan-Amer. Expo., Buffalo, 1901; silver medal, St. Louis Expo., 1904. Work: "The Window," Lenox Library; "Catskill Brook," Corcoran Gallery, Washington. Honorary Member, Metro. Museum.

WHISNER, G. A., Columbus, Ohio (I. T.) b. Jan. 30, 1889, Columbus. With Terry Engraving Co., Columbus. Member: PPC.

WICKEY, HARRY, 54 West 74th Street; h. 350 West 21st Street, New York, N. Y. (E.) b. Stryker, Ohio, Oct. 14, 1892. Member: Salma. C.; Brooklyn SE. Awards: Logan prize, Chicago SE; Shaw prize, Salma. C., 1925; bronze medal, Sesquicentennial Expo., Philadelphia, 1926. Work: "Midsummer Night," "Snug Harbor," and "The Park," Metropolitan Museum of Art, New York; "Midsummer Night," Art Institute of Chicago.

WIESSLER, WILLIAM (JR.), 131 East Third St., Cincinnati, Ohio (P. T.) b. Cincinnati, June 14, 1887. Pupil of Frank Duveneck, L. H. Meakin, Vincent Nowottny. Member: Cin. AC; Valley of the Moon Soc. P.; Duveneck Soc. PS.

WILCOX, FRANK NELSON, Cleveland School of Art, Cleveland, Ohio; h. 2072 Cornell Rd., East Cleveland. (P. E. T.) b. Cleveland, Oct. 3, 1887. Pupil of H. G. Keller, F. C. Gottwald. Member: Cleveland SA; NYWCC. Award: Penton medal, Cleveland, 1920. Work: "The Old Market," Cleveland MA; Brooklyn Mus.

WILLARD, ARCHIBALD M.* (P.) b. Bedford, Ohio, Aug. 22, 1836; d. Cleveland, Oct. 11, 1918. Studied with J. O. Eaton, in N. Y. Work: "Pluck' series of lithographs; "The Spirit of '76," in Marblehead, Mass.; landscapes.

WILLIAMS, JOHN INSCO* (P.) b. Dayton, Ohio, May 3, 1813. Pupil McMicken School of Design, Cincinnati. Painted panoramas.

WILLIAMS, LAWRENCE S., 121 Engle St., Tenafly, N. J. (P.) b. Columbus, Ohio, July 24, 1878. Pupil of Carroll Beckwith, William M. Chase, F. C. Du Mond. Member: Salma. C.

WILMES, FRANK, 1560 Elm St., Cincinnati, Ohio (P. C.) b. Cincinnati, Oct. 4, 1858. Pupil of L. H. Meakin; Vincent Nowottny; Frank Duveneck. Member: Cin. AC.

WILSON, HENRIETTA, Art Academy, Cincinnati, Ohio; h. 2215 Monroe Ave., Norwood, Ohio (P. T.) b. Cincinnati. Pupil of Cincinnati Art Academy. Member: Cincinnati WAC; Ohio-Born WA; Ohio WCS. Instructor, Cincinnati Art Academy. Work: "Autumn Flowers."

WILSON, KATE, 2215 Monroe Ave., Norwood, Ohio (P. T.) b. Cincinnati. Member: Cin. WAC. Studied with Barnhorn.

WILSON, MRS. LUCY ADAMS, 2266 Northwest 33rd St., Miami, Fla (P.) b. Warren, Ohio, 1855. Pupil of Herron Art Inst., Indianapolis; ASL of NY; William Forsyth and Steele. Member: Miami Lg. A; Tropical Lg. A; SSAL; AFA. Represented in Herron Art Inst.

WIMMER, MRS. SUE A., Hagerstown, Ind. (P.) b. Eaton, Ohio.

WINKLER, AGNES CLARK (MRS. G. A. M.), 4468 Lake Park Ave., Chicago, Ill. (P. L. T. I. C.) b. Cincinnati, Ohio, Apr. 3, 1893. Pupil of Leon Lundmark, Edward J. F. Timmons of AIC; Watson and Mary Helen Stubbs. Member: Allied AA. Represented: La Revue Moderne, Paris; Revue du Vrai et du Beau, Paris.

WISER, GUY BROWN, 100 West Duncan St., Columbus, Ohio (P. T.) b. Marion, Ind., Feb. 10, 1895. Pupil of Despujols, Gorguet, Hugh H. Breckenridge, Charles Hawthorne, J. R. Hopkins. Member: Hoosier Art Patrons' Assoc.; Columbus AL; Nor. Ind. AL. Awards: Walter Lippincott prize, PAFA, Philadelphia, 1927; Union Trust prize, Nor. Ind. AL, 1927; George T. Buckingham prize, Hoosier Salon, Chicago, 1929, 1930; first prize, Columbus AL, 1929.

WITT, JOHN H.* (P.) b. Dublin, Ind., 1840; d. 1901. Studied with J. O. Eaton, Cincinnati. Settled in Columbus, 1862; painted portraits and had many pupils there. Many portraits in State House, Columbus. Elected ANA, 1885.

WOELFLE, ARTHUR W., 261 Madison Ave., Flushing, N. Y. (P. T.) b. Trenton, N. J. Ten years in Ohio. Studied Brooklyn Inst.; ASL of NY; NA; Paris; Munich. Awards: hon. men., Munich; Grant prize; Irvin Hanson prize; silver medal, Allied AA. Member: ANA; NAC; Grand Central Galleries; Salma. C.; Allied AA. Work: portraits; 125-ft. mural, Courthouse, Youngstown, Ohio; mural, "Bouquet's Expedition," Coshocton, Ohio. Instructor, Castle School, Tarrytown, N. Y., five years; Mechanics' Institute, N. Y., five years; Grand Central Galleries, N. Y.; Provincetown, Mass.

WOOLRYCH, BERTHA HEWIT (MRS. F. HUMPHREY WOOLRYCH), 3855 Hartford Street, St. Louis, Mo.; summer, Sherman, Mo. (P. I.) b. in Ohio, in 1868. Pupil of St. Louis School of Fine Arts; Morot, Collin and Courtois in Paris. Member: St. Louis AG; St. Louis Art Students' Association. Awards: medal, Lewis and Clark Expo., Portland, 1905; gold and silver medals, St. Louis School of Fine Arts; silver medal, 1908, St. Louis District, General Federation of Women's Clubs.

WOOTTON, DON, 12505 Edgewater Drive, Cleveland, Ohio (News A.) b. Mt. Vernon, Ohio, Jan. 15, 1896. Studied Landon School, Cleveland; Cleveland Art School. Work: caricatures and cartoons. Work appears in: *Cleveland Press, Cleveland Plain-Dealer, Literary Digest, Review of Reviews, Cosmopolitan,* NEA Syndicate.

WORTHLEY, CAROLINE BONSALL (MRS. IRVING TUPPER WORTHLEY), R.F.D. 3, Phoenixville, Pa. (P. C.) b. Cincinnati, Ohio, Dec. 25, 1880. Pupil of Cincinnati Art Academy; Pennsylvania School of Industrial Art; Fred Wagner; F. G. Copeland. Member: Plastic C.; Philadelphia Alliance.

WRENN, CHARLES LEWIS, 18 East 8th Street, New York, N. Y.; Wilson Point, So. Norwalk, Conn. (P. I.) b. Cincinnati, Ohio, Sept. 18, 1880. Pupil of Chase and ASL of NY. Member: SI; Salma. C. Specialty: portraits.

WRIGHT, RUFUS* (P.) b. Cleveland, Ohio, 1832. Worked in Akron in the '70's. Work: portraits of Chief Justice Taney, Secretary Seward, Stanton, and others. In State House, Columbus, Gov. Wood; "The Heathen Chinee," an interpretation of Bret Harte's poem.

WUICHET, MRS. ABBY LYTLE, 22 North Robert Blvd., Dayton, Ohio (P. T.) Studied with Laura Birge; with Duveneck at Cin. AA; with Chase and Cox, in New York. Work: flowers, still life, portraits, landscapes of New Orleans. Member: Cin. WAA. Teacher: Purdue Univ., Western Univ.; Dayon Art Inst.

WYANT, ALEXANDER H.* (Ldscp. P.) b. Evans Creek, Tuscarawas County, Ohio, 1836; d. Catskill Mountains, 1892. Studied Cincinnati; with Hans Gude, Carlsruhe, Germany; London. Member: NA, 1869. One of founders of AWCS. Hon. men., Paris Expo., 1889. Represented: "View in County Kerry, Ireland," "Mohawk Valley,"

"Forenoon in the Adirondacks," "A Glimpse of the Sea," "Broad, Silent Valley," Metropolitan Museum, N. Y. Elected, NA, 1869.

WYANT, MRS. ALEXANDER H.* (P.) d. Oct. 27, 1919, Ashville, N. Y. Studied with her husband. Member: NA Women PS; NAC.

WYNKOOP, JOHN* (Arch.) b. Ohio, 1883; d. New York, Dec. 13, 1923. Studied Columbia Univ.; N. Y. Beaux Arts Society winning the Paris prize entitling him to admission to the École des Beaux Arts, Paris, without examination. Awards: three, first medals in Paris. Work: Christian Science Church, 110th Street, N. Y. Professor of Architecture, Univ. of Pa.

YATES, CULLEN, Shawnee-on-Delaware, Monroe Co., Pa. (Ldscp. P.) b. Bryan, Ohio, Jan. 24, 1866. Pupil of NAD; Chase, Ochtman, N. Y.; École des Beaux Arts; Colarossi, Julian Academies, Paris. Member: ANA, 1908; NA, 1919; AWCS; NYWCS; Lotos C; Salma. C.; NAC; Allied AA. Awards: bronze medal, St. Louis, 1904; Inness prize, Salma. C., 1907; Isador prize, Salma. C., 1921. Work: "Rock-Bound Coast, Cape Ann," Nat'l Gallery, Washington; "Gloucester Harbor," St. Louis Mus.; "Early Evening," AC, Philadelphia; "The Harbor," Montclair, N. J. Gallery; landscape, Brooklyn Institute; "Mountain Stream," Butler Art Inst., Youngstown, Ohio; "The Cove, Ogunquit, Maine," Harrison Gallery, Los Angeles, Calif.

YOST, JOSEPH WARREN* (Arch.) b. Clarington, Ohio, 1847; d. Avalon, Pa., Nov. 24, 1924.

ZANETTA, CLOTILDE, Cincinnati Art Academy, Cincinnati, Ohio (S.) Studied with Bourdelle, Rodin's successor, and Barnhorn. Member: Cin. WAC.

ZARING, MRS. LOUISE A., Greencastle, Ind. (P.) b. Cincinnati, Ohio. Pupil ASL of NY; Académie Vitti, Paris, under Merson and MacMonnies; Aman-Jean, Raphael Colin, Julien Dupré; Cape Cod Art School under Chas. W. Hawthorne; William Forsyth. Awards: bronze medal and hon. men., from Académie Vitti; hon. men., Richmond, Ind. Member: SS of Indiana.

ZARSKY, ERNEST, 1218 Rozelle Ave., East Cleveland, Ohio (P.) b. Germany, Sept. 19, 1864. Pupil of F. C. Gottwald; Henry Keller; Henry R. Poore; Cleveland School of Art. Member: Cleveland SA; Cleveland MA; AFA.

ZEHRUNG, SAMUEL D., San-Rae Gardens, Dayton, Ohio (Ldscp. Arch.) b. Roseville, Ohio, Jan. 23, 1892. Studied: Ohio State Univ.; Mass. State College; Harvard Univ. Work: landscape architecture, many private estates. Member: Dayton AI.

ZELL, ERNEST N., 1171 Westwood Ave., Columbus, Ohio (P.) b. in Dayton, Ohio, Oct. 16, 1874. Pupil of Columbus Art School; Cincinnati Art Academy; Shinnecock Summer School; summer school, Ohio State University at Columbus; under Chase in Holland. Member: Columbus AL; PPC. Director of Art School for the Deaf, Columbus.

ZIEGLER, SUSAN S., 2510 Moorman Ave., Walnut Hills, Cincinnati, Ohio (C.) Work: decorative china, conventionalized luster. Member: Cin. WAC.

INDEX